COMPUTERIZED ACCOUNTING
WITH
CA-SIMPLY ACCOUNTING FOR WINDOWS

Janet Horne, MS
Los Angeles Pierce College

and

Sylvia Hearing, MBA, PA
Clackamas Community College

From Janet: To my husband and our sons
with thanks for their support, patience, and understanding
and to my parents
with thanks for the gift of an education and the love of accounting

From Sylvia: In memory of my friend Huey Gene Hatten

Acquisitions Editor: Alana Bradley
Assistant Editor: Fran Toepfer
Editor-in-Chief: P.J. Boardman
Marketing Manager: Beth Toland
Production Editor: Marc Oliver
Associate Managing Editor: Sondra Greenfield
Manufacturing Buyer: Lisa DiMaulo
Senior Manufacturing Supervisor: Paul Smolenski
Senior Manufacturing/Prepress Manager: Vincent Scelta
Cover Designer: Lorraine Castellano

© 2001 by Prentice Hall, Inc.

Upper Saddle River, New Jersey 07458

Printed in the United States of America

10 9 8 7 6 5 4 3 2

Prentice-Hall International (UK) Limited, London
Prentice-Hall of Australia Pty. Limited, Sydney
Prentice-Hall Canada Inc., Toronto
Prentice-Hall Hispanoamericana, S.A., Mexico
Prentice-Hall of India Private Limited, New Delhi
Prentice-Hall of Japan, Inc., Tokyo
Prentice-Hall (Singapore) Pte Ltd
Editora Prentice-Hall do Brasil, Ltda., Rio de Janeiro

CONTENTS

CONTENTS

SECTION 2—MERCHANDISING BUSINESSES

CONTENTS

CONTENTS

CONTENTS

Chapter 11 Computerizing a Manual Accounting System—Budgeting

PREFACE

Computerized Accounting with CA-Simply Accounting for Windows is a comprehensive instructional and learning resource that responds to the growing business trend to adopt Windows applications and to computerize accounting systems. As a result of this trend, this text provides training using Windows and the popular *CA-Simply Accounting* program.

SOFTWARE AND ORGANIZATIONAL FEATURES

The educational version of the commercially popular CA-Simply Accounting for Windows program is (identical to the commercial version except that it will not accept dates after January 1, 1997) is packaged with this text ready for installation. No special site licenses are required.

CA-Simply Accounting for Windows includes six fully-integrated accounting modules: General Ledger, Payables Ledger, Receivables Ledger, Payroll Ledger, Inventory and Services Ledger, and Project Ledger. The text introduces each module gradually so that students can gain experience working with each of the program's components independently prior to working with the entire program. The text begins with an introduction to computerized accounting systems as used in a service business using the Receivables, Payables, and General modules (Section 1). It continues to use these modules while it builds on this foundation by introducing the use of the Inventory, Payroll, and Project modules in a merchandising business (Section2). Additional skills are developed in each module through the conversion process from a manual to a computerized accounting system. Budgeting is also included in this section (Section 3). Finally, the multitasking and data sharing capabilities of CA-Simply Accounting for Windows are examined and explored in the appendix.

Student data files containing the companies used in Section 1 and Section 2 of the textbook are included on the CD-ROM that accompanies this text. In Section 3, students will create their own companies for use in training. These companies are not contained on the CD-ROM.

DISTINGUISHING FEATURES

Extensive assignment material in the form of tutorials, questions, exercises, and three comprehensive practice sets are included in the text.

A step-by-step, extensively illustrated tutorial format is used to introduce the material in each chapter. The tutorials build student confidence and expertise, which can then be applied to the more challenging exercise and comprehensive practice set assignments.

Each chapter includes thought-provoking questions designed to develop and enhance critical thinking skills. The questions address alternative software techniques and ask the student to explain how typical customer, vendor, and employee inquiries could be answered using the software.

To give students realistic exposure to an actual business environment, source documents representative of actual business documents are used to illustrate transactions throughout the text. The combined use of commercial accounting software and realistic business source documents creates a powerful, effective learning tool.

The text includes a tutorial on how to send and share accounting data with other applications using the CA-Simply Accounting for Windows for Export and Dynamic Data Exchange (DDE) features. Is also includes a tutorial covering Microsoft Office integration of Excel, Word, and Simply Accounting. Data sharing among applications emphasizes the important role of accounting data in management information systems.

Report transmittals for each tutorial, exercise, and practice set help students keep the paper flow of the course organized and provide convenient checkpoints to verify the accuracy of their work.

STUDENT PREREQUISITES

No prior knowledge of computers, Windows, or computerized accounting systems is required. Students should be familiar with the accounting cycle for both service and merchandising businesses through either college course work or accounting experience.

LEARNING OBJECTIVES

Computerized Accounting with CA-Simply Accounting for Windows is designed to provide students with a sound basic knowledge of how computerized integrated accounting systems function to the extent that students will be prepared to work with any accounting software package using its reference manual as a guide to unique features. Furthermore, the text builds the foundation for exploring, using, and designing computerized management information systems of which computerized accounting systems form a large part.

SUPPLEMENT FOR THE INSTRUCTOR

Solutions Manual and Teaching Guide with Tests provides a comprehensive answer key to all questions, exercises, and practice sets including teaching suggestions, a sample course outline, and advice on creating your own assignments. Test for use after Section 1, Section 2, Section 3, and a comprehensive final exam are included.

ABOUT THE AUTHORS

Janet Horne has been teaching and writing about accounting and computerized accounting systems for over 20 years. Other published texts by Janet Horne include *Computerized Accounting with QuickBooks 5.0.*

Sylvia Hearing, too, has been teaching and writing about accounting and computerized accounting systems for over 20 years. Other published texts by Sylvia Hearing include *Computerized Accounting an Integrated Skills Approach.* She is also a contributing and consulting author on computerized accounting systems for *College Accounting*, sixth edition, by Jeffrey Slater.

ACKNOWLEDGEMENTS

We wish to thank our colleagues for testing and reviewing the manuscript for this and previous editions of the text. Their comments and suggestions are greatly appreciated.

INTRODUCTION TO COMPUTERIZED ACCOUNTING SYSTEMS

INTRODUCTION TO COMPUTERIZED ACCOUNTING SYSTEMS

LEARNING OBJECTIVES

After studying this chapter, you will be able to:
- Define and understand the components of a computer system
- Define various types of user interfaces
- Name several different types of operating systems software
- Name several different types of applications software
- Describe the characteristics of integrated accounting software
- Compare the manual and computerized accounting cycles
- List the advantages of computerized accounting systems
- Use a mouse to navigate within the Windows operating environment

COMPUTERS HAVE BECOME A NECESSITY IN INFORMATION PROCESSING

The revolution signaled by the advent of the microcomputer continues to bring changes to the information systems environment of modern business organizations. The microcomputer is rapidly becoming a standard information-processing component in both large and small organizations with computer-processed accounting data forming the hub of the management information wheel. As day-to-day business transactions are summarized in an accounting system they become the information base for financial reporting, budgeting, marketing, strategic planning, and decision making.

WHAT IS A SYSTEM?

The term *system* is often associated with computers, but it actually refers to a wider concept of any group of related elements or components that work together to perform a specific task or function or to achieve a specific goal. For example, an automobile is a system. Its components are an engine, a body, tires, and so forth. These components work together for the purpose of providing transportation.

An information system is a collection of components that work together to process data and provide information within an organization. An information system does not have to include the use of a computer. For example, people can process data manually or by using equipment such as adding machines.

The term *management information system* refers to a system that gathers, condenses, and filters data until it becomes information, and then makes it available in a timely, useful form for use in decision making at various levels of management. Again, a management information system does not necessarily imply the use of a computer. Some businesses employ people to review newspapers, select articles of interest, and edit them into a daily report for management.

A computer system is an electronic device that consists of several components that together have the ability to accept user-supplied data; input, store, and execute programmed instructions; and output results according to user specifications. The physical computer and its related devices are the hardware, while the stored program that supplies the instructions is called the software.

The decisions confronting management today are complex. Many organizations have found it essential to incorporate new information technologies to respond to an increasingly complex business environment. Initially, businesses reacted by installing computerized data processing systems to transform raw data into useful information. The next step in the evolution was the creation of computerized management information systems (MIS). The change from simple data processing systems to MIS affected the entire spectrum of computing operations. The data processing division in many instances became the MIS department. Its function was no longer only to process data, but also to provide the kind of summarized information that was essential to operational decision making at all levels of management.

Decision support systems (DSS) represent the next stage in the evolution of computerized tools for management. DSS use historical data to project the future and enable top level management to evaluate alternative strategies and options in decision-making situations. Both MIS and DSS rely on computerized systems to manage data; however, the systems differ in the way management uses this data. With MIS, processed data are typically used to carry out routine, repetitive decision-making tasks. In the case of DSS, processed data are used to answer the "what if" exploratory questions that influence the strategic planning process in an organization. Although there is a tendency for the two systems to overlap, there is a class of software that is presented as decision support software. While some software is specialized for DSS, many decision support systems make use of general-purpose software.

TYPES OF COMPUTERS

Computers are classified in three groups: mainframe computers, minicomputers, and microcomputers or personal computers. Distinctions among these classifications are based on the speed and internal memory capacity of a computer. As computer technology advances, these distinctions are constantly redefined. The microcomputers of the 1990s are as fast and have more memory than the mainframe computers first used by business in the 1950s. Hence, the microcomputer of today would have been considered a mainframe computer in the 1950s. The computer procedures discussed in this text will focus on the use of microcomputers in business. However, the concepts and practices covered are equally applicable to minicomputers and mainframe computers.

COMPUTER COMPONENTS

As mentioned earlier, a computer system is an electronic device that consists of several components that provide the capability of following instructions, performing operations on data, storing the results, and making the results available as output. To understand how this is accomplished by a computer system, we must first look at a conceptual computer that demonstrates the major components and functions of a computer system. The conceptual computer shown below has four major elements—input devices, processing/internal memory unit, secondary storage devices, and output devices. The illustration also shows the flow of data into the computer and of processed information out of the computer.

Conceptual Computer

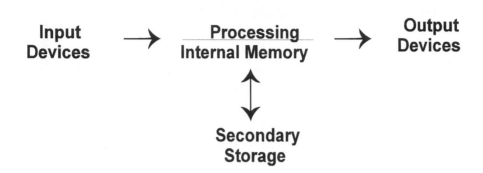

Input devices are used to feed data and instructions into the computer. Once the data and instructions are entered, the computer must be able to store them internally and then process the data based on the instructions. Storage and processing occur in the processing/internal memory unit.

There are two types of internal computer memory: random-access memory (RAM) and read-only memory (ROM). RAM is the largest portion of the memory but still has limited capacity; consequently, secondary storage devices are needed. In addition, RAM is temporary—anything stored in RAM is erased when power to the computer is interrupted. Therefore, data stored in RAM must be saved to a secondary storage medium through the use of a secondary storage device before the power is turned off. ROM is permanent memory and consists of those instruction sets necessary to start the computer and receive initial messages from input devices. ROM takes up only a small portion of the total internal memory capacity of a computer system.

Finally, the results of processing must be made available to computer users through output devices. These components form a collection of devices referred to as computer hardware because they have physical substance.

In a typical microcomputer or personal computer system a keyboard and mouse are used for input and a printer and monitor are used for output. The processing/internal memory unit is housed inside a box along with secondary storage devices consisting of a hard drive unit and one or more floppy disk drives. Other system devices may include a modem, which sends and receives information between computers over telephone lines, and optical disk drives that function as high-capacity secondary storage devices.

Typical Configuration of a Microcomputer System

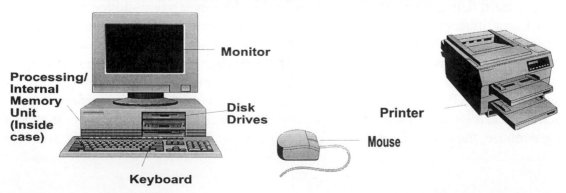

Computer hardware cannot do anything unless it is given instructions. These instructions are provided in computer software programs. Computer programs are supplied on disks, which are a secondary storage medium used in floppy disk drives. Programs also come on CD-ROMs, which are used in CD-ROM drives. The following illustration shows a 3.5-inch disk, which is the most common type of disk used in floppy disk drives.

Handle diskettes carefully! Do not bend them, fold them, or touch any of the exposed surfaces with your fingers!

3.5-inch disk

To operate a particular computer program, you must first load the program into the system's internal memory (RAM) by accessing the program which has been installed and stored on the system's hard drive. Once a program is accessed by RAM, the computer can execute the program instructions and process data as directed by the user through an input device. At the end of a processing session, the results may be viewed on the monitor, printed on the printer, and/or stored permanently on a secondary storage medium through the use of a secondary storage device.

COMPUTER SOFTWARE

Computer programs (also referred to as computer software) control the input, processing, storage, and output operations of a computer. Computer programmers write the instructions that tell the computer to execute certain procedures and process data. There are two broad categories of computer software: systems software and applications software.

Systems software provides the link between the computer hardware, applications software, and the computer user. It consists of programs that start up the computer, retrieve applications programs, and allow the computer operator to store and retrieve data. An integral part of systems software is the operating system. Operating system software controls access to input and output devices and access to other computer programs. The style of the link between the user and an operating system is referred to as the user interface. There are three common types of user interfaces: command-driven, menu-driven, and graphical.

Command-driven interfaces require that the user know exactly what operation is to be done, the command required to invoke the action, and the precise format of the command. Command-driven interfaces are difficult to learn and use but are more direct and faster to use once the commands are learned.

Menu-driven interfaces present the user with a list of options and then wait for the user to make a choice. Once the choice is made, the program performs the required processing. Menu-driven interfaces are generally easier to learn than are command-driven interfaces. However, menu-driven interfaces often require the user to continue working through the menu system long after the use of the system has been mastered. Consequently, menu-driven programs are slower to operate than command-driven programs once the user knows the commands. Some programs permit the use of either commands or menus.

Graphical user interfaces (GUIs) use pictures and graphic symbols (called icons) to represent commands, choices, or actions. Each icon represents some function the software can perform. By pointing to an icon, often by using a mouse, the user can select the desired operation. The advantage of icons over commands and menus is that the user can quickly grasp what the icon means, creating a more intuitive learning and working environment.

User interfaces can also be designed so that different parts of the screen can be used for different purposes at the same time. For example, one part of the screen may be used for a menu, another part for data entry, still another part to display a report, and a fourth part to display a graph. This multiple part display can be the result of a single program executing in the computer or because several programs are executing at the same time. This is achieved by dividing the screen into variable-sized rectangular sections called windows.

OPERATING SYSTEMS SOFTWARE

When IBM first introduced the personal computer, the company turned to a little-known firm, Microsoft, to develop the set of instructions linking the user with the computer hardware. The systems software developed was the Disk Operating System (DOS), which uses a command-driven interface. For new computer users, DOS commands are often cumbersome and difficult to understand. Consequently, Microsoft developed an operating system enhancement program called Windows. Windows is an operating environment that makes use of a GUI and derives its name from the extensive use of windowed screen displays. In addition to using GUI, Windows 95, 98, and NT permit two or more tasks or programs to execute at the same time in separate windows (called multitasking), support the sharing of data among various applications (called Dynamic Data Exchange, or DDE), and allow long file names.

APPLICATIONS SOFTWARE

Applications software refers to programs designed for a specific use. The three most common types of business applications software are spreadsheets, word processing, and database management. Spreadsheet software allows the manipulation of data and has the ability to project answers to "what if"-type questions. For example, a spreadsheet program could project a company's profit next year if sales increased by 10% and expenses increased by 6%. Spreadsheets may also be described as decision support tools because of their modeling and simulation capabilities. Word processing software enables the user to write and print letters, memos, and other documents. Database management software stores, retrieves, sorts, and updates an organized body of information. Most computerized accounting systems are designed as database management software. Accounting information is data that must be organized and stored in a common base of data. This allows the entry of data and the retrieval of information in an organized and systematic way.

Applications software is linked to a particular operating system. Database management, spreadsheet, word processing, accounting, and other software applications are available in versions that work with most of the popular operating systems. For example, if your computer system is using Windows, you would purchase the Windows version of a word processing program. If you were using a Macintosh computer and operating system, you would purchase the Macintosh version of a spreadsheet program.

COMMON USER INTERFACE

One of the most significant benefits of the Windows operating environment is the common user interface imposed on all Windows applications. This means that if you are already familiar with one Windows application, such as a Windows spreadsheet application or a Windows word processing application, it will be much easier to learn another application because all Windows applications work in basically the same way.

ACCOUNTING SOFTWARE PROGRAMS

Most computerized accounting software is organized into modules. Each module is designed to process a particular type of accounting data such as accounts receivable, accounts payable, inventory, or payroll. Each module is also designed to work in conjunction with the other modules. When modules are designed to work together in this manner, they are referred to as integrated software. In an integrated accounting system, each module handles a different function but also communicates with the other modules. For example, to record a sale on account, you would make an entry into the accounts receivable module. The integration feature automatically records this entry in the sales journal, updates the customer's account in the accounts receivable subsidiary ledger, and records the inventory reduction in the inventory module. All general ledger accounts affected would also be automatically posted. Thus, in an integrated accounting system, transaction data are entered only once. All of the other accounting procedures required to bring the accounting records up-to-date are performed automatically through the integration function.

Many different types of accounting packages are available. High-end (and therefore high-cost) accounting packages are sold by individual modules ($500 to $2,500 per module). Low-end (and therefore lower-cost) accounting packages do not offer some of the more sophisticated features of high-end packages but are generally considered adequate for use by small businesses.

Accounting packages designed to meet the needs of a specific business or industry are referred to as vertical accounting packages. Accounting software designed to be useful to a variety of businesses is called horizontal or general-purpose accounting software. Most vertical accounting packages are designed to run on minicomputers and are frequently priced in the high-end price range. However, there has been a general industry trend to design vertical accounting software for use on microcomputers. Horizontal or general-purpose accounting software is available in all price ranges and for use on all sizes of computer systems.

Some low-end and most high-end accounting software packages are available in multiuser and network system versions. For businesses that require several employees to be working with the accounting data at the same time, the accounting software selection process should focus on accounting packages that have these capabilities. Small businesses generally select single-user, single-system computerized accounting packages, and find that these systems quite adequately meet their needs.

High-end and low-end accounting software is available in separate versions that work with Windows, the Macintosh operating system, and other operating systems. The greatest variety of low-end, general-purpose accounting software for microcomputers is available in Windows versions.

MANUAL VERSUS COMPUTERIZED ACCOUNTING SYSTEMS

Accounting procedures are essentially the same whether they are performed manually or on the computer. The following is a list of the accounting cycle steps in manual accounting system as compared to the steps in a computerized accounting system.

The Accounting Cycle		
Step	**Manual System**	**Computerized System**
1	Analyze transaction in terms of the accounts to be debited and credited	Analyze transaction in terms of the accounts used in the transaction
2	Record transaction in a journal	Enter transaction into the computer
3	Post to accounts in the general ledger	Posting performed automatically
4	Prepare trial balance	Trial balance prepared automatically
5	Compile adjustment data and record adjusting entries on the worksheet	Compile adjustment data and enter into the computer
6	Complete the worksheet	No worksheet necessary
7	Prepare the financial statements	Financial statements prepared automatically
8	Journalize and post the adjusting entries	Posting is automatic; adjusting entries recorded in Step 5
9	Journalize and post the closing entries	Journalizing and posting performed automatically
10	Prepare postclosing trial balance	Trial balance prepared automatically

The accounting cycle comparison shows that the accountant's task of initially analyzing transactions (both routine business transactions and adjusting entries) is required in both manual and computerized accounting systems. However, in a computerized accounting system, the "drudge" work of posting transactions, creating and completing worksheets and financial statements, and performing the closing procedures is all handled automatically by the accounting software.

In addition, computerized accounting systems can perform accounting procedures at higher speeds and with greater accuracy than can be achieved in a manual accounting system. It is important to recognize, however, that the computer is only a tool that can accept and process data supplied by the accountant or other user. Each transaction must first be analyzed and recorded correctly; otherwise, the financial reports generated by the program will contain errors and will not be useful for decision-making purposes. Accountants or other users must use extreme care in providing the program with the proper initial accounting data. If such care is not exercised, the advantages of computer processing can be lost.

Beyond increased speed and accuracy, computerized accounting systems offer several other advantages:

Volume	More data can be processed in less time.
Posting	Immediate and automatic posting of transactions keeps the account balances current.
Errors	Mistakes such as unbalanced entries, duplicate entries, or invalid account numbers can be detected and corrected at the time transactions are entered.
Reports	Financial statements, ledgers, journals, and other special reports can be produced on demand.
Documents	Customer statements, invoices, checks, and other documents can be prepared automatically.
Audit Trail	Account balance changes can be traced back to initial transaction data.

The advantages of computerized accounting systems are appreciated by both accountants and managers in an organization. Managers can rely on the information produced by the accounting system with more confidence, and they can respond more rapidly to changes in the business environment as the result of more timely reports. Accountants are freed from repetitive tasks and can turn their attention to the more challenging and satisfying work of analyzing financial data.

CA-SIMPLY ACCOUNTING FOR WINDOWS

CA-Simply Accounting for Windows has been selected for use in this text to demonstrate and help you learn how to use computerized accounting software. The program contains many of the features you will find in both high-end and low-end accounting software packages. CA-Simply Accounting for Windows is designed to meet the accounting needs of small businesses in a single-user, single-system environment. The educational version can be installed in a network environment for use in your school's computer lab, or on a single-user system at your school, or on your own microcomputer system. CA-Simply Accounting for Windows is easy to use, fully integrated, and makes use of the DDE—the sharing of information between different computer programs—capabilities and common user interface features of Windows applications.

CA-Simply Accounting for Windows includes six modules: General Ledger, Receivables Ledger, Payables Ledger, Inventory Ledger, Payroll Ledger, and Project Ledger. The procedures for all components of the program are discussed and demonstrated in this text. Two modes of operation are available in CA-Simply Accounting for Windows: **Ready** and **Not Ready**. The **Not Ready** mode is used when you are converting a manual accounting system to a computerized accounting system. The **Ready** mode is used for regular accounting purposes. In addition, the use of CA-Simply Accounting for Windows export feature, DDE feature, and bank reconciliation feature will be examined. These special features facilitate the sharing of accounting data with other applications so that accountants, managers, and other users can continue to use the power of the computer to analyze and interpret the financial condition of a business.

SYSTEM REQUIREMENTS AND RESTRICTIONS

The minimum software and hardware your computer system needs to run both Windows and CA-Simply Accounting for Windows are:

- Simply Accounting for Microsoft Windows
- Microsoft Windows 95 or Windows 3.1 or 3.11
- A personal computer with an 80486/33 processor
- A hard disk with 25 megabytes (Mb) of free space, and one floppy-disk drive or a CD-ROM drive
- 8 Mb of memory (RAM)
- A VGA or similar high-resolution monitor that is supported by Windows
- A printer supported by windows
- A mouse supported by windows

The educational version of CA-Simply Accounting for Windows has been supplied with this text. The educational version is a complete program package with one restriction: The program will not accept dates after January 1, 1998. The payroll functions of the educational version are based on the federal and state tax laws in effect as of July 1, 1997. When sold commercially, the CA-Simply Accounting for Windows is year 2000 compliant and the package includes a *User Guide*, a *Getting Started Manual*, a *Workbook*, and an *Accounting Manual*. For educational purposes, this text replaces the documentation supplied with the commercial version.

WORKING IN WINDOWS

When you are running Windows, your work takes place on the desktop. Think of this area as resembling the surface of a desk. There are physical objects on your real desk and there are windows and icons on the Windows desktop. You can move work items around on the Windows desktop, bring new ones onto it, and remove those you do not need.

A mouse is an essential input device for all Windows applications. A mouse is a pointing device that assumes different shapes on your monitor as you move the mouse on your desk. According to the nature of the current action, the mouse pointer may appear as a small arrowhead, an I-beam, or a hand. The mouse pointer will also change to an hourglass to indicate Windows is processing your last command and that no further commands may be issued until the action is completed. There are four basic mouse techniques:

Click	To quickly press and release the left mouse button
Double-click	To click the left mouse button twice in rapid succession
Drag	To hold down the left mouse button while you move the mouse
Point	To move the mouse until the mouse pointer on the screen rests on the item of choice

THE WINDOWS DESKTOP

When you turn on the computer, Windows 95, 98, or NT will automatically be in use and icons will be visible on the desktop. Your desktop may be different from the one displayed below, just as your real desk is arranged differently from that of your colleagues. Regardless of the windows that are open on your desktop, most windows have certain elements in common, but not all windows will have every element. In this text, illustrations will be provided for the Windows 95 desktop.

Windows 95 Desktop

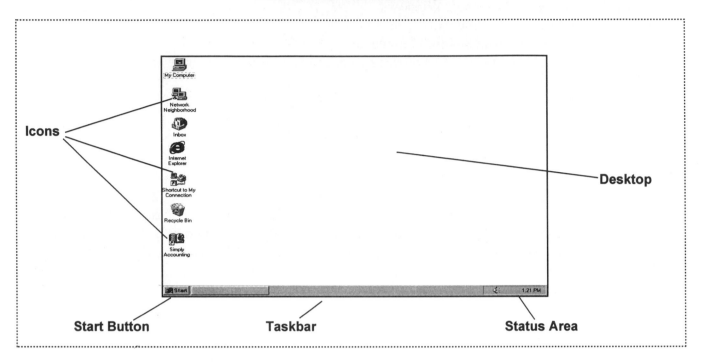

Terms used in conjunction with the Windows desktop are:

Desktop: The primary work area and covers the entire screen.

Icons: Pictorial representations of objects. Some icons on the desktop are "shortcuts" used to access programs and/or documents. Other icons are used to access information regarding your computer or to delete files/programs from the computer.

Taskbar: The major focal point of Windows. It usually appears at the bottom of your screen. The taskbar contains the **Start** button, which is used to launch (open) programs, access documents, alter the appearance of the desktop, and shut down the computer when you are finished working.

Taskbar buttons: Indicate the names of any programs/files that are currently open.

Status area: On the right side of the taskbar. Programs can place information or notification of events in the status area. Windows places information in the status area: the time and (if available on your computer) a sound icon, which is used to control the volume of the computer's sound system.

APPLICATIONS WINDOW

As you work with CA-Simply Accounting for Windows, two kinds of windows will appear on your desktop: the application window (called the home window), and windows contained within the home window. In Windows, an application window contains a running application. The name of the application and the application's menu bar appear at the top of the application window.

In order to use Windows 95 effectively, it is helpful to understand the terminology used in describing the various Windows elements while in the applications window.

CA-Simply Accounting for Windows
Application (Home) Window

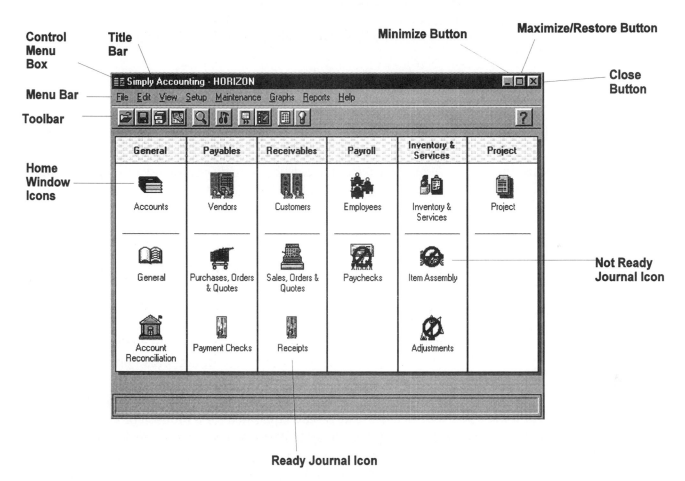

Ready Journal Icon

Minimize button: Clicking on this button reduces a window to an icon.

Maximize button: Clicking on this button enlarges the active window so that it fills the entire desktop.

Restore button (icon not shown): After you enlarge a window, the **maximize** button is replaced by the **restore** button that returns the window back to its original size.

Control menu box: Double-clicking on this box will close the window. A single click will present a menu to resize, move, maximize, minimize, close the window, or switch to another window.

Title bar: Displays the name of the window.

Menu bar: Lists the available menus for the window.

Toolbar: Provides icons/pictures for giving program commands.

Window title: Provides the name of the window. It appears in the title bar.

Home window icons: The icons in the home window let you open the program's records and transaction entry windows.

Highlighted (selected) icon: The active icon in the home window has the name of the selection in a different color.

Ready Journal icon: A Journal icon is shown without the locked symbol ⊘ if its status is **Ready.**

Not Ready Journal icon: A Journal icon is shown with the locked symbol ⊘ if its status is **Not Ready**.

CHOOSE AND SELECT

In Windows applications, the terms *choose* and *select* have different and specific meanings. Selecting an item means marking the item so that it appears as a highlight or in a dotted rectangle, or both. Selecting alone does not initiate an action.

You choose an item to carry out an action. For example, choosing an icon might start an application, open a window, or carry out a command. You can also choose an item from a menu. You often need to select an item before you can choose it.

You can use a combination of mouse and keyboard techniques to select and choose. For example, you can click on an item to select it, and then press the ENTER key to choose it, or you can just double-click on the item. CA-Simply Accounting for Windows is designed for a mouse, but it also provides keyboard equivalents for almost every command. It may seem confusing at first that there are several different ways to do the same thing; however, you will find this flexibility useful. For example, if your hands are already on the keyboard, it may be faster to use the keyboard equivalent of a mouse command. Alternatively, if your hand is already on the mouse, it may be faster to use a mouse technique to carry out a command. When a procedure in this text says to select or choose an item, generally use whichever method you prefer. Alternative procedures are often provided as well. It is not necessary to memorize any particular technique, just be flexible and willing to experiment. As you gain experience with the program, you will develop personal preferences, and the various techniques become second nature.

DIALOG BOXES

A dialog box appears when additional information is needed to execute a command. There are different ways to supply that information; consequently, there are different types of dialog boxes. Most dialog boxes contain options you can select. After you specify options, you can choose a command button to carry out a command. Other dialog boxes may display additional information, warnings, or messages indicating why a requested task cannot be accomplished.

Dialog Box 1

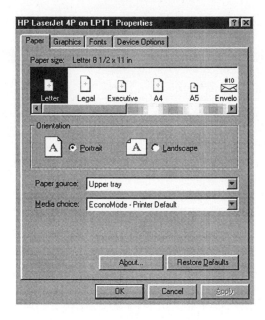

Option buttons: A small circle that represents an option. When you select (click on the button) an option from a group, that button contains a large black dot; the remaining buttons in the group are blank. Option buttons represent mutually exclusive options. You can select only one option button at a time.

Check box: A small square that represents an option. When you select an option (click on the empty check box), the check box contains an X; when you turn off the option (click on the check box to remove the X), it is blank (not shown on the above).

Scroll arrow: A small arrow at the end of a scroll bar that you click on to move to the next item in the list. The top and left arrows scroll to the previous item; the bottom and right arrows scroll to the next item.

Scroll bar: A bar that may appear at the bottom or right side of a window or dialog box if there is more text than can be displayed at one time.

Scroll box: A small box in a scroll bar. When it is highlighted, you can press the arrow keys to move through a list. You can also use the mouse to drag the scroll box left or right, or up or down. The scroll box also indicates the relative position in the list.

Dialog Box 2

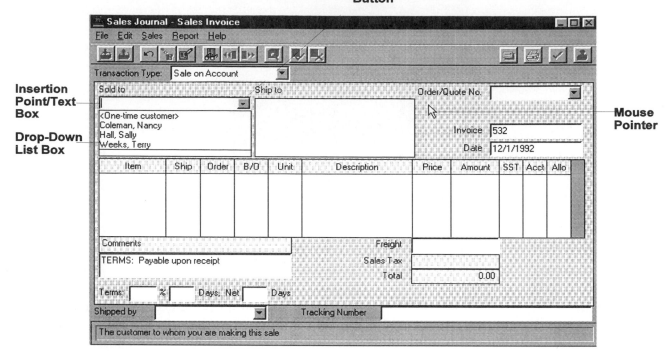

Insertion point: Shows where you are in the dialog box. It marks the place where text will appear when you begin typing.

Text box: When you move to an empty text box, an insertion point appears at the far left side of the box. The text you type starts at the insertion point. If the box you move to already contains text, this text is selected (highlighted), and any text you type replaces it. You can also delete the selected text by pressing the DELETE key or the BACKSPACE key.

Drop-down list box: Displays a list of choices. It will appear initially as a text box. When you click the **arrow** button to the right of the box, a list of available choices will appear. If there are more choices than can fit in the box, scroll bars are provided so you can move quickly through the list.

Mouse pointer: Shown as a small arrowhead in this example.

USING MENUS

Windows commands are listed on menus. Each application has its own menus, which are listed on the **Application menu bar**. To display a complete menu, click the **menu title**. When a menu is displayed, choose a command by clicking on it or by typing the **underlined letter** to execute the command. You can also bypass the menu entirely if you know the **keystroke equivalent** shown to the right of the command when the menu is displayed.

A dimmed command indicates that a command is not currently executable; some additional action has to be taken for the command to become available. Some commands are followed by an **ellipsis (...)** to indicate that more information is required to execute the command. The additional information can be entered into a dialog box, which will appear immediately after the command has been selected.

Sample Menu

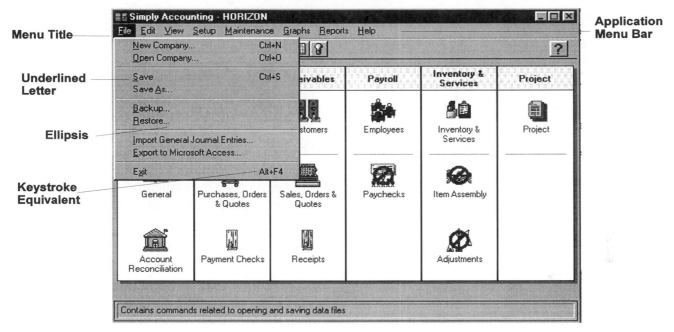

THE HELP MENU

The Help menu provides access to on-screen Help. Use Help for quick information about CA-Simply Accounting for Windows and the task you are performing or to look up information about other parts of the program.

The Help Menu

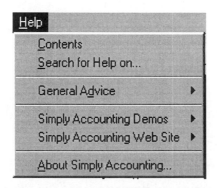

Contents: Choose Contents to display the main Help index. The books displayed allow the user to click on a topic and read information about the program.

Search for Help on...: Allows information to be located according to alphabetical entries in an index.

General Advice: Provides information on general accounting topics.

Simply Accounting Demos: Shows many of the program's features and provides instruction on how to do something in CA-Simply Accounting.

Simply Accounting Web Site: Gives access to program information, ordering, and technical support via the Internet.

About Simply Accounting: Displays the program version number and product ID.

TEXT ORGANIZATION

This text is organized into three major sections followed by an appendix. The text is designed to gradually introduce you to the CA-Simply Accounting for Windows program through the use of tutorials, exercises, and practice sets. In Section 1, you will learn to use the General, Receivables, and Payables components of the program for a service business. In Section 2, you will learn to use the General, Receivables, Payables, Inventory, Payroll, and Project components of the program for a merchandising business. In both Sections 1 and 2, you will be working with the program in the Ready mode. In Section 3, you will have the opportunity to use the CA-Simply Accounting for Windows program in the Not Ready mode while you learn to convert a manual accounting system to a computerized accounting system. In Sections 1 and 2, you will reconcile a bank statement, and in Section 3, you will work with budgeting. In the appendix, you will explore the export of data, DDE, and Microsoft Office Integration capabilities of CA-Simply Accounting for Windows.

Three practice sets are included in the text: Image Art Appraisal, Camera Corner, and Firelight Stoves. Image Art Appraisal is a service business practice set in business paper format and is designed for use after studying the material in Section 1. Camera Corner is a merchandising practice set in business paper format and is designed for use after studying the material in Section 2. A final comprehensive merchandising practice set, Firelight Stoves, is for use after studying Section 3. It requires you to convert a manual accounting system to a computerized accounting system. Once the conversion process is complete, merchandising transactions are presented.

ABOUT THE CD-ROM

A CD-ROM is included with your text. It contains the CA-Simply Accounting for Windows Program. (Because of the CA-Simply Accounting for Windows date restriction in the educational version, all assignments contain dates prior to January 1, 1998. Other than this date restriction, the program will work exactly as it would in a real business situation.)

In addition to the program, the CD-ROM also contains folders that have the company files that will be used in completing each tutorial, exercise, and practice set. The following is a list of the companies you will be working with and the folder names under which they are stored on the CD-ROM.

Folder Name	File Name	Company Name	Type of Assignment
\Horizon	Horizon.asc	Horizon Events	Tutorial, Chapters 2–4
\Harmony	Harmony.asc	Harmony Piano Works	Exercise, Chapters 2–4
\Image	Image.asc	Image Art Appraisal	Practice Set
\Explorer	Explorer.asc	Oregon Explorer Maps	Tutorial, Chapters 5–8
\Windmill	Windmill.asc	Windmill Wheels	Exercise, Chapters 5–8
\Camera	Camera.asc	Camera Corner	Practice Set
\Clocks	Clocks.asc	Classic Clocks	Tutorial, Chapters 9–11
\Paint	Paint.asc	The Paint Place	Exercise, Chapters 9–11
\Firelight	Firelight.asc	Firelight Stoves	Practice Set

PREPARING TO WORK WITH CA-SIMPLY ACCOUNTING FOR WINDOWS

Before you begin to work with CA-Simply Accounting for Windows, you need to accomplish the tasks listed on the following checklist. As you complete an item, place a check in the box to the left of the list.

Check box	Preparing to Work with CA-Simply Accounting for Windows Checklist	
☐	Make working copies of the company files.	You need to make working copies of the company files stored on the CD-ROM by copying each file to a data disk.
☐	Install the CA-Simply Accounting for Windows program.	You need to install the CA-Simply Accounting for Windows program (if you will be using your own microcomputer system to complete the assignments in this text) or verify with your instructor that the program has been installed in your school's computer lab.
☐	Verify that the CA-Simply Accounting for Windows print and display settings work with your computer system.	If you will be using your school's computer lab to complete the assignments in this text, check with your instructor to see if there are any special procedures required to access the program and/or print the reports requested in the assignments. If you will be using your own computer to complete the assignments in this text, you will need to test the default printer and display settings in the CA-Simply Accounting for Windows program to see if they work with your system; and, if necessary, adjust the printer and display settings.
☐	Add your name to the company name for each set of company data files.	It is important for you to be able to identify the specific reports that you print for each assignment as your own, particularly if you are using a computer that shares a printer with other computers. The CA-Simply Accounting for Windows program prints the name of the company you are working with at the top of each report. To personalize your reports so that you can identify both the company and your printed reports, each company name needs to be modified to include your name as well. It is important to add your name to each company name prior to starting on any of the assignments in the text. This will be done for Horizon Events in Chapter 2.
☐	You are now ready to begin.	Go to Chapter 2.

SUMMARY

In this chapter, you have learned that computerized accounting systems have many advantages over manual accounting systems. The increased speed and accuracy of computerized accounting systems allow accountants and others to spend more time analyzing accounting data and give management more timely reports. You have also learned about computer hardware, operating systems, Windows, and Windows application programs.

The remaining chapters in this text will discuss the specific procedures used to operate CA-Simply Accounting for Windows for both service and merchandising businesses. In the latter part of the text, you will learn how to convert a manual accounting system to a computerized accounting system. You will also have the opportunity to explore how to send CA-Simply Accounting for Windows data to other Windows programs.

QUESTIONS

1. List the accounting cycle steps that a computerized accounting system performs automatically.

2. Describe the advantages that computerized accounting systems have over manual accounting systems.

3. List and define the four components of a computer system.

4. List the types of ledgers used in CA-Simply Accounting for Windows.

5. Explain the difference between the terms *choose* and *select* as used in a Windows environment.

6. What does the term *integrated accounting software* mean?

7. List the appendix located at the end of this text and the information it includes.

8. Define the following terms:

    A. System
    B. Information system
    C. Management information system
    D. Computer system
    E. Decision support system
    F. Operating system software
    G. Application software

For answers to the following questions, talk with your instructor, lab assistant, or someone else at your school who is knowledgeable about the computer system you will be using to complete the assignments in this text; then answer each of the following questions. If you will be using your own personal computer system to complete the assignments, answer the questions based on the characteristics of your own system.

9. Describe your system:

    A. What input and output devices are connected to your computer system?
    B. How much RAM is installed in your computer system?
    C. What is the capacity of your hard drive?
    D. What version of Windows is installed on your system?
    E. How do you access Windows on your computer system?
    F. What applications are installed on your system?
    G. What type of printer is connected to your system?
    H. What procedures do you follow to make sure your printer is ready to print?

SECTION 1:

SERVICE BUSINESSES

SERVICE BUSINESSES—RECEIVABLES

SERVICE BUSINESSES— RECEIVABLES

LEARNING OBJECTIVES

After studying this chapter, you will be able to:
- Open the Sales and Receipts Journals
- Customize the company by adding the student's name to the company name
- Open the Receivables Ledger
- Enter sales transactions
- Enter cash receipt transactions
- Make bank deposits
- Enter partial payments made by customers
- Enter cash sales
- Review and edit Sales and Receipts Journal transactions
- Post transactions in the Sales and Receipts Journals
- Correct errors to posted transactions
- Create, modify, and remove customer records using the Receivables Ledger
- Display and print reports from the Sales and Receipts Journals
- Display and print a Customer List, Customer Aged report, and mailing labels
- Display and print a Trial Balance
- Back up company data file
- Observe and understand Receivables-related integration accounts

SERVICE BUSINESSES REQUIRE COMPUTERIZED ACCOUNTING

Major changes have taken place in the structure and complexity of the American economy during the 1900s. The early part of the 20th century was characterized by the industrial revolution, when the majority of jobs were concentrated in manufacturing. Over the past few decades, the character of the American economy has gradually changed from a manufacturing emphasis to a service emphasis. It is predicted that 90% of all jobs in the 1990s will be in service industries and that 90% of all new jobs created during the 1990s will also be in the service-related sectors of the economy. It follows that the majority of accounting positions will also be in the area of providing accounting services to service-based organizations. For this reason, your study of computerized accounting systems will begin with a look at the accounting needs of a service business.

ACCOUNTING FOR RECEIVABLES

Three components of CA-Simply Accounting for Windows are used to account for receivables transactions and to maintain customer records: Sales, Orders & Quotes; Receipts; and Customers. The icons for these items appear beneath Receivables on the home window. Sales on account and cash sales are recorded as Sales, Orders & Quotes, which is the Sales Journal. Cash receipts from credit customers are recorded as Receipts, which is the Receipts Journal, and customer records (name, address, phone number, etc.) and subsidiary ledger information are maintained by accessing Customers, which is the

Receivables Ledger. A variety of reports are available through the use of each component. All Receivables functions in CA-Simply Accounting for Windows are fully integrated with or linked to the General Ledger. For example, when a sale on account is recorded in Sales, Orders & Quotes, the program automatically records the entry in the General Journal, posts to the related accounts in Accounts (the General Ledger), and updates the customer's accounts receivable subsidiary ledger in Customers (the Receivables Ledger). Consequently, once a Receivables-related transaction is posted, its effect on the overall financial condition of the company is reflected immediately and automatically throughout the company's financial records.

HORIZON EVENTS TUTORIAL

The following tutorial is a step-by-step guide to recording routine transactions for Horizon Events within the Receivables components of CA-Simply Accounting for Windows. The procedures required to record transactions using the Payables components will be discussed in Chapter 3. The procedures required to record adjusting entries, prepare financial statements, reconcile bank statements, and close the accounting records at the end of the fiscal year are functions of the General components and will be discussed in Chapter 4. The Horizon Events Tutorial will be continued in both Chapters 3 and 4 to give you a comprehensive overview of how CA-Simply Accounting for Windows can be used to maintain the accounting records for a service business.

Study Tips

To get the most educational value out of the Horizon Events Tutorial in Chapters 2, 3, and 4, the following study steps are recommended for each chapter:

1. Read the entire chapter.
2. Answer the questions at the end of the chapter.
3. Complete all of the Horizon Events Tutorial steps (indicated by the word ACTION) in the chapter using your computer. Hint: Place a check mark (✔) in the box next to each ACTION item as you complete it.
4. Enter all of the Additional Transactions (represented in narrative form) as they occur throughout the chapter.
5. As you work through the tutorial, compare your displays/reports to those illustrated in the text to determine the accuracy of your work. If you detect an error in an unposted transaction, follow the Editing Tips (highlighted in special boxes) to correct the transaction. If you detect an error in a posted transaction, refer to the procedures illustrated in the chapter to correct/adjust the transaction.
6. Complete the Horizon Events Tutorial Transmittal located at the end of the chapter.
7. Review the LEARNING OBJECTIVES stated at the beginning of the chapter to ensure that you have accomplished each objective.
8. Complete the Harmony Piano Works Exercise at the end of the chapter.

HORIZON EVENTS COMPANY PROFILE

Horizon Events is an event planning business owned and operated by Seth Hunter as a sole proprietorship in Portland, Oregon. Horizon Events plans and oversees special events for individuals and organizations, ranging from birthday parties to fund-raising events for nonprofit organizations to neighborhood festivals. Services include desktop publishing of invitations and announcements, bulk mailings, publicity when appropriate, and logistical support for entertainment, food service, facilities, and decorations. The business does not have any employees; Seth hires support staff on a contractual basis as needed for individual events.

Seth maintains his own accounting records using CA-Simply Accounting for Windows. As a service business, he uses the General, Receivables, and Payables components of the software. Seth charges his clients by the hour, issuing invoices payable upon receipt as work progresses for a particular event. As a small business with limited cash flow, Seth arranges for specific services such as printing or entertainment on behalf of his clients; however, the client is the contracting party for these services and is responsible for the payment of related charges.

A Trial Balance for Horizon Events as of December 1, 1997, appears below:

Horizon Events/Your Name
Trial Balance As At 12/1/1997

		Debits	Credits
1010	Cash	$ 5,124.36	-
1020	Accounts Receivable	3,155.29	-
1030	Prepaid Insurance	375.00	-
1040	Office Supplies	2,563.00	-
1050	Software	4,695.00	-
1060	Acc. Dep.- Software	-	$ 2,999.62
1080	Computer Equipment	15,145.00	-
1090	Acc. Dep.- Computer Equip.	-	8,944.43
2010	Accounts Payable	-	1,886.70
3010	Seth Hunter, Capital	-	13,636.18
3020	Seth Hunter, Drawing	15,400.00	-
4010	Revenue From Services	-	36,810.61
5010	Advertising Expense	1,575.00	-
5020	Utilities Expense	525.00	-
5030	Rent Expense	3,600.00	-
5040	Office Supplies Expense	2,013.00	-
5050	Depreciation Exp.-Software	1,434.62	-
5060	Depreciation Exp.-Comp. Eq.	4,277.77	-
5070	Insurance Expense	687.50	-
5080	Professional Services Exp.	2,545.00	-
5150	Misc. Expense	1,162.00	-
		$64,277.54	$64,277.54

OPEN SIMPLY ACCOUNTING AND LOAD THE DATA FILES

Prior to entering transactions for Horizon, CA-Simply Accounting for Windows must be opened and the correct data file must be loaded for use by the computer.

   ACTION: Follow your professor's directions to copy the data file for Horizon from the CD-ROM to a floppy disk. Once your copy of the company file has been made, insert the disk containing the file for Horizon into floppy disk drive A:. Open CA-Simply Accounting for Windows by clicking the **Start** button, pointing to Programs, and pointing to Simply. Your screen will look like this:

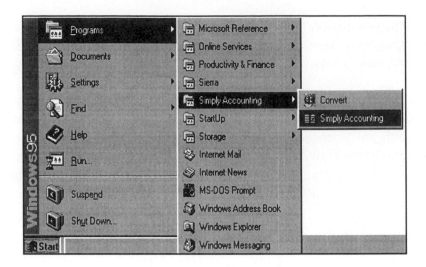

ACTION: Click **Simply Accounting**. To open the data files for Horizon Events (A:\HORIZON\Horizon.asc), click **Select an existing company**, then click **OK**. Your screen will appear as follows:

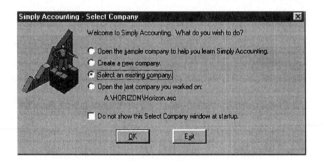

ACTION: Before a company file will be opened, you must tell Simply where the company file is located. If your screen does not look like the one below, click the drop-down list arrow next to the Look in: text box and click **A:** to identify the disk location. In the center section of the text box, you should see a folder named Horizon; click the **Horizon folder**, then click **Open**. Your screen should then look like the one below.

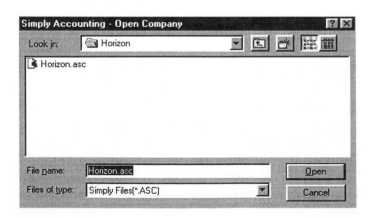

ACTION: Complete the procedures to open a company file by clicking **Horizon.asc** in the center portion of the text box or keying *Horizon.asc* in the File name: text box, then click **Open**. The program will respond with a request for the Date for this Session, as shown in the following dialog box:

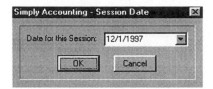

Explanation: The session date is the date associated with the current work session and will be offered as the default date in the journals when you record transactions. Many businesses, especially small businesses, batch their accounting work. To record transactions in batches, a session date that is the same date as the end of the week (or month or quarter) is selected as the session date for the current work session. All transactions occurring during the prior week (or month or quarter) are recorded in the journals under the actual date they occurred. This is accomplished by overriding the default session date offered and entering the actual date of the transaction. Consequently, the session date does not have to agree with the actual date of a transaction. The actual date of the transaction can be prior to or the same as the session date, but it cannot be after the session date.

The session date can only be advanced. This is to ensure the integrity of the company's accounting data. When you enter a session date, the program checks to see if more than seven days have elapsed since the last session date. If the date you enter is more than seven days past the previous session date, the program will alert you via a screen message in case you have accidentally entered an incorrect session date. The program also checks to see whether the session date you have entered is a significant date, such as the end of an accounting year. If the session date that you entered is a significant date, the program will alert you via a screen message so that you can perform period-end procedures or take other appropriate actions before advancing the session date.

 ACTION: Click the drop-down list arrow to the right of the **Date for this Session** field. Your screen will look like this:

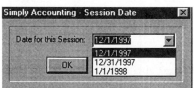

Explanation: A list of default dates will appear. In many cases, throughout the program, date fields will appear with a drop-down list arrow to the right of the field. The list of dates will vary, depending on what area of the program you are working with, and when. The list may include the current year's **fiscal start** date, the **earliest transaction** date, the **session** date, the current year's **fiscal end** date, and/or the first day in the next fiscal year. The fiscal start date is the first day of the company's accounting year. The earliest transaction date is the date that the company converted from its former accounting system to CA-Simply Accounting for Windows. The fiscal end date is the last day of the company's accounting year.

In this example, the program is offering three default dates as potential new session dates. The most recent session date (12/1/1997); Horizon Events' fiscal end date (12/31/1997), and the first day in Horizon Events' next fiscal year (1/1/1998).

Horizon Events records its accounting transactions in weekly batches, and would like to enter 12/5/1997 as the session date for the current work session. Consequently, none of the default dates offered are appropriate and the session date desired must be entered directly.

 ACTION: Enter *12/5/1997* as the new date for this session. Your screen will look like this:

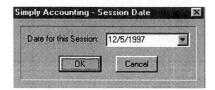

Explanation: Date fields in CA-Simply Accounting for Windows accept dates in most standard formats, as long as you include a separator between the numbers. For example, you can enter December 5, 1997 as 12/5/97, 12/05/97, 12-5-97, or 12-05-97. CA-Simply Accounting for Windows uses the short-date format set in your Windows operating environment. To change the date format in Windows, choose the International icon in the Windows Control Panel; then set the options you want in the Short Date Format box. For more information on date formats in Windows, consult the Microsoft Windows User's Guide. For consistency, dates will be entered as 12/5/97 but will appear as 12/5/1997. Because CA-Simply Accounting for Windows is year 2000 compliant, the four-digit year is displayed.

 ACTION: Choose OK by clicking the **OK** button. The main window for CA-Simply Accounting for Windows, called the home window, will appear:

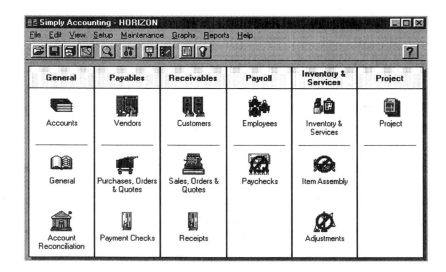

Explanation: When you start CA-Simply Accounting for Windows, the file name for the company's data files (in this case Horizon for Horizon Events) will appear in the title bar at the top of the home window.

The home window displays the objects (icons) that represent a company's accounting records, the various ledgers and journals that are used to maintain accounting records and to record accounting transactions. The top row contains the headings. The second row contains the lists or ledgers—Accounts, which is the General Ledger; Vendors, which is the Accounts Payable Ledger; and Customers, which is the Accounts Receivable Ledger. The bottom two rows contain icons for Journals and Account Reconciliation. In the General column, the General icon represents the General Journal, and the Account Reconciliation icon is used to reconcile various accounts. In the Payables column, the Purchases, Orders & Quotes icon is used to represent the Purchases Journal, and the Payment Checks icon represents the Cash Disbursements/Payments Journal. In the Receivables column, the icon for Sales, Orders & Quotes represents the Sales Journal, and the Receipts icon represents the Cash Receipts Journal. As indicated, the journals are aligned vertically with their corresponding ledgers.

Note: The journal icons for the Payroll and Inventory & Services columns are in the locked position. As a service business with no employees, Horizon Events does not use the Payroll or the Inventory & Services components of CA-Simply Accounting for Windows. The Payroll and Inventory & Services components of CA-Simply Accounting for Windows are discussed in Section 2—Merchandising Businesses.

 ACTION: Customize the Horizon company file by adding your name to the company name. On the home window, click the **Setup** menu and point to Company Information. Your screen will appear as follows:

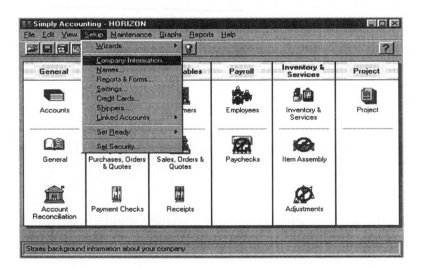

 ACTION: Click **Company Information** to open the Company Information dialog box. Click after Horizon Events in the **Name** box. Key */Your Name*. Your screen will appear as follows but will include your actual name, not the words *your name*.

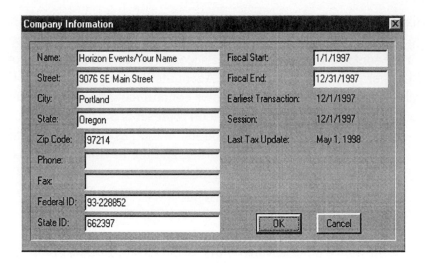

Explanation: For example, the Company Information screen for Melissa Kim would have "Horizon Events/Melissa Kim" in the **Name** box.

SALES JOURNAL—RECORDING SALES ON ACCOUNT

Sales on account are recorded in the Sales Journal. Seth Hunter uses a time log to keep track of the number of billable hours he works on behalf of each client. The following memo summarizes the hours he has worked on Sally Hall's event.

Horizon Events—Document 1   **Session Date: 12/5/1997**

Memo:

Date: December 3, 1997

Record 18 hours at $50.00 per hour for event planning services provided to Sally Hall.

ACTION: Open the Sales Journal dialog box by double-clicking the **Sales, Orders & Quotes** icon. Your screen will look like this:

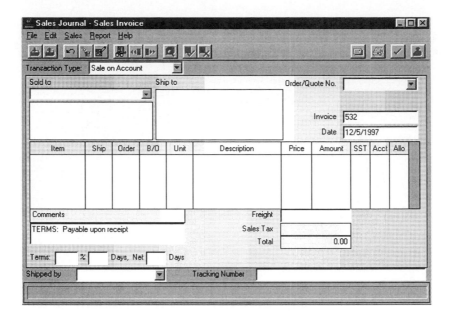

Explanation: The Sales Journal - Sales Invoice is used to record sales on account, cash sales, and certain types of correcting entries for transactions posted in error.

ACTION: Click the drop-down list arrow to the right of the **Sold to** field to display Horizon Events' customer list. Your screen will look like this:

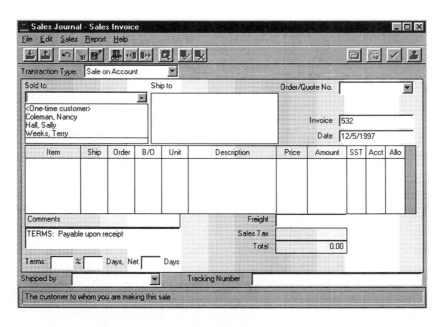

Explanation: A drop-down list box displaying an alphabetical list of Horizon Events' customers will appear along with the <One-time customer> option. The customer list contains the names of all the customers in the Accounts Receivable Ledger. Use of the one-time customer option is discussed later in this chapter.

ACTION: Click **Hall, Sally** to select the customer. Your screen will look like this:

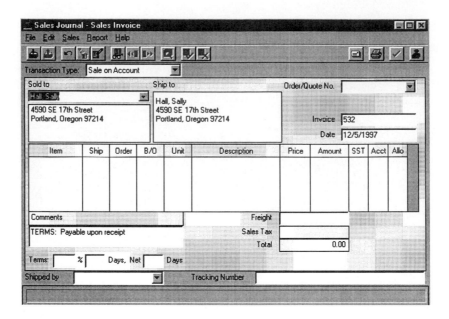

Explanation: The program has automatically filled in the customer's address in the **Sold to** and **Ship to** fields. The **Invoice** field is also completed automatically. Horizon Events has elected to use the CA-Simply Accounting for Windows automatic invoice preparation and numbering feature. Invoice 532 represents the next invoice in the automatic sequence. You can enter a different invoice number before printing, as long as it does not duplicate a number already used for the same customer. If you enter a duplicate invoice number, the program will alert you via a screen message. For companies that do not use the program to print invoices, invoice numbers are entered individually as sales are recorded.

 ACTION: Double-click the **Date** field; enter the transaction date of *12/3/97*; then press the TAB key. Your screen will look like this:

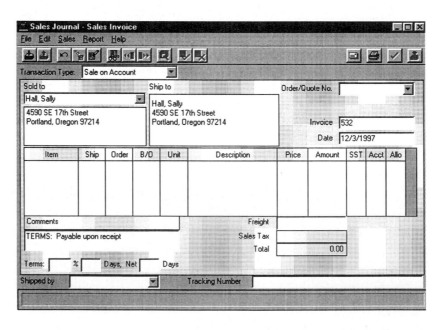

Explanation: After accepting the new transaction date, the program will position a flashing insertion point in the **Item** field. The **Item** field is used primarily by merchandising businesses to list the internal item number associated with a specific inventory unit. As a service business, Horizon Events does not use this field.

 ACTION: To move the cursor, press the TAB key or click in the **Ship** field; enter *18*; then press the TAB key. Your screen will look like this:

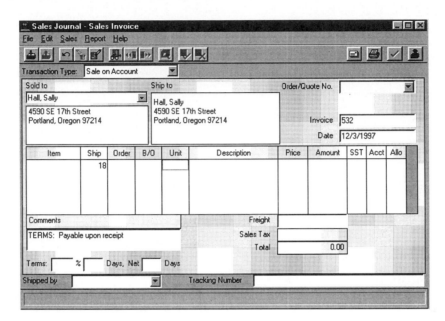

Explanation: The **Ship** field is used to record the number of units you are selling. You may use up to four decimal places in this field. Because this is a service business, you will skip the **Order** and **B/O** (back order) fields.

 ACTION: Enter the word *Hours* into the **Unit** field; then press the TAB key and enter *Event Planning Services* into the **Description** field. Press the TAB key. Your screen will look like this:

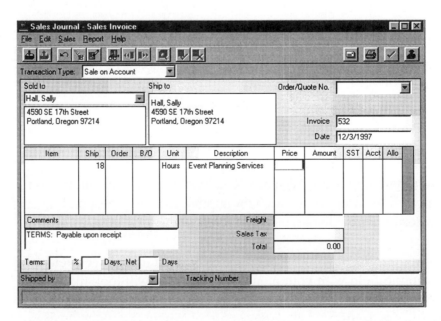

Explanation: A flashing insertion point is positioned in the **Price** field. Seth Hunter is charging $50.00 per hour for the event planning services he has performed for Sally Hall.

■ **ACTION:** Enter *50.00* into the **Price** field; then press the TAB key until the cursor is positioned in the **Acct** field. Your screen will look like this:

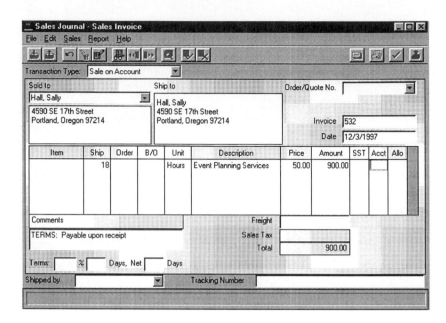

Explanation: The program has automatically multiplied the number entered in the **Ship** field (18) by the amount entered in the **Price** field (50.00) and entered the result in the **Amount** field (900.00).

Dollar amounts can be entered in several ways in CA-Simply Accounting for Windows. For example, to enter $50.00, type 50, 50., or 50.00. To enter an amount containing a decimal point, type the decimal point as part of the amount. For example, enter five dollars and twenty-five cents as 5.25.

A flashing insertion point is positioned in the **Acct** field and the program has skipped the **SST** (state sales tax) field because there is no sales tax associated with the sale of services in Oregon. This transaction is a sale on account. The standard journal entry to record a sale on account is:

	Debit	**Credit**
Accounts Receivable	xxx	
Revenue From Services		xxx

The program will automatically debit Accounts Receivable through its integration/linking feature, but needs to be supplied with the appropriate account number for the corresponding credit portion of the entry. This can be determined by displaying a list of accounts.

■ **ACTION:** With the flashing insertion point positioned in the **Acct** field, press the ENTER key or double-click in the field with your mouse. Your screen will look like this:

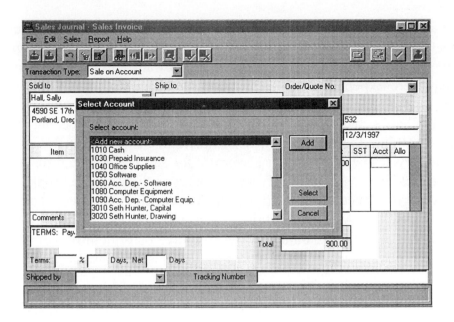

Explanation: A display listing Horizon Events' chart of accounts will appear in the Select Account dialog box. Use this list to determine the account to be entered into the **Acct** field for the credit portion of the journal entry. If you receive an error message stating an unknown account number, click the **OK** button to display the Select Account dialog box.

 ACTION: Scroll through the list by dragging your mouse or by using the scroll bar until the Revenue From Services account (account number 4010) is highlighted. Select the Revenue From Services account (account number 4010) by double-clicking on the account or by highlighting the account and clicking the **Select** button. Your screen will look like this:

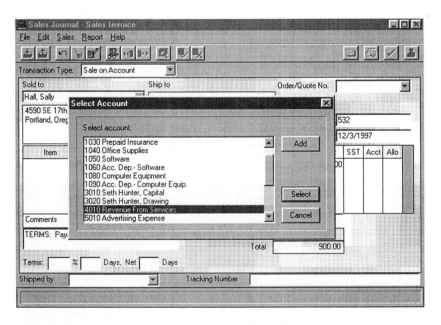

Explanation: CA-Simply Accounting for Windows uses the following account numbering system:

Asset accounts	1000–1999	Equity accounts	3000–3999	Expense accounts	5000–5999
Liability accounts	2000–2999	Revenue accounts	4000–4999		

Note: To move quickly through the list of accounts to the area where Revenue accounts appear, press the number 4. This will advance the list to the start of the section where accounts beginning with the number 4 (Revenue accounts) are listed. Alternatively, if you wanted to move quickly through the list of accounts to the area where Expense accounts appear, you would press the number 5.

Once the Select button has been clicked, the program automatically enters account number 4010 (Revenue From Services) into the **Acct** field. This completes the data you need to enter into the Sales Invoice to record the services Seth Hunter has performed for Sally Hall. You were not given access to the **Allo** (Allocation) field because Horizon Events is not currently using the Project component of the program; nor were you given access to the **Shipped by** or **Tracking Number** fields because nothing was shipped in this transaction. Also note that the default statement for Horizon Events "TERMS: Payable upon receipt" appears in the **Comments** field. Before you print this invoice or post the transaction, you need to verify that the transaction data is correct by viewing the journal entry.

ACTION: Click **Report** on the Sales Journal menu bar. Your screen will look like this:

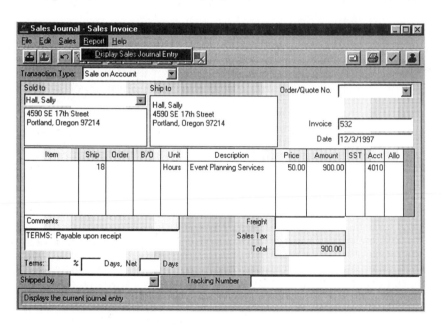

ACTION: Click **Display Sales Journal Entry**. Your screen will look like this:

12/3/1997	Debits	Credits	Project
1020 Accounts Receivable	900.00	-	
4010 Revenue From Services	-	900.00	
	900.00	900.00	

Explanation: The journal entry representing the data you have recorded in the Sales Journal - Sales Invoice is displayed. Review the journal entry for accuracy, noting any errors.

ACTION: Close the Sales Journal Entry display by clicking the **Exit** button on the title bar. If you made an error, use the following editing techniques to correct the error:

Editing Tips
Editing a Sales Journal Entry

Move to the field that contains the error by either pressing the TAB key to move forward through each field or the SHIFT and TAB keys together to move to a previous field. This will highlight the selected field information so you can change it. Alternatively, you can use the mouse to point to a field and drag through the incorrect information to highlight it.

Type the correct information; then press the TAB key to enter it.

If you have associated a transaction with the incorrect customer, select the correct customer from the customer list display after clicking the drop-down list arrow to the right of the **Sold to** field.

If you have associated this transaction with an incorrect account number, select the correct account number from the chart of accounts display after double-clicking the **Acct** field.

To discard an entry and start over, either choose **Undo Entry** from Edit on the Sales Journal menu bar, or click the **Exit** button. Click the **Yes** button in response to the question "Are you sure you want to discard this journal entry?"

Review the journal entry for accuracy after any corrections by choosing **Display Sales Journal Entry** from Report on the Sales Journal menu bar.

It is IMPORTANT TO NOTE that a transaction may be edited after it is posted by adjusting the entry and entering the correct transaction. To correct transactions posted in error, see the correction for Terry Weeks later in this chapter.

 ACTION: After verifying that the journal entry is correct, select **File** from the Sales Journal menu bar and click **Print** to print the invoice. Compare your invoice to the one shown below:

Horizon Events/Your Name
9076 SE Main Street
Portland, Oregon 97214

                                                                         532

                                                                         12/3/1997

                                                                         1 of 1

Hall, Sally   Hall, Sally
4590 SE 17th Street   4590 SE 17th Street
Portland, Oregon 97214   Portland, Oregon 97214

          18   Hours   Event Planning Services   50.00   900.00

TERMS: Payable upon receipt   900.00

Explanation: Verify that the invoice is correct. If you detect an error, refer to the Editing Tips for Editing a Sales Journal Entry for information on corrective action. Editing Tips for Editing a Sales Journal Entry appears in a special box earlier in this chapter.

If you made a mistake on the invoice, you can correct the invoice information and print a new invoice. The program does not make any journal entries when it prints invoices, so printing copies of the same invoice does not affect the company's records or the invoice numbers of subsequent invoices. For the purposes of this text, you may destroy incorrect invoices; however, in an actual business situation, incorrect invoices would be retained as an internal control measure.

 ACTION: After a correct invoice is printed and all information is verified, click the **Post** button to post this transaction.

Explanation: A blank Sales Journal dialog box is displayed, ready for additional Sales Journal transactions to be recorded.

ADDITIONAL SALES ON ACCOUNT TRANSACTIONS

Record the following additional sales on account transactions:

Document 2 December 5—Bill Nancy Coleman for 10 hours of event planning services at $50.00 per hour (automatic Invoice 533). Print the invoice.

Document 3 December 5—Bill Terry Weeks for 18 hours of event planning services at $50.00 per hour (automatic Invoice 534). Print the invoice.

Compare your invoices to the ones shown below:

Horizon Events/Your Name
9076 SE Main Street
Portland, Oregon 97214

                                                                              533

                                                                              12/5/1997

                                                                              1 of 1

Coleman, Nancy   Coleman, Nancy
5600 SE 82nd Street   5600 SE 82nd Street
Portland, Oregon 97214   Portland, Oregon 97214

          10   Hours   Event Planning Services   50.00   500.00

TERMS: Payable upon receipt   500.00

Horizon Events/Your Name
9076 SE Main Street
Portland, Oregon 97214

                                                            534

                                                        12/5/1997

                                                          1 of 1

Weeks, Terry	Weeks, Terry			
2390 SE Madison Blvd.	2390 SE Madison Blvd.			
Portland, Oregon 97214	Portland, Oregon 97214			

18	Hours	Event Planning Services	50.00	900.00

TERMS: Payable upon receipt   900.00

ACTION: After you have printed the invoices and posted the journal entries for Documents 2 and 3, close the Sales Journal dialog box by clicking the **Exit** button. You will return to the home window and your screen will look like this:

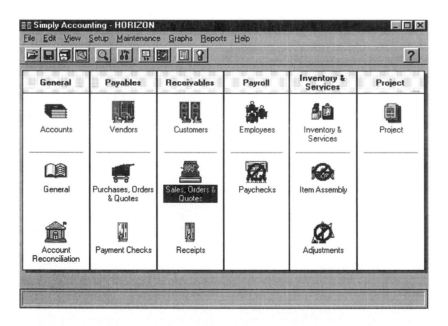

ACTION: Upon examining the printed copy of Invoice 534, you realize that event planning services for Terry Weeks should have been recorded for 20 hours rather than 18 hours. In order to correct this invoice, double-click the **Sales, Orders & Quotes** icon on the home window. In the Sales Journal - Sales Invoice window, click the **Adjust Invoice** button. On the Adjust an invoice screen, click the drop-down list arrow for Customer Name and click **Weeks, Terry** to select him as the customer.

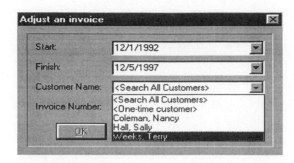

ACTION: After Terry Weeks has been selected as the customer, click the **Browse** button.

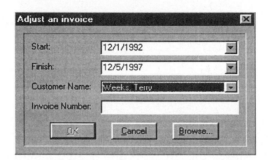

ACTION: CA-Simply Accounting will browse through all the invoices and display the following invoice information for Terry Weeks:

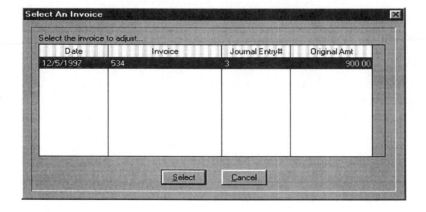

ACTION: With the invoice information highlighted, click the **Select** button. The original invoice will appear on the screen. Click **18** in the **Ship** field to highlight. Type *20* to change the hours from 18 to 20, and tab to have Simply recalculate the total amount for the invoice. The invoice will appear as follows:

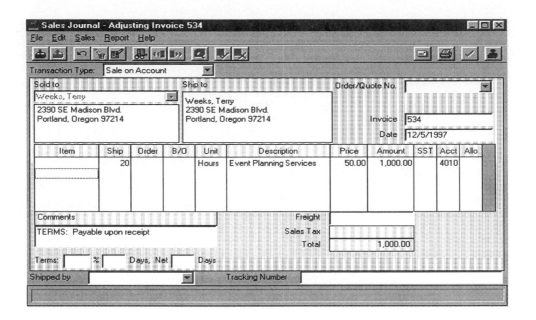

 ACTION: Print Adjusting Invoice 534 and compare with the following:

Horizon Events/Your Name
9076 SE Main Street
Portland, Oregon 97214

534

12/5/1997

1 of 1

Weeks, Terry	Weeks, Terry
2390 SE Madison Blvd.	2390 SE Madison Blvd.
Portland, Oregon 97214	Portland, Oregon 97214

20	Hours	Event Planning Services	50.00	1,000.00

TERMS: Payable upon receipt   1,000.00

 ACTION: Click the **Post** button and return to the home window. With the **Sales, Orders & Quotes** icon highlighted, click **Report** on the home window menu bar. Point to Journal Entries, Sales. Your screen will look like this:

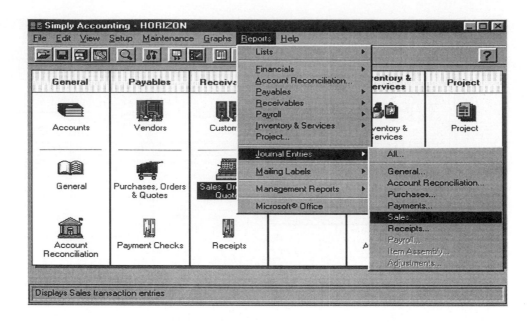

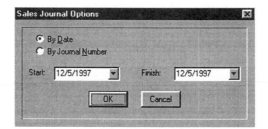

ACTION: Click **Sales**. The Sales Journal Options dialog box will appear, and your screen will appear as follows:

Explanation: The Sales Journal Options dialog box appears, asking you to define the information you want displayed.

If you select **By Date**, a report listing all entries between the start and finish dates you specify will be prepared. The start date must be between the earliest transaction date and the session date inclusive. The finish date must be between the start date and the session date inclusive. Default options for start and finish dates are automatically displayed, and additional default options are available by clicking the drop-down list arrows next to the **Start** and **Finish** fields. You can override the default options by specifying the posting dates in the **Start** and **Finish** fields.

If you select **By Journal Number**, a report listing all the entries between the start and finish journal numbers you enter will be prepared. Journal entries made anywhere in the program are stored in the General Journal. The program automatically assigns a sequential reference number to each journal entry. Default options for start and finish journal entry numbers are automatically displayed in the Sales Journal Options dialog box. Additional default options are available by clicking the drop-down list arrow buttons next to the **Start** and **Finish** fields.

ACTION: Select **By Date**; key *12/1/1997* or click the drop-down list arrow next to start and click **12/1/1997** to enter the start date; leave the finish date set at 12/5/1997; then click the **OK** button. The following Sales Journal Display will appear on your screen:

Sales Journal Display					
File Help					
12/1/1997 to 12/5/1997				Debits	Credits
12/3/1997	J1	532, Hall, Sally			
		1020	Accounts Receivable	900.00	-
		4010	Revenue From Services	-	900.00
12/5/1997	J2	533, Coleman, Nancy			
		1020	Accounts Receivable	500.00	-
		4010	Revenue From Services	-	500.00
12/5/1997	J3	534, Weeks, Terry			
		1020	Accounts Receivable	900.00	-
		4010	Revenue From Services	-	900.00
12/5/1997	J4	ADJ534, Reversing J3. Correction is J5.			
		4010	Revenue From Services	900.00	-
		1020	Accounts Receivable	-	900.00
12/5/1997	J5	534, Weeks, Terry			
		1020	Accounts Receivable	1,000.00	-
		4010	Revenue From Services	-	1,000.00
				4,200.00	4,200.00
Double-click to display Vendor or Customer Aged Report or Employee Report					

Explanation: Review the display for accuracy, verifying that journal entry dates, customer names, invoice numbers, account names and numbers, and amounts are correct. Notice the reversing entry that was automatically prepared by CA-Simply Accounting when Terry Weeks' Invoice 534 was adjusted. If you have posted any other incorrect transactions, refer to the steps listed to adjust Terry Weeks' invoice earlier in the chapter and correct your errors.

 ACTION: Select **File** from the Sales Journal Display menu bar. Click **Print** to print the report; then compare your report to the one shown below:

Horizon Events/Your Name
Sales Journal 12/1/1997 to 12/5/1997

			Debits	**Credits**
12/3/1997	J1	532, Hall, Sally		
		1020 Accounts Receivable	900.00	-
		4010 Revenue From Services	-	900.00
12/5/1997	J2	533, Coleman, Nancy		
		1020 Accounts Receivable	500.00	-
		4010 Revenue From Services	-	500.00
12/5/1997	J3	534, Weeks, Terry		
		1020 Accounts Receivable	900.00	-
		4010 Revenue From Services	-	900.00
12/5/1997	J4	ADJ534, Reversing J3, Correction is J5		
		4010 Revenue From Services	900.00	-
		1020 Accounts Receivable	-	900.00
12/5/1997	J5	534, Weeks, Terry		
		1020 Accounts Receivable	1,000.00	-
		4010 Revenue From Services	-	1,000.00
			4,200.00	4,200.00

Explanation: If you detect an error, refer to the steps listed for the correction of Invoice 534 and make any necessary corrections.

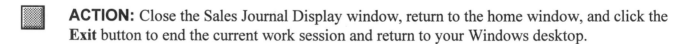 **ACTION:** Close the Sales Journal Display window, return to the home window, and click the **Exit** button to end the current work session and return to your Windows desktop.

ALTERNATIVE ACTION: If you wish to continue the tutorial without exiting from the program, choose **Advance Session Date** from the home window setup menu. Enter *12/12/1997* as the new session date; then skip the next ACTION and continue with the tutorial.

RECEIPTS JOURNAL—RECORDING CASH RECEIPTS FROM CREDIT CUSTOMERS

Payments received for outstanding invoices are recorded in the Sales, Orders & Quotes. The steps to enter Check 1542 from Nancy Coleman are listed below.

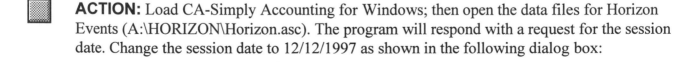 **ACTION:** Load CA-Simply Accounting for Windows; then open the data files for Horizon Events (A:\HORIZON\Horizon.asc). The program will respond with a request for the session date. Change the session date to 12/12/1997 as shown in the following dialog box:

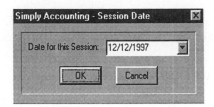

ACTION: Horizon Events has received the following check as a payment on account:

Horizon Events—Document 4   **Session Date: 12/12/1997**

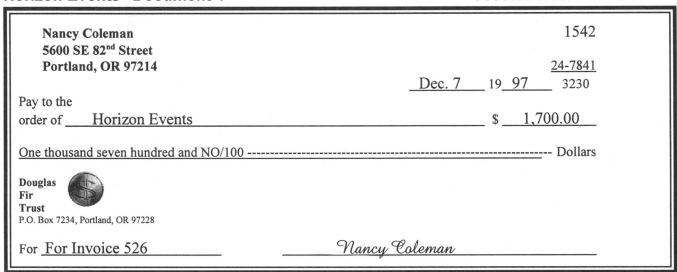

Nancy Coleman   1542
5600 SE 82nd Street
Portland, OR 97214   24-7841
                                              Dec. 7   19 97   3230

Pay to the
order of ____Horizon Events_____ $ ___1,700.00___

One thousand seven hundred and NO/100 -- Dollars

Douglas
Fir
Trust
P.O. Box 7234, Portland, OR 97228

For For Invoice 526   Nancy Coleman

ACTION: Record Check 1542 for payment of Invoice 526 by double-clicking the **Receipts** icon. Your screen will look like this:

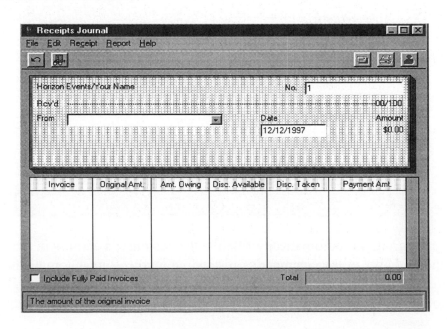

Explanation: The Receipts Journal dialog box is used to record payments received for outstanding invoices and certain types of correcting entries for transactions posted in error.

ACTION: Click the drop-down list arrow to the right of the **From** field. Your screen will look like this:

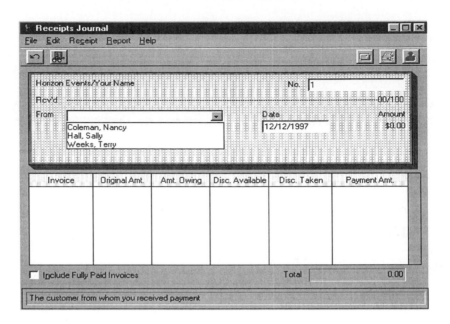

ACTION: Click **Coleman, Nancy**. Your screen will look like this:

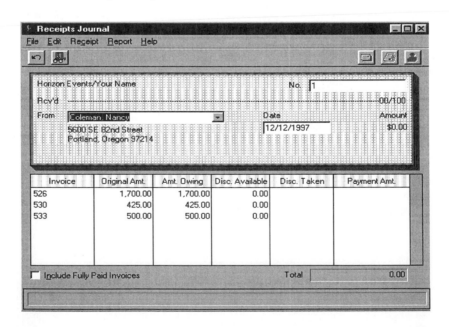

Explanation: The program has automatically filled in the customer's address in the **From** field. The invoice numbers and amounts of the customer's outstanding invoices are automatically listed in the lower part of the Receipts Journal dialog box. The **Invoice** field lists the invoice number; the **Original Amt.** (original amount) field shows the invoice amount; and the **Amt. Owing** (amount owing) field shows the unpaid portion of the invoice. The invoices are displayed in date order, with the oldest one at the top of the list.

 ACTION: Position the flashing insertion point in the **No.** (number) field using the mouse or by pressing the TAB key; enter Nancy Coleman's check number of *1542*; then press the TAB key. With the **Date** field highlighted; enter *12/7/1997*; then press the TAB key until the cursor is positioned in the **Payment Amt.** column. Your screen will look like this:

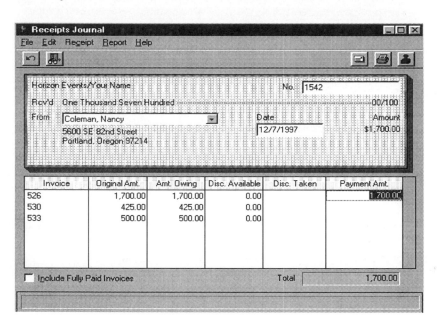

Explanation: The full amount of Invoice 526 is highlighted and offered as the default **Payment Amt**. If a customer is making a partial payment, you can type over the amount displayed, entering the lesser amount. You cannot enter an amount greater than the amount owed.

This completes the data you need to enter into the Receipts Journal dialog box to record the check received from Nancy Coleman. Before you post this entry, you need to verify that the transaction data is correct by viewing the journal entry. You do not need to check the **Include Fully Paid Invoices** check box. This box is used for correcting transactions posted in error or to account for a customer's NSF check.

 ACTION: Tab once more to remove the highlighting from the payment amount and to enter that amount as the total. Select **Report** from the Receipts Journal menu bar. Your screen will look like this:

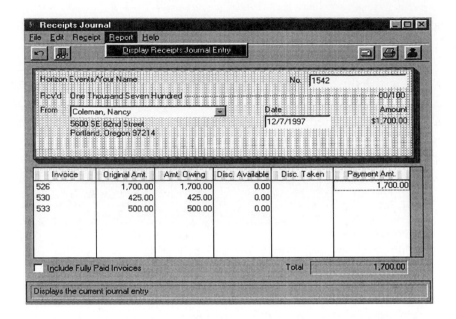

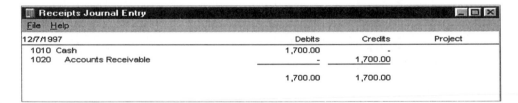

ACTION: Click **Display Receipts Journal Entry**. Your screen will look like this:

Explanation: The journal entry reflecting the information you have recorded in the Receipts Journal dialog box is displayed. The integration/linking feature of CA-Simply Accounting for Windows has created the standard entry for a cash receipt on account:

	Debit	**Credit**
Cash	xxx	
Accounts Receivable		xxx

Review the journal entry for accuracy, noting any errors.

ACTION: Close the Receipts Journal Entry window. If you have made an error, use the following editing techniques to correct the error:

Editing Tips
Editing a Receipts Journal Entry

Move to the field that contains the error by either pressing the TAB key to move forward through each field or the SHIFT and TAB keys together to move to a previous field. This will highlight the field information so that you can change it. Alternatively, you can use the mouse to point to a field and drag through the incorrect information to highlight it. Type the correct information; then press the TAB key to enter it.

If you have associated the transaction with an incorrect customer, select the correct customer from the customer list display after clicking the drop-down list arrow to the right of the **From** field. You will be asked to confirm that you want to discard the current transaction. Click the **Yes** button to discard the incorrect entry and display the outstanding invoices for the correct customer.

To completely discard an entry and start over, either choose **Undo Entry** from Edit on the Receipts Journal menu bar or double-click on the control menu box. Click the **Yes** button in response to the question "Are you sure you want to discard this journal entry?"

Review the journal entry for accuracy after any corrections by choosing **Display Receipts Journal Entry** from Report on the Receipts Journal menu bar.

It is IMPORTANT TO NOTE that a transaction may be edited after it is posted by adjusting the entry and entering the correct transaction. To correct transactions posted in error, see the transaction for Sally Hall later in this chapter.

ACTION: After you have verified that all of the transaction data are correct, print the Receipt Journal for Nancy Coleman. When printing is complete, post the entry by clicking the **Post** button. If you get a dialog box regarding the receipt numbering, click **No**.

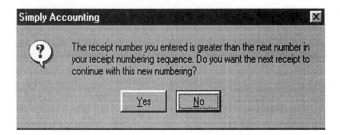

Once posting is complete, your screen will look like this:

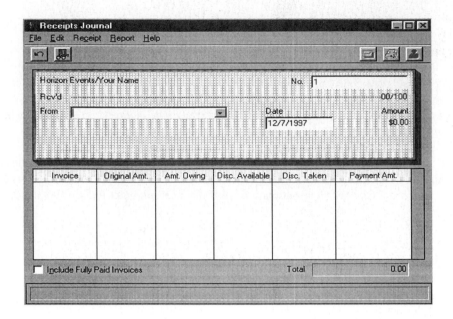

Explanation: A blank Receipts Journal dialog box is displayed, ready for additional Receipts Journal transactions to be recorded.

BANK DEPOSITS OF CASH RECEIPTS

ACTION: Cash receipts should be deposited in the bank frequently. Deposit the check received from Nancy Coleman by closing the Sales Journal - Sales Invoice screen. Click **Account Reconciliation** on the home window to highlight. Your screen will appear as follows:

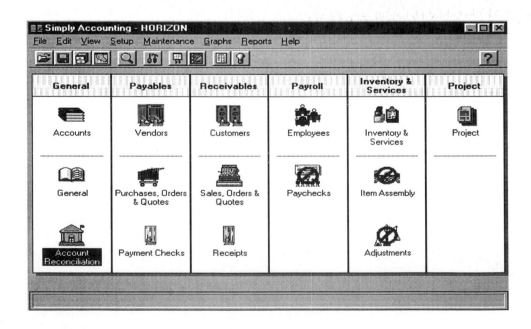

ACTION: Double-click the **Account Reconciliation** icon. When the Account Reconciliation Journal appears, click the drop-down list arrow next to Account. Your screen will look like the following:

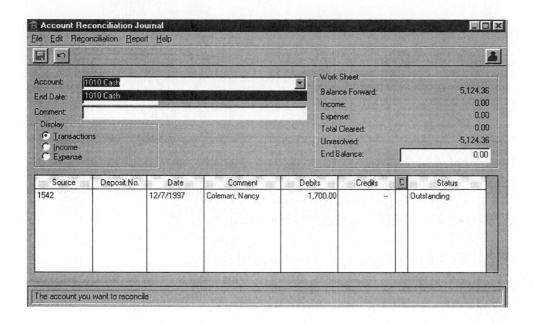

ACTION: Click **1010 Cash** to select this as the account to be reconciled. Beneath the **Comment** text box, **Display** should have Transactions selected. Click the column for **Deposit No.** next to Source 1542, which is the number of Nancy Coleman's check. Enter *7257* as the number of the deposit slip used for the deposit. Your screen will look like the following:

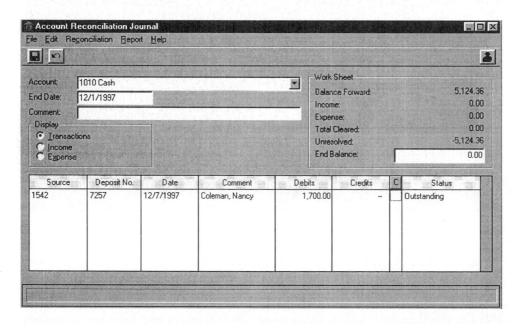

Explanation: Whenever a bank deposit is made, the number of the deposit slip is entered on the account reconciliation. When the bank statement is received with the deposit listed, the deposit will be marked cleared during the reconciliation process. The amount listed as the balance forward is the same amount as the beginning balance of the Cash account. That amount also reflects the end balance of the previous bank reconciliation. The bank reconciliation will be completed in Chapter 4.

ACTION: Since the account reconciliation is not being completed at this time, click the **Save** icon 🖫 to save the transaction. **DO NOT CLICK THE POST ICON**. Click the **Close** button to exit the Account Reconciliation Journal and return to the home window.

ADDITIONAL CASH RECEIPTS TRANSACTIONS

Record the following additional cash receipts transactions:

Document 5 December 10—Received Check 4525 in the amount of $350.29 from Sally Hall in full payment of Invoice 521. Print the completed receipt.

Document 6 December 12—Received Check 624 in the amount of $250.00 from Terry Weeks in partial payment of Invoice 531. Print the completed receipt.

 ACTION: Upon examining the printed copy of the receipt for Check 4525 from Sally Hall, you realize that the amount of the check should have been $450.29. In order to correct this receipt, double-click the **Receipts** icon on the home window. In the Receipts Journal, record *4525 REV* in the **No.** text box to indicate a reversal of check number 4525. In the **Payment Amt.** column for Invoice 521, enter *-350.29* (don't forget to precede the number with a minus sign). Your screen will appear as follows:

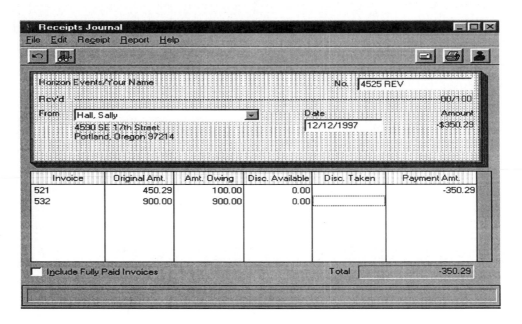

Explanation: This entry will reverse the previous receipt recorded for Invoice 521. Note: If the invoice had been fully paid, the check box next to Include Fully Paid Invoices would have to be marked in order for the invoice to be displayed.

 ACTION: On the Receipts Journal menu bar, click **Report** and **Display Receipts Journal Entry**. Your screen will show the following:

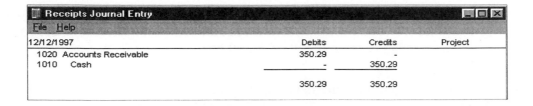

Explanation: This reverses the previous receipt entry by debiting Accounts Receivable and crediting Cash.

ACTION: Click the **Print** icon on the toolbar. Click **OK** on the message box that states "The receipt cannot be printed unless the amount is positive."

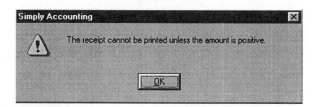

ACTION: Click the **Post** icon on the toolbar. Re-enter the receipt, using *4525 C* as the **No.** and making sure to enter the correct amount of *$450.29*. Your screen will appear as follows:

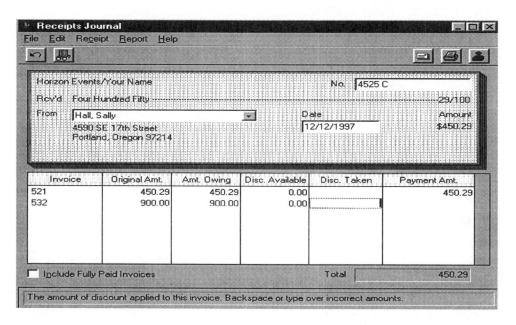

ACTION: Verify the information entered, print the Receipt, and click the **Post** button to post the transaction. Click the **Exit** button to close the Receivables Journal. You will return to the home window and Receipts will be highlighted. With the **Receipts** icon highlighted, select **Report** from the home window menu bar. Point to Journal Entries, Receipts. Your screen will look like this:

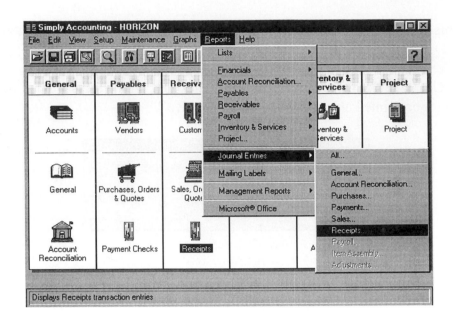

ACTION: Click **Receipts**. Your screen will look like this:

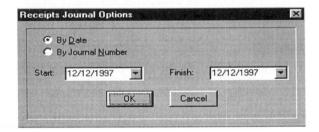

Explanation: A Receipts Journal Options dialog box, similar to the Sales Journal Options dialog box, will appear, asking you to define the information you want displayed.

ACTION: Select **By Date**; enter 1*2/1/1997* as the start date; leave the finish date set at 12/12/1997; then click the **OK** button. The following Receipts Journal Display will appear:

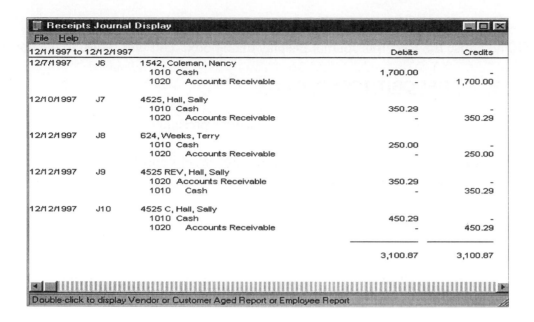

Explanation: Review the display for accuracy, verifying that journal entry dates, customer names, check numbers, account names and numbers, and amounts are correct. If you have posted an incorrect transaction, refer to the corrections made for Sally Hall on Invoice 521.

 ACTION: Select **File** from the Receipts Journal Display menu. Click **Print** to print the report; then compare your report to the one shown below:

Horizon Events/Your Name
Sales Journal 12/1/1997 to 12/12/1997

			Debits	**Credits**
12/7/1997	J6	1542, Coleman, Nancy		
		1010 Cash	1,700.00	-
		1020 Accounts Receivable	-	1,700.00
12/10/1997	J7	4525, Hall, Sally		
		1010 Cash	350.29	-
		1020 Accounts Receivable	-	350.29
12/12/1997	J8	624, Weeks, Terry		
		1010 Cash	250.00	-
		1020 Accounts Receivable	-	250.00
12/12/1997	J9	4525 REV, Hall, Sally		
		1020 Accounts Receivable	350.29	-
		1010 Cash	-	350.29
12/12/1997	J10	4525 C, Hall, Sally		
		1010 Cash	450.29	-
		1020 Accounts Receivable	-	450.29
			3,100.87	3,100.87

ACTION: Close the Receipts Journal Display dialog box. You will return to the home window.

ADDITIONAL BANK DEPOSIT TRANSACTION

Record the following bank deposit following the instructions presented earlier in the chapter.

Document 7 December 12—Deposit Check 624 from Terry Weeks and Check 4525 C from Sally Hall using Deposit Slip 7258 for both checks. (Remember to SAVE the transaction. DO NOT POST!)

 ACTION: Click the **Exit** button to end the current work session and return to your Windows desktop.

 ALTERNATIVE ACTION: You may continue with the tutorial without exiting from the program if you wish. The next steps are recorded under the same session date as the prior steps. Skip the next ACTION, and continue with the tutorial.

SALES JOURNAL—RECORDING CASH SALES AND ONE-TIME CUSTOMER SALES

It is not uncommon for service businesses to make cash sales of services or to provide services to a customer on a one-time basis. CA-Simply Accounting for Windows provides a short-cut method of accounting for these types of transactions through two special features in the Sales Journal - Sales Invoice dialog box: One-time customer option in the customer drop-down list, and the Sale with Payment option from the Transaction Type drop-down list.

The one-time customer option is used to enter an invoice for a customer who is not listed in the Receivables Ledger as a recurring customer. When you choose <One-time customer> from the customer list, you have the option of entering the customer's name and address in the box below or skipping this field. Once you leave the **Sold to** field, the program automatically selects the Sale with Payment option as the Transaction type and a **Paid by** field will appear. The word Cash will automatically appear in the **Paid by** field. You can accept Cash or click the drop-down list arrow next to Cash and select Check. If Check is selected, a check number box appears, and the check number is entered in this field (up to seven characters are allowed). Payment must be received from one-time customers at the time the sale is made. The program does not keep a permanent record of the one-time customer's name and address information, but it will include a description of this transaction in the General Ledger, General Journal, and Sales Journal.

The Sale with Payment box can be used independently of the one-time customer option in instances in which the business is receiving payment for services at the time they are rendered to an established customer of the business. This feature allows you to post the invoice and the payment received at the same time, without having to open Receipts to record the payment. After choosing the established customer from the customer list in the **Sold to** field, select Sale with Payment as the transaction type, then either accept the word Cash in the **Paid by** field or select Check from the drop-down list and enter the customer's check number in the **Check** field.

Horizon Events—Document 8   **Session Date: 12/12/1997**

> *Memo*
> Date: December 12, 1997
>
> Record 2 hours at $35.00 per hour for graphic design services provided to Kathy Quin,
> 239 SW Broadway, Portland, Oregon, 97205, and the receipt of her Check 6832 for $70.00.

 ACTION: Load CA-Simply Accounting for Windows; then open the data files for Horizon Events (A:\HORIZON\Horizon.asc). The program will respond with a request for the session date. The session date for the prior work session 12/12/1997 is offered as a default. Accept the date by clicking the **OK** button. The home window will appear as shown below:

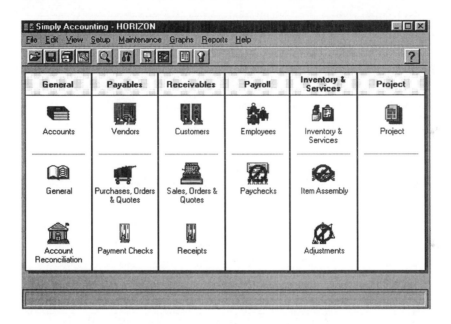

 ACTION: Open the Sales Journal - Sales Invoice dialog box by double-clicking the **Sales, Orders & Quotes** icon. Click the drop-down list arrow to the right of the **Sold to** field to display the customer list. Your screen will look like this:

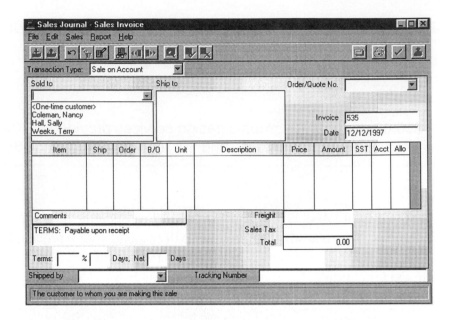

ACTION: Choose **<One-time customer>**; then press the TAB key. (Note: If your cursor does not move into the area below the customer list, click **One-time customer** in the **Sold to** box; cursor down one time to Coleman, Nancy; allow Nancy's address to display; cursor back up to One-time customer; and click in the box below One-time customer.) Your screen will look like this:

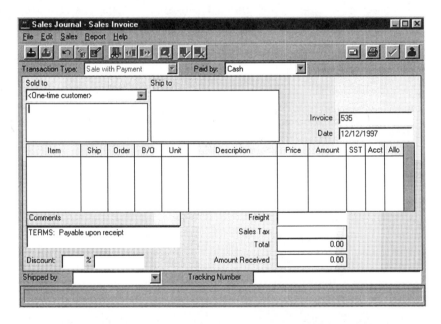

Explanation: A flashing insertion point should appear in the area below the customer list box.

ACTION: Enter *Kelly Quin*; then press the TAB key. Enter Kelly Quin's address, pressing the TAB key at the end of each line. Your screen will look like this:

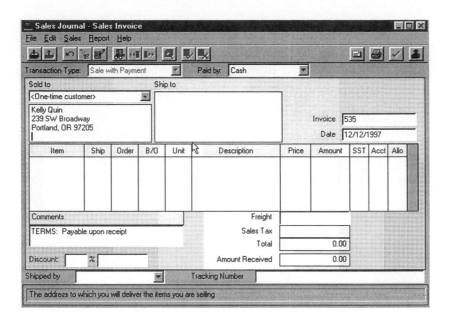

ACTION: Click the drop-down list arrow next to **Paid by**. Click **Check**. Click in the check box that appears and enter Kelly Quin's check number *6832*; press the TAB key. Your screen will appear as follows:

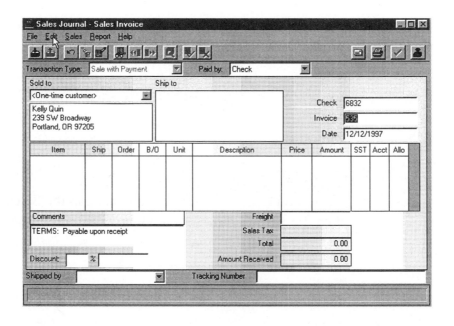

ACTION: Tab to or click in **Ship**. Enter *2*. Tab to or click in **Unit**. Enter the word *Hours*. Tab to or click in **Description**, and enter *Graphic Design Services*. Tab to or click in **Price**, and enter *35*. Tab to or click in **Acct**, and enter *4010*. Your Sales Journal - Sales Invoice should agree with the one shown below:

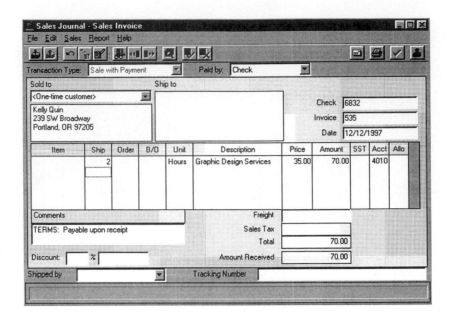

Explanation: This completes the information that you need to enter into the Sales Journal dialog box to record a one-time customer sale. Before you post this entry, you need to verify that the transaction data is correct by viewing the journal entry.

 ACTION: Select **Report** from the Sales Journal menu bar; then click **Display Sales Journal Entry**. Compare your display to the one shown below:

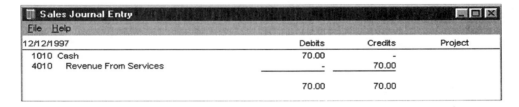

Explanation: The journal entry representing the data you have recorded in the Sales Journal Entry dialog box is displayed. The program has recorded the standard journal entry for a cash sale.

	Debit	**Credit**
Cash	xxx	
Revenue From Services		xxx

Review the journal entry for accuracy noting any errors. If you made an error, refer to the Editing Tips for Editing a Sales Journal Entry, which appears in a special box earlier in this chapter, for information on corrective action.

 ACTION: After verifying that the journal entry is correct, close the Sales Journal Entry dialog box. Choose **Print** from the Sales Journal File menu. Compare your invoice with the following:

Horizon Events/Your Name
9076 SE Main Street
Portland, Oregon 97214

535

12/12/1997

1 of 1

Kelly Quin
239 SW Broadway
Portland, OR 97205

2	Hours	Graphic Design Services	35.00	70.00

TERMS: Payable upon receipt   70.00

Explanation: Verify that the invoice is correct. If you detect an error, refer to the Editing Tips for Editing a Sales Journal Entry for information on corrective action.

 ACTION: After a correct invoice has been printed, click the **Post** button to post the transaction. A blank Sales Journal dialog box is displayed, ready for additional Sales Journal transactions to be recorded.

Additional Cash Sales and One-time Customer Transactions

Record the following additional transactions:

Document 9 December 12—Received Check 7821 in the amount of $50.00 from one-time customer Mary Wilson (no address given) for 1 hour of event planning services. Issued automatic Invoice 536. Print the invoice.

Document 10 December 12—Received $35.00 in cash from established customer Nancy Coleman for 1 hour of graphic design services. Issued automatic Invoice 537. Print the invoice.

Compare your invoices to the ones shown below:

Horizon Events/Your Name
9076 SE Main Street
Portland, Oregon 97214

536

12/12/1997

1 of 1

Mary Wilson

| | 1 | Hour | Event Planning Services | 50.00 | 50.00 |

TERMS: Payable upon receipt   50.00

Horizon Events/Your Name
9076 SE Main Street
Portland, Oregon 97214

537

12/12/1997

1 of 1

Coleman, Nancy   Coleman, Nancy
5600 SE 82nd Street   5600 SE 82nd Street
Portland, Oregon 97214   Portland, Oregon 97214

| | 1 | Hour | Graphic Design Services | 35.00 | 35.00 |

TERMS: Payable upon receipt   35.00

Note: If you detect an error after printing and posting an invoice, refer to the steps illustrated for correcting/adjusting Terry Weeks' invoice earlier in the chapter.

 ACTION: After you have printed the invoices and posted the transaction data associated with Documents 9 and 10, close the Sales Journal - Sales Invoice dialog box. With the Sales, Orders & Quotes icon highlighted, choose **Journal Entries, Sales** from the home window Report menu. Your screen will look like this:

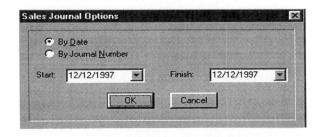

Explanation: The Sales Journal Options dialog box will appear, asking you to define the information you want displayed.

 ACTION: Select **By Date**; enter *12/1/1997* as the start date; leave the finish date set at 12/12/1997; click the **OK** button. The following Sales Journal Display will appear on your screen:

```
 Sales Journal Display
File  Help
12/1/1997 to 12/12/1997                                    Debits        Credits
12/3/1997      J1      532, Hall, Sally
                       1020  Accounts Receivable          900.00            -
                       4010     Revenue From Services        -          900.00

12/5/1997      J2      533, Coleman, Nancy
                       1020  Accounts Receivable          500.00            -
                       4010     Revenue From Services        -          500.00

12/5/1997      J3      534, Weeks, Terry
                       1020  Accounts Receivable          900.00            -
                       4010     Revenue From Services        -          900.00

12/5/1997      J4      ADJ534, Reversing J3. Correction is J5.
                       4010  Revenue From Services        900.00            -
                       1020     Accounts Receivable          -          900.00

12/5/1997      J5      534, Weeks, Terry
                       1020  Accounts Receivable        1,000.00           -
                       4010     Revenue From Services        -        1,000.00

12/12/1997     J11     535, 6832, Kelly Quin
                       1010  Cash                          70.00           -
                       4010     Revenue From Services        -           70.00

12/12/1997     J12     536, 7821, Mary Wilson
                       1010  Cash                          50.00           -
                       4010     Revenue From Services        -           50.00

12/12/1997     J13     537, Cash, Coleman, Nancy
                       1010  Cash                          35.00           -
                       4010     Revenue From Services        -           35.00
                                                        _____      _____
                                                        4,355.00       4,355.00
```

Explanation: Review the display for accuracy, verifying that journal entry dates, customer names, invoice numbers, account names and numbers, and amounts are correct. Use the scroll bar to advance through the display. If you have posted an incorrect transaction, see the previous invoice adjustment for Terry Weeks.

 ACTION: Print the report by choosing **Print** from the Sales Journal Display File menu. Compare your report to the one shown below:

Horizon Events/Your Name
Sales Journal 12/1/1997 to 12/12/1997

				Debits	Credits
12/3/1997	J1	532, Hall, Sally			
		1020	Accounts Receivable	900.00	-
		4010	Revenue From Services	-	900.00
12/5/1997	J2	533, Coleman, Nancy			
		1020	Accounts Receivable	500.00	-
		4010	Revenue From Services	-	500.00
12/5/1997	J3	534, Weeks, Terry			
		1020	Accounts Receivable	900.00	-
		4010	Revenue From Services	-	900.00
12/5/1997	J4	ADJ534, Reversing J3. Correction is J5			
		4010	Revenue From Services	900.00	-
		1020	Accounts Receivable	-	900.00
12/5/1997	J5	534, Weeks, Terry			
		1020	Accounts Receivable	1,000.00	-
		4010	Revenue From Services	-	1,000.00
12/12/1997	J11	535, 6832, Kelly Quin			
		1010	Cash	70.00	-
		4010	Revenue From Services	-	70.00
12/12/1997	J12	536, 7821, Mary Wilson			
		1010	Cash	50.00	-
		4010	Revenue From Services	-	50.00
12/12/1997	J13	537, Cash, Coleman, Nancy			
		1010	Cash	35.00	-
		4010	Revenue From Services	-	35.00
					4,355.00	4,355.00

Explanation: If you detect an error, see the invoice adjustment for Terry Weeks earlier in the chapter.

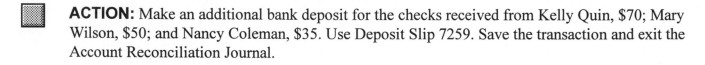   **ACTION:** Close the Sales Journal Display window.

ADDITIONAL BANK DEPOSIT TRANSACTION

ACTION: Make an additional bank deposit for the checks received from Kelly Quin, $70; Mary Wilson, $50; and Nancy Coleman, $35. Use Deposit Slip 7259. Save the transaction and exit the Account Reconciliation Journal.

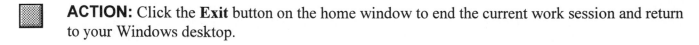   **ACTION:** Click the **Exit** button on the home window to end the current work session and return to your Windows desktop.

ALTERNATIVE ACTION: You may continue with the tutorial without exiting from the program if you wish. The next steps are recorded under the same session date as the prior steps. Skip the next ACTION; then continue with the tutorial.

RECEIVABLES LEDGER—MAINTAINING CUSTOMER RECORDS

In the Receivables Column, transactions can be entered only through the Journals components of the program—Sales, Orders & Quotes, and Receipts. The Receivables Ledger component—Customers—is used to maintain customer records. Each record contains the customer's address, amount owed, and the total sales to that customer for the prior year and the current year. You can create, modify, or remove customer records through the Receivables Ledger dialog box.

Creating a Customer Record

Seth Hunter has had a preliminary discussion with a new client and would like to add the client to his list of customers.

Horizon Events—Document 11   **Session Date: 12/12/1997**

Memo
Date: December 12, 1997

Add the following new customer to the customer list:

Roger Takamura
8519 SE 19th Street
Portland, Oregon 97214
503-231-4312

 ACTION: Load CA-Simply Accounting for Windows; open the data files for Horizon Events (A:\HORIZON\Horizon.asc); then leave the session date set at 12/12/1997. Open the Receivables Ledger by double-clicking **Customers**. Your screen will look like this:

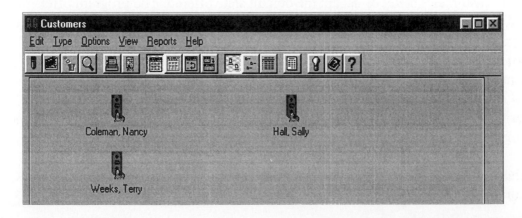

Explanation: The names of all of Horizon Events' customers are displayed.

ACTION: Click the **Create** button on the Customers toolbar. Your screen will look like this:

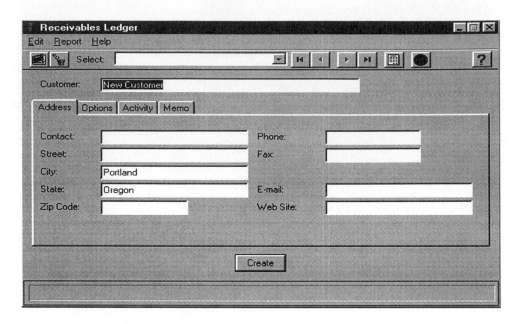

Explanation: A blank Receivables Ledger dialog box is presented with tabs for Address, Options, Activity, and Memo. Fields are defined as follows:

Address Tab
Customer: Enter the customer's name, up to 35 characters.

Contact: Enter the name of the person the business usually deals with when calling or corresponding with this customer.

Street: Enter the customer's street address.

City: Enter the customer's city, up to 18 characters, or accept the default city offered. The program offers the city portion of the company's address as a default under the assumption that a company is most likely to do business with customers residing in the same city.

State: Enter the customer's state, or accept the default state offered. The program offers the state portion of the company's address as a default under the assumption that a company is most likely to do business with customers residing in the same state.

Zip Code: Enter the customer's zip code.

Phone: Enter the customer's phone number, including area code if you wish. You do not need to type parentheses or hyphens; the program fills these in when you move to another field.

Fax: Enter the customer's fax number, including area code if you wish. You do not need to type parentheses or hyphens; the program fills these in when you move to another field.

E-mail: Enter the customer's e-mail address. The e-mail address may be used to send invoices, and so forth to the customer by e-mail.

Web Site: Enter the customer's Web site. When in the Customers window, choose **Web Site** from the Edit menu or toolbar to go to the Web site associated with this customer record.

Options Tab

Early Payment Terms: Complete this information if you allow the customer to take a discount for early payment.

Clear Invoices When Paid: Check this box if you want invoices to be removed from the Receivables Ledger immediately after they are fully paid. Leave this box unchecked if you want to retain invoices on file after they are fully paid. **For all sample companies in this text, this box will remained unchecked so that paid invoices will appear on customer statements, in the Customer Aged Report, and in the Receipts Journal**. This technique will produce a complete audit trail for all Receivables transactions, facilitating the detection and correction of any errors posted in the Sales and Receipts Journals.

Print Statements for this Customer: Check this box to print statements for customers. For businesses that do not send printed statements to customers, this box should not be checked.

Print or E-mail Forms for this Customer: Click the drop-down list arrow to select whether to print or to e-mail forms for this customer.

Activity Tab

Balance Owing: The program fills in this amount; you cannot change it. It is the difference between the total amount sold to and the total payments received from this customer. This field is updated every time a sale is recorded or a payment is received.

YTD Sales (Year-to-Date Sales): This field is used when a company is first converting to CA-Simply Accounting for Windows after the start of its fiscal year and the Receivables Ledger of the program is in the Not Ready mode. The total amount of sales made to this customer prior to the Conversion date is entered, and the program updates it every time a new sale is made after the earliest transaction date. Once the Receivables Ledger of the program is in the Ready mode, you cannot modify the amount listed in this field.

Last Year's Sales: This field is used when a company is first converting to CA-Simply Accounting for Windows and the Receivables Ledger of the program is in the Not Ready mode. The total amount of sales made to this customer in the last fiscal year may be entered for reference purposes. Once the Receivables Ledger of the program is in the Ready mode, you cannot modify the amount listed in this field.

Credit Limit: Enter a credit limit for this customer. The program warns you before you post a sale that will exceed this limit. If there is no credit limit, leave this field blank.

Memo Tab

Memo: Enter any memo you would like to appear in the To-Do Lists.

To-Do Date: If the reminder is date sensitive, type a due date in the To-Do Date field.

 ACTION: Enter the available information about the new customer, Roger Takamura, onto the Receivables Ledger Address tab. Your screen will look like this:

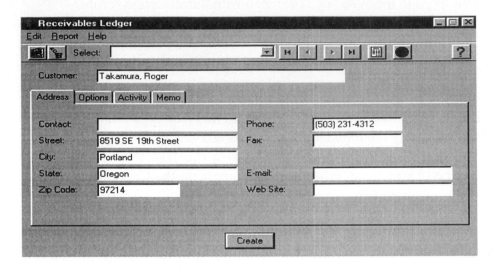

Explanation: Verify that all of the information is correct. If you have made an error, use the following editing techniques to correct the error:

Editing Tips
Editing a Receivables Ledger Record

Move to the field that contains the error by either pressing the TAB key to move forward through each field or press the SHIFT and TAB keys together to move to a previous field. This will highlight the selected field information so that you can change it. Alternatively, you can use the mouse to point to a field and drag through the incorrect information to highlight it.

Type the correct information; then press the TAB key to enter it.

Click on the check boxes to select or deselect as required.

To discard a record and start over, choose Undo Changes from Edit on the Receivables Ledger menu bar; then click the **Yes** button in response to the question "Are you sure you want to undo changes to this ledger page?" Alternatively, double-click the control menu box; then click the **No** button in response to the question "Do you still want to create this ledger page?"

It is IMPORTANT TO NOTE that the only way to edit a Receivables Ledger record after it is created is to either modify the record or remove it and create a new Receivables Ledger record.

 ACTION: When the ledger page is correct, click the **Create** button. Your screen will look like this:

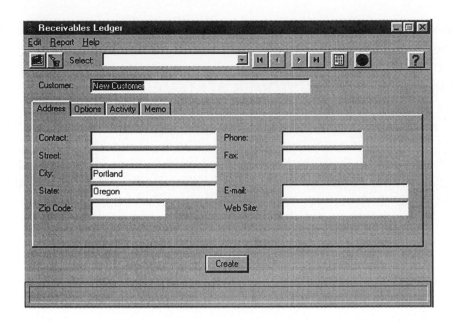

Explanation: The program has added the new customer to Horizon Events' records and has cleared the Receivables Ledger dialog box in preparation for creating another customer record.

Modifying a Customer Record

If you made an error in a customer record or need to change some information about a customer, choose **Find** from the Receivables Ledger Edit menu; then choose the customer from the list presented. Make corrections as necessary using the Editing Tips for Editing a Receivables Ledger Record. To accept the changes, either use the scroll bar to move to another ledger page or close the dialog box by clicking the **Exit** button. Note that only descriptive information, **Customer**, **Contact**, **Street**, **City**, **State**, **Zip Code**, **Phone**, **Fax**, **E-mail**, **Web Site**, and **Credit Limit** text boxes and the **Clear Invoices When Paid** and **Print Statements for this Customer** check boxes can be modified. **Balance Owing**, **YTD Sales**, and **Last Year's Sales** are under program control once the Receivables Ledger is in the Ready mode.

Removing a Customer Record

You cannot remove a customer record unless its outstanding balance is zero. To remove a customer, choose **Find** from the Receivables Ledger Edit menu; then choose the customer from the list presented. Choose **Remove** from the Receivables Ledger Edit menu. The program will ask you if you are sure you want to remove the customer record. Choose **Yes** to remove it; then close the dialog box by clicking the **Exit** button.

Additional Receivables Ledger Maintenance Items

Enter the following additional maintenance items:

Document 12 December 12—Create a new Receivables Ledger record for the Sunnyside Neighborhood Association, 3421 SE Salmon, Portland, Oregon 97214; Telephone: 503-280-6226, Fax: 503-280-2626; Contact: Cindy Galbraith.

Document 13 December 12—Modify Nancy Coleman's address. She has moved to 4301 NE Tillamook Street, Portland, Oregon 97213; new phone: 503-288-0460.

RECEIVABLES REPORTS AND CUSTOMER STATEMENTS

A variety of Receivables-related reports are available in CA-Simply Accounting for Windows. The procedures required to generate invoices and to print and display Sales Journal and Receipts Journal reports were demonstrated throughout this chapter. In addition to these reports, the program can print or display a Customer List and a Customer Aged report. Mailing labels and customer statements can be printed, but not displayed. However, you can display similar information in a Customer Aged Detail report and in a Customer List. Use the scroll bars at the bottom or right side of a displayed report to view reports that contain more text than can be displayed at one time.

Horizon Events—Document 14   **Session Date: 12/12/1997**

> *Memo*
> Date: December 12, 1997
>
> Prepare and print the following: Customer List, Customer Aged Detail report, a statement for Nancy Coleman, mailing labels, and a Trial Balance.

ACTION: Close the Receivables Ledger; then select Report from the Customers window menu bar. Your screen will look like this:

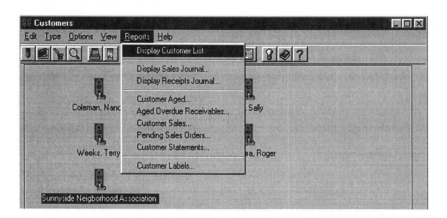

ACTION: Choose **Display Customer List**. Your screen will look like this:

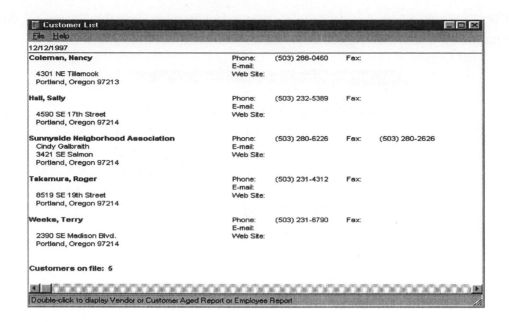

![ACTION icon] **ACTION:** Choose **Print** from the Customer List File menu. Compare your report to the one shown below:

Horizon Events/Your Name
Customer List 12/12/1997

Coleman, Nancy

	Phone: (503) 288-0460	Fax:
4301 NE Tillamook Street	E-mail:	
Portland, Oregon 97213	Web Site:	

Hall, Sally

	Phone: (503) 232-5389	Fax:
4590 SE 17th Street	E-mail:	
Portland, Oregon 97214	Web Site:	

Sunnyside Neighborhood Association

Cindy Galbraith	Phone: (503) 280-6226	Fax: (503) 280-2626
3421 SE Salmon	E-mail:	
Portland, Oregon 97214	Web Site:	

Takamura, Roger

	Phone: (503) 231-4312	Fax:
8519 SE 19th Street	E-mail:	
Portland, Oregon 97214	Web Site:	

Weeks, Terry

	Phone: (503) 231-6790	Fax:
2390 SE Madison Blvd.	E-mail:	
Portland, Oregon 97214	Web Site:	

Customers on file: 5

ACTION: Close the Customer List dialog box; select **Report** from the Customers window menu bar; then choose **Customer Aged**. Your screen will look like this:

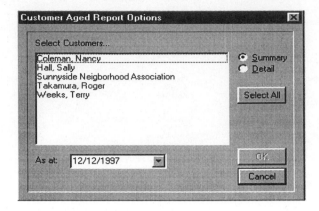

Explanation: The Customer Aged dialog box presents several options. A Customer Aged report lists all outstanding invoices and payments for either all customers or for the individual customers you specify. To display total, current, and aged amounts that customers owe, select **Summary**. To display all outstanding invoices and payments for the customers, select **Detail**.

 ACTION: Click **Detail**, **Select All**, and **OK**. Your screen will look like this:

Customer Aged Detail							
File Help							
As at 12/12/1997			Total	Current	31 to 60	61 to 90	91+
Coleman, Nancy							
526	11/24/1997	Invoice	1,700.00	1,700.00	-	-	-
1542	12/7/1997	Payment	-1,700.00	-1,700.00	-	-	-
530	11/29/1997	Invoice	425.00	425.00	-	-	-
533	12/5/1997	Invoice	500.00	500.00	-	-	-
537	12/12/1997	Invoice	35.00	35.00	-	-	-
Cash	12/12/1997	Payment	-35.00	-35.00	-	-	-
			925.00	925.00	-	-	-
Hall, Sally							
521	11/21/1997	Invoice	450.29	450.29	-	-	-
4525	12/10/1997	Payment	-350.29	-350.29	-	-	-
4525 REV	12/12/1997	Payment	350.29	350.29	-	-	-
4525 C	12/12/1997	Payment	-450.29	-450.29	-	-	-
532	12/3/1997	Invoice	900.00	900.00	-	-	-
			900.00	900.00	-	-	-
Weeks, Terry							
531	11/29/1997	Invoice	580.00	580.00	-	-	-
624	12/12/1997	Payment	-250.00	-250.00	-	-	-
534	12/5/1997	Invoice	1,000.00	1,000.00	-	-	-
			1,330.00	1,330.00	-	-	-
			3,155.00	3,155.00	-	-	-

ACTION: Choose **Print** from the Customer Aged Detail File menu. Compare your report to the one shown below:

Horizon Events/Your Name
Customer Aged Detail As at 12/12/1997

			Total	Current	31 to 60	61 to 90	91+
Coleman, Nancy							
526	11/24/1997	Invoice	1,700.00	1,700.00	-	-	-
1542	12/7/1997	Payment	-1,700.00	-1,700.00	-	-	-
530	11/29/1997	Invoice	425.00	425.00	-	-	-
533	12/5/1997	Invoice	500.00	500.00	-	-	-
537	12/12/1997	Invoice	35.00	35.00	-	-	-
Cash	12/12/1997	Payment	-35.00	-35.00	-	-	-
			925.00	925.00	-	-	-
Hall, Sally							
521	11/21/1997	Invoice	450.29	450.29	-	-	-
4525	12/10/1997	Payment	-350.29	-350.29	-	-	-
4525REV	12/10/1997	Payment	350.29	350.29	-	-	-
4525C	12/10/1997	Payment	-450.29	-450.29	-	-	-
532	12/3/1997	Invoice	900.00	900.00	-	-	-
			900.00	900.00	-	-	-
Weeks, Terry							
531	11/29/1997	Invoice	580.00	580.00	-	-	-
624	12/12/1997	Payment	-250.00	-250.00	-	-	-
534	12/5/1997	Invoice	1,000.00	1,000.00	-	-	-
			1,330.00	1,330.00	-	-	-
			3,155.00	3,155.00	-	-	-

ACTION: Close the Customer Aged Detail dialog box; select **Report** from the Customers window menu bar; then choose **Customer Statements**. Your screen will look like this:

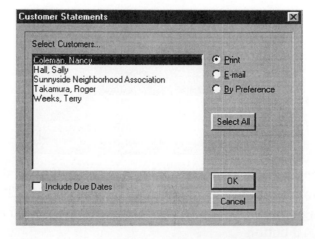

Explanation: The Print Customer Statements dialog box presents several options. Customer statements can be printed or e-mailed for either all customers or for the individual customers you specify. To print or e-mail statements for individual customers, highlight the appropriate customer names. To print statements for all customers, click the **Select All** button.

 ACTION: Highlight Nancy Coleman's name; then click the **OK** button. Compare your statement to the one shown below:

Horizon Events/Your Name
9076 SE Main Street
Portland, Oregon 97214

12/12/1997

    Coleman, Nancy   Coleman, Nancy
    4301 NE Tillamook Street
    Portland, Oregon 97213

12/12/97

11/24/1997	526	Invoice	1,700.00			
12/7/1997	1542	Payment	-1,700.00			
				0.00	526	0.00
11/29/1997	530	Invoice		425.00	530	425.00
12/5/1997	533	Invoice		500.00	533	500.00
12/12/1997	537	Invoice	35.00			
12/12/1997	Cash	Payment	-35.00			
				0.00	537	0.00

Current	31-60	Over 60		
925.00	0.00	0.00	925.00	925.00

 ACTION: Choose **Mailing Labels** from the Customers window Report menu. Click **Select All**. Your screen will look like this:

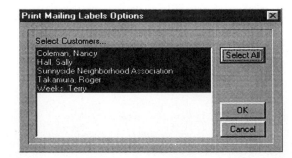

Explanation: The Print Mailing Labels Option dialog box presents several options. Mailing labels can be printed either for all customers or for the individual customers you specify. To print mailing labels for individual customers, highlight the appropriate customer names. To print mailing labels for all customers, click the **Select All** button.

ACTION: With all the customer names selected, click the **OK** button. Compare your mailing labels with the ones shown below:

Coleman, Nancy
4301 NE Tillamook Street
Portland, Oregon 97213

Hall, Sally
4590 SE 17th Street
Portland, Oregon 97214

Sunnyside Neighborhood Association
Cindy Galbraith
3421 SE Salmon
Portland, Oregon 97214

Takamura, Roger
8519 SE 19th Street
Portland, Oregon 97214

Weeks, Terry
2390 SE Madison Blvd.
Portland, Oregon 97214

 ACTION: Close the Customer window. Click the **Reports** menu on the home window. Point to Financials and Trial Balance. Your screen will look like this:

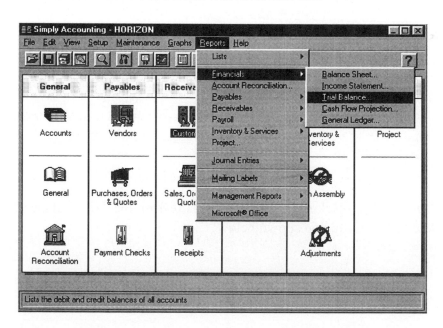

 ACTION: Click **Trial Balance**. Your screen will show the following:

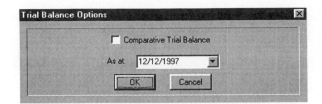

Explanation: The program is requesting the as at date for the Trial Balance. The date must be between the earliest transaction date and the session date inclusive. Additional default date options are available by clicking the drop-down list arrow to the right of the **As at** date field. You can override the default option by specifying the as at date.

 ACTION: Accept the default date of 12/12/1997 for the Trial Balance by clicking the **OK** button. Your screen will look like this:

Trial Balance

File   Help

As At 12/12/1997		Debits	Credits
1010	Cash	7,679.65	-
1020	Accounts Receivable	3,155.00	-
1030	Prepaid Insurance	375.00	-
1040	Office Supplies	2,563.00	-
1050	Software	4,695.00	-
1060	Acc. Dep.- Software	-	2,999.62
1080	Computer Equipment	15,145.00	-
1090	Acc. Dep.- Computer Equip.	-	8,944.43
2010	Accounts Payable	-	1,886.70
3010	Seth Hunter, Capital	-	13,636.18
3020	Seth Hunter, Drawing	15,400.00	-
4010	Revenue From Services	-	39,365.61
4020	Interest Income	-	0.00
5010	Advertising Expense	1,575.00	-
5020	Utilities Expense	525.00	-
5030	Rent Expense	3,600.00	-
5040	Office Supplies Expense	2,013.00	-
5050	Depreciation Exp.-Software	1,434.62	-
5060	Depreciation Exp.-Comp. Eq	4,277.77	-
5070	Insurance Expense	687.50	-
5080	Professional Services Exp.	2,545.00	-
5090	Bank Charges	0.00	-
5150	Misc. Expense	1,162.00	-
		66,832.54	66,832.54

 ACTION: Print the Trial Balance by choosing **Print** from the Trial Balance File menu. Compare your Trial Balance with the one shown below:

Horizon Events/Your Name
Trial Balance As At 12/12/1997

		Debits	Credits
1010	Cash	7,679.65	-
1020	Accounts Receivable	3,155.00	-
1030	Prepaid Insurance	375.00	-
1040	Office Supplies	2,563.00	-
1050	Software	4,695.00	-
1060	Acc. Dep.- Software	-	2,999.62
1080	Computer Equipment	15,145.00	-
1090	Acc. Dep.- Computer Equip.	-	8,944.43
2010	Accounts Payable	-	1,886.70
3010	Seth Hunter, Capital	-	13,636.18
3020	Seth Hunter, Drawing	15,400.00	-
4010	Revenue From Services	-	39,365.61
4020	Interest Income	-	0.00
5010	Advertising Expense	1,575.00	-
5020	Utilities Expense	525.00	-
5030	Rent Expense	3,600.00	-
5040	Office Supplies Expense	2,013.00	-
5050	Depreciation Exp.-Software	1,434.62	-
5060	Depreciation Exp.-Comp. Eq	4,277.77	-
5070	Insurance Expense	687.50	-
5080	Professional Services Exp.	2,545.00	-
5090	Bank Charges	0.00	-
5150	Misc. Expense	1,162.00	-
		66,832.54	66,832.54

ACTION: Close the Trial Balance window; back up your work for the chapter by clicking the **File** menu on the home window menu bar; point to Backup. Your screen will appear as follows:

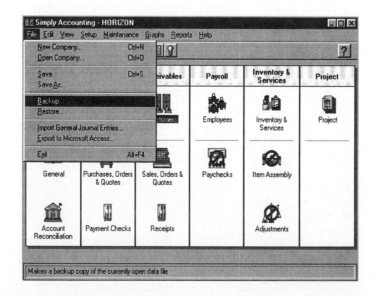

ACTION: Click **Backup**. Highlight the information shown in the Backup File Name dialog box. Change the information for the Backup File Name to match the following screen:

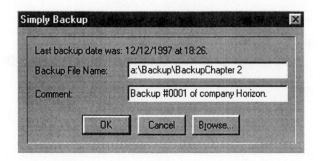

 ACTION: Click **OK** to back up your data. Once the backup of the company data files is complete, click the **Exit** button on the home window to end the current work session and return to your Windows desktop.

SUMMARY

This chapter has explored the Receivables components of CA-Simply Accounting for Windows as they would typically be used by a service business. Use of the Sales, Orders & Quotes (Sales Journal), Receipts (Receipts Journal), and the Customers (Receivables Ledger) to record cash and credit sales, cash receipts, and to maintain customer records has been explained in detail. In addition, the procedures used to correct errors; to display and print a Sales Journal, Receipts Journal, invoice, Customer List, Customer Aged report, mailing labels, customer statement, and Trial Balance; and to back up data files have been demonstrated. By examining the methods used to record Receivables-related transactions, various integration/linking features of CA-Simply Accounting for Windows were illustrated.

QUESTIONS

QUESTIONS ABOUT THE SOFTWARE

1. In CA-Simply Accounting for Windows all Receivables functions are fully integrated with and linked to the General Ledger. Explain this statement and give an example.

2. Define the following terms:
   Session date:
   Fiscal start date:
   Fiscal end date:
   Earliest transaction date:

3. Customer Aged reports can be prepared on a summary or detail basis. How does a summary report differ from a detail report?

4. Sales Journal and Receipts Journal reports can be prepared by posting date or by journal entry number. How does a posting date report differ from a journal entry number report?

QUESTIONS ABOUT DAILY OPERATIONS

5. A customer has called to inquire about his bill. He has wants to know how much he owes the business. How would you use the CA-Simply Accounting for Windows program to answer his question?

6. A former customer has called to ask about the total amount she paid to the business last year. How would you use the CA-Simply Accounting for Windows program to answer her question?

7. You would like to know the total current balance in Accounts Receivable. How would you use the CA-Simply Accounting for Windows program to answer your question?

8. Why is it important for a business to make frequent backup copies of a company's data files?

EXPLORING ALTERNATIVE SOFTWARE TECHNIQUES

9. Why might it be to a business's advantage to create Receivables Ledger records for all customers and not use the CA-Simply Accounting for Windows one-time customer option?

10. The CA-Simply Accounting for Windows program can adapt its Inventory components to meet the needs of a service industry. For example, a service business that charges a consistent rate for a particular service can list that service as an inventory item. When the sale of the service is recorded in the Sales Journal - Sales Invoice, a unit (such as hours) is entered; then the program computes the total cost by multiplying the quantity indicated in the **Shipped** column times the amount indicated in the **Price** column to determine the amount due. Adjusted rates and nonstandard services can continue to be recorded using the methods you learned in this chapter. Discuss the value of this approach for use by Seth Hunter in his Horizon Events business.

TRANSMITTAL

Horizon Events   **Name:**_____
Chapter 2

Attach the following documents and reports:

1. Invoice 532
2. Invoice 533
3. Invoice 534
4. Corrected Invoice 534
5. Sales Journal 12/1/1997 to 12/5/1997
6. Payment receipt for Invoice 526
7. Payment receipt for Invoice 521
8. Payment receipt for Invoice 531
9. Corrected payment receipt for Invoice 521
10. Receipts Journal 12/2/1997 to 12/12/1997
11. Invoice 535
12. Invoice 536
13. Invoice 537
14. Sales Journal 12/1/1997 to 12/12/1997
15. Customer List 12/12/1997
16. Customer Aged Detail As at 12/12/1997
17. Customer statement: Nancy Coleman
18. Mailing labels
19. Trial Balance As at 12/12/1997

EXERCISE—Harmony Piano Works

COMPANY PROFILE

Harmony Piano Works is owned and operated by Sara Montage as a sole proprietorship in Portland, Oregon. Services include piano tuning, refinishing, and repairs. Sara maintains her own accounting records using CA-Simply Accounting for Windows. As a service business, she uses the General, Receivables, and Payables components of the program. Each job Sara accepts is individual in nature and is bid and charged separately; payment is due upon receipt of an invoice. Sara uses the CA-Simply Accounting for Windows automatic invoice, check, and customer statement preparation features.

1. Load CA-Simply Accounting for Windows; open the data files for Harmony Piano Works (A:\HARMONY\Harmony.acs). Add your actual name to the company name. Record the following transactions under the session date of 12/5/1997. Print all invoices and receipts as they are recorded.

   December 1—Issue Invoice 292 to Ron Johnson in the amount of $275.00 for piano tuning.

   December 3—Issue Invoice 293 to a new customer in the amount of $180.00 for a keyboard repair.

New Customer:	Engles, Joe
	1472 SW 14th Avenue
	Portland, Oregon 97204
	503-221-6824

   December 4—Record the receipt of Check 567 in the amount of $800.00 from Ron Johnson in payment of Invoice 289.

   December 5—Issue Invoice 294 to Carol Rodgers in the amount of $745.00 for piano repairs.

   December 5—Record the receipt of Check 1476 in the amount of $500.00 from Pam Grayson in partial payment of Invoice 291.

   December 5—Deposit all checks received into the Cash account.

2. Advance the **Session** date to 12/12/1997; then record the following transactions.

   December 7—Issue Invoice 295 to Don Otten, a one-time customer, for a sale with payment in the amount of $215.00. Record his Check 768 for $215.00 as payment for refinishing work.

   December 8—Record the receipt of Check 8768 in the amount of $180.00 from Joe Engles in payment of Invoice 293.

   December 9—Record the receipt of Check 572 from Ron Johnson in the amount of $175.00 in partial payment of Invoice 292.

   December 10—Issue Invoice 296 to Pam Grayson in the amount of $115.00 for a keyboard repair.

December 11—Issue Invoice 297 to Joe Engles in the amount of $145.00 for piano repair work.

December 11—Adjust Invoice 297 to Joe Engles. The amount for the piano repair work should have been $165.00.

December 12—Deposit all checks received from December 6 through December 12.

3. Print the following reports:

   1. Sales Journal (By posting date) 12/1/1997 to 12/12/9197
   2. Receipts Journal (By posting date) 12/1/1997 to 12/12/1997
   3. Customer Aged report (Select All, Detail) As at 12/12/1997
   4. Trial Balance As at 12/12/1997

4. Make a backup copy of Harmony Piano Works' data files. Exit from the program.

5. Complete the Harmony Piano Works Transmittal.

TRANSMITTAL

Harmony Piano Works   **Name:**_____
Chapter 2

A.   Attach the following documents and reports:

 1. Invoice 292
 2. Invoice 293
 3. Payment receipt for Invoice 289
 4. Invoice 294
 5. Payment receipt for Invoice 291
 6. Invoice 295
 7. Payment receipt for Invoice 293
 8. Payment receipt for Invoice 292
 9. Invoice 296
10. Invoice 297
11. Corrected Invoice 297
12. Sales Journal 12/1/1997 to 12/12/1997
13. Receipts Journal 12/1/1997 to 12/12/1997
14. Customer Aged report As at 12/12/1997
15. Trial Balance As at 12/12/1997

B.   Refer to your reports to list the amounts requested below:

1. How much does Joe Engles owe Harmony Piano Works on 12/12/1997? $_____

2. How much does Pam Grayson owe Harmony Piano Works on 12/12/1997? $_____

3. What is the balance of the Cash account on 12/12/1997? $_____

4. What is the balance of the Revenue From Services account on 12/12/1997? $_____

5. What is the balance of the Accounts Receivable account on 12/12/1997? $_____

SERVICE BUSINESSES— PAYABLES

SERVICE BUSINESSES—
PAYABLES

LEARNING OBJECTIVES

After studying this chapter, you will be able to:
- Open the Purchases and Payments Journals
- Open the Payables Ledger
- Enter purchases transactions
- Enter payment transactions
- Enter partial payments made to vendors
- Enter cash purchases
- Review and edit Purchases and Payments Journal transactions
- Post transactions in the Purchases and Payments Journals
- Create, modify, and remove vendor records using the Payables Ledger
- Display and print reports from the Purchases and Payments Journals
- Display and print a Vendor List, Vendor Aged Report, and mailing labels
- Display and print a Trial Balance
- Make a backup of a company data file
- Observe and understand Payables-related integration accounts

In this chapter, you will continue working with the Horizon Events company files. The features of the Payables components of CA-Simply Accounting for Windows will be discussed in detail.

ACCOUNTING FOR PAYABLES

Three components of CA-Simply Accounting for Windows are used to account for Payables transactions and to maintain vendor records: Purchases, Orders & Quotes (Purchases Journal); Payment Checks (Payments Journal); and Vendors (Payables Ledger). Purchases on account and cash purchases are recorded in the Purchases Journal, cash payments to credit vendors are recorded in the Payments Journal, and vendor records (name, address, phone number, etc.) and subsidiary ledger information are maintained in the Payables Ledger. A variety of reports is available through the use of each component. All Payables functions in CA-Simply Accounting for Windows are fully integrated with and linked to the General Ledger. For example, when a purchase on account is recorded in the Purchases Journal the program automatically records the entry in the General Journal, posts the related accounts in the General Ledger, and updates the vendor's accounts payable subsidiary ledger in the Payables Ledger. Consequently, once a Payables-related transaction is posted, its effect on the overall financial condition of the company is reflected immediately and automatically throughout the company's financial records.

HORIZON EVENTS TUTORIAL

The following tutorial is a step-by-step guide to recording routine transactions for Horizon Events within the Payables components of CA-Simply Accounting for Windows. The procedures required to record transactions using the Receivables components were discussed in Chapter 2. The procedures required to record adjusting entries, prepare financial statements, and close the accounting records at the end of the fiscal year are functions of the General components and will be discussed in Chapter 4. The Horizon Events Tutorial is continued in Chapters 3 and 4 to give you a comprehensive overview of how CA-Simply Accounting for Windows can be used to maintain the accounting records for a service business.

PURCHASES JOURNAL—RECORDING PURCHASES ON ACCOUNT

Purchases on account are recorded in the Purchases Journal.

Horizon Events—Document 15   **Session Date: 12/19/1997**

Portland Weekly   Invoice # ____6842____
8900 SE Ladd Blvd.   To: Horizon Events
Portland, Oregon 97214   9076 SE Main Street
Phone: 232-5612 FAX: 232-5688   Portland, Oregon 97214

Date	Description	Amount
12/14/1997	Advertising	$410.00
	TOTAL	$410.00

 ACTION: Load CA-Simply Accounting for Windows; open the data files for Horizon Events (A:\HORIZON\Horizon.asc); then advance the session date to 12/19/1997. The Horizon Events home window will appear as shown below:

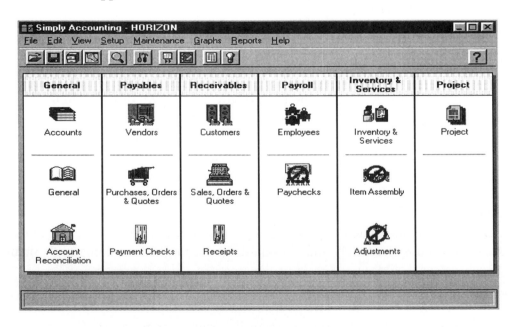

 ACTION: Open the Purchases Journal - Purchase Invoice dialog box by double-clicking the **Purchases, Orders & Quotes** icon. Your screen will look like this:

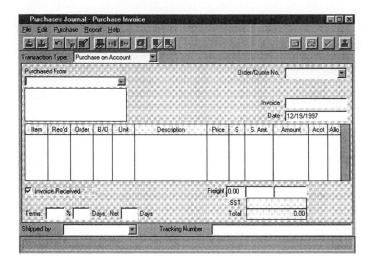

Explanation: The Purchases Journal - Purchase Invoice dialog box is used to record purchases on account, cash purchases, and certain types of correcting entries for transactions posted in error.

ACTION: Click the drop-down list arrow to the right of the **Purchased from** field to display Horizon Events' vendor list. Your screen will look like this:

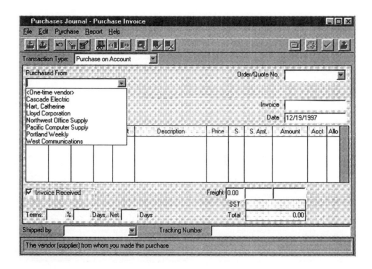

Explanation: A drop-down list box displaying an alphabetical list of Horizon Events' vendors will appear along with the <One-time vendor> option. Use of the one-time vendor option is discussed later in this chapter.

ACTION: Click **Portland Weekly** to choose it. Your screen will look like this:

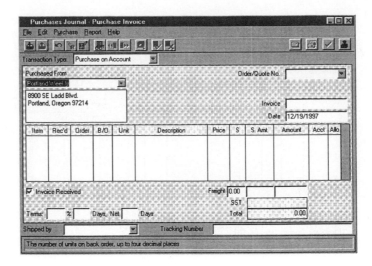

Explanation: The program has automatically filled in the vendor's address in the **Purchased From** field. The transaction type is shown as Purchase on Account.

ACTION: Click the **Invoice** field; enter Portland Weekly's invoice number of *6842*; then press the TAB key. Your screen will look like this:

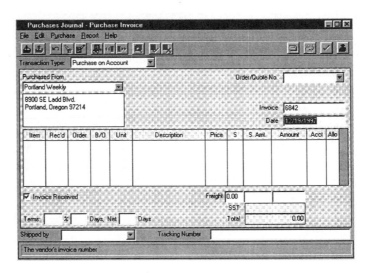

ACTION: Enter the transaction date of *12/14/1997* in the **Date** field; then press the TAB key. Your screen will look like this:

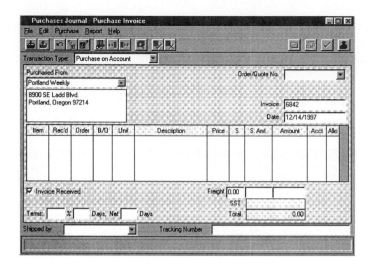

Explanation: After accepting the new transaction date, the program will position a flashing insertion point in the **Item** field. The **Item** field is used primarily by merchandising businesses to list the internal item number associated with a specific inventory unit. As a service business, Horizon Events does not enter information into this field when recording invoices received from vendors.

 ACTION: Click in the **Amount** column or use the TAB key to advance through the various columns until the flashing insertion point is positioned in the **Amount** field. Enter *410* into the **Amount** field; then press the TAB key. Your screen will look like this:

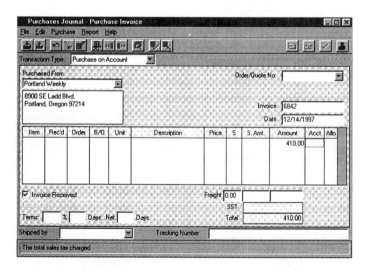

Explanation: When entering a dollar amount without any cents, there is no need to type a decimal point and two zeros. Once the TAB key is pressed, the flashing insertion point is positioned in the **Acct** field. This is a purchase on account. The standard journal entry to record the purchase of advertising on account is:

	Debit	**Credit**
Advertising Expense	xxx	
Accounts Payable		xxx

The program will automatically credit Accounts Payable through its integration/linking feature but needs to be supplied with the appropriate account number for the corresponding debit portion of the entry. This can be determined by displaying a list of accounts.

ACTION: With the flashing insertion point positioned in the **Acct** field, press the ENTER key or double-click in the field with your mouse. Your screen will look like this:

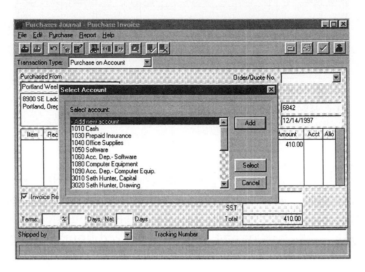

Explanation: A display listing Horizon Events' chart of accounts will appear in the Select Account dialog box. Use this list to determine the account to be entered into the **Acct** field for the debit portion of the journal entry. If you receive an error message stating an unknown account number, click the **OK** button to display the Select Account dialog box.

ACTION: Scroll through the list by dragging your mouse or by using the scroll bar until 5010 Advertising Expense is highlighted. Your screen will look like this:

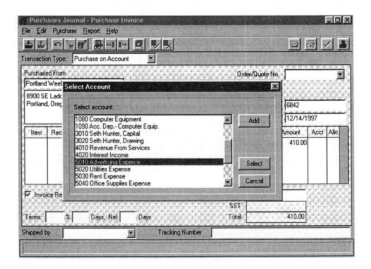

ACTION: Select 5010 Advertising Expense by double-clicking on the account or by highlighting the account and clicking the **Select** button. Your screen will appear as follows:

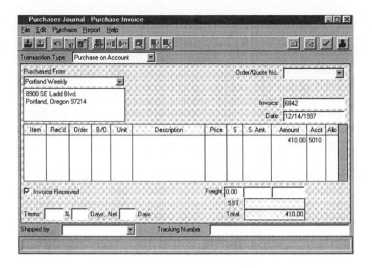

Explanation: The program automatically enters account number 5010 (Advertising Expense) into the **Acct** field. This completes the data you need to enter into the Purchases Journal dialog box to record the purchase of advertising. **Note:** You were not given access to the **Allo** (Allocation) field because Horizon Events is not currently using the Project component of the program; nor were you given access to the **Freight** field because there were no freight charges associated with this transaction.

Before posting this transaction, you need to verify that the transaction data is correct by viewing the journal entry.

 ACTION: Choose **Display Purchases Journal Entry** from Report on the Purchases Journal menu bar. Your screen will look like this:

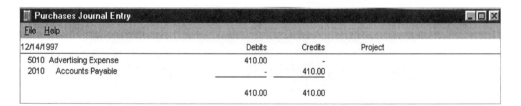

Explanation: The journal entry representing the data you have recorded in the Purchases Journal dialog box is displayed. Review the journal entry for accuracy, noting any errors.

 ACTION: Close the Purchases Journal Entry display and return to the Purchases Journal - Purchase Invoice by clicking the **Exit** button on the right side of the Purchases Journal Entry title bar.

Explanation: If you made an error, use the following editing techniques to correct the error:

Editing Tips
Editing a Purchases Journal Entry

Move to the field that contains the error by pressing the TAB key to move forward through each field or the SHIFT and TAB keys together to move to a previous field. This will highlight the selected field information so you can change it. Alternatively, you can use the mouse to point to a field and drag through the incorrect information to highlight it.

Type the correct information; then press the TAB key to enter it.

If you have associated a transaction with the incorrect vendor, select the correct vendor from the vendor list display after clicking the drop-down list arrow to the right of the **Purchased From** field.

If you have associated this transaction with an incorrect account number, select the correct account number from the chart of accounts display after double-clicking in the **Acct** field.

To discard an entry and start over, either choose **Undo Entry** from Edit on the Purchases Journal menu bar, or double-click the exit button on the title bar. Click on the **Yes** button in response to the question "Are you sure you want to discard this journal entry?"

Review the journal entry for accuracy after any corrections by choosing **Display Purchases Journal Entry** from Report on the Purchases Journal menu bar.

It is IMPORTANT TO NOTE that the only way to edit a transaction after it is posted is to reverse the entry and enter the correct transaction. To correct transactions posted in error, refer to the correcting transaction for Northwest Office Supply later in this chapter.

 ACTION: After verifying that the journal entry is correct, click the **Post** button to post this transaction. Your screen will look like this:

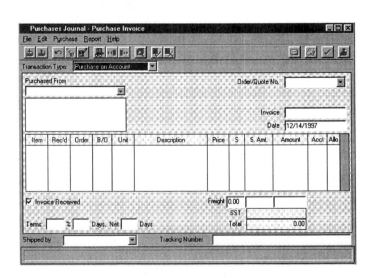

Explanation: A blank Purchases Journal dialog box is displayed, ready for additional Purchases Journal transactions to be recorded.

Additional Purchases on Account Transactions

Record the following additional purchases on account transactions:

Document 16 December 16—Received Invoice 8467 for the purchase of office supplies from Pacific Computer Supply for $187.95. (Debit Account 1040 Office Supplies—remember that office supplies are an asset until the supplies are used.)

Document 17 December 16—Received Invoice 12372 for the purchase of office supplies from Northwest Office Supply for $609.33. (Debit Account 1040 Office Supplies.)

 ACTION: After you have posted the journal entries for Documents 16 and 17, close the Purchases Journal dialog box by clicking the **Exit** button. Your screen will look like this:

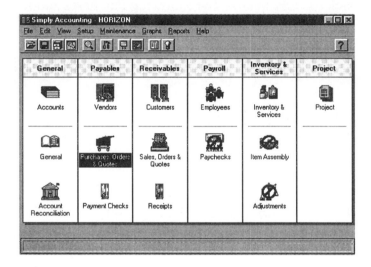

Explanation: This will restore the home window, and the Purchases Journal icon will remain highlighted.

 ACTION: With the Purchases Journal icon highlighted, click **Report** on the home window menu bar. Point to Journal Entries; then point to Purchases. Your screen will look like this:

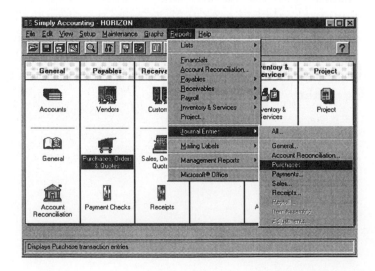

ACTION: Click **Purchases**. Your screen will show the following Purchases Journal Options dialog box:

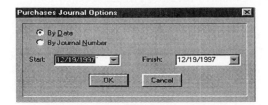

Explanation: The Purchases Journal Options dialog box appears, asking you to define the information you want displayed.

 ACTION: Select **By Date**; enter *12/1/1997* as the start date; leave the finish date set at 12/19/1997; then click the **OK** button. The following Purchases Journal Display will appear on your screen:

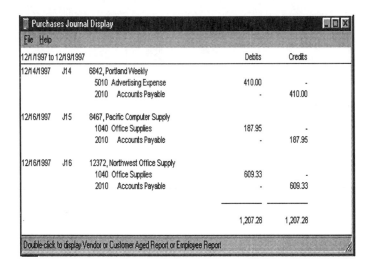

Explanation: Review the display for accuracy verifying that journal entry dates, vendor names, invoice numbers, account names and numbers, and amounts are correct.

 ACTION: Upon examining the Purchases Journal Display, you realize that the transaction for Northwest Office Supply should be for $629.33. In order to correct the purchase invoice, double-click the **Purchases, Orders & Quotes** icon on the home window. In the Purchases Journal - Purchase Invoice window, click the **Adjust invoice** button. On the Adjust an invoice screen, click the drop-down list arrow next to Vendor Name; then click **Northwest Office Supply** to select the vendor.

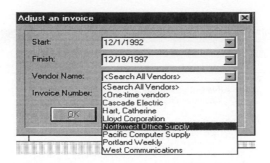

ACTION: After Northwest Office Supply has been selected, click the **Browse** button. The following Select An Invoice screen will appear:

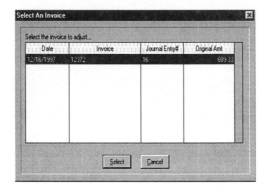

ACTION: If Invoice 12372 is not highlighted, click the Invoice to highlight. Click the **Select** button. Click the **Amount** column and change the amount to *$629.33*. Your screen will appear as follows:

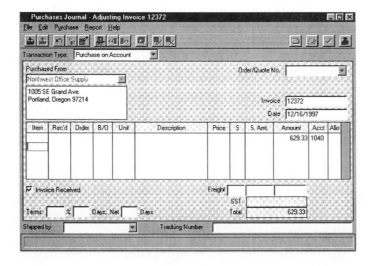

ACTION: Click the **Post** button to post, then close the Purchase Journal - Adjusting Invoice 12372 screen. On the home window, click **Report**, point to Journal Entries, and click **Purchases** to prepare the Purchases Journal Display.

```
 Purchases Journal Display
 File  Help
12/1/1997 to 12/19/1997                                        Debits        Credits
12/14/1997    J14     6842, Portland Weekly
                      5010  Advertising Expense              410.00             -
                      2010    Accounts Payable                   -          410.00

12/16/1997    J15     8467, Pacific Computer Supply
                      1040  Office Supplies                  187.95             -
                      2010    Accounts Payable                   -          187.95

12/16/1997    J16     12372, Northwest Office Supply
                      1040  Office Supplies                  609.33             -
                      2010    Accounts Payable                   -          609.33

12/16/1997    J17     ADJ12372, Reversing J16. Correction is J18.
                      2010  Accounts Payable                 609.33             -
                      1040    Office Supplies                    -          609.33

12/16/1997    J18     12372, Northwest Office Supply
                      1040  Office Supplies                  629.33             -
                      2010    Accounts Payable                   -          629.33
                                                          _____      _____
                                                           2,445.94        2,445.94
```

Explanation: All entries and corrections recorded for the Purchases Journal are displayed.

ACTION: Print the Purchases Journal by choosing **Print** from the Purchases Journal Display File menu. Compare your report to the one shown below:

Horizon Events/Your Name
Purchases Journal 12/1/1997 to 12/19/1997

				Debits	Credits
12/14/1997	J14	6842, Portland Weekly			
		5010	Advertising Expense	410.00	-
		2010	Accounts Payable	-	410.00
12/16/1997	J15	8467, Pacific Computer Supply			
		1040	Office Supplies	187.95	-
		2010	Accounts Payable	-	187.95
12/16/1997	J16	12372, Northwest Office Supply			
		1040	Office Supplies	609.33	-
		2010	Accounts Payable	-	609.33
12/16/1997	J17	ADJ12372, Reversing J16, Correction is J18.			
		2010	Accounts Payable	609.33	-
		1040	Office Supplies	-	609.33
12/16/1997	J18	12372, Northwest Office Supply			
		1040	Office Supplies	629.33	-
		2010	Accounts Payable	-	629.33
				2,445.94	2,445.94

Explanation: If you detect an error, refer to the correction made for Northwest Office Supply.

▒ **ACTION:** Close the Purchases Journal Display window and return to the home window. Choose **Exit** from the home window File menu to end the current work session and return to your Windows desktop.

▒ **ALTERNATIVE ACTION:** If you wish to continue the tutorial without exiting from the program, choose **Advance Session Date** from the home window Setup menu. Enter *12/26/1997* as the new session date; then skip the next ACTION and continue with the tutorial.

PAYMENTS JOURNAL—RECORDING CASH PAYMENTS TO CREDIT VENDORS

Payments made on outstanding invoices are recorded by clicking the **Payment Checks** icon (Payments Journal). Horizon Events needs to issue a check to Pacific Computer Supply for an outstanding invoice as described in the following memo.

Horizon Events—Document 18   **Session Date: 12/26/1997**

Memo

Date: December 21, 1997

Pay Pacific Computer Supply Invoice 8120 in the amount of $558.43.

ACTION: Load CA-Simply Accounting for Windows; open the data files for Horizon Events (A:\HORIZON\Horizon.asc); then advance the session date to 12/26/1997. The Horizon Events home window will appear. Open the Payments Journal by double-clicking the **Payment Checks** icon. Your screen will look like this:

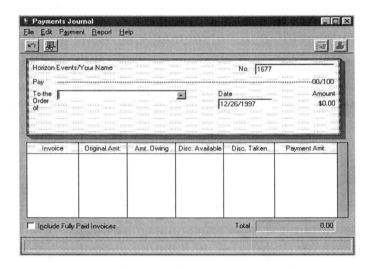

Explanation: The Payments Journal dialog box is used to record payments made on outstanding invoices, to issue checks, and for certain types of correcting entries for transactions posted in error.

ACTION: Click the drop-down list arrow to the right of the **To the Order of** field. Your screen will look like this:

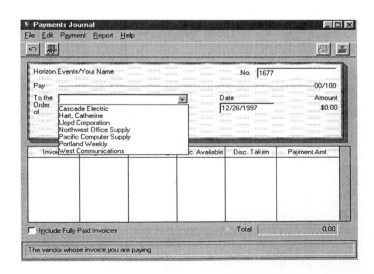

ACTION: Choose **Pacific Computer Supply**. Your screen will look like this:

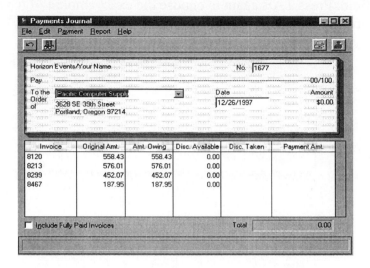

Explanation: The program has automatically filled in the vendor's address in the **To the Order of** field. The invoice numbers and amounts of Horizon Events' outstanding invoices with Pacific Computer Supply are automatically listed in the lower part of the Payments Journal dialog box. The **Invoice** field lists the vendor's invoice number; the **Original Amt.** (original amount) field shows the invoice amount; and the Amt. Owing (amount owing) shows the unpaid portion of the invoice. The **Disc. Available** field shows any discount amounts available, the **Disc. Taken** field allows the amount of the discount taken to be entered, and **Payment Amt.** is used to enter the amount of the payment. The invoices are displayed in date order, with the oldest one at the top of the list. The **No.** (number) field is completed automatically. Horizon Events has elected to use the CA-Simply Accounting for Windows automatic check preparation and numbering feature. Check number 1677 represents the next check in the automatic sequence. You can enter a different check number before printing, as long as it does not duplicate a number already used for the same vendor. If you enter a duplicate check number, the program will alert you via a screen message. For companies that do not use the program to print checks, check numbers are entered individually as payments are recorded.

 ACTION: Highlight the **Date** field; enter *12/21/1997*; then press the TAB key. Your screen will look like this:

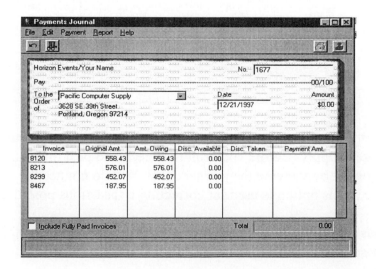

ACTION: Press the TAB key until the Payment Amount for Invoice 8120 appears in the **Payment Amt.** field. Press TAB again to choose the exact amount of the outstanding balance of Invoice 8120. Your screen will look like this:

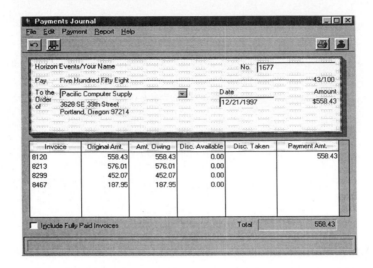

Explanation: The full amount of Invoice 8120 is highlighted and offered as the default payment amount. To record partial payments, type over the amount displayed, entering the lesser amount. You cannot enter an amount greater than the amount owed.

 ACTION: If the program highlights the full amount of the next invoice as a payment amount, press the DELETE key to remove the amount offered for Invoice 8213. Because Invoice 8213 is not yet due, the amount should not be selected. Your screen will look like this:

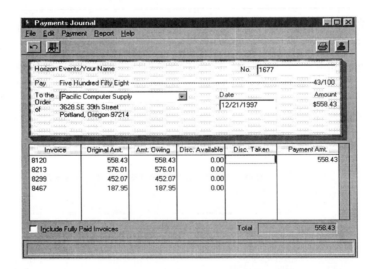

Explanation: This completes the data you need to enter into the Payments Journal dialog box to issue a check to Pacific Computer Supply. Before you print the check and post this entry, you need to verify that the transaction data is correct by viewing the journal entry. You do not need to check the **Include Fully Paid Invoices** check box. This option is used for correcting transactions posted in error.

 ACTION: Choose **Display Payments Journal Entry** from Report on the Payments Journal menu bar. Your screen will look like this:

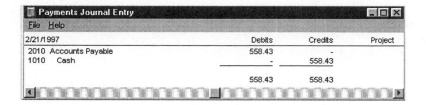

Explanation: The journal entry reflecting the information you have recorded in the Payments Journal dialog box is displayed. The integration/linking feature of CA-Simply Accounting for Windows has created the standard entry for the payment of an outstanding invoice.

	Debit	**Credit**
Accounts Payable	xxx	
Cash		xxx

Review the journal entry for accuracy noting any errors.

 ACTION: Close the Display Payments Journal Entry window and return to the Payments Journal.

Explanation: If you made an error, use the following editing techniques to correct the error:

Editing Tips
Editing a Payments Journal Entry

Move to the field that contains the error by pressing the TAB key to move forward through each field or the SHIFT and TAB keys together to move to a previous field. This will highlight the field information so that you can change it. Alternatively, you can use the mouse to point to a field and drag through the incorrect information to highlight it.

Type the correct information; then press the TAB key to enter it.

If you have associated the transaction with an incorrect vendor, select the correct vendor from the vendor list display after clicking the drop-down list arrow to the right of the **To the Order of** field. You will be asked to confirm that you want to discard the current transaction. Click the **Yes** button to discard the incorrect entry and display the outstanding invoices for the correct vendor.

To completely discard an entry and start over, either choose **Undo Entry** from Edit on the Payments Journal menu bar, or click the exit button on the Payments Journal title bar. Click the **Yes** button in response to the question "Are you sure you want to discard this journal entry?"

Review the journal entry for accuracy after any corrections by choosing **Display Payments Journal Entry** from Report on the Payments Journal menu bar.

It is IMPORTANT TO NOTE that the only way to edit a transaction after it is posted is to reverse the entry and enter the correct transaction. To correct transactions posted in error, refer to the transaction for Pacific Computer Supply later in the chapter.

 ACTION: After verifying that the journal entry is correct, choose **Print** from the Payments Journal File menu. Compare your check with the one shown below:

Horizon Events/Your Name
9076 SE Main Street
Portland, Oregon 97214   1677

Five Hundred Fifty Eight--43/100

                                                12/21/1997 $************558.43

Pacific Computer Supply
3628 SE 39th Street
Portland, Oregon 97214

Horizon Events/Your Name

Pacific Computer Supply   12/21/1997   1677

8120....................................558.43

Explanation: Verify that the check is correct. If you detect an error, refer to the Editing Tips for Editing a Payments Journal Entry for information on corrective action.

If you have made a mistake on the check, you can correct the payment information and print a new check prior to posting. The program does not make any journal entries when it prints checks, so printing copies of the same check does not affect the company's records or the check numbers of subsequent checks. For the purposes of this text, you may destroy incorrect checks; however, in an actual business situation incorrect checks would be retained as an internal control measure.

 ACTION: After a correct check is printed, click the **Post** button to post this transaction. You will get a blank Payments Journal screen that appears as follows:

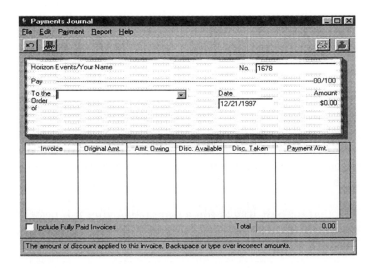

Explanation: A blank Payments Journal dialog box is displayed, ready for additional Payments Journal transactions to be recorded.

Additional Cash Payments Transactions

Record the following additional cash payments transactions:

Document 19 December 22—Pay Invoice K00324 in the amount of $62.80 from Cascade Electric. Print Check 1678.

Document 20 December 22—Make a partial payment on Invoice 8213 in the amount of $400.99 from Pacific Computer Supply. Print Check 1679.

Compare your checks with the ones shown below:

```
Horizon Events/Your Name
9076 SE Main Street
Portland, Oregon 97214                                              1678

Sixty Two------------------------------------------------------------------------------------------80/100

                                     12/22/1997                  $***********62.80

Cascade Electric
890 SE Stark Street
Portland, Oregon 97214

Horizon Events/Your Name

Cascade Electric              12/22/1997              1678

K00324.............................62.80
```

```
Horizon Events/Your Name
9076 SE Main Street
Portland, Oregon 97214                                              1679

Four Hundred----------------------------------------------------------------------------------------99/100

                                     12/22/1997                  $**********400.99

Pacific Computer Supply
3628 SE 39th Street
Portland, Oregon 97214

Horizon Events

Pacific Computer Supply              12/22/1997              1679

8213...................................400.99
```

ACTION: After you have printed the checks and posted the journal entries associated with Documents 19 and 20, close the Payments Journal dialog box. This will restore the home window, and the Payment Checks icon will remain highlighted. With the Payment Checks icon highlighted, choose **Reports**, point to Journal Entries, and click **Payments** on the home window menu bar. Your screen will look like this:

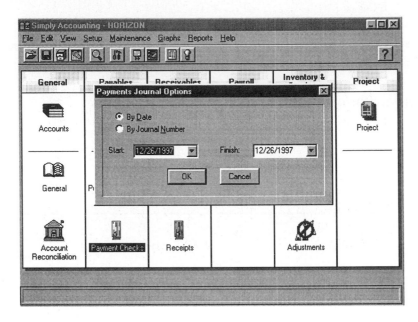

Explanation: A Payments Journal Options dialog box, similar to the Purchases Journal Options dialog box, will appear asking you to define the information you want displayed.

 ACTION: Select **By Date**; enter *12/1/1997* as the start date; leave the finish date set at 12/26/1997; then click the **OK** button. The following Payments Journal Display will appear on your screen:

Payments Journal Display				
File Help				
12/1/1997 to 12/26/1997			Debits	Credits
12/21/1997	J19	1677, Pacific Computer Supply		
		2010 Accounts Payable	558.43	-
		1010 Cash	-	558.43
12/22/1997	J20	1678, Cascade Electric		
		2010 Accounts Payable	62.80	-
		1010 Cash	-	62.80
12/22/1997	J21	1679, Pacific Computer Supply		
		2010 Accounts Payable	400.99	-
		1010 Cash	-	400.99
			1,022.22	1,022.22

Explanation: Review the display for accuracy verifying that journal entry dates, vendor names, check numbers, account names and numbers, and amounts are correct.

ACTION: Upon examining the Payments Journal Display, you realize that the transaction J21 for Pacific Computer Supply should be for $400.00. In order to correct the amount of the check, close the Payments Journal and double-click the **Payment Checks** icon on the home window. In the window, click the drop-down list arrow next to Vendor Name; then click **Pacific Computer**

Supply to select the vendor. Enter *1679 COR* as the number. Change the date to *12/22/1997*. Your screen will appear as follows:

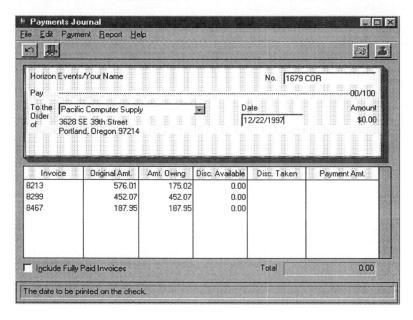

Explanation: Entering the check number of the incorrect transaction followed by COR represents the fact that this is a correcting entry. The letters ADJ could also be used next to the check number.

ACTION: TAB to or click in **Payment Amt.** for Invoice 8213. To correct the amount, key in the wrong amount preceded by a minus sign (*-400.99*). TAB to enter the amount as the total. Your screen should look like the following:

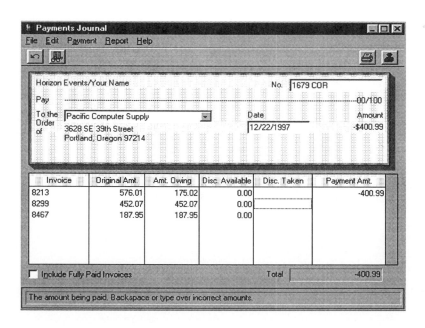

ACTION: Click **Report, Display Payments Journal Entry**. Your screen should show the following report:

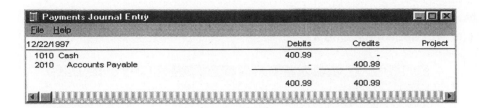

Explanation: The correcting entry for Check 1679 should show a debit to Cash and a credit to Accounts Payable for $400.99.

 ACTION: If your report appears as the above, close the Payments Journal Entry report. Click the **Post** button to post then enter the original transaction correctly with a check number of *1679 C* and an amount of *$400.00.* Your correct payment will appear as follows:

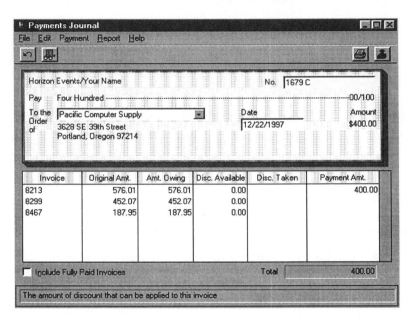

Explanation: The letter C (or some other designation representing a corrected transaction) must be added to **No.** Otherwise, you will not be able to print the corrected check. If you are using prenumbered checks, you will want to use the next available check number for the correction. If you receive a dialog box regarding the check, simply click **OK**.

ACTION: Compare your check with the one shown below:

Horizon Events/Your Name
9076 SE Main Street
Portland, Oregon 97214   1679 C

Four Hundred---00/100

                                        12/22/1997 $**********400.00

Pacific Computer Supply
3628 SE 39th Street
Portland, Oregon 97214

Horizon Events

Pacific Computer Supply   12/22/1997   1679 C

8213....................................400.00

 ACTION: If the check is correct, post the transaction, close the Payments Journal, and print the Payments Journal report for 12/1/1997 to 12/26/1997 by following the steps in previous transactions. Print the Payments Journal. Compare your report with the one shown below:

Horizon Events/Your Name
Payments Journal 12/1/1997 to 12/26/1997

			Debits	Credits
12/21/1997	J19	1677, Pacific Computer Supply		
		2010 Accounts Payable	558.43	-
		1010 Cash	-	558.43
12/22/1997	J20	1678, Cascade Electric		
		2010 Accounts Payable	62.80	-
		1010 Cash	-	62.80
12/22/1997	J21	1679, Pacific Computer Supply		
		2010 Accounts Payable	400.99	-
		1010 Cash	-	400.99
12/22/1997	J22	1679 COR, Pacific Computer Supply		
		1010 Cash	400.99	-
		2010 Accounts Payable	-	400.99
12/22/1997	J23	1679 C, Pacific Computer Supply		
		2010 Accounts Payable	400.00	-
		1010 Cash	-	400.00
			1,823.21	1,823.21

▦ **ACTION:** Close the Payments Journal Display and return to the home window. Choose **Exit** from the home window to end the current work session and return to your Windows desktop.

▦ **ALTERNATIVE ACTION:** Close the Payments Journal display and return to the home window. You can continue with the tutorial without exiting from the program if you wish. The next steps are recorded under the same session date as the prior steps. Skip the next ACTION; then continue with the tutorial.

PURCHASES JOURNAL—RECORDING CASH PAYMENTS AND ONE-TIME VENDOR PURCHASES

It is not uncommon for service businesses to make cash purchases or pay vendors on a one-time basis. CA-Simply Accounting for Windows provides a short-cut method of accounting for these types of transactions through two special features in the Purchases Journal - Purchase Invoice dialog box: One-time vendor option in the vendor list drop-down box and the choice of Purchase with Payment when completing the Purchases Journal - Purchase Invoice.

The one-time vendor option is used to enter an invoice for a vendor who is not listed in the Payables Ledger as a recurring vendor. When you choose <One-time vendor> from the vendor list, you will have the option of entering the vendor's name and address in the box below or skipping this field. Once you leave the **Purchased From** field, the program automatically selects Purchase with Payment as the transaction type and a **Check** field appears. The next number in the company's automatic check sequence will appear in the **Check** field. Payment must be made to one-time vendors at the time the purchase is made. The program does not keep a permanent record of the one-time vendor's name and address information, but it will include a description of this transaction in the General Ledger, General Journal, and Purchases Journal.

The Purchase with Payment Transaction type can be used independently of the one-time vendor option in instances in which the business is making payment for an item at the same time the item is received from an established vendor of the business. This feature allows you to post the invoice and issue the check at the same time, without having to open the Payments Journal dialog box. Select the transaction type as Purchase with Payment and choose an established vendor from the vendor list in the **Purchased From** field.

Horizon Events—Document 21   **Session Date: 12/26/1997**

Conversion Technologies
6655 SW Hampton Street
Portland, Oregon 97223
Phone: 598-0180
FAX: 598-0188
			Invoice # ___9863___
			
			To: Horizon Events
			       9076 SE Main Street
			       Portland, Oregon 97214

Date	Description		Amount
12/23/97	Data Conversion from old system to new system		$65.00
		TOTAL	$65.00

ACTION: Load CA-Simply Accounting for Windows; open the data files for Horizon Events (A:\HORIZON\Horizon.asc). Leave the session date set at 12/26/1997. The home window will appear. Open the Purchases Journal dialog box by double-clicking on the **Purchases, Orders & Quotes** icon. Your screen will look like this:

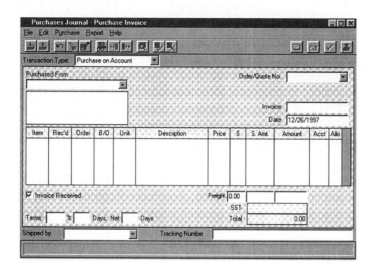

ACTION: Click the drop-down list arrow to the right of the **Purchased From** field to display the vendor list. Your screen will look like this:

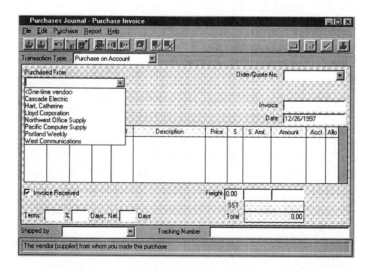

ACTION: Choose <One-time vendor>; then press the TAB key. Your screen will look like this:

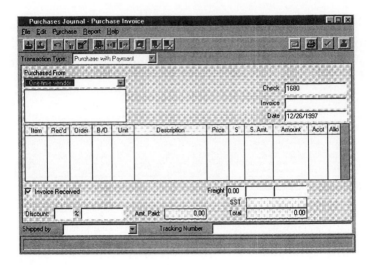

Explanation: A flashing insertion point moves to the area below the vendor list box. Notice that the transaction type is gray in color and shows "Purchase with Payment." Also note the text box for the **Check** field with the next available check number 1680 inserted.

ACTION: Enter Conversion Technologies' name and address, pressing the TAB key at the end of each line; then press the TAB key until the flashing insertion point is positioned in the **Invoice** field. Your screen will look like this:

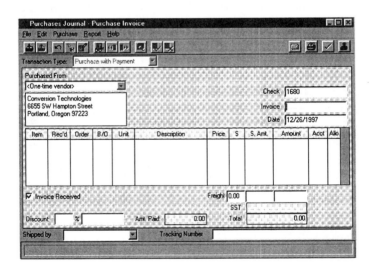

ACTION: Enter Conversion Technologies' invoice number of *9863* into the **Invoice** field and press the TAB key. Enter the invoice date of *12/23/1997* and press the TAB key. Your screen will look like this:

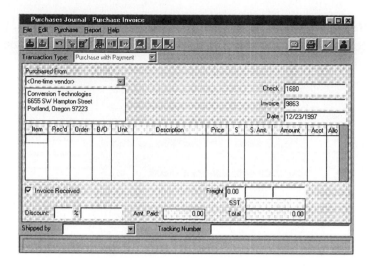

ACTION: Use the TAB key to move through the **Item**, **Rec'd**, **Order**, **B/O**, **Unit**, **Description**, **Price**, **S** (sales tax percentage), and **S. Amt.** (sales tax amount) fields until the flashing insertion point is positioned in the **Amount** field; enter *65.00* and press the TAB key. Your screen will appear as follows:

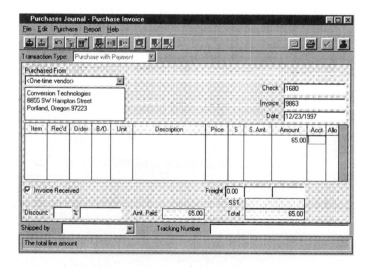

Explanation: A flashing insertion point is positioned in the **Acct** field. This is a cash purchase for a miscellaneous expense. The standard journal entry to record a cash purchase for a miscellaneous expense is:

	Debit	**Credit**
Misc. Expense	xxx	
Cash		xxx

The program will automatically credit cash through its integration/linking feature but needs to be supplied with the appropriate account number for the corresponding debit portion of the entry. This can be determined by displaying a list of accounts.

ACTION: With the flashing insertion point positioned in the **Acct** field, press the ENTER key or double-click in the field with your mouse. Your screen will look like this:

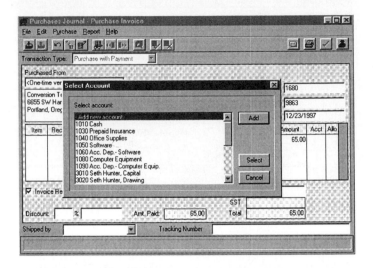

Explanation: A display listing Horizon Events' chart of accounts will appear in the Select Account dialog box. Use this list to determine the account to be entered into the **Acct** field for the debit portion of the journal entry. If you receive an error message stating an unknown account number, click the **OK** button to display the Select Account dialog box.

ACTION: Scroll through the list by dragging your mouse or by using the scroll bar until the Misc. Expense account (account number 5150) is highlighted. Your screen will look like this:

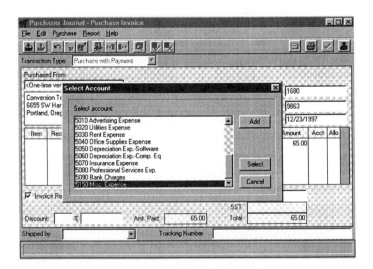

ACTION: Select the **Misc. Expense** account (account number 5150) by double-clicking on the account or by highlighting the account and clicking the **Select** button. Your screen will look like this:

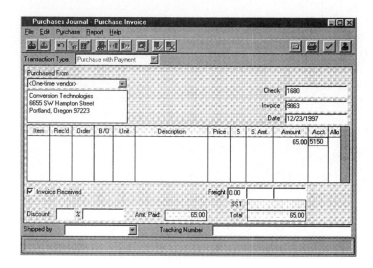

Explanation: The program automatically enters account number 5150 (Misc. Expense) into the **Acct** field. This completes the data you need to enter into the Purchases Journal dialog box to record the miscellaneous expense. Before posting this transaction, you need to verify that the transaction data is correct by viewing the journal entry.

 ACTION: Select **Report** from the Purchases Journal menu bar; then click **Display Purchases Journal Entry**. Compare your display to the one shown below:

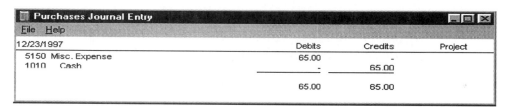

Purchases Journal Entry			
12/23/1997	Debits	Credits	Project
5150 Misc. Expense	65.00	-	
1010　Cash	-	65.00	
	65.00	65.00	

Explanation: The journal entry representing the data you have recorded in the Purchases Journal dialog box is displayed. Review the journal entry for accuracy noting any errors.

 ACTION: Close the Purchases Journal Entry dialog box. **Note:** If you made an error, refer to the Editing Tips for Editing a Purchases Journal Entry, which appears in a special box earlier in this chapter, for information for corrective action. After verifying that the journal entry is correct, choose **Print** from the Purchases Journal File menu. Compare your check with the one shown below:

Horizon Events/Your Name
9076 SE Main Street
Portland, Oregon 97214   1680

Sixty Five--00/100

                                        12/23/1997 $***********65.00

Conversion Technologies
6655 SW Hampton Street
Portland, Oregon 97223

Horizon Events/Your Name

Conversion Technologies   12/23/1997   1680

9863.................................65.00

Explanation: If you detect an error, refer to the Editing Tips for Editing a Purchases Journal Entry for information on corrective action.

 ACTION: Click the **Post** button to post this transaction. Your screen will look like this:

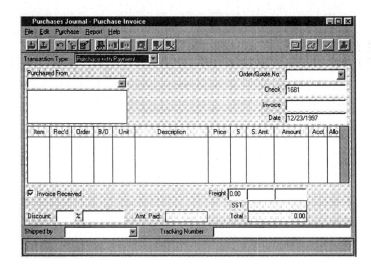

Explanation: A blank Purchases Journal dialog box is displayed, ready for additional Purchases Journal transactions to be recorded.

Additional One-Time Vendor and Cash Purchases Transactions

Record the following additional transactions:

Document 22 December 23—Record the purchase and payment of advertising from a one-time vendor, Buckman Voice, 5409 SE 14th Avenue, Portland, Oregon 97214; Invoice 1246, in the amount of $75.00. Print Check 1681.

Document 23 December 26—Record the receipt of Invoice 12637 from an established vendor, Northwest Office Supply, in the amount of $28.79 for office supplies and the issuance of a check in the amount of $28.79 to Northwest Office Supply. Print Check 1682.

Compare your checks with the ones shown below:

```
Horizon Events/Your Name
9076 SE Main Street
Portland, Oregon 97214                                              1681

Seventy Five--------------------------------------------------------------------00/100

                                    12/23/1997          $***********75.00

Buckman Voice
5409 SE 14th Avenue
Portland, Oregon 97214

Horizon Events/Your Name

Buckman Voice                 12/23/1997            1681

1246.............................75.00
```

```
Horizon Events/Your Name
9076 SE Main Street
Portland, Oregon 97214                                              1682

Twenty Eight-------------------------------------------------------------------79/100

                                    12/26/1997          $***********28.79

Northwest Office Supply
1005 SE Grand Ave.
Portland, Oregon 97214

Horizon Events/Your Name

Northwest Office Supply         12/26/1997            1682

12637.............................28.79
```

 ACTION: After you have printed the checks and posted the transaction information associated with Documents 22 and 23, close the Purchases Journal - Purchase Invoice dialog box and return to the home window. With the **Purchases Journal** icon highlighted, click the **Report** menu on the home window, point to Journal Entries, and click **Purchases**. Your screen will look like this:

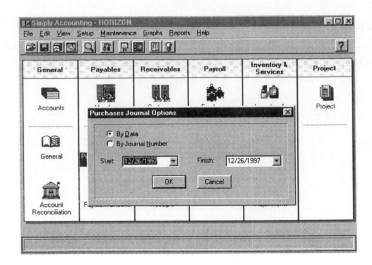

Explanation: The Purchases Journal Options dialog box will appear, asking you to define the information you want displayed.

 ACTION: Select **By Date**; enter *12/1/1997* as the start date; leave the finish date set at 12/26/1997; then click the **OK** button. The following Purchases Journal Display will appear on your screen:

Purchases Journal Display			Debits	Credits
12/1/1997 to 12/26/1997				
12/14/1997	J14	6842, Portland Weekly		
		5010 Advertising Expense	410.00	-
		2010 Accounts Payable	-	410.00
12/16/1997	J15	8467, Pacific Computer Supply		
		1040 Office Supplies	187.95	-
		2010 Accounts Payable	-	187.95
12/16/1997	J16	12372, Northwest Office Supply		
		1040 Office Supplies	609.33	-
		2010 Accounts Payable	-	609.33
12/16/1997	J17	ADJ12372, Reversing J16. Correction is J18.		
		2010 Accounts Payable	609.33	-
		1040 Office Supplies	-	609.33
12/16/1997	J18	12372, Northwest Office Supply		
		1040 Office Supplies	629.33	-
		2010 Accounts Payable	-	629.33
12/23/1997	J24	9863, 1680, Conversion Technologies		
		5150 Misc. Expense	65.00	-
		1010 Cash	-	65.00
12/23/1997	J25	1246, 1681, Buckman Voice		
		5010 Advertising Expense	75.00	-
		1010 Cash	-	75.00
12/23/1997	J26	12637, 1682, Northwest Office Supply		
		1040 Office Supplies	28.79	-
		1010 Cash	-	28.79
			2,614.73	2,614.73

Explanation: Review the display for accuracy, verifying that journal entry dates, vendor names, invoice and check numbers, account names and numbers, and amounts are correct. Use the scroll bar to advance through the display. When checking your Purchases Journal Display, you notice that the amount of the check for Northwest Office Supply should be $26.79 rather than $28.79.

ACTION: Prepare a correcting entry by double-clicking the **Purchases, Orders & Quotes** icon. Once a blank purchase invoice appears on the screen, click the **Find** button. 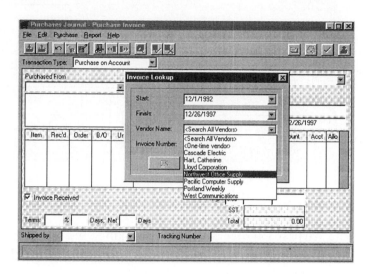 On the Invoice Lookup dialog box that appears, click the drop-down list arrow next to Vendor Name. Your screen will look like the following:

ACTION: Click **Northwest Office Supply**; then click the **Browse** button. Make sure Invoice 12637 is highlighted on the Select An Invoice screen. You should see the following:

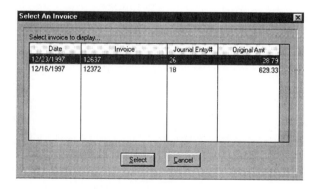

ACTION: With Invoice 12637 highlighted, click the **Select** button. Your screen will look like the following:

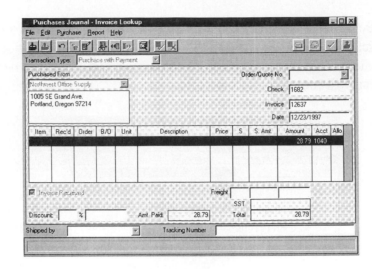

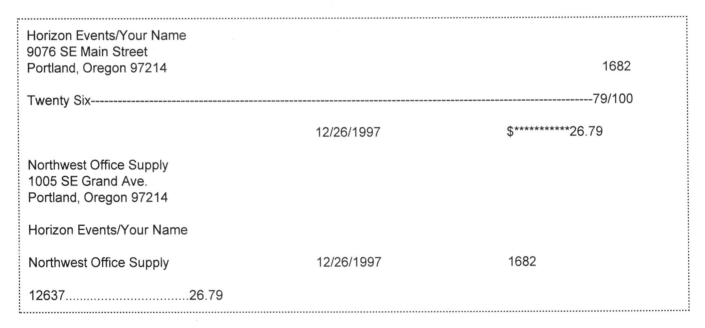

ACTION: Click the **Adjust Invoice** button. Change the amount of the invoice to *26.79* and press the TAB key to insert the change. Print the new check. It should appear as follows:

Horizon Events/Your Name
9076 SE Main Street
Portland, Oregon 97214   1682

Twenty Six--79/100

                                          12/26/1997 $***********26.79

Northwest Office Supply
1005 SE Grand Ave.
Portland, Oregon 97214

Horizon Events/Your Name

Northwest Office Supply   12/26/1997   1682

12637................................26.79

ACTION: Compare your check with the above; if it matches the above, click the **Post** button. If you get the following dialog box regarding duplicate check numbers, click **Yes**.

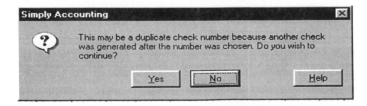

ACTION: After you have printed the check and posted the transaction information to correct the error for the Northwest Office Supply transaction, close the Purchases Journal - Purchase Invoice dialog box and return to the home window. With the **Purchases Journal** icon highlighted, choose **Journal Entries, Purchases** from the Report menu on the home window. Your screen will show:

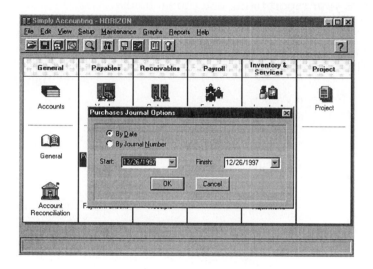

Explanation: The Purchases Journal Options dialog box will appear, asking you to define the information you want displayed.

ACTION: Select **By Date**; enter *12/1/1997* as the start date; leave the finish date set at 12/26/1997; then click the **OK** button. The following Purchases Journal Display will appear:

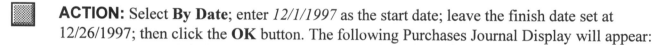

Purchases Journal Display			Debits	Credits
12/1/1997 to 12/26/1997				
12/14/1997	J14	6842, Portland Weekly		
		5010 Advertising Expense	410.00	-
		2010 Accounts Payable	-	410.00
12/16/1997	J15	8467, Pacific Computer Supply		
		1040 Office Supplies	187.95	-
		2010 Accounts Payable	-	187.95
12/16/1997	J16	12372, Northwest Office Supply		
		1040 Office Supplies	609.33	-
		2010 Accounts Payable	-	609.33
12/16/1997	J17	ADJ12372, Reversing J16. Correction is J18.		
		2010 Accounts Payable	609.33	-
		1040 Office Supplies	-	609.33
12/16/1997	J18	12372, Northwest Office Supply		
		1040 Office Supplies	629.33	-
		2010 Accounts Payable	-	629.33
12/23/1997	J24	9863, 1680, Conversion Technologies		
		5150 Misc. Expense	65.00	-
		1010 Cash	-	65.00
12/23/1997	J25	1246, 1681, Buckman Voice		
		5010 Advertising Expense	75.00	-
		1010 Cash	-	75.00
12/23/1997	J26	12637, 1682, Northwest Office Supply		
		1040 Office Supplies	28.79	-
		1010 Cash	-	28.79
12/23/1997	J27	ADJ12637, Reversing J26. Correction is J28.		
		1010 Cash	28.79	-
		1040 Office Supplies	-	28.79
12/23/1997	J28	12637, 1682, Northwest Office Supply		
		1040 Office Supplies	26.79	-
		1010 Cash	-	26.79
			2,670.31	2,670.31

Explanation: Review the display for accuracy, verifying that journal entry dates, vendor names, invoice and check numbers, account names and numbers, and amounts are correct. Use the scroll bar to advance through the display. Notice the correcting entry for Northwest Office Supply.

 ACTION: Print the Purchases Journal by choosing **Print** from the Purchases Journal Display File menu. Compare your report to the one shown below:

Horizon Events/Your Name
Purchases Journal 12/1/1997 to 12/26/1997

				Debits	Credits
12/14/1997	J14	6842, Portland Weekly			
		5010	Advertising Expense	410.00	-
		2010	Accounts Payable	-	410.00
12/16/1997	J15	8467, Pacific Computer Supply			
		1040	Office Supplies	187.95	-
		2010	Accounts Payable	-	187.95
12/16/1997	J16	12372, Northwest Office Supply			
		1040	Office Supplies	609.33	-
		2010	Accounts Payable	-	609.33
12/16/1997	J17	ADJ12372, Reversing J16, Correction is J18.			
		2010	Accounts Payable	609.33	-
		1040	Office Supplies	-	609.33
12/16/1997	J18	12372, Northwest Office Supply			
		1040	Office Supplies	629.33	-
		2010	Accounts Payable	-	629.33
12/23/1997	J24	9863, 1680, Conversion Technologies			
		5150	Misc. Expense	65.00	-
		1010	Cash	-	65.00
12/23/1997	J25	1246, 1681, Buckman Voice			
		5010	Advertising Expense	75.00	-
		1010	Cash	-	75.00
12/23/1997	J26	12637, 1682, Northwest Office Supply			
		1040	Office Supplies	28.79	-
		1010	Cash	-	28.79
12/23/1997	J27	ADJ12637, Reversing J26. Correction is J28.			
		1010	Cash	28.79	-
		1040	Office Supplies	-	28.79
12/23/1997	J28	12637, 1682, Northwest Office Supply			
		1040	Office Supplies	26.79	-
		1010	Cash	-	26.79
				2,670.31	2,670.31

Explanation: If you detect an error, follow the instructions given for previous corrections and correct the error.

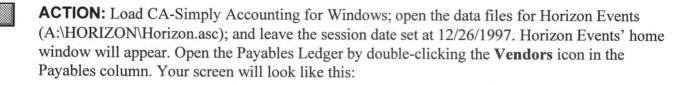 **ACTION:** Close the Purchases Journal Display window and return to the home window.

ACTION: Choose **Exit** from the home window File menu to end the current work session and return to your Windows desktop.

ALTERNATIVE ACTION: You can continue with the tutorial without exiting from the program if you wish. The next steps are recorded under the same session date as the prior steps. Skip the next ACTION; then continue with the tutorial.

PAYABLES LEDGER—MAINTAINING VENDOR RECORDS

Transactions can be entered only through the Journals component of the program. The Payables Ledger component is used to maintain vendor records. Each record contains the vendor's address, the amount Horizon Events owes the vendor, and the total purchases from that vendor for the prior year and the current year. You can create, modify, or remove vendor records through the Payables Ledger dialog box.

Creating a Vendor Record

Seth Hunter has had a preliminary discussion with Jim Hart regarding future contract support staff work for several events he is planning. He would like to add Jim Hart as a new vendor.

Horizon Events—Document 24   **Session Date: 12/26/1997**

> *Memo*
> Date: December 26, 1997
>
> Add the following new vendor to the vendor list:
>
> Jim Hart
> 410 NW 18th, #303
> Portland, Oregon 97209
> 503-223-6590

ACTION: Load CA-Simply Accounting for Windows; open the data files for Horizon Events (A:\HORIZON\Horizon.asc); and leave the session date set at 12/26/1997. Horizon Events' home window will appear. Open the Payables Ledger by double-clicking the **Vendors** icon in the Payables column. Your screen will look like this:

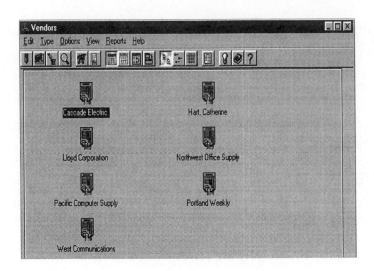

Explanation: The icon for the first vendor in Horizon Events' vendor list, Cascade Electric, is highlighted.

ACTION: Click the **Create** button [icon] on the toolbar. Your screen will look like this:

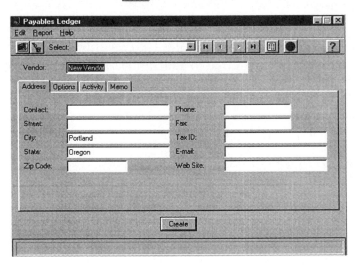

Explanation: A blank Payables Ledger dialog box is presented. Fields are defined as follows:

Address Tab
Vendor: Enter the vendor's name, up to 35 characters.

Contact: Enter the name of the person the business usually deals with when calling or corresponding with this vendor.

Street: Enter the vendor's street address.

City: Enter the vendor's city, up to 18 characters, or accept the default city offered. The program offers the city portion of the company's address as a default under the assumption that a company is most likely to do business with vendors residing in the same city.

State: Enter the vendor's state, or accept the default state offered. The program offers the state portion of the company's address as a default under the assumption that a company is most likely to do business with vendors residing in the same state.

Zip Code: Enter the vendor's zip code.

Phone: Enter the vendor's phone number, including area code if you wish. You do not need to type parentheses or hyphens; the program fills these in when you move to another field.

Fax: Enter the vendor's fax number, including area code if you wish. You do not need to type parentheses or hyphens; the program fills these in when you move to another field.

Tax ID: Enter the vendor's tax identification number.

E-mail: Enter the vendor's e-mail address, if known.

Web Site: If the vendor has a Web Site, enter the Web address. When in the Vendors window, choose **Web Site** from the Edit menu or toolbar to go to the Web site associated with this vendor record.

Options Tab
Early Payment Terms: Enter any early payment terms allowed by the vendor.

Calculate Discounts Before Tax: Check the box if the vendor calculates the discount before adding the tax.

Print 1099s for this Vendor: Check this box to print 1099s for the vendor.

Print the Amount in the Box for: Select the revenue box in which to print the vendor's income.

Clear Invoices When Paid: Check this box if you want invoices to be removed from the Payables Ledger immediately after they are fully paid. Leave this box unchecked if you want to retain invoices on file after they are fully paid. **For all sample companies in this text, this box will remain unchecked so that paid invoices will appear in the Vendor Aged report and in the Payments Journal.** This technique will produce a complete audit trail for all Payables transactions, facilitating the detection and correction of any errors posted in the Purchases and Payments Journals.

Print Contact on Checks: Select if you want to print the contact person's name on checks for the vendor.

Print or E-mail Forms for this Vendor: Click the drop-down list arrow to select whether to print or to e-mail forms for this vendor.

Activity Tab
Balance owing: The program fills in this amount; you cannot change it. It is the difference between the total amount purchased from and the total payments made to this vendor. This field is updated every time a purchase is recorded or a payment is issued.

Fiscal Year-to-Date Purchases: This field is used when a company is first converting to CA-Simply Accounting for Windows after the start of its fiscal year. The Payables component of the program must be in the Not Ready mode. The total amount of purchases from this vendor prior to the Earliest Transaction date is entered, and the program updates it every time a new purchase is made after the Earliest Transaction date. Once the Payables Ledger of the program is in the Ready mode, you cannot modify the amount listed in this field.

Last Fiscal Year's Purchases: This field is used when a company is first converting to CA-Simply Accounting for Windows and the Payables Ledger of the program is in the Not Ready mode. The total amount of purchases from this vendor in the last fiscal year may be entered for reference purposes. Once the Payables Ledger of the program is in the Ready mode, you cannot modify the amount listed in this field.

Current Calendar Year-to-Date Payments: Indicates the year-to-date total payments made to the vendor for this calendar year.

Previous Calendar Year's Payments: Indicates the total amount paid to the vendor in the last calendar year.

<u>Memo Tab</u>
Memo: Enter any memo you would like to appear in the To-Do Lists.

To-Do Date: If the reminder is date sensitive, type a due date in the **To-Do Date** field.

ACTION: Enter the available information about the new vendor, Jim Hart, into the Payables Ledger dialog box. Your screen will look like this:

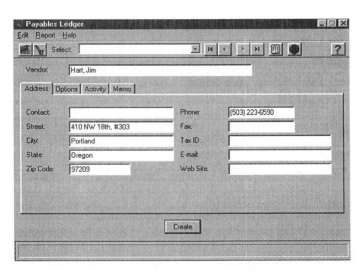

Explanation: Verify that all of the information is correct. If you have made an error, use the following editing techniques to correct the error:

Editing Tips
Editing a Payables Ledger Record

Move to the field that contains the error by either pressing the TAB key to move forward through each field or the SHIFT and TAB keys together to move to a previous field. This will highlight the selected field information so that you can change it. Alternatively, you can use the mouse to point to a field and drag through the incorrect information to highlight it.

Type the correct information; then press the TAB key to enter it.

Click check boxes to select or deselect as required.

To discard a record and start over, choose **Undo Changes** from Edit on the Payables Ledger menu bar; then click the **Yes** button in response to the question "Are you sure you want to undo changes to this ledger page?" Alternatively, double-click the control menu box; then click the **No** button in response to the question "Do you still want to create this ledger page?"

It is IMPORTANT TO NOTE that the only way to edit a Payables Ledger record after it is created is to either modify the record or remove it and create a new Payables Ledger record.

 ACTION: When the ledger page is correct, click the **Create** button. You will get a blank Payables Ledger screen.

Explanation: The program has added the new vendor to Horizon Events' records and has cleared the Payables Ledger dialog box in preparation for creating another vendor record.

Modifying a Vendor Record

If you made an error in a vendor record after you have created it, or need to change some information about a vendor, choose **Find** from the Payables Ledger Edit menu; then choose the vendor from the list presented. Make corrections as necessary, using the Editing Tips for Editing a Payables Ledger Record. To record the changes, either use the scroll bar to move to another ledger page, or close the dialog box by clicking the **Close** button. **Note:** Only descriptive information can be changed. Items such as last fiscal year's purchases, fiscal year-to-date purchases, and balance owing are under program control once the Payables Ledger is in the Ready mode and cannot be changed.

Removing a Vendor Record

You cannot remove a vendor record unless its outstanding balance is zero. To remove a vendor, choose **Find** from the Payables Ledger Edit menu; then choose the vendor from the list presented. Choose **Remove** from the Payables Ledger Edit menu. The program will ask you if you are sure you want to remove the vendor record. Choose **Yes** to remove it. Close the dialog box by clicking the close button.

Additional Payables Ledger Maintenance Items

Enter the following additional maintenance items:

Document 25 December 26—Create a new vendor: Josh Campton, 2874 NW Luray Terrace, Portland, Oregon 97210; 503-228-2575. (**Note:** Enter as Campton, Josh to ensure that vendor records are listed in alphabetical order.)

Document 26 December 26—Modify Catherine Hart's address. She has moved to 1025 SE Oak Grove Road, Milwaukie, Oregon 97222; 503-659-8499.

PAYABLES REPORTS

A variety of Payables-related reports are available in CA-Simply Accounting for Windows. The procedures required to generate checks and to print and display Purchases Journal and Payments Journal reports were demonstrated throughout this chapter. In addition to these reports, the program can print or display a Vendor List and a Vendor Aged report. Mailing labels can be printed, but not displayed. However, you can display similar information in a Vendor List. Use the scroll bars at the bottom or right side of a displayed report to view reports that contain more text than can be displayed at one time.

 ACTION: Close the Payables Ledger dialog box; then choose **Display Vendor List** from Report on the Vendor window menu bar. (An alternate method is to click **Reports** on the home window menu bar, point to Lists, click **Vendors**.) Your screen will look like this:

Vendor List					
File Help					
12/26/1997					
Campton, Josh		Phone:	(503) 228-2575	Fax:	
		E-mail:			
2874 NW Luray Terrace		Web Site:			
Portland, Oregon 97210					
Tax ID:					
Cascade Electric		Phone:	(503) 232-1292	Fax:	(503) 232-1290
Karen Pearson		E-mail:			
890 SE Stark Street		Web Site:			
Portland, Oregon 97214					
Tax ID:					
Hart, Catherine		Phone:	(503) 659-8499	Fax:	
		E-mail:			
1025 SE Oak Grove Road		Web Site:			
Milwaukie, Oregon 97222					
Tax ID:					
Hart, Jim		Phone:	(503) 223-6590	Fax:	
		E-mail:			
410 NW 18th, #303		Web Site:			
Portland, Oregon 97209					
Tax ID:					
Lloyd Corporation		Phone:	(503) 287-3000	Fax:	(503) 287-3020
Arlene Simpson		E-mail:			
4567 NE 15th Street		Web Site:			
Portland, Oregon 97232					
Tax ID:					

Northwest Office Supply   Phone: (503) 231-5600   Fax: (503) 231-5510
    Martin King   E-mail:
    1005 SE Grand Ave.   Web Site:
    Portland, Oregon 97214
    Tax ID:

Pacific Computer Supply   Phone: (503) 231-7890   Fax: (503) 231-7893
    Jose Gonzalez   E-mail:
    3628 SE 39th Street   Web Site:
    Portland, Oregon 97214
    Tax ID:

Portland Weekly   Phone: (503) 232-5612   Fax: (503) 232-5688
    Yi Chen   E-mail:
    8900 SE Ladd Blvd.   Web Site:
    Portland, Oregon 97214
    Tax ID:

West Communications   Phone: (503) 222-3555   Fax: (503) 222-3500
    Rahman Abdullah   E-mail:
    4298 SW 10th Avenue   Web Site:
    Portland, Oregon 97205
    Tax ID:

Vendors on file: 9

ACTION: Choose **Print** from the Vendor List File menu. Compare your report to the one shown above.

ACTION: Close the Vendor List dialog box; select **Report** from the Vendor window menu bar; then choose **Vendor Aged**. Your screen will look like this:

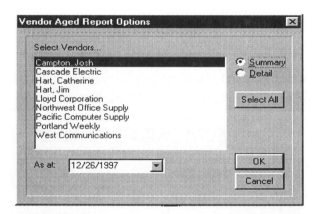

Explanation: The Vendor Aged dialog box presents several options. A Vendor Aged report lists all outstanding invoices and payments for either all vendors or for the individual vendors you specify. To display total, current, and aged amounts that are owed to vendors, select **Summary**. To display all outstanding invoices and payments for the vendors, select **Detail**.

ACTION: Click the **Detail** option button; click **Select All**, then click **OK**. Your screen will look like this:

Vendor Aged Detail

File   Help

As at 12/26/1997			Total	Current	31 to 60	61 to 90	91+
Cascade Electric							
K00324	11/21/1997	Invoice	62.80	-	62.80	-	-
1678	12/22/1997	Payment	-62.80	-	-62.80	-	-
			-		-		
Northwest Office Supply							
12372	12/16/1997	Invoice	629.33	629.33	-	-	-
12637	12/23/1997	Invoice	26.79	26.79	-	-	-
1682	12/23/1997	Payment	-26.79	-26.79	-	-	-
			629.33	629.33	-	-	-
Pacific Computer Supply							
8120	11/14/1997	Invoice	558.43	-	558.43	-	-
1677	12/21/1997	Payment	-558.43	-	-558.43	-	-
8213	11/19/1997	Invoice	576.01	-	576.01	-	-
1679	12/22/1997	Payment	-400.99	-	-400.99	-	-
1679 COR	12/22/1997	Payment	400.99	-	400.99	-	-
1679 C	12/22/1997	Payment	-400.00	-	-400.00	-	-
8299	11/26/1997	Invoice	452.07	452.07	-	-	-
8467	12/16/1997	Invoice	187.95	187.95	-	-	-
			816.03	640.02	176.01	-	-
Portland Weekly							
6677	11/29/1997	Invoice	175.00	175.00	-	-	-
6842	12/14/1997	Invoice	410.00	410.00	-	-	-
			585.00	585.00	-	-	-
West Communications							
68-891	11/29/1997	Invoice	62.39	62.39	-	-	-
			2,092.75	1,916.74	176.01	-	-

ACTION: Chose **Print** from the Vendor Aged Detail File menu. Compare your report to the one shown above.

ACTION: Close the Vendor Aged Detail dialog box; then choose **Vendor Labels** from the Vendor window Report menu. Your screen will look like this:

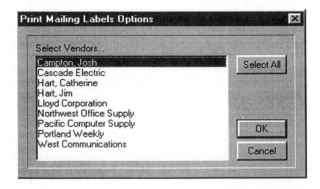

Print Mailing Labels Options

Select Vendors...

Campton, Josh
Cascade Electric
Hart, Catherine
Hart, Jim
Lloyd Corporation
Northwest Office Supply
Pacific Computer Supply
Portland Weekly
West Communications

[Select All]   [OK]   [Cancel]

Explanation: The Print Mailing Labels Option dialog box presents several options. Mailing labels can be printed either for all vendors or for the individual vendors you specify. To print mailing labels for individual vendors, highlight the appropriate vendor names. To print mailing labels for all vendors, click the **Select All** button.

ACTION: Josh Campton should already be highlighted. To highlight a second vendor, click **Lloyd Corporation** to select this company; then click **OK**. Compare your mailing labels with the ones shown below:

Campton, Josh
2874 NW Luray Terrace
Portland, Oregon 97210

Lloyd Corporation
Arlene Simpson
4567 NE 15th Street
Portland, Oregon 97232

ACTION: Close the Vendor window. Click **Report** on the home window menu bar. Point to Financials and click **Trial Balance**. Your screen will show the following dialog box:

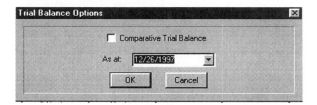

Explanation: The program is requesting the as at date for the Trial Balance. The date must be between the earliest transaction date and the session date inclusive. Additional default date options are available by clicking the drop-down list arrow to the right of the **As at** date field. You can override the default option by specifying the as at date.

ACTION: Accept the default date of 12/26/1997 for the Trial Balance by clicking the **OK** button. Your screen will look like this:

Trial Balance

File   Help

As At 12/26/1997		Debits	Credits
1010	Cash	6,491.63	-
1020	Accounts Receivable	3,155.00	-
1030	Prepaid Insurance	375.00	-
1040	Office Supplies	3,407.07	-
1050	Software	4,695.00	-
1060	Acc. Dep.- Software	-	2,999.62
1080	Computer Equipment	15,145.00	-
1090	Acc. Dep.- Computer Equip.	-	8,944.43
2010	Accounts Payable	-	2,092.75
3010	Seth Hunter, Capital	-	13,636.18
3020	Seth Hunter, Drawing	15,400.00	
4010	Revenue From Services	-	39,365.61
4020	Interest Income	-	0.00
5010	Advertising Expense	2,060.00	-
5020	Utilities Expense	525.00	-
5030	Rent Expense	3,600.00	-
5040	Office Supplies Expense	2,013.00	-
5050	Depreciation Exp.-Software	1,434.62	-
5060	Depreciation Exp.-Comp. Eq	4,277.77	-
5070	Insurance Expense	687.50	-
5080	Professional Services Exp.	2,545.00	-
5090	Bank Charges	0.00	-
5150	Misc. Expense	1,227.00	-
		67,038.59	67,038.59

ACTION: Print the Trial Balance by choosing **Print** from the Trial Balance File menu. Compare your Trial Balance to the one shown below:

Horizon Events
Trial Balance As at 12/26/1997

		Debits	Credits
1010	Cash	6,491.63	-
1020	Accounts Receivable	3,155.00	-
1030	Prepaid Insurance	375.00	-
1040	Office Supplies	3,407.07	-
1050	Software	4,695.00	-
1060	Acc. Dep.- Software	-	2,999.62
1080	Computer Equipment	15,145.00	-
1090	Acc. Dep.- Computer Equip.	-	8,944.43
2010	Accounts Payable	-	2,092.75
3010	Seth Hunter, Capital	-	13,636.18
3020	Seth Hunter, Drawing	15,400.00	-
4010	Revenue From Services	-	39,365.61
4020	Interest Income		0.00
5010	Advertising Expense	2,060.00	-
5020	Utilities Expense	525.00	-
5030	Rent Expense	3,600.00	-
5040	Office Supplies Expense	2,013.00	-
5050	Depreciation Exp.-Software	1,434.62	-
5060	Depreciation Exp.-Comp. Eq	4,277.77	-
5070	Insurance Expense	687.50	-
5080	Professional Services Exp.	2,545.00	-
5090	Bank Charges	0.00	
5150	Misc. Expense	1,227.00	-
		67,038.59	67,038.59
		==========	==========

ACTION: Close the Trial Balance window; backup your work for the chapter by clicking the File menu on the home window menu bar; point to Backup; click **Backup**. Highlight the information shown in the Backup File Name dialog box. Change the information for the Backup File Name to match the following screen:

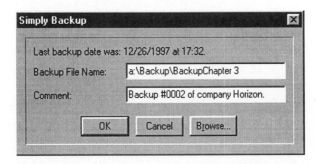

ACTION: Click **OK** to back up your data. Once the backup of the company data files is complete, click the **Exit** button to end the current work session and return to your Windows desktop.

SUMMARY

This chapter has explored the Payables components of CA-Simply Accounting for Windows as they would typically be used by a service business. Use of the Purchases, Orders & Quotes (Purchases Journal), Payment Checks (Payments Journal), and Vendors (Payables Ledger) to record cash and credit purchases, cash payments, and to maintain vendor records has been explained in detail. In addition, the procedures used to display and print a Purchases Journal, Payments Journal, check, Vendor List, Vendor Aged Report, mailing labels, and a Trial Balance have been demonstrated. By examining the methods used to record Payables-related transactions, various integration features of CA-Simply Accounting for Windows were illustrated.

QUESTIONS

QUESTIONS ABOUT THE SOFTWARE

1. In CA-Simply Accounting for Windows, all Payables functions are fully integrated with and linked to the General Ledger. Explain this statement and give an example.

2. If you entered an incorrect amount for a purchase transaction prior to posting the transaction, what steps would you follow to edit the entry?

3. Describe how the program prevents the use of duplicate check numbers.

4. Describe how partial payments made to vendors are recorded in the Payments Journal.

QUESTIONS ABOUT DAILY OPERATIONS

5. You would like to know the total amount paid to a vendor to date for the current fiscal year. How would you use the CA-Simply Accounting for Windows program to answer this question?

6. You have just received an invoice from a vendor that you think might be a duplicate of an invoice you have already recorded in CA-Simply Accounting for Windows. How would you use the CA-Simply Accounting for Windows program to determine if the invoice has already been recorded?

7. You would like to know the total current balance in Accounts Payable. How would you use the CA-Simply Accounting for Windows program to answer your question?

8. You are looking into the current financial status of the business and are concerned about the ability of the business to pay its current obligations. What report(s) would be of use to you in researching the answer to this question? Why?

9. You would like to know the total amount of advertising purchased by the company to date this fiscal year. How would you use the CA-Simply Accounting for Windows program to answer your question?

EXPLORING ALTERNATIVE SOFTWARE TECHNIQUES

10. CA-Simply Accounting for Windows supports both the accrual and cash basis accounting methods. Although generally accepted accounting principles (GAAP) require that businesses use the accrual basis, many small service businesses use the cash basis of accounting because it is an acceptable accounting method for income tax purposes; and it is more easily understood by business owners and managers that do not have an accounting background. Under the cash basis of accounting, revenues are recorded when cash is received regardless of when a sale is made, and expenses are recorded when cash is paid regardless of when the expense was incurred. The following example demonstrates the difference between the accrual and cash accounting methods for a Payables-related transaction, and explains how CA-Simply Accounting for Windows would account for the transaction under its cash-based accounting option.

Manual or Computerized System Accrual Method			**Manual System Cash Method**		
Date	**Debit**	**Credit**		**Debit**	**Credit**
12/15/1997 Phone Expense	$98.00		No entry		
Accounts Payable		$98.00			
Phone bill for November					
1/15/1998 Accounts Payable	$98.00		Phone Expense	$98.00	
Cash		$98.00	Cash		$98.00
Phone bill paid			Phone bill paid		

If a business elected to use the cash-based accounting option in CA-Simply Accounting for Windows, the program would record the above described transaction as follows:

CA-Simply Accounting for Windows Cash Basis

Date	**Debit**	**Credit**	
12/15/1997 Phone Expense	$98.00		**Unposted Entry**
Cash		$98.00	
Phone bill for November			

The above entry would be recorded in the Purchases Journal; however, the **Post** button would be replaced with a **Record** button. The transaction would be recorded in a special cash-based accounting data file (accessed through a menu option called Display Unpaid Entries under Report in the home window when the Purchases Journal icon is highlighted), and the purchase would be reflected in the vendors' Payables Ledger record. The program does not post the transaction to the General Ledger until the invoice is paid. The Vendor Aged report would reflect the entry, but the balance of Accounts Payable in the Trial Balance would not include the unposted $98.00 amount of the invoice.

The following entry would be posted when the invoice is selected for payment in the Payments Journal.

CA-Simply Accounting for Windows Cash Basis

Date	**Debit**	**Credit**	
1/15/93 Phone Expense	$98.00		**Posted Entry**
Cash		$98.00	
Phone bill for November			

Discuss the advantages and disadvantages of Seth Hunter's using the cash basis method in his Horizon Events business.

TRANSMITTAL

Horizon Events   **Name**_____
Chapter 3

Attach the following documents and reports:

1. Purchases Journal 12/1/1997 to 12/19/1997
2. Check 1677
3. Check 1678
4. Check 1679
5. Check 1679C
6. Payments Journal 12/1/1997 to 12/26/1997
7. Check 1680
8. Check 1681
9. Check 1682
10. Check 1682 (corrected check)
11. Purchases Journal 12/1/1997 to 12/26/1997
12. Vendor List 12/26/1997
13. Vendor Aged Detail report As at 12/26/1997
14. Mailing labels
15. Trial Balance As at 12/26/1997

EXERCISE—Harmony Piano Works
(CONTINUED FROM CHAPTER 2)

1. Load CA-Simply Accounting for Windows; open the data files for Harmony Piano Works (a:\HARMONY\Harmony.acs); then record the following transactions under the session date of 12/19/1997:

   December 14—Record the receipt of Invoice 1293 from Portland Piano in the amount of $334.95 for supplies.

   December 15—Record the receipt of Invoice 7724 from a new vendor in the amount of $302.90 for supplies:

New Vendor:	Piano City Refinishers
	Contact: Laurent Bourgeois
	8026 SW 61st Street
	Portland, Oregon 97219
	Phone: 503-244-2267
	Fax: 503-244-2270

   December 18—Record the receipt of Invoice 2514 from Hardware Northwest in the amount of $362.90 for tools.

   December 19—Issue Check 1020 to West Communications in full payment of their Invoice 2290.

   December 19—Issue Check 1021 to Northwest Gas in full payment of their Invoice X346.

   December 19—Correct Invoice 7724 from Piano City Refinishers. The amount of the invoice should be $496.55. Use 12/15/1997 as the date for the correcting entry.

2. Advance the session date to 12/26/1997; then record the following transactions:

   December 21—Record the receipt of Invoice X485 from Northwest Gas in the amount of $164.00 for gas and oil expense.

   December 22—Record the receipt of Invoice 7821 from Piano City Refinishers in the amount of $926.50 for supplies.

   December 26—Issue Check 1022 to Hardware Northwest in the amount of $425.00 in partial payment of Invoice 2390.

   December 26—Record the purchase and payment (Check 1023) of advertising from the Southeast Times, Invoice 943, a one-time vendor, in the amount of $57.00.

   December 26—Issue Check 1024 to Portland Piano in full payment of their Invoice 1276.

December 26—Correct the amount of Check 1023 for Invoice 943 to Southeast Times. The correct amount is $75.00

December 26—Correct the amount of Check 1022 to Hardware Northwest. The actual amount should be $400.00.

December 26—Issue Check 1025 to Hardware Northwest in full payment of their Invoice 2514.

3. Print the following reports:

   A. Purchases Journal (by posting date) 12/1/1997 to 12/26/1997
   B. Payments Journal (by posting date) 12/1/1997 to 12/26/1997
   C. Vendor Aged report (Select All, Detail) 12/1/1997 to 12/26/1997
   D. Trial Balance As at 12/26/1997

4 Make a backup copy of Harmony Piano Works' data files. Exit from the program.

5. Complete the Harmony Piano Works Transmittal.

TRANSMITTAL

Harmony Piano Works   **Name:**_____
Chapter 3

A. Attach the following documents and reports:

1. Check 1020
2. Check 1021
3. Check 1022
4. Check 1023
5. Check 1024
6. Corrected Check 1023
7. Corrected Check 1022 C
8. Check 1025
9. Purchases Journal 12/1/1997 to 12/26/1997
10. Payments Journal 12/1/1997 to 12/26/1997
11. Vendor Aged Detail report As at 12/26/1997
12. Trial Balance As at 12/26/1997

B. Refer to your reports to list the amounts requested below:

1. How much does Harmony Piano Works owe Portland Piano on 12/26/1997? $_____

2. How much does Harmony Piano Works owe Piano City Refinishers on 12/26/1997? $_____

3. What is the balance of the Cash account on 12/26/1997? $_____

4. What is the balance of the Supplies account on 12/26/1997? $_____

5. What is the balance of the Accounts Receivable account on 12/26/1997? $_____

SERVICE BUSINESSES—GENERAL

SERVICE BUSINESSES—GENERAL

LEARNING OBJECTIVES

After studying this chapter, you will be able to:
- Open the General Journal
- Open the General Ledger
- Enter General Journal entry transactions
- Review and edit General Journal transactions
- Post transactions in the General Journal
- Create, modify, and remove accounts using the General Ledger
- Perform a bank reconciliation
- Display and print reports from the General Journal
- Display and print a Chart of Accounts, General Ledger, Income Statement, and Balance Sheet
- Perform a year-end closing of the accounting records
- Observe and understand General-related integration accounts

GENERAL ACCOUNTING FOR A SERVICE BUSINESS

In this chapter, you will continue working with the Horizon Events company files. The features of the General components of CA-Simply Accounting for Windows will be discussed in detail. A bank reconciliation will be prepared, and year-end accounting procedures will be demonstrated. At the conclusion of this chapter, a practice set for Image Art Appraisal will give you an opportunity to work with the Receivables, Payables, and General components of CA-Simply Accounting for Windows all at the same time to record transactions and to perform the year-end procedures for a service business. Source documents similar to those illustrated throughout the Horizon Events Tutorial are used to represent transactions in the Image Art Appraisal practice set.

ACCOUNTING FOR GENERAL TRANSACTIONS

Three components of CA-Simply Accounting for Windows are used to account for general transactions and to maintain a company's chart of accounts: Journal (General Journal), Account Reconciliation, and Accounts (General Ledger). The General Journal is used to record journal entries that are not appropriately recorded in any of the other journals, for example, adjusting entries and closing entries. Journal entries can be made to all General Ledger accounts except for the Accounts Payable and Accounts Receivable integration/linking accounts. Journal entries affecting these integration/linking accounts can be posted only through the use of the appropriate subsidiary journals. This is to ensure that the Receivables and Payables subsidiary records are always in balance with the Accounts Receivable and Accounts Payable control accounts in the General Ledger. The Account Reconciliation Journal is used to perform a bank reconciliation, which reconciles the cash account with the bank account. Information about all accounts (account name, number, balance, etc.) are maintained in Accounts, which is the General Ledger. A variety of reports are available through the use of each component. All components of the program are fully integrated with and linked to the General Ledger. For example, when a General Journal entry is recorded in the General Journal, the program automatically posts the entry to the General Ledger. Consequently, once a general transaction is posted, its effect on the overall financial condition of the company is reflected immediately and automatically throughout the company's financial records.

HORIZON EVENTS TUTORIAL

The following tutorial is a step-by-step guide to recording General transactions for Horizon Events within the General components of CA-Simply Accounting for Windows. In addition, the procedures used to record adjusting entries, to perform a bank reconciliation, to prepare the financial statements, and to close the accounting records at the end of the year will be discussed. The procedures required to record transactions in the Receivables and Payables components were discussed in Chapters 2 and 3. The Horizon Events Tutorial will be continued and concluded in Chapter 4 to give you a comprehensive overview of how CA-Simply Accounting for Windows can be used to maintain the accounting records for a service business.

GENERAL JOURNAL—RECORDING GENERAL TRANSACTIONS

At the end of each accounting period, a business must make adjusting entries to update the accounting records prior to preparing its financial statements. Some businesses choose to make adjusting entries annually, others choose to make adjusting entries monthly. Seth Hunter records adjusting entries monthly for depreciation, expired insurance, and office supplies used during the past month. Seth Hunter has provided the following memo regarding the December adjusting entry for computer equipment depreciation.

Horizon Events—Document 27   **Session Date: 12/31/1997**

Memo:

Date: December 31, 1997

Record $388.89 in depreciation expense for the computer equipment for the month ending December 31, 1997.

 **ACTION:** Load CA-Simply Accounting for Windows; open the data files for Horizon Events (A:\HORIZON\Horizon.asc); then advance the session date to 12/31/1997. The Horizon Events home window will appear as shown below:

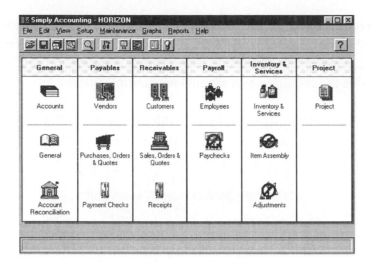

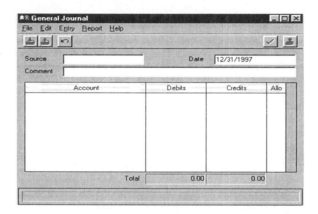

ACTION: Open the General Journal dialog box by double-clicking the **General** icon. Your screen will look like this:

Explanation: The General Journal dialog box is used to record General Journal entries, adjusting entries, closing entries, and certain types of correcting entries for transactions posted in error.

ACTION: Enter the word *Memo* in the **Source** field; then press the TAB key. Your screen will look like this:

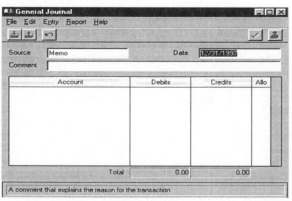

Explanation: The **Source** text box can be used for any reference number or notation you wish to associate with a General Journal entry and the source document that authorizes the entry. The **Comment** text box can be used for comments related to the journal entry in much the same way that an explanation is used when journal entries are recorded in a manual accounting system.

 ACTION: Press the TAB key to accept 12/31/1997 in the **Date** field; enter *Dec. adj. entry for Comp. Equip. dep.* in the **Comment** text box; then press the TAB key. Your screen will look like this:

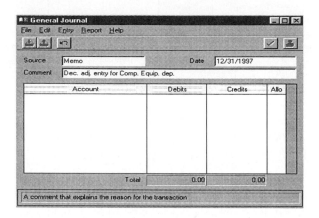

Explanation: A flashing cursor is positioned in the **Account** field.

 ACTION: With the flashing cursor positioned in the **Account** field, either press the ENTER key or double-click in the field with your mouse. Your screen will look like this:

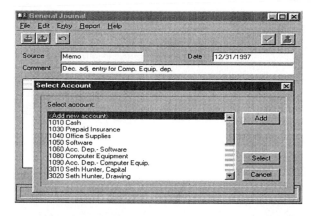

Explanation: The standard journal entry to record depreciation expense is:

	Debit	**Credit**
Depreciation Expense	xxx	
Accumulated Depreciation		xxx

The General Journal is used to record a variety of journal entries; consequently, you need to select the accounts to be debited and credited from the Select Account dialog box.

ACTION: Select **Depreciation Exp.-Comp. Eq.** (account number 5060) from the Select Account dialog box. Your screen will look like this:

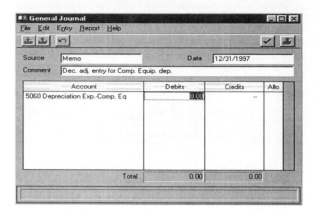

Explanation: The program has positioned the flashing insertion point in the **Debits** field.

ACTION: Enter *388.89* in the **Debits** field; then press the TAB key. Your screen will look like this:

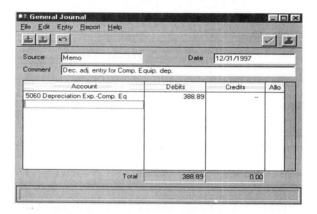

Explanation: The flashing insertion point is positioned in the **Account** field, ready for the selection of the account to be credited for this adjusting entry.

ACTION: With the flashing insertion point positioned in the **Account** field, either press the ENTER key or double-click in the field with your mouse. Select **Acc. Dep.-Computer Equip.** (account number 1090) from the Select Account dialog box. Your screen will look like this:

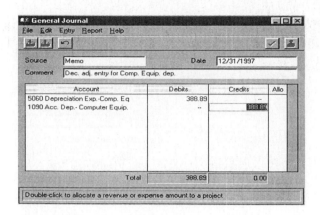

Explanation: The program has offered the same amount as the debit portion of the entry as a default amount in the **Credits** field. The credit amount remains highlighted. This feature is designed to facilitate entering compound journal entries. To enter compound journal entries, override the default amount offered; enter the correct amount; then select the other accounts affected by the transaction from the Select Account dialog box.

 ACTION: Press the TAB key to accept the default amount in the **Credits** field. Your screen will look like this:

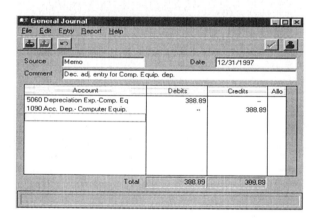

Explanation: This completes the data you need to enter into the General Journal dialog box to record Computer Equipment depreciation for the month. Note that you did not use the **Allo** field. Horizon Events is not currently using the Project components of CA-Simply Accounting for Windows, so the transaction is not allocated to a project. Before posting this transaction, you need to verify that the transaction data is correct by viewing the journal entry.

 ACTION: Click **Report** on the General Journal menu, choose **Display General Journal Entry**. Your screen will look like this:

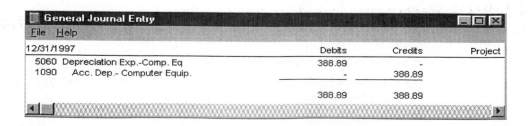

Explanation: The journal entry representing the data you have recorded in the General Journal dialog box is displayed. Review the journal entry for accuracy, noting any errors. If you have made an error, use the following editing techniques to correct the error:

Editing Tips
Editing a General Journal Entry

Move to the field that contains the error either by pressing the TAB key to move forward through each field or by pressing the SHIFT and TAB keys together to move to a previous field. This will highlight the selected field information so you can change it. Alternatively, you can use the mouse to point to a field and drag through the incorrect information to highlight it.

Type the correct information; then press the TAB key to enter it.

If you have associated a transaction with an incorrect account, double-click the incorrect account; then select the correct account from the **Select Account** dialog box. This will replace the incorrect account with the correct account.

Note that the **Post** button will be dimmed (unavailable) until the journal entry is in balance.

To discard an entry and start over, either choose **Undo Entry** from Edit on the General Journal menu, or click the **Exit** button on the title bar. Click **Yes** in response to the question "Are you sure you want to discard this journal entry?"

Review the journal entry for accuracy after any corrections by choosing **Display General Journal Entry** from Report on the General Journal menu bar.

It is **IMPORTANT TO NOTE** that the only way to edit a transaction after it is posted is to reverse the entry and enter the correct transaction. To correct transactions posted in error, refer to the transaction for software depreciation presented later in this chapter.

 ACTION: Close the General Journal Entry window and return to the General Journal transaction. If necessary, make corrections to the transaction. After verifying that the journal entry is correct, click the **Post** button to post this transaction. Your screen will look like this:

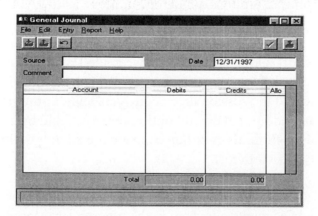

Explanation: A blank General Journal dialog box is displayed, ready for additional General Journal transactions to be recorded.

Additional General Journal Transactions

Record the following additional General Journal transactions:

Document 28 December 31—Record $130.42 as the amount of depreciation expense for the software for the month ending December 31, 1997.

Document 29 December 31—Record expired insurance in the amount of $26.50 for the month ending December 31, 1997.

Document 30 December 31—Record the use of $256.00 in office supplies for the month ending December 31, 1997.

 ACTION: After you have posted the journal entries for Documents 28, 29, and 30, close the General Journal dialog box. This will restore the home window, and the **General Journal** icon will remain highlighted. With the **General Journal** icon highlighted, click **Report** on the home window menu, point to Journal, and click **General**. Your screen will look like this:

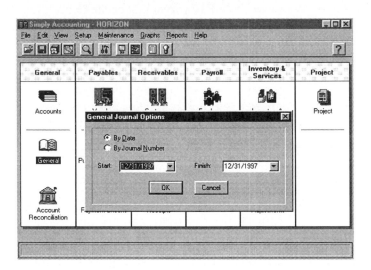

Explanation: The General Journal Options dialog box appears, asking you to define the information you want displayed.

Select **By Date** to display a report listing all entries between the start and finish dates you specify. The start date must be between the earliest transaction date and the session date inclusive. The finish date must be between the start date and the session date inclusive. Default options for start and finish dates are automatically displayed and additional default options are available by clicking the drop-down list arrows next to the **Start** and **Finish** fields. You can override the default options by specifying the posting dates in the **Start** and **Finish** fields.

Select **By Journal Number** to display a report listing all the entries between the start and finish journal numbers you enter. Journal entries made anywhere in the program are stored in the General Journal. The program automatically assigns a reference number to each journal entry. It assigns entry numbers sequentially from 00001 to 65000, then resets the counter when it reaches 65000. If you have posted entries in the current work session, the program displays the first journal entry number of the session. If you have not posted entries, it displays the first journal entry number on file. Default options for start and finish journal entry numbers are automatically displayed, and additional default options are available by clicking the drop-down list arrows next to the **Start** and **Finish** fields. You can override the default options by specifying the posting dates in the **Start** and **Finish** fields.

If you select the first and last journal entries of the current work session, the report lists all journal entries made during the session, including entries for which you entered an earlier date.

 ACTION: Select **By Date**; enter *12/1/1997* as the start date; leave the finish date set at 12/31/1997; then click the **OK** button. The following General Journal Display will appear on your screen:

<table>
<tr><td colspan="4">**General Journal Display**</td></tr>
<tr><td colspan="4">File   Help</td></tr>
<tr><td>12/1/1997 to 12/31/1997</td><td></td><td>Debits</td><td>Credits</td></tr>
<tr><td>12/31/1997   J29</td><td>Memo, Dec. adj. entry for Comp. Equip. dep.</td><td></td><td></td></tr>
<tr><td></td><td>5060 Depreciation Exp.-Comp. Eq</td><td>388.89</td><td>-</td></tr>
<tr><td></td><td>1090   Acc. Dep.- Computer Equip.</td><td>-</td><td>388.89</td></tr>
<tr><td>12/31/1997   J30</td><td>Memo, Dec. adj. entry for Software Dep.</td><td></td><td></td></tr>
<tr><td></td><td>5050 Depreciation Exp.-Software</td><td>310.42</td><td>-</td></tr>
<tr><td></td><td>1060   Acc. Dep.- Software</td><td>-</td><td>310.42</td></tr>
<tr><td>12/31/1997   J31</td><td>Memo, Dec. adj. entry for Prepaid Insurance</td><td></td><td></td></tr>
<tr><td></td><td>5070 Insurance Expense</td><td>62.50</td><td>-</td></tr>
<tr><td></td><td>1030   Prepaid Insurance</td><td>-</td><td>62.50</td></tr>
<tr><td>12/31/1997   J32</td><td>Memo, Dec. adj. entry for Off. Supplies used</td><td></td><td></td></tr>
<tr><td></td><td>5040 Office Supplies Expense</td><td>256.00</td><td>-</td></tr>
<tr><td></td><td>1040   Office Supplies</td><td>-</td><td>256.00</td></tr>
<tr><td></td><td></td><td>1,017.81</td><td>1,017.81</td></tr>
</table>

Explanation: Review the display for accuracy verifying that journal entry dates, account names and numbers, and amounts are correct.

 ACTION: Upon examining the General Journal Display, you realize that the adjustment for the software depreciation in J30 was entered incorrectly. The correct amount of the transaction should be $130.42. In order to correct the adjusting entry, double-click the **General** icon on the home window. This will open the General Journal. Enter *J30 COR* as the source. Your screen will appear as follows:

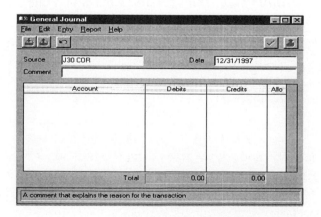

ACTION: Enter the comment *Reverse adj. entry for software dep.* Your screen will appear as follows:

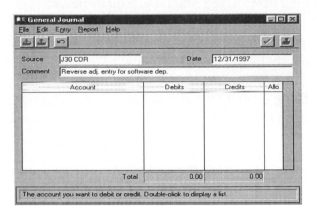

ACTION: Debit account 1060 for *$310.42* and credit account 5050 for *$310.42* to reverse the error. Your screen should appear as follows:

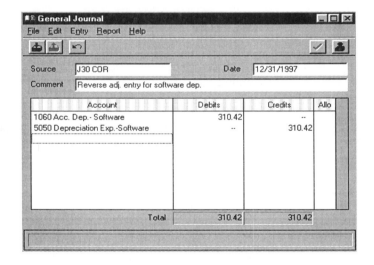

ACTION: If you entered everything correctly, click the **Post** button. Re-enter the transaction as a debit of *$130.42* to account 5050 and a credit of *$130.42* to account 1060. The source is *J30* and the explanation is *Correction of adj. entry for software dep.* Your screen will look like this:

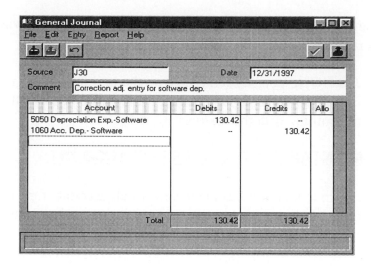

Explanation: This entry is the correct entry for the depreciation of software.

ACTION: If your transaction matches the above, click the **Post** button. Close the General Journal by clicking the **Close** button.

ACTION: On the home window, click **Report**, point to Journals, click **General**. Select **By Date** and use the start date of 12/1/1997 and a finish date of 12/31/1997. Click **OK** to display the General Journal. Your screen should appear as follows:

General Journal Display

File Help

12/1/1997 to 12/31/1997			Debits	Credits
12/31/1997	J29	Memo, Dec. adj. entry for Comp. Equip. dep.		
		5060 Depreciation Exp.-Comp. Eq	388.89	-
		1090 Acc. Dep.- Computer Equip.	-	388.89
12/31/1997	J30	Memo, Dec. adj. entry for Software Dep.		
		5050 Depreciation Exp.-Software	310.42	-
		1060 Acc. Dep.- Software	-	310.42
12/31/1997	J31	Memo, Dec. adj. entry for Prepaid Insurance		
		5070 Insurance Expense	62.50	-
		1030 Prepaid Insurance	-	62.50
12/31/1997	J32	Memo, Dec. adj. entry for Off. Supplies used		
		5040 Office Supplies Expense	256.00	-
		1040 Office Supplies	-	256.00
12/31/1997	J33	J30 COR, Reverse adj. entry for software dep.		
		1060 Acc. Dep.- Software	310.42	-
		5050 Depreciation Exp.-Software	-	310.42
12/31/1997	J34	J30 , Correction adj. entry for software dep.		
		5050 Depreciation Exp.-Software	130.42	-
		1060 Acc. Dep.- Software	-	130.42
			1,458.65	1,458.65

ACTION: If your screen matches the above, print the General Journal by choosing **Print** from the General Journal Display File menu. Compare your printed report to the one shown above.

Explanation: If you detect an error, refer to the steps presented above and correct your error.

■   **ACTION:** Close the General Journal Display window; close the home window to end the current work session and return to your Windows desktop.

■   **ALTERNATIVE ACTION:** You can continue with the tutorial without exiting from the program if you wish. The next steps are recorded under the same session date as the prior steps. Skip the next ACTION; then continue with the tutorial.

GENERAL LEDGER—MAINTAINING THE CHART OF ACCOUNTS

The General Ledger is the main ledger, it holds the records of all accounts for a company. Each account record contains the account number, account name, account balance, and account type. You can create, modify, or remove accounts through the General Ledger dialog box.

Creating a New General Ledger Account

In the process of preparing his financial records for the year-end closing, Seth Hunter has decided to add a new account to his chart of accounts.

Horizon Events—Document 31   **Session Date: 12/31/1997**

Memo

Date: December 31, 1997

Add account number 5015 Dues and Membership Expense to the chart of accounts.

■   **ACTION:** Load CA-Simply Accounting for Windows; open the data files for Horizon Events (A:\HORIZON\Horizon.asc); leave the session date set at 12/31/1997. Horizon Events home window will appear. Open the General Ledger by double-clicking the **Accounts** icon. Your screen will show large icons and the account names as shown in the partial account listing below: Accounts

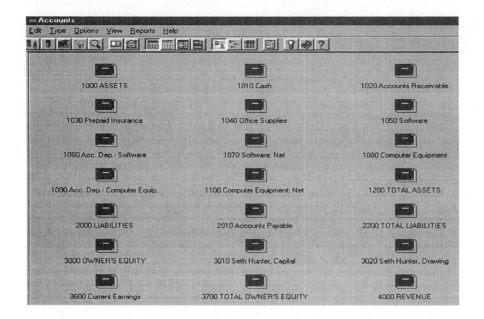

 ACTION: Change the screen to display all the accounts by clicking the **Display by small icon** button on the toolbar. Your screen will show the following:

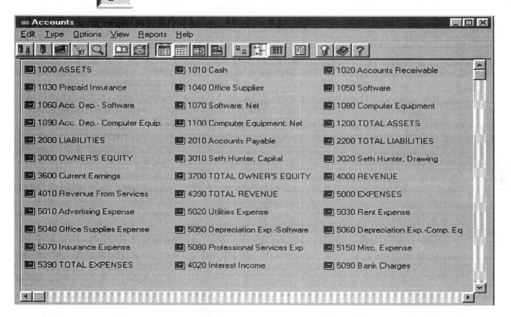

ACTION: Click the **Create** button on the toolbar. Your screen will show a blank General Ledger dialog box.

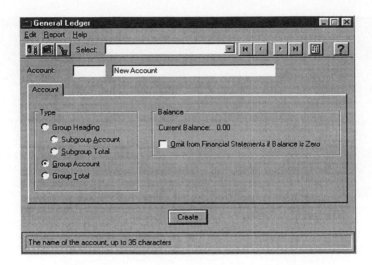

Explanation: CA-Simply Accounting for Windows uses a system of account numbers and account types to maintain the chart of accounts, create headings and subtotals in the financial statements, and to control the placement of headings, subtotals, and account balances on the financial statements. The section on the screen used to identify the type of account allows an account to be identified as a Group Heading, Subgroup Account, Subgroup Total, Group Account, and Group Total. Account types are not related to debits and credits. Financial statement design techniques will be discussed in detail in Section 3—Computerizing a Manual Accounting System. For now, all new accounts added to Horizon Events' chart of accounts will be assigned an account type of Group Account. In the blank General Ledger dialog box, fields are defined as follows:

Account: Enter the account number in the left part of the field; enter the account name in the right part of the field. The name can be up to 35 characters.

Balance: This field is used to enter account balances when the General Ledger is in the Not Ready mode. When the General Ledger is ready, this field displays the account's current balance for information only, you cannot change it.

Account type: Select the account type. See Section 3—Computerizing a Manual Accounting System for more information on account types. For now, all new accounts will be assigned a Group Account designation.

Omit from Financial Statements if Balance is Zero: Check this box if you do not want the account to be listed on the Balance Sheet or Income Statement if it has a zero balance. Leave the box unchecked if you want it to appear even if it has a zero balance.

 ACTION: Enter the information about the new account, Dues and Membership Expense, into the General Ledger dialog box. Your screen will look like this:

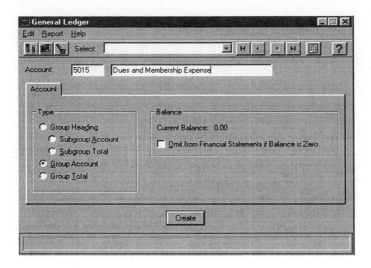

Explanation: Verify that all of the information is correct. If you have made an error, use the following editing techniques to correct the error:

Editing Tips
Editing a General Ledger Record

Move to the field that contains the error either by pressing the TAB key to move forward through each field or by pressing the SHIFT and TAB keys together to move to a previous field. This will highlight the selected field information so that you can change it. Alternatively, you can use the mouse to point to a field and drag through the incorrect information to highlight it.

Type the correct information; then press the TAB key to enter it.

Click the check box and/or option buttons to select or deselect as required.

To discard a record and start over, choose **Undo Changes** from Edit on the General Ledger menu bar; then click the **Yes** button in response to the question "Are you sure you want to undo changes to this ledger page?" Alternatively, click the **Exit** button on the title bar; then click the **No** button in response to the question "Do you still want to create this ledger page?"

It is IMPORTANT TO NOTE that the only way to edit a General Ledger record after it is created is to either modify the record or remove it and create a new General Ledger record.

 ACTION: When the ledger page is correct; click **Create**. Your screen will look like this:

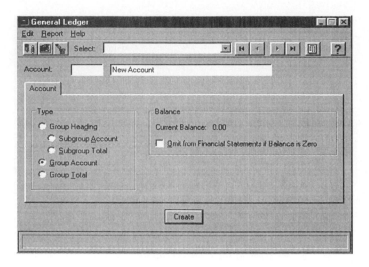

Explanation: The program has added the new account to Horizon Events' chart of accounts and has cleared the General Ledger dialog box in preparation for creating another account.

Modifying a General Ledger Account

If you made an error in a General Ledger account after you have created it, or need to change some information about an account, choose **Find** from the General Ledger Edit menu and choose the account from the list presented or click the account on the Accounts window and click the **Edit** button on the toolbar. Make corrections as necessary using the Editing Tips for Editing a General Ledger Record. To record the changes, either use the scroll bar to move to another ledger page or close the dialog box by clicking the **Exit** button on the title bar. Note that you cannot change the number of an account unless it has not been used since the earliest transaction date and that you cannot change a Subgroup Account or a Group Account to a Group Heading, Subgroup Total, or Group Total Account. To make this change, remove the account; then recreate the account. Once the General Ledger is in the Ready mode, the balance of an account is under program control and cannot be changed.

 ACTION: Change the name of Account 5060 from Depreciation Exp.-Comp. Eq to Depreciation Exp.-Comp. Equip. by clicking the drop-down list arrow next to select. Scroll through the account list until you see Account 5060. Point to Account 5060 to highlight. Your screen will appear as follows:

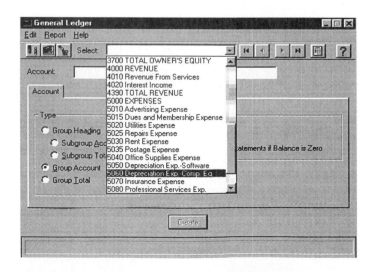

ACTION: Click **5060 Depreciation Exp.-Comp. Eq** to insert into the Account dialog box on the General Ledger screen. Position the cursor after Eq and type *uip.* to complete the name. Your screen will appear as follows:

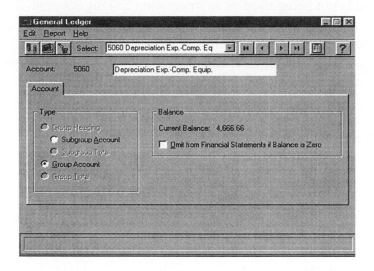

ACTION: Click the **Close** button on the title bar to save the change and exit the General Ledger. Display the account names and the account balances of all accounts by clicking the **Display by Name** button ▦ on the Accounts tool bar. A listing of accounts and balances will appear on the screen and ▦ Account 5060 Depreciation Exp.-Comp. Equip. will be highlighted. Your screen will look like the following:

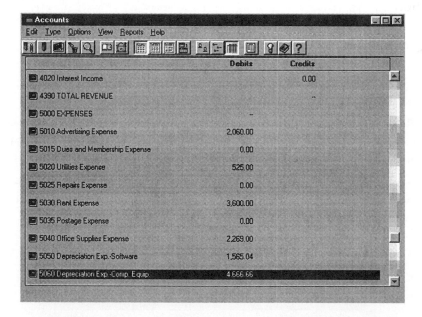

Explanation: Displaying the accounts by name allows you to see all the account names in full and the debit or credit balance of each account. Scroll through the chart of accounts and view the accounts and their balances.

Removing a General Ledger Account

You cannot remove a General Ledger account unless its balance is zero, it has not been used since the earliest transaction date, and is not being used as an integration/linking account. To remove a General Ledger account, choose **Find** from the General Ledger Edit menu and choose the account from the list presented or click the account on the Accounts window and click the **Remove** button on the toolbar. Choose **Remove** from the General Ledger Edit menu. The program will ask you if you are sure you want to remove the account. Choose **Yes** to remove it; then close the dialog box by clicking the **Exit** button.

Additional General Ledger Maintenance Items

Enter the following additional maintenance items:

Document 32 December 31—Add accounts 5025 Repairs Expense and 5035 Postage Expense to the chart of accounts. Both accounts are Group Accounts and have a zero balance.

Document 33 December 31—Add accounts 2020 Loans Payable and 5045 Interest Expense: Loans to the chart of accounts. Both accounts are Group Accounts and have a zero balance.

Document 34 December 31—Change the name of Account 1060 Acc. Dep.-Software to Accum. Dep.-Software.

Document 35 December 31—Change the name of Account 1090 Acc. Dep.-Computer Equip. to Accum. Dep.-Computer Equip.

ADDITIONAL TRANSACTIONS

Enter the following additional transactions:

Document 36 December 31—Use the Journal to record the purchase of computer equipment in the amount of $3,000 on account. Use Memo as the source. The Comment is "Purch. of and Loan for Comp. Equip." Use 2020 Loans Payable for the liability account. (Monthly payments including interest will be automatically deducted from the checking account by the bank.) Compare your transaction with the following General Journal entry. Make any changes necessary. When your transaction is correct, post the transaction and close the General Journal.

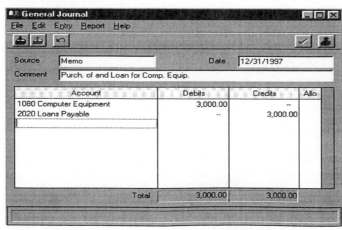

Document 37 December 31—Record the receipt of Check 801 from Viv Andrews, a one-time customer, for the sale of two hours of design service at $35.00 per hour. (Refer to Chapter 2 if you need assistance with this transaction.) Compare your transaction with the following Sales Journal - Sales Invoice. Make any changes necessary. When your transaction is correct, print the Sales Invoice and post the transaction.

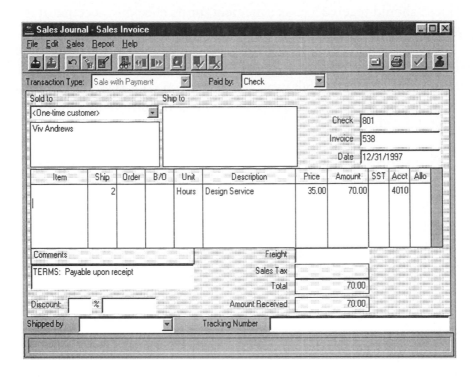

Document 38 December 31—Use Check 1683 to pay for Invoice 27-987 from a one-time vendor, Mail Service, for an $18.75 postage expense. (Refer to Chapter 3 if you need assistance with this transaction.) Compare your transaction with the following Purchase Journal - Purchase Invoice. Make any changes necessary. When your transaction is correct, print the Purchase Invoice and post the transaction.

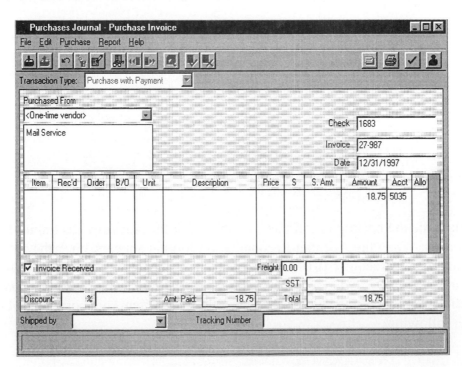

Document 39 December 31—Record the deposit of Viv Andrew's check on Deposit Slip 7260. (If necessary, refer to Chapter 2 for additional instructions.)

BANK RECONCILIATION

Each month, a business should receive a bank statement for its checking account. It is extremely important that this bank statement be reconciled with the account to which it is linked. Simply Accounting has a reconciliation feature that may be used to reconcile a bank or credit card account. There are five main tasks to complete when reconciling the bank statement: identify the bank account to be reconciled; clear the deposits and withdrawals that appear on your statement; identify any differences between the statement and your account, and adjust or correct the differences; process the reconciled information; and print the Account Reconciliation reports.

Horizon Events—Document 40   **Session Date: 12/31/1997**

Memo
December 31, 1997

Reconcile the Cash account using the December bank statement from Oregon Gold Bank.

Preparing to Reconcile the Bank Statement

Before beginning the bank reconciliation, a backup of the company files should be made.

ACTION: Click the **File** menu; then click **Backup**. The Simply Backup dialog box will appear. Fill in the Backup File name as *A:\Backup\12-31 Prior to Bank Reconciliation*. The comment should be *Backup #003 of company Horizon*. When your screen looks like the following, click **OK**.

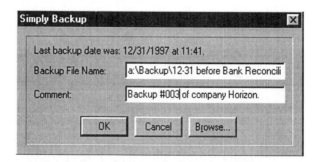

ACTION: Once the backup is complete, double-click the **Account Reconciliation** icon in the home window. When the Account Reconciliation Journal appears, click the drop-down list arrow for Account. Click **Account 1010 Cash** to select it as the account to be reconciled. Change the end date to 12/31/1997. Complete the comment as *Bank Reconciliation December*. Make sure **Transactions** has been selected for Display. When these items are complete, your screen should match the following:

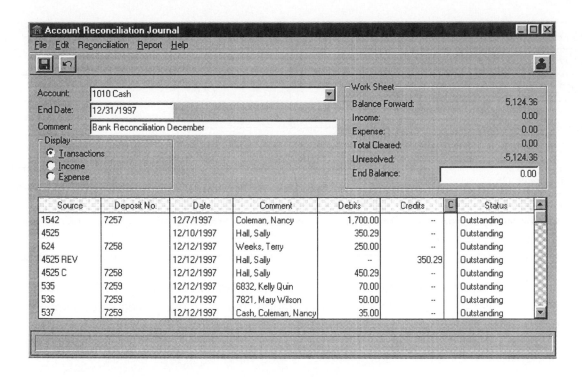

Reconcile the Bank Statement: Clearing Deposits

The first part of the reconciliation process is to compare the bank statement with the items recorded in the cash account. Simply Accounting uses the Account Reconciliation window to facilitate this process. When an item matches on both the bank statement and in the account, it is marked cleared in the Account Reconciliation window.

 ACTION: Refer to the following bank statement to complete the reconciliation:

OREGON GOLD BANK
2931 SE 25th Street
Portland, OR 97214
(503) 555-1122

Horizon Events
9076 SE Main
Portland, OR 97214

Acct. # 123-098			December, 1997
12/1/1997 Beginning Balance			$5,124.36
12/7/1997 Deposit 7257	$1,700.00		6,824.36
12/12/1997 Deposit 7258	700.29		7,524.65
12/12/1997 Deposit 7259	155.00		7,679.65
12/21/1997 Check 1677		$558.43	7,121.22
12/22/1997 Check 1678		62.80	7,058.42

12/22/1997 Check 1679 C		400.00	6,658.42
12/23/1997 Check 1680		65.00	6,593.42
12/23/1997 Check 1681		75.00	6,518.42
12/23/1997 Check 1682		26.79	6,491.63
12/31/1997 Computer Equip. Loan Pmt.: $29.17 Principal, $53.39 Interest		82.56	6,409.07
12/31/1997 Service Chg.		8.00	6,401.07
12/31/1997 Interest	3.22		6,404.29
12/31/1997 Ending Balance			$6,404.29

 ACTION: Enter the ending balance from the bank statement into the **End Balance** box in the Work Sheet section of the Account Reconciliation Journal. Your screen should appear as follows:

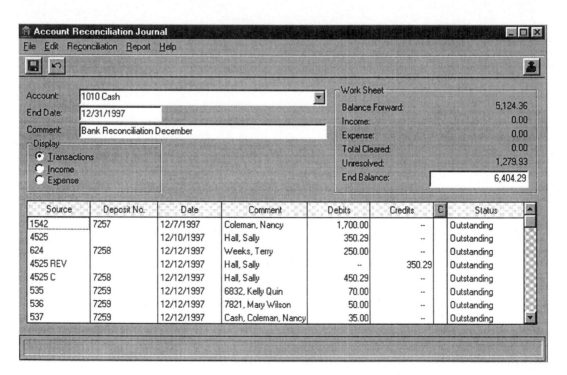

Explanation: The Work Sheet section of the Account Reconciliation Journal shows the balance forward (beginning balance) for the cash account. When the end balance is entered from the bank statement, the unresolved difference between the balance forward and the end balance is automatically calculated by Simply Accounting. When deposits and checks are cleared and when service charges, automatic payments, and interest income are recorded, the amount shown as unresolved should be 0.00.

 ACTION: Clear Deposit 7257 by comparing the amount shown on the bank statement with the amount shown in the Account Reconciliation Journal. If both items show 1,700.00, click the **C** column. This will place a ✔ in the column and change the status from outstanding to cleared. Once this is complete, your screen will look like the following:

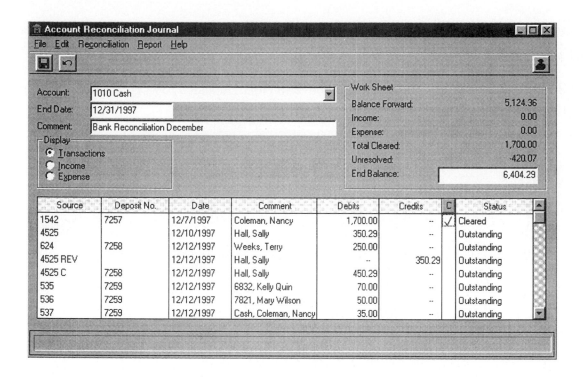

Explanation: Notice the change in the **Status** column from outstanding to cleared. Also notice the changes in the Work Sheet area of the Journal. The total cleared is $1,700.00 and the unresolved amount is -$420.07.

 ACTION: Clear both items deposited on Deposit 7258 by clicking the **C** column next to either of the checks deposited on this deposit slip. Then click the **C** column heading two times. This should place check marks next to the $250.00 amount deposited for the check from Terry Weeks and the $450.29 amount deposited for the check from Sally Hall. Your screen should appear as follows:

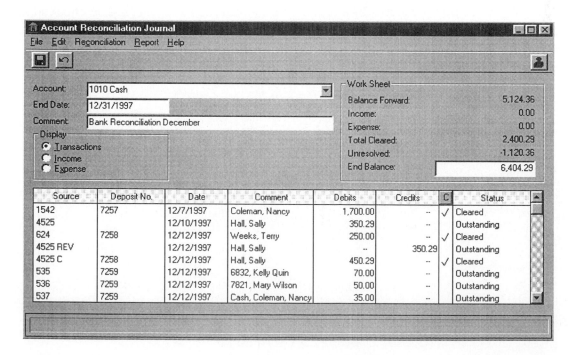

Explanation: The shortcut illustrated above can save time when several items have been deposited on one deposit slip.

ACTION: Repeat the steps illustrated above to clear Deposit 7259. Your screen will appear as follows:

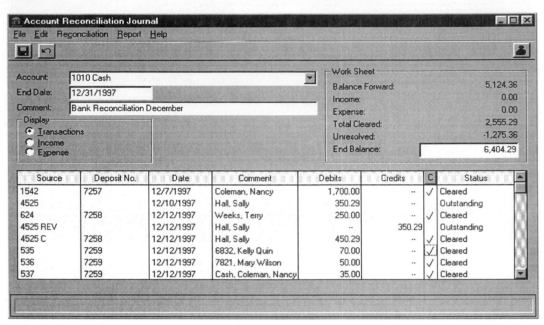

Explanation: All the deposits that were shown on the bank statement have been marked "Cleared." Notice the correction made to the transaction for Sally Hall appears in the Account Reconciliation Journal. Even though the two $350.29 transactions for Sally Hall were a correction, Simply still records and displays them as part of the Account Reconciliation Journal so that no cash transaction is hidden. These corrections must also be changed from the status of outstanding.

ACTION: To change the status of a correction, the transaction must first be checked and changed from a status of outstanding to cleared. Click the **C** column to mark both of the corrections for Sally Hall to cleared. Your screen will appear as follows:

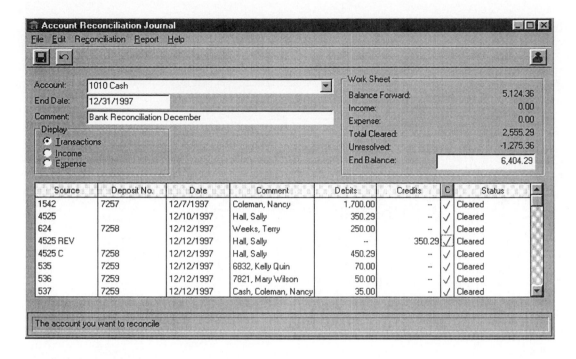

Explanation: Once the status is cleared, it may be changed to something more appropriate.

ACTION: Because the original transaction of $350.29 for Sally Hall was corrected by using a reversing entry, the status of this transaction should be changed from cleared to reversed. Do this by double-clicking **Outstanding** in the **Status** column to get the Select Transaction Status dialog box as shown below:

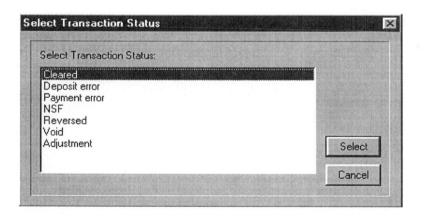

ACTION: Click **Reversed** in the Select Transaction Status dialog box; then click the **Select** button. This will change the status of the original entry for Sally Hall to reversed. Repeat the procedures indicated to change the status of the $350.29 credit for Sally to adjustment. When these steps have been completed, your screen will appear as follows:

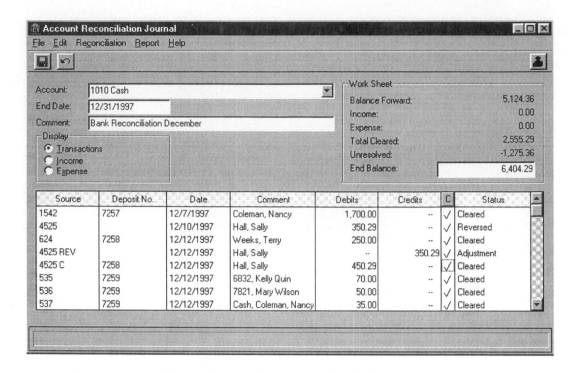

Source	Deposit No.	Date	Comment	Debits	Credits	C	Status
1542	7257	12/7/1997	Coleman, Nancy	1,700.00	--	√	Cleared
4525		12/10/1997	Hall, Sally	350.29	--	√	Reversed
624	7258	12/12/1997	Weeks, Terry	250.00	--	√	Cleared
4525 REV		12/12/1997	Hall, Sally	--	350.29	√	Adjustment
4525 C	7258	12/12/1997	Hall, Sally	450.29	--	√	Cleared
535	7259	12/12/1997	6832, Kelly Quin	70.00	--	√	Cleared
536	7259	12/12/1997	7821, Mary Wilson	50.00	--	√	Cleared
537	7259	12/12/1997	Cash, Coleman, Nancy	35.00	--	√	Cleared

Reconcile the Bank Statement: Clearing Checks

Once the deposits have been reconciled, the next step in the reconciliation process is to clear all the checks that have been processed by the bank.

ACTION: If necessary, use the scroll button next to the **Status** column to scroll down through the transactions until you see the checks. Check 1677 has been cleared by the bank. Clear Check 1677 in the amount of $558.43 by clicking next to the check in the **C** column. This will place a check mark in the column and change the status to cleared. Your screen will appear as follows:

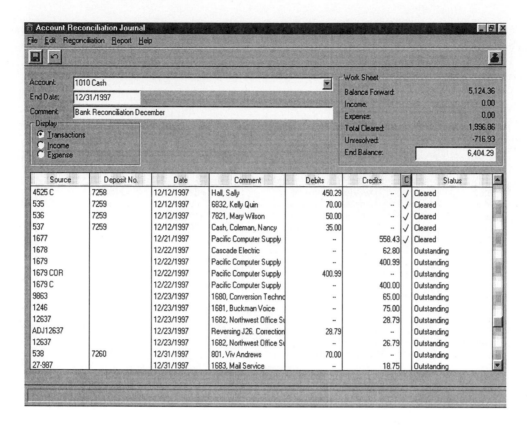

Explanation: The above procedure clears the check that has been paid by the bank and changes the amount for the total cleared and the amount for unresolved. Because all the deposits were cleared first, you may have noticed that the unresolved amount is a negative number. As the checks are cleared, the amount that is unresolved will change from a negative into a positive amount.

ACTION: Repeat the steps listed above until all the checks shown on the bank statement have been cleared. When this is complete, your screen will appear as follows:

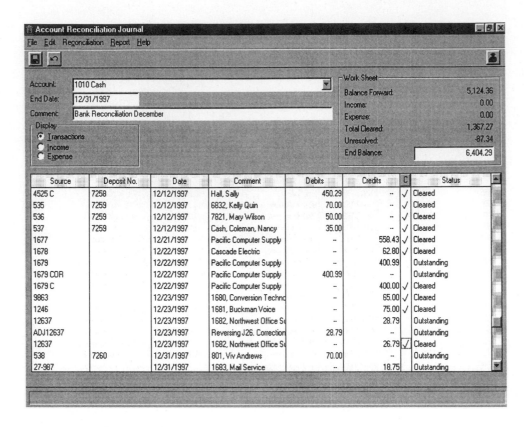

Explanation: All the checks paid by the bank have been cleared, yet there is still an unresolved amount. As you look at the Account Reconciliation Journal, you will notice that there are some correcting entries that were made but still show a status of outstanding. Since the transaction for Pacific Computer Supply in the amount of $400.99 was entered in error and subsequently corrected, Check 1679 should have a status of reversed, and the debit entry for $400.99 that was made to correct the error should have a status of adjustment.

 ACTION: To change the status of a correction, the transaction must first be checked and changed from a status of outstanding to cleared. Click the **C** column to mark both of the corrections for Pacific Computer Supply to cleared. Your screen will appear as follows:

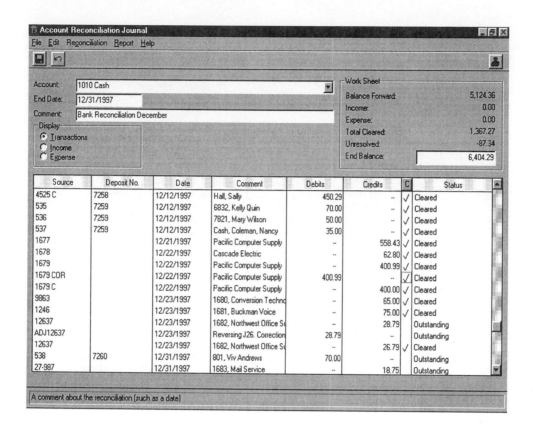

Explanation: Once the status is cleared, it may be changed to something more appropriate.

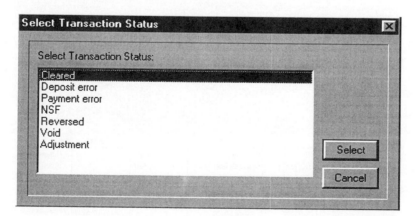

ACTION: Because the original transaction of $400.99 for Pacific Computer Supply was corrected by using a reversing entry, the status of this transaction should be changed from cleared to reversed. Do this by double-clicking **Outstanding** in the **Status** column to get the Select Transaction Status dialog box as shown below:

ACTION: Click **Reversed** in the Select Transaction Status dialog box; then click the **Select** button. This will change the status of the original entry for Pacific Computer Supply to reversed. Repeat the procedures indicated to change the status of the $400.99 debit to Pacific Computer Supply to adjustment. When these steps have been completed, your screen will appear as follows:

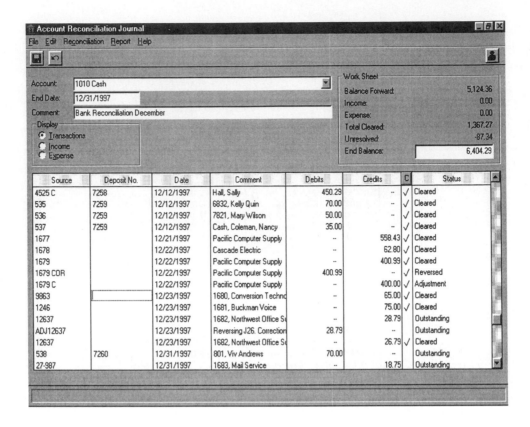

ACTION: Repeat the steps above to change the status of the correction for Northwest Office Supply in the amount of $28.79. The original credit entry should have a status of reversed and the debit transaction should have a status of adjustment. When this is complete, your screen will appear as follows:

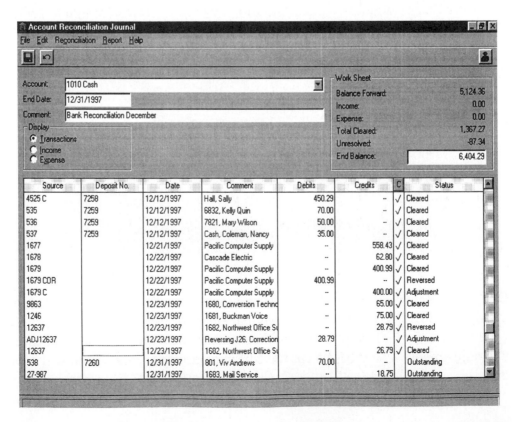

Explanation: At this point, all deposits, cleared checks, and correcting entries have been removed from a status of outstanding. Yet, there is still an amount shown as unresolved. As you look at the Account Reconciliation Journal, you will notice two transactions listed as outstanding. When you look at the bank statement, you will notice amount listed for an automatic loan payment, a bank service charge, and interest paid by the bank. All of these items must be accounted for as part of the reconciliation process.

Reconcile the Bank Statement: Outstanding Checks and Deposits in Transit

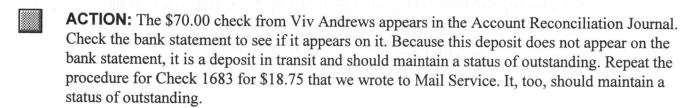 **ACTION:** The $70.00 check from Viv Andrews appears in the Account Reconciliation Journal. Check the bank statement to see if it appears on it. Because this deposit does not appear on the bank statement, it is a deposit in transit and should maintain a status of outstanding. Repeat the procedure for Check 1683 for $18.75 that we wrote to Mail Service. It, too, should maintain a status of outstanding.

Explanation: No change is made to the Account Reconciliation Journal for any checks or deposits that have not yet been cleared by the bank.

Reconcile the Bank Statement: Recording Bank Statement Transactions

The next part of the bank reconciliation requires entering any transaction that appears on the bank statement but does not appear in the Account Reconciliation Journal.

ACTION: Make an entry in the General Journal to record the automatic loan payment for the computer equipment. As stated in the bank statement, the loan payment amount (principal) is $29.17 and the amount of interest paid is $53.39 for a total payment of $82.56. Use Memo as the source of the Journal transaction. Save the Account Reconciliation prepared up to this point by clicking the **Save** icon on the Account Reconciliation toolbar. Switch from the Account Reconciliation window to the home window by clicking the **Simply Accounting** button on the Windows taskbar.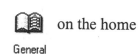

Explanation: Clicking the **Simply Accounting** button on the taskbar switches between windows within Simply without having to close the Account Reconciliation Journal.

ACTION: Open the General Journal by double-clicking the **General** icon on the home window. Your screen should look like the following:

General

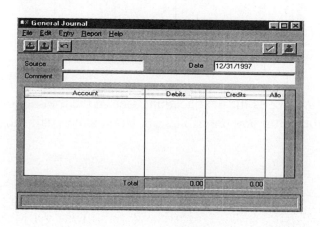

Explanation: A blank General Journal dialog box is on the screen ready to have the adjusting entry recorded for the loan payment.

ACTION: Enter the transaction for the automatic loan payment. The source is Memo. The comment is "December Loan Pmt. Computer Equip." Use the date of 12/31/1997. Because this is a compound entry, you will debit 2020 Loans Payable for *$29.17* and you will debit 5045 Interest Expense: Loans for *$53.39*. When the first debit amount is entered, Simply automatically credits the second account for the same amount. Your screen will appear as follows:

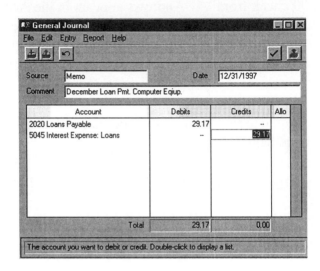

ACTION: Eliminate the credit to Interest Expense by deleting the credit amount, clicking in the **Debit** column, and entering *$53.39*. Your screen should look like the following:

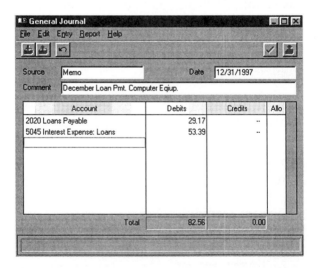

ACTION: Enter *1010 Cash* as the next account used in the transaction. Simply will automatically enter the credit amount of $82.56. Your screen will show the following:

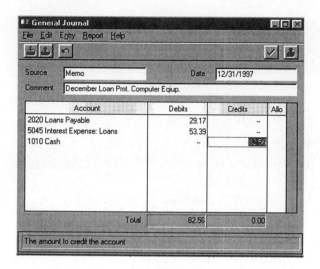

ACTION: TAB to enter the credit amount into the Total at the bottom of the screen. Compare your transaction to the above. If you have used the correct accounts and amounts, click the **Post** button. When the transaction has been posted, close the General Journal and return to the Account Reconciliation Journal by clicking the **Account Reconciliation** button on the Windows taskbar.

Explanation: If necessary, scroll through the transactions displayed for the cash account until you see the entry for the automatic loan payment. The entry is now on the bank statement and in the Account Reconciliation Journal, so it must be marked "Cleared."

ACTION: Follow the procedures indicated earlier to mark the December Loan Payment as cleared. Your screen should look like the following:

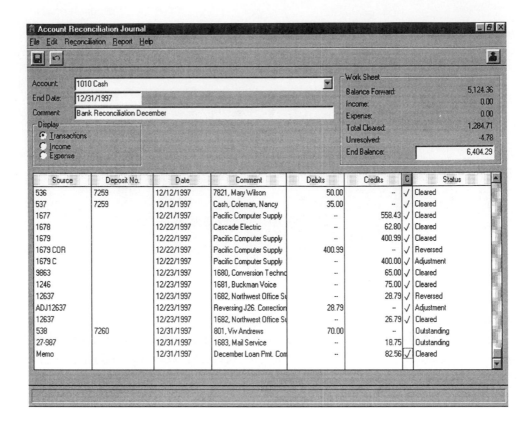

Explanation: The automatic loan payment has been cleared. Yet, there is still an unresolved amount of -$4.78; and there are still two items on the bank statement that have not been reconciled. In addition to displaying transactions, the Account Reconciliation Journal can also display a window for income or expense. Both the Income display and the Expense display show a window in which up to three transactions may be recorded for items that have been added to or deducted from the account.

ACTION: Enter the $8.00 service charge by clicking **Expense** in the Display area of the Account Reconciliation Journal. Your screen will appear as follows:

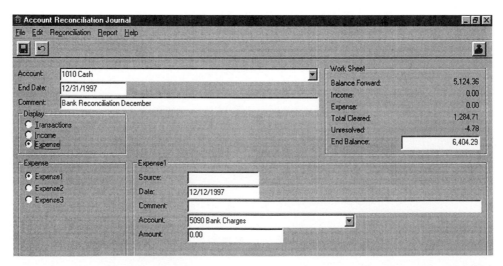

Explanation: The Account Reconciliation Journal displays the screen used to enter expenses. Notice Expense1 is shown. Simply will allow two other expense transactions to be recorded as part of the bank reconciliation.

ACTION: Complete the recording of the $8.00 bank service charge. Enter *Bank Statemnt* as the source, *12/31/1997* as the date, *December Service Charge* as the comment, and *8* for the amount. When finished, your screen will show the following:

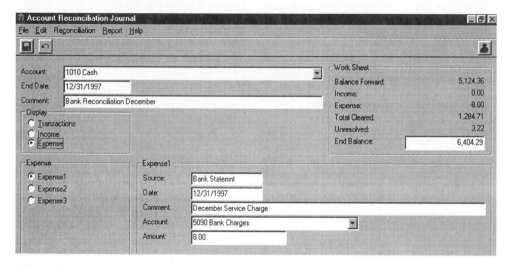

Explanation: The amount of the service charge has been entered. Notice that the unresolved amount is now $3.22. The final item to be entered from the bank statement is the $3.22 interest earned on the account.

ACTION: In the Display section of the Account Reconciliation Journal window, click **Income**. Income1 should be selected and appear in the Income1 section of the window. If it does not appear automatically, click **Income1** in the **Income** column. Your screen will appear as follows:

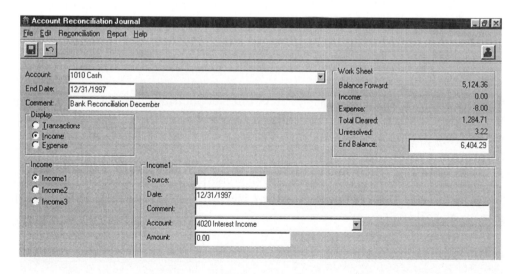

ACTION: Enter the $3.22 interest income received from the bank. Use *Bank Statemnt* as the source, *12/31/1997* as the date, and *December Interest* as the comment. Enter *3.22* as the amount. When complete, your screen should appear as follows:

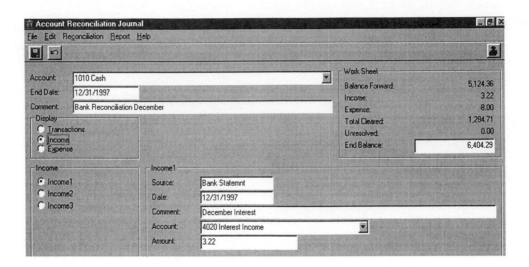

Explanation: All items on the bank statement have been entered. Notice that the unresolved amount is now equal to 0.00.

Reconcile the Bank Statement: Reports, Printing, and Processing

Once you have reconciled every item on the statement and matched or checked everything in the Account Reconciliation window, the Unresolved amount will be zero if everything in the reconciliation has been done correctly. When you reconcile an account and process the reconciliation, Simply updates the income and expense accounts you selected and entered in the Account Reconciliation window. In addition, all transactions whose status you updated are removed from the Account Reconciliation window. Only the transactions with a status of outstanding remain in the transaction window. Finally, the Account Reconciliation window is updated to prepare for the next reconciliation by advancing the ending date by one month and changing the ending balance in the Work Sheet area to the new balance forward.

To complete the bank reconciliation process, an Account Reconciliation report should be printed so you have a record of your work. This printout should be filed along with the bank statement. The last part of the bank reconciliation is to back up your work.

 ACTION: To see the transactions for the service charges and the interest income, click **Report** on the menu bar. Then click **Display Account Reconciliation Journal Entry**. Your screen should appear as follows:

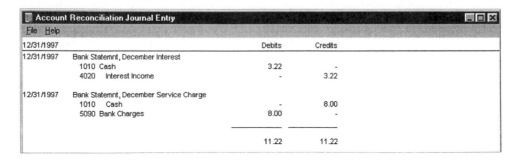

ACTION: Click **File** on the Account Reconciliation Journal Entry menu bar. Click **Print** to print a copy of the journal entries. Close the Account Reconciliation Journal Entry. If your entries do not match the above, make the appropriate changes to Expense1 and/or Income1 to correct.

ACTION: Prior to processing the Account Reconciliation, it is a good idea to print an Account Reconciliation detail report. (This report may also be printed after the reconciliation has been processed.) In order to print this report, you need to access the Report menu on the home window toolbar. Do not close the Account Reconciliation Journal. Click the **Simply Accounting** button on the Windows taskbar. 🖳 Simply Acco...

Explanation: Clicking the button for the home window on the Windows taskbar switches you from one part of the program to another. Notice that the Simply Accounting button looks like it is pressed in (this means it is the active window—the one on the screen) and the Account Reconciliation button looks like it is pushed out (it is inactive—open but not in use).

ACTION: Click **Report** on the home window, click **Account Reconciliation.** Your screen will show the following Account Reconciliation Report Options dialog box:

ACTION: Complete the Account Reconciliation Report Options dialog box by clicking the drop-down list arrow for Accounts. Click **1010 Cash** and TAB to select. Verify that **Detail** is selected and that the start date is 12/1/1997 and the finish date is 12/31/1997. When your screen matches the following, click **OK**.

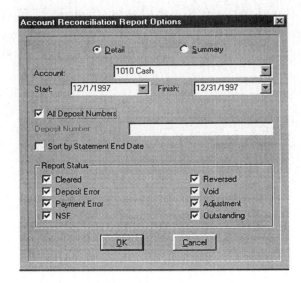

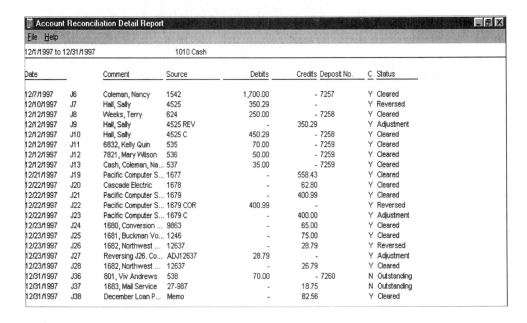

ACTION: The following Account Reconciliation Detail Report will appear on your screen. Compare your report with the one shown. If it matches, click **File** and **Print** to print the report. If it does not match, return to the Account Reconciliation window and make any changes necessary; then print the report.

Explanation: This report shows all of the items reconciled on the Transaction display of the Account Reconciliation Journal. The Account Reconciliation Journal Entry Report shows the transactions entered on the Income and Expense displays.

ACTION: If all items printed are correct, close the Account Reconciliation Detail Report and return to the Account Reconciliation Journal by clicking the **Account Reconciliation** button on the taskbar. If the items are not correct, return to the Account Reconciliation Journal to make any corrections necessary and print the report. Once the report has been printed, click the **Post** button to process the account reconciliation. When the processing is complete, your screen should show the following:

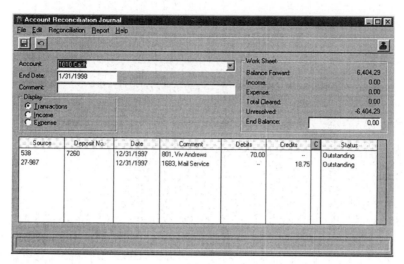

Explanation: The only items shown are the two transactions with an outstanding status. Notice that the end date has been changed and that the end balance of the previous reconciliation is now shown as the balance forward on this Account Reconciliation Journal.

ACTION: The bank reconciliation is complete. Close the Account Reconciliation Journal and return to the home window. Back up your work by clicking **File** on the menu bar. Click **Backup**. Name your backup file *A:\Backup\Backup Chapter 4 Bank Reconciliation Complete*. The comment should be *Backup #004 of company Horizon*. Click **OK** to back up your work.

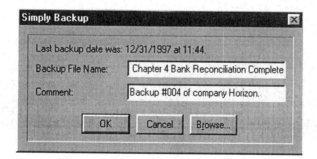

GENERAL REPORTS AND FINANCIAL STATEMENTS

A variety of General-related reports are available in CA-Simply Accounting for Windows. The procedures required to print and display a General Journal report were demonstrated earlier in this chapter. In addition to the General Journal report, the program can print or display a Chart of Accounts, General Ledger, Trial Balance, Income Statement, and Balance Sheet. Use the scroll bars at the bottom or right side of a displayed report to view reports that contain more text than can be displayed at one time.

ACTION: Close the Simply Backup dialog box; on the home window menu bar, click **Report**, point to List, and click **Chart of Accounts**. Scroll through the Chart of Accounts. You will see the accounts listed below; however, Revenue and Expenses will appear below Owner's Equity:

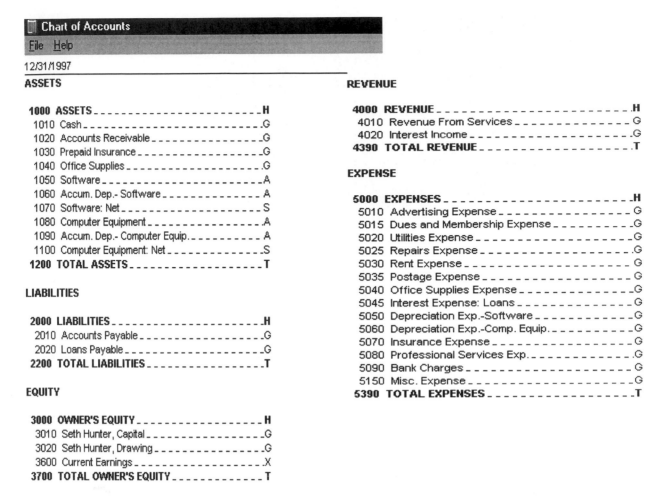

 ACTION: Choose **Print** from the Chart of Accounts File menu. Compare your report to the one shown above.

Explanation: The Chart of Accounts lists all General Ledger accounts in ascending order by account code. Code abbreviations are defined as follows: Group Heading—H, Group Account—G; Subgroup Account—A; Subgroup Total—S; Current Earnings—X; Group Total—T. Current Earnings is a linked account within the General portion of the program. It is the account that is used to list the company's net income in the owner's equity section of the Balance Sheet and is linked to the owner's capital account. During the closing process, the balance of the Current Earnings account is transferred to the owner's capital account. For more information on the use of linking accounts and account codes, see Section 3—Computerizing a Manual Accounting System.

 ACTION: Close the Chart of Accounts dialog box; select **Report** from the home window menu bar; then point to Financials and click **General Ledger**. Your screen will look like this:

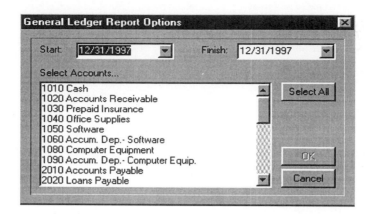

Explanation: The General Ledger Report Options dialog box presents several options. General Ledger reports can be prepared for all accounts or for the individual accounts you specify. To prepare reports for individual accounts, highlight the appropriate account names. To prepare a report listing all accounts, click the **Select All** button. Specify the start and finish dates of the period to be covered by the General Ledger report. The start date must be between the earliest transaction date and the session date. The finish date must be between the start date and the session date. Default options for start and finish dates are automatically displayed, and additional default options are available by clicking the drop-down list arrow buttons next to the **Start** and **Finish** fields. You can override the default options by specifying the posting dates in the **Start** and **Finish** fields.

 ACTION: Enter *12/1/1997* as the start date; leave the finish date set at 12/31/1997; click account **1040 Office Supplies** to select; then click the **OK** button. Your screen will look like this:

General Ledger Report

File Help

12/1/1997 to 12/31/1997

				Debits	Credits	Balance
1040	**Office Supplies**					2,563.00 Dr
12/16/1997	Pacific Computer Supply	8467	J15	187.95	-	2,750.95 Dr
12/16/1997	Northwest Office Supply	12372	J16	609.33	-	3,360.28 Dr
12/16/1997	Reversing J16. Correction is J...	ADJ12372	J17	-	609.33	2,750.95 Dr
12/16/1997	Northwest Office Supply	12372	J18	629.33	-	3,380.28 Dr
12/23/1997	1682, Northwest Office Supply	12637	J26	28.79	-	3,409.07 Dr
12/23/1997	Reversing J26. Correction is J...	ADJ12637	J27	-	28.79	3,380.28 Dr
12/23/1997	1682, Northwest Office Supply	12637	J28	26.79	-	3,407.07 Dr
12/31/1997	Dec. adj. entry for Off. Suppli...	Memo	J32	-	256.00	3,151.07 Dr
				1,482.19	894.12	

Double-click to display the record on this line

 ACTION: Choose **Print** from the General Ledger Report File menu. Compare your report to the one shown above. Close the General Ledger Report dialog box; from Report on the home window menu bar point to Financials and click **Trial Balance**. Your screen will look like this:

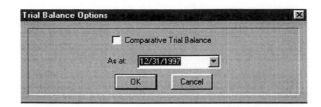

Explanation: The Trial Balance Options dialog box allows you to specify the as at date for the Trial Balance. The date must be between the earliest transaction date and the session date inclusive.

ACTION: Accept the default date of 12/31/1997 for the Trial Balance by clicking the **OK** button. Your screen will look like this:

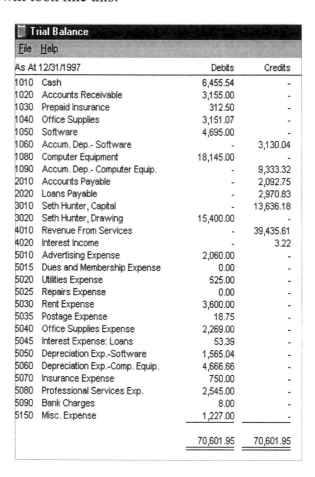

Trial Balance		
File Help		
As At 12/31/1997	Debits	Credits
1010 Cash	6,455.54	-
1020 Accounts Receivable	3,155.00	-
1030 Prepaid Insurance	312.50	-
1040 Office Supplies	3,151.07	-
1050 Software	4,695.00	-
1060 Accum. Dep.- Software	-	3,130.04
1080 Computer Equipment	18,145.00	-
1090 Accum. Dep.- Computer Equip.	-	9,333.32
2010 Accounts Payable	-	2,092.75
2020 Loans Payable	-	2,970.83
3010 Seth Hunter, Capital	-	13,636.18
3020 Seth Hunter, Drawing	15,400.00	-
4010 Revenue From Services	-	39,435.61
4020 Interest Income	-	3.22
5010 Advertising Expense	2,060.00	-
5015 Dues and Membership Expense	0.00	-
5020 Utilities Expense	525.00	-
5025 Repairs Expense	0.00	-
5030 Rent Expense	3,600.00	-
5035 Postage Expense	18.75	-
5040 Office Supplies Expense	2,269.00	-
5045 Interest Expense: Loans	53.39	-
5050 Depreciation Exp.-Software	1,565.04	-
5060 Depreciation Exp.-Comp. Equip.	4,666.66	-
5070 Insurance Expense	750.00	-
5080 Professional Services Exp.	2,545.00	-
5090 Bank Charges	8.00	-
5150 Misc. Expense	1,227.00	-
	70,601.95	70,601.95

ACTION: Print the Trial Balance by choosing **Print** from the Trial Balance File menu. Compare your Trial Balance to the one shown above. Close the Trial Balance window; select **Report** from the home window menu bar; point to Financials and click **Income Statement**. Your screen will look like this:

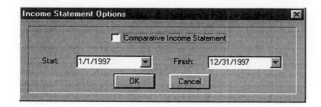

Explanation: The Income Statement Options dialog box presents **Start** and **Finish** date fields. The start date can be same as the fiscal start date, or any date between the earliest transaction date and the session date inclusive. It cannot be between the fiscal start date and the earliest transaction date. The finish date can be any date between the earliest transaction date and the session date inclusive. Default options for start and finish dates are automatically displayed and additional default options are available by clicking the drop-down list arrow buttons next to the **Start** and **Finish** fields. You can override the default options by specifying the posting dates in the **Start** and **Finish** fields.

 ACTION: Accept 1/1/1997 as the start date; accept 12/31/1997 as the finish date; click the **OK** button. Your screen will look like this:

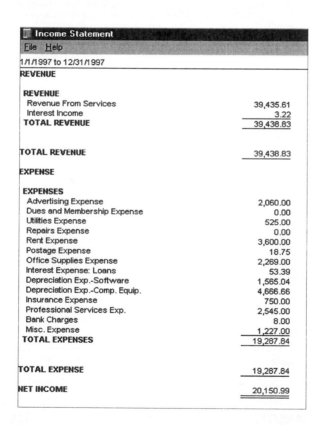

 ACTION: Choose **Print** from the Income Statement File menu. Compare your report to the one shown above. Close the Income Statement dialog box; then choose **Balance Sheet** from the Financials option on the home window Report menu. Your screen will look like this:

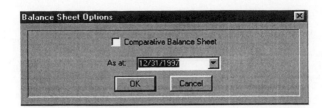

Explanation: The Balance Sheet Options dialog box presents an **As at** date field. Balance Sheets can be prepared for any date between the earliest transaction date and the session date inclusive. The session date is displayed automatically and additional default date options are available by clicking the drop-down list arrow button to the right of the **As at** date field. You can override the default option by specifying the as at date.

 ACTION: Accept the as at date of 12/31/1997 by clicking the **OK** button. Your screen will look like this:

Balance Sheet
File   Help

As At 12/31/1997

ASSETS

ASSETS		
Cash		6,455.54
Accounts Receivable		3,155.00
Prepaid Insurance		312.50
Office Supplies		3,151.07
Software	4,695.00	
Accum. Dep.- Software	-3,130.04	
Software: Net		1,564.96
Computer Equipment	18,145.00	
Accum. Dep.- Computer Equip.	-9,333.32	
Computer Equipment: Net		8,811.68
TOTAL ASSETS		23,450.75
TOTAL ASSETS		23,450.75
LIABILITIES		
LIABILITIES		
Accounts Payable		2,092.75
Loans Payable		2,970.83
TOTAL LIABILITIES		5,063.58
TOTAL LIABILITIES		5,063.58
OWNER'S EQUITY		
Seth Hunter, Capital		13,636.18
Seth Hunter, Drawing		-15,400.00
Current Earnings		20,150.99
TOTAL OWNER'S EQUITY		18,387.17
TOTAL EQUITY		18,387.17
LIABILITIES AND EQUITY		23,450.75

ACTION: Choose **Print** from the Balance Sheet File menu. Compare your Balance Sheet to the one shown above. Close the Balance Sheet dialog box; select **File** from the home window menu bar; then choose **Exit** to end the current work session and return to your Windows desktop.

YEAR-END CLOSING PROCEDURES

At the end of an accounting year, a business must close its revenue and expense accounts to owner's equity. The closing process clears the revenue and expense accounts so that transactions for the following year can be accumulated in these accounts. In addition, if the business uses an owner's drawing account, this temporary owner's equity account must also be closed. CA-Simply Accounting for Windows can automatically close all revenue and expense accounts to owner's equity but does not have the capability of automatically closing an owner's drawing account. Horizon Events uses a drawing account; therefore, a closing entry for the drawing account must be entered directly into the General Journal.

All of Horizon Events' routine transactions for 1997 have been recorded. The accounting records have also been adjusted for 1997, and the 1997 financial statements have been printed. It is time to close the accounting records for the year. In an actual business situation several other reports, such as a General Journal (including all ledger entries) and a General Ledger (selecting all accounts) would be printed for the entire year, and a backup copy of the company's 1997 data files would be made. In this tutorial, we will omit the printing of these additional reports; however, it is important that you make a backup copy of Horizon Events' data files prior to performing the closing procedures. In actual practice, the backup of the data files would be on a separate disk and a duplicate of the backup disk would be made and stored off site as a precaution against fire, theft, and so on. In this tutorial, we will make one backup copy of the data files using the working data disk location in A:.

 ACTION: Make a backup copy of Horizon Event's data files following the steps previously provided. Name this backup file *A:\Backup\12-31-1997*.

Horizon Events—Document 41 **Session Date: 12/31/1997**

Memo:

Date: December 31, 1997

Close the Seth Hunter, Drawing account to the Seth Hunter, Capital account.

 ACTION: Load CA-Simply Accounting for Windows; open the data files for Horizon Events (A:\HORIZON\Horizon.asc); leave the session date set at 12/31/1997. The Horizon Events home window will appear. Open the General Journal dialog box; then enter the following entry to close the Seth Hunter, Drawing account to the Seth Hunter, Capital account. Your screen should agree with the one shown below:

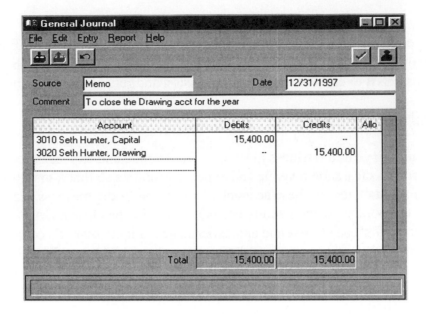

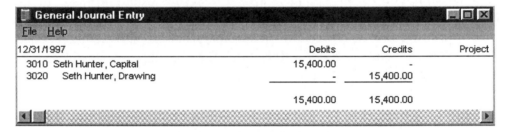

ACTION: Choose **Display General Journal Entry** from the General Journal Report menu. Compare your display to the one shown below:

Explanation: Review the journal entry noting any errors.

ACTION: Close the General Journal Entry dialog box. If you have made an error, refer to the Editing Tips for Editing a General Journal Entry presented earlier in the chapter for information on corrective action. Once the journal entry is correct, click the **Post** button to post the closing entry; close the General Journal dialog box. On the home window menu bar, click **Maintenance**; then choose **Advance Session Date**. Your screen will look like this:

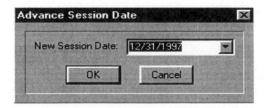

Explanation: The final step in the closing process requires advancing the session date to the first day of the next fiscal year, in this case 1/1/1998. During the closing process the program will permanently remove the following details from Horizon Events' data files: all journal entries from all journals and all individual postings of journal entries to the General Ledger accounts.

The ending balances for assets, liabilities, and the updated owner's equity accounts will become the beginning balances in 1998 for these accounts. All revenue and expense accounts will show zero balances, and the 1997 income will be transferred to the General linking account designated in the company's data files. Horizon Events has established 3010 Seth Hunter, Capital as the General linking account.

The program will retain the following data after the closing process is complete:

1. Ending balances in asset, liability, and owner's equity accounts
2. Unpaid sales invoices
3. Unpaid purchases invoices
4. All details of fully paid sales and purchases invoices since the last use of the Clear Journal Entries choice on the home window Maintenance menu

 **ACTION:** Advance the session date to 1/1/1998; click the **OK** button. Your screen will look like this:

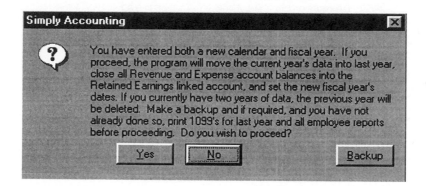

Explanation: The warning message states that the revenue and expense accounts will be closed to an account titled Retained Earnings. This is the account that corporations use to accumulate earnings. Horizon Events is a sole proprietorship, and the program will correctly close the revenue and expense accounts to the Seth Hunter, Capital account even though the message used a different account name. The backup copy of Horizon Events' data files that you made at the beginning of this section will serve as the backup copy suggested in the warning message.

ACTION: Click the **Yes** button in response to the warning message. Choose **Trial Balance** from the home window Report menu; accept the default as at date of 1/1/1998; then click the **OK** button. Your screen will look like this:

Trial Balance		
File Help		
As At 1/1/1998	Debits	Credits
1010 Cash	6,455.54	-
1020 Accounts Receivable	3,155.00	-
1030 Prepaid Insurance	312.50	-
1040 Office Supplies	3,151.07	-
1050 Software	4,695.00	-
1060 Accum. Dep.- Software	-	3,130.04
1080 Computer Equipment	18,145.00	-
1090 Accum. Dep.- Computer Equip.	-	9,333.32
2010 Accounts Payable	-	2,092.75
2020 Loans Payable	-	2,970.83
3010 Seth Hunter, Capital	-	18,387.17
3020 Seth Hunter, Drawing	-	0.00
4010 Revenue From Services	-	0.00
4020 Interest Income	-	0.00
5010 Advertising Expense	0.00	-
5015 Dues and Membership Expense	0.00	-
5020 Utilities Expense	0.00	-
5025 Repairs Expense	0.00	-
5030 Rent Expense	0.00	-
5035 Postage Expense	0.00	-
5040 Office Supplies Expense	0.00	-
5045 Interest Expense: Loans	0.00	-
5050 Depreciation Exp.-Software	0.00	-
5060 Depreciation Exp.-Comp. Equip.	0.00	-
5070 Insurance Expense	0.00	-
5080 Professional Services Exp.	0.00	-
5090 Bank Charges	0.00	-
5150 Misc. Expense	0.00	-
	35,914.11	35,914.11

Explanation: Notice that all the expenses in the Trial Balance have a zero balance. Also notice that the drawing account is zero. Compare the amount of Seth Hunter's capital account with the earlier Trial Balance. The previous account balance was $13,636.18 and the current account balance is $18,387.17. This represents the addition of the $20,150.99 net income less the $15,400 transferred from the drawing account.

 ACTION: Choose **Print** from the Trial Balance File menu. Compare your Trial Balance to the one shown above. Close the Trial Balance dialog box. Prepare an Income Statement for 01/01/1998 through 01/01/1998. Your screen should show the following:

```
┌──────────────────────────────────────────────────┐
│ ▌ Income Statement                                 │
├──────────────────────────────────────────────────┤
│ File  Help                                         │
├──────────────────────────────────────────────────┤
│ 1/1/1998 to 1/1/1998                               │
│ REVENUE                                            │
│                                                    │
│  REVENUE                                           │
│   Revenue From Services                  0.00      │
│   Interest Income                        0.00      │
│  TOTAL REVENUE                           0.00      │
│                                                    │
│                                                    │
│ TOTAL REVENUE                            0.00      │
│                                                    │
│ EXPENSE                                            │
│                                                    │
│  EXPENSES                                          │
│   Advertising Expense                    0.00      │
│   Dues and Membership Expense            0.00      │
│   Utilities Expense                      0.00      │
│   Repairs Expense                        0.00      │
│   Rent Expense                           0.00      │
│   Postage Expense                        0.00      │
│   Office Supplies Expense                0.00      │
│   Interest Expense: Loans                0.00      │
│   Depreciation Exp.-Software             0.00      │
│   Depreciation Exp.-Comp. Equip.         0.00      │
│   Insurance Expense                      0.00      │
│   Professional Services Exp.             0.00      │
│   Bank Charges                           0.00      │
│   Misc. Expense                          0.00      │
│  TOTAL EXPENSES                          0.00      │
│                                                    │
│                                                    │
│ TOTAL EXPENSE                            0.00      │
│                                                    │
│ NET INCOME                               0.00      │
└──────────────────────────────────────────────────┘
```

Explanation: Notice that everything has been closed and all expense and revenue account balances are zero.

ACTION: Choose **Print** from the Income Statement File menu. Compare your Income Statement to the one shown above. Close the Income Statement dialog box. Prepare a Balance Sheet as at 01/01/1998. Your screen should show the following:

Balance Sheet

File   Help

As At 1/1/1998

ASSETS

ASSETS
Cash		6,455.54
Accounts Receivable		3,155.00
Prepaid Insurance		312.50
Office Supplies		3,151.07
Software	4,695.00	
Accum. Dep.- Software	-3,130.04	
Software: Net		1,564.96
Computer Equipment	18,145.00	
Accum. Dep.- Computer Equip.	-9,333.32	
Computer Equipment: Net		8,811.68
TOTAL ASSETS		23,450.75

TOTAL ASSETS	23,450.75

LIABILITIES

LIABILITIES
Accounts Payable	2,092.75
Loans Payable	2,970.83
TOTAL LIABILITIES	5,063.58

TOTAL LIABILITIES	5,063.58

EQUITY

OWNER'S EQUITY
Seth Hunter, Capital	18,387.17
Seth Hunter, Drawing	0.00
Current Earnings	0.00
TOTAL OWNER'S EQUITY	18,387.17

TOTAL EQUITY	18,387.17

LIABILITIES AND EQUITY	23,450.75

Explanation: Notice that both the drawing account and the current earnings account have zero balances.

 ACTION: Select **File** from the home window menu bar; choose **Exit** to end the current work session and return to your Windows desktop.

SUMMARY

This chapter has explored the General components of CA-Simply Accounting for Windows as they would typically be used by a service business. Use of the General Journal and the General Ledger to record General Journal entries and to maintain General Ledger accounts has been explained in dctail. A bank reconciliation has been performed and items appearing on the bank statement that did not appear in the cash account have been entered. The procedures used to display and print a General Journal, an

Account Reconciliation report, a Chart of Accounts, a Balance Sheet, an Income Statement, a General Ledger report, and a Trial Balance have been demonstrated. In addition, the procedures required to close the accounting records at the end of the fiscal year have been explained. By examining the methods used to record General-related transactions and to adjust and close the accounting records at the end of the year, the various integration/linking features of CA-Simply Accounting for Windows have been illustrated.

QUESTIONS

QUESTIONS ABOUT THE SOFTWARE

1. How does the program prevent the posting of unbalanced journal entries?

2. Name three different ways to determine the current account balance for an account using the CA-Simply Accounting for Windows program.

3. Why must you specify both a start and a finish date when preparing an income statement?

4. What conditions does the program impose for the removal of a General Ledger account? What might happen to the accounting records if these conditions were not in place?

5. Describe the type of information that is available in a General Ledger report.

6. What restriction does the program impose on the types of journal entries that can be recorded in the General Journal? What might happen to the accounting records if this restriction were not in place?

QUESTIONS ABOUT YEAR-END CLOSING PROCEDURES

7. Why do you have to enter the closing entry for an owner's drawing account prior to advancing the session date to a new fiscal year?

8. What effect does advancing the session date to a new fiscal year have on the accounting records maintained by the program?

9. Based on your answer to the above question, why is it especially important to make a backup copy of a company's data files prior to advancing the session date to a new fiscal year?

EXPLORING ALTERNATIVE SOFTWARE TECHNIQUES

10. CA-Simply Accounting for Windows can maintain separate data files for an unlimited number of companies. In addition, the program requires only that the General Ledger be in Ready status prior to recording accounting transactions. How might Horizon Event's sole proprietor, Seth Hunter, make use of these features of the program?

TRANSMITTAL

Horizon Events   **Name**_____
Chapter 4

Attach the following and reports:

1. General Journal (General Journal entries only) 12/1/1997 to 12/31/1997
2. Invoice 538, Viv Andrews
3. Check 1683, Mail Service
4. Account Reconciliation Journal entry 12/31/1997
5. Account Reconciliation Detail report 12/1/1997 to 12/31/1997
6. Chart of Accounts 12/31/1997
7. General Ledger report (1040 Office Supplies) 12/1/1997 to 12/31/1997
8. Trial Balance As at 12/31/1997
9. Income Statement 1/1/1997 to 12/31/1997
10. Balance Sheet As at 12/31/1997
11. Trial Balance As at 1/1/1998
12. Income Statement 1/1/1998 to 1/1/1998
13. Balance Sheet 1/1/1998

EXERCISE—Harmony Piano Works
(CONTINUED FROM CHAPTER 3)

1. Load CA-Simply Accounting for Windows; open the data files for Harmony Piano Works (A:\HARMONY\Harmony.acs); then record the following transactions under the session date of 12/31/1997:

    December 31—Modify the following accounts:
    Change 1120 Acc. Dep.- Tools to 1120 Accum. Dep.-Tools
    Change 1150 Acc. Dep.-Truck to 1150 Accum. Dep.-Truck

    December 31—Add the following accounts to the chart of accounts:
    2020 Loans Payable
    5080 Interest Expense: Loans
    5090 Rent Expense
    5100 Postage Expense

    December 31— Print the Chart of Accounts

    December 31—Record the following adjusting entries and transactions:

    A. Tool depreciation for the year in the amount of $1,666.66.
    B. Truck depreciation for the year in the amount of $2,000.00.
    C. Supplies used during the year of $1,146.00.
    D. Expired insurance for the year in the amount of $400.00.
    E. Purchase tools on account for $500. The source is Memo. Monthly payments including interest will be automatically deducted from the checking account by the bank.
    F. Record the receipt of Check 729 for $125 from Matthew Ericsons, a one-time customer, for the repair of a piano. Print Sales Invoice 298.
    G. Add a new vendor: Larry's Postal Service, 7890 SE Main, Portland, Oregon 97214, 503-555-1289. Use Check 1026 to pay for Invoice 123 from Larry's Postal Service, for a $12.25 postage expense. Print the check.

    December 31—Back up Harmony. Name the file *A:\Backup\12-31 Prior to Bank reconciliation.*

    December 31—When the backup is complete, use the following bank statement to complete the reconciliation of Account 1010 Cash. Print the Account Reconciliation Journal Entry for 12/31/1997 and the Account Reconciliation Detail report 12/1/1997 to 12/31/1997.

OREGON GOLD BANK
2931 SE 25th Street
Portland, OR 97214
(503) 555-1122

Harmony Piano Works
5698 SE Ladds Addition
Portland, OR 97214

Acct. # 11-563   December, 1997

12/1/1997 Beginning Balance			$4567.84
12/5/1997 Deposit 406	$1,300.00		5,867.84
12/12/1997 Deposit 407	470.00		6,437.84
12/19/1997 Check 1020		$62.25	6,375.59
12/19/1997 Check 1021		267.90	6,107.69
12/26/1997 Check 1022 C		400.00	5,707.69
12/26/1997 Check 1023		75.00	5,632.69
12/26/1997 Check 1024		956.59	4,676.10
12/26/1997 Check 1025		362.90	4,313.20
12/31/1997 Tools Loan Pmt.: $2.17 Principal, $20.68 Interest		22.85	4,290.35
12/31/1997 Service Chg.		8.00	4,282.35
12/31/1997 Interest	6.15		4,288.50
12/31/1997 Ending Balance			$4,288.50

2. Print the following reports:

    A. General Journal (General Journal entries only) 12/1/1997 to 12/31/1997
    B. General Ledger report (supplies) 12/1/1997 to 12/31/1997
    C. Trial Balance As at 12/31/1997
    D. Income Statement 1/1/1997 to 12/31/1997
    E. Balance Sheet As at 12/31/1997

3. Make a backup copy of Harmony Piano Works' data files. The name of the backup is *A:\Backup\12-31-1997*.

4. Record the closing entry for the drawing account.

    December 31—Record the closing entry for Sara Montage's Drawing account. Print the General Journal entry for this transaction.

5.   Advance the session date to 1/1/1998. Print the following reports:

     A. Trial Balance As at 1/1/1998
     B. Income Statement 1/1/1998 to 1/1/1998
     C. Balance Sheet 1/1/1998

6.   Exit from the program.

7.   Complete the Harmony Piano Works' Transmittal.

TRANSMITTAL

Harmony Piano Works   Name:_____
Chapter 4

A. Attach the following and reports:

1. Chart of Accounts
2. Sales Invoice 298
3. Check 1026
4. Account Reconciliation Journal entry 12/31/1997
5. Account Reconciliation Detail report 12/1/1997 to 12/31/1997
6. General Journal (General Journal entries only) 12/1/1997 to 12/31/1997
7. General Ledger report (supplies) 12/1/1997 to 12/31/1997
8. Trial Balance As at 12/31/1997
9. Income Statement 1/1/1997 to 12/31/1997
10. Balance Sheet As at 12/31/1997
11. General Journal entry to close drawing
12. Trial Balance As at 1/1/1998
13. Income Statement 1/1/1998 to 1/1/1998
14. Balance Sheet 1/1/1998

B. Refer to your reports to list the amounts requested below:

1. What are total assets at 12/31/1997? $_____

2. What is net income for the year? $_____

3. How much did Sara Montage withdraw from the business during the year? $_____

4. What is the balance of the Supplies account on 12/31/1997? $_____

5. What is the balance of Sara Montage's Capital account on 1/1/1998? $_____

END-OF-SECTION 1—
IMAGE ART APPRAISAL
PRACTICE SET: SERVICE BUSINESS

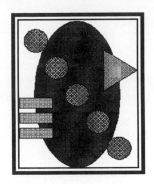

COMPANY PROFILE

Image Art Appraisal is owned and operated by Margaret Graven as a sole proprietorship in Portland, Oregon. Services include research and value estimation for various art objects. The majority of Margaret's business is concentrated in the area of appraising the value of paintings and sculptures for insurance companies and individual collectors.

Margaret uses the services of the Financial Services Group to maintain her accounting records. She submits a packet of business documents each week for processing. As a new employee of the Financial Services Group, you are responsible for recording Image Art Appraisal's December transactions, and for performing the month-end and year-end accounting procedures using CA-Simply Accounting for Windows.

The Financial Services Group uses the General, Receivables, and Payables components of CA-Simply Accounting for Windows to record transactions for Image Art Appraisal and has established the following accounting procedures and policies in cooperation with Margaret Graven.

SALES

Due to the nature of Margaret's work, all sales are made on a credit basis with payment terms of net 30 days. When Margaret wants to bill a client for services rendered, she prepares a memo to that effect and forwards it to the Financial Services Group. The Financial Services Group prepares an invoice using the CA-Simply Accounting for Windows automatic invoicing preparation feature, listing all services as "Art Appraisal Services" on the invoice. If Margaret is requesting that a new client be billed for the first time, she will list the name and address of the client in her memo so a new customer record can be created; consequently the one-time customer option within the CA-Simply Accounting for Windows program is not used. Margaret does not issue monthly statements and wishes to retain all details regarding fully paid invoices in her accounting data files.

RECEIPTS

When Margaret receives payment from a customer on account, she makes a photocopy of the check and deposits the original in the bank. She will include a photocopy of the check in her weekly packet of materials for your use in recording the transaction.

PURCHASES

Vendor records have been established for those vendors that Image Art Appraisal deals with on a frequent basis; all details of fully paid invoices are retained in the company's accounting data files. Occasionally, Margaret will make a purchase or receive a bill from a new vendor. She may or may not want to establish a Payables Ledger record for the new vendor and payment may or may not be due immediately. Therefore, Margaret uses the following notations on vendor invoices and bills to indicate how she would like the purchase handled.

1. *Approved*. Record purchase in the Purchases Journal under the established vendor's name. Payment is not yet due.
2. *New vendor*. Create a Payables Ledger record for the vendor.
3. *Issue check*. Issue a check using the cash purchase option in the Purchases Journal.
4. *One-time vendor*. Issue a check using the one-time vendor and cash purchase option in the Purchases Journal.
5. *Create account*. Create a new General Ledger account using the title and number indicated.

Review Purchases source documents carefully; Margaret may use more than one notation on a source document.

PAYMENTS

When Margaret wants a check issued to a credit vendor, she prepares a memo to that effect and forwards it to the Financial Services Group. The Financial Services Group prepares checks using the CA-Simply Accounting for Windows automatic check preparation feature. Printed checks are returned to Margaret to sign and mail.

MONTH-END AND YEAR-END ACCOUNTING PROCEDURES

At the end of each month, Margaret completes a bank reconciliation and forwards a copy of it to the Financial Services Group so any related journal entries can be recorded in her financial records. She also includes a memo at this time informing the Financial Services Group of any monthly adjusting entries required. If the month just ending is also the year-end for the business, Margaret will request that the year-end financial statements be prepared and that her Drawing account be closed along with the revenue and expense accounts in preparation for recording transactions in the new fiscal year.

Image Art Appraisal's 12/1/1997 trial balance appears below:

Image Art Appraisal
Trial Balance As At 12/1/1997

		Debits	Credits
1010	Cash	4,295.92	-
1020	Accounts Receivable	13,155.29	-
1030	Prepaid Insurance	1,500.00	-
1040	Office Supplies	1,067.45	-
1050	Office Equipment	6,250.00	-
1051	Acc. Dep.- Office Equipment	-	3,500.00
1060	Office Gallery	27,000.00	-
1061	Acc. Dep.- Office Gallery	-	6,416.63
1080	Car	21,000.00	-
1081	Acc. Dep.- Car	-	10,222.17
2010	Accounts Payable	-	2,886.70
3010	Margaret Graven, Capital	-	42,283.63
3020	Margaret Graven, Drawing	33,000.00	-
4010	Income From Services	-	81,576.45
4020	Interest Income		0.00
5010	Advertising Expense	8,960.00	-
5020	Utilities Expense	525.00	-
5030	Rent Expense	13,200.00	-
5040	Office Supplies Expense	1,485.00	-
5050	Depreciation Exp.- Office Equipment	1,100.00	-
5060	Depreciation Exp.- Office Gallery	2,016.63	-
5070	Depreciation Exp.- Car	4,888.84	-
5080	Professional Services Exp.	620.00	-
5090	Financial Services Expense	2,635.00	-
5110	Insurance Expense	1,375.00	-
5120	Dues and Membership Expense	1,925.00	-
5130	Security Monitoring Expense	549.45	-
5140	Bank Charges	0.00	-
5190	Professional Education Expense	175.00	-
5200	Misc. Expense	162.00	-
		146,885.58	146,885.58

Packet 1: Week Ending 12/5/1997

The first packet for December contains several source documents and memos from Margaret that you need to record using CA-Simply Accounting for Windows. Examine each source document carefully, referring to the accounting procedures and policies described above if you have questions concerning how to record a transaction. To begin the practice set, load CA-Simply Accounting for Windows; open the data files for Image Art Appraisal (A:\IMAGE\Image.asc); then advance the session date to 12/5/1997.

Image Art Appraisal—Document 1   **Session Date 12/5/1997**

Memo:

December 1, 1997

Add two new accounts: 2020 Loans Payable and 5150 Interest Expense: Loans. Print the chart of accounts. Record the purchase of $2,000 of office equipment on account. Payments will be automatically deducted from the cash account by the bank and will appear each month on the bank statement.

Image Art Appraisal—Document 2   **Session Date: 12/5/1997**

Memo:

Date: December 1, 1997

Bill Art Forum $396.00 for art appraisal services.

Image Art Appraisal—Document 3   **Session Date: 12/5/1997**

Winningstad Insurance	1650
2390 SE Madison Blvd.	
Portland, OR 97214	Dec. 1 , 19 97

Pay to the
order of _____Image Art Appraisal_____ $ 5,580.00

Five thousand five hundred eighty and NO/100 _____Dollars

Portland
Bank
P. O. 981, Portland, OR 97212

For ___Invoice #531___   *Janice Winningstad*

Use Deposit Slip 102 to deposit this check.

Image Art Appraisal—Document 4   **Session Date: 12/5/1997**

Memo:

Date: December 4, 1997

Bill new customer Alan Holman, P. O. Box 1283, Vancouver, Washington 98665, 206-281-0999, $560.00 for art appraisal services. *Note:* Don't forget to enter the last name first.

Image Art Appraisal—Document 5   **Session Date: 12/5/1997**

Yes! Sign me up for a one-year subscription (12 issues) of

ART TODAY Magazine

___X___ Enclosed is my check for $76.00

_____ Bill me later

Send to:
ART TODAY Magazine
P. O. Box 7983
Denver, CO 80201
303-292-6866

Name __Image Art Appraisal_____

Address ___3600 SE Hawthorne Blvd._____

City __Portland__ State __OR__ Zip __97214__

NOTE:

Pay as a new vendor and create a new Account
#5100 Subscription Expense
Margaret 12/5/1997

Because there is no invoice for the magazine subscription, use the word *Bill* rather than an invoice number when entering the transaction above.

Image Art Appraisal—Document 6   **Session Date: 12/5/1997**

Memo:

To: Accountant
From: Margaret
Date: December 5, 1997

Please issue a $50.00 check to Cascade Electric in *partial* payment of Invoice K00324.

End-of-Session Procedures

A. Print the following reports:

1. Journal entries (Print <u>All</u> ledger entries, By posting date) 12/1/1997 to 12/5/1997
2. Customer Aged report (Select All, Detail) As at 12/5/1997
3. Vendor Aged report (Select All, Detail) As at 12/5/1997
4. Trial Balance As at 12/5/1997

B. Make a backup copy of Image Art Appraisal's data files. Name it *Backup 12-5*.

C. Complete the Image Art Appraisal Transmittal.

TRANSMITTAL

Image Art Appraisal   **Name**_____
Packet 1   **Session Date: 12/5/1997**

A. Attach the following documents and reports:

   1. Chart of Accounts
   2. Invoice 532
   3. Receipt of Check 1650 in payment of Invoice 531
   4. Invoice 533
   5. Check 1677
   6. Check 1678
   7. General Journal (All ledger entries, By posting date) 12/1/1997 to 12/5/1997
   8. Customer Aged report (Select All, Detail) As at 12/5/1997
   9. Vendor Aged report (Select All, Detail) As at 12/5/1997
  10. Trial Balance As at 12/5/1997

B. Refer to your reports to list the amounts requested below:

1. Accounts Payable balance $_____

2. Accounts Receivable balance $_____

3. Cash balance $_____

4. Amount Image Art Appraisal owes Cascade Electric $_____

5. Amount Alan Holman owes Image Art Appraisal $_____

Packet 2: Week Ending 12/12/1997

If you exited the program, load CA-Simply Accounting for Windows; open the data files for Image Art Appraisal (A:\IMAGE\Image.asc); then advance the session date to 12/12/1997. Record the following transactions:

Image Art Appraisal—Document 7   **Session Date: 12/12/1997**

Alan Holman	1245
P. O. Box 1283	
Vancouver, WA 98665	Dec. 7 , 19 97

Pay to the
order of _____ Image Art Appraisal _____ $ 560.00

Five hundred sixty and NO/100 _____ Dollars

Washington Federal Bank
P. O. 1762, Vancouver, WA 98665

For   Invoice 533   *Alan Holman*

Image Art Appraisal—Document 8   **Session Date: 12/12/1997**

Memo:

Date: December 8, 1997

Bill Corporate Art Design $558.00 for art appraisal services.

Image Art Appraisal—Document 9   **Session Date: 12/12/1997**

Pacific Office Supply
3628 SE 39ᵗʰ Ave.
Portland, OR 97214

PACIFIC OFFICE SUPPLY

Invoice #   8324

To: Image Art Appraisal
3600 SE Hawthorne Blvd.
Portland, OR 97214

Date	Item	Quantity	Description	Unit Price	Amount
12/08/97					$56.95
			Terms: N/30	**TOTAL**	$56.95

Office Supplies Approved. *Margaret*

Image Art Appraisal—Document 10   **Session Date: 12/12/1997**

```
Portland Center Stage                                    276
4590 SE 17th Street
Portland, OR 97214                       Dec. 9 , 19 97    24-7841
                                                            440
Pay to the
order of _____ Image Art Appraisal _____   $  2,450.29

  Two thousand four hundred fifty and 29/100 _____ Dollars

     (  )  Douglas Fir Trust
          P. O. Box 7234, Portland, OR 97228

  For   Invoice 521            Thomas Anderson
```

Image Art Appraisal—Document 11   **Session Date: 12/12/1997**

Memo:

DATE: December 9, 1997

Make a correction to the sales invoice for Corporate Art Design. The correct amount of the bill should be $588.00. Leave the date of the sales invoice as 12/8/1997.

Image Art Appraisal—Document 12   **Session Date: 12/12/1997**

Memo:

Date: December 10, 1997

Bill new customer, Ted Nelson, 4276 SE 9th Street, Portland, Oregon 97214, 503-232-1289, $592.00 for art appraisal services.

Image Art Appraisal—Document 13   **Session Date: 12/12/1997**

Corporate Art Design   832
5600 SE 82nd Street
Portland, OR 97214   Dec. 11 , 19 _97_   24-7841

                                               440

Pay to the
order of _____ Image Art Appraisal _____ $ _1,700.00_

One thousand seven hundred and NO/100 _____ Dollars

Douglas Fir Trust
P. O. Box 7234, Portland, OR 97228

For ___Invoice 526___   *Sally Mannington*

Image Art Appraisal—Document 14   **Session Date: 12/12/1997**

Memo:

Date: December 11, 1997

Bill James Blanchard $2,500.00 for art appraisal services.

Image Art Appraisal—Document 15   **Session Date: 12/12/1997**

 Tidy Up
9847 SW 11th Ave.
Portland, OR 97205
Phone: (503) 222-3611

Invoice # ___3012___
To: Image Art Appraisal
3600 SE Hawthorne Blvd.
Portland, OR 97214

Date	Item	Quantity	Description	Unit Price	Amount
12/12/97			Weekly Cleaning Services		$55.00
				TOTAL	$55.00

Create a new vendor and a new account: **5160 Cleaning Services Expense.** Issue check for payment.

Margaret

Image Art Appraisal—Document 16   **Session Date: 12/12/1997**

> # Memo:
>
> **To:**   Accountant
> **From:** Margaret
> **Date:** December 12, 1997
>
> Please issue a check to West Communications for the November phone bill in the amount of $62.39. Invoice 68-891.

Image Art Appraisal—Document 17   **Session Date: 12/12/1997**

> # Memo:
>
> **To:**   Accountant
> **From:** Margaret
> **Date:** December 12, 1997
>
> Please issue a check to Pacific Office Supply in the amount of $1,134.44 in payment of Invoices 8120 ($558.43) and 8213 ($576.01).

Image Art Appraisal—Document 18   **Session Date: 12/12/1997**

> # Memo:
>
> Date: December 12, 1997
>
> Deposit checks received, using Deposit Slip 103.

End-of-Session Procedures

A. Print the following reports:

1. General Journal (All ledger entries, By posting date) 12/6/1997 to 12/12/1997
2. Customer Aged report (Select All, Detail) As at 12/12/1997
3. Vendor Aged report (Select All, Detail) As at 12/12/1997
4. Trial Balance As at 12/12/1997

B. Make a backup copy of Image Art Appraisal's data files. Name it *Backup 12-12*.

C. Complete the Image Art Appraisal Transmittal.

TRANSMITTAL

Image Art Appraisal   **Name**_____
Packet 2
                                                 Session Date: 12/12/1997

A. Attach the following documents and reports:

1. Receipt of Check 1245 in payment of Invoice 533
2. Invoice 534
3. Receipt of Check 276 in payment of Invoice 521
4. Corrected Invoice 534
5. Invoice 535
6. Receipt of Check 832 in payment of Invoice 526
7. Invoice 536
8. Check 1679
9. Check 1680
10. Check 1681
11. General Journal (All ledger entries, By posting date) 12/6/1997 to 12/12/1997
12. Customer Aged report (Select All, Detail) As at 12/12/1997
13. Vendor Aged report (Select All, Detail) As at 12/12/1997
14. Trial Balance As at 12/12/1997

B. Refer to your reports to list the amounts requested below:

1. Accounts Payable balance $_____

2. Accounts Receivable balance $_____

3. Cash balance $_____

4. Amount Image Art Appraisal owes Pacific Office Supply $_____

5. Amount Corporate Art Design owes Image Art Appraisal $_____

Packet 3: Week Ending 12/19/1997

If you exited the program, load CA-Simply Accounting for Windows; open the data files for Image Art Appraisal (A:\IMAGE\Image.asc); then advance the session date to 12/19/1997. Record the following transactions:

Image Art Appraisal—Document 19   **Session Date: 12/19/1997**

Hawthorne Business Association

1931 SE Stark Street
Portland, OR 97214
Phone: (503) 232-7890

Invoice # ___B-17___

To: Image Art Appraisal
3600 SE Hawthorne Blvd.
Portland, OR 97214

Date	Item	Quantity	Description	Unit Price	Amount
12/14/97			1998 Annual Dues		$150.00
				TOTAL	$150.00

Create a new vendor. Payable by 01-31-1998   *Margaret*

Image Art Appraisal—Document 20   **Session Date: 12/19/1997**

INFO-TECH

90 Ford Blvd.
Portland, OR 97212
Phone: (503) 222-8000

Invoice # ___10026___

To: Image Art Appraisal
3600 SE Hawthorne Blvd.
Portland, OR 97214

Date	Description	Unit Price	Amount
12/15/97	Technical Services and Consultation		$1,800.00
	TOTAL $1,800.00		

Create a new vendor. Approved as a professional services exp. Payable by 01/15/1998. *Margaret*

Image Art Appraisal—Document 21   **Session Date: 12/19/1997**

Corporate Art Design   841
5600 SE 82nd Street
Portland, OR 97214   Dec. 16 , 19 97   24-7841
                                                                                      440

Pay to the
order of _____ Image Art Appraisal _____ $ 3,425.00

Three thousand four hundred twenty-five and NO/100 _____ Dollars

Douglas Fir Trust
P. O. Box 7234, Portland, OR 97228

For   Invoice 530   *Sally Mannington*

Image Art Appraisal—Document 22   **Session Date: 12/19/1997**

PACIFIC OFFICE SUPPLY

Pacific Office Supply   Invoice #   8351
3628 SE 39th Ave.   **To:** Image Art Appraisal
Portland, OR 97214   3600 SE Hawthorne Blvd.
                                                                    Portland, OR 97214

Date	Item	Quantity	Description	Unit Price	Amount
12/16/97					$125.95
			Terms: N/30	TOTAL	$125.95

Office supplies approved. *Margaret*

Image Art Appraisal—Document 23   **Session Date: 12/19/1997**

Memo:

Date: December 17, 1997

Bill Portland Center Stage $1,360.00 for art appraisal services.

Image Art Appraisal—Document 24   **Session Date: 12/19/1997**

Memo:

Date: December 17, 1997

Bill Art Forum $758.50 for art appraisal services.

Image Art Appraisal—Document 25   **Session Date: 12/19/1997**

Ted Nelson   307
4276 SE 9th Street
Portland, OR 97214   Dec. 18 , 19 97

Pay to the
order of _____ Image Art Appraisal _____ $ 592.00

Five hundred ninety-two and NO/100 _____ Dollars

Portland
Bank
P. O. 981, Portland, OR 97212

For   Invoice 535   *Ted Nelson*

Image Art Appraisal—Document 26   **Session Date: 12/19/1997**

 Tidy Up
9847 SW 11th Ave.
Portland, OR 97205
Phone: (503) 222-3611

Invoice #   3089
To: Image Art Appraisal
3600 SE Hawthorne Blvd.
Portland, OR 97214

Date	Item	Quantity	Description	Unit Price	Amount
12/19/97			Weekly Cleaning Services		$55.00
				TOTAL	**$55.00**

Issue check for payment.   *Margaret*

Image Art Appraisal—Document 27 **Session Date: 12/19/1997**

Memo:

To: Accountant
From: Margaret
Date: December 19, 1997

Please issue a check to Pacific Office Supply in the amount of $95.00 in *partial* payment of Invoice 8299.

Image Art Appraisal—Document 28 **Session Date: 12/19/1997**

Memo:

Date: December 19, 1997

Deposit checks received, using Deposit Slip 104.

Image Art Appraisal—Document 29 **Session Date: 12/19/1997**

Memo:

To: Accountant
From: Margaret
Date: December 19, 1997

Check 1683 issued to Pacific Office Supply in the amount of $95.00 as a partial payment of Invoice 8299 should be for $100.00. Please make the necessary corrections and reissue the check using Check 1683 C.

End-of-Session Procedures

A. Print the following reports:

1. General Journal (All ledger entries, By posting date) 12/13/1997 to 12/19/1997
2. Customer Aged report (Select All, Detail) As at 12/19/1997
3. Vendor Aged report (Select All, Detail) As at 12/19/1997
4. Trial Balance As at 12/19/1997

B. Make a backup copy of Image Art Appraisal's data files. Name it *Backup 12-19*.

C. Complete the Image Art Appraisal Transmittal.

TRANSMITTAL

Image Art Appraisal   **Name**_____

Packet 3   **Session Date: 12/19/1997**

A. Attach the following documents and reports:

  1. Receipt of Check 841 in payment of Invoice 530
  2. Invoice 537
  3. Invoice 538
  4. Receipt of Check 307 in payment of Invoice 535
  5. Check 1682
  6. Check 1683
  7. Check 1683 C
  8. General Journal (All ledger entries, By posting date) 12/13/1997 to 12/19/1997
  9. Customer Aged report (Select All, Detail) As at 12/19/1997
10. Vendor Aged report (Select All, Detail) As at 12/19/1997
11. Trial Balance As at 12/19/1997

B. Refer to your reports to list the amounts requested below:

1. Accounts Payable balance $_____

2. Accounts Receivable balance $_____

3. Cash balance $_____

4. Amount Image Art Appraisal owes Info-Tech $_____

5. Amount Portland Center Stage owes Image Art Appraisal $_____

Packet 4: Week Ending 12/26/1997

If you exited the program, load CA-Simply Accounting for Windows; open the data files for Image Art Appraisal (A:\IMAGE\Image.asc); then advance the session date to 12/26/1997. Record the following transactions:

Image Art Appraisal—Document 30　　　　　　　**Session Date: 12/26/1997**

Northwest Power

1234 SE 12th Ave.
Portland, OR 97214

Image Art Appraisal
3600 SE Hawthorne Blvd.
Portland, OR 97214

December Service:

Invoice K010023
Date 12/21/1997
Due 01/04/1998

TOTAL DUE: $85.76

Usage: Meter Number 12-0932　　　Readings: 58659-39204　　　Usage 545kWh

New vendor.　Approved to record transaction for payment later.　*Margaret*

Image Art Appraisal—Document 31　　　　　　　**Session Date: 12/26/1997**

Portland Center Stage
4590 SE 17th Street
Portland, OR 97214

292

Dec. 22 , 19 97　24-7841
440

Pay to the
order of _____Image Art Appraisal_____　$ 1,200.00

One thousand two hundred and NO/100 _____Dollars

Douglas Fir Trust
P. O. Box 7234, Portland, OR 97228

For ___Invoice 537 partial pmt.___　*Thomas Anderson*

Image Art Appraisal—Document 32   **Session Date: 12/26/1997**

Memo:

Date: December 23, 1997

Bill Winningstad Insurance $427.00 for art appraisal services.

Image Art Appraisal—Document 33   **Session Date: 12/26/1997**

Corporate Art Design   922
5600 SE 82nd Street
Portland, OR 97214   Dec. 23 , 19 97   24-7841
                                                           440

Pay to the
order of _____ Image Art Appraisal _____ $ 588.00

 Five hundred eighty-eight and NO/100 _____ Dollars

Douglas Fir Trust
P. O. Box 7234, Portland, OR 97228

For   Invoice 534   *Sally Mannington*

Image Art Appraisal—Document 34   **Session Date: 12/26/1997**

Pacific Office Supply   Invoice #   8362
PACIFIC OFFICE SUPPLY   **3628 SE 39th Ave.**   **To:** Image Art Appraisal
                          Portland, OR 97214   3600 SE Hawthorne Blvd.
                                                        Portland, OR 97214

Date	Item	Quantity	Description	Unit Price	Amount
12/24/97					$238.55
			Terms: N/30	TOTAL	$238.55

Office supplies approved. *Margaret*

Image Art Appraisal—Document 35   **Session Date: 12/26/1997**

Memo:

Date: December 24, 1997

Bill Art Forum $590.00 for art appraisal services.

Image Art Appraisal—Document 36   **Session Date: 12/26/1997**

Memo:

Date: December 24, 1997

Bill Ted Nelson $726.00 for art appraisal services.

Image Art Appraisal—Document 37   **Session Date: 12/26/1997**

Tidy Up
9847 SW 11th Ave.
Portland, OR 97205
Phone: (503) 222-3611

Invoice # ___3102___

To: Image Art Appraisal
3600 SE Hawthorne Blvd.
Portland, OR 97214

Date	Item	Quantity	Description	Unit Price	Amount
12/26/97			Weekly Cleaning Services		$55.00
				TOTAL	**$55.00**

Issue check for payment.   *Margaret*

Image Art Appraisal—Document 38   **Session Date: 12/26/1997**

Memo:

To: Accountant
From: Margaret
Date: December 26, 1997

Please issue a check payable to A & E Advertising in the amount of $1,175.00 in payment of their Invoice 6677.

Image Art Appraisal—Document 39   **Session Date: 12/26/1997**

Memo:

Date: December 26, 1997

Deposit checks received, using Deposit Slip 105.

End-of-Session Procedures

A. Print the following reports:

1. General Journal (All ledger entries, By posting date) 12/20/1997 to 12/26/1997
2. Customer Aged report (Select All, Detail) As at 12/26/1997
3. Vendor Aged report (Select All, Detail) As at 12/26/1997
4. Trial Balance As at 12/26/1997

B. Make a backup copy of Image Art Appraisal's data files. Name it *Backup 12-26*.

C. Complete the Image Art Appraisal Transmittal.

TRANSMITTAL

Image Art Appraisal   **Name**_____
Packet 4
                                   Session Date: 12/26/1997

A. Attach the following documents and reports:

1. Receipt of Check 292 in payment of Invoice 537
2. Invoice 539
3. Receipt of Check 922 in payment of Invoice 534
4. Invoice 540
5. Invoice 541
6. Check 1684
7. Check 1685
8. General Journal (All ledger entries, By posting date) 12/20/1997 to 12/26/1997
9. Customer Aged report (Select All, Detail) As at 12/26/1997
10. Vendor Aged report (Select All, Detail) As at 12/26/1997
11. Trial Balance As at 12/26/1997

B. Refer to your reports to list the amounts requested below:

1. Accounts Payable balance $_____

2. Accounts Receivable balance $_____

3. Cash balance $_____

4. Amount Image Art Appraisal owes Cascade Electric $_____

5. Amount Winningstad Insurance owes Image Art Appraisal $_____

Packet 5: Partial Week Ending 12/31/1997

If you exited the program, load CA-Simply Accounting for Windows; open the data files for Image Art Appraisal (A:\IMAGE\Image.asc); then advance the session date to 12/31/1997. Record the following transactions:

Image Art Appraisal—Document 39   **Session Date: 12/31/1997**

West Communications ✻ 4298 SW 10ᵗʰ ✻ Portland, OR ✻ 97205

INVOICE: 69-201   **DATE:** 12-29-97   **DUE DATE:** 1-4-98

CURRENT CHARGES:
WEST TELEPHONE CHARGES
   Monthly Service and Equipment $50.50
   Itemized Calls 10.78
         WEST TELEPHONE CURRENT CHARGES **$61.28**
WEST COMMUNICATION CHARGES
   Itemized Calls 21.32
         WEST COMMUNICATION CURRENT CHARGES **$21.32**

TOTAL CURRENT CHARGES **$82.60**

CUSTOMER INFORMATION:
   Image Art Appraisal
   3600 SE Hawthorne Blvd.
   Portland, OR 97214

Approved to record transaction for payment later. *Margaret*

Image Art Appraisal—Document 40   **Session Date: 12/31/1997**

ALERT Security

                                        Invoice # __AB226__

3411 NE King Road   **To:** Image Art Appraisal
Portland, OR 97232   3600 SE Hawthorne Blvd.
Phone: (503) 287-1100   Portland, OR 97214

Date	Description		Amount
12/31/97	Monthly Monitor Fee		$55.00
	Due 1/31/97	**TOTAL**	**$55.00**

Approved for recording.   *Margaret*

Image Art Appraisal—Document 41   **Session Date: 12/31/1997**

Memo:

Date: December 31, 1997

Bill Alan Holman $1,685.00 for art appraisal services.

Image Art Appraisal—Document 42   **Session Date: 12/31/1997**

Memo:

Date: December 31, 1997

Bill Art Forum $250.00 for art appraisal services.

Image Art Appraisal—Document 43   **Session Date: 12/31/1997**

A & E Advertising
8900 Ladd Blvd. ✳ Portland, OR ✳ 97214

To: Image Art Appraisal
3600 SE Hawthorne Blvd.
Portland, OR 97214

Invoice #   6821

Date	Description		Amount
12/31/97	December Advertising		$150.00
	Terms: N/30	**TOTAL**	$150.00

Approved for recording. *Margaret*

Image Art Appraisal—Document 44   **Session Date: 12/31/1997**

Financial Services Group
600 SW Broadway, #1000
Portland, OR 97201

To: Image Art Appraisal
3600 SE Hawthorne Blvd.
Portland, OR 97214

Invoice #   7226

Date	Description		Amount
12/31/97	December Accounting Services		$175.00
	Terms: N/30	**TOTAL**	$175.00

Approved for recording.   *Margaret*

Image Art Appraisal—Document 45   **Session Date: 12/31/1997**

REGISTRATION APPLICATION

[✔] $80 Enclosed (Registrations accepted in order received. Class size is <u>limited</u>.)

[ ] Salem	Jan. 16	[ ] Everett WA	Jan. 18	[ ] Medford OR	Jan. 23
[ ] Eugene	Jan. 24	[✔] Portland-West	Jan. 27	[ ] Tumwater WA	Jan. 31

Topic: Native American Art

Name: Margaret Graven

Firm: Image Art Appraisal

Address: 3600 SE Hawthorne Blvd.

City, State Zip: Portland, OR 97214

Phone (Day):   234-9021   **Phone (Evening):**   232-1292

Date Submitted: 12/31/1997

NORTHWEST ART PROFESSIONALS ✳ 12604 SE Stark ✳ Portland, OR 97233 ✳ (503) 253-9002

Pay as a one-time vendor. Use Bill as the invoice number.   *Margaret*

Image Art Appraisal—Document 46   **Session Date: 12/31/1997**

Cheryl Thomas   726
4135 SE 123rd Street
Portland, OR 97214   Dec. 31 , 19 97

Pay to the
order of _____ Image Art Appraisal _____ $ 75.00

 Seventy-five and NO/100 _____ Dollars

Portland
 Bank   (**One-time customer**)
  P. O. 981, Portland, OR 97212

For   Art Appraisal Services   *Cheryl Thomas*

Image Art Appraisal—Document 47   **Session Date: 12/31/1997**

Memo:

Date: December 31, 1997

Deposit checks received, using Deposit Slip 106.

Image Art Appraisal—Document 48   **Session Date: 12/31/1997**

Memo:

Date: December 31, 1997

Reconcile the cash account with the following bank statement. Enter any transactions shown on the bank statement that have not been entered into the company's accounts. There is an owner withdrawal for $3,000.00 shown on the bank statement. Use a General Journal entry to record this transaction. Print the Account Reconciliation Journal entry and the Account Reconciliation Detail report.

Portland Bank
P. O. 981, Portland, OR 97212

Statement Date: 12/31/1997 Account: 0113499			Image Art Appraisal 3600 SE Hawthorne Blvd. Portland, OR 97214
12/1/1997 Beginning Balance			$4,295.92
12/1/1997 Deposit 102	$5,580.00		9,875.92

12/5/1997 Check 1677		$76.00	9,799.92
12/5/1997 Check 1678		50.00	9,749.92
12/11/1997 Deposit 103	4,710.29		14,460.21
12/12/1997 Check 1679		55.00	14,405.21
12/12/1997 Check 1680		62.39	14,342.82
12/12/1997 Check 1681		1,134.44	13,208.38
12/16/1997 Deposit 104	4,017.00		17,225.38
12/19/1997 Check 1682		55.00	17,170.38
12/19/1997 Check 1683		100.00	17,070.38
12/23/1997 Deposit 105	1,788.00		18,858.38
12/26/1997 Check 1684		55.00	18,803.38
12/26/1997 Check 1685		1,175.00	17,628.38
12/31/1997 Office Equipment Loan Pmt: $5.36 Principal; $58.24 Interest		63.60	17,564.78
12/31/1997 Withdrawal		3,000.00	14,564.78
12/31/1997 Interest	62.45		14,627.23
12/31/1997 Service Charge		25.00	14,602.23
12/31/1997 Ending Balance			$14,602.23

End-of-Session Procedures

A. Print the following reports:

1. General Journal (By posting date, All ledger entries) 12/27/1997 to 12/31/1997
2. Customer Aged report (Select All, Detail) As at 12/31/1997
3. Vendor Aged report (Select All, Detail) As at 12/31/1997
4. Trial Balance As at 12/31/1997

B. Make a backup copy of Image Art Appraisal's data files. Name it *Backup 12-31 Bank Rec*.

C. Complete the Image Art Appraisal Transmittal.

TRANSMITTAL

Image Art Appraisal   **Name**_____
Packet 5
                                                         Session Date: 12/31/1997

A. Attach the following documents and reports:

   1. Invoice 542
   2. Invoice 543
   3. Check 1686
   4. Invoice 544
   5. Account Reconciliation Journal entry, 12/31/1997
   6. Account Reconciliation Detail report, 12/1/1997 to 12/31/1997
   7. General Journal (All ledger entries, By posting date) 12/27/1997 to 12/31/1997
   8. Customer Aged report (Select All, Detail) As at 12/31/1997
   9. Vendor Aged report (Select All, Detail) As at 12/31/1997
  10. Trial Balance As at 12/31/1997

B. Refer to your reports to list the amounts requested below:

1. Accounts Payable balance $_____

2. Accounts Receivable balance $_____

3. Cash balance $_____

4. Amount Image Art Appraisal owes A & E Advertising $_____

5. Amount Art Forum owes Image Art Appraisal $_____

Packet 6: Month-End and Year-End Procedures 12/31/1997 and 1/1/1998

If you exited the program, load CA-Simply Accounting for Windows; open the data files for Image Art Appraisal (A:\IMAGE\Image.asc); leave the session date set at 12/31/1997. Record the adjusting entries authorized by the following memo:

Image Art Appraisal—Document 49   **Session Date: 12/31/1997**

> ## Memo:
> Date: December 31, 1997
>
> Please record the following adjusting entries for December:
>
> 1. Expired insurance, $125.00
> 2. Office supplies used, $356.00
> 3. Office equipment depreciation, $100.00
> 4. Office gallery depreciation, $183.33
> 5. Car depreciation, $444.44

A. Print the following reports:

1. General Journal (By posting date, All ledger entries) 12/1/1997 to 12/31/1997
2. Trial Balance As at 12/31/1997
3. Income Statement 1/1/1997 to 12/31/1997
4. Balance Sheet As at 12/31/1997

B. Make a backup copy of Image Art Appraisal's data files. Name it *12-31-97.*

Record the closing entry authorized by the following memo:

Image Art Appraisal—Document 50   **Session Date: 12/31/1997**

> ## Memo:
> Date: December 31, 1997
>
> Please record the entry to close my drawing account for the year.

End-of-Session Procedures:

A. Advance the session date to 1/1/1998

B. Print the following reports:

1. Trial Balance As at 1/1/1998
2. Income Statement 1/1/1998 to 1/1/1998
3. Balance Sheet As at 1/1/1998

C. Exit from the program.

D   Complete the Image Art Appraisal Transmittal.

TRANSMITTAL

Image Art Appraisal   Name_____
Packet 6   Session Date: 12/31/1997 and 1/1/1998

A. Attach the following reports:

1. General Journal (All ledger entries, By posting date) 12/1/1997 to 12/31/1997
2. Trial Balance As at 12/31/1997
3. Income Statement 1/1/1997 to 12/31/1997
4. Balance Sheet As at 12/31/1997
5. Trial Balance As at 1/1/1998
6. Income Statement 1/1/1998 to 1/1/1998
7. Balance Sheet As at 1/1/1998

B. Refer to your reports to list the amounts requested below:

1. What are total assets at 12/31/1997? $_____

2. How much is the net income for 1997? $_____

3. How much are total expenses for 1997? $_____

4. How much did Margaret Graven withdraw from the business during 1997? $_____

5. What is the balance of prepaid insurance on 1/1/1998? $_____

6. What is net value of the office gallery on 12/31/1997? $_____

7. How much revenue did the business generate during 1997? $_____

8. How much was office supplies expense for 1997? $_____

9. What is the balance of the Margaret Graven, Capital account on 1/1/1998? $_____

10. What is the amount of the total liabilities on 12/31/1997? $_____

SECTION 2:

MERCHANDISING BUSINESSES

MERCHANDISING BUSINESSES—
RECEIVABLES AND PROJECTS

MERCHANDISING BUSINESSES— RECEIVABLES AND PROJECTS

LEARNING OBJECTIVES

After studying this chapter, you will be able to:
- Enter inventory sales on account transactions
- Enter credit memo transactions
- Enter cash receipt transactions
- Enter credit card transactions
- Enter sales discount transactions
- Enter cash sales transactions
- Enter project allocations in the Sales Journal
- Review and edit inventory-related Sales Journal transactions
- Correct errors to posted transactions
- Make bank deposits for cash, check, and credit card receipts
- Process NSF checks
- Observe and understand receivables and inventory integration/linking accounts

ACCOUNTING FOR A MERCHANDISING BUSINESS

Merchandising businesses are a vital part of the American economy. The purchase and resale of consumer goods generate billions of dollars in economic activity each year. The accounting procedures for a merchandising business are more complex than the accounting procedures for a service business. Merchandising businesses require accounting procedures designed to accurately account for inventory purchases, inventory levels, reorder points, and sales. For this reason, the discussion of computerized inventory procedures was deferred until you were generally familiar with CA-Simply Accounting for Windows.

ACCOUNTING FOR INVENTORY

Merchandise inventory can be accounted for under either a periodic or perpetual inventory system. Periodic inventory systems require a physical count of the inventory remaining on hand at the end of an accounting period before financial statements can be prepared. The ending inventory value is used to calculate cost of goods sold for the income statement and is used as the amount reported for inventory as an asset on the balance sheet. When inventory is sold in a periodic inventory system, a single journal entry is required:

	Debit	Credit
Accounts Receivable (or Cash)	xxx	
Sales		xxx

Under a perpetual inventory system, a continuous record of the quantity and cost of all goods on hand is maintained. Each time an inventory item is sold, the resulting cost and reduction in inventory is also recorded. This process requires two journal entries each time an item is sold:

	<u>Debit</u>	<u>Credit</u>
1. Accounts Receivable (or Cash)	xxx	
Sales		xxx
2. Cost of Goods Sold	xxx	
Inventory		xxx

Perpetual inventory systems allow the preparation of financial statements at any time during the year, not just at the end of an accounting period when a physical inventory is taken. In a perpetual inventory system, the current inventory levels and values are always available in the accounting records for use in preparing the financial statements.

Prior to the extensive use of computers in business, many small and medium-sized businesses—especially those marketing a high volume of low-priced goods—were limited to periodic inventory systems because the cost of maintaining perpetual inventory records on a manual basis was prohibitive. Now, through computer processing, virtually all merchandising businesses—regardless of size—can enjoy the advantages of a perpetual inventory system. A physical count of the inventory is still required in a perpetual inventory system, but the information is used to verify the perpetual inventory records and to authorize adjustments for any discrepancies between the accounting records and the physical inventory records.

CA-Simply Accounting for Windows maintains inventory records on a fully integrated, perpetual basis. Through the program's integration/linking feature, the inventory records in the Inventory Ledger are updated each time an inventory item is purchased, sold, transferred, or adjusted. For example, when an inventory sale on account is recorded in the Sales Journal, the program automatically records the entry in the General Journal, posts the related accounts in the General Ledger, updates the customer's accounts receivable subsidiary ledger in the Receivables Ledger, and updates the inventory records in the Inventory Ledger for the inventory items sold.

The valuation of inventory is also an important aspect of accounting for merchandising businesses. The prices paid for merchandise are subject to frequent change. Identical lots of merchandise can be purchased throughout an accounting period, but each lot may be acquired at a different cost. Several alternative methods are permitted for assigning costs to identical units of inventory purchased at different prices and remaining on hand at year-end. Each costing method assumes a different flow of purchase costs through the accounting system and will lead to a different value for inventory in the financial statements. The four most common inventory valuation methods are: (1) specific identification, (2) first in, first out (FIFO), (3) last in, first out (LIFO), and (4) average cost. CA-Simply Accounting for Windows uses the average cost method. Under this method, the cost of merchandise available for sale is recalculated each time a purchase is made; consequently, the average cost of an item is matched against its current sales price when the item is sold.

ACCOUNTING FOR PROJECTS

The financial accounting system of a business is designed to report on the result of operations (income statement) and the solvency position (balance sheet) of an organization as a whole. However, management often finds it useful to analyze financial accounting data for the different parts or segments of the organization separately. Many businesses are organized into a number of separate segments.

Different names may be used to describe these segments. For example, a business may be organized by departments, divisions, product lines, job contracts, stores, branches, or geographic regions. Regardless of how the segments of an organization are defined, management will find it useful to analyze data in such a way as to determine the efficiency of each segment and how each segment contributes to the overall performance of the company.

CA-Simply Accounting for Windows facilitates the segmentation of accounting information through the Project component. Each segment of an organization is assigned a project title in the Project Ledger. As revenue and expense transactions are recorded in the General, Purchases, Sales, Payroll, and Adjustments Journals, an Allocate button is made available to assign all or part of the revenue or expense to a specific project. The Project Ledger does not have its own journal; allocation information is stored with journal entries in the originating journal. Consequently, the Project Ledger serves a reporting role only in CA-Simply Accounting for Windows and its status does not need to be changed from Not Ready to Ready prior to use.

OREGON EXPLORER MAPS TUTORIAL

The following tutorial is a step-by-step guide to recording merchandising transactions and related project allocations for Oregon Explorer Maps within the Receivables components of CA-Simply Accounting for Windows. The procedures required to record merchandising transactions and project allocations in the Payables components will be discussed in Chapter 6, and payroll procedures will be addressed in Chapter 7. The procedures required to record adjusting entries (including inventory), prepare financial statements, perform bank reconciliations, and close the accounting records at the end of the fiscal year are functions of the Inventory and General components and will be discussed in Chapter 8. The Oregon Explorer Maps Tutorial will be continued in Chapters 6, 7, and 8 to give you a comprehensive overview of how CA-Simply Accounting for Windows can be used to maintain the accounting records for a merchandising business.

Study Tips

To get the most educational value out of the Oregon Explorer Maps Tutorial in Chapters 5, 6, 7, and 8, the following study steps are recommended for each chapter:

1. Read the entire chapter.
2. Answer the Questions at the end of the chapter.
3. Complete all of the Oregon Explorer Maps Tutorial steps (indicated by the word ACTION) in the chapter, using your computer. **Hint:** Place a check mark (✔) in the box as you complete each ACTION.
4. Enter all of the Additional Transactions (represented in narrative and document form) as they occur throughout the chapter.
5. As you work through the tutorial, compare your displays/reports to those illustrated in the text to determine the accuracy of your work. If you detect an error in an unposted transaction, follow the Editing Tips (highlighted in special boxes) to correct the transaction. If you detect an error in a posted transaction, refer to the procedures illustrated within the chapter to correct the transaction.
6. Complete the Oregon Explorer Maps Transmittal located at the end of the chapter.

7. Review the LEARNING OBJECTIVES stated at the beginning of the chapter to ensure that you have accomplished each objective.
8. Complete the Windmill Wheels Exercise at the end of the chapter.

OREGON EXPLORER MAPS COMPANY PROFILE

Oregon Explorer Maps was established in 1990 as a sole proprietorship with the intent of creating maps to meet the need of Oregon's growing tourist industry. Three specialized maps, focusing on golf courses, wineries, and ski resorts were designed along with a general tourist information map describing other Oregon attractions. All four maps were designed during 1990 and began selling in 1991. The maps were updated in 1995, and the revised second edition began to be sold in 1996. The products were well received, and the need for long-range planning on map updates was established. New golf courses, wineries, ski resorts, and other attractions are opening frequently, and the current growth trend is expected to continue. Consequently, as each edition of the maps is sold, research and design on the next updated version of each product occurs simultaneously. As of December 1, 1997, the new second edition of the attractions map is selling well and the new second editions of the wine and ski maps have just been delivered by the printer in time for the holiday sales period. The new second edition of the golf map is expected to be completed soon. In addition to the maps, Oregon Explorer Maps sells three types of display racks for the maps. Due to the varied types of outlets, plastic, wood, and wire racks have been selected.

Oregon Explorer Maps markets its products to large distributors of books and maps and directly to other retail outlets on a wholesale basis. For management information purposes, Oregon Explorer Maps maintains separate inventory, cost of goods sold, and sales accounts in its chart of accounts for each type of map (attractions, ski, wine, and golf) and a single inventory, cost of goods sold, and sales account for all type of racks. In addition, sales accounts are further subdivided by type of customer: distributor and wholesale.

A trial balance for Oregon Explorer Maps as of December 1, 1997, appears below:

Oregon Explorer Maps/Your Name
Trial Balance As At 12/1/1997

		Debits	Credits
1060	Cash	36,202.94	-
1200	Accounts Receivable	30,174.90	-
1210	Golf Map Inventory	710.00	-
1220	Ski Map Inventory	16,382.65	-
1230	Wine Map Inventory	14,258.40	-
1240	Attraction Map Inventory	4,979.43	-
1250	Rack Inventory	1,675.00	-
1300	Office Supplies	347.60	-
1310	Shipping Supplies	246.73	-
1320	Prepaid Insurance	450.00	-
1550	Office Equipment	7,000.00	-
1560	Accum Dep: Office Equipment	-	4,152.71
1600	Vehicle	16,000.00	-
1610	Accum Dep: Vehicle	-	5,366.63
2200	Accounts Payable	-	31,963.60
2310	FIT Payable	-	546.31
2320	SIT Payable	-	361.62

2330	Social Security Tax Payable	-	792.60
2340	Medicare Tax Payable	-	185.36
2350	FUTA Payable	-	23.24
2360	SUTA Payable	-	272.64
2400	Medical Insurance Payable	-	125.00
2700	Loans Payable	-	0.00
3560	Karen Bailey, Capital	-	78,185.62
3570	Karen Bailey, Drawing	27,500.00	-
4210	Wholesale Golf Map Sales	-	8,641.59
4220	Wholesale Ski Map Sales	-	6,484.19
4230	Wholesale Wine Map Sales	-	6,478.19
4240	Wholesale Attraction Map Sales	-	21,603.97
4310	Distributor Golf Map Sales	-	43,212.79
4320	Distributor Ski Map Sales	-	32,420.84
4330	Distributor Wine Map Sales	-	32,398.34
4340	Distributor Attraction Map Sales	-	108,031.97
4500	Rack Sales	-	1,417.49
4600	Sales Discounts	864.16	-
4700	Sales Returns and Allowances	2,028.75	-
5010	COGS-Golf Maps	15,681.19	-
5020	COGS-Ski Maps	13,503.48	-
5030	COGS-Wine Maps	12,423.48	-
5040	COGS-Attraction Maps	30,368.52	-
5050	COGS-Racks	1,181.25	-
5060	Purchase Discounts	0.00	-
5070	Purchase Returns and Allowances	0.00	-
5301	Wages	70,095.00	-
5310	Social Security Tax Expense	4,345.89	-
5320	Medicare Tax Expense	1,016.38	-
5330	FUTA Expense	224.00	-
5340	SUTA Expense	2,180.36	-
5400	Phone Expense	1,376.92	-
5410	Postage Expense	976.29	-
5420	Shipping Expense	18,974.32	-
5430	Advertising Expense	8,476.20	-
5440	Vehicle Expense	627.46	-
5450	Utilities Expense	1,176.42	-
5460	Rent Expense	30,000.00	-
5470	Membership and Dues Expense	973.20	-
5480	Subscription Expense	267.50	-
5490	Interest Expense: Loans	0.00	-
5500	Dep. Expense: Office Equipment	1,986.05	-
5510	Dep. Expense: Vehicle	2,566.63	-
5610	Insurance Expense	1,650.00	-
5620	Office Supplies Expense	2,219.95	-
5630	Shipping Supplies Expense	1,011.42	-
5650	Bank Service Charge Expense	295.00	-
5660	Credit Card Fees Expense	0.00	0
5800	Misc. Expense	247.23	-
		382,664.70	382,664.70

Inventory Pricing

The suggested retail price for all maps is $4.99. Maps are sold to distributors for $2.25 each (a 55% discount off the suggested retail price) and to wholesale customers for $3.00 each (a 40% discount off the suggested retail price). The prices for racks are the same for both types of customers (distributors and wholesale): plastic, $5.95; wire, $4.75; wood, $4.95. An Inventory Synopsis report for Oregon Explorer Maps as of December 1, 1997, appears below:

Inventory Synopsis							
File Help							
12/1/1997			Price	Quantity	Cost	Value	Margin (%)
Attr2-D	Explore Oregon-Attra...	Each	2.25	7,646	0.54	4,128.91	76.00
Attr2-W	Explore Oregon-Attra...	Each	3.00	1,575	0.54	850.52	82.00
Golf1	Explore Oregon-Golf	Each	3.00	1,028	0.6907	710.00	76.98
RPlast	Plastic Racks	Each	5.95	100	5.0	500.00	15.97
RWire	Wire Racks	Each	4.75	100	3.75	375.00	21.05
RWood	Wood Racks	Each	4.95	200	4.0	800.00	19.19
Ski1	Explore Oregon-Ski	Each	3.00	320	0.82	262.40	72.67
Ski2-D	Explore Oregon-Ski	Each	2.25	18,000	0.75	13,500.00	66.67
Ski2-W	Explore Oregon-Ski	Each	3.00	3,494	0.7499	2,620.25	75.00
Wine1	Explore Oregon-Wine	Each	3.00	456	0.76	346.56	74.67
Wine2-D	Explore Oregon-Wine	Each	2.25	17,525	0.68	11,916.72	69.78
Wine2-W	Explore Oregon-Wine	Each	3.00	2,934	0.68	1,995.12	77.33
						38,005.48	

The following inventory numbering system has been established for Oregon Explorer Maps' products: Inventory numbers are interpreted as follows:

Example 1:

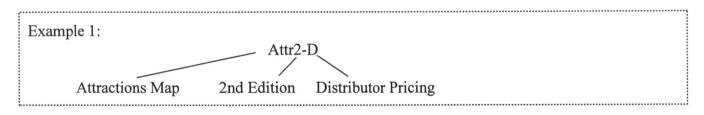

Attr2-D

Attractions Map   2nd Edition   Distributor Pricing

Example 2:

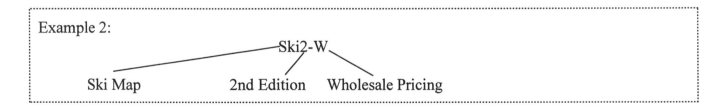

Ski2-W

Ski Map   2nd Edition   Wholesale Pricing

Example 3:

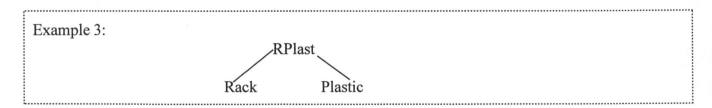

RPlast

Rack   Plastic

Note: The Golf 1, Ski1, and Wine1 maps listed in the inventory synopsis are obsolete (dated) inventory items and are not shown in the above inventory numbering examples. Oregon Explorer Maps plans to adjust these inventory items at the end of the current fiscal year.

Project Accounting

The Project component of CA-Simply Accounting allows income and expenses to be allocated to a specific project. This is useful if you want to allocate income and expenses to a specific job/contract or to isolate information about a particular area of your business. Beginning December 1, Oregon Explorer Maps will begin using the Project component of CA-Simply Accounting for Windows on an experimental basis. Five projects have been established:

1. Attraction Map Sales Summary
2. Golf Map Sales Summary
3. Rack Sales Summary
4. Ski Map Sales Summary
5. Wine Map Sales Summary

Revenues and expenses associated with each type of map sale, regardless of the type of customer the map is sold to, will be allocated to the appropriate project. All revenues and expenses associated with rack sales will be allocated to the Rack Sales Summary project. Oregon Explorer Maps plans to evaluate the usefulness of the project reports at the end of December.

Payroll and Employee Information

Oregon Explorer Maps employs four people in addition to the owner, Karen Bailey, who acts as the business manager for the company. Joyce Graham is employed as the research and design specialist for new and existing products. Arlie Richman is the sales manager working with both the distributors and various wholesale customers. Alice White is the accountant, and Sam York is the shipping clerk. The job functions of each employee contribute equally to generating all types of sales and cannot be specifically identified with a particular product. Therefore, payroll transactions will not be allocated to projects. Employees are paid monthly on the last working day of each month. Medical insurance is provided, with a small co-payment required of each employee for personal coverage; coverage for additional family members is at the expense of the employee.

OPEN SIMPLY ACCOUNTING AND CUSTOMIZE COMPANY INFORMATION

 ACTION: Follow the steps learned in earlier chapters to Load CA-Simply Accounting for Windows. Open the data files for Oregon Explorer Maps (A:\EXPLORER\Explorer.asc); then advance the session date to 12/5/1997. The home window for Oregon Explorer Maps will appear as shown below:

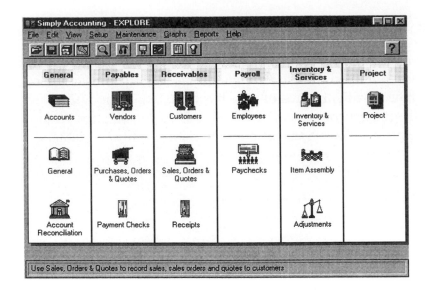

Note: Notice that all the components of the program are set as ready. None of the icons on the screen are identified as locked. A component that is locked has an icon with a red circle and a slash through it.

ACTION: Customize the Explorer company file by adding your name to the company name. On the home window, click the **Setup** menu and point to Company Information. Your screen will appear as follows:

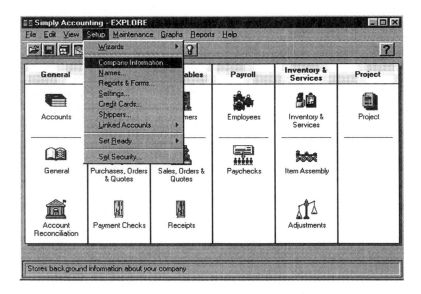

ACTION: Click **Company Information** to open the Company Information dialog box. Click after Oregon Explorer Maps in the **Name** box. Key a diagonal and your name. Your screen will appear as follows but will include your actual name, not the words *your name*.

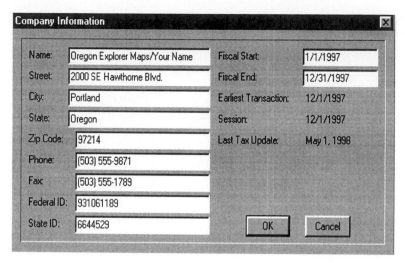

Company Information	
Name: Oregon Explorer Maps/Your Name	Fiscal Start: 1/1/1997
Street: 2000 SE Hawthorne Blvd.	Fiscal End: 12/31/1997
City: Portland	Earliest Transaction: 12/1/1997
State: Oregon	Session: 12/1/1997
Zip Code: 97214	Last Tax Update: May 1, 1998
Phone: (503) 555-9871	
Fax: (503) 555-1789	
Federal ID: 931061189	
State ID: 6644529	OK Cancel

Explanation: For example, the Company Information screen for Ray Bailey would have "Oregon Explorer Maps/Ray Bailey" in the **Name** box.

 ACTION: Click the **OK** button to add your name to the company name and to close the Company Information dialog box. You will return to the home window.

SALES JOURNAL—RECORDING INVENTOR Y SALES ON ACCOUNT

Inventory sales on account are recorded in the Sales Journal. Most distributor and wholesale customer sales orders are taken by phone. A phone order form is given to the accountant to prepare the invoice, which is shipped with the order.

Oregon Explorer Maps—Document 1   Session Date: 12/5/1997

Phone Order
Customer: Northewest Pipeline   **Date:** December 1, 1997

Item	Qty.	Description	Price	Amount
Ski2-D	1200	Explore Oregon-Ski	2.25	$ 2,700.00
Attr2-D	4200	Explore Oregon-Attractions	2.25	9,450.00
Wine2-D	1000	Explore Oregon-Wine	2.25	2,250.00
RPlast	20	Plastic Racks	5.95	119.00
RWire	15	Wire Racks	4.75	71.25
		TOTAL		$14,590.25

 ACTION: Open the Sales Journal by double-clicking the **Sales, Orders & Quotes** icon on the home window. Click the drop-down list arrow to the right of the **Sold to** field, select **Northwest Pipeline** from the customer list; enter *12/1/1997* in the **Date** field; then press the TAB key. Your screen will look like this:

Sales, Orders & Quotes

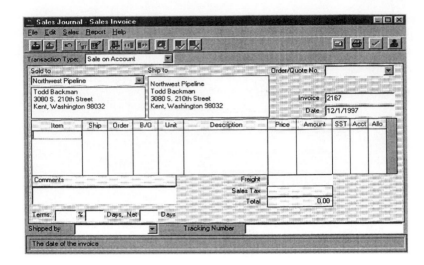

Explanation: The program has automatically filled in the customer's address in the **Sold to** and **Ship to** fields. The **Invoice** field is also completed automatically. Oregon Explorer Maps has elected to use the CA-Simply Accounting for Windows automatic invoice preparation and numbering feature. Invoice 2167 represents the next invoice in the automatic sequence. After accepting the new transaction date, the program will position a flashing insertion point in the **Item** field.

> **ACTION:** With the flashing insertion point positioned in the **Item** field, press the ENTER key or double-click in the field with your mouse. Your screen will look like this:

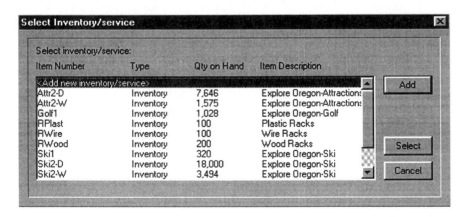

Explanation: A display listing Oregon Explorer Maps' inventory items will appear in the Select Inventory/Service dialog box. The scroll bar on the right side of dialog box can be used to advance the inventory item list. Use this list to determine the inventory item to be entered into the **Item** field. **CAUTION!** Oregon Explorer Maps uses special identification numbers to identify its various inventory products and the sales prices and accounts associated with each product. **USE SPECIAL CARE** to select the correct inventory item. For example, Attr2-D for Explore Oregon-Attractions maps sold to distributors or Ski2-W for Explore Oregon-Ski maps sold to wholesale customers.

> **ACTION:** Select Item number **Ski2-D** by double-clicking the item or by highlighting the item and clicking the **Select** button. Your screen will look like this:

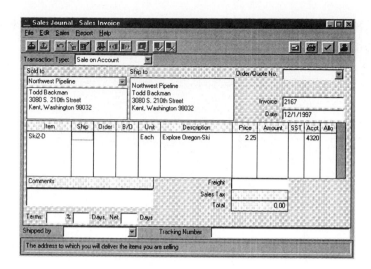

Explanation: The program has automatically completed the **Unit** (Each), **Description** (Explore Oregon-Ski), **Price** (2.25—the distributor sales price), and **Acct** (4320—Distributor Ski Map Sales) fields associated with this inventory item. The flashing insertion point is positioned in the **Ship** field.

ACTION: Enter *1200* into the **Ship** field; then press the TAB key. Your screen will look like this:

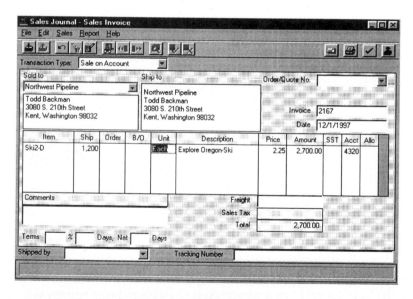

Explanation: The program has automatically multiplied the number entered in the **Ship** field (1200) by the amount entered in the **Price** field (2.25) and entered the result in the **Amount** field (2700.00). Note that the program has highlighted the word *Each* in the **Unit** field and that the **Allocate** button is now available (no longer dimmed). You can activate the **Allocate** button for an inventory line item by highlighting any completed field for that inventory line item. Allocating an inventory line item to a project may be completed by clicking the **Allocation** button or by clicking in the **Allo** column as illustrated below.

ACTION: With the word *Each* in the **Unit** field highlighted (or by highlighting any other completed field for the Ski2-D inventory item), TAB to or click the **Allo** column. This will move the insertion point into the **Allo** column. To show a Project Allocation screen, double-click in the **Allo** column. Your screen will look like this:

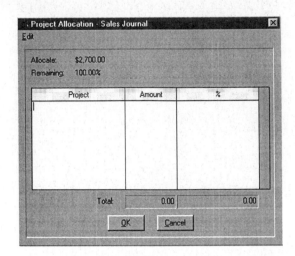

Explanation: The Project Allocation dialog box is displayed. Revenues and expenses can be allocated to projects by dollar amounts or by percentages. Oregon Explorer Maps has elected to use the percentage method.

ACTION: With the flashing insertion point positioned in the **Project** field, press the ENTER key or double-click with your mouse. Your screen will look like this:

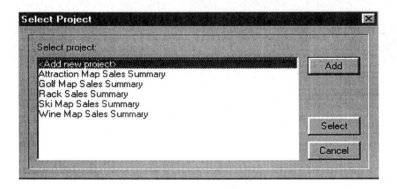

Explanation: A display listing Oregon Explorer Maps' Projects will appear.

ACTION: Select the **Ski Map Sales Summary** project by double-clicking in the **Project** field or by highlighting the project and clicking the **Select** button. Your screen will look like this:

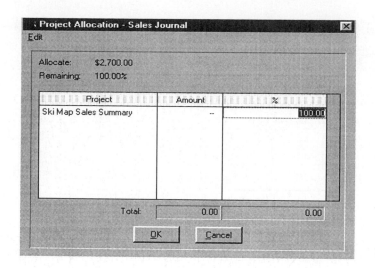

Explanation: The flashing insertion point is positioned in the **%** field, and 100.00 is automatically displayed as the percentage. It is Oregon Explorer Maps' policy to allocate 100% of a revenue or expense to a project unless otherwise noted.

 ACTION: Click the **OK** button. Your screen will look like this:

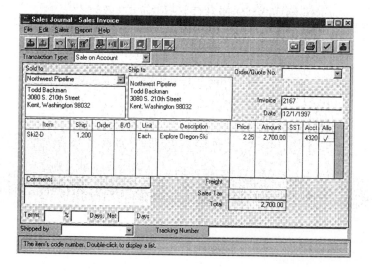

Explanation: The full amount of the sales price ($2,700.00) for this item has been allocated to the Ski Map Sales Summary project. Notice the check mark (✔) in the **Allo** column, which indicates that this item has been allocated to a project.

 ACTION: Click the **Item** field and enter the remaining items listed on the phone order for Northwest Pipeline, allocating 100% of each inventory line item to the appropriate project. Your screen will look like this:

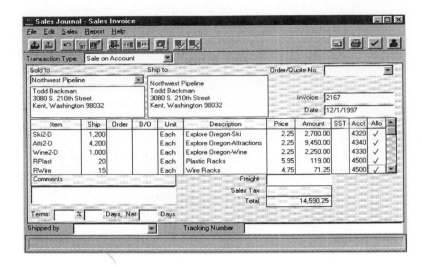

Explanation: This completes the information that you need to enter into the Sales Journal dialog box to record an inventory sale on account to Northwest Pipeline. **Note:** The program has automatically entered the account number associated with each inventory item selected in the **Acct** field, and the **Freight**, **Sales Tax**, and **Terms** fields have been left blank because there were no freight charges, sales tax (the state of Oregon does not charge sales tax), or special terms associated with this transaction. Before you print this invoice or post the transaction, you need to verify that the transaction data are correct by viewing the journal entry.

 ACTION: Choose **Display Sales Journal Entry** from the Sales Journal Report menu. Your screen will look like this:

Sales Journal Entry

File   Help

12/1/1997		Debits	Credits	Project
1200	Accounts Receivable	14,590.25	-	
5020	COGS-Ski Maps	900.00	-	
	- Ski Map Sales Summary			900.00
5030	COGS-Wine Maps	679.98	-	
	- Wine Map Sales Summary			679.98
5040	COGS-Attraction Maps	2,268.04	-	
	- Attraction Map Sales Summary			2,268.04
5050	COGS-Racks	156.25	-	
	- Rack Sales Summary			156.25
1220	Ski Map Inventory	-	900.00	
1230	Wine Map Inventory	-	679.98	
1240	Attraction Map Inventory	-	2,268.04	
1250	Rack Inventory	-	156.25	
4320	Distributor Ski Map Sales	-	2,700.00	
	- Ski Map Sales Summary			2,700.00
4330	Distributor Wine Map Sales	-	2,250.00	
	- Wine Map Sales Summary			2,250.00
4340	Distributor Attraction Map Sales	-	9,450.00	
	- Attraction Map Sales Summary			9,450.00
4500	Rack Sales	-	190.25	
	- Rack Sales Summary			190.25
		18,594.52	18,594.52	

Explanation: The journal entry representing the data you have recorded in the Sales Journal dialog box is displayed. Use the scroll bar to the right of the display to advance the display or click the maximize button on the title bar to display the entire transaction. The standard journal entry for an inventory sale on account in a perpetual inventory system is displayed:

	Debit	**Credit**
Accounts Receivable	xxx	
Cost of Goods Sold	xxx	
Inventory		xxx
Sales		xxx

Through its integration/linking feature, the program will automatically debit Accounts Receivable and the cost of goods sold account associated with each inventory item selected. In addition, the inventory and sales accounts associated the each inventory item selected will be credited. Remember, the amount recorded in the transaction for cost of goods sold and inventory represents the average cost of the inventory item to the company, and the amount recorded in the transaction for accounts receivable and sales represents the amount the customer is charged for the item. Review the journal entry and project allocations for accuracy, noting any errors.

 ACTION: Close the Sales Journal Entry window. You will return to the sales invoice. Print the invoice by choosing **Print** from the Sales Journal File menu. Compare your invoice to the one shown below:

Oregon Explorer Maps/Your Name
2000 SE Hawthorne Blvd.
Portland, Oregon 97214

2167

12/1/1997

1 of 1

Northwest Pipeline	Northwest Pipeline
Todd Backman	Todd Backman
3080 S. 210th Street	3080 S. 210th Street
Kent, Washington 98032	Kent, Washington 98032

Ski2-D	1,200	Each	Explore Oregon-Ski	2.25	2,700.00
Attr2-D	4,200	Each	Explore Oregon-Attractions	2.25	9,450.00
Wine2-D	1,000	Each	Explore Oregon-Wine	2.25	2,250.00
RPlast	20	Each	Plastic Racks	5.95	119.00
RWire	15	Each	Wire Racks	4.75	71.25

14,590.25

 ACTION: If you have made an error, use the following editing techniques to correct the error:

Editing Tips
Editing Inventory-Related Sales Journal Entries and Project Allocations

Move to the field that contains the error by either pressing the TAB key to move forward through each field or the SHIFT and TAB keys together to move to a previous field. This will highlight the selected field information so you can change it. Alternatively, you can use the mouse to point to a field and drag through the incorrect information to highlight it.

Type the correct information; then press the TAB key to enter it.

If an inventory item is incorrect, select the correct item from the Select Inventory Item dialog box after double-clicking on the incorrect item in the **Item** field.

If you have associated the transaction with the incorrect customer, select the correct customer from the customer list display after clicking the drop-down list arrow button to the right of the **Sold to** field.

If you have associated an inventory item with an incorrect account number, select the correct account number from the chart of accounts display after double-clicking on the incorrect account number in the **Acct** field.

If you have associated an inventory item with an incorrect project or have allocated an incorrect amount to a project, double-click in the **Allo** column to display the Project Allocation dialog box. To correct the project, select the correct project from the Select Project dialog box after double-clicking on the incorrect project in the **Project** field; then click the **OK** button. To correct the allocated amount or percentage, highlight the incorrect amount or percentage; enter the correct amount or percentage; then click the **OK** button.

To discard an entry and start over, either choose **Undo Entry** from Edit on the Sales Journal menu bar, or click the close button on the titlebar. Click the **Yes** button in response to the question, "Are you sure you want to discard this journal entry?"

Review the journal entry and allocations for accuracy after any corrections by choosing **Display Sales Journal Entry** from the Sales Journal Report menu.

It is IMPORTANT TO NOTE that the only way to edit a transaction after it is posted is to reverse the entry and enter the correct transaction. To correct transactions posted in error, see the transaction for **Applegate Vineyard Winery** later in this chapter.

 ACTION: After a correct invoice is printed, click the **Post** button to post this transaction. Your screen will look like this:

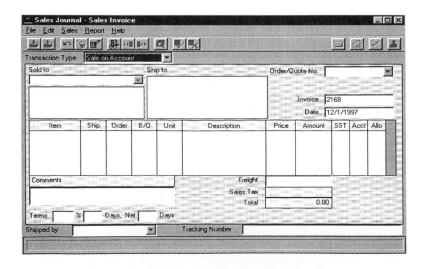

Explanation: A blank Sales Journal dialog box is displayed, ready for additional Sales Journal transactions to be recorded. If you receive an error message stating that an account has not been fully allocated, do not post the entry. For information on corrective action, refer to Editing Tips for Editing Inventory-Related Sales Journal Entries and Project Allocations, which appears in a special box earlier in this chapter.

Additional Inventory Sales on Account Transactions

Record the following additional inventory sales on account transactions, allocating 100% of each inventory item sold to the appropriate project and printing each invoice:

Oregon Explorer Maps—Document 2   Session Date: 12/5/1997

Phone Order
Customer: Applegate Vineyard Winery   **Date:** December 2, 1997

Item	Qty.	Description	Price	Amount
Wine2-W	30	Explore Oregon-Wine	3.00	$ 90.00
RWire	1	Wire Rack	4.75	4.75
		TOTAL		$ 94.75

Oregon Explorer Maps—Document 3   Session Date: 12/5/1997

Phone Order
Customer: Pacific Crest Maps   **Date:** December 3, 1997

Item	Qty.	Description	Price	Amount
Attr2-D	2500	Explore Oregon-Attractions	2.25	$ 5,625.00
Ski2-D	900	Explore Oregon-Ski	2.25	2,025.00
Wine2-D	650	Explore Oregon-Wine	2.25	1,462.50
		TOTAL		$ 9,112.50

Compare your invoices to the ones shown below:

Oregon Explorer Maps/Your Name
2000 SE Hawthorne Blvd.
Portland, Oregon 97214

2168

12/2/1997

1 of 1

Applegate Vineyard Winery	Applegate Vineyard Winery
Jane Martin	Jane Martin
7927 Caves Hwy.	7927 Caves Hwy.
Cave Junction, Oregon 97523	Cave Junction, Oregon 97523

Wine2-W	30	Each	Explore Oregon-Wine	3.00	90.00
RWire	1	Each	Wire Racks	4.75	4.75
					94.75

Oregon Explorer Maps/Your Name
2000 SE Hawthorne Blvd.
Portland, Oregon 97214

2169

12/3/1997

1 of 1

Pacific Crest Maps	Pacific Crest Maps
Elaine Nelson	Elaine Nelson
25177 NE 61st Street	25177 NE 61st Street
Redmond, Washington 98052	Redmond, Washington 98052

Attr2-D	2500	Each	Explore Oregon-Attractions	2.25	5,625.00
Ski2-D	900	Each	Explore Oregon-Ski	2.25	2,025.00
Wine2-D	650	Each	Explore Oregon-Wine	2.25	1,462.50
			TOTAL		9,112.50

Note: If you detect an error after printing and posting an invoice, refer to Editing Tips for Editing Inventory-Related Sales Journal Entries and Project Allocations, that appears in a special box earlier in this chapter, for information on corrective action.

 ACTION: After you have printed the invoices and posted the journal entries for Documents 2 and 3, close the Sales Journal dialog box and return to the home window. Upon examining the printed copy of Invoice 2168, you realize that Applegate Vineyards has an item listed as RWood and it should have been RWire. In order to correct this invoice, double-click **Sales, Orders & Quotes** icon on the home window. In the Sales Journal - Sales Invoice window, click the **Adjust Invoice** button. On the Adjust an invoice screen, click the drop-down list arrow next to Customer Name and click **Applegate Vineyard Winery** to select the customer.

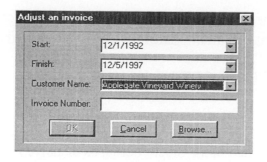

ACTION: After Applegate Vineyard Winery has been selected as the customer, click the **Browse** button. CA-Simply Accounting will browse through all the invoices and display the following invoice information for Applegate Vineyard Winery:

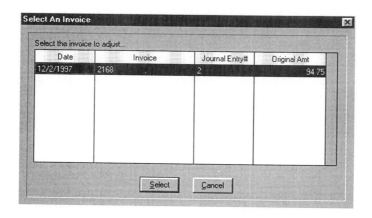

ACTION: With the invoice information highlighted, click the **Select** button. The original invoice will appear on the screen. Double-click **RWire**. Click **RWood** on the Select Inventory/Service screen. Enter *1* in the **Shipped** column and re-enter the allocation to the rack project. The invoice will appear as follows:

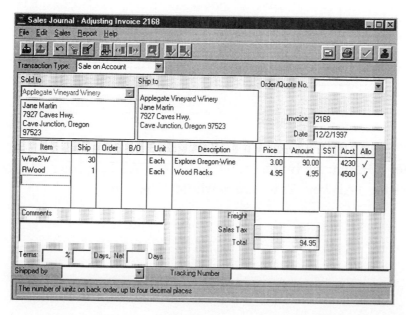

Explanation: This will change the invoice. Notice the total is now $94.95 rather than $94.75.

ACTION: Verify that the information on the revised invoice is correct. Print the invoice, post the invoice, and close the Sales Journal - Sales Invoice to return to the home window screen.

SALES JOURNAL—RECORDING CREDIT MEMOS

Oregon Explorer Maps has a policy of allowing customers to return merchandise for credit if they are dissatisfied with their purchase or if the product is damaged. When items are returned, a credit memo is prepared. Credit memos are recorded in the Sales Journal as negative invoices. This has the effect of reducing the customer's outstanding accounts receivable balance and increasing the inventory quantity for the item returned.

Oregon Explorer Maps—Document 4   **Session Date: 12/5/1997**

Credit Memo 56
Customer: Springwater Country Club   **Date:** December 4, 1997

Record the return of 2 Golf1 maps at $3.00 each for a total of $6.00.

 ACTION: Open the Sales Journal - Sales Invoice dialog box; click the drop-down list arrow to the right of the **Sold to** field; then select **Springwater County Club** from the customer list. Your screen will look like this:

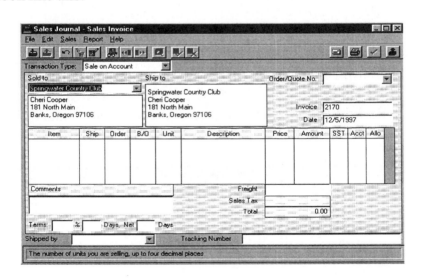

 ACTION: Enter *CM56* in the **Invoice** field; press the TAB key; enter *12/4/1997* in the **Date** field; then press the TAB key. Your screen will look like this:

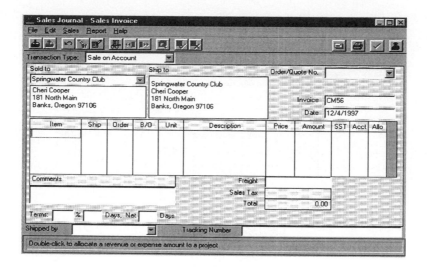

ACTION: With the flashing insertion point positioned in the **Item** field, press the ENTER key or double-click with your mouse; select the **Golf1** inventory item from the Select Inventory Item dialog box. Your screen will look like this:

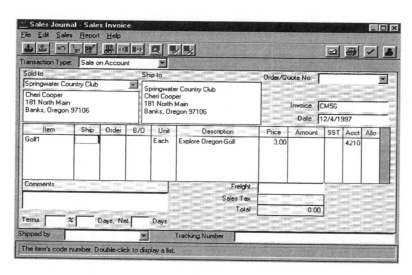

ACTION: Enter *-2* in the **Ship** field; then press the TAB key until the **Acct** field is highlighted. Your screen will look like this:

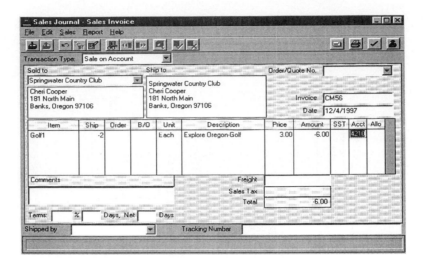

Explanation: The standard journal entry to record a credit memo is:

	Debit	Credit
Inventory	xxx	
Sales Returns and Allowances	xxx	
Accounts Receivable		xxx
Cost of Goods Sold		xxx

Through its integration/linking feature, the program will automatically debit the inventory account associated with the inventory item returned, credit Accounts Receivable, and credit the cost of goods sold account associated with the returned inventory item. To record this transaction as a sales return, the 4700 Sales Returns and Allowances account needs to be selected from the chart of accounts to replace to default account offered (4210 Wholesale Golf Map Sales).

 ACTION: Press the ENTER key; then select account number **4700 Sales Returns and Allowances** from the Select Account dialog box. Allocate the sales return to the Golf Map Sales Summary project. Your screen will look like this:

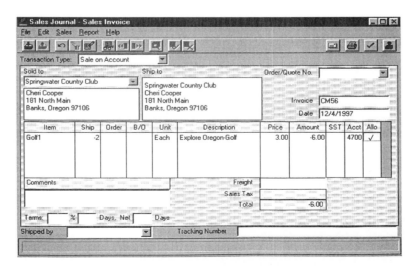

Explanation: This completes the information that you need to enter into the Sales Journal dialog box to record the credit memo. Before you print the credit memo and post this entry, you need to verify that the transaction data are correct by viewing the journal entry.

 ACTION: Choose **Display Sales Journal Entry** from the Sales Journal Report menu. Compare your display to the one shown below:

Sales Journal Entry			
File Help			
12/4/1997	Debits	Credits	Project
1210 Golf Map Inventory	1.38	-	
4700 Sales Returns and Allowances	6.00	-	
- Golf Map Sales Summary			-6.00
1200 Accounts Receivable	-	6.00	
5010 COGS-Golf Maps	-	1.38	
- Golf Map Sales Summary			-1.38
	7.38	7.38	

Explanation: The journal entry representing the data you have recorded in the Sales Journal dialog box is displayed. Review the journal entry and allocations for accuracy noting any errors.

ACTION: Close the Sales Journal Entry window. If you made an error, refer to the Editing Tips for Editing Inventory-Related Sales Journal Entries and Project Allocations, which appears in a special box earlier in this chapter, for information on corrective action.

ACTION: After verifying that the journal entry and allocations are correct, choose **Print** from the Sales Journal File menu; then compare your credit memo to the one shown below:

Oregon Explorer Maps/Your Name
2000 SE Hawthorne Blvd.
Portland, Oregon 97214

CM56

12/4/1997

1 of 1

Springwater County Club   Springwater County Club
Cheri Cooper   Cheri Cooper
181 North Main   181 North Main
Banks, Oregon 97106   Banks, Oregon 97106

Golf1   -2   Each   Explore Oregon-Golf   3.00   -6.00

-6.00

ACTION: Verify that the credit memo is correct. If you detect an error, refer to the Editing Tips for Editing Inventory-Related Sales Journal Entries and Project Allocations for information on corrective action.

ACTION: After a correct credit memo has been printed, click the **Post** button to post the transaction. A blank Sales Journal dialog box is displayed, ready for additional Sales Journal transactions to be recorded.

Additional Credit Memo Transactions

Record the following additional credit memo transactions, allocating 100% of each inventory item returned to the appropriate project and printing each credit memo:

Oregon Explorer Maps—Document 5   Session Date: 12/5/1997

> **Credit Memo 57**
> **Customer:** Applegate Vineyard Winery   **Date:** December 4, 1997
>
> Use CR57 to record the return of 3 Wine1 maps at $3.00 each for a total of $9.00.

Oregon Explorer Maps—Document 6   Session Date: 12/5/1997

> **Credit Memo 58**
> **Customer:** Lost Lake Lodge   **Date:** December 5, 1997
>
> Use CM58 to record the return of 5 Ski1 maps at $3.00 each for a total of $15.00.

Compare your credit memos to the ones shown below:

> Oregon Explorer Maps/Your Name
> 2000 SE Hawthorne Blvd.
> Portland, Oregon 97214   CR57
>
>   12/4/1997
>
>   1 of 1
>
>
> Applegate Vineyard Winery   Applegate Vineyard Winery
> Jane Martin   Jane Martin
> 7927 Caves Hwy.   7927 Caves Hwy.
> Cave Junction, Oregon 97523   Cave Junction, Oregon 97523
>
>
> Wine1   -3   Each   Explore Oregon-Wine   3.00   -9.00
>
>   -9.00

Oregon Explorer Maps/Your Name
2000 SE Hawthorne Blvd.
Portland, Oregon 97214

CM58

12/5/1997

1 of 1

Lost Lake Lodge   Lost Lake Lodge
Ken Ho   Ken Ho
P. O. Box 94   P. O. Box 94
Lost Lake, Oregon 97028   Lost Lake, Oregon 97028

Ski1   -5   Each   Explore Oregon-Ski   3.00   -15.00

                                                                              -15.00

If you detect an error after printing and posting a credit memo, refer to Editing Tips for Editing Inventory-Related Sales Journal Entries and Project Allocations for information on corrective action.

 ACTION: After you have printed the credit memos and posted the transaction data associated with Documents 5 and 6, close the Sales Journal dialog box. This will restore the home window screen, and the Sales Journal icon will remain highlighted. With the Sales Journal icon highlighted, select **Journal Entries** and **Sales** from the home window Report menu. Your screen will look like this:

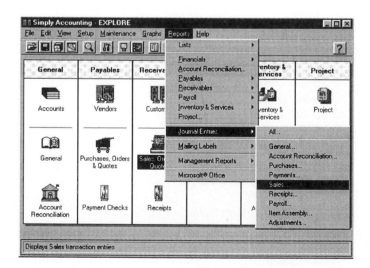

Explanation: The Sales Journal Options dialog box appears, asking you to define the information you want displayed.

 ACTION: Select **By date**; check the Project allocations check box; enter *12/1/1997* as the start date; leave the finish date set at 12/5/1997; then click the **OK** button. The following Sales Journal Display will appear on your screen:

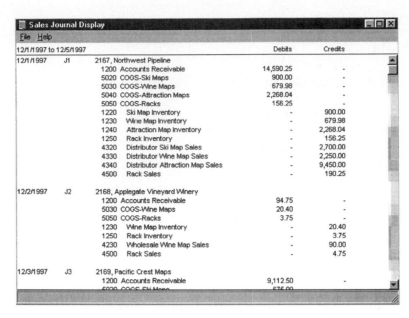

Explanation: Review the display for accuracy, verifying that journal entry dates, project allocations, customer names, invoice numbers, account names and numbers, and amounts are correct. Use the scroll bars at the bottom and to the right of the display to advance the display. If you have posted an incorrect transaction, correct your transactions by following the instructions for the Applegate Vineyard Winery correction you made earlier in the chapter.

 ACTION: Print the Sales Journal by choosing **Print** from the Sales Journal Display File menu. Compare your report to the one shown below:

Oregon Explorer Maps/Your Name
Sales Journal 12/1/1997 to 12/5/1997

					Debits	**Credits**
12/1/1997	J1	2167, Northwest Pipeline				
		1200	Accounts Receivable		14,590.25	-
		5020	COGS-Ski Maps		900.00	-
		5030	COGS-Wine Maps		679.98	-
		5040	COGS-Attraction Maps		2,268.04	-
		5050	COGS-Racks		156.25	-
		1220	Ski Map Inventory		-	900.00
		1230	Wine Map Inventory		-	679.98
		1240	Attraction Map Inventory		-	2,268.04
		1250	Rack Inventory		-	156.25
		4320	Distributor Ski Map Sales		-	2,700.00
		4330	Distributor Wine Map Sales		-	2,250.00
		4340	Distributor Attraction Map Sales		-	9,450.00
		4500	Rack Sales		-	190.25
12/2/1997	J2	2168, Applegate Vineyard Winery				
		1200	Accounts Receivable		94.75	-
		5030	COGS-Wine Maps		20.40	-
		5050	COGS-Racks		3.75	-
		1230	Wine Map Inventory		-	20.40
		1250	Rack Inventory		-	3.75
		4230	Wholesale Wine Map Sales		-	90.00
		4500	Rack Sales		-	4.75

12/3/1997	J3	2169, Pacific Crest Maps			
		1200 Accounts Receivable	9,112.50	-
		5020 COGS-Ski Maps	675.00	-
		5030 COGS-Wine Maps	441.99	-
		5040 COGS-Attraction Maps	1,350.02	-
		1220 Ski Map Inventory	-	675.00
		1230 Wine Map Inventory	-	441.99
		1240 Attraction Map Inventory	-	1,350.02
		4320 Distributor Ski Map Sales	-	2,025.00
		4330 Distributor Wine Map Sales	-	1,462.50
		4340 Distributor Attraction Map Sales	-	5,625.00
12/2/1997	J4	ADJJ2168, Reversing J2. Correction is J5.		
		1230 Wine Map Inventory	20.40	-
		1250 Rack Inventory	3.75	-
		4320 Wholesale Wine Map Sales	90.00	-
		4500 Rack Sales	4.75	-
		1200 Accounts Receivable	-	94.75
		5030 COGS-Wine Maps	-	20.40
		5050 COGS-Racks	-	3.75
12/2/1997	J5	2168, Applegate Vineyard Winery		
		1200 Accounts Receivable	94.95	-
		5030 COGS-Wine Maps	20.40	-
		5050 COGS-Racks	4.00	-
		1230 Wine Map Inventory	-	20.40
		1250 Rack Inventory	-	4.00
		4230 Wholesale Wine Map Sales	-	90.00
		4500 Rack Sales	-	4.95
12/4/1997	J6	CM56, Springwater Country Club		
		1210 Golf Map Inventory	1.38	-
		4700 Sales Returns and Allowances	6.00	-
		1200 Accounts Receivable	-	6.00
		5010 COGS-Golf Maps	-	1.38
12/4/1997	J7	CR57 Applegate Vineyard Winery		
		1230 Wine Map Inventory	2.28	-
		4700 Sales Returns and Allowances	9.00	-
		1200 Accounts Receivable	-	9.00
		5030 COGS-Wine Maps	-	2.28
12/5/1997	J8	CM58, Lost Lake Lodge		
		1220 Ski Map Inventory	4.10	-
		4700 Sales Returns and Allowances	15.00	-
		1200 Accounts Receivable	-	15.00
		5020 COGS-Ski Maps	-	4.10
			30,568.94	30,568.94

Explanation: If you detect an error, refer to the material presented earlier in the chapter for corrections.

▨ **ACTION:** Close the Sales Journal Display window and return to the home window.

ACTION: Choose **Exit** from the home window File menu to end the current work session and return to your Windows desktop.

ALTERNATIVE ACTION: If you wish to continue the tutorial without exiting from the program, choose **Advance Session Date** from the home window Setup menu. Enter *12/12/1997* as the new session date; then skip the next ACTION and continue with the tutorial.

RECEIPTS JOURNAL—RECORDING CASH RECEIPTS FROM CREDIT CUSTOMERS

Payments received for outstanding invoices are recorded in the Receipts Journal. Oregon Explorer Maps has received the following check as a payment on account.

Oregon Explorer Maps—Document 7   **Session Date: 12/12/1997**

Northwest Pipeline	17634
3080 S. 210th Street	
Kent, WA 98032	Dec. 7 , 19 97 98-57
	1233
Pay to the	
order of _____ Oregon Explorer Maps _____	$ 18,000.00
Eighteen thousand and NO/100 _____Dollars	
Washington Federal Bank, P. O. 1762, Kent, WA 98032	
For __Invoice 2049__ *Todd Backman*	

ACTION: Load CA-Simply Accounting for Windows; open the data files for Oregon Explorer Maps (A:\EXPLORER\Explorer.asc); then advance the session date to 12/12/1997. Open the Receipts Journal dialog box; click the drop-down list arrow to the right of the **From** field; select **Northwest Pipeline** from the customer list; enter *17634* in the **No.** field; press the TAB key; enter *12/7/1997* in the **Date** field; then press the TAB key. Your screen will look like this:

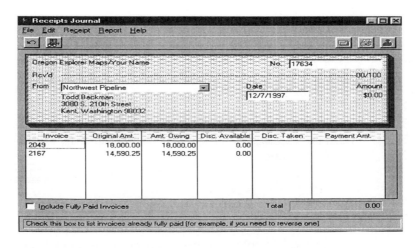

ACTION: Press the TAB key to choose the exact amount of the outstanding balance of Invoice 2049. Your screen will look like this:

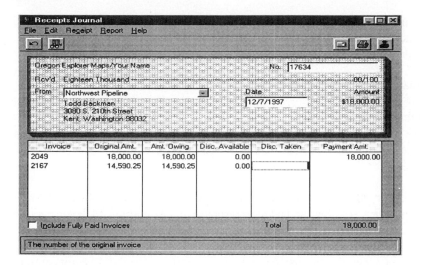

Explanation: This completes the data you need to enter into the Receipts Journal dialog box to record the check received from Northwest Pipeline. Before you post this entry, you need to verify that the transaction data are correct by viewing the journal entry.

 ACTION: Choose **Display Receipts Journal Entry** from the Receipts Journal Report menu. Your screen will look like this:

12/7/1997	Debits	Credits	Project
1060 Cash	18,000.00	-	
1200 Accounts Receivable	-	18,000.00	
	18,000.00	18,000.00	

Explanation: The journal entry reflecting the information you have recorded in the Receipts Journal dialog box is displayed. Through its integration/linking feature, the program has created the standard journal entry for a cash receipt on account:

	Debit	**Credit**
Cash	xxx	
Accounts Receivable		xxx

Note: The Receipts Journal dialog box does not have an allocation column. Project allocations can be made only to revenue and expense accounts. Cash and Accounts Receivable are both asset accounts.

Review the journal entry for accuracy noting any errors.

 ACTION: Close the Receipts Journal Entry window. You will return to the Receipts Journal.

Explanation: If you have made an error, use the following editing techniques to correct the error:

Editing Tips
Editing a Receipts Journal Entry

Move to the field that contains the error by either pressing the TAB key to move forward through each field or the SHIFT and TAB keys together to move to a previous field. This will highlight the field information so that you can change it. Alternatively, you can use the mouse to point to a field and drag through the incorrect information to highlight it.

Type the correct information; then press the TAB key to enter it.

If you have associated the transaction with an incorrect customer, select the correct customer from the customer list display after clicking the drop-down list arrow to the right of the **From** field. You will be asked to confirm that you want to discard the current transaction. Click the **Yes** button to discard the incorrect entry and display the outstanding invoices for the correct customer.

To completely discard an entry and start over, either choose **Undo Entry** from the Receipts Journal Edit menu, or click the **Exit** button on the title bar. Click the **Yes** button in response to the question, "Are you sure you want to discard this journal entry?"

Review the journal entry for accuracy after any corrections by choosing **Display Receipts Journal Entry** from the Receipts Journal Report menu.

It is IMPORTANT TO NOTE that the only way to edit a transaction after it is posted is to reverse the entry and enter the correct transaction. To correct transactions posted in error, see the transaction to correct the error for Sheriden Vineyards later in this chapter.

 ACTION: After you have verified that all of the transaction data are correct, print the Receipts Journal for Northwest Pipeline. Your printout should appear as follows:

Oregon Explorer Maps/Your Name
2000 SE Hawthorne Blvd.
Portland, Oregon 97214   17634
                                                                              12/7/1997

                                                                                    $18,000.00

Northwest Pipeline
3080 S. 210th Street
Kent, Washington 98032

Oregon Explorer Maps/Your Name

Northwest Pipeline   12/7/1997   17634

2049 . . . .   18,000.00

 ACTION: Post the entry by clicking the **Post** button. A blank Receipts Journal dialog box is displayed, ready for additional Receipts Journal transactions to be recorded.

BANK DEPOSITS OF CASH RECEIPTS

ACTION: Cash receipts should be deposited in the bank frequently. Deposit the check received from Northwest Pipeline by closing the Sales Journal - Sales Invoice screen. Click **Account Reconciliation** on the home window to highlight. Your screen will appear as follows:

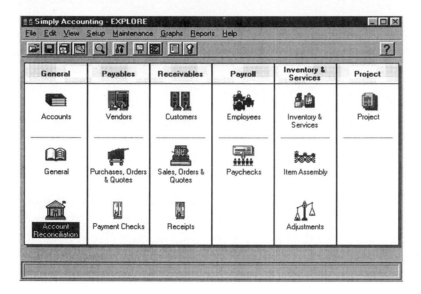

ACTION: Double-click the **Account Reconciliation** icon. When the Account Reconciliation Journal appears, click the drop-down list arrow next to **Account**. Your screen will look like the following:

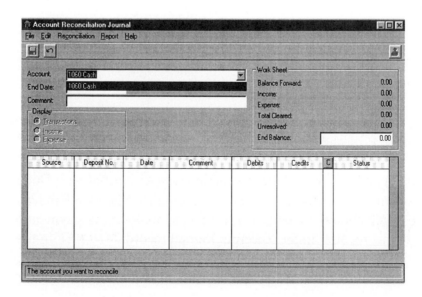

ACTION: Click **1060 Cash** to select this as the account to be reconciled. Beneath the Comment text box, Display should have Transactions selected. Click the column for **Deposit No.** next to Source 17634, which is the number of Northwest Pipeline's check. Enter *2138* as the number of the deposit slip used for the deposit. Your screen will look like the following:

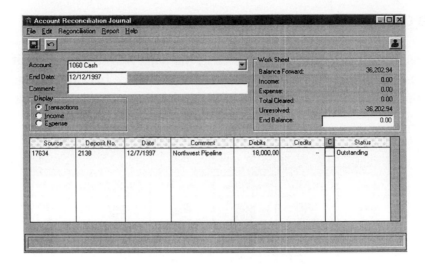

Explanation: Whenever a bank deposit is made, the number of the deposit slip is entered on the account reconciliation. When the bank statement is received with the deposit listed, the deposit will be marked cleared during the reconciliation process. The amount listed as the balance forward is the same amount as the beginning balance of the cash account. That amount also reflects the end balance of the previous bank reconciliation. The bank reconciliation will be completed in Chapter 8.

 ACTION: Because the account reconciliation is not being completed at this time, click the **Save** icon 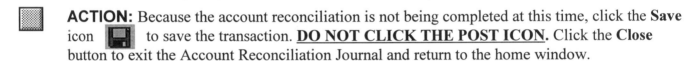 to save the transaction. **DO NOT CLICK THE POST ICON.** Click the **Close** button to exit the Account Reconciliation Journal and return to the home window.

ADDITIONAL CASH RECEIPTS TRANSACTIONS

Record the following additional cash receipts transactions:

Document 8 December 8—Received Check 64325 in the amount of $11,250.00 from Pacific Crest Maps in full payment of Invoice 2089. Print the receipt.

Document 9 December 8—Received Check 3410 in the amount of $100.00 from Sheriden Vineyards in payment of Invoice 2146. Print the receipt.

ACTION: After you have posted the transaction data associated with Documents 8 and 9, you realize you have made an error in the amount entered for Sheriden Vineyards. The correct amount of the check should have been entered as $150.00 in full payment of Invoice 2146. In order to correct this receipt, in the Receipts Journal record *3410 REV* in the **No.** text box to indicate a reversal of Check 3410. In the **Payment Amt.** column for Invoice 2146, enter *-100.00* (don't forget to precede the number with a minus sign). Your screen will appear as follows:

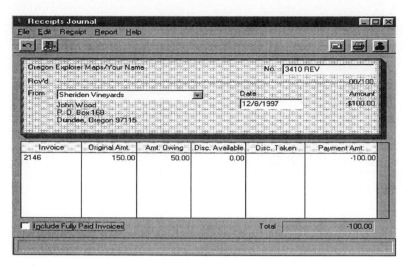

Explanation: This entry will reverse the previous receipt recorded for Invoice 2146. **Note:** If the invoice had been fully paid, the check box next to Include Fully Paid Invoices would have to be marked in order for the invoice to be displayed.

ACTION: On the Receipts Journal menu bar, click **Report** and **Display Receipts Journal Entry**. Your screen will show the following:

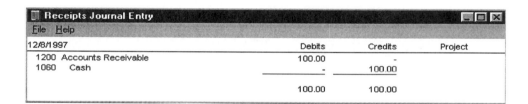

Explanation: This reverses the previous receipt entry by debiting Accounts Receivable and crediting Cash.

ACTION: Click the **Print** icon on the toolbar. Click **OK** on the message box that states "The receipt cannot be printed unless the amount is positive."

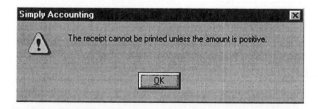

ACTION: Click the **Post** icon on the toolbar. Re-enter the receipt, using *3410C* as the number and making sure to enter the correct amount of *$150.00*. Your screen will appear as follows:

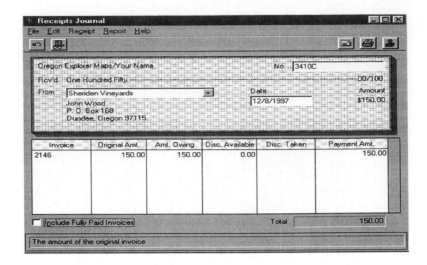

ACTION: Verify the information entered, print the receipt, and click the **Post** button to post the transaction. Click the **Exit** button to close the Receivables Journal. You will return to the home window, and Receipts will be highlighted. With the Receipts icon highlighted, select **Report** from the home window menu bar. Point to Journal Entries, Receipts. Your screen will look like this:

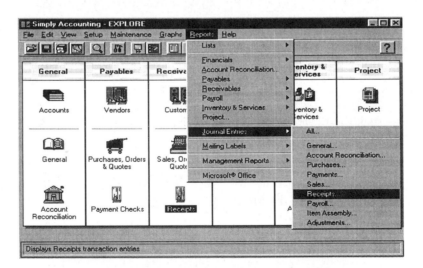

ACTION: Click **Receipts**. Your screen will look like this:

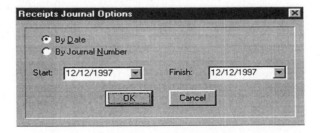

Explanation: A Receipts Journal Options dialog box (similar to the Sales Journal Options dialog box) will appear, asking you to define the information you want displayed.

▨ **ACTION:** Select **By Date**; enter *12/1/97* as the start date; leave the finish date set at 12/12/1997; then click the **OK** button. The following Receipts Journal Display will appear:

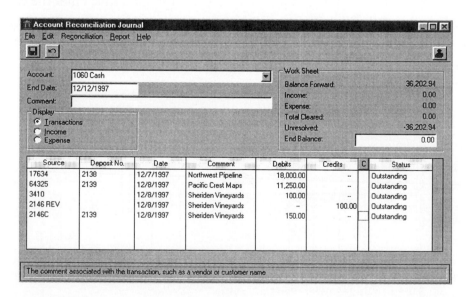

Explanation: Review the display for accuracy verifying that journal entry dates, customer names, check numbers, account names and numbers, and amounts are correct. If you have posted an incorrect transaction, refer to the corrections made for Sheriden Vineyards on Invoice 2146.

▨ **ACTION:** Close the Receipts Journal dialog box. You will return to the home window. Use the Account Reconciliation for Cash and deposit the checks received, using Deposit Slip 2139. Your screen will look like this:

Explanation: You have indicated the deposits made using Deposit Slip 2139. Notice that the error and adjustment were not marked.

ACTION: Because the account reconciliation is not being completed at this time, click the **Save** icon to save the transaction. **DO NOT CLICK THE POST ICON.** Click the **Close** button to exit the Account Reconciliation Journal and return to the home window.

SALES JOURNAL—RECORDING SALES DISCOUNTS

Businesses sometimes offer special payment terms to customers as an incentive for early payment of invoices. Oregon Explorer Maps offers payment terms of 2/15, n/30 to all wholesale customers. These terms allow wholesale customers to deduct 2% of the amount of the invoice from their payment if payment is made within 15 days of the invoice date. Only early-payment discounts are included in the Sales Discounts account. Simply calculates the discount automatically when terms for a sales discount are entered. There are three ways in which you can enter discount terms. If all customers will receive a discount for early payment, you may set up the discount in your Customers and Sales options, using the Settings menu on the home window. You may set up discount terms for individual customers when the customer is created. Finally, you may record discount terms on an invoice as it is recorded. This chapter will use the last method for discount terms.

Oregon Explorer Maps—Document 10   **Session Date: 12/10/1997**

Phone Order
Customer: Blue Mountain Slopes   **Date:** December 10, 1997

Item	Qty.	Description	Price	Amount
Ski2-2	55	Explore Oregon-Ski	3.00	$165.00
		TOTAL		$165.00

Terms 2/15, N/30

 ACTION: Open the Sales Journal dialog box. Except for the terms, enter the invoice information as previously instructed. Click **Terms**. Enter *2* for the percentage; press the TAB key; enter *15* for the number of days; press the TAB key; enter *30* for the net days. Your screen will look like this:

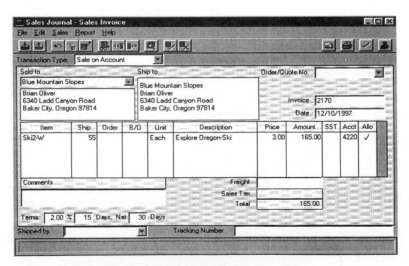

Explanation: The discount terms have been recorded as part of the invoice.

ACTION: Check the invoice for errors and correct any errors. When everything is correct, print the invoice. When the invoice has been printed, compare it to the invoice shown below:

Oregon Explorer Maps/Your Name
2000 SE Hawthorne Blvd.
Portland, Oregon 97214   2170

         12/10/1997

         1 of 1

Blue Mountain Slopes	Blue Mountain Slopes
Brian Oliver	Brian Oliver
6340 Ladd Canyon Road	6340 Ladd Canyon Road
Baker City, Oregon 97814	Baker City, Oregon 97814

Ski2-W	55	Each	Explore Oregon-Ski	3.00	165.00

Terms: 2%/15, Net 30. Due 1/9/1998.   165.00

Explanation: When comparing your invoice to the one above, notice that Simply records the terms of the invoice and the net due date.

 ACTION: Post the invoice and close the Sales Journal. You will return to the home window.

Additional Sales Discount Transactions

Record the following additional sales discount transactions:

Document 11 December 10—Invoice 2171: Sold to Portland Saturday Market 75 Explore Oregon-Attractions maps. Allow the discount for a wholesale transaction. Print the sales invoice.

Document 12 December 10—Invoice 2172: Sold to Sheriden Vineyards Winery 50 Explore Oregon-Attractions maps. Allow the discount for a wholesale transaction. Print the sales discount invoice.

RECEIPTS JOURNAL—RECEIPTS INCLUDING SALES DISCOUNTS

The sales discount is subtracted from the total amount due for an invoice when the payment is received. The payment receipt is recorded using the Receipts icon on the home window and the amount of the discount is entered and applied at that time.

Oregon Explorer Maps—Document 13   **Session Date: 12/12/1997**

Blue Mountain Slopes   4245
6340 Ladd Canyon Road
Baker City, OR 97814   Dec. 12 , 19 97   98-55
                                                                   1244

Pay to the
order of _____ Oregon Explorer Maps _____ $ 161.70

_ One hundred sixty-one and 71/100 _____Dollars

Oregon State Bank, P. O. 165, Baker City, OR 97814
For _ Invoice 2170 ____   *Brian Oliver* _____

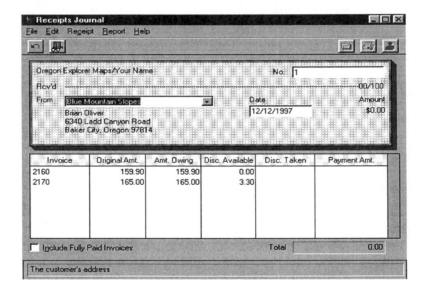

ACTION: Open the Receipts Journal by clicking the **Receipts** icon on the home window. Click the drop-down list arrow next to **From**. Click **Blue Mountain Slopes** to select the company. Your screen will appear as follows:

ACTION: TAB to or click in **No.** and enter *4245* as the number of the check. Click in the column **Disc. Taken** in the line for Invoice 2170. (Make sure you do not highlight or enter any payment information for Invoice 2160.) Your screen will look like this:

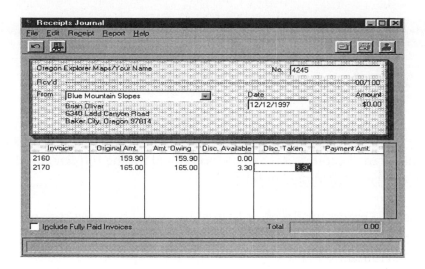

Explanation: When an invoice qualifies to receive a discount, the amount of the discount is shown in the **Disc. Available** column. Tabbing to or clicking in the **Disc. Taken** column allows Simply to insert the amount of the discount that has been taken and deduct the amount of the discount from the payment amount without leaving a remaining balance for the invoice. If a customer takes a discount and it is not recorded as a discount taken, Simply will leave the amount of the discount as an amount due on the invoice. If a customer did not pay in time to qualify for the discount, you would not insert anything in the **Disc. Taken** column and the full amount of the invoice would be due.

 ACTION: TAB to or click in the **Payment Amt.** column. TAB again to insert the amount shown by Simply as the payment amount received. Your screen will appear as follows:

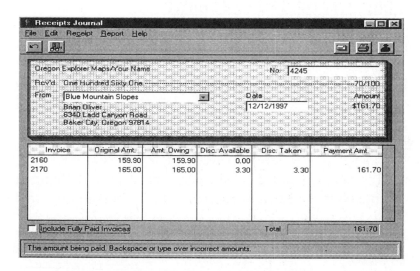

Explanation: Simply entered $161.70 as the payment amount. This should be the same amount as the check from Blue Mountain Slopes.

 ACTION: Click **Report** on the Receipts Journal menu bar. Click **Display Receipts Journal Entry**. Your screen will appear as follows:

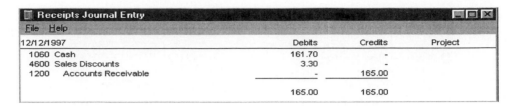

Explanation: Simply automatically debits Cash for the amount received and Sales Discounts for the amount of the discount taken. Accounts Receivable is credited for the full amount due. Once the receipt is posted, the invoice will be marked paid in full.

 ACTION: Close the report for Receipts Journal Entry and print the receipt. If everything is correct on the receipt, click the **Post** button. If it is not, make any corrections, reprint the receipt, and then post the transaction.

Additional Receipts with Sales Discounts

Record the following additional sales discount transactions:

Document 14 December 12—Received Check 5249 in the amount of $294.00 from Portland Saturday Market in payment of Invoice 2171 within the discount period. Print the receipt.

Document 15 December 12—Received Check 3624 in the amount of $147.00 from Sheriden Vineyards Winery in payment of Invoice 2172 within the discount period. Print the receipt.

ADDITIONAL BANK DEPOSIT OF CASH RECEIPTS

Deposit the checks received for invoices with sales discounts.

Document 16 December 12—Deposit the three checks received for invoices with sales discounts. Use Deposit Slip 2140.

RECEIPTS JOURNAL—INVOICES WITH CREDIT MEMOS

When payment is received for an invoice and a deduction is made for a credit memo that was previously issued, the transaction is entered in the Receipts Journal and the amount of the credit memo is applied at that time.

Oregon Explorer Maps—Document 17   **Session Date: 12/12/1997**

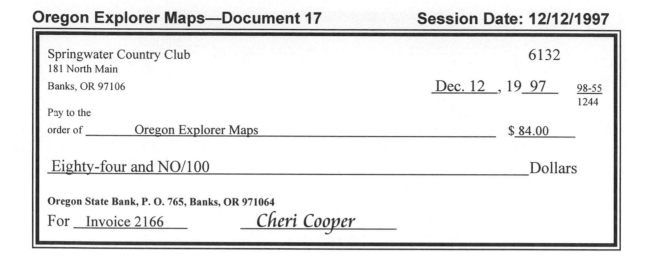

Springwater Country Club   6132
181 North Main
Banks, OR 97106   Dec. 12 , 19 97   98-55
                                                      1244

Pay to the
order of   Oregon Explorer Maps $ 84.00

Eighty-four and NO/100   Dollars

Oregon State Bank, P. O. 765, Banks, OR 971064
For   Invoice 2166   *Cheri Cooper*

ACTION: Open the Receipts Journal and select **Springwater Country Club** from the drop-down list for **From**. Your screen will appear as follows:

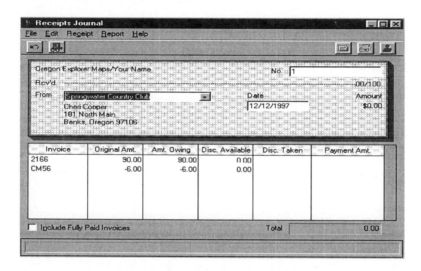

Explanation: Invoice 2166 and CM56 both appear in the detail section of the Receipts Journal for Springwater Country Club. Refer to the **Disc. Available** column. You should note that neither the invoice nor the credit memo is eligible for a discount.

ACTION: Enter *6132* for the check number. The date remains 12/12/1997. Click the **Payment Amt.** column for Invoice 2166 and for CM56. Your screen will appear as follows:

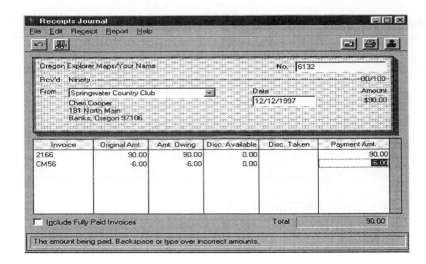

Explanation: The payment amount of $90.00 has been applied to Invoice 2166 and the amount of the receipt is shown as $90.00 even though the $6.00 amount for Credit Memo 56 is highlighted. As in earlier receipt transactions, you must TAB or click in the next line to apply the amount shown in the **Payment Amt.** column.

ACTION: TAB or click in the next line to apply the amount of the credit memo. Your screen will appear as follows:

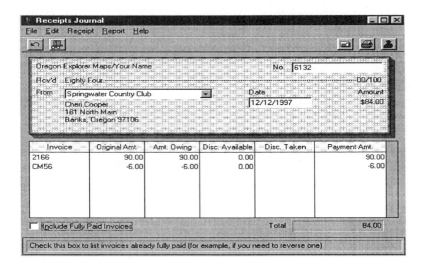

Explanation: Both **Amount** (in the upper portion of the Receipts Journal) and **Total** (in the lower portion of the Receipts Journal) show $84.00 as the total payment amount. The credit memo amount has been applied and the invoice is now paid in full.

ACTION: Click **Report** on the Receipts Journal menu bar. Click **Display Receipts Journal Entry**. Your report should look like the following:

```
Receipts Journal Entry                                              _ □ ×
File  Help

12/12/1997                              Debits      Credits      Project
    1060  Cash                           84.00          -
    1200     Accounts Receivable            -          84.00
                                        _____    _____
                                          84.00        84.00
```

Explanation: Cash has been debited and Accounts Receivable has been credited for the amount received. When the credit memo was recorded, Accounts Receivable had been reduced by $6.00.

ACTION: Close the Receipts Journal Entry report. Check your receipt for errors. When everything on the receipt is correct, print the receipt. Once the receipt has been printed, post the transaction and close the Receipts Journal.

ACTION: Verify the status of Springwater Country Club's account by preparing a Customer Aged Detail report for Springwater Country Club. Do this by clicking **Reports**, **Receivables**, **Customer Aged** on the home window.

ACTION: Scroll through the customer list and click **Springwater Country Club** to select. Click **Detail**. Your screen should appear as follows:

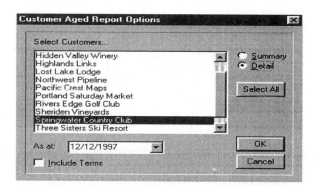

ACTION: Click **OK**. Your Customer Aged Detail report for Springwater Country Club should appear as follows:

```
Customer Aged Detail                                                       _ □ ×
File  Help

As at 12/12/1997                Total      Current    31 to 60    61 to 90    91+
Springwater Country Club
2166      11/30/1997  Invoice    90.00      90.00         -           -        -
6132      12/12/1997  Payment   -90.00     -90.00         -           -        -
CM56      12/4/1997   Invoice    -6.00      -6.00         -           -        -
6132      12/12/1997  Payment     6.00       6.00         -           -        -
```

ACTION: Close the Customer Aged Detail report and return to the home window.

CORRECT ERRORS IN A CREDIT MEMO

It is possible to make an error when a credit memo is recorded. Frequently, the error is not discovered immediately after posting. Instead it is found at a later date. The following correction will be made to Credit Memo 57 for Applegate Vineyard Winery. In this instance, the incorrect inventory item was selected. Even though the price of the incorrect item is the same as the correct item, leaving the incorrect item on the credit memo would result in an error in the inventory for both Wine1 maps and Wine2-W maps.

ACTION: Upon further examination, you discover that CR57 for Applegate Vineyard Winery for the return of three Wine1 maps should be CM57 for the return of three Wine2-W maps. The price of the maps is the same but the error on the credit memo number and the item should be corrected. Open the Sales Journal by clicking the **Sales, Orders & Quotes** icon on the home window. Click the **Adjust Invoice** button ![icon] on the Sales Journal toolbar. Click the drop-down list arrow next to **Customer Name**. Click **Applegate Vineyard Winery** to select. Key *CR57* for the invoice number. Your screen will look like this:

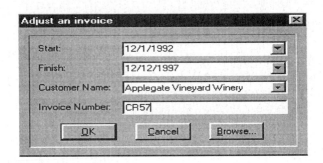

ACTION: Click the **OK** button to display the credit memo. Your screen will appear as follows:

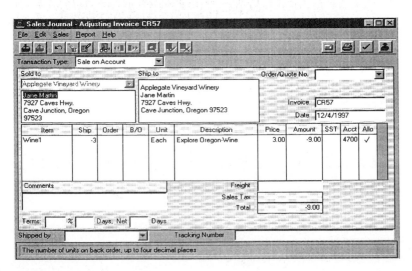

ACTION: Change the invoice from CR57 to *CM57*. Click in the **Item** column and change the item from Wine1 to Wine2-W. In the **Ship** column, re-enter *-3* as the number shipped. Re-enter the allocation as 100% to Wine Map Sales Summary. Your screen should look like the following:

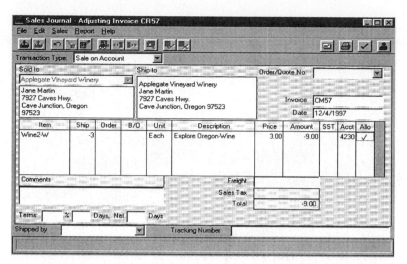

Explanation: Simply will automatically create an adjusting entry using the 12/4/1997 date of the original entry. This adjustment will offset the original CR57 and will enter the corrected CM57 for Applegate Vineyard Winery.

 ACTION: Check the adjustment for errors. Make any corrections necessary and print the invoice. Once the invoice has printed successfully, post the transaction.

Additional Transactions for Invoices with Credit Memos and Bank Deposits of Receipts

Document 18 December 12—Record the receipt of Check 7237 for $85.95 as payment from Applegate Vineyard Winery for Invoice 2168. Apply the amount of CM57 to the receipt. Print the receipt.

Document 19 December 12—Record the receipt of Check 351 for $135.00 as payment from Lost Lake Lodge for Invoice 2157. Apply the amount of CM58 to the receipt. Print the receipt.

Document 20 December 12—Use Deposit Slip 2141 to deposit the three checks received for payments of invoices with credit memos.

RECEIPT OF A NONSUFFICIENT FUNDS (NSF) CHECK

Occasionally, a business will receive a check from a customer who does not have enough money in his or her checking account to cover the amount of the check. When the bank discerns the lack of funds, it sends the check back to the business that deposited it and charges a bank fee for processing the NSF (nonsufficient funds) check, and so does Oregon Explorer Maps.

Oregon Explorer Maps—Document 21   **Session Date: 12/12/1997**

Memo: **Date:** December 12, 1997

The bank returned the check received from Northwest Pipeline marked NSF (shown below). Record the NSF check. Also, combine Oregon Explorer Maps' $10 fee for an NSF check and the bank's fee of $15 for an NSF check. Enter the combined charges as part of the NSF transaction.

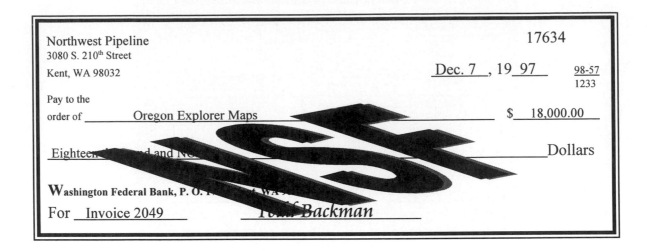

ACTION: Record the NSF check by clicking the **Receipts** icon on the home window. Select **Northwest Pipeline** as the customer and enter *17634 NSF* as the check number. Leave the date as 12/12/1997. In order to view Invoice 2049, click the check box for **Include Fully Paid Invoices** at the bottom of the Receipts Journal. Your screen will appear as follows:

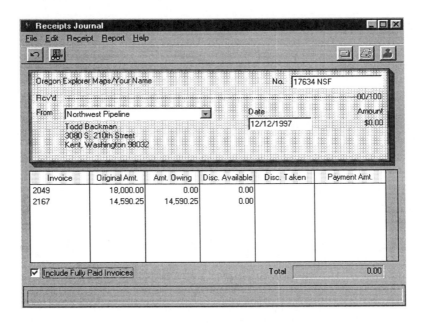

ACTION: Enter *-18,000.00* as the payment amount for Invoice 2049. Your screen will show the following:

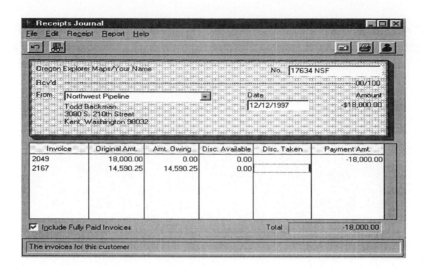

ACTION: Display the Receipt Transaction report to make sure you are debiting Accounts Receivable and crediting Cash. Your screen will appear as follows:

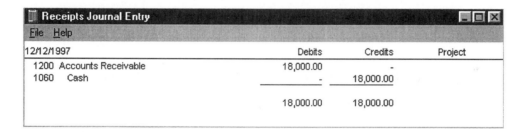

ACTION: Correct any errors. Because a negative receipt cannot be printed, post the receipt when corrections, if any, have been made. Close the Receipts Journal, and return to the home window. Before recording the charges for the bad check, some new accounts need to be added to the chart of accounts. Click the **Accounts** icon on the home window. Click the **Create** button on the Accounts menu bar. Your screen will look like this:

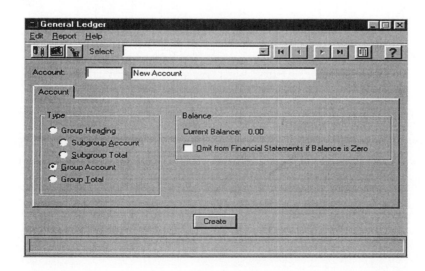

ACTION: Enter *4820* as the account number and *Bad Check Charges* as the account name. The type of account is Group Account. Your screen will show the following:

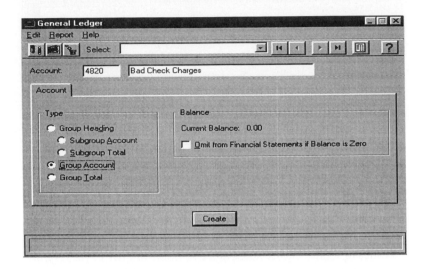

ACTION: Click the **Create** button to create the account. Close the General Ledger and return to the home window.

ACTION: Open the Sales Journal. Select **Northwest Pipeline** as the customer. Use the invoice number shown and the date of 12/12/1997. Your screen will look like this:

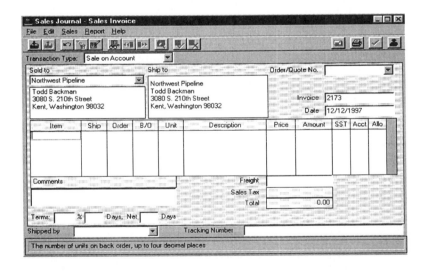

ACTION: Position the cursor in the **Item** column and double-click. Because there are no items for Bad Check Charges, create one by clicking **<Add new inventory/service>** to highlight. Your screen will show the following:

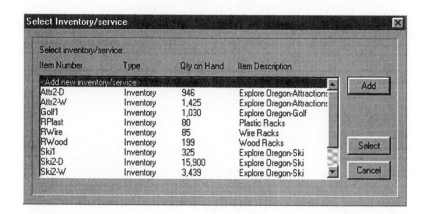

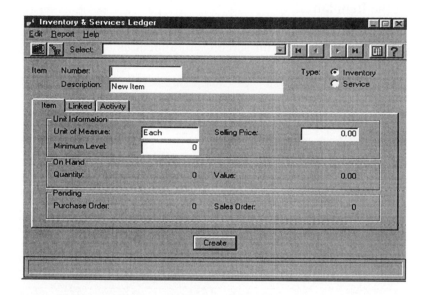

ACTION: Click the **Add** button. The Inventory & Services Ledger will appear, and your screen will look like this:

Explanation: The Inventory & Services Ledger is used to create new inventory and/or service items. The items are linked to specific accounts, which appear automatically when an item is used in an invoice.

ACTION: Key *Chg1* as the item number and *Charges for Bad Checks* as the description. Click **Service** to indicate the type of item. Your screen will appear as follows:

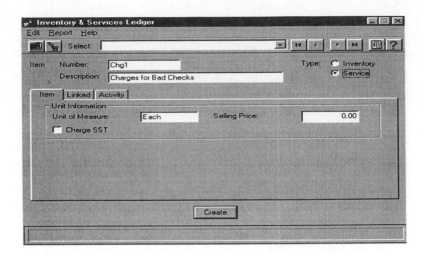

Explanation: The item number and description have been entered. Because this is a service item, nothing is completed on the Item tab.

ACTION: Click the **Linked** tab. Your screen will appear as follows:

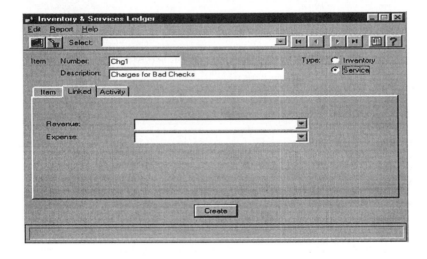

ACTION: Click the drop-down list arrow next to **Revenue**. Scroll through the accounts and select **Account 4820 Bad Check Charges**. Your screen will show the following:

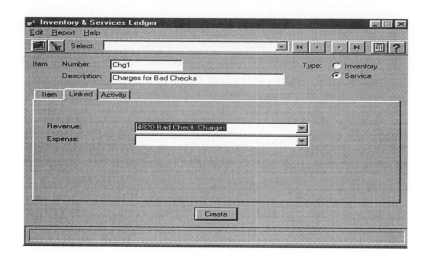

Explanation: Linking an account to this item will allow the account to be selected automatically when the item is used in a transaction.

ACTION: Click the **Create** button to create the item. Enter *25.00* in the **Amount** column. The sales invoice will appear as follows:

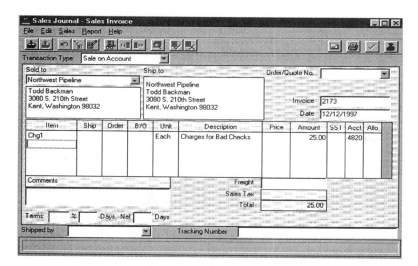

Explanation: When Chg1 is entered in the **Item** column, the **Description** and **Acct.** columns are automatically completed, using the information provided when the item was created.

ACTION: Check your sales invoice for accuracy and correct any errors. Print Sales Invoice 2173. Display the Sales Journal Entry and compare it with the one shown below.

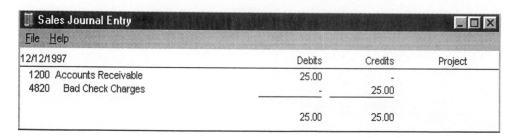

Explanation: Accounts Receivable is credited for the amount due from Northwest Pipeline for the bad check charges, and the income account Bad Check Charges is credited for the amount of the bad check charges. When the bank statement is received, an adjustment will be made to remove the amount of the bank charges from the income account and transfer it into an expense account.

ACTION: Close the Sales Journal Entry and post the transaction. You will get a Simply Accounting dialog box that appears as follows:

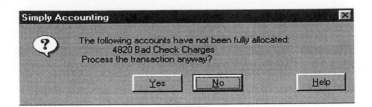

Explanation: This transaction was not allocated to a project because Oregon Explorer Maps chose not to create a project showing the amount of bad check charges. Because inventory items have been allocated to projects, Simply prompts you when you try to post a transaction without allocating it to a project.

ACTION: Click **Yes** to process the transaction anyway. Exit the Sales Journal and return to the home window. Prepare a Customer Aged Detail report by clicking **Reports** on the home window. Point to Receivables and Customer Aged. Your screen will look like this:

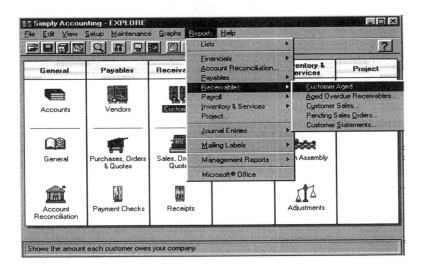

ACTION: Click **Customer Aged.** Complete the Customer Aged Report Options as shown below:

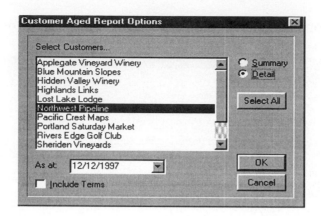

ACTION: Click **OK** to display the Customer Aged Detail report for Northwest Pipeline. Your screen should show the following report:

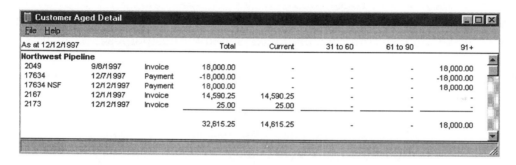

ACTION: Print the report by clicking **File** on the menu bar and **Print** on the file menu. Close the Customer Aged Detail report and return to the home window.

SALES JOURNAL—RECORDING INVENTORY SALES WITH PAYMENT BY CREDIT CARD

While most of Oregon Explorer Maps' customers have accounts with the company, there are some customers who would like to use a credit card at the time of purchase. The chart of accounts contains Account 5660 Credit Card Fees Expense, which is designed to be used to record the cost of the fees charged by the credit card companies. Because the credit card companies charge a fee to companies accepting their card, the credit card company assumes all risks and expenses involved in collecting from customers who do not pay their bills. There are primarily two types of credit cards: bank credit cards, such as Visa and MasterCard, and nonbank credit cards such as American Express. Oregon Explorer Maps has decided to accept only bank credit cards. Simply must be set up to record credit card sales, make deposits of bank credit card receipts, and record the credit card company's fees.

Oregon Explorer Maps—Document 22   **Session Date: 12/12/1997**

Memo: **Date:** December 12, 1997

Set up the accounting program so we can accept credit card sales. The Credit Card Fees Expense account has already been created.

ACTION: On the home window, click **Setup** and **Credit Cards**. Your screen will look like this:

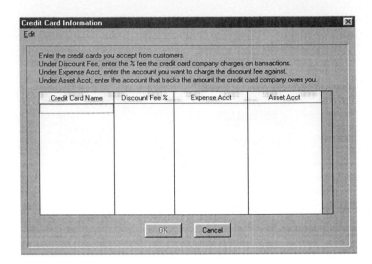

Explanation: Simply needs to set up the appropriate accounts, fees, and so on before it can record credit card sales. The Credit Card Information screen is used for this purpose.

ACTION: In the **Credit Card Name** column, key *MasterCard*. Your screen will show the following:

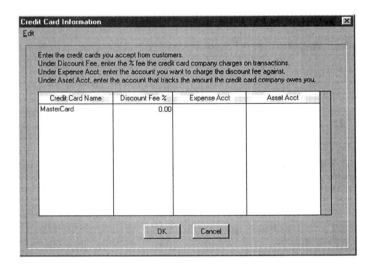

Explanation: The name of the credit card accepted is entered in this column.

ACTION: Enter *6.00* in the **Discount Fee %** column. The expense account used is 5660 Credit Card Fees Expense, and the asset account is 1060 Cash. Enter these accounts in the appropriate columns. Your screen will show the following:

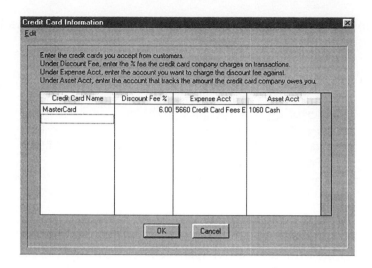

Explanation: As previously stated, the discount fee percentage is the amount or percentage of the sale that the credit card company charges Oregon Explorer Maps for being allowed to accept the bank credit card for payment. When a sale is made and a credit card is used, Simply automatically debits the expense account specified for the amount of the fee that is charged and debits the asset account specified with the remaining amount collected from the sale. As usual, Simply credits the appropriate sales account and adjusts the inventory and cost of goods sold accounts. Since only bank credit cards are being accepted, cash has been chosen as the asset account because Oregon Explorer Maps will deposit the charge card receipts along with any checks it receives.

 ACTION: Use the accounts and percentages listed above and establish the use of a Visa card. Your screen will show the following:

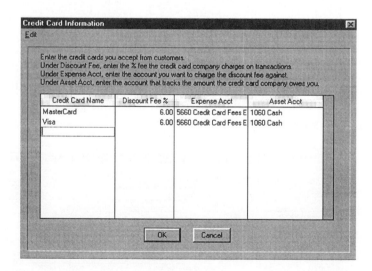

Explanation: Two credit cards have been established. You may return to the Credit Card Information screen at any time to establish other credit cards.

ACTION: Click **OK** to save the information and return to the home window.

Oregon Explorer Maps—Document 23   **Session Date: 12/12/1997**

Order
Customer: One-Time Customer   **VISA Sale**   **Date:** December 12, 1997

Item	Qty.	Description	Price	Amount
Golf1	25	Explore Oregon-Golf	3.00	75.00
RPlast	2	Plastic Racks	5.95	11.90
		TOTAL		$86.90

ACTION: Click **Sales, Orders & Quotes**. Record the above transaction. The transaction type is Sale with Payment. Click the drop-down list arrow for **Paid by** and point to Visa. Your screen will show the following:

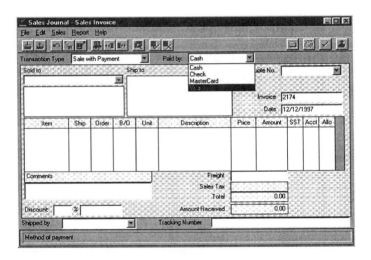

ACTION: Click **Visa** to select. Complete the invoice for a one-time customer by selecting **<One-time customer>** for **Sold to**. Use Invoice 2174 as the invoice number and use 12/12/1997 as the date. Fill out the sales information and allocation as previously instructed for other invoices. Your screen should appear as follows:

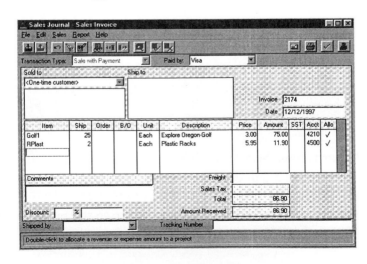

Explanation: The sales invoice looks like the other invoices prepared, except under the Total there is a new item, Amount Received, which indicates the amount received for the sale.

 ACTION: Display the Sales Journal Entry for this transaction. Your screen should show the following:

Sales Journal Entry			_ □ ×
File Help			
12/12/1997	Debits	Credits	Project
1060 Cash	81.69	-	
5010 COGS-Golf Maps	17.27	-	
- Golf Map Sales Summary			17.27
5050 COGS-Racks	10.00	-	
- Rack Sales Summary			10.00
5660 Credit Card Fees Expense	5.21	-	
1210 Golf Map Inventory	-	17.27	
1250 Rack Inventory	-	10.00	
4210 Wholesale Golf Map Sales	-	75.00	
- Golf Map Sales Summary			75.00
4500 Rack Sales	-	11.90	
- Rack Sales Summary			11.90
	114.17	114.17	

Explanation: Notice that Cash was debited for $81.69, which is the amount of cash received after the credit card fees had been subtracted. Credit Card Fees Expense was debited for $5.21, which is the 6% fee charged by the bank. The other debits and credits reflect the inventory adjustments, cost of goods sold, and sales portions of the transaction. Regardless of the method of payment, revenue and expenses are allocated to a project. As you review the transaction, note that the portions of the transaction debiting Cost of Goods Sold and crediting Sales show an allocation to a project.

 ACTION: Close the Sales Journal Entry report. Make sure any errors in the transaction have been corrected. Print and post the sales invoice.

Oregon Explorer Maps—Document 24   **Session Date: 12/12/1997**

New Customer ORDER

Customer: Mary's Travel Boutique   <u>MasterCard Sale</u>   **Date:** December 12, 1997
                 1237 NE 20th Street
                 Portland, OR 97214

Item	**Qty.**	**Description**	**Price**	**Amount**
Attr2-W	25	Explore Oregon-Attractions	3.00	75.00
Golf1	25	Explore Oregon-Golf	3.00	75.00
Ski2-W	25	Explore Oregon-Ski	3.00	75.00
Wine2-W	25	Explore Oregon-Wine	3.00	75.00
RPlast	2	Plastic Racks	5.95	11.90
		TOTAL		$316.90

ACTION: Use the information in the above order to prepare Sales Invoice 2175 for Mary's Travel Boutique. Because Mary's Travel Boutique is not an established customer, key in the company name in **Sold to**. Your screen will appear as follows:

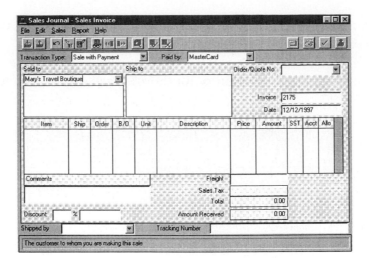

ACTION: Press the TAB key. You will get the following message:

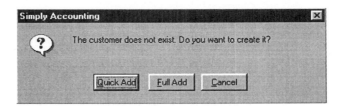

ACTION: Click **Full Add**. You will get the following screen:

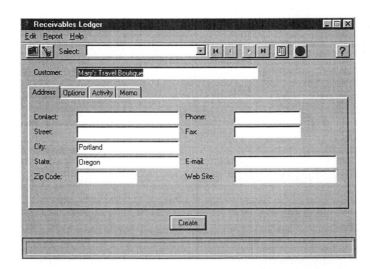

ACTION: Enter the street and zip code shown in the order. When complete, your screen will appear as follows:

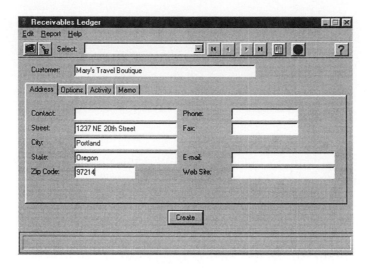

Explanation: Since information regarding a contact person, telephone numbers, e-mail, or Web address was not provided, leave those areas blank. It is not essential to have that information for credit card customers. If Mary's Travel Boutique becomes a regular customer, that information may be obtained at that time.

ACTION: Click **Create** to add the customer. Complete the invoice using the information provided on the order form. Your complete invoice should appear as follows:

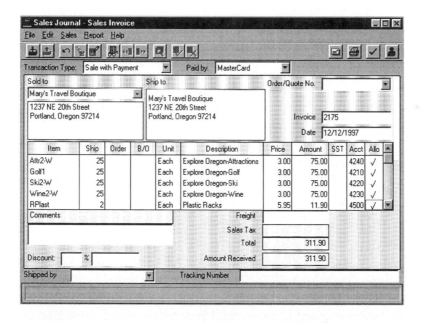

ACTION: If everything is correct on the invoice, print and post the invoice. If you discover any errors, correct them prior to printing and posting. Close the Sales Journal. If the following screen appears, click where it says **[Click here to close.]**:

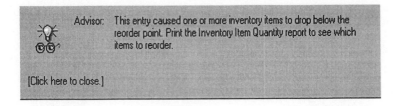

Advisor: This entry caused one or more inventory items to drop below the
reorder point. Print the Inventory Item Quantity report to see which
items to reorder.

[Click here to close.]

Explanation: Whenever an inventory items goes below a preset limit, Simply will remind you to check to see which item to reorder. Ordering items will be covered in Chapter 6.

ACTION: Close the Sales Journal and return to the home window. Open the Reconciliation for Cash and record the deposit of the credit card receipts (just as you would deposit checks) using Deposit Slip 2142. Your screen will appear as follows:

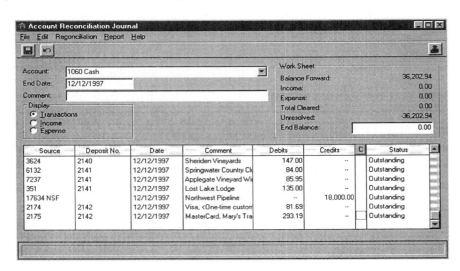

ACTION: Save the Reconciliation and return to the home window.

SALES JOURNAL—RECORDING CASH SALES

Frequently, businesses will make sales and will require customers to pay for the items using cash. Oregon Explorer Maps does not have a lot of cash customers but does expect to have some cash sales. To keep track of the amount of cash sales, a new customer named Cash Sales will be used as the customer name when the sales invoice is recorded. Cash will be used for the method of payment. Deposits of cash are made into the bank account using the Cash account.

Oregon Explorer Maps—Document 25   **Session Date: 12/5/1997**

Order
Customer: Cash Sale   **Date:** December 12, 1997

Item	Qty.	Description	Price	Amount
Golf1	2	Explore Oregon-Golf	3.00	6.00
		TOTAL		$6.00

ACTION: Record the cash sale listed in the above order. Use Cash Sale as the customer and cash as the method of payment. Click the **Sales, Orders & Quotes** icon to open the Sales Journal. Key *Cash Sale* as the customer name. Your screen will show the following:

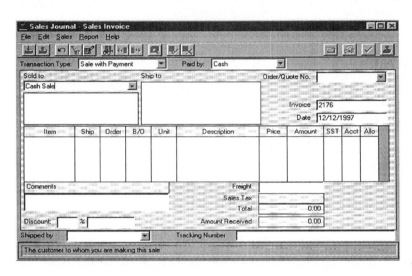

ACTION: Press the TAB key. You will get the following dialog box:

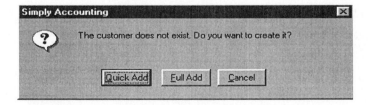

ACTION: Click **Quick Add** and complete the invoice. The completed invoice will appear as follows:

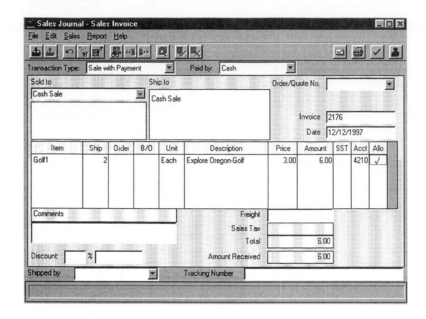

Explanation: The sale has been entered for a cash customer. Notice the **Amount Received** box beneath **Total**. These two amounts should be the same.

ACTION: Correct any errors you may have made. Print and post the invoice.

ACTION: Close the Sales Journal and return to the home window. Open the Reconciliation for Cash and record the deposit of the cash received in the cash sale transaction (just as you would deposit checks) using Deposit Slip 2143. Your screen will appear as follows:

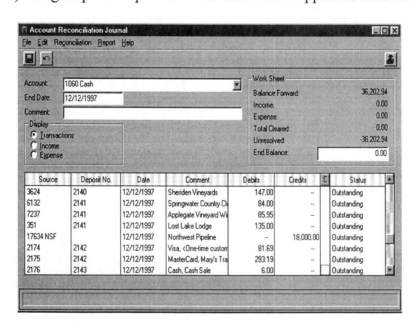

Additional Cash Sale and Deposit Transactions

Record the following additional cash sale transactions:

Document 26 December 12—Sold 3 Ski1 maps to a cash customer. Print the invoice.

Document 27 December 12—Sold 1 Golf1 map and 1 Ski1 map to a cash customer. Print the invoice.

Document 28 December 12—Record the deposit of the two cash sale transactions using Deposit Slip 2144.

REPORTS FOR RECEIVABLES TRANSACTIONS

Oregon Explorer Maps—Document 29　　　　　　　　**Session Date: 12/12/1997**

Memo:　　　　　　　　　　　　　　　　　　　**Date:** December 12, 1997

Prepare and print the following reports: All Journal Entries from 12/1/1997 to 12/12/1997; Customer Aged Detail report for all customers as at 12/12/1997; Inventory Synopsis as at 12/12/1997; and a Trial Balance as at 12/12/1997.

 ACTION: Prepare the journal report for all entries by clicking **Reports** on the home window menu bar, pointing to Journal Entries, and clicking **All**. You will get the following:

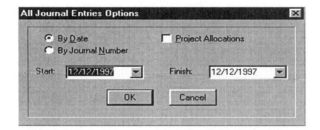

Explanation: The All Journal Entries Options dialog box appears, asking you to define the information you want displayed.

 ACTION: Select **By posting date**; check **Project Allocations**; enter *12/1/1997* as the start date; leave the finish date set at 12/12/1997; then click the **OK** button. The following journal display will appear on your screen:

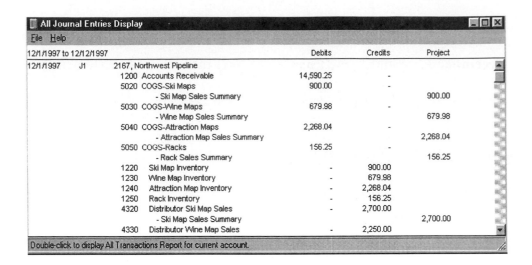

Explanation: Review the display for accuracy, verifying that journal entry dates; account names and numbers; project allocations, customer names; check, invoice, and credit memo numbers; and amounts are correct. Use the scroll bars at the bottom and to the right of the display to advance the display. If you have posted an incorrect transaction, refer to the material presented earlier in the chapter to correct your errors.

 ACTION: Print the General Journal by choosing **Print** from the All Journal Entries Display File menu. Compare your report to the one shown below:

Oregon Explorer Maps
All Journal Entries 12/1/1997 to 12/12/1997

				Debits	Credits	Project
12/1/1997	J1	2167, Northwest Pipeline				
		1200	Accounts Receivable	14,590.25	-	
		5020	COGS-Ski Maps	900.00	-	
			-Ski Map Sales Summary			900.00
		5030	COGS-Wine Maps	679.98	-	
			-Wine Map Sales Summary			679.98
		5040	COGS-Attraction Maps	2,268.04	-	
			-Attraction Map Sales Summary			2,268.04
		5050	COGS-Racks	156.25	-	
			-Rack Sales Summary			156.25
		1220	Ski Map Inventory	-	900.0	
		1230	Wine Map Inventory	-	679.98	
		1240	Attraction Map Inventory	-	2,268.04	
		1250	Rack Inventory	-	156.25	
		4320	Distributor Ski Map Sales	-	2,700.00	
			-Ski Map Sales Summary			2,700.00
		4330	Distributor Wine Map Sales	-	2,250.00	
			-Wine Map Sales Summary			2,250.00
		4340	Distributor Attraction Map Sales	-	9,450.00	
			-Attraction Map Sales Summary			9,450.00
		4500	Rack Sales	-	190.25	
			-Rack Sales Summary			190.25

12/2/1997	J2	2168, Applegate Vineyard Winery			
		1200	Accounts Receivable	94.75	-	
		5030	COGS-Wine Maps	20.40	-	
			-Wine Map Sales Summary			20.40
		5050	COGS-Racks	3.75	-	
			-Rack Sales Summary			3.75
		1230	Wine Map Inventory	-	20.40	
		1250	Rack Inventory	-	3.75	
		4230	Wholesale Wine Map Sales	-	90.00	
			-Wine Map Sales Summary			90.00
		4500	Rack Sales	-	4.75	
			-Rack Sales Summary			4.75

12/3/1997	J3	2169, Pacific Crest Maps			
		1200	Accounts Receivable	9,112.50	-	
		5020	COGS-Ski Maps	675.00	-	
			-Ski Map Sales Summary			675.00
		5030	COGS-Wine Maps	441.99	-	
			-Wine Map Sales Summary			441.99
		5040	COGS-Attraction Maps	1,350.02	-	
			-Attraction Map Sales Summary			1,350.02
		1220	Ski Map Inventory	-	675.00	
		1230	Wine Map Inventory	-	441.99	
		1240	Attraction Map Inventory	-	1,350.02	
		4320	Distributor Ski Map Sales	-	2,025.00	
			-Ski Map Sales Summary			2,025.00
		4330	Distributor Wine Map Sales	-	1,462.50	
			-Wine Map Sales Summary			1,462.50
		4340	Distributor Attraction Map Sales	-	5,625.00	
			-Attraction Map Sales Summary			5,625.00

12/2/1997	J4	ADJ2168, Reversing J2. Correction is J5.			
		1230	Wine Map Inventory	20.40	-	
		1250	Rack Inventory	3.75	-	
		4230	Wholesale Wine Map Sales	90.00	-	
			-Wine Map Sales Summary			-90.00
		4500	Rack Sales	4.75	-	
			-Rack Sales Summary			-4.75
		1200	Accounts Receivable	-	94.75	
		5030	COGS-Wine Maps	-	20.40	
			-Wine Map Sales Summary			-20.40
		5050	COGS-Racks	-	3.75	
			-Rack Sales Summary			-3.75

12/2/1997	J5	2168, Applegate Vineyard Winery			
		1200	Accounts Receivable	94.95	-	
		5030	COGS-Wine Maps	20.40	-	
			-Wine Map Sales Summary			20.40
		5050	COGS-Racks	4.00	-	
			-Rack Sales Summary			4.00
		1230	Wine Map Inventory	-	20.40	
		1250	Rack Inventory	-	4.00	
		4230	Wholesale Wine Map Sales	-	90.00	
			-Wine Map Sales Summary			90.00
		4500	Rack Sales	-	4.95	
			-Rack Sales Summary			4.95

12/4/1997	J6	CM56, Springwater Country Club		
		1210 Golf Map Inventory	1.38	-
		4700 Sales Returns and Allowances	6.00	-
		-Golf Map Sales Summary		-6.00
		1200 Accounts Receivable	-	6.00
		5010 COGS-Golf Maps	-	1.38
		-Golf Map Sales Summary		-1.38
12/4/1997	J7	CR57, Applegate Vineyard Winery		
		1230 Wine Map Inventory	2.28	-
		4700 Sales Returns and Allowances	9.00	-
		-Wine Map Sales Summary		-9.00
		1200 Accounts Receivable	-	9.00
		5030 COGS-Wine Maps	-	2.28
		-Wine Map Sales Summary		-2.28
12/5/1997	J8	CM58, Lost Lake Lodge		
		1220 Ski Map Inventory	4.10	-
		4700 Sales Returns and Allowances	15.00	-
		-Ski Map Sales Summary		-15.00
		1200 Accounts Receivable	-	15.00
		5020 COGS-Ski Maps	-	4.10
		-Ski Map Sales Summary		-4.10
12/7/1997	J9	17634, Northwest Pipeline		
		1060 Cash	18,000.00	-
		1200 Accounts Receivable	-	18,000.00
12/8/1997	J10	64325, Pacific Crest Maps		
		1060 Cash	11,250.00	-
		1200 Accounts Receivable	-	11,250.00
12/8/1997	J11	3410, Sheriden Vineyards		
		1060 Cash	150.00	-
		1200 Accounts Receivable	-	150.00
12/8/1997	J12	3410 REV, Sheriden Vineyards		
		1200 Accounts Receivable	100.00	-
		1060 Cash	-	100.00
12/8/1997	J13	3410C, Sheriden Vineyards		
		1060 Cash	150.00	-
		1200 Accounts Receivable	-	150.00
12/10/1997	J14	2170, Blue Mountain Slopes		
		1200 Accounts Receivable	165.00	-
		5020 COGS-Ski Maps	41.25	-
		-Ski Map Sales Summary		41.25
		1220 Ski Map Inventory	-	41.25
		4220 Wholesale Ski Map Sales	-	165.00
		-Ski Map Sales Summary		165.00
12/10/1997	J15	2171, Portland Saturday Market		
		1200 Accounts Receivable	300.00	-
		5040 COGS-Attraction Maps	54.00	-
		-Attraction Map Sales Summary		54.00

		1240	Attraction Map Inventory	-	54.00	
		4240	Wholesale Attraction Map Sales	-	300.00	
			-Attraction Map Sales Summary			300.00

12/10/1997	J16	2172, Sheriden Vineyards				
		1200	Accounts Receivable	150.00	-	
		5040	COGS-Attraction Maps	27.00	-	
			-Attraction Map Sales Summary			27.00
		1240	Attraction Map Inventory	-	27.00	
		4240	Wholesale Attraction Map Sales	-	150.00	
			-Attraction Map Sales Summary			150.00

12/12/1997	J17	4245, Blue Mountain Slopes			
		1060	Cash	161.70	-
		4600	Sales Discounts	3.30	-
		1200	Accounts Receivable	-	165.00

12/12/1997	J18	5249, Portland Saturday Market			
		1060	Cash	294.00	-
		4600	Sales Discounts	6.00	-
		1200	Accounts Receivable	-	300.00

12/12/1997	J19	3624, Sheriden Vineyards			
		1060	Cash	147.00	-
		4600	Sales Discounts	3.00	-
		1200	Accounts Receivable	-	150.00

12/12/1997	J20	6132, Springwater Country Club			
		1060	Cash	84.00	-
		1200	Accounts Receivable	-	84.00

12/12/1997	J21	ADJCR57, Reversing J7. Correction is J22.				
		1200	Accounts Receivable	9.00	-	
		5030	COGS-Wine Maps	2.28	-	
			-Wine Map Sales Summary			2.28
		1230	Wine Map Inventory	-	2.28	
		4700	Sales Returns and Allowances	-	9.00	
			-Wine Map Sales Summary			9.00

12/12/1997	J22	CM57, Applegate Vineyard Winery				
		1230	Wine Map Inventory	2.04	-	
		4230	Wholesale Wine Map Sales	9.00	-	
			-Wine Map Sales Summary			-9.00
		1200	Accounts Receivable	-	9.00	
		5030	COGS-Wine Maps	-	2.04	
			-Wine Map Sales Summary			-2.04

12/12/1997	J23	7237, Applegate Vineyard Winery			
		1060	Cash	85.95	-
		1200	Accounts Receivable	-	85.95

12/12/1997	J24	351, Lost Lake Lodge			
		1060	Cash	135.00	-
		1200	Accounts Receivable	-	135.00

12/12/1997	J25	17634 NSF, Northwest Pipeline			
		1200	Accounts Receivable	18,000.00	-
		1060	Cash	-	18,000.00

12/12/1997	J26	2173, Northwest Pipeline				
		1200	Accounts Receivable	25.00	-	
		4820	Bad Check Charges	-	25.00	
12/12/1997	J27	2174, Visa, <One-time customer>				
		1060	Cash	81.69	-	
		5010	COGS-Golf Maps	17.27	-	
			-Golf Map Sales Summary			17.27
		5050	COGS-Racks	10.00	-	
			-Rack Sales Summary			10.00
		5660	Credit Card Fees Expense	5.21	-	
		1210	Golf Map Inventory	-	17.27	
		1250	Rack Inventory	-	10.00	
		4210	Wholesale Golf Map Sales	-	75.00	
			-Golf Map Sales Summary			75.00
		4500	Rack Sales	-	11.90	
			-Rack Sales Summary			11.90
12/12/1997	J28	2175, MasterCard, Mary's Travel Boutique				
		1060	Cash	293.19	-	
		5010	COGS-Golf Maps	17.27	-	
			-Golf Map Sales Summary			17.27
		5020	COGS-Ski Maps	18.75	-	
			-Ski Map Sales Summary			18.75
		5030	COGS-Wine Maps	17.00	-	
			-Wine Map Sales Summary			17.00
		5040	COGS-Attraction Maps	13.50	-	
			-Attraction Map Sales Summary			13.50
		5050	COGS-Racks	10.00	-	
			-Rack Sales Summary			10.00
		5660	Credit Card Fees Expense	18.71	-	
		1210	Golf Map Inventory	-	17.27	
		1220	Ski Map Inventory	-	18.75	
		1230	Wine Map Inventory	-	17.00	
		1240	Attraction Map Inventory	-	13.50	
		1250	Rack Inventory	-	10.00	
		4210	Wholesale Golf Map Sales	-	75.00	
			-Golf Map Sales Summary			75.00
		4220	Wholesale Ski Map Sales	-	75.00	
			-Ski Map Sales Summary			75.00
		4230	Wholesale Wine Map Sales	-	75.00	
			-Wine Map Sales Summary			75.00
		4240	Wholesale Attraction Map Sales	-	75.00	
			-Attraction Map Sales Summary			75.00
		4500	Rack Sales	-	11.90	
			-Rack Sales Summary			11.90
12/12/1997	J29	2176, Cash, Cash Sale				
		1060	Cash	6.00	-	
		5010	COGS-Golf Maps	1.38	-	
			-Golf Map Sales summary			1.38
		1210	Golf Map Inventory	-	1.38	
		4210	Wholesale Golf Map Sales	-	6.00	
			-Golf Map Sales Summary			6.00

12/12/1997	J30	2177, Cash, Cash Sale			
		1060 Cash	9.00	-	
		5020 COGS-Ski Maps	2.46	-	
		-Ski Map Sales summary			2.46
		1220 Ski Map Inventory	-	2.46	
		4220 Wholesale Ski Map Sales	-	9.00	
		-Ski Map Sales Summary			9.00

12/12/1997	J31	2178, Cash, Cash Sale			
		1060 Cash	6.00	-	
		5010 COGS-Golf Maps	0.69	-	
		-Golf Map Sales summary			0.69
		5020 COGS-Ski Maps	0.82	-	
		-Ski Map Sales Summary			0.82
		1210 Golf Map Inventory	-	0.69	
		1220 Ski Map Inventory	-	0.82	
		4210 Wholesale Golf Map Sales	-	3.00	
		-Golf Map Sales Summary			3.00
		4220 Wholesale Ski Map Sales	-	3.00	
		-Ski Map Sales Summary			3.00

80,402.40	80,402.40

Explanation: If you detect an error, refer to the materials presented earlier in the chapter on making corrections.

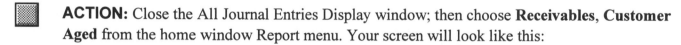 **ACTION:** Close the All Journal Entries Display window; then choose **Receivables**, **Customer Aged** from the home window Report menu. Your screen will look like this:

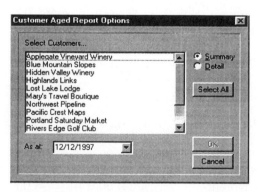

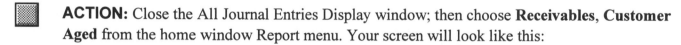 **ACTION:** Click **Detail**; click **Select All** button; then click the **OK** button. Your screen will look like this:

ACTION: Choose **Print** from the Customer Aged Detail File menu. Compare your report to the one shown below:

Oregon Explorer Maps
Customer Aged Detail As at 12/12/1997

			Total	Current	31 to 60	1 to 90	91+
Applegate Vineyard Winery							
2168	12/2/1997	Invoice	94.95	94.95	-	-	-
7237	12/12/1997	Payment	-94.95	-94.95	-	-	-
CM57	12/4/1997	Invoice	-9.00	-9.00	-	-	-
7237	12/12/1997	Payment	9.00	.00	-	-	-
			-	-	-	-	-
Blue Mountain Slopes							
2160	11/29/1997	Invoice	159.90	159.90	-	-	-
2170	12/10/1997	Invoice	165.00	165.00	-	-	-
4245	12/12/1997	Discount	-3.30	-3.30	-	-	-
4245	12/12/1997	Payment	-161.70	-161.70	-	-	-
			159.90	159.90	-	-	-
Cash Sale							
2176	12/12/1997	Invoice	6.00	6.00	-	-	-
Cash	12/12/1997	Payment	-6.00	-6.00	-	-	-
2177	12/12/1997	Invoice	9.00	9.00	-	-	-
Cash	12/12/1997	Payment	-9.00	-9.00	-	-	-
2178	12/12/1997	Invoice	6.00	6.00	-	-	-
Cash	12/12/1997	Payment	-6.00	-6.00	-	-	-
			-	-	-	-	-
Lost Lake Lodge							
2157	11/28/1997	Invoice	150.00	150.00	-	-	-
351	12/12/1997	Payment	-150.00	-150.00	-	-	-
CM58	12/5/1997	Invoice	-15.00	-15.00	-	-	-
351	12/12/1997	Payment	15.00	15.00	-	-	-
			-	-	-	-	-
Mary's Travel Boutique							
2175	12/12/1997	Invoice	311.90	311.90	-	-	-
MasterCard	12/12/1997	Payment	-311.90	-311.90	-	-	-
			-	-	-	-	-

Northwest Pipeline

2049	9/8/1997	Invoice	18,000.00	-	-	-	18,000.00
17634	12/7/1997	Payment	-18,000.00	-	-	-	-18,000.00
17634 NSF	12/12/1997	Payment	18,000.00	-	-	-	-18,000.00
2167	12/1/1997	Invoice	14,590.25	14,590.25	-	-	-
2173	12/12/1997	Invoice	25.00	25.00	-	-	-
			32,615.25	14,615.25	-	-	-18,000.00

Pacific Crest Maps

2089	9/12/1997	Invoice	11,250.00	-	-	-	11,250.00
64325	12/8/1997	Payment	-11,250.00	-	-	-	-11,250.00
2169	12/3/1997	Invoice	9,112.50	9,112.50	-	-	-
			9,112.50	9,112.50	-	-	-

Portland Saturday Market

2171	12/10/1997	Invoice	300.00	300.00	-	-	-
5249	12/12/1997	Discount	-6.00	-6.00	-	-	-
5249	12/12/1997	Payment	-294.00	-294.00	-	-	-
			–	-	-	-	-

Rivers Edge Golf Club

2165	11/30/1997	Invoice	75.00	75.00	-	-	-

Sheriden Vineyards

2146	11/17/1997	Invoice	150.00	150.00	-	-	-
3410	12/8/1997	Payment	-100.00	-100.00	-	-	-
3410 REV	12/8/1997	Payment	100.00	100.00	-	-	-
3410C	12/8/1997	Payment	-150.00	-150.00	-	-	-
2172	12/10/1997	Invoice	150.00	150.00	-	-	-
3624	12/12/1997	Discount	-3.00	-3.00	-	-	-
3624	12/12/1997	Payment	-147.00	-147.00	-	-	-
			–	-	-	-	-

Springwater Country Club

2166	11/30/1997	Invoice	90.00	90.00	-	-	-
6132	12/12/1997	Payment	-90.00	-90.00	-	-	-
CM56	12/4/1997	Invoice	-6.00	-6.00	-	-	-
6132	12/12/1997	Payment	6.00	6.00	-	-	-
			–	-	-	-	-

Three Sisters Ski Resort

2123	11/2/1997	Invoice	300.00	-	300.00	-	-
			42,262.65	23,962.65	300.00	-	18,000.00

▓ **ACTION:** Close the Customer Aged Detail report. From the home window menu bar, select **Reports, Inventory & Services**, and **Inventory**. Your screen will show the following Inventory Report Options:

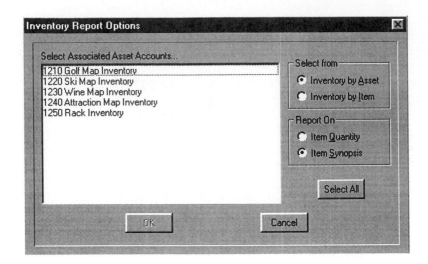

Explanation: The Inventory Report Options dialog box appears, asking you to define the information you want displayed. You can choose to display items associated with one or more asset accounts (Select from Inventory by Asset), with individual inventory items (Select from Inventory by Item), or for all items (Select All). The Inventory Quantity report shows item number, item description, unit, quantity of stock on hand, minimum stock level, and the number of items that have fallen below the minimum stock level. The inventory synopsis report shows item number, item description, unit, price, quantity of stock on hand, cost, and value (quantity multiplied by cost). In addition, the Inventory Synopsis report shows the margin percentage of each inventory item.

 ACTION: Make the following choices: Select from **Inventory by Asset**, Report on **Item Synopsis**, **Select All** to highlight all the Select Associated Asset Accounts. Then, click **OK**. Your screen will show the following report.

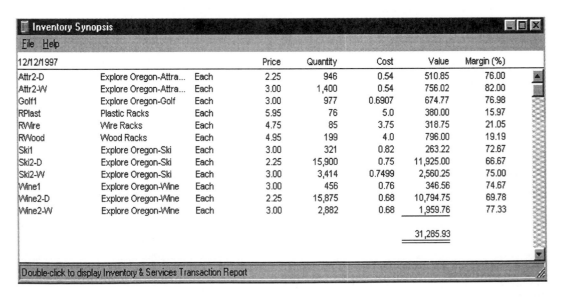

Inventory Synopsis			Price	Quantity	Cost	Value	Margin (%)
12/12/1997							
Attr2-D	Explore Oregon-Attra...	Each	2.25	946	0.54	510.85	76.00
Attr2-W	Explore Oregon-Attra...	Each	3.00	1,400	0.54	756.02	82.00
Golf1	Explore Oregon-Golf	Each	3.00	977	0.6907	674.77	76.98
RPlast	Plastic Racks	Each	5.95	76	5.0	380.00	15.97
RWire	Wire Racks	Each	4.75	85	3.75	318.75	21.05
RWood	Wood Racks	Each	4.95	199	4.0	796.00	19.19
Ski1	Explore Oregon-Ski	Each	3.00	321	0.82	263.22	72.67
Ski2-D	Explore Oregon-Ski	Each	2.25	15,900	0.75	11,925.00	66.67
Ski2-W	Explore Oregon-Ski	Each	3.00	3,414	0.7499	2,560.25	75.00
Wine1	Explore Oregon-Wine	Each	3.00	456	0.76	346.56	74.67
Wine2-D	Explore Oregon-Wine	Each	2.25	15,875	0.68	10,794.75	69.78
Wine2-W	Explore Oregon-Wine	Each	3.00	2,882	0.68	1,959.76	77.33
						31,285.93	

Double-click to display Inventory & Services Transaction Report

 ACTION: Print the Inventory Synopsis report and compare it to the one shown above.

ACTION: Close the Inventory Synopsis report. Choose **Reports** from the home window Report menu; select **Financials**, **Trial Balance**. Accept the default as at date of 12/12/1997; click the **OK** button. Your screen will look like this:

```
┌─────────────────────────────────────────────────────────────┐
│ ⊡ Trial Balance                                    _ ☐ ✕     │
├─────────────────────────────────────────────────────────────┤
│ File   Help                                                   │
├─────────────────────────────────────────────────────────────┤
│ As At 12/12/1997                    Debits      Credits       │
│ 1060  Cash                        48,906.47        -      ▲   │
│ 1200  Accounts Receivable         42,262.65        -          │
│ 1210  Golf Map Inventory             674.77        -          │
│ 1220  Ski Map Inventory           14,748.47        -          │
│ 1230  Wine Map Inventory          13,101.07        -          │
│ 1240  Attraction Map Inventory     1,266.87        -          │
│ 1250  Rack Inventory               1,494.75        -          │
│ 1300  Office Supplies                347.60        -          │
│ 1310  Shipping Supplies              246.73        -          │
│ 1320  Prepaid Insurance              450.00        -          │
│ 1550  Office Equipment             7,000.00        -          │
│ 1560  Accum Dep:  Office Equipment      -       4,152.71      │
│ 1600  Vehicle                     16,000.00        -          │
│ 1610  Accum Dep:  Vehicle               -       5,366.63      │
│ 2200  Accounts Payable                  -      31,963.60      │
│ 2310  FIT Payable                       -         546.31  ▼   │
├─────────────────────────────────────────────────────────────┤
│ Double-click to display All Transactions Report for current account. │
└─────────────────────────────────────────────────────────────┘
```

ACTION: Print the trial balance by choosing **Print** from the Trial Balance File menu. Compare your trial balance to the one shown below:

Oregon Explorer Maps
Trial Balance As At 12/12/1997

		Debits	Credits
1060	Cash	48,906.47	-
1200	Accounts Receivable	42,262.65	-
1210	Golf Map Inventory	674.77	-
1220	Ski Map Inventory	14,748.47	-
1230	Wine Map Inventory	13,101.07	-
1240	Attraction Map Inventory	1,266.87	-
1250	Rack Inventory	1,494.75	-
1300	Office Supplies	347.60	-
1310	Shipping Supplies	246.73	-
1320	Prepaid Insurance	450.00	-
1550	Office Equipment	7,000.00	-
1560	Accum Dep: Office Equipment	-	4,152.71
1600	Vehicle	16,000.00	-
1610	Accum Dep: Vehicle	-	5,366.63
2200	Accounts Payable	-	31,963.60
2310	FIT Payable	-	546.31
2320	SIT Payable	-	361.62
2330	Social Security Tax Payable	-	792.60
2335	Medicare Tax Payable	-	185.36
2340	FUTA Payable	-	23.24
2350	SUTA Payable	-	272.64
2400	Medical Insurance Payable	-	125.00
2710	Loans Payable		0.00
3560	Karen Bailey, Capital	-	78,185.62
3570	Karen Bailey, Drawing	27,500.00	-

4210	Wholesale Golf Map Sales	-	8,800.59
4220	Wholesale Ski Map Sales	-	6,736.19
4230	Wholesale Wine Map Sales	-	6,634.19
4240	Wholesale Attraction Map Sales	-	22,128.97
4310	Distributor Golf Map Sales	-	43,212.79
4320	Distributor Ski Map Sales	-	37,145.84
4330	Distributor Wine Map Sales	-	36,110.84
4340	Distributor Attraction Map Sales	-	123,106.97
4500	Rack Sales	-	1,636.49
4600	Sales Discounts	876.46	-
4700	Sales Returns and Allowances	2,049.75	-
4810	Interest income	-	0.00
4820	Bad Check Charges	-	25.00
5010	COGS-Golf Maps	15,716.42	-
5020	COGS-Ski Maps	15,137.66	-
5030	COGS-Wine Maps	13,580.81	-
5040	COGS-Attraction Maps	34,081.08	-
5050	COGS-Racks	1,361.50	-
5060	Purchase Discounts	0.00	-
5070	Purchase Returns and Allowances	0.00	-
5301	Wages	70,095.00	-
5310	Social Security Tax Expense	4,345.89	-
5315	Medicare Tax Expense	1,016.38	-
5320	FUTA Expense	224.00	-
5330	SUTA Expense	2,180.36	-
5400	Phone Expense	1,376.92	-
5410	Postage Expense	976.29	-
5420	Shipping Expense	18,974.32	-
5430	Advertising Expense	8,476.20	-
5440	Vehicle Expense	627.46	-
5450	Utilities Expense	1,176.42	-
5460	Rent Expense	30,000.00	-
5470	Membership and Dues Expense	973.20	-
5480	Subscription Expense	267.50	-
5490	Interest Expense: Loans	0.00	-
5500	Dep. Expense: Office Equipment	1,986.05	-
5510	Dep. Expense: Vehicle	2,566.63	-
5610	Insurance Expense	1,650.00	-
5620	Office Supplies Expense	2,219.95	-
5630	Shipping Supplies Expense	1,011.42	-
5650	Bank Service Charge Expense	295.00	-
5660	Credit Card Fees Expense	23.92	-
5800	Misc. Expense	247.23	-
		407,513.20	407,513.20

 ACTION: Close the Trial Balance, backup Oregon Explorer Maps' data files, exit the program, and return to the windows desktop.

SUMMARY

This chapter has explored the Receivables and Project components of CA-Simply Accounting for Windows as they would typically be used by a merchandising business. Use of the Sales and Receipts Journals to record inventory sales on account, credit memos, cash receipts, credit card sales, cash sales, and sales discounts have been explained in detail. By examining the methods used to record inventory-related receivables transactions, various integration/linking features of the program were illustrated.

QUESTIONS

QUESTIONS ABOUT THE SOFTWARE

1. In CA-Simply Accounting for Windows, all receivables and inventory functions are fully integrated with and linked to the General Ledger. Explain this statement and give an example.

2. CA-Simply Accounting for Windows uses the perpetual inventory system. Describe the differences between the periodic and perpetual inventory systems.

3. Name the four most common inventory valuation methods. Which method does the CA-Simply Accounting for Windows program use?

4. Describe several different ways that a business might define or organize its business segments for use with the Project component of CA-Simply Accounting for Windows.

5. Explain how project allocations are recorded in CA-Simply Accounting for Windows.

6. The Receipts Journal dialog box does not present an allocation column. Why?

QUESTIONS ABOUT DAILY OPERATIONS

7. A customer has called to inquire about an invoice he recently received. He was shipped 30 Explore Oregon-Ski maps as ordered, yet his invoice lists 30 Explore Oregon-Attraction maps. The charges on the invoice are correct. How might this error of occurred and how would you use the CA-Simply Accounting for Windows program to correct the error?

8. A customer has called to inquire about her account balance. She would like to know the total amount she owes to the business. How would you use the CA-Simply Accounting for Windows program to answer her question?

9. A customer has called to inquire about the statement she recently received. Her records show that she sent a check for $1,350.00 within the company's 2/10, net 30 discount period in payment of her $1,500.00 invoice, yet the statement lists the following items:

3/21/1997	4590	Invoice	1,500.00
3/31/1997	3223	Payment	1,350.00
Balance Due:			150.00

How might this error occur and how would you use the CA-Simply Accounting for Windows program to correct the error?

EXPLORING ALTERNATIVE SOFTWARE TECHNIQUES

10. Describe three methods of applying and recording sales discounts. Indicate which method would be used to enter discount terms for Oregon Explorer Maps' wholesale customers, which method would be used for all customers, and which method would be used for individual invoices.

TRANSMITTAL

Oregon Explorer Maps   **Name:** _____
Chapter 5

Attach the following documents and reports:

1. Invoice 2167
2. Invoice 2168
3. Invoice 2169
4. Invoice 2168
5. CM56
6. CR57
7. CM58
8. Sales Journal 12/1/1997 to 12/5/1997
9. Receipt of Check 17634
10. Receipt of Check 64325
11. Receipt of Check 3410
12. Corrected Check 3410C
13. Invoice 2170
14. Invoice 2171
15. Invoice 2172
16. Receipt of Check 4245
17. Receipt of Check 5249
18. Receipt of Check 3624
19. Receipt of Check 6132
20. CM57
21. Receipt of Check 7237
22. Receipt of Check 351
23. Invoice 2173
24. Customer Aged Detail report: Northwest Pipeline
25. Invoice 2174
26. Invoice 2175
27. Invoice 2176
28. Invoice 2177
29. Invoice 2178
30. All Journal Entries 12/1/1997 to 12/12/1997
31. Customer Aged Detail As at 12/12/1997
32. Inventory Synopsis 12/12/1997
33. Trial Balance As at 12/12/1997

EXERCISE—Windmill Wheels

Company Profile

Windmill Wheels is owned and operated by Alton Long as a sole proprietorship in Portland, Oregon. Alton operates two retail bicycle shops under the Windmill Wheels name. Merchandise at both stores, the main store and the branch store, include a variety of bikes. Alton maintains his own accounting records using CA-Simply Accounting for Windows. As a merchandising business with employees and two stores, he uses the General, Receivables, Payables, Inventory, Payroll, and Project components of the program. Alton has elected to use the CA-Simply Accounting for Windows automatic invoice, check, and customer statement preparation features. He allocates 100% of revenue and expenses to main store and branch store projects unless otherwise indicated. Cash sales from each of the two stores are reported on a Weekly Cash Sales Summary form. Alton uses the cash sale option in the Sales Journal to record cash sales under the Cash Sales customer name. If you make any errors, correct them following the procedures learned in the chapter and in previous chapters.

1. Load CA-Simply Accounting for Windows; open the data files for Windmill Wheels (A:\WINDMILL\Windmill.acs). Record the following transactions under the session date of 12/5/1997.

    December 1—Sold 1 road bike (Item 1) to Northwest Touring; Terms: 2/10, n/30; Project: Main Store. Print the invoice.

    December 1—Sold 2 children's bikes (Item 5) to Cycle Oregon; Terms: 2/10, n/30; Project: Main Store. Print the invoice.

    December 1— Sold 3 city bikes (Item 3) to Cycle Club; Terms: 2/10, n/30; Project: Branch Store. Print the invoice.

    December 2— Northwest Touring purchased 2 more road bikes; Terms: 2/10, n/30; Project: Main Store. Print the invoice.

    December 3—Issued Credit Memo 16 to Northwest Touring for the return of 1 road bike. Credit their account $350.00; Project: Main Store. Print the credit memo.

    December 3—Received Check 2389 from Alameda Sports Program Invoice 627. The original invoice was for $3,500.00. Print the payment receipt.

    December 5—Received Check 8392 from Cycle Club in full payment of Invoice 634 within the discount period. Print the payment receipt.

    December 5—Use Deposit Slip 2137 to deposit checks received for payments.

December 5—Weekly Cash Sales Summary 47; Project: Main Store. (**Note:** Enter *Sum47* in the Invoice field.) Print Sum47.

Item	Quantity	Description	Unit Price	Amount
3	6	City Bike	$ 275.00	$ 1,650.00
1	4	Road Bike	350.00	1,400.00
6	1	Tandem Bike	375.00	375.00
				$ 3,425.00

December 5—Use Deposit Slip 2138 to deposit the cash received in the main store.

December 5—Weekly Cash Sales Summary 48; Project: Branch Store. Print Sum48.

Item	Quantity	Description	Unit Price	Amount
2	2	Mountain Bike	$ 450.00	$ 900.00
4	1	Racing Bike	750.00	750.00
3	3	City Bike	275.00	825.00
				$ 2,475.00

December 5—Use Deposit Slip 2139 to deposit the cash received in the branch store.

December 5—Mr. Long decides to accept bank credit cards for payment from customers. Set up Simply to receive both Visa and MasterCard credit cards. Use Expense Account 5660 Credit Card Fees Expense, Asset Account 1060 Cash, and a fee of 6%.

December 5—Sold 2 mountain bikes to a one-time customer using a Visa credit card in the branch store. Print the invoice.

December 5—Sold 1 racing bike to a new customer: Racers Unlimited, 382 NE 20th Street, Portland, Oregon 97204. A MasterCard was used for this sale in the main store. Print the invoice.

December 5—Use Deposit Slip 2140 to deposit the credit card receipts from both stores.

2. Advance the session date to 12/12/1997; then record the following transactions:

December 7—Sold 2 city bikes to Courier Express; Terms: n/30; Project: Main Store. Print the invoice.

December 8—Received Check 567 from Cycle Club in the amount of $2,250.00 in full payment of Invoice 617. Print the receipt.

December 9—Received Check 8990 from Cycle Oregon within Windmill Wheels' 2/10, n/30 discount period for Invoice 633 and for full payment of Invoice 631. Total amount of the check received was $5,691.00. Print the receipt.

December 10—Issued Credit Memo 17 to Courier Express for the return of 1 city bike. Credit their account $275.00; Project: Main Store. Print the credit memo.

December 11—Received Check 125 for $686.00 from Northwest Touring for Invoice 632 and 635. Apply CM16 and take the discount allowed. Print the receipt.

December 12—Received Check 9-1023 from Courier Express for payment of Invoice 612. Apply CM17. Print the receipt.

December 12—Weekly Cash Sales Summary 49; Project: Main Store. Print Sum49.

Item	Quantity	Description	Unit Price	Amount
2	6	Mountain Bike	$ 450.00	$ 2,700.00
1	2	Road Bike	350.00	700.00
5	10	Children's Bike	225.00	2,250.00
				$ 5,650.00

December 12—Weekly Cash Sales Summary 50; Project: Branch Store. Print Sum50.

Item	Quantity	Description	Unit Price	Amount
6	1	Tandem Bike	$ 375.00	$ 375.00
4	2	Racing Bike	750.00	1,500.00
				$ 1,875.00

December 12—Use Deposit Slip 2141 to deposit all checks received and the cash sales from both stores.

December 12—Sold 3 children's bikes to a one-time customer using a MasterCard in the branch store. Print the invoice.

December 12—Sold 1 racing bike to Racers Unlimited in the main store. Payment was made with a Visa. Print the invoice.

December 12—Use Deposit Slip 2142 to deposit the credit card sales from both stores.

December 12—Received a returned check from the bank marked NSF. Check 567 was from Cycle Club in payment of Invoice 617. Create any necessary accounts and/or items to record the return of the check and the $25 charges for the NSF check (the bank charges $15 and we charge $10 for NSF checks). Print the invoice created in this transaction.

3. Print the following reports:

   A. All Journal Entries (Project allocations) 12/1/1997 to 12/12/1997
   B. Customer Aged report (Select All, Detail) As at 12/12/1997
   C. Trial Balance As at 12/12/1997

4. Back up Windmill Wheels' data files and exit from the program. Complete the Windmill Wheels Transmittal.

TRANSMITTAL

Windmill Wheels   Name: _____
Chapter 5

A. Attach the following documents and reports:

1. Invoice 632
2. Invoice 633
3. Invoice 634
4. Invoice 635
5. CM16
6. Receipt of Check 2389
7. Receipt of Check 8392
8. Sum47
9. Sum48
10. Invoice 636
11. Invoice 637
12. Invoice 638
13. Receipt of Check 567
14. Receipt of Check 8990
15. CM17
16. Receipt of Check 125
17. Receipt of Check 9-1023
18. Sum49
19. Sum50
20. Invoice 639
21. Invoice 640
22. Invoice 641
23. All Journal Entries 12/1/1997 to 12/12/1997
24. Customer Aged report As at 12/12/1997
25. Trial Balance As at 12/12/1997

B. Refer to your reports to list the amounts requested below:

1. How much does Northwest Touring owe Windmill Wheels on 12/12/1997? $ _____

2. How much does Cycle Oregon owe Windmill Wheels on 12/12/1997? $ _____

3. What is the balance of the Sales Returns and Allowances account on 12/12/1997? $ _____

4. What is the balance of the Accounts Receivable account on 12/12/1997? $ _____

5. What is the balance of the Sales Discounts account on 12/12/1997? $ _____

MERCHANDISING BUSINESSES—
PAYABLES AND PROJECTS

MERCHANDISING BUSINESSES— PAYABLES AND PROJECTS

LEARNING OBJECTIVES

After studying this chapter, you will be able to:
- Enter inventory purchases
- Enter noninventory purchases
- Enter debit memo transactions
- Enter purchase orders and merchandise receipts
- Enter payment transactions to credit vendors
- Enter payment transactions for current liabilities
- Enter purchase discount transactions
- Enter project allocations in the Purchases Journal
- Review and edit inventory-related Purchases Journal transactions
- Observe and understand payables and inventory integration/linking accounts

PURCHASES

In this chapter, you will continue working with the Oregon Explorer Maps' company files. The features of the Payables components of CA-Simply Accounting for Windows will be discussed in detail.

CA-Simply Accounting for Windows maintains inventory records on a fully integrated, perpetual basis. Through the program's integration/linking feature, which links accounts together, the inventory records in the Inventory Ledger are updated each time an inventory item is purchased, sold, transferred, or adjusted. For example, when an inventory purchase on account is recorded in the Purchases Journal dialog box, the program automatically records the entry in the Purchases Journal, posts to the related accounts in the General Ledger, updates the vendor's account in the Vendors' Ledger (Accounts Payable Subsidiary Ledger), and updates the inventory records in the Inventory & Services Ledger for the inventory items purchased.

OREGON EXPLORER MAPS TUTORIAL

The following tutorial is a step-by-step guide to recording merchandising transactions and related project allocations for Oregon Explorer Maps within the Payables components of CA-Simply Accounting for Windows. The procedures required to record merchandising transactions and project allocations using the Receivables components were discussed in Chapter 5. Payroll procedures will be discussed in Chapter 7. The procedures required to record adjusting entries (including inventory), prepare financial statements, and close the accounting records at the end of the fiscal year are functions of the Inventory and General components and will be discussed in Chapter 8. The Oregon Explorer Maps Tutorial will be continued in Chapters 7 and 8 to give you a comprehensive overview of how CA-Simply Accounting for Windows can be used to maintain the accounting records for a merchandising business.

PURCHASES JOURNAL—RECORDING INVENTORY PURCHASES ON ACCOUNT

Inventory purchases on account are recorded in the Purchases Journal.

Oregon Explorer Maps—Document 30   **Session Date: 12/19/1997**

SG Supply Co.

S. Glade Supply Co.
3628 SE 39ᵗʰ Ave.
Portland, OR 97214

Invoice ___8643___

To: Oregon Explorer Maps

2000 SE Hawthorne Blvd.
Portland, OR 97214

Date	Code	Quantity	Description	Unit Price	Amount
12/14/97	X7224	100	4.25 Plastic Rack	$5.00	$500.00
				TOTAL	**$500.00**

Shipping: FOB Destination   Approved. *K. B.*

ACTION: Load CA-Simply Accounting for Windows; open the data files for Oregon Explorer Maps (A:\EXPLORER\Explorer.asc); then advance the session date to 12/19/1997. The Oregon Explorer Maps' home window will appear as shown below:

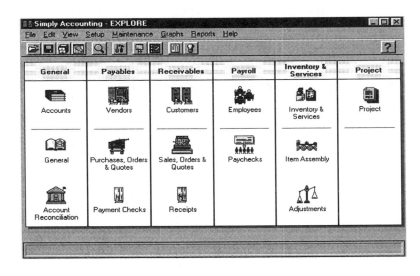

ACTION: Open the Purchases Journal dialog box by clicking the **Purchases, Orders & Quotes** icon on the home window. Click the drop-down list arrow to the right of the **Purchased from** field; select **S. Glade Supply Company** from the vendor list. Your screen will look like this:

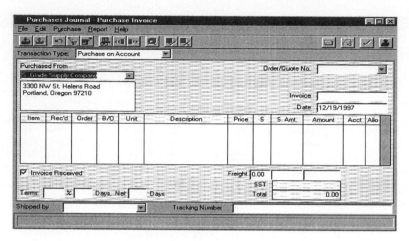

Explanation: The program has automatically filled in the vendor's address in the **Purchased From** field.

ACTION: Click in the **Invoice** field; enter S. Glade Company's invoice number of *8643*; press the TAB key; enter *12/14/1997* in the **Date** field; then press the TAB key. Your screen will look like this:

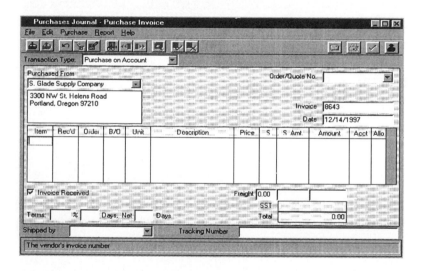

Explanation: After accepting the new transaction date, the program will position a flashing insertion point in the **Item** field.

ACTION: With the flashing insertion point positioned in the **Item** field, press the ENTER key or double-click in the field with your mouse. Your screen will look like this:

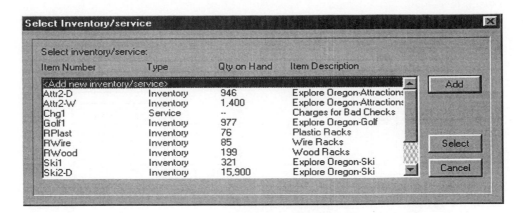

Explanation: A display listing Oregon Explorer Maps' inventory and service items will appear in the Select Inventory/service dialog box. The scroll bar on the right side of the dialog box can be used to advance the item list.

ACTION: Select Item Number **RPlast** by double-clicking on the item or by highlighting the item and clicking the **Select** button. Your screen will look like this:

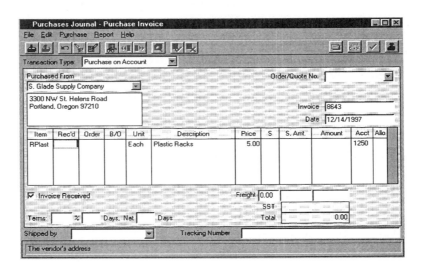

Explanation: The program has automatically completed the **Unit** (Each), **Description** (Plastic Racks), **Price** (5.00), and **Acct** (1250 Rack Inventory) fields associated with this inventory item. The flashing insertion point is positioned in the **Rec'd** field. The default price offered is the current average cost of the item based on the data in the Inventory Ledger. If the purchase price is different from this amount you can enter a different price.

ACTION: Enter *100* in the **Rec'd** field; press the TAB key. Your screen will look like this:

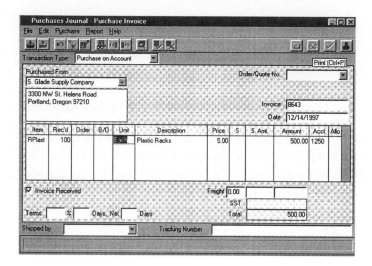

Explanation: The program has automatically multiplied the number entered in the **Rec'd** field (100) by the amount entered in the **Price** field (5.00) and entered the result in the **Amount** field (500.00). The program calculates the amount by multiplying the price by the number entered in the **Rec'd** column. If you enter a different amount in the **Amount** column, the program will calculate the new price by dividing the new amount by the number in the **Rec'd** column.

This completes the data you need to enter into the Purchases Journal dialog box to record the purchase of inventory on account. Before posting this transaction, you need to verify that the transaction data are correct by viewing the journal entry.

 ACTION: Choose **Display Purchases Journal Entry** from the Purchases Journal Report menu. Your screen will look like this:

Purchases Journal Entry			
File Help			
12/14/1997	Debits	Credits	Project
1250 Rack Inventory	500.00	-	
2200 Accounts Payable	-	500.00	
	500.00	500.00	

Explanation: The journal entry representing the data you have recorded in the Purchases Journal dialog box is displayed. Through its integration/linking feature, the program has created the standard journal entry to record the purchase of inventory on account:

	Debit	**Credit**
Inventory	xxx	
Accounts Payable		xxx

Note that the **Allo** column is not used in the Purchases Journal for this transaction and that there is no project listed in the Purchases Journal Entry report. Project allocations can be made only to revenue and expense accounts. Inventory is an asset account and Accounts Payable is a liability account.

Review the journal entry for accuracy, noting any errors.

ACTION: Close the Purchases Journal Entry window. If you have made an error, use the following editing techniques to correct the error:

Editing Tips
Editing Inventory and Noninventory Purchases Journal Entries and Project Allocations

Move to the field that contains the error by pressing either the TAB key to move forward through each field or the SHIFT and TAB keys together to move to a previous field. This will highlight the selected field information so that you can change it. Alternatively, you can use the mouse to point to a field and drag through the incorrect information to highlight it. Type the correct information; then press the TAB key to enter it.

If you have associated a transaction with the incorrect vendor, select the correct vendor from the vendor list display after clicking the drop-down list arrow to the right of the **Purchased From** field.

If an inventory item is incorrect, select the correct item from the Select Inventory Item dialog box after double-clicking on the incorrect item in the **Item** field.

If you have associated this transaction with an incorrect account number, select the correct account number from the chart of accounts display after double-clicking in the **Acct** field.

If you have associated an item with an incorrect project or have allocated an incorrect amount to a project, double-click in the **Allo** column to display the Project Allocation dialog box. To correct the project, select the correct project from the Select Project dialog box after double-clicking on the incorrect project in the **Project** field; then click the **OK** button. To correct the allocated amount or percentage, highlight the incorrect amount or percentage; enter the correct amount or percentage; then click the **OK** button.

To discard an entry and start over, either choose **Undo Entry** from the Purchases Journal Edit menu or double-click the **Close** button on the title bar. Click the **Yes** button in response to the question, "Are you sure you want to discard this journal entry?"

Review the journal entry for accuracy after any corrections by choosing **Display Purchases Journal Entry** from the Purchases Journal Report menu.

It is IMPORTANT TO NOTE that the only way to edit a transaction after it is posted is to reverse the entry and enter the correct transaction. To correct transactions posted in error, see the transaction for Engineered Shelving later in this chapter.

 ACTION: After verifying that the journal entry is correct, click the **Post** button to post this transaction. A blank Purchases Journal dialog box is displayed, ready for additional Purchases Journal transactions to be recorded.

Additional Inventory Purchases on Account Transactions

Record the following additional inventory purchases on account transactions:

Document 31 December 14—Received Invoice 12763 in the amount of $750.00 from Interstate Racking Systems for the purchase of 200 wire racks at $3.75 each.

Document 32 December 14—Received Invoice 634 in the amount of $20.00 from Engineered Shelving for the purchase of 5 wood racks at $4.00 each.

ACTION: After you have posted the journal entries for Documents 31 and 32, close the Purchases Journal dialog box. You will return to the home window. You realize that the Purchase Invoice for wood racks should have been for 50 racks rather than 5 racks. To correct this invoice, double-click the **Purchases, Orders & Quotes** icon on the home window. In the Purchases Journal - Purchase Invoice window click the **Adjust Invoice** button. On the Adjust an invoice screen, click the drop-down list next to **Vendor Name** and click **Engineered Shelving** to select the vendor.

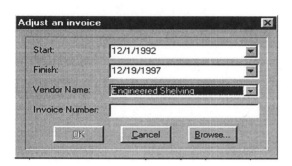

ACTION: After Engineered Shelving has been selected as the vendor, click the **Browse** button. CA-Simply Accounting will browse through all the invoices and display the following invoice information for Engineered Shelving:

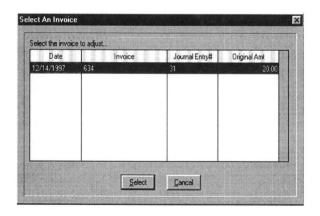

ACTION: With the invoice information highlighted, click the **Select** button. The original invoice will appear on the screen. Change the number of wood racks from 5 to 50 by highlighting or deleting 5 in the **Rec'd** column and inserting *50*. TAB so Simply can recalculate the total for the purchase invoice. The invoice will appear as follows:

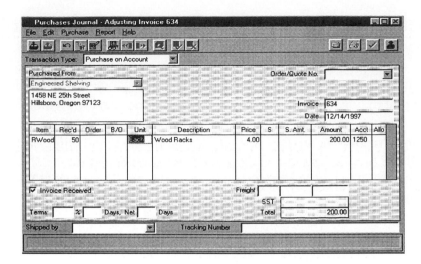

Explanation: This will change the invoice. Notice that the **Rec'd** column shows 50 and the total is now $200.00 rather than $20.00.

 ACTION: Verify that the information on the revised invoice is correct. Print the invoice, post the invoice, and close the Purchases Journal to return to the home window.

PURCHASES JOURNAL—RECORDING INVENTORY PURCHASES ON ACCOUNT WITH PURCHASE DISCOUNT

Businesses sometimes offer special payment terms to customers as an incentive for early payment of invoices. As a customer, Oregon Explorer Maps may be eligible for a discount. When you receive a discount for paying for a purchase, it is called a purchase discount. Payment/discount terms may be offered in a variety of forms. One of the most common discount/payment terms is 2/10, n/30, which means the customer may deduct 2% of the amount of the invoice from the payment if payment is made within 10 days of the invoice date. Only early-payment discounts are included in the purchases discounts account. CA-Simply Accounting for Windows calculates the discount automatically when terms for a purchase discount are entered. There are three ways in which you can enter discount terms. You may set up discount terms for individual vendors when the vendor is created add discount terms for an existing vendor by accessing the Options tab in the vendor record and entering the discount terms, or record discount terms on an invoice as it is recorded. This chapter will use the last method for discount terms.

Oregon Explorer Maps—Document 33 **Session Date: 12/19/1997**

Canyon Litho
10900 SW 5th Street
Beaverton, OR 97005

Invoice # _98726_

To: Oregon Explorer Maps
2000 SE Hawthorne Blvd.
Portland, OR 97214

Date	Code	Quantity	Description	Unit Price	Amount
12/14/97	AM74	1,000	Explore Oregon Attraction Maps	$0.54	$540.00
			Terms: 2/10, N/30	**TOTAL**	**$540.00**

Shipping: FOB Destination Approved. *K. B.*

NOTE: Create a new inventory item for retail sales of attraction maps— Attr2-R Explore Oregon-Attractions selling for $4.50 each. The minimum to have on hand is 100.

 ACTION: A new item will be added for this purchase invoice. Prior to completing the invoice, a new account must be created for Attraction Map Retail Sales. Click the **Accounts** icon on the home window. Click the **Display by Name** button on the Accounts toolbar. 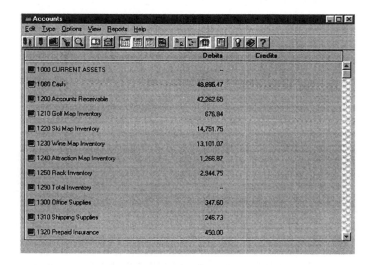 Your screen will show the following:

Explanation: The Display by Name button displays the accounts in numerical order and shows the debit or credit balances of each account.

 ACTION: Click the **Create** button. Your screen will show the following:

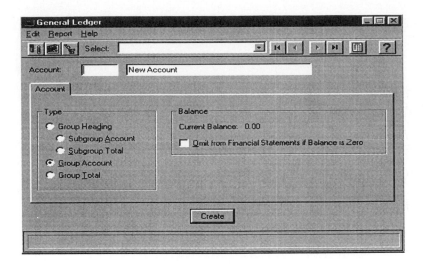

ACTION: Enter *4410* as the account number. The account name is Retail Attraction Map Sales. The type of account is Subgroup Account. Your screen will show the following:

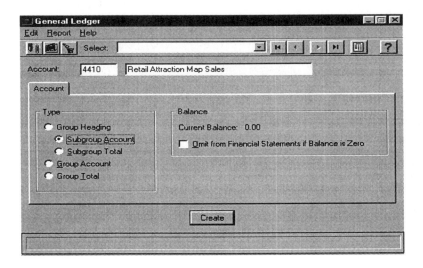

Explanation: In preparation for adding other types of retail sales accounts, Oregon Explorer is creating a subgroup for retail sales. This will allow all the different accounts for retail sales to be displayed and a total shown for all the retail sales accounts. This makes an income statement easier to read and to use when determining the amount of sales generated within a specific category.

ACTION: Click **Create** to create this account. Add a Subgroup Total Account for Total Retail Sales. This account is numbered 4490. When the above information is entered, your screen will show the following:

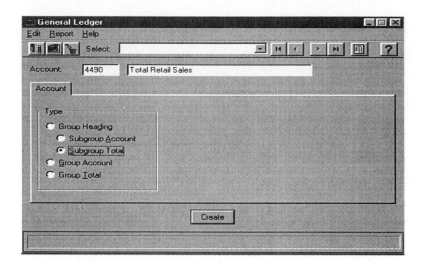

Explanation: This account will be used to display the total of all the retail sales accounts on reports.

ACTION: Click the **Create** button to create the account. Close the General Ledger. Your screen will show the following:

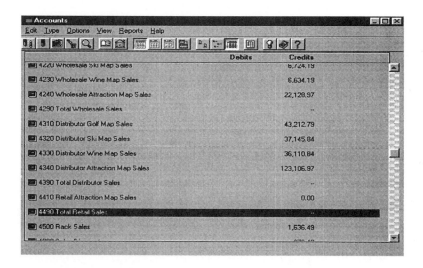

Explanation: Notice the two new accounts. The last account entered should be highlighted.

ACTION: Close Accounts. Prepare a purchase invoice, inserting the vendor, invoice number, and date as previously instructed. Double-click in the **Item** column. Your screen will show the following:

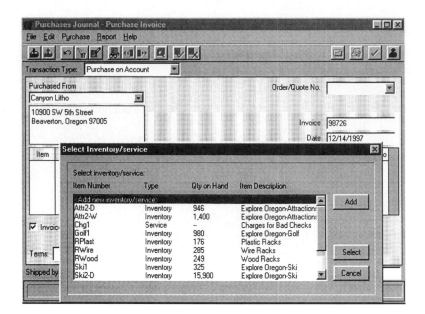

Explanation: The information for **Purchased From**, **Invoice**, and **Date** has been entered and the Select Inventory/service dialog box is open. Because the purchase of 1,000 attractions maps for retail sales has been authorized, a new inventory item will need to be added.

ACTION: With **<Add new inventory/service>** highlighted, click the **Add** button. Your screen will show the following:

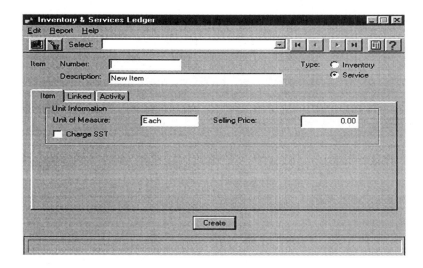

Explanation: Notice that Service is the type of item indicated on the above screen. When the item is identified as an inventory item, the screen will change. If your screen is different than the one above, check to see if the type of item is Inventory. If it is, do not change it.

ACTION: Enter *Attr2-R* as the item number and *Explore Oregon-Attractions* as the description. If necessary, click **Inventory** as the type of item. Your screen will show the following:

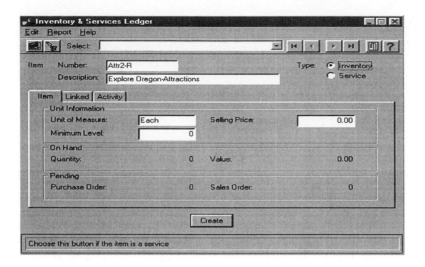

Explanation: Notice the additional information provided and required for an inventory item.

ACTION: The unit of measure is Each, the selling price is $4.50, and the minimum level is 100. Enter this information in the appropriate areas. Your screen will show the following:

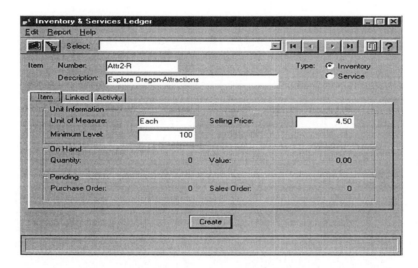

Explanation: The item information has been entered. The linking information must be entered so that Simply can automatically post transactions to the appropriate accounts.

ACTION: Click the **Linked** tab. Your screen will show the following:

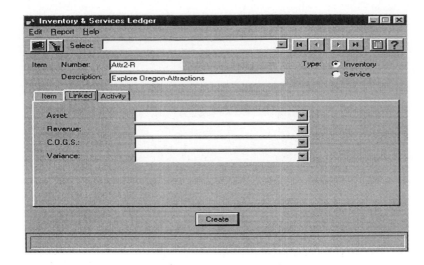

Explanation: This screen allows you to indicate which accounts will automatically be used by Simply when a transaction is recorded for this item.

ACTION: Click the drop-down list arrow for **Asset**. Your screen will show the following:

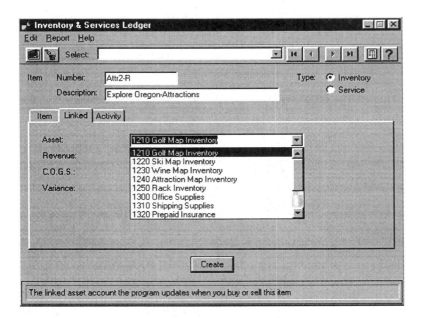

Explanation: A listing of some of the asset accounts appears.

ACTION: Click **1240 Attraction Map Inventory** to select it as the asset account used in inventory transactions. Click the drop-down list arrow for **Revenue**. Your screen will show the following:

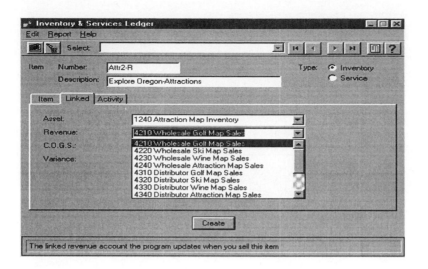

Explanation: A partial listing of revenue accounts is displayed.

ACTION: Scroll through the list of revenue accounts. Click **Account 4410** to select. Click the drop-down list arrow next to **C.O.G.S.** Your screen will show the following:

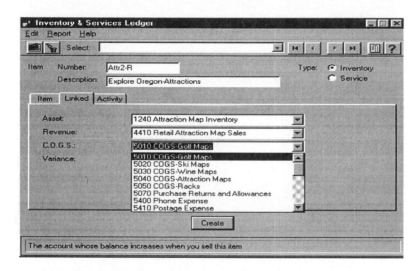

Explanation: A list of cost of goods sold accounts is displayed.

ACTION: Click **Account 5040** to select. Your screen will show the following:

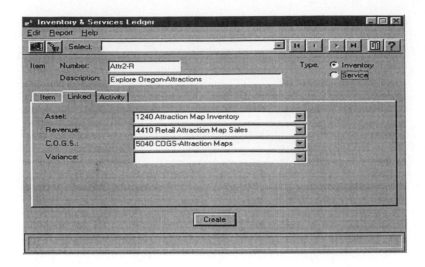

Explanation: The accounts that will be linked to retail sales of attraction maps have been identified.

ACTION: Click the **Activity** tab. Your screen will show the following:

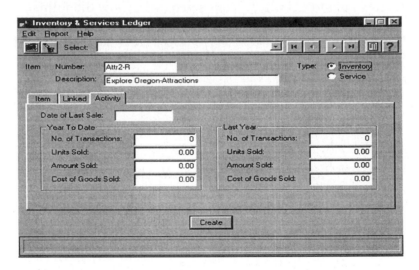

Explanation: If any historical sales information existed for this item, it would be entered at this point. Once the item is created, historical data may no longer be added. Once an item is established, checking the activity of the item provides information regarding the number of transactions, units sold, amount sold, and cost of goods sold for the item for the year to date and for the previous year.

ACTION: Since no historical data is being input at this time, click **Create** to create the inventory item. Your screen will show the purchase order with the item information completed:

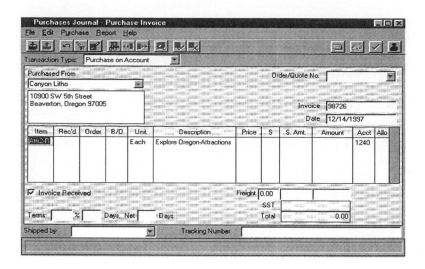

 ACTION: TAB to **Rec'd** and enter *1,000.* TAB to or click in the **Price** column. Enter *0.54* for the price. Press the TAB key. Your screen will show the following:

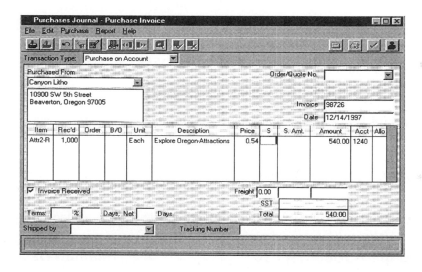

Explanation: Normally, Simply calculates the price by dividing the quantity of the item on hand by the value of the item and automatically inserts the price in the purchase invoice. Because this is a new item, the price Oregon Explorer is paying for the maps had to be inserted on the invoice. The selling price indicated when the item was created is the amount Oregon Explorer will charge when it sells the item, not the amount it pays when it buys the item. **Note**: If the purchase price is different than the price calculated by Simply, highlight the price Simply inserted in the **Price** column and key in the price the vendor is charging.

 ACTION: To enter the payment terms for this invoice, click in the box next to terms and enter *2* as the discount percentage. TAB to or click in the box for **Days** and enter *10*. Enter *30* for **Net Days**. Your completed purchase invoice will appear as follows:

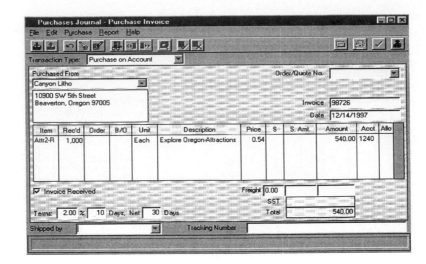

ACTION: Check your invoice carefully. If you find any mistakes, correct them. Post the transaction.

Additional Inventory Purchases on Account with Purchases Discounts Transactions

Document 34 December 14—Invoice 2937: Purchase 25 Wine2-W maps from Oregon Wine Press. Terms 2/10, n/30.

Document 35 December 14—Invoice 33-1057: Purchase 50 Ski2-W maps from Metro Graphics. Terms 2/10, n/30.

PURCHASES JOURNAL—RECORDING NONINVENTORY PURCHASES

Noninventory purchases and any related project allocations are also recorded in the Purchases Journal.

Oregon Explorer Maps—Document 36   **Session Date: 12/19/1997**

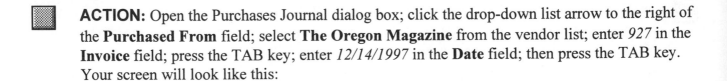

The Oregon Magazine		**CUSTOMER:**	Oregon Explorer Maps
P. O. Box 336			2000 SE Hawthorne Blvd.
Roseburg, OR 97470	**Invoice 927**		Portland, OR 97214
12/14/1997	November Ad—Attraction Map		$300.00
	Approved—K. B.		

ACTION: Open the Purchases Journal dialog box; click the drop-down list arrow to the right of the **Purchased From** field; select **The Oregon Magazine** from the vendor list; enter *927* in the **Invoice** field; press the TAB key; enter *12/14/1997* in the **Date** field; then press the TAB key. Your screen will look like this:

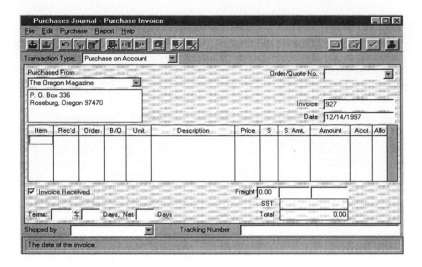

Explanation: After accepting the new transaction date, the program will position a flashing insertion point in the **Item** field.

 ACTION: Use the TAB key to advance through the **Item**, **Rec'd**, **Unit**, **Description**, and **Price** fields until the flashing insertion point is positioned in the **Amount** field. Enter *300.00* into the **Amount** field; then press the TAB key. Your screen will look like this:

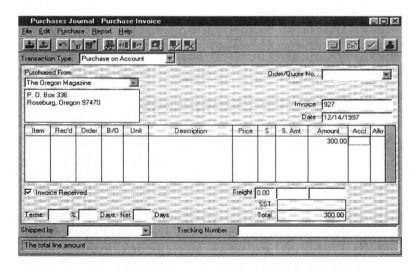

Explanation: The flashing insertion point is positioned in the **Acct** field. This is a noninventory purchase on account. The standard journal entry to record the purchase of advertising on account is:

	Debit	**Credit**
Advertising Expense	xxx	
Accounts Payable		xxx

The program will automatically credit Accounts Payable through its integration/linking feature but needs to be supplied with the appropriate account number for the corresponding debit portion of the entry (advertising expense).

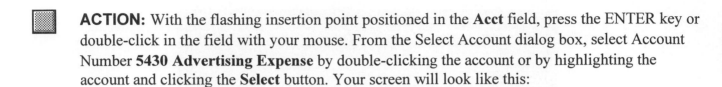 **ACTION:** With the flashing insertion point positioned in the **Acct** field, press the ENTER key or double-click in the field with your mouse. From the Select Account dialog box, select Account Number **5430 Advertising Expense** by double-clicking the account or by highlighting the account and clicking the **Select** button. Your screen will look like this:

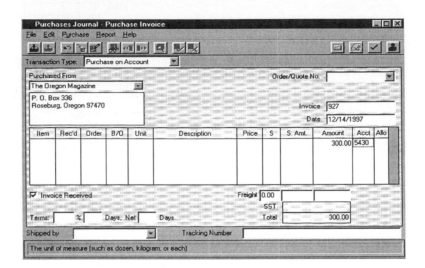

Explanation: If you receive an error message stating an unknown account number, click the **OK** button to display the Select Account dialog box. After the correct account has been selected, the program will automatically enter account number 5430 (advertising expense) into the **Acct** field.

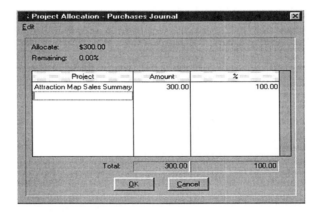 **ACTION:** Click in the **Allo** column; then allocate 100% of the advertising expense to the Attraction Map Sales Summary project. Your screen will look like this:

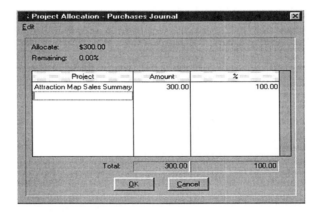

ACTION: Click **OK** and return to the Purchases Journal. Your screen will show the following:

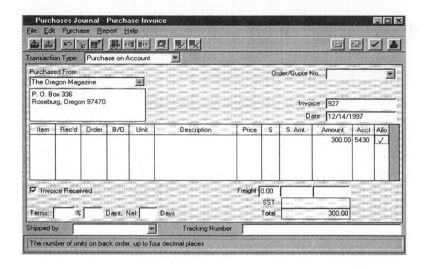

Explanation: Note that a check mark (✔) has been placed in the **Allo** column indicating that the advertising expense has been allocated to a project. This completes the information that you need to enter into the Purchases Journal dialog box to record the advertising expense. Before you post this entry, you need to verify that the transaction data and project allocations are correct by viewing the journal entry.

ACTION: Choose **Display Purchases Journal Entry** from the Purchases Journal Report menu. Your screen will look like this:

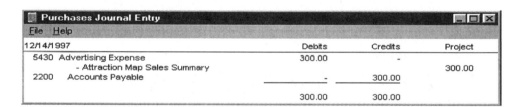

Explanation: The journal entry representing the data you have recorded in the Purchases Journal dialog box is displayed. Review the journal entry for accuracy noting any errors.

ACTION: Close the Purchases Journal Entry window. If you made an error, refer to Editing Tips for Editing Inventory and Noninventory Purchases Journal Entries and Project Allocations, which appears in a special box earlier in this chapter, for information on corrective action.

ACTION: After verifying that the journal entry and allocation are correct, click the **Post** button to post this transaction.

Explanation: A blank Purchases Journal dialog box is displayed, ready for additional Purchases Journal transactions to be recorded. If you receive an error message stating that an account has not been fully allocated, do not post the entry. Refer to Editing Tips for Editing Inventory and Noninventory Purchases Journal Entries and Project Allocations for information on corrective action.

Additional Noninventory Purchases Transactions

Record the following additional noninventory purchases and project allocation transactions, distributing 100% of each invoice amount to the appropriate project:

Document 37 December 14—Received Invoice 8743 from Northwest Slopes in the amount of $1,500.00 for Explore Oregon-Ski map advertising.

Document 38 December 14—Received Invoice 1497 from Oregon Wine Press in the amount of $600.00 for Explore Oregon-Wine map advertising.

 ACTION: After you have posted the journal entries for Documents 37 and 38, close the Purchases Journal dialog box and return to the home window.

PURCHASES JOURNAL—RECORDING DEBIT MEMOS

Debit memos are prepared when Oregon Explorer Maps returns damaged products to a vendor. Debit memos are recorded in the Purchases Journal as negative invoices. This has the effect of reducing the vendor's Accounts Payable balance and decreasing the inventory quantity for the item returned. When using a perpetual inventory, the inventory account is always kept up to date. Because a return reduces the amount of inventory available, the inventory account is decreased.

Oregon Explorer Maps—Document 39   **Session Date 12/19/1997**

> **Debit Memo 24**   **Date:** December 14, 1997
> **Vendor:** S. Glade Supply Company
>
> Returning 3 damaged plastic racks purchased at $5.00 each for a total of $15.00.

ACTION: Open the Purchases Journal dialog box; click the drop-down list arrow to the right of the **Purchased From** field; select **S. Glade Supply Company** from the vendor list. Your screen will look like this:

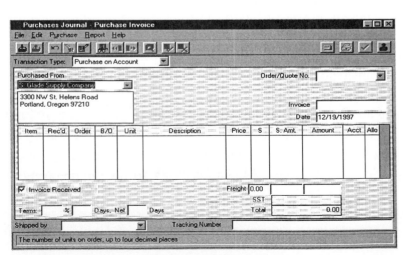

ACTION: Enter *DM24* in the **Invoice** field; press the TAB key; enter *12/14/1997* in the **Date** field; then press the TAB key. With the flashing insertion point positioned in the **Item** field, press the ENTER key or double-click with your mouse; then select the plastic rack (**RPlast**) inventory item from the **Select Inventory Item** dialog box. Your screen will look like this:

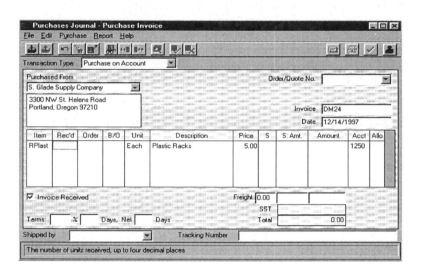

Explanation: The program has automatically completed the **Unit** (Each), **Description** (Plastic Racks), **Price** (5.00), and **Acct** (1250 Rack Inventory) fields associated with this inventory item. The flashing insertion point is positioned in the **Rec'd** field. The default price offered is the current average cost of the item based on the data in the Inventory Ledger. If the original purchase price of the returned item was an amount different than the default amount offered, enter the original price.

ACTION: Enter *-3* in the **Rec'd** field (don't forget the minus sign before the number); press the TAB key. Your screen will look like this:

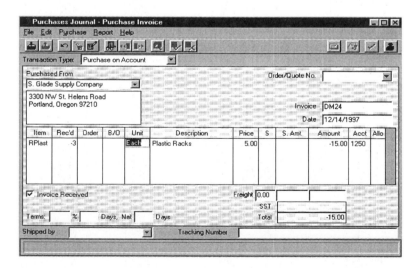

Explanation: The program has automatically multiplied the number entered in the **Rec'd** field (-3) by the amount entered in the **Price** field (5.00) and entered the result in the **Amount** field (-15.00). The program calculates the amount by multiplying the price by the number entered in **Rec'd**. If you enter a different amount, the program will calculate the new price by dividing the amount by the number entered in **Rec'd**.

This completes the data you need to enter into the Purchases Journal dialog box to record the debit memo. Before posting this transaction, you need to verify that the transaction data are correct by viewing the journal entry.

 ACTION: Choose **Display Purchases Journal Entry** from the Purchases Journal Report menu. Compare your display to the one shown below:

Purchases Journal Entry			
File Help			
12/14/1997	Debits	Credits	Project
2200 Accounts Payable	15.00	-	
1250 Rack Inventory	-	15.00	
	15.00	15.00	

Explanation: The journal entry representing the data you have recorded in the Purchases Journal dialog box is displayed. The standard journal entry to record a debit memo is:

	Debit	**Credit**
Accounts Payable	xxx	
Inventory		xxx

Through its integration/linking feature, the program will automatically debit Accounts Payable, and credit the inventory account associated with the inventory item returned. When an item is returned, it is recorded as a credit to inventory because it is removed from the inventory and is no longer available for sale. Remember, the perpetual inventory system keeps the inventory account up to date at all times. Note that the **Allo** column is not available in the Purchases Journal for this transaction. Project allocations can be made only to revenue and expense accounts; and this transaction used Inventory, which is an asset account, and Accounts Payable, which is a liability account.

Review the journal entry for accuracy, noting any errors.

 ACTION: Close the Purchases Journal Entry window. Your screen will look like this:

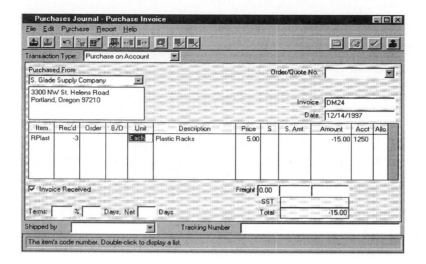

Explanation: If you made an error, refer to the Editing Tips for Editing Inventory and Noninventory Purchases Journal Entries and Project Allocations, which appears in a special box earlier in this chapter, for information on corrective action.

ACTION: After verifying that the journal entry is correct, click the **Post** button to post the transaction.

Additional Debit Memo Transactions

Record the following additional debit memo transactions:

Document 40 December 14—Record Debit Memo 25 for the return of 12 wire racks to Interstate Racking Systems at $3.75 each for a total of $45.00.

Document 41 December 14—Record Debit Memo 26 for the return of 2 wood racks to Engineered Shelving at $4.00 each for a total of $8.00.

ACTION: After recording the journal entries for Documents 40 and 41, close the Purchases Journal dialog box. This will restore the home window and the Purchases Journal icon will remain highlighted.

ACTION: With the Purchases Journal icon highlighted, select **Journal Entries and Purchases** from the home window Report menu. Your screen will look like this:

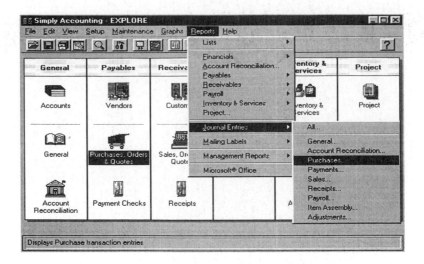

ACTION: After you select Purchases, you will get the following screen:

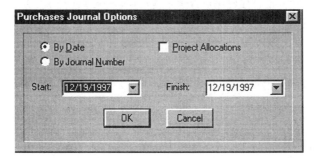

Explanation: The Purchases Journal Options dialog box appears, asking you to define the information you want displayed.

ACTION: Select **By Date**; check the Project Allocations check box; enter 1*2/1/1997* as the start date; leave the finish date set at 12/19/1997; then click the **OK** button. The following Purchases Journal Display will appear on your screen:

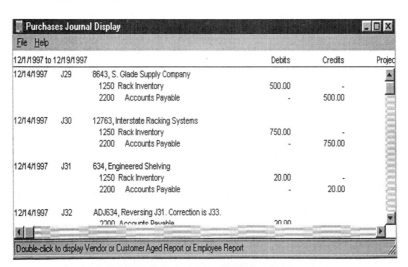

Explanation: Review the display for accuracy verifying that journal entry dates, vendor names, invoice numbers, account names and numbers, allocations, and amounts are correct. Use the scroll bars at the bottom and to the right of the display to advance the display. If you have posted an incorrect transaction, refer to the correction made for Engineered Shelving earlier in the chapter.

 ACTION: Print the Purchases Journal by choosing **Print** from the Purchases Journal Display File menu. Compare your report to the one shown below:

Oregon Explorer Maps

Purchases Journal 12/1/1997 to 12/19/1997			Debits	Credits	Project
12/14/1997	J29	8643, S. Glade Supply Company			
		1250 Rack Inventory	500.00	-	
		2200 Accounts Payable	-	500.00	
12/14/1997	J30	12763, Interstate Racking Systems			
		1250 Rack Inventory	750.00	-	
		2200 Accounts Payable	-	750.00	
12/14/1997	J31	634, Engineered Shelving			
		1250 Rack Inventory	20.00	-	
		2200 Accounts Payable	-	20.00	
12/14/1997	J32	ADJ634, Reversing J31. Correction is J33.			
		2200 Accounts Payable	20.00	-	
		1250 Rack Inventory	-	20.00	
12/14/1997	J33	634, Engineered Shelving			
		1250 Rack Inventory	200.00	-	
		2200 Accounts Payable	-	200.00	
12/14/1997	J34	98726, Canyon Litho			
		1240 Attraction Map Inventory	540.00	-	
		2200 Accounts Payable	-	540.00	
12/14/1997	J35	2937, Oregon Wine Press			
		1230 Wine Map Inventory	17.00	-	
		2200 Accounts Payable	-	17.00	
12/14/1997	J36	33-1057, Metro Graphics			
		1220 Ski Map Inventory	37.50	-	
		2200 Accounts Payable	-	37.50	
12/14/1997	J37	927, The Oregon Magazine			
		5430 Advertising Expense	300.00	-	
		-Attraction Map Sales Summary			300.00
		2200 Accounts Payable	-	300.00	
12/14/1997	J38	8743, Northwest Slopes			
		5430 Advertising Expense	1,500.00	-	
		-Ski Map Sales Summary			1,500.00
		2200 Accounts Payable	-	1,500.00	

12/14/1997	J39	1497, Oregon Wine Press			
		5430 Advertising Expense	600.00	-	
		-Wine Map Sales Summary			600.00
		2200 Accounts Payable	-	600.00	
12/14/1997	J40	DM24, S. Glade Supply Company			
		2200 Accounts Payable	15.00	-	
		1250 Rack Inventory	-	15.00	
12/14/1997	J41	DM25, Interstate Racking Systems			
		2200 Accounts Payable	45.00	-	
		1250 Rack Inventory	-	45.00	
12/14/1997	J42	DM26, Engineered Shelving			
		2200 Accounts Payable	8.00	-	
		1250 Rack Inventory	-	8.00	
			4,552.50	4,552.50	

ACTION: If you detect an error, refer to the editing tips and the correction made for Engineered Shelving earlier in the chapter. Close the Purchases Journal Display window.

PURCHASES JOURNAL—PURCHASE ORDERS

In addition to purchasing items on account, CA-Simply Accounting also has a purchase order feature that is used to place orders with vendors. When the merchandise is received, the purchase order is converted into a purchase invoice.

Oregon Explorer Maps—Document 42   **Session Date 12/19/1997**

Purchase Order #1   **Date:** December 15, 1997
Vendor: Storage Systems, Inc.

Order 3 wood racks at $4.00 each.

ACTION: Click the drop-down list arrow for **Transaction Type**. Your screen will show the following:

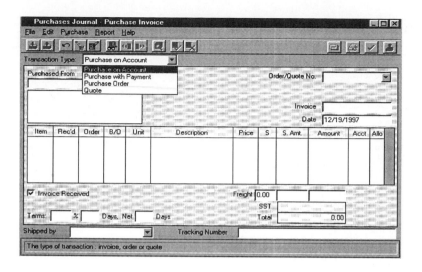

ACTION: Click **Purchase Order**. Your screen will change and show the following:

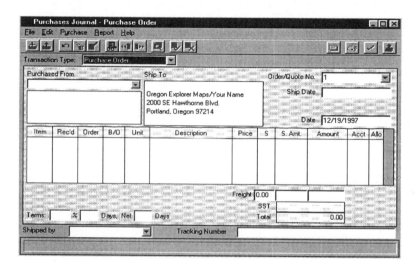

ACTION: Click the drop-down list arrow for **Purchased From** and select **Storage Systems, Inc.** TAB to or click in the **Date** field. Change the date to *12/15/1997*. Your screen will show the following:

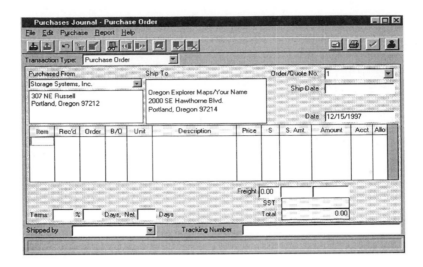

Explanation: Simply automatically fills in the **Ship To** information for Oregon Explorer and numbers the purchase order.

    ACTION: Double-click in the **Item** column to display the list of items for Oregon Explorer. Double-click **RWood** to select wood racks as the item on order. When the item is selected, the cursor is positioned in the order column. Enter *3* as the number of items ordered, and press the TAB key. Your screen will appear as follows:

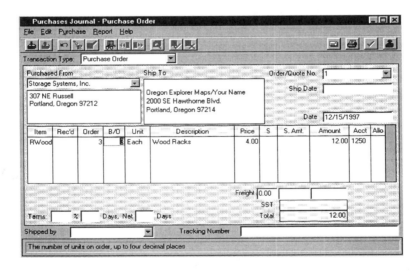

Explanation: When the number of items ordered is inserted and the TAB key is pressed, Simply inserts the same number in the **B/O** (back-ordered) column, and inserts the amount for the order in the **Amount** column.

    ACTION: Click the **Print** button and print the purchase order. Check your work and correct any errors. When everything is correct, click the **Post** button to record the purchase order.

Explanation: The printed purchase order may be mailed to the vendor. A purchase order may also be e-mailed to a vendor by clicking the **E-Mail** button ⬛ on the Purchases Journal toolbar. When a purchase order is posted, Simply updates your 🖥 inventory records to include the details of the order, but it does not update the Transaction List or account balances, because no inventory or money has changed hands.

Additional Purchase Order Transactions

Record the following additional purchase order transactions:

Document 43 December 15—Record Purchase Order 2 for 5 wire racks from Northwest Steel at $3.75 each. Print and post the purchase order.

Document 44 December 15—Record Purchase Order 3 for 3 plastic racks from Engineered Shelving at $5.00 each. Print and post the purchase order.

PURCHASES JOURNAL—PURCHASE ORDERS RECEIPT OF MERCHANDISE

When merchandise ordered by issuing a purchase order is received, the purchase order is converted to an invoice. This allows you to convert the order into an actual transaction, which will debit the inventory asset account and credit accounts payable or cash.

Oregon Explorer Maps—Document 45   **Session Date 12/19/1997**

Invoice 7810-3   **Date:** December 16, 1997
Storage Systems, Inc.   Oregon Explorer Maps
307 NE Russell   2000 SE Hawthorne Blvd.
Portland, Oregon 97212   Portland, Oregon 97214

| 3 | Wood Racks | $4.00 each | $12.00 |

ACTION: Convert Purchase Order 1 to an invoice. All items ordered are received. Match the invoice above with the purchase order issued. Prepare a report listing all pending purchase orders by clicking **Reports** and pointing to Payables and Pending Purchase Orders. Your screen will show the following:

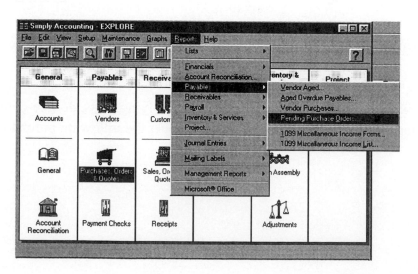

▨ **ACTION:** Click **Pending Purchase Orders**. Your screen will show the following report:

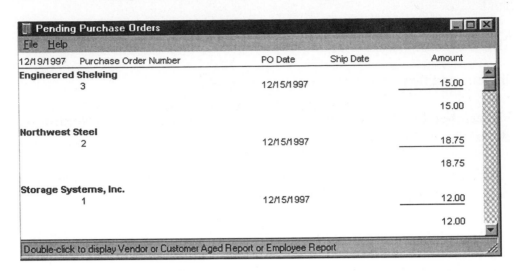

Explanation: The Pending Purchase Orders report shows the purchase order number, date, and amount for each vendor.

▨ **ACTION:** To see the actual purchase order for Storage Systems, Inc., point to the listing for the vendor/purchase order you want to display. Your mouse pointer will turn into a magnifying glass with a + in it as shown below:

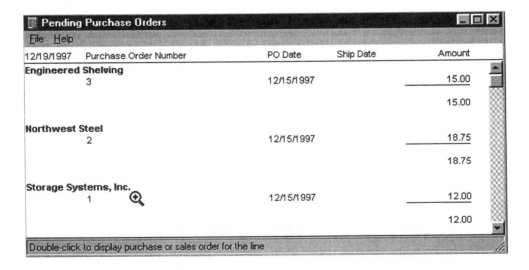

▨ **ACTION:** With the mouse pointer shown as a magnifying glass, double-click anywhere on the purchase order for Storage Systems, Inc. You will get the following purchase order displayed on the screen:

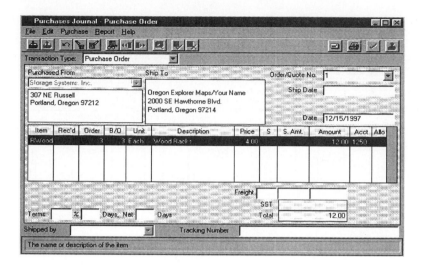

ACTION: Now that you have verified the purchase order for the invoice received, close Purchase Order 1 and the Pending Purchase Order report by clicking the close button for each. Double-click the **Purchases, Orders & Quotes** icon. Select **Purchase Order** as the transaction type. Click the drop-down list arrow next to **Order/Quote No**. Your screen will show the following:

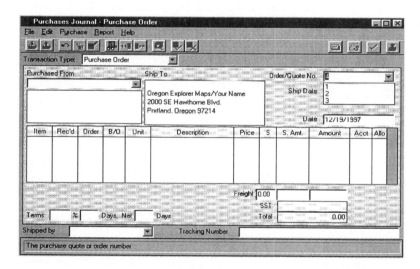

ACTION: Click **1** to select Purchase Order 1 and press the TAB key. Your screen will appear as follows:

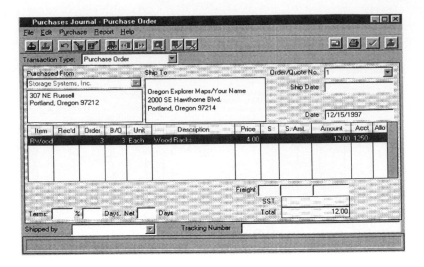

Explanation: The original purchase order is displayed on the screen. Notice that the vendor name is in a light gray color.

ACTION: With Purchase Order 1 on the screen, change the transaction type to Purchase on Account by clicking the drop-down list arrow next to **Transaction Type**. Enter Invoice Number *7810-3* in the invoice text box. Change the date to *12/16/1997*. Make sure the check box for Invoice Received has a check mark in it. Your screen will show the following:

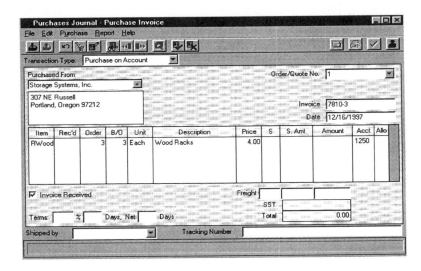

ACTION: TAB to or click in the **Rec'd** column. Enter *3* as the number of items received. Your screen will look like the following:

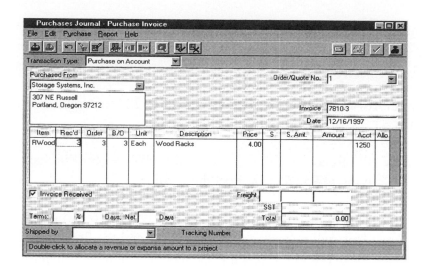

ACTION: Press the TAB key. Your screen will show the following:

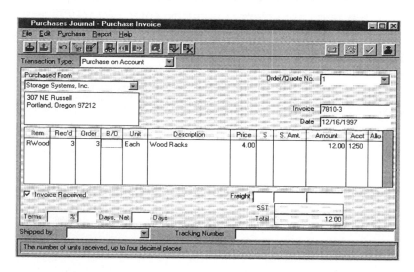

Explanation: Notice the amount in the **B/O** (back-ordered) column is removed. This indicates that the order has been received in full. If you received a partial shipment of your order, you would enter the number you received in the **Rec'd** column and enter the number still on order in the **B/O** column. An alternate method to use when the purchase order items are received in full is to click the **Fill Back Ordered Quantities** button. This will enter the number (3) listed in the **B/O** column into the **Rec'd** column and clear the **B/O** column.

ACTION: Make sure everything has been entered correctly. When everything is correct, click the **Post** button to post the transaction. When you get the following screen, click **OK.**

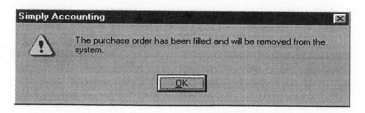

Additional Purchase Order Receipt of Merchandise Transactions

Record the following additional purchase order receipt of merchandise transactions:

Document 46 December 16—Record the receipt of Invoice 2122 for Purchase Order 2 for 5 wire racks from Northwest Steel at $3.75 each. Post invoice.

Document 47 December 19—Record the receipt of Invoice 003-295 for Purchase Order 3 for 3 plastic racks from Engineered Shelving at $5.00 each. Post the invoice.

ACTION: After recording the journal entries for Documents 46 and 47, close the Purchases Journal dialog box. This will restore the home window and the Purchases Journal icon will remain highlighted. With the Purchases Journal icon highlighted, select **Journal Entries and Purchases** from the home window Report menu. After you select Purchases, you will get the Purchases Journal Options screen.

ACTION: Select **By Date** and check the Project Allocations check box. To display only the transactions to convert purchase orders to invoices, enter *12/15/1997* as the start date; leave the finish date set at 12/19/1997; then click the **OK** button. The following Purchases Journal Display will appear on your screen:

Purchases Journal Display				
File Help				
12/15/1997 to 12/19/1997		Debits	Credits	Project
12/16/1997 J43	7810-3, Storage Systems, Inc.			
	1250 Rack Inventory	12.00	-	
	2200 Accounts Payable	-	12.00	
12/16/1997 J44	2122, Northwest Steel			
	1250 Rack Inventory	18.75	-	
	2200 Accounts Payable	-	18.75	
12/19/1997 J45	003-295, Engineered Shelving			
	1250 Rack Inventory	15.00	-	
	2200 Accounts Payable	-	15.00	
		45.75	45.75	

Explanation: Review the display for accuracy verifying that journal entry dates, vendor names, invoice numbers, account names and numbers, and amounts are correct.

ACTION: After reviewing the above report, you realize the date for Engineered Shelving should have been 12/16/1997. Follow the steps provided earlier in the chapter to correct the invoice. When the error has been corrected, prepare a new Purchases Journal Display report. It should look like the following:

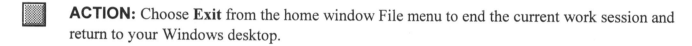

Purchases Journal Display			Debits	Credits	Project
File Help					
12/15/1997 to 12/19/1997			Debits	Credits	Project
12/16/1997	J43	7810-3, Storage Systems, Inc.			
		1250 Rack Inventory	12.00	-	
		2200 Accounts Payable	-	12.00	
12/16/1997	J44	2122, Northwest Steel			
		1250 Rack Inventory	18.75	-	
		2200 Accounts Payable	-	18.75	
12/19/1997	J45	003-295, Engineered Shelving			
		1250 Rack Inventory	15.00	-	
		2200 Accounts Payable	-	15.00	
12/19/1997	J46	ADJ003-295, Reversing J45. Correction is J47.			
		2200 Accounts Payable	15.00	-	
		1250 Rack Inventory	-	15.00	
12/16/1997	J47	003-295, Engineered Shelving			
		1250 Rack Inventory	15.00	-	
		2200 Accounts Payable	-	15.00	
			75.75	75.75	

Double-click to display Vendor or Customer Aged Report or Employee Report

ACTION: Print the Purchases Journal by choosing **Print** from the Purchases Journal Display **File** menu. Compare your report to the one shown above.

ACTION: Choose **Exit** from the home window File menu to end the current work session and return to your Windows desktop.

ALTERNATIVE ACTION: You can continue with the tutorial without exiting from the program if you wish. The next steps are recorded under the same session date as the prior steps. Skip the next ACTION; then continue with the tutorial.

PAYMENTS JOURNAL—RECORDING PAYMENTS TO CREDIT VENDORS

Payments made on outstanding invoices are recorded in the Payments Journal. Oregon Explorer Maps needs to issue a check to Edwards Business Supply for an outstanding invoice as described in the following memo.

Oregon Explorer Maps—Document 48   **Session Date: 12/19/1997**

Memo   **Date:** December 16, 1997

Pay Edwards Business Supply's Invoice 27361 in the amount of $57.60.

ACTION: Load CA-Simply Accounting for Windows; open the data files for Oregon Explorer Maps (A:\EXPLORER\Explorer.asc); then leave the session date set at 12/19/1997. The Oregon

Explorer Maps' home window will appear. Open the Payments Journal dialog box by double-clicking the **Payment Checks** icon on the home window. When the Payments Journal appears, click the drop-down list arrow to the right of the **To the order of** field; then select **Edwards Business Supply** from the vendor list. Your screen will look like this:

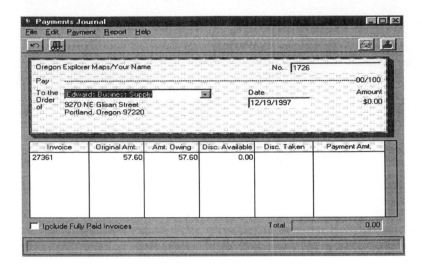

Explanation: The program has automatically filled in the vendor's address in the **To the order of** field. The invoice number and amount of Oregon Explorer Maps' outstanding invoice with Edwards Business Supply is automatically listed in the lower part of the Payments Journal dialog box. The **Invoice** field lists the vendor's invoice number; the **Original Amt.** (original amount) field shows the invoice amount; and the **Amt. Owing** (amount owing) field shows the unpaid portion of the invoice. The **No.** (number) field is also completed automatically. Oregon Explorer Maps has elected to use the CA-Simply Accounting for Windows automatic check preparation and numbering feature. Check number 1726 represents the next check in the automatic sequence.

 ACTION: Highlight the **Date** field; enter *12/16/1997*; press the TAB key; then press the TAB key until the exact amount of the outstanding balance of Invoice 27361 is shown as the payment amount. Your screen will look like this:

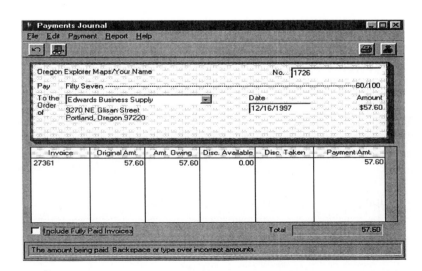

Explanation: This completes the data you need to enter into the Payments Journal dialog box to issue a check to Edwards Business Supply. Before you print the check and post this entry, you need to verify that the transaction data are correct by viewing the journal entry.

 ACTION: Choose **Display Payments Journal Entry** from the Payments Journal Report menu. Your screen will look like this:

Payments Journal Entry			_ □ ⊠
File Help			
12/16/1997	Debits	Credits	Project
2200 Accounts Payable	57.60	-	
1060 Cash	-	57.60	
	57.60	57.60	

Explanation: The journal entry reflecting the information you have recorded in the Payments Journal dialog box is displayed. The integration/linking feature of CA-Simply Accounting for Windows has created the standard journal entry for the payment of an outstanding invoice:

	Debit	**Credit**
Accounts Payable	xxx	
Cash		xxx

Note that the **Allo** column is not available in the Payments Journal. Project allocations can be made only to revenue and expense accounts. This transaction uses Accounts Payable, which is a liability account, and Cash, which is an asset account.

Review the journal entry for accuracy noting any errors.

 ACTION: Close the Payments Journal Entry window to return to the Payments Journal. If you have made an error, use the following editing techniques to correct the error:

Editing Tips
Editing a Payments Journal Entry

Move to the field that contains the error by either pressing the TAB key to move forward through each field or the SHIFT and TAB keys together to move to a previous field. This will highlight the field information so that you can change it. Alternatively, you can use the mouse to point to a field and drag through the incorrect information to highlight it.

Type the correct information; then press the TAB key to enter it.

If you have associated the transaction with an incorrect vendor, select the correct vendor from the vendor list display after clicking on the arrow button to the right of the **To the order of** field. You will be asked to confirm that you want to discard the current transaction. Click on the **Yes** button to discard the incorrect entry and display the outstanding invoices for the correct vendor.

To completely discard an entry and start over, either choose **Undo Entry** from the Payments Journal Edit menu, or double-click on the control menu box. Click on the **Yes** button in response to the question "Are you sure you want to discard this journal entry?"

Review the journal entry for accuracy after any corrections by choosing **Display Payments Journal Entry** from the Payments Journal Report menu.

It is IMPORTANT TO NOTE that the only way to edit a transaction after it is posted is to reverse the entry and enter the correct transaction. To correct transactions posted in error, see the transaction for Metro Graphics later in this chapter.

 ACTION: After verifying that the journal entry is correct, choose **Print** from the Payments Journal File menu. Compare your check to the one shown below:

Oregon Explorer Maps/Your Name
2000 SE Hawthorne Blvd.
Portland, Oregon 97214   1726

Fifty Seven ---60/100

                                            12/16/1997 $**********57.60
Edwards Business Supply
9270 NE Glisan Street
Portland, Oregon 97220

Oregon Explorer Maps/Your Name

Edwards Business Supply   12/16/1997   1726

27361..................................57.60

Explanation: Verify that the check is correct. If you detect an error, refer to the Editing Tips for Editing a Payments Journal Entry, which appears in a special box earlier in this chapter, for information on corrective action.

If you have made a mistake on the check, you can correct the payment information and print a new check. The program does not make any journal entries when it prints checks, so printing copies of the same check does not affect the company's records or the check numbers of subsequent checks. For the purposes of this text, you may destroy incorrect checks; however, in an actual business situation incorrect checks would be retained as an internal control measure.

 ACTION: After a correct check is printed, click the **Post** button to post this transaction. A blank Payments Journal dialog box is displayed, ready for additional Payments Journal transactions to be recorded.

Additional Cash Payments Transactions

Record the following additional cash payments transactions:

Document 49 December 16—Pay Invoice 382087 from Metro Graphics in the amount of $16,000.00. Print Check 1727.

Document 50 December 15—Pay Invoice 5621 from Storage Systems, Inc., in the amount of $250.00. Print Check 1728.

Compare your checks to the ones shown below:

Oregon Explorer Maps/Your Name
2000 SE Hawthorne Blvd.
Portland, Oregon 97214   1727

Sixteen Thousand --00/100

                                                12/16/1997 $***********16,000.00

Metro Graphics
1726 SW Parkway
Portland, Oregon 97219

Oregon Explorer Maps/Your Name

Metro Graphics   12/16/1997   1727

            Discount   Amount Paid
382087... 16,000.00
33-1057................0.75...........................0.00

Explanation: If you TAB to Invoice 33-1057, the cursor will be positioned in the **Discount** column. Even though you do not enter a payment, the invoice and the discount amount appear on the printed check as shown above. You can avoid this if you TAB to enter the payment for Invoice 382087, delete the discount amount for Invoice 33-1057, and then position the cursor back on the amount paid (16,000.00) for Invoice 382087. If you do this, make sure the total still appears as $16,000.00.

Oregon Explorer Maps/Your Name
2000 SE Hawthorne Blvd.
Portland, Oregon 97214   1728

Two Hundred Fifty ---00/100

                                            12/16/1997 $**********250.00

Storage Systems Inc.
307 NE Russell
Portland, Oregon 97212

Oregon Explorer Maps/Your Name

Storage Systems Inc.   12/16/1997   1728

5621...................................250.00

 ACTION: After you have printed the checks and posted the journal entries associated with Documents 49 and 50, you realize that Check 1727 to Metro Graphics should be for $16,742.00. In the Payments Journal, click the drop-down list arrow for **To the Order of** and click **Metro Graphics** to select the vendor. Enter *1727 COR* as the number. Change the date to 12/16/1997. Your screen will appear as follows:

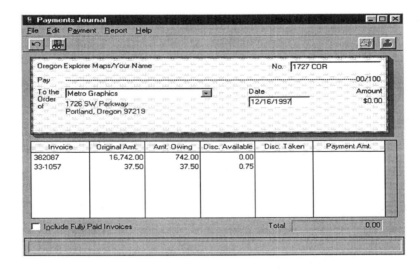

Explanation: Entering the check number of the incorrect transaction followed by COR represents the fact that this is a correcting entry. The letters ADJ could also be used next to the check number.

 ACTION: TAB to or click in the **Payment Amt** column for Invoice 382087. To correct the amount, key in the wrong amount preceded by a minus sign (*-16,000.00*). TAB to enter the amount as the total. Your screen should look like the following:

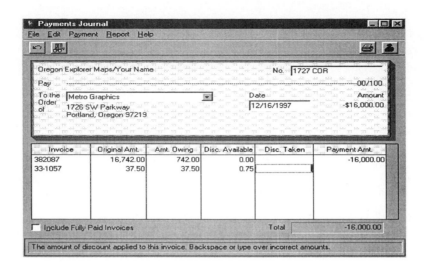

ACTION: Click **Report, Display Payments Journal Entry**. Your screen should show the following report:

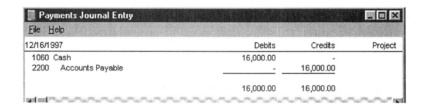

Explanation: The correcting entry for Check 1727 should show a debit to Cash and a credit to Accounts Payable for $16,000.00.

ACTION: If your report appears as the above, close the Payments Journal Entry report. Click the **Post** button to post. Enter the original transaction correctly with a check number of *1727 C* and an amount of *$16,742.00*. Print the corrected check. Click **OK** if you get the following error message:

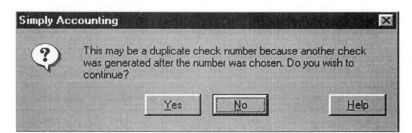

Explanation: The letter C (or some other designation representing a corrected transaction) must be added to the number. Otherwise, you will not be able to print the corrected check. If you are using prenumbered checks, you will want to use the next available check number for the correction.

ACTION: Compare your check with the one shown below:

Oregon Explorer Maps/Your Name
2000 SE Hawthorne Blvd.
Portland, Oregon 97214   1727C

Sixteen Thousand Seven Hundred Forty Two--00/100

                                                              12/16/1997 $*******16,742.00

Metro Graphics
1726 SW Parkway
Portland, Oregon 97219

Oregon Explorer Maps/Your Name

Metro Graphics   12/16/1997   1727C

                        Discount   Amount Paid
382087...16,742.00
33-1057.............................0.75............................0.00

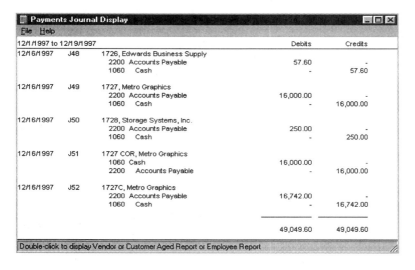 **ACTION:** If the check is correct, post the transaction, close the Payments Journal, and print the Payments Journal report for 12/1/1997 to 12/19/1997. Compare your report with the one shown below:

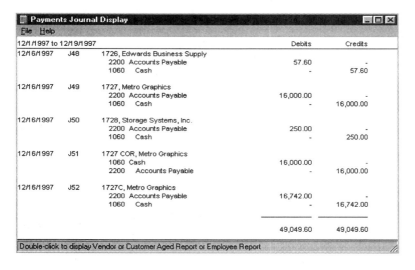

 ACTION: If your report is correct, print the Payments Journal. Close the Payments Journal Display and return to the home window.

PURCHASES AND PAYMENTS JOURNALS—RECORDING PURCHASE DISCOUNTS

Vendors sometimes offer special payment terms as an incentive for early payment of invoices. Several invoices with terms allowing for early payment discounts were entered earlier in the chapter. Canyon Litho gave the terms of 2/10, n/30, which means that these terms allow Oregon Explorer Maps to reduce the cost of the merchandise purchased by 2% if payment is received within 10 days of the invoice date. Oregon Explorer Maps has a policy of taking advantage of all purchase discounts offered.

Oregon Explorer Maps—Document 51   **Session Date: 12/19/1997**

Memo   **Date:** December 16, 1997

Pay Canyon Litho's Invoice 98726 in the amount of $540.00. Be sure to take the $10.80 discount.

ACTION: Open the Payments Journal by double-clicking the **Payment Checks** icon on the home window. Click the drop-down list arrow for **Pay to the Order of** and select **Canyon Litho.** Accept the default check number (1729) and change the date to *12/16/1997*. Your screen should show the following:

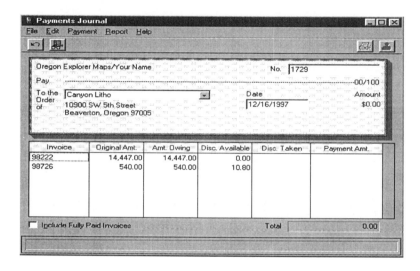

ACTION: Click in the **Disc. Taken** column for Invoice 98726. TAB two times to insert the payment amount into the **Payment Amt.** column and for the total. Your screen will look like this:

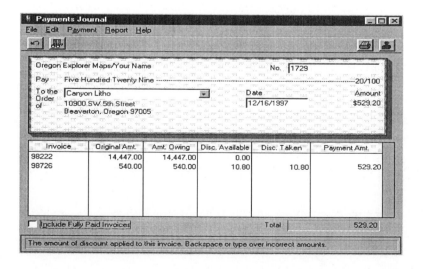

Explanation: Once you click in the **Disc. Taken** field, Simply automatically subtracts the amount of the discount, and when you TAB to **Payment Amt.**, Simply inserts the amount of the check (amount owing minus the discount).

ACTION: Display the Payments Journal Entry following the instructions given earlier in the chapter. Your screen should show the following:

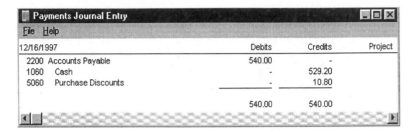

Explanation: The invoice has been paid in full so Accounts Payable is debited for the full amount ($540.00) owed, Cash is credited for the actual amount of the check ($529.20), and Purchase Discounts is credited for the amount of the discount ($10.80).

ACTION: Check your entries. Close the Payments Journal Entry report. Make any corrections necessary to the check. When everything is correct, print the check. Click **OK** when you see the following screen.

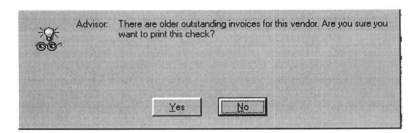

Explanation: Normally, a business will pay its oldest invoices first; however, in order to take advantage of discount terms, it is possible to pay for a discounted invoice first. Remember, with terms of 2/10, you will save 2% on your purchase if you pay for the invoice within 10 days.

ACTION: When the check has been printed, post the transaction. Close the Payments Journal. Determine which invoices are eligible for discounts by selecting **Reports, Payables, Vendor Aged** from the home window. When you click **Vendor Aged**, you will get the following dialog box:

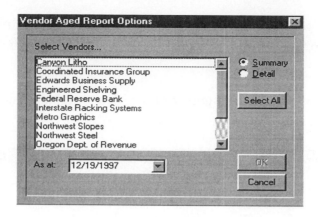

ACTION: Click **Detail** and **Select All**. Leave the as at date of 12/19/1997. Your screen will show the following:

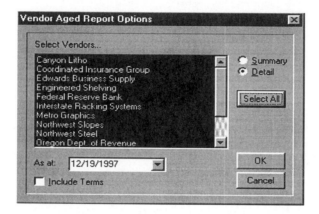

Explanation: When Detail is selected, you will notice a new check box for Include Terms. When this is selected, invoice terms will be displayed.

ACTION: Click **Include Terms** to select this option. Click the **OK** button. You will get the Vendor Aged Detail report shown below:

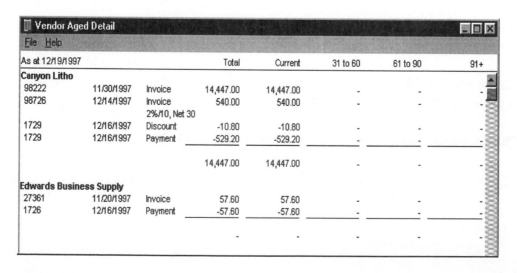

Explanation: Notice the information for Canyon Litho. Invoice 96726 shows terms of 2/10, net 30. The vendor information also shows Check 1729 with a $10.80 discount and a payment amount of $529.20.

 ACTION: Scroll through the report until you see Metro Graphics and Oregon Wine Press, as shown below:

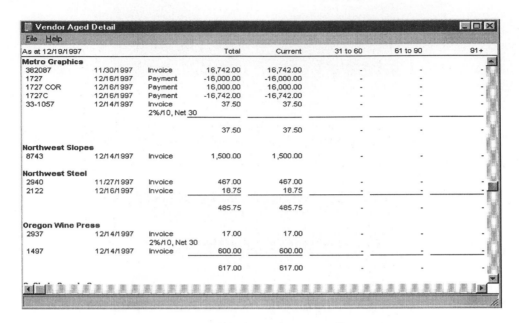

Vendor Aged Detail							
File Help							
As at 12/19/1997			Total	Current	31 to 60	61 to 90	91+
Metro Graphics							
382087	11/30/1997	Invoice	16,742.00	16,742.00	-	-	-
1727	12/16/1997	Payment	-16,000.00	-16,000.00	-	-	-
1727 COR	12/16/1997	Payment	16,000.00	16,000.00	-	-	-
1727C	12/16/1997	Payment	-16,742.00	-16,742.00	-	-	-
33-1057	12/14/1997	Invoice	37.50	37.50	-	-	-
		2%/10, Net 30					
			37.50	37.50	-	-	-
Northwest Slopes							
8743	12/14/1997	Invoice	1,500.00	1,500.00	-	-	-
Northwest Steel							
2940	11/27/1997	Invoice	467.00	467.00	-	-	-
2122	12/16/1997	Invoice	18.75	18.75	-	-	-
			485.75	485.75	-	-	-
Oregon Wine Press							
2937	12/14/1997	Invoice	17.00	17.00	-	-	-
		2%/10, Net 30					
1497	12/14/1997	Invoice	600.00	600.00	-	-	-
			617.00	617.00	-	-	-

Explanation: The two vendors showing discount terms for invoices not yet paid are Metro Graphics and Oregon Wine Press.

 ACTION: Close the Vendor Aged Detail report and return to the home window.

Additional Payment with Purchase Discounts Transactions

Record the following additional transactions:

Document 52 December 16—Record the payment of Invoice 33-1057 to Metro Graphics. Take the discount and print the check.

Document 53 December 16—Record the payment of Invoice 2937 to Oregon Wine Press. Take the discount and print the check.

PAYMENTS JOURNAL—RECORDING PAYMENTS WITH DEBIT MEMOS

When a debit memo has been prepared for merchandise returned, it is deducted from the amount paid on an invoice.

Oregon Explorer Maps—Document 54

Session Date: 12/19/1997

Memo

Date: December 16, 1997

Pay S. Glade Supply Company for Invoice 8643. Apply DM24 to this payment.

ACTION: With the Payments Journal still on the screen, click the drop-down list arrow for **To the Order of** and select **S. Glade Supply Company**. Make sure the date is 12/16/1997. Your screen will show the following:

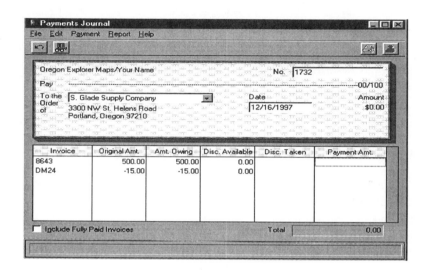

ACTION: TAB to or click **Payment Amt**. Press the TAB key two times. Your payment will look like this:

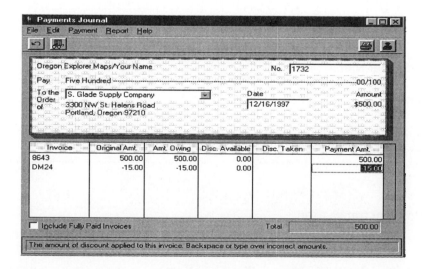

Explanation: This inserts the full payment amount as the total. The debit memo amount is highlighted but has not been deducted.

ACTION: Press the TAB key again. Simply will deduct the debit memo from the total. Your payment will look like this:

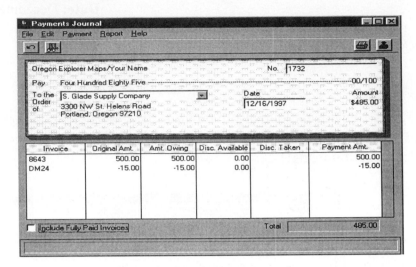

Explanation: The amount of the debit memo has been deducted from the total.

ACTION: Verify that everything entered on the check is correct. If everything is correct, print the check. It should look like the following:

Oregon Explorer Maps/Your Name
2000 SE Hawthorne Blvd.
Portland, Oregon 97214   1732

Four Hundred Eighty Five --00/100

                        12/16/1997 $*********485.00

S. Glade Supply Company
3300 NW St. Helens Road
Portland, Oregon 97210

Oregon Explorer Maps/Your Name

S. Glade Supply Company   12/16/1997   1732

8643....................................500.00
DM24...................................-15.00

ACTION: Post the transaction.

Additional Payment with Debit Memo Transactions

Record the following additional transactions:

Document 55 December 16—Pay Interstate Racking Systems for Invoice 12763. Include DM25. The total payment should be $705.00. Print the check.

Document 56 December 16—Pay Engineered Shelving for Invoice 634. Include DM26. The total payment should be $192.00. Print the check.

PAYMENTS JOURNAL—RECORDING PAYMENTS FOR LIABILITIES

Most businesses maintain current liability accounts other than Accounts Payable. For Oregon Explorer Maps, these current liability accounts include the accounts associated with payroll liabilities: FIT Payable, SIT Payable, Social Security Tax Payable, Medicare Tax Payable, FUTA Payable, SUTA Payable, and Medical Insurance Payable. CA-Simply Accounting for Windows provides a shortcut method of making payments for these types of liabilities through the Purchase with Payment transaction type in the Purchases Journal. The Purchase with Payment feature allows you to issue a check and debit a liability account other than Accounts Payable. Consequently, you need not access the Payments Journal; the complete transaction can be recorded in the Purchases Journal using the Purchase with Payment option.

Oregon Explorer Maps—Document 57   **Session Date 12/19/1997**

Memo   **Date:** December 16, 1997

Issued a check to the Federal Reserve Bank for payment of the November payroll liabilities and taxes:

FIT Payable	$ 546.31
Social Security Tax Payable	792.60
Medicare Tax Payable	185.36
	$1,524.27

ACTION: Open the Purchases Journal, click the drop-down list arrow to the right of **Transaction Type**; select **Purchase with Payment**. In the **Purchased From** field; select **Federal Reserve Bank** from the vendor list. Change the date to *12/16/1997*. Your screen will look like this:

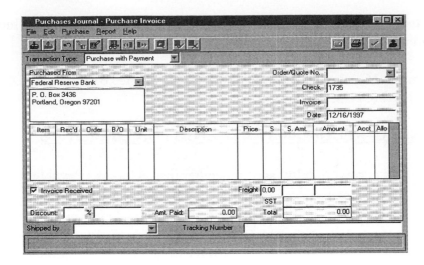

Explanation: Note that the next check number (1735) automatically appears when Purchase with Payment is selected as the transaction type.

ACTION: Enter *NovTax* into the **Invoice** field; click in the **Amount** column; enter *546.31* as the amount and press the TAB key. Your screen will look like this:

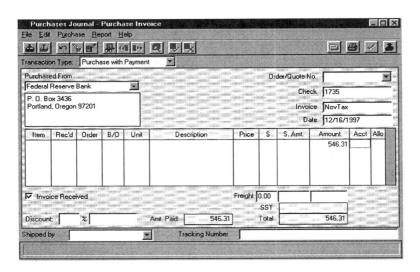

Explanation: A flashing insertion point is positioned in the **Acct** field. This is the payment of the November payroll liabilities and payroll taxes to the Federal Reserve Bank. The standard journal entry to record the payment of these liabilities is:

	Debit	**Credit**
FIT Payable	xxx	
Social Security Tax Payable	xxx	
Medicare Tax Payable	xxx	
Cash		xxx

The program will automatically credit cash through its integration/linking feature, but needs to be supplied with the appropriate account numbers for the corresponding debits to the liability accounts. This can be determined by displaying a list of accounts.

 ACTION: With the flashing insertion point positioned in the **Acct** field, press the ENTER key or double-click in the field with your mouse. Your screen will look like this:

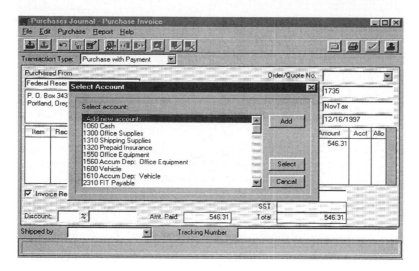

Explanation: A display listing Oregon Explorer Maps' chart of accounts will appear in the Select Account dialog box. Use this list to determine the account to be entered into the **Acct** field for the debit portions of this journal entry. If you receive an error message stating an unknown account number, click the **OK** button to display the Select Account dialog box.

 ACTION: Select **FIT Payable** (account number 2310) by double-clicking on the account or by highlighting the account and clicking the **Select** button. Your screen will look like this:

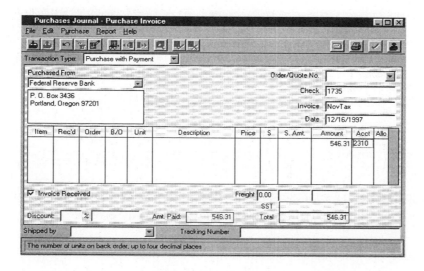

Explanation: The program automatically enters account number 2310 (FIT Payable) into the **Acct** field.

ACTION: Enter the information for payment of the other payroll liabilities. Your screen will look like this:

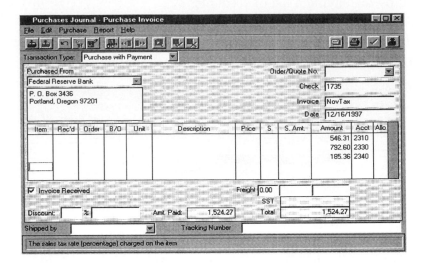

Explanation: This completes the data you need to enter into the Purchases Journal dialog box to record the payment of the payroll liabilities to the Federal Reserve Bank. Note that the **Allo** column is not used in the Purchases Journal for this transaction. Project allocations can be made only to revenue and expense accounts. This transaction involved entries to current liability accounts and to the asset account Cash.

Before printing and posting this transaction, you need to verify that the transaction data are correct by viewing the journal entry.

 ACTION: Select **Display Purchases Journal Entry** from the Purchases Journal Report menu. Compare your display to the one shown below:

Purchases Journal Entry			
File Help			
12/16/1997	Debits	Credits	Project
2310 FIT Payable	546.31	-	
2330 Social Security Tax Payable	792.60	-	
2340 Medicare Tax Payable	185.36	-	
1060 Cash	-	1,524.27	
	1,524.27	1,524.27	

Explanation: The journal entry representing the data you have recorded in the Purchases Journal dialog box is displayed. Review the journal entry for accuracy noting any errors.

 ACTION: Close the Purchases Journal Entry dialog box.

Explanation: If you have made an error, refer to the Editing Tips for Editing Inventory and Noninventory Purchases Journal Entries and Project Allocations, which appears in a special box earlier in this chapter, for information on corrective action.

ACTION: After verifying that the journal entry is correct, choose **Print** from the Purchases Journal File menu. Compare your check to the one shown below:

Oregon Explorer Maps/Your Name
2000 SE Hawthorne Blvd.
Portland, Oregon 97214   1735

One Thousand Five Hundred Twenty Four --27/100

                                                         12/16/1997 $***********1,524.27

Federal Reserve Bank
P. O. Box 3436
Portland, Oregon 97201

Oregon Explorer Maps/Your Name

Federal Reserve Bank   12/16/1997   1735

NovTax.................................1,524.27

Explanation: If you detect an error, refer to Editing Tips for Editing Inventory and Noninventory Purchases Journal Entries and Project Allocations for information on corrective action.

 ACTION: After any errors have been corrected and a correct check has been printed, click the **Post** button to post this transaction.

Explanation: A blank Purchases Journal dialog box is displayed, ready for additional Purchases Journal transactions to be recorded.

Additional Current Liability Payment Transactions

Record the following additional transactions:

Document 58 December 16—Record the payment of the SIT Payable liability of $361.62 to the Oregon Dept. of Revenue (Invoice: NovTax). Print Check 1736.

Document 59 December 16—Record the payment of the Medical Insurance Payable liability of $125.00 to Coordinated Insurance Group (Invoice: NovPrem). Print Check 1737.

If you detect an error after printing and posting a check, refer to the editing tips and error correction presented earlier in the chapter.

 ACTION: After you have printed the checks and posted the transaction information associated with Documents 58 and 59, close the Purchases Journal dialog box. This will restore the home window.

ACTION: From the home window Reports menu, select **Journal Entries** and **All**. Your screen will look like this:

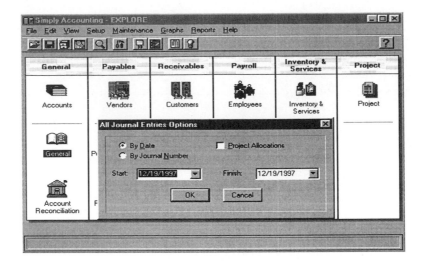

Explanation: The All Journal Entries Options dialog box appears, asking you to define the information you want displayed.

 ACTION: Select **By Date**; check the Project Allocations check box; enter *12/14/1997* as the start date; leave the finish date set at 12/19/1997; then click the **OK** button. The following Journal Display will appear on your screen:

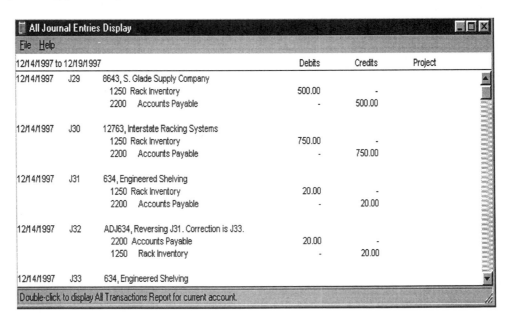

Explanation: Review the display for accuracy, verifying that journal entry dates, account names and numbers, project allocations, and amounts are correct. Use the scroll bars at the bottom and to the right of the display to advance the display. If you have posted an incorrect transaction, refer to the editing tips and error corrections presented earlier in the chapter.

▨ **ACTION:** Print the Journal by choosing **Print** from the All Journal Entries Display File menu. Compare your report to the one shown below:

Oregon Explorer Maps/Your Name
All Journal Entries 12/14/1997 to 12/19/1997

			Debits	Credits	Project
12/14/1997	J29	8643, S. Glade Supply Company			
		1250 Rack Inventory	500.00	-	
		2200 Accounts Payable	-	500.00	
12/14/1997	J30	12763, Interstate Racking Systems			
		1250 Rack Inventory	750.00	-	
		2200 Accounts Payable	-	750.00	
12/14/1997	J31	634, Engineered Shelving			
		1250 Rack Inventory	20.00	-	
		2200 Accounts Payable	-	20.00	
12/14/1997	J32	ADJ634, Reversing J31. Correction is J33.			
		2200 Accounts Payable	20.00	-	
		1250 Rack Inventory	-	20.00	
12/14/1997	J33	634, Engineered Shelving			
		1250 Rack Inventory	200.00	-	
		2200 Accounts Payable	-	200.00	
12/14/1997	J34	98726, Canyon Litho			
		1240 Attraction Map Inventory	540.00	-	
		2200 Accounts Payable	-	540.00	
12/14/1997	J35	2937, Oregon Wine Press			
		1230 Wine Map Inventory	17.00	-	
		2200 Accounts Payable	-	17.00	
12/14/1997	J36	33-1057, Metro Graphics			
		1220 Ski Map Inventory	37.50	-	
		2200 Accounts Payable	-	37.50	
12/14/1997	J37	927, The Oregon Magazine			
		5430 Advertising Expense	300.00	-	
		-Attraction Map Sales Summary			300.00
		2200 Accounts Payable	-	300.00	
12/14/1997	J38	8743, Northwest Slopes			
		5430 Advertising Expense	1,500.00	-	
		-Ski Map Sales Summary			1,500.00
		2200 Accounts Payable	-	1,500.00	
12/14/1997	J39	1497, Oregon Wine Press			
		5430 Advertising Expense	600.00	-	
		-Wine Map Sales Summary			600.00
		2200 Accounts Payable	-	600.00	

12/14/1997	J40	DM24, S. Glade Supply Company			
		2200	Accounts Payable	15.00	-
		1250	Rack Inventory	-	15.00
12/14/1997	J41	DM25, Interstate Racking Systems			
		2200	Accounts Payable	45.00	-
		1250	Rack Inventory	-	45.00
12/14/1997	J42	DM26, Engineered Shelving			
		2200	Accounts Payable	8.00	-
		1250	Rack Inventory	-	8.00
12/16/1997	J43	7810-3, Storage Systems, Inc.			
		1250	Rack Inventory	12.00	-
		2200	Accounts Payable	-	12.00
12/16/1997	J44	2122, Northwest Steel			
		1250	Rack Inventory	18.75	-
		2200	Accounts Payable	-	18.75
12/16/1997	J45	003-295, Engineered Shelving.			
		1250	Rack Inventory	15.00	-
		2200	Accounts Payable	-	15.00
12/16/1997	J46	ADJ003-295, Reversing J45. Correction is J47.			
		2200	Accounts Payable	15.00	-
		1250	Rack Inventory	-	15.00
12/16/1997	J47	003-295, Engineered Shelving.			
		1250	Rack Inventory	15.00	-
		2200	Accounts Payable	-	15.00
12/16/1997	J48	1726, Edwards Business Supply			
		2200	Accounts Payable	57.60	-
		1060	Cash	-	57.60
12/16/1997	J49	1727, Metro Graphics			
		2200	Accounts Payable	16,000.00	-
		1060	Cash	-	16,000.00
12/16/1997	J50	1728, Storage Systems Inc.			
		2200	Accounts Payable	250.00	-
		1060	Cash	-	250.00
12/16/1997	J51	1727 COR, Metro Graphics			
		1060	Cash	16,000.00	-
		2200	Accounts Payable	-	16,000.00
12/16/1997	J52	1727C, Metro Graphics			
		2200	Accounts Payable	16,742.00	-
		1060	Cash	-	16,742.00

12/16/1997	J53	1729, Canyon Litho			
		2200	Accounts Payable	540.00	-
		1060	Cash	-	529.20
		5060	Purchase Discounts	-	10.80

12/16/1997	J54	1730, Metro Graphics			
		2200	Accounts Payable	37.50	-
		1060	Cash	-	36.75
		5060	Purchase Discounts	-	0.75

12/16/1997	J55	1731, Oregon Wine Press			
		2200	Accounts Payable	17.00	-
		1060	Cash	-	16.66
		5060	Purchase Discounts	-	0.34

12/16/1997	J56	1732, S. Glade Supply Company			
		2200	Accounts Payable	485.00	-
		1060	Cash	-	485.00

12/16/1997	J57	1733, Interstate Racking Systems			
		2200	Accounts Payable	705.00	-
		1060	Cash	-	705.00

12/16/1997	J58	1734, Engineered Shelving			
		2200	Accounts Payable	192.00	-
		1060	Cash	-	192.00

12/16/1997	J59	NovTax, 1735, Federal Reserve Bank			
		2310	FIT Payable	546.31	-
		2330	Social Security Tax Payable	792.60	-
		2335	Medicare Tax Payable	185.36	-
		1060	Cash	-	1,524.27

12/15/1997	J60	NovTax, 1736, Oregon Dept. of Revenue			
		2320	SIT Payable	361.62	-
		1060	Cash	-	361.62

12/15/1997	J61	NovPrem, 1737, Coordinated Insurance Group			
		2400	Medical Insurance Payable	125.00	-
		1060	Cash	-	125.00
				57,665.24	57,665.24

Explanation: If you detect an error, refer to the materials presented earlier in the chapter for information on corrective action.

 ACTION: Close the All Journal Entries Display window; then select Payables and Vendor Aged from the home window Report menu. Your screen will look like this:

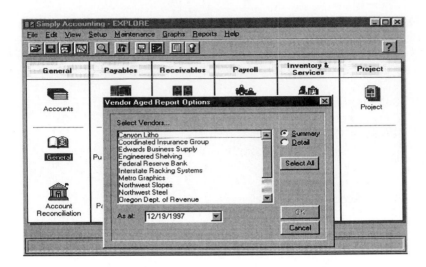

ACTION: Leave the as at date of 12/19/1997. Click **Detail**; click the **Select All** button; then click the **OK** button. Your screen will look like this:

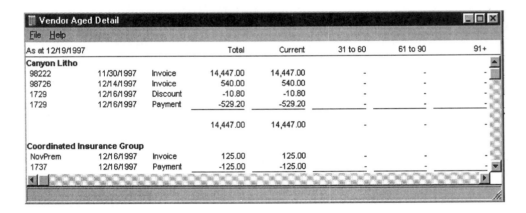

ACTION: Choose **Print** from the Vendor Aged Detail File menu. Compare your report to the one shown below:

Oregon Explorer Maps/Your Name
Vendor Aged Detail As at 12/19/1997

			Total	Current	31 to 60	61 to 90	91+
Canyon Litho							
98222	11/30/1997	Invoice	14,447.00	14,447.00	-	-	-
98726	12/14/1997	Invoice	540.00	540.00	-	-	-
1729	12/16/1997	Discount	-10.80	-10.80	-	-	-
1729	12/16/1997	Payment	-529.20	-529.20	-	-	-
			14,447.00	14,447.00	-	-	-
Coordinated Insurance Group							
NovPrem	12/16/1997	Invoice	125.00	125.00	-	-	-
1737	12/16/1997	Payment	-125.00	-125.00	-	-	-
			-	-	-	-	-

Edwards Business Supply

27361	11/20/1997	Invoice	57.60	57.60	-	-	-
1726	12/15/1997	Payment	-57.60	-57.60	-	-	-
			-	-	-	-	-

Engineered Shelving

634	12/14/1997	Invoice	200.00	200.00	-	-	-
1734	12/16/1997	Payment	-200.00	-200.00	-	-	-
DM26	12/14/1997	Invoice	-8.00	-8.00	-	-	-
1734	12/16/1997	Payment	8.00	8.00	-	-	-
003-295	12/16/1997	Invoice	15.00	15.00	-	-	-
			15.00	15.00			

Federal Reserve Bank

NovTax	12/16/1997	Invoice	1,524.27	1,524.27	-	-	-
1735	12/15/1997	Payment	-1,524.27	-1,524.27	-	-	-
			-	-	-	-	-

Interstate Racking Systems

12763	12/14/1997	Invoice	750.00	750.00	-	-	-
1733	12/16/1997	Payment	-750.00	-750.00	-	-	-
DM25	12/14/1997	Invoice	-45.00	-45.00	-	-	-
1733	12/16/1997	Payment	45.00	45.00	-	-	-
			-	-	-	-	-

Metro Graphics

382087	11/30/1997	Invoice	16,742.00	16,742.00	-	-	-
1727	12/16/1997	Payment	-16,000.00	-16,000.00	-	-	-
1727 COR	12/16/1997	Payment	16,000.00	16,000.00	-	-	-
1727C	12/16/1997	Payment	-16,742.00	16,742.00	-	-	-
33-1057	12/14/1997	Invoice	37.50	37.50	-	-	-
1730	12/16/1997	Discount	-0.75	-0.75	-	-	-
1730	12/16/1997	Payment	-36.75	-36.75	-	-	-
			-	-	-	-	-

Northwest Slopes

8743	12/14/1997	Invoice	1,500.00	1,500.00	-	-	-

Northwest Steel

2940	11/27/1997	Invoice	467.00	467.00	-	-	-
2122	12/16/1997	Invoice	18.75	18.75	-	-	-
			485.75	485.75	-	-	-

Oregon Dept. of Revenue

NovTax	12/16/1997	Invoice	361.62	361.62	-	-	-
1736	12/16/1997	Payment	-361.62	-361.62	-	-	-
			-	-	-	-	-

Oregon Wine Press

2937	12/14/1997	Invoice	17.00	17.00	-	-	-
1731	12/16/1997	Discount	-0.34	-0.34	-	-	-
1737	12/16/1997	Payment	-16.66	-16.66	-	-	-
1497	12/14/1997	Invoice	600.00	600.00	-	-	-
			-	-	-	-	-

S. Glade Supply Company

8643	12/14/1997	Invoice	500.00	500.00	-	-	-
1732	12/16/1997	Payment	-500.00	-500.00	-	-	-
DM24	12/14/1997	Invoice	-15.00	-15.00	-	-	-
1732	12/16/1997	Payment	15.00	15.00	-	-	-
			-	-	-	-	-

Storage Systems Inc.

5621	11/19/1997	Invoice	250.00	250.00	-	-	-
1728	12/16/1997	Payment	-250.00	-250.00	-	-	-
7810-3	12/16/1997	Invoice	12.00	12.00	-	-	-
			-	-			

The Oregon Magazine

927	12/14/1997	Invoice	300.00	300.00	-	-	-
			17,359.75	17,359.75	-	-	-

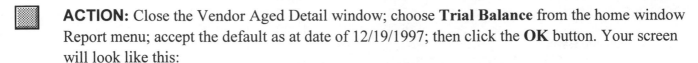 **ACTION:** Close the Vendor Aged Detail window; choose **Trial Balance** from the home window Report menu; accept the default as at date of 12/19/1997; then click the **OK** button. Your screen will look like this:

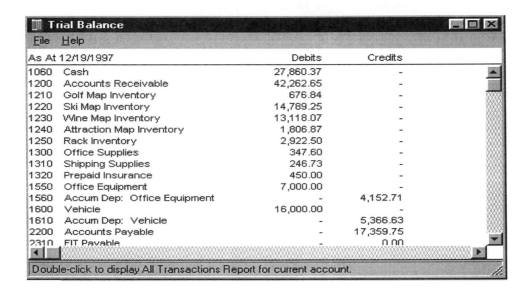

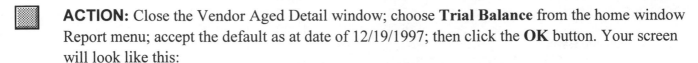 **ACTION:** Print the Trial Balance by choosing **Print** from the Trial Balance File menu. Compare your Trial Balance to the one shown below:

Oregon Explorer Maps/Your Name
Trial Balance As At 12/19/1997

		Debits	Credits
1060	Cash	27,860.37	-
1200	Accounts Receivable	42,262.65	-
1210	Golf Map Inventory	676.84	-
1220	Ski Map Inventory	14,789.25	-
1230	Wine Map Inventory	13,118.07	-
1240	Attraction Map Inventory	1,806.87	-
1250	Rack Inventory	2,922.50	-
1300	Office Supplies	347.60	-
1310	Shipping Supplies	246.73	-
1320	Prepaid Insurance	450.00	-
1550	Office Equipment	7,000.00	-
1560	Accum Dep: Office Equipment	-	4,152.71
1600	Vehicle	16,000.00	-
1610	Accum Dep: Vehicle	-	5,366.63
2200	Accounts Payable	-	17,359.75
2310	FIT Payable	-	0.00

Account	Name	Debit	Credit
2320	SIT Payable	-	0.00
2330	Social Security Tax Payable	-	0.00
2340	Medicare Tax Payable	-	0.00
2350	FUTA Payable	-	23.24
2360	SUTA Payable	-	272.64
2400	Medical Insurance Payable	-	0.00
2710	Loans Payable	-	0.00
3560	Karen Bailey, Capital	-	78,185.62
3570	Karen Bailey, Drawing	27,500.00	-
4210	Wholesale Golf Map Sales	-	8,791.59
4220	Wholesale Ski Map Sales	-	6,724.19
4230	Wholesale Wine Map Sales	-	6,634.19
4240	Wholesale Attraction Map Sales	-	22,128.97
4310	Distributor Golf Map Sales	-	43,212.79
4320	Distributor Ski Map Sales	-	37,145.84
4330	Distributor Wine Map Sales	-	36,110.84
4340	Distributor Attraction Map Sales	-	123,106.97
4410	Retail Attraction Map Sales	-	0.00
4500	Rack Sales	-	1,636.49
4600	Sales Discounts	876.46	-
4700	Sales Returns and Allowances	2,049.75	-
4810	Interest Income	-	0.00
4820	Bad Check Charges	-	25.00
5010	COGS-Golf Maps	15,714.35	-
5020	COGS-Ski Maps	15,134.38	-
5030	COGS-Wine Maps	13,580.81	-
5040	COGS-Attraction Maps	34,081.08	-
5050	COGS-Racks	1,361.50	-
5060	Purchase Discounts	-	11.89
5070	Purchase Returns and Allowances	0.00	-
5301	Wages	70,095.00	-
5310	Social Security Tax Expense	4,345.89	-
5320	Medicare Tax Expense	1,016.38	-
5330	FUTA Expense	224.00	-
5340	SUTA Expense	2,180.36	-
5400	Phone Expense	1,376.92	-
5410	Postage Expense	976.29	-
5420	Shipping Expense	18,974.32	-
5430	Advertising Expense	10,876.20	-
5440	Vehicle Expense	627.46	-
5450	Utilities Expense	1,176.42	-
5460	Rent Expense	30,000.00	-
5470	Membership and Dues Expense	973.20	-
5480	Subscription Expense	267.50	-
5490	Interest Expense: Loans	0.00	-
5500	Dep. Expense: Office Equipment	1,986.05	-
5510	Dep. Expense: Vehicle	2,566.63	-
5610	Insurance Expense	1,650.00	-
5620	Office Supplies Expense	2,219.95	-
5630	Shipping Supplies Expense	1,011.42	-
5650	Bank Service Charge Expense	295.00	-
5660	Credit Card Fees Expense	23.92	-
5800	Misc. Expense	247.23	-
		390,889.35	390,889.35

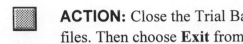 **ACTION:** Close the Trial Balance window. Make a backup copy of Oregon Explorer Maps' data files. Then choose **Exit** from the home window File menu to end the current work session and return to your Windows desktop.

SUMMARY

This chapter has explored the Payables and Project components of CA-Simply Accounting for Windows as they would typically be used by a merchandising business. Use of the Purchases and Payments Journals to record inventory and noninventory purchases, debit memos, payments for accounts payable and current liabilities, and purchase discounts have been explained in detail. By examining the methods used to record inventory-related Payables transactions, various integration/linking features of CA-Simply Accounting for Windows were illustrated.

QUESTIONS

QUESTIONS ABOUT THE SOFTWARE

1. In CA-Simply Accounting for Windows, all payables and inventory functions are fully integrated with and linked to the General Ledger. Explain this statement and give an example.

2. If you entered an incorrect inventory item number for an inventory purchase transaction prior to posting the transaction, what steps would you follow to edit the entry?

3. When an inventory item is selected from the Select Inventory Item dialog box, the program automatically enters the current average cost of the item based on the data in the Inventory Ledger into the Price field. If the transaction you are recording is the purchase of additional inventory items at a different cost than the current average cost, what steps would you take to record the new price?

4. The Payments Journal dialog box does not present an allocation column. Why?

5. Describe the process required to issue a check to a vendor within the discount period offered.

QUESTIONS ABOUT DAILY OPERATIONS

6. You would like to know the total amount currently owed to a specific vendor. How would you use the CA-Simply Accounting for Windows program to answer this question?

7. You have just received an inquiry from a vendor (Acme Inc.) regarding a check they recently received from your company. The check was received within the 2/10, net 30 discount period that they offer, but their records show that your company owes $1,176.00 rather than the $1,097.60 they received. The check stub lists the following information:

   Acme Inc.   2/28/1997   734

   1634...........................1, 200.00
   DM46.......................   -80.00
   D1634........................   -22.40

   What is the most likely explanation for the discrepancy?

8. You would like to know the total current balance in Accounts Payable. How would you use the CA-Simply Accounting for Windows program to answer your question?

9. A new part-time accountant has been hired to assist in recording accounting data in the CA-Simply Accounting for Windows program for your company. You are explaining the company's chart of accounts. The new accountant points out that the chart of accounts includes a Sales Returns and Allowances account and a Sales Discounts account, but does not include a Purchase Returns and Allowances account or a Purchase Discounts account. How would you answer her question? (**Hint:**

The new accountant's prior work experience has been with a company that uses the periodic inventory method.)

EXPLORING ALTERNATIVE SOFTWARE TECHNIQUES

10. Controlling the cost of inventory is a major concern of most merchandising businesses. An aspect of inventory cost control is the manner in which purchase discounts are recorded by a business. There are two ways of recording purchase discounts: The gross method (illustrated in this chapter) and the net method. Under the net method it is assumed that payment will be made within the discount period. Consequently, the purchase is recorded initially at the net cost rather than the gross cost. If the payment is made beyond the discount period, the cost difference is debited to an expense account titled Purchase Discounts Lost. The balance in the Purchase Discounts Lost account reflects the financial impact of overlooking a purchase discount opportunity.

The two methods can be compared as follows (3/10, net 30 terms assumed):

		Gross Method			**Net Method**		
		Debit	**Credit**		**Debit**	**Credit**
12/1/1997	Inventory	1,000.00		Inventory	970.00	
	Accounts Payable		1,000.00	Accounts Payable		970.00
	Purchased Inventory			Purchased Inventory		
12/10/1997	Accounts Payable	1,000.00		Accounts Payable	970.00	
	Cash		970.00	Cash		970.00
	Inventory		30.00			
	Paid within discount period			Paid within discount period		
12/31/1997	Accounts Payable	1,000.00		Accounts Payable	970.00	
	Cash		1,000.00	Purchase Discounts Lost	30.00	
				Cash		1,000.00
	Paid beyond discount period			Paid beyond discount period		

Discuss the advantages of Oregon Explorer Maps' using the net method, and how data entry would differ if they elected to use the net method.

TRANSMITTAL

Oregon Explorer Maps   Name: _____
Chapter 6

Attach the following documents and reports:

1. Purchases Journal 12/1/1997 to 12/19/1997
2. Purchase Order 1
3. Purchase Order 2
4. Purchase Order 3
5. Purchases Journal 12/15/1997 to 12/19/1997
6. Check 1726
7. Check 1727
8. Check 1728
9. Check 1727C
10. Payments Journal 12/1/1997 to 12/19/1997
11. Check 1729
12. Check 1730
13. Check 1731
14. Check 1732
15. Check 1733
16. Check 1734
17. Check 1735
18. Check 1736
19. Check 1737
20. All Journal Entries 12/14/1997 to 12/19/1997
21. Vendor Aged Detail report As at 12/19/1997
22. Trial Balance As at 12/19/1997

EXERCISE—Windmill Wheels
(Continued from Chapter 5)

1. Load CA-Simply Accounting for Windows; open the data files for Windmill Wheels
    (A:\WINDMILL\Windmill.acs); then record the following transactions under the session date of
    12/19/1997:

    December 14—Received Invoice M967 from Circle Cycles in the amount of $687.50 for 5 city
    bikes.

    December 15—Received Invoice 2678 from Bike and Hike, Inc., in the amount of $675.00 for
    3 mountain bikes. Terms 2/10, net 30.

    December 15—Issue Check 3467 to the Federal Reserve Bank for the payment of the November
    payroll liabilities and taxes as follows:

FIT Payable	$ 591.76
Social Security Tax Payable	830.18
Medicare Tax Payable	194.18
Total amount due	$1,616.12

    December 15—Issue Check 3468 to the Oregon Dept. of Revenue for the payment of the November
    SIT Payable in the amount of $384.79.

    December 15—Issue Check 3469 to Managed Care Inc. for the payment of the November Medical
    Insurance Payable in the amount of $125.00.

    December 15—Prepare Purchase Order 1 to Orbit Bikes for 1 tandem bike at $187.50.

    December 15—Prepare Purchase Order 2 to Bike and Hike, Inc., for 2 mountain bikes at $225
    each.

    December 17—Received Invoice 1846 from the Multnomah Village Post in the amount of $250.00
    for a branch store advertisement. (Project: Branch Store)

    December 17—Issue Debit Memo 11 in the amount of $137.50 to Circle Cycles for the return of
    1 city bike.

    December 19—Issue Check 3470 to NW Lights in full payment of Invoice K009.

    December 19—Issue Check 3471 to Bike and Hike, Inc., in the amount of $661.50 in full payment
    of Invoice 2678 less a 2% discount.

2.   Advance the session date to 12/26/1997; then record the following transactions:

December 20—Received Invoice 2701 from Hike and Bike, Inc. for the 2 mountain bikes ordered in Purchase Order 2.

December 21—Record the receipt of Invoice 8241 from Orbit Bikes for Purchase Order 1 in the amount of $187.50 for 1 tandem bike. Terms 2/10, net 30.

December 22—Received Invoice 6273 from Northwest Review in the amount of $500.00 for main store advertising. (Project: Main Store)

December 23—Issued Debit Memo 12 to Bike and Hike, Inc., in the amount of $225.00 for the return of 1 mountain bike.

December 26—Issue Check 3472 to Orbit Bikes in the amount of $183.75 in payment of Invoice 8241 less a 2% discount.

December 26—Issue Check 3473 to West Telephone in full payment of their Invoice L4560.

3.   Print the following reports:

A. All Journal Entries (Project allocations) 12/14/1997 to 12/26/1997
B. Vendor Aged report (Select All, Detail, Include Terms) As at 12/26/1997
C. Trial Balance As at 12/26/1997

4.   Make a backup copy of Windmill Wheels' data files. Exit from the program. Complete the Windmill Wheels Transmittal.

TRANSMITTAL

Windmill Wheels   **Name:** _____
Chapter 6

A. Attach the following documents and reports:

1. Check 3467
2. Check 3468
3. Check 3469
4. Purchase Order 1
5. Purchase Order 2
6. Check 3470
7. Check 3471
8. Check 3472
9. Check 3473
10. All Journal Entries 12/14/1997 to 12/26/1997
11. Vendor Aged Detail report As at 12/26/1997
12. Trial Balance As at 12/26/1997

B. Refer to your reports to list the amounts requested below:

1. How much does Windmill Wheels owe Circle Cycle on 12/26/1997? $_____

2. How much does Windmill Wheels owe Bike and Hike, Inc., on 12/26/1997? $_____

3. What is the balance of the Cash account on 12/26/1997? $_____

4. What is the balance of the Accounts Payable account on 12/26/1997? $_____

5. What is the balance of the Inventory account on 12/26/1997? $_____

MERCHANDISING BUSINESSES— PAYROLL

MERCHANDISING BUSINESSES— PAYROLL

LEARNING OBJECTIVES

After studying this chapter, you will be able to:
- Open the Payroll Journal
- Enter payroll transactions and issue payroll checks
- Review and edit Payroll Journal transactions
- Post payroll transactions in the Payroll Journal
- Create, modify, and remove employee records using the Payroll Ledger
- Display and print payroll-related reports
- Observe and understand payroll-related integration/linking accounts

AUTOMATING PAYROLL

Payroll is one of the oldest and most useful applications of computers in business. Employers must maintain a detailed and accurate payroll accounting system for three reasons. First, businesses must be able to collect the data necessary to compute the compensation and payroll deductions for each employee each payroll period. Second, businesses must be able to generate the information needed to complete the various governmental reports that are required of all employers. Third, businesses must remit employee payroll deductions and payroll taxes on a periodic basis as specified by law. In order to accomplish these payroll activities, payroll information must be maintained for both the business as a whole and for individual employees. Governmental agencies require businesses to withhold taxes from employees' compensation, remit payments on a timely basis, and submit reports on a periodic basis. Specific penalties are imposed on employers if these requirements are not met. Clearly, the increased speed and accuracy of a computerized payroll system can assist an organization in meeting its payroll responsibilities.

ACCOUNTING FOR PAYROLL

The various types of payroll information that must be maintained by a business are best explained by the two journal entries required to record payroll. The first journal entry records the wage or salary expense to the employer, and the second records the payroll taxes assessed on the employer:

Employee Payroll Entry—To record an employee's gross pay, taxes withheld, and net pay:

	Debit	Credit
Wages	xxx	
FIT Payable		xxx
SIT Payable		xxx
Social Security Tax Payable		xxx
Medicare Tax Payable		xxx

Other Deductions Payable	xxx	
Cash (net pay)	xxx	

Employer Payroll Entry—To record an employer's obligation for payroll taxes:

	Debit	**Credit**
Social Security Tax Expense	xxx	
Medicare Tax Expense	xxx	
FUTA Expense	xxx	
SUTA Expense	xxx	
Social Security Tax Payable		xxx
Medicare Tax Payable		xxx
FUTA Payable		xxx
SUTA Payable		xxx

Employee Payroll Entry

Wages: Wages represent all taxable earnings of the employee. Depending on the type of business, wages may include salaries, regular and overtime pay to hourly employees, tips, commissions, taxable benefits, vacation pay, or other income categories defined by the employer. The amount debited to the Wages account represents the gross pay of the employee.

FIT Payable: Federal income tax (FIT) is the amount of tax that must be withheld from an employee's wages based on the employee's rate of pay, frequency of payment, marital status, and withholding allowances claimed. The employer determines wages and the frequency of payment. The employee reports his or her marital status and number of withholding allowances claimed to the employer on Federal Form W-4. Amounts withheld from employee wages for FIT must be remitted on a timely, periodic basis and reported quarterly on Federal Form 941. The total of an employee's earnings and deductions for the year must be reported annually to the federal government and to the employee on Federal Form W-2.

SIT Payable: State income tax (SIT) is the amount of tax that must be withheld from an employee's wages based on the income tax statutes of a specific state. Amounts withheld from employee wages for SIT must be remitted periodically to the state and reported periodically (usually quarterly) to the state assessing the tax.

Social Security Tax Payable: Sometimes called FICA, Social Security tax is assessed on the taxable gross earnings of an employee at a certain rate and up to a certain amount of maximum gross earnings each year. The Social Security tax rate and maximum gross earnings subject to the tax are set by Congress and are subject to frequent change. Social Security tax must be withheld from the employee's wages and matched on a dollar-for-dollar basis by the employer. Social Security tax withheld from an employee's wages plus the employer's matching contribution must be remitted with FIT on a timely basis and reported quarterly on Federal Form 941.

Medicare Tax Payable: Medicare tax is assessed on the taxable gross earnings of an employee at a specified rate. The Medicare tax rate is set by Congress. Medicare tax must be withheld from the employee's wages and matched on a dollar-for-dollar basis by the employer. Medicare tax withheld from an employee's wages plus the employer's matching contribution must be remitted with Social Security tax and FIT on a timely basis and reported quarterly on Federal Form 941.

Other Deductions Payable: Other deductions, usually voluntary in nature, are designated by the employee and may include deductions for such items as union dues or medical and dental insurance premiums. Reporting and remittance responsibilities for other deductions vary on an item-by-item basis.

Cash: The credit to cash represents the net pay to the employee after the required and other deductions have been subtracted from the employee's gross wages for the pay period.

Employer Payroll Entry

The Employer Payroll Entry records the taxes assessed directly on the employer for the pay period. Payroll taxes represent an expense to the business above and beyond the wages paid to employees. Employer payroll taxes include the employer's matching contribution for Social Security tax and Medicare tax as well as federal and state unemployment taxes. Federal unemployment taxes are the sole responsibility of the employer; they are not deducted from employee earnings. Depending on the state, state unemployment taxes may be either an employee deduction or an employer payroll tax expense. In Oregon, state unemployment taxes are an employer payroll tax expense.

Social Security Tax Expense: Social Security tax expense represents the employer's matching contribution for the employee's Social Security tax.

Medicare Tax Expense: Medicare tax expense represents the employer's matching contribution for the employee's Medicare tax.

FUTA Expense: Federal unemployment tax (FUTA) is levied on employers to finance the federal unemployment compensation program. Only employers are subject to this tax; it is not deducted from an employee's gross earnings. As in the case of Social Security tax, FUTA tax is imposed at a specified rate on a specified employee earnings base and is subject to modification by Congress. FUTA taxes must be remitted on a periodic basis and reported annually on Federal Form 940.

SUTA Expense: In some states, state unemployment tax (SUTA) is an employee deduction; however, in most states, SUTA is assessed directly on employers for the purpose of paying unemployment compensation benefits. In Oregon, SUTA is an employer expense. As in the case of FUTA, SUTA tax payments are the responsibility of the employer and are not deducted from employee earnings. There is considerable variation among the states concerning the tax rate and employee earnings base subject to the tax and methods of collection. Each state has established guidelines for when this tax must be remitted and when reports must be submitted.

From the previous discussion, it is clear that a payroll system must be able to maintain payroll information in a variety of formats in order to issue accurate payroll checks, remit deductions and payroll taxes on a timely basis, and prepare the various governmental payroll reports. Payroll records must be maintained for each employee in order to prepare accurate payroll checks and to produce the annual W-2 forms. In addition, payroll records must be maintained for the entire company in order to remit the amounts for FIT, SIT, SUTA, FUTA, Social Security tax, and Medicare tax on timely basis. Finally, payroll records must be maintained on a quarterly and annual basis to facilitate the preparation of Federal Forms 941 and 940 and to meet the quarterly and annual filing requirements of the state for SIT and SUTA taxes.

All payroll functions in CA-Simply Accounting for Windows are fully integrated/linked with the General Ledger. For example, when a payroll check is recorded in the Payroll Journal dialog box, the program automatically records the entry in the Payroll Journal, posts the related accounts in the General Ledger, and updates the employee's record in the Payroll ledger. Consequently, once a payroll-related transaction is posted, its effect on the overall financial condition of the company is reflected immediately and automatically throughout the company's financial records.

OREGON EXPLORER MAPS TUTORIAL

The Payroll components of the CA-Simply Accounting for Windows program are designed to meet all of the payroll record-keeping responsibilities required by law. The Oregon Explorer Maps Tutorial is continued in this chapter to demonstrate the use of the Payroll components of the program.

PAYROLL JOURNAL—RECORDING PAYROLL CHECKS

Oregon Explorer Maps' payroll information for employee Joyce Graham's December payroll check is summarized in the following memo:

Oregon Explorer Maps—Document 60   **Session Date: 12/31/1997**

Memo: **Date:** December 31, 1997

Issue a payroll check to Joyce Graham for her regular salary, deducting $25.00 for medical insurance. Print Check 1738.

ACTION: Load CA-Simply Accounting for Windows; open the data files for Oregon Explorer Maps (A:\EXPLORE\Explore.asc); then advance the session date to 12/31/1997. If you get the following screen, click **OK.**

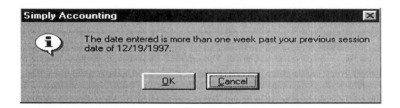

ACTION: The Oregon Explorer Maps home window will appear as shown below:

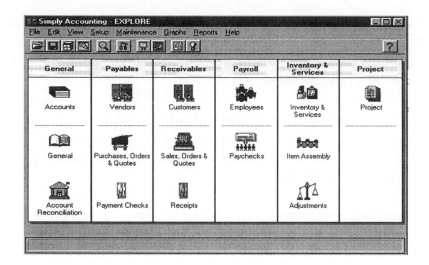

▦ **ACTION:** Open the Payroll Journal by double-clicking the **Paychecks** icon on the home window. Click the drop-down list arrow to the right of the **To the Order of** field; select **Joyce Graham** from the employee list; press the TAB key. Your screen will show the following:

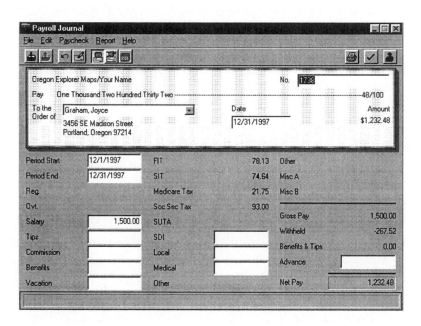

Explanation: Oregon Explorer Maps has elected to use the CA-Simply Accounting for Windows automatic payroll calculation and payroll check printing features. When these features are selected, the program calculates and fills in most of the payroll information automatically.

No.: The next check number in the program's automatic check sequence is displayed.

Date: The session date is displayed, which also represents the posting date for this payroll period.

Period Start: This is the starting date of the pay period to be covered by this payroll check.

Period End: This is the ending date of the pay period covered by this payroll check.

Reg.: For employees who are paid on an hourly basis, this field will be activated. Enter the number of regular hours worked in the first field. The program multiplies this number by the regular hourly rate stored in the employee's record in the Payroll Ledger, then displays the amount in the second field when you move the insertion point to another field.

Ovt.: For employees who are paid on an hourly basis, this field will be activated. Enter the number of overtime hours worked in the first field. The program multiplies this number by the overtime hourly rate stored in the employee's record in the Payroll Ledger, then displays the amount in the second field when you move the insertion point to another field.

Salary: This field is completed automatically for salaried employees based on the salary amount stored in the employee's record in the Payroll Ledger.

Tips: Enter the amount of tips reported by the employee for the pay period. The program adds the value of the tips to any other earnings for the pay period and calculates taxes on the total; however, because the employer does not pay the tips, the tips are deducted from the gross pay before calculating the net pay.

Commission: Enter the amount of commission to be paid to the employee for the pay period.

Benefits: Enter the amount of taxable benefits received by the employee during the pay period. The program adds the value of the benefits to the gross pay before calculating taxes; however, because benefits are not paid in cash, they are deducted from the gross pay before calculating the net pay.

Vacation: Enter the amount of vacation pay for this pay period.

FIT: The program automatically calculates this amount using the current FIT rate.

SIT: The program automatically calculates this amount using the current SIT rate.

Medicare Tax: The program automatically calculates this amount using the current Medicare tax rate.

Soc Sec Tax: The program automatically calculates this amount using the current Social Security tax rate.

SUTA: In some states, SUTA is an employee deduction rather than an employer expense. In states in which SUTA is an employee deduction, the program automatically calculates this amount using the current state rate. This field is not accessible in states in which SUTA is an employer expense. SUTA is an employer expense in Oregon and therefore is not accessible.

SDI: Enter the amount of state disability insurance (SDI) premiums the employee owes (if any) for this pay period. If the employer pays the SDI premium (as Oregon Explorer Maps does), enter zero or leave this field blank.

Local: Enter the amount of any local income tax to be withheld from the employee for the pay period.

Medical, Other, Other, Misc A, Misc B: Enter the amount of the medical insurance premiums to be withheld from the employee for the pay period and any other deductions requested. The program calculates the taxes payable before deducting these amounts from gross income as required by the Internal Revenue Service.

Gross Pay, Withheld, Benefits, and Tips: These fields summarize the payroll information entered and cannot be changed directly.

Advance: Enter the amount advanced to the employee. The program does not calculate tax or deductions on advances. When the advance is paid back, enter a negative amount in this field; the program will deduct this amount from the employee's net payroll check (after taxes have been calculated) and reduce the advances paid amount in the employee's record in the Payroll Ledger.

Net Pay: The net amount of the payroll check the employee will receive.

ACTION: Click in the **Medical** field; enter *25.00*; and press the TAB key. Your screen will show the following:

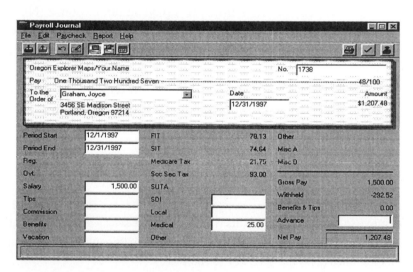

Explanation: This completes the data that you need to enter into the Payroll Journal dialog box to record Joyce Graham's December earnings and print her paycheck. Oregon Explorer Maps does not allocate payroll entries to projects. Due to the nature of each employee's duties and the way in which the company uses the Project component of CA-Simply Accounting for Windows, Oregon Explorer Maps does not find it useful to allocate payroll entries.

For businesses that choose to allocate payroll amounts to projects, the procedures used to record distributions are identical to those used in the Purchases and Sales Journals. After clicking the **Allocate** button, select the Project; then allocate the amount or percentage desired. CA-Simply Accounting for Windows also permits the distribution of payroll amounts by employee hours if a business finds this method useful.

Before you print the payroll check and post this entry, you need to verify that the transaction data are correct by viewing the journal entry.

ACTION: Choose **Display Payroll Journal Entry** from the Payroll Journal Report menu. Your screen will show the following:

12/31/1997		Debits	Credits	Project
5301	Wages	1,500.00	-	
5310	Social Security Tax Expense	93.00	-	
5320	Medicare Tax Expense	21.75	-	
5340	SUTA Expense	52.50	-	
1060	Cash	-	1,207.48	
2310	FIT Payable	-	78.13	
2320	SIT Payable	-	74.64	
2330	Social Security Tax Payable	-	186.00	
2340	Medicare Tax Payable	-	43.50	
2360	SUTA Payable	-	52.50	
2400	Medical Insurance Payable	-	25.00	
		1,667.25	1,667.25	

Explanation: Note that the two required payroll journal entries are combined into a single entry recording both the employee's wages and the employer's payroll tax expense. Note that FUTA Expense and FUTA Payable do not appear in the journal entry. Joyce Graham's earnings for the year have exceeded the annual FUTA wage base. Review the journal entry for accuracy, noting any errors.

 ACTION: Close the Payroll Journal Entry window. You will return to the Payroll Journal. If you made an error, use the following editing techniques to correct the error:

Editing Tips
Editing Payroll Journal Entries

Move to the field that contains the error by either pressing the TAB key to move forward through each field or the SHIFT and TAB keys together to move to a previous field. This will highlight the selected field information so that you can change it. Alternatively, you can use the mouse to point to a field and drag through the incorrect information to highlight it. Type the correct information; then press the TAB key to enter it.

If you have associated a transaction with an incorrect employee, select the correct employee from the employee list display after clicking the drop-down list arrow to the right of the **To the Order of** field.

To discard an entry and start over, either choose **Undo Entry** from the Payroll Journal Edit menu, or double-click the **Close** button on the title bar. Click the **Yes** button in response to the question, "Are you sure you want to discard this journal entry?"

Review the journal entry for accuracy after any corrections by choosing **Display Payroll Journal Entry** from the Payroll Journal Report menu.

It is IMPORTANT TO NOTE that the only way to edit a transaction after it is posted is to reverse the entry and enter the correct transaction. To correct transactions posted in error, see the transaction for Sam York later in this chapter.

ACTION: Make any necessary corrections following the information above. After verifying that the journal entry is correct, print the payroll check by choosing **Print** from the Payroll Journal File menu. Compare your payroll check to the one shown below:

Oregon Explorer Maps/Your Name
2000 SE Hawthorne Blvd.
Portland, Oregon 97214   1738

One Thousand Two Hundred Seven --00/100

                                                       12/31/1997 $*******1,207.48

Graham, Joyce
3456 SE Madison Street
Portland, Oregon 97214

Oregon Explorer Maps/Your Name

Graham, Joyce   12/31/1997   1738

For Pay Period: 12/1/1997 to 12/31/1997   SSN: 541 51 5066
Salary . . . . 1,500.00   FIT . . . . 78.13   Gross 1,500.00
                                                SIT . . . . 74.64   Withheld . . . . -292.52
Gross . . . . 1,500.00   Medicare Tax 21.75
                                                Soc Sec Tax . . . . 93.00   Net 1,207.48
                                                Medical 25.00
                                                Withheld 292.52

Explanation: Verify that the check is correct. If you detect an error, refer to the Editing Tips for Editing Payroll Journal Entries for information on corrective action.

You cannot print a payroll check after a transaction is posted. However, if you have made a mistake on a payroll check, you can correct the payroll information and print a new payroll check prior to posting the transaction. The program does not make any journal entries when it prints payroll checks, so printing copies of the same payroll check does not affect the company's records or the check numbers of subsequent checks. For the purposes of this text, you may destroy incorrect payroll checks; however, in an actual business situation, incorrect payroll checks would be retained as an internal control measure.

 ACTION: After a correct check is printed, click the **Post** button to post the transaction. The program will alert you via a screen message that the payroll entry has not been allocated. As follows:

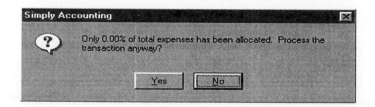

ACTION: Click the **Yes** button in response to the question, "Process the transaction anyway?" A blank Payroll Journal dialog box will be displayed.

Additional Payroll Check Transactions

Record the following additional payroll transactions:

Document 61 December 31—Issue a payroll check to Arlie Richman for his regular salary, deducting $75.00 for medical insurance. Print and post Check 1739.

Document 62 December 31—Issue a payroll check to Alice White for her regular salary, deducting $25.00 for medical insurance. Print and post Check 1740.

Document 63 December 31—Issue a payroll check to Sam York for 135 regular hours at his regular hourly rate. Print and post Check 1741. (Note that the only difference between completing the payroll for an hourly employee and a salaried employee is that an hourly employee must have regular hours and any overtime hours entered in the boxes for **Reg**. and **Ovt**.) Refer to the following illustration for assistance:

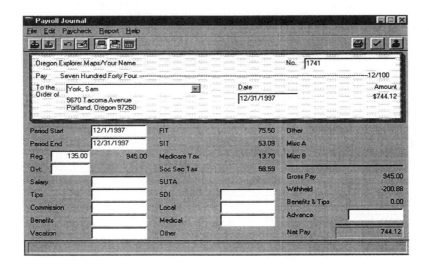

Compare your printed checks to the ones shown below:

Oregon Explorer Maps/Your Name
2000 SE Hawthorne Blvd.
Portland, Oregon 97214   1739

One Thousand Six Hundred Eighty Three --03/100

                         12/31/1997 $*******1,683.03

Richman, Arlie
2029 SW Vermont Street
Portland, Oregon 97209

Oregon Explorer Maps/Your Name

Richman, Arlie   12/31/1997   1739

For Pay Period: 12/1/1997 to 12/31/1997   SSN: 542 78 1234

Salary 2,200.00	FIT 150.00	Gross 2,200.00
	SIT 123.67	Withheld .... -516.97
Gross 2,200.00	Medicare Tax 31.90	
	Soc Sec Tax 136.40	Net 1,683.03
	Medical 75.00	
	Withheld 516.97	

Oregon Explorer Maps/Your Name
2000 SE Hawthorne Blvd.
Portland, Oregon 97214   1740

One Thousand One Hundred Seventy Five--65/100

                         12/31/1997 $*******1,175.65

White, Alice
3456 SE 65th Avenue
Portland, Oregon 97206

Oregon Explorer Maps/Your Name

White, Alice   12/31/1997   1740

For Pay Period: 12/1/1997 to 12/31/1997   SSN: 542 78 2756

Salary 1,600.00	FIT 173.75	Gross 1,600.00
	SIT 103.20	Withheld .... -424.35
Gross 1,600.00	Medicare Tax 23.20	
	Soc Sec Tax 99.20	Net 1,175.65
	Medical 25.00	
	Withheld 424.35	

Oregon Explorer Maps/Your Name
2000 SE Hawthorne Blvd.
Portland, Oregon 97214   1741

Seven Hundred Forty Four---12/100

                                        12/31/1997 $***********744.12

York, Sam
5670 Tacoma Avenue
Portland, Oregon 97260

Oregon Explorer Maps/Your Name

York, Sam   12/31/1997   1741

For Pay Period: 12/1/1997 to 12/31/1997   SSN: 541 67 0093
Salary .... 945.00   FIT .... 75.50   Gross 1,500.00
                                 SIT .... 53.09   Withheld .... -200.88
Gross .... 945.00   Medicare Tax 13.70
                                 Soc Sec Tax .... 58.59   Net 744.12
                                 Withheld 200.88

Regular 135.00 Hours @ $7.00 per Hour

 ACTION: After printing and posting the checks, you realize that the hours for Sam York were transposed and should have been 153 rather than 135. To correct the error, click the **Adjust Check** button 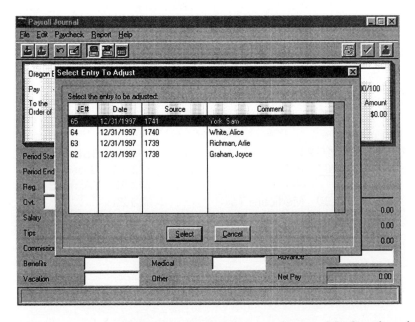 on the toolbar. Your screen will show the following:

Explanation: All the checks processed for the employees are shown. Notice that the most recent check processed is shown first.

ACTION: Select **Sam York**. Your Payroll Journal will appear as follows:

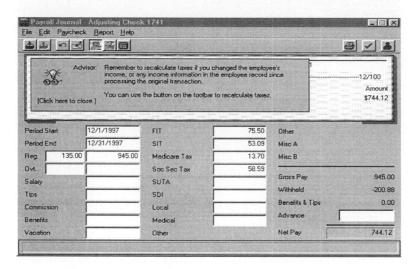

Explanation: Note the Advisor box reminding you to recalculate taxes when the check amount is changed.

ACTION: Close the Advisor by clicking where it says **[Click here to close.]** Change Sam's regular hours from 135 to *153*. Press TAB. Your screen will show the following:

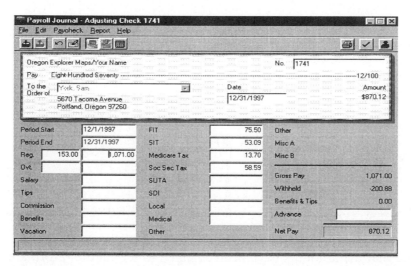

Explanation: The amount of pay for regular hours changed from $945.00 to $1,071.00. The taxes have not been changed.

ACTION: Recalculate the amount of taxes by clicking the **Recalculate Taxes** button. Your screen will show the following:

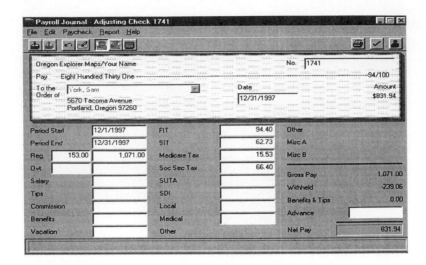

Explanation: The taxes have been recalculated by Simply based on the new amount for regular earnings.

ACTION: To verify your entries, display the Payroll Journal Entry and check your work. Your entry should appear as follows:

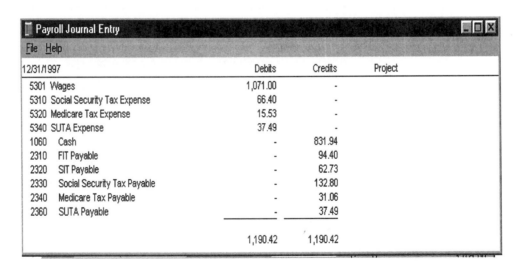

Explanation: Notice that the amounts have been changed to reflect the information for 153 regular hours. The check has been corrected.

ACTION: Close the Payroll Journal Entry display. Print the check. If you get the following dialog box, click **Yes**.

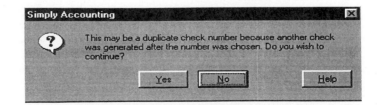

ACTION: Compare your check with the one shown below:

Oregon Explorer Maps/Your Name
2000 SE Hawthorne Blvd.
Portland, Oregon 97214   1741C

Eight Hundred Thirty One--94/100

                                        12/31/1997 $***********831.94

York, Sam
5670 Tacoma Avenue
Portland, Oregon 97260

Oregon Explorer Maps/Your Name

York, Sam   12/31/1997   1741C

For Pay Period: 12/1/1997 to 12/31/1997   SSN: 541 67 0093

Salary . . . . 1,071.00   FIT . . . . 94.40   Gross 1,071.00

                                       SIT . . . . 62.73   Withheld . . . . -239.06

Gross . . . . 1,071.00   Medicare Tax 15.53

                                       Soc Sec Tax . . . . 66.40   Net 831.94

                                       Withheld 239.06

Regular 153.00 Hours @ $7.00 per Hour

 ACTION: Post the check.

 ACTION: Now that the payroll transactions have been posted and corrected, close the Payroll Journal dialog box; from the Reports menu on the home window, select **Journal Entries** and point to Payroll. Your screen will show the following:

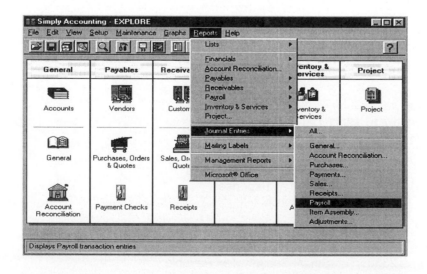

 ACTION: Click **Payroll**. Your screen will show the following:

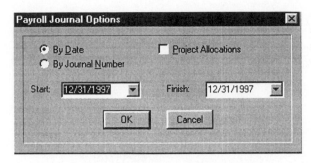

Explanation: The Payroll Journal Options dialog box appears, asking you to define the information you want displayed.

 ACTION: Select **By Date**; leave the start and finish dates set at 12/31/1997; click **OK.** The following Payroll Journal display will appear on your screen:

Payroll Journal Display		Debits	Credits
File Help			
12/31/1997 to 12/31/1997		Debits	Credits
12/31/1997 J62 1738, Graham, Joyce			
	5301 Wages	1,500.00	-
	5310 Social Security Tax Expense	93.00	-
	5320 Medicare Tax Expense	21.75	-
	5340 SUTA Expense	52.50	-
	1060 Cash	-	1,207.48
	2310 FIT Payable	-	78.13
	2320 SIT Payable	-	74.64
	2330 Social Security Tax Payable	-	186.00
	2340 Medicare Tax Payable	-	43.50
	2360 SUTA Payable	-	52.50
	2400 Medical Insurance Payable	-	25.00
12/31/1997 J63 1739, Richman, Arlie			
	5301 Wages	2,200.00	-
	5310 Social Security Tax Expense	136.40	-

Explanation: Review the display for accuracy, verifying that journal entry dates, account names and numbers, check numbers, and employee names are correct. Use the scroll bar to the right of the display to advance the display. If you have posted an incorrect transaction, refer to the correcting entry for Sam York earlier in the chapter.

 ACTION: Print the Payroll Journal by choosing **Print** from the Payroll Journal Display File menu. Compare your report to the one shown below:

Oregon Explorer Maps

Payroll Journal 12/31/1997 to 12/31/1997		**Debits**	**Credits**
12/31/1997 J62 1738, Graham, Joyce			
	5301 Wages	1,500.00	-
	5310 Social Security Tax Expense	93.00	-
	5320 Medicare Tax Expense	21.75	-
	5340 SUTA Expense	52.50	-
	1060 Cash	-	1,207.48
	2310 FIT Payable	-	78.13
	2320 SIT Payable	-	74.64
	2330 Social Security Tax Payable	-	186.00
	2340 Medicare Tax Payable	-	43.50
	2360 SUTA Payable	-	52.50
	2400 Medical Insurance Payable	-	25.00

Date	Ref	Account		Debit	Credit
12/31/1997	J63	1739, Richman, Arlie			
		5301	Wages	2,200.00	-
		5310	Social Security Tax Expense	136.40	-
		5320	Medicare Tax Expense	31.90	-
		5340	SUTA Expense	77.00	-
		1060	Cash	-	1,683.03
		2310	FIT Payable	-	150.00
		2320	SIT Payable	-	123.67
		2330	Social Security Tax Payable	-	272.80
		2340	Medicare Tax Payable	-	63.80
		2360	SUTA Payable	-	77.00
		2400	Medical Insurance Payable	-	75.00
12/31/1997	J64	1740, White Alice			
		5301	Wages	1,600.00	-
		5310	Social Security Tax Expense	99.20	-
		5320	Medicare Tax Expense	23.20	-
		5340	SUTA Expense	56.00	-
		1060	Cash	-	1,175.65
		2310	FIT Payable	-	173.75
		2320	SIT Payable	-	103.20
		2330	Social Security Tax Payable	-	198.40
		2340	Medicare Tax Payable	-	46.40
		2360	SUTA Payable	-	56.00
		2400	Medical Insurance Payable	-	25.00
12/31/1997	J65	1741, York, Sam			
		5301	Wages	945.00	-
		5310	Social Security Tax Expense	58.59	-
		5320	Medicare Tax Expense	13.70	-
		5340	SUTA Expense	33.08	-
		1060	Cash	-	744.12
		2310	FIT Payable	-	75.50
		2320	SIT Payable	-	53.09
		2330	Social Security Tax Payable	-	117.18
		2340	Medicare Tax Payable	-	27.40
		2360	SUTA Payable	-	33.08
12/31/1997	J66	ADJ1741 Reversing J65. Correction is J67.			
		1060	Cash	744.12	-
		2310	FIT Payable	75.50	-
		2320	SIT Payable	53.09	-
		2330	Social Security Tax Payable	117.18	-
		2340	Medicare Tax Payable	27.40	-
		2360	SUTA Payable	33.08	-
		5301	Wages	-	945.00
		5310	Social Security Tax Expense	-	58.59
		5320	Medicare Tax Expense	-	13.70
		5340	SUTA Expense	-	33.08
12/31/1997	J67	1741, York, Sam			
		5301	Wages	1,071.00	-
		5310	Social Security Tax Expense	66.40	-
		5320	Medicare Tax Expense	15.53	-
		5340	SUTA Expense	37.49	-
		1060	Cash	-	831.94
		2310	FIT Payable	-	94.40
		2320	SIT Payable	-	62.73

2330	Social Security Tax Payable	-	132.80
2340	Medicare Tax Payable	-	31.06
2360	SUTA Payable	-	37.49
		9,182.11	9,182.11

ACTION: Close the Payroll Journal Display window and return to the home window.

ACTION: Chose **Exit** from the home window File menu or click the **Close** button on the title bar to end the current work session and return to your Windows desktop.

ALTERNATIVE ACTION: You can continue with the tutorial without exiting from the program if you wish. The next steps are recorded under the same session date as the prior steps. Skip the next ACTION and continue with the tutorial.

PAYROLL LEDGER—MAINTAINING EMPLOYEE RECORDS

Transactions can be entered only through the Journals components of the program, which is accessed by clicking the **Paycheck** icon on the home window. The Payroll Ledger component is used to maintain employee records and is accessed by clicking the **Employees** icon on the home window. Each record contains the employee's address, salary or hourly wage information, and withholding allowance information. You can create, modify, or remove employee records through the Payroll Ledger dialog box.

Creating an Employee Record

Oregon Explorer Maps has hired a new employee and would like to add her to the Payroll Ledger.

Oregon Explorer Maps—Document 64   **Session Date: 12/31/1997**

Memo   **Date:** December 31, 1997

Add the following employee to the employee list:

Susan Hudson   SSN# 542 78 9246
6127 SW Corbett Avenue   Birth Date: 8/18/1972
Portland, Oregon 97201   Hire Date: 12/31/1997
503-246-2710
Reg. Per Hour: 7.00   Tax Table: Oregon
Overtime Per Hour: 10.50   Federal Allowances: 1   State Allowances: 1
Pay Periods: 12   Federal Status: Single   State Status: Single

---

ACTION: Load CA-Simply Accounting for Windows; open the data files for Oregon Explorer Maps (A:\EXPLORE\Eplore.asc); leave the session date set at 12/31/1997. The Oregon Explorer Maps home window will appear.

ACTION: Open the Payroll Ledger dialog box by clicking the **Employees** icon on the home window. Your screen will show the following:

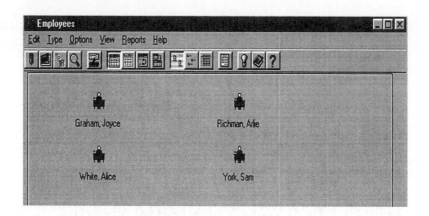

ACTION: Click the **Create** icon on the toolbar. Your screen will look like this:

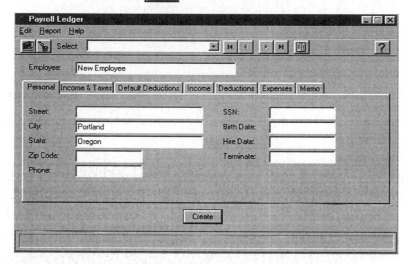

Explanation: A blank Payroll Ledger dialog box is presented. Various tabs are shown for entering employee data.

Employee: Enter the employee's name, up to 35 characters. Enter the last name, followed by a comma and a space; then enter the first name.

Personal Tab

Street: Enter the employee's street address, up to 30 characters.

City: Enter the employee's city, up to 18 characters. The program fills in this field with the city in the company's address as the default. You can accept this city or type a different one.

State: Enter the employee's state. The program fills in this field with the state in the company's address as the default. You can accept this state or type a different one.

Zip Code: Enter the employee's zip code.

Phone: Enter the employee's phone number, including the area code if you wish. You do not need to type parentheses or hyphens; the program fills these in when you move to another field.

SSN: Enter the employee's Social Security number. The program prints the number on payroll checks.

Birth Date: Enter the employee's birth date. You cannot leave this field blank.

Hire Date: Enter the employee's first day of employment.

Terminate: Enter the employee's last day of employment. Leave this field blank until the employee leaves the company.

Income and Taxes Tab

Regular Per Hour: Enter the employee's regular per hour pay rate. If the employee is paid a salary per pay period rather than a wage per hour, leave this field blank.

Overtime Per Hour: Enter the employee's overtime per hour pay rate.

Salary Per Period: Enter the employee's salary per pay period. If an employee is paid by the hour, leave this field blank.

Pay Periods Per Year: Click the drop-down list arrow to the right of the field to display a list of pay periods. Choose the number of times per year the company pays this employee. You cannot leave this field blank.

Tax Table: Click the drop-down list arrow to the right of the field to display a list of states; select the state in the employee's address. You cannot leave this field blank.

Federal Allowances: Enter the number of federal allowances (exemptions) the employee claims on Federal Form W-4.

Federal Status: Click the drop-down list arrow to the right of the field to display a list of marital statuses; select the one that applies to the employee as reported on Federal Form W-4.

State Allowances: Enter the number of state allowances (exemptions) the employee claims.

State Status: Click the drop-down list arrow to the right of the field to display a list of marital statuses; select the one that applies to the employee. You cannot leave this field blank.

Soc Sec/Medicare Tax Exempt: Check this box if the employee is exempt from Social Security and Medicare tax.

Dependents: If the state requires it, enter the number of dependents the employee claims on the state form.

Default Deductions Tab

Default Deductions Per Pay Period: Medical, Other, Misc. A, Misc. B: Use to record deductions made from an employee. Frequently used for employee-paid medical insurance. Other and miscellaneous deductions may be used for items such as employee-paid dental insurance, union dues, credit union deductions, and so on.

Additional Tax Per Pay Period: Federal and State: Allows an employee to have addition federal and/or state tax withheld from a paycheck.

Income, Deductions, and Expenses Tabs

Income: Shows quarter-to-date (QTD) and year-to-date (YTD) amounts for the employee.

Deductions: Shows QTD and YTD amounts for the employee.

Expenses: Shows QTD and YTD amounts for the employee.

Memo Tab

Memo: Allows a memo to be created for this employee.

To-Do Date: For memos to be displayed in the To-Do List, this is the action's due date. You also need to place a check mark in the check box for **Display this Memo in the To-Do List.**

 ACTION: Enter the available information about the new employee, Susan Hudson, into the Payroll Ledger. Complete the Personal Tab information first. Your screen will show the following:

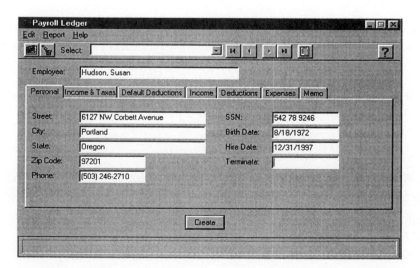

Explanation: The personal information for Susan Hudson has been entered. Verify that all the information has been entered correctly.

ACTION: Click the **Income & Taxes** tab. Enter the available information about the new employee. Your screen will show the following:

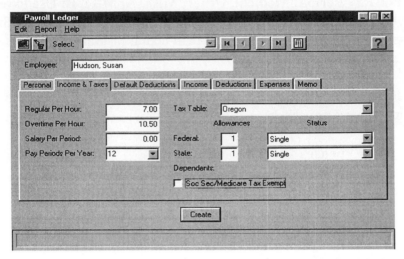

Explanation: The tax information for Susan Hudson has been entered. Verify that all the information has been entered correctly.

Editing Tips
Editing a Payroll Ledger Record

Move to the field that contains the error by either pressing the TAB key to move forward through each field or the SHIFT and TAB keys together to move to a previous field. This will highlight the selected field information so that you can change it. Alternatively, you can use the mouse to point to a field and drag through the incorrect information to highlight it. Type the correct information; then press the TAB key to enter it.

Click the drop-down list arrow as needed to select field information. Click the check boxes to select or deselect as required.

To discard an entry and start over, choose **Undo Changes** from the Payroll Ledger Edit menu. Click the **Yes** button in response to the question, "Are you sure you want to undo changes to this ledger page?" Alternatively, double-click the **Close** button on the title bar. Click **No** in response to the question, "Do you still want to create this ledger page?"

It is IMPORTANT TO NOTE that the only way to edit a Payroll Ledger record after it is created is to either modify the record or remove it, if possible, and create a new Payroll Ledger record.

 ACTION: There is no other information to be entered for Susan Hudson. Again, verify the entries made for Susan and correct any errors. Refer to the above Editing Tips if you made an error entering the information for Susan. When the Payroll Ledger is correct, click the **Create** button. Your screen will look like this:

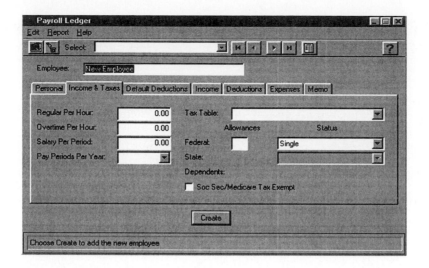

Explanation: The program has added the new employee to Oregon Explorer Maps' employee records, and has cleared the Payroll Ledger dialog box in preparation for creating another employee record. Note that the Income & Taxes tab is displayed. Simply shows the last tab that was used rather than returning to the Personal tab.

Modifying an Employee Record

If you make an error in an employee record after it has been created, or need to change some information about an employee, click the drop-down list arrow next to **Select** to display all the employees. Select the employee whose information needs to be changed. Make any necessary changes to the employee and select a different employee or close the Payroll Ledger. Either of the two will save the changes to the employee selected.

Oregon Explorer Maps—Document 65   **Session Date: 12/31/1997**

Memo   **Date:** December 31, 1997

Change the telephone number for Joyce Graham. The new number is 503-231-7772.

ACTION: Click the drop-down list arrow next to **Select**. Click **Graham, Joyce** to select Joyce as the employee. Click in the text box for **Phone**. Change the telephone number to *503-231-7772*. Your screen will show the following:

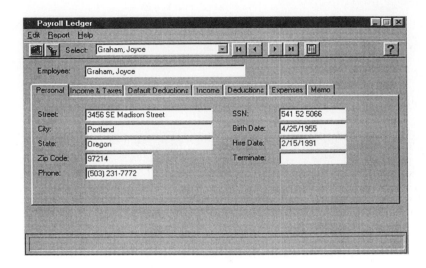

ACTION: Click the **Close** button on the title bar. This will close the Payroll Ledger and save the change for Joyce Graham.

Removing an Employee Record

It is important to use caution before removing an employee record. Generally, it is a good idea to wait until the start of a new calendar year before removing any employee records. Do not remove an employee record until you have printed the W-2 forms and the 940 and 941 summaries at the end of the calendar year. To remove an employee, select the employee from the drop-down list for **Select**, click the employee's name to select, and click the **Remove Current Employee** icon on the Payroll Ledger toolbar.

Additional Payroll Ledger Maintenance Items

Enter the following additional maintenance items:

Document 66 December 31—Create a new Payroll Ledger record for Bob Martinsen, 8235 SW 30th Street, Portland, Oregon 97219, 503-244-0750. SSN# 541-63-5027; Birth Date: 2/12/1975; Hire Date: 12/31/1997; Regular Rate: 6.00; Overtime Rate: 9.00; Pay Periods: 12; Tax Table: Oregon; Federal Allowances: 1; Federal Status: Single; State Allowances: 1; State Status: Single.

Document 67 December 31—Modify Sam York's address. He has moved to 4713 SW Vermont Street, Portland, Oregon 97219, 503-246-5497.

PAYROLL REPORTS

A variety of payroll-related reports are available in CA-Simply Accounting for Windows. The procedures required to generate payroll checks and to print and display a Payroll Journal report were demonstrated earlier in this chapter. In addition to the Payroll Journal report, the program can print or display an Employee List, Employee QTD or YTD Summary, Detail Employee report, SUTA Summary, 941 Summary, and 940 Summary. W-2 forms and employee labels may also be printed. Use scroll bars at the bottom or right side of a displayed report to view reports that contain more text than can be displayed at one time.

 ACTION: Close the Payroll Ledger dialog box. Choose **Display Employee List** from the Reports menu on the Employees window. Your screen will show the following:

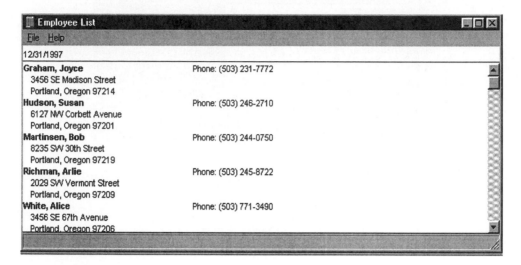

Explanation: Employee reports are also available on the home window. Just click the **Reports** menu, point to Payroll, and select from among the employee reports listed.

 ACTION: Choose **Print** from the Employee List File menu. Compare your report to the one shown below:

Oregon Explorer Maps
Employee List 12/31/1997

Graham, Joyce   Phone: (503) 231-7772
     3456 SE Madison Street
     Portland, Oregon 97214
Hudson, Susan   Phone: (503) 246-2710
     6127 NW Corbett Avenue
     Portland, Oregon 97201
Martinsen, Bob   Phone: (503) 244-0750
     8235 SW 30th Street
     Portland, Oregon 97219
Richman, Arlie   Phone: (503) 245-8722
     2029 SW Vermont Street
     Portland, Oregon 97209
White, Alice   Phone: (503) 771-3490
     3456 SE 67th Avenue
     Portland, Oregon 97206
York, Sam   Phone: (503) 246-5497
     4713 Vermont Street
     Portland, Oregon 97219

Employees on file: 6

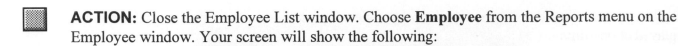 **ACTION:** Close the Employee List window. Choose **Employee** from the Reports menu on the Employee window. Your screen will show the following:

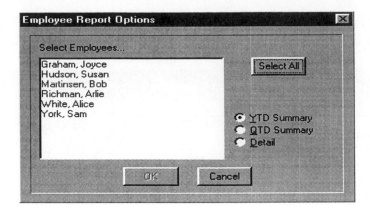

Explanation: A list of all employee names and report selections is shown. **Note**: There is no problem if one of your employee names is highlighted.

The selections available on the Employee Report Options dialog box are:

YTD Summary: Lists the selected employee's personal information, such as address, hire date, number of pay periods, year-to-date earnings and deductions, and the employer's associated payroll tax expenses.

QTD Summary: Lists the selected employee's personal information, such as address, hire date, number of pay periods, quarter-to-date earnings and deductions, and the employer's associated payroll tax expenses.

Detail: Allows you to select the information to report. Lists the items selected for each employee selected or for all employees.

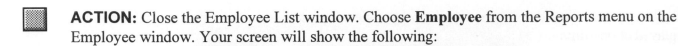 **ACTION:** Click **YTD Summary** to select. Click **Select All** button to choose all the employees. Click **OK.** Your screen will show the following:

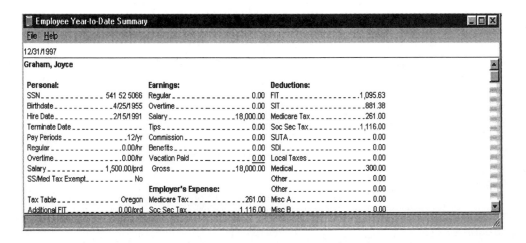

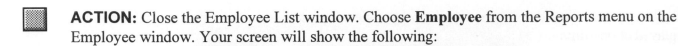 **ACTION:** Print the report and compare it with the following:

Oregon Explorer Maps
Employee Year-to-Date Summary 12/31/1997

Graham, Joyce

Personal:

SSN	541 52 5066
Birthdate	4/25/1955
Hire Date	2/15/1991
Terminate Date	
Pay Periods	12/yr
Regular	0.00/hr
Overtime	0.00/hr
Salary	1,500.00/prd
SS/Med Tax Exempt	No

Tax Table	Oregon
Additional FIT	0.00/prd
Federal Allowances	2
Federal Status	Married
Additional SIT	0.00/prd
Dependents	0
State Allowances	2, 0
State Status	Married

Earnings:

Regular	0.00
Overtime	0.00
Salary	18,000.00
Tips	0.00
Commission	0.00
Benefits	0.00
Vacation Paid	0.00
Gross	18,000.00

Employer's Expense:

Medicare Tax	261.00
Soc Sec Tax	1,116.00
FUTA	56.00
SUTA	630.00
SDI	0.00
Expense	2,063.00

Deductions:

FIT	1,095.63
SIT	881.38
Medicare Tax	261.00
Soc Sec Tax	1,116.00
SUTA	0.00
SDI	0.00
Local Taxes	0.00
Medical	300.00
Other	0.00
Other	0.00
Misc A	0.00
Misc B	0.00
Withheld	3,654.01
Advance Paid	0.00
Net Pay	14,345.99

Hudson, Susan

Personal:

SSN	542 78 9246
Birthdate	8/18/1972
Hire Date	12/31/1997
Terminate Date	
Pay Periods	12/yr
Regular	7.00/hr
Overtime	10.50/hr
Salary	0.00/prd
SS/Med Tax Exempt	No

Tax Table	Oregon
Additional FIT	0.00/prd
Federal Allowances	1
Federal Status	Single
Additional SIT	0.00/prd
Dependents	0
State Allowances	1, 0
State Status	Single

Earnings:

Regular	0.00
Overtime	0.00
Salary	0.00
Tips	0.00
Commission	0.00
Benefits	0.00
Vacation Paid	0.00
Gross	0.00

Employer's Expense:

Medicare Tax	0.00
Soc Sec Tax	0.00
FUTA	0.00
SUTA	0.00
SDI	0.00
Expense	0.00

Deductions:

FIT	0.00
SIT	0.00
Medicare Tax	0.00
Soc Sec Tax	0.00
SUTA	0.00
SDI	0.00
Local Taxes	0.00
Medical	0.00
Other	0.00
Other	0.00
Misc A	0.00
Misc B	0.00
Withheld	0.00
Advance Paid	0.00
Net Pay	0.00

Martinsen, Bob

Personal:

SSN	541 63 5027
Birthdate	2/12/1970
Hire Date	12/31/1997
Terminate Date	
Pay Periods	12/yr
Regular	6.00/hr
Overtime	9.00/hr

Earnings:

Regular	0.00
Overtime	0.00
Salary	0.00
Tips	0.00
Commission	0.00
Benefits	0.00
Vacation Paid	0.00

Deductions:

FIT	0.00
SIT	0.00
Medicare Tax	0.00
Soc Sec Tax	0.00
SUTA	0.00
SDI	0.00
Local Taxes	0.00

Salary 0.00/prd	Gross 0.00	Medical 0.00
SS/Med Tax Exempt . . . . No		Other 0.00
	Employer's Expense:	Other 0.00
Tax Table . . . . Oregon	Medicare Tax 0.00	Misc A 0.00
Additional FIT 0.00/prd	Soc Sec Tax 0.00	Misc B 0.00
Federal Allowances 1	FUTA 0.00	Withheld 0.00
Federal Status . . . . Single	SUTA 0.00	
Additional SIT 0.00/prd	SDI 0.00	Advance Paid 0.00
Dependents 0	Expense 0.00	
State Allowances 1, 0		Net Pay 0.00
State Status . . . . . . Single		

Richman, Arlie

Personal:	**Earnings:**	**Deductions:**
SSN 542 78 1234	Regular 0.00	FIT 2,006.25
Birthdate 10/3/1950	Overtime 0.00	SIT 1,465.45
Hire Date 12/1/1991	Salary 26,400.00	Medicare Tax 382.80
Terminate Date	Tips 0.00	Soc Sec Tax 1,636.80
Pay Periods 12/yr	Commission 0.00	SUTA 0.00
Regular 0.00/hr	Benefits 0.00	SDI 0.00
Overtime 0.00/hr	Vacation Paid 0.00	Local Taxes 0.00
Salary 2,200.00/prd	Gross 26,400.00	Medical 900.00
SS/Med Tax Exempt . . . . No		Other 0.00
	Employer's Expense:	Other 0.00
Tax Table . . . . Oregon	Medicare Tax 382.80	Misc A 0.00
Additional FIT 0.00/prd	Soc Sec Tax 1,636.80	Misc B 0.00
Federal Allowances 3	FUTA 56.00	Withheld 6,391.30
Federal Status . . . . Married	SUTA 672.00	
Additional SIT 0.00/prd	SDI 0.00	Advance Paid 0.00
Dependents 0	Expense 2,747.60	
State Allowances 3, 0		Net Pay 20,008.70
State Status . . . . . Married		

White, Alice

Personal:	**Earnings:**	**Deductions:**
SSN 542 78 2756	Regular 0.00	FIT 2,160.68
Birthdate 2/15/1970	Overtime 0.00	SIT 1,231.58
Hire Date 2/1/1991	Salary 19,200.00	Medicare Tax 278.40
Terminate Date	Tips 0.00	Soc Sec Tax 1,190.40
Pay Periods 12/yr	Commission 0.00	SUTA 0.00
Regular 0.00/hr	Benefits 0.00	SDI 0.00
Overtime 0.00/hr	Vacation Paid 0.00	Local Taxes 0.00
Salary 1,600.00/prd	Gross 19,200.00	Medical 300.00
SS/Med Tax Exempt . . . . No		Other 0.00
	Employer's Expense:	Other 0.00
Tax Table . . . . Oregon	Medicare Tax 278.40	Misc A 0.00
Additional FIT 0.00/prd	Soc Sec Tax 1,190.40	Misc B 0.00
Federal Allowances 1	FUTA 56.00	Withheld 5,161.06
Federal Status . . . . Single	SUTA 651.00	
Additional SIT 0.00/prd	SDI 0.00	Advance Paid 0.00
Dependents 0	Expense 2,175.80	
State Allowances 1, 0		Net Pay 14,038.94
State Status . . . . . . Single		

York, Sam

Personal:
SSN 541 67 0093
Birthdate 3/21/1963
Hire Date 6/12/1991
Terminate Date ....
Pay Periods 12/yr
Regular 7.00/hr
Overtime 10.50/hr
Salary 0.00/prd
SS/Med Tax Exempt .... No

Tax Table .... Oregon
Additional FIT 0.00/prd
Federal Allowances 1
Federal Status .... Single
Additional SIT 0.00/prd
Dependents 0
State Allowances 1, 0
State Status ...... Single

Earnings:
Regular 12,866.00
Overtime 0.00
Salary 0.00
Tips 0.00
Commission 0.00
Benefits 0.00
Vacation Paid 0.00
  Gross 12,866.00

Employer's Expense:
Medicare Tax 186.56
Soc Sec Tax 797.69
FUTA 56.00
SUTA 450.35
SDI 0.00
  Expense 1,490.60

Deductions:
FIT 1,210.58
SIT 747.01
Medicare Tax 186.56
Soc Sec Tax 797.69
SUTA 0.00
SDI 0.00
Local Taxes 0.00
Medical 0.00
Other 0.00
Other 0.00
Misc A 0.00
Misc B 0.00
  Withheld 2,941.84

Advance Paid 0.00

Net Pay 9,924.16

 ACTION: Close the Employee Year-to-Date Summary report. Choose **Employee** from the Employee window Reports menu. Select **All employees**; click **Detail**. Click the following options to include in the report: **FIT**, **SIT**, **SUTA**, **Medicare**, **Soc. Sec.**, and **SDI.** Your screen will show the following:

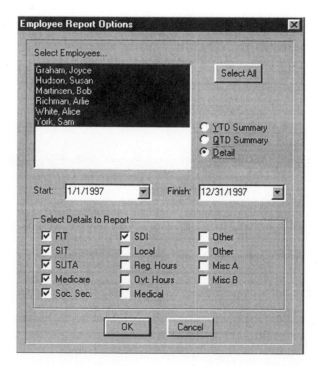

 ACTION: Click **OK** to process the report. Your screen will look like the following:

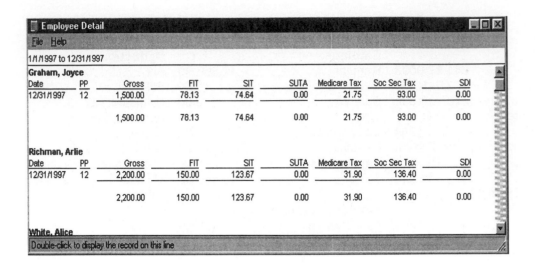

ACTION: Use Simply's zoom feature to see the employee record for Sam York. Scroll through the report until you see Sam's information. Point to his name. Your mouse will turn into a magnifying glass. As shown in the following:

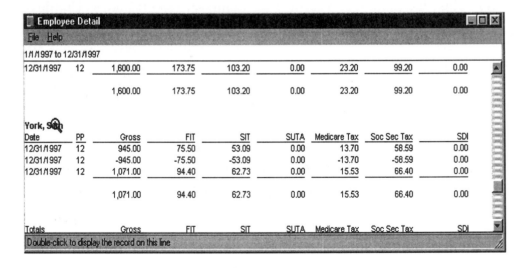

ACTION: Double-click **York, Sam**. The Payroll Ledger listing for Sam York will be displayed as follows:

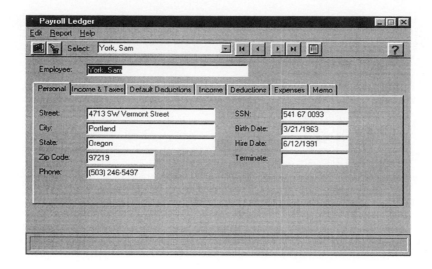

ACTION: Close the Payroll Ledger for Sam York. Print the Employee Detail Report and compare it with the following:

Oregon Explorer Maps/Your Name
Employee Detail 1/1/1997 to 12/31/1997

Graham, Joyce

Date	PP	Gross	FIT	SIT	SUTA	Medicare Tax	Soc Sec Tax	SDI
12/31/1997	12	1,500.00	78.13	74.64	0.00	21.75	93.00	0.00
		1,500.00	78.13	74.64	0.00	21.75	93.00	0.00

Richman, Arlie

Date	PP	Gross	FIT	SIT	SUTA	Medicare Tax	Soc Sec Tax	SDI
12/31/1997	12	2,200.00	150.00	123.67	0.00	31.90	136.40	0.00
		2,200.00	150.00	123.67	0.00	31.90	136.40	0.00

White, Alice

Date	PP	Gross	FIT	SIT	SUTA	Medicare Tax	Soc Sec Tax	SDI
12/31/1997	12	1,600.00	173.75	103.20	0.00	23.20	99.20	0.00
		1,600.00	173.75	103.20	0.00	23.20	99.20	0.00

York, Sam

Date	PP	Gross	FIT	SIT	SUTA	Medicare Tax	Soc Sec Tax	SDI
12/31/1997	12	945.00	75.50	53.09	0.00	13.70	58.58	0.00
12/31/1997	12	-945.00	-75.50	-53.09	0.00	-13.70	-58.59	0.00
12/31/1997	12	1,071.00	94.40	62.73	0.00	15.53	66.40	0.00
		1,071.00	94.40	62.73	0.00	15.53	66.40	0.00

Totals

	Gross	FIT	SIT	SUTA	Medicare Tax	Soc Sec Tax	SDI
	6,371.00	496.28	364.24	0.00	92.38	395.00	0.00

ACTION: Close the Employee Detail report. Choose **SUTA Summary** from the Reports Menu on the Employees window. Your screen will show the following:

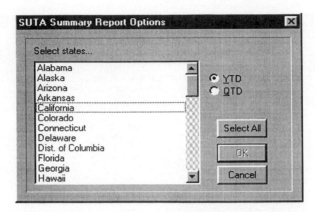

Explanation: The SUTA Summary Report Options dialog box presents several options. SUTA Summary reports can be prepared for either YTD or QTD information based on the state(s) selected.

ACTION: Scroll through the states until Oregon is highlighted. Make sure YTD has been selected. Click **OK.** Your screen will show the following:

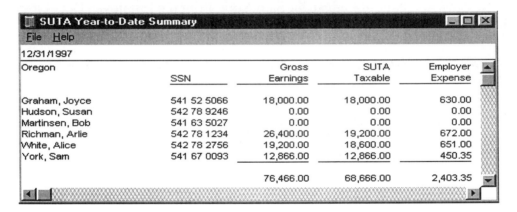

ACTION: Print your report and compare it with the one shown above.

ACTION: Close the SUTA Year-to-Date Summary Report. Choose **940 Summary** from the Reports menu. Your screen will show the following:

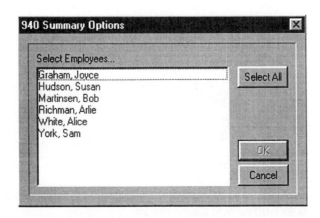

Explanation: The 940 Summary Options dialog box allows you to specify the employees to be included in the report. The 940 Summary lists the selected employees, their gross earnings, their FUTA taxable earnings, and the FUTA tax expense.

ACTION: Click **Select All** and **OK.** Your screen will display the following report:

940 Summary						
File Help						
12/31/1997	Gross Earnings		FUTA Taxable Earnings		FUTA Tax Expense	
	QTD	YTD	QTD	YTD	QTD	YTD
Graham, Joyce	4,500.00	18,000.00	0.00	7,000.00	0.00	56.00
Hudson, Susan	0.00	0.00	0.00	0.00	0.00	0.00
Martinsen, Bob	0.00	0.00	0.00	0.00	0.00	0.00
Richman, Arlie	6,600.00	26,400.00	0.00	7,000.00	0.00	56.00
White, Alice	4,800.00	19,200.00	0.00	7,000.00	0.00	56.00
York, Sam	3,262.00	12,866.00	0.00	7,000.00	0.00	56.00
	19,162.00	76,466.00	0.00	28,000.00	0.00	224.00

Explanation: The program zeros the current quarter-to-date amounts when the session date is advanced to a new calendar quarter. Year-to-date amounts accumulate over the calendar year and are set to zero when the session date is advanced to a new calendar year.

ACTION: Print the 940 Summary report and compare it with the one shown above.

ACTION: Close the 940 Summary and choose **941 Summary** from the Reports menu. Your screen will show the following:

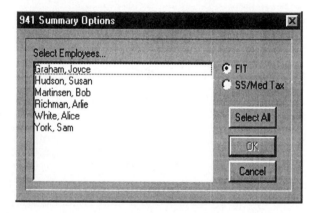

Explanation: The 941 Summary Options dialog box presents several options. The 941 Summary report can be prepared for selected employees or for all employees, and reports can be prepared listing either FIT or SS/Med Tax information (Social Security/Medicare). The 941 Summary report includes quarter-to-date information only. The program zeros the current quarter-to-date amounts when the session date is advanced to the next calendar quarter so that the next quarter's amounts can be accumulated for these reports.

ACTION: Click **Select All**. Make sure FIT has been chosen. Click **OK.** You will see the following report:

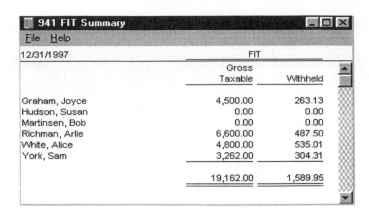

Explanation: The 941 FIT Summary shows the gross taxable income for the quarter for federal income taxes and the amount of taxes withheld for the quarter.

ACTION: Choose **Print** from the 941 FIT Summary File menu. Compare your report to the one shown above.

ACTION: Close the 941 FIT Summary window; choose **941 Summary** from the Employees window Reports Menu; click the **SS/Med Tax** option button; click **Select All** and **OK.** You will see the following report:

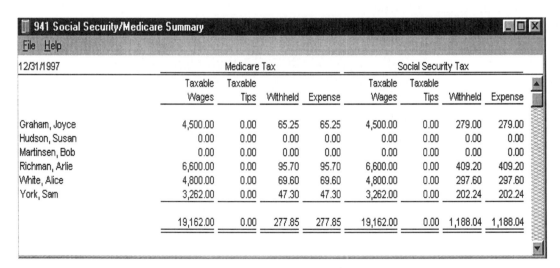

Explanation: The 941 Social Security/Medicare Summary lists the employees' taxable wages and taxable tips, the amount withheld from the employees, and the amount of employer expense incurred for both Medicare tax and Social Security tax for the quarter.

ACTION: Choose **Print** from the 941 Social Security/Medicare Summary File menu. Compare your report with the one shown above.

ACTION: Close the 941 Social Security/Medicare Summary window. You will get the following screen:

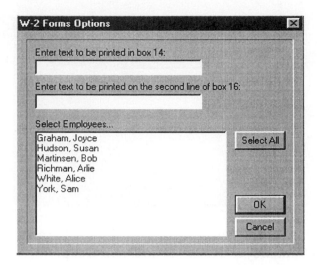

Explanation: W-2 forms list the employee earnings and tax information you must submit to the federal government at the end of the calendar year. This includes employer's identification number, employer's name and address, employer's state ID number, employee Social Security number, name, wages, tips and other compensation, federal income tax withheld, Social Security wages, and Social Security tax withheld.

 ACTION: Leave the information for text to be printed in boxes 14 and 16 blank. Select **York, Sam** and click **OK.** You will not get the W-2 displayed on the screen. Simply will automatically print the W-2 for Sam York. Compare your printed W-2 with the one shown below:

93-1061189	12866.00	1210.58
Oregon Explorer Maps/Your Name	12866.00	797.69
2000 SE Hawthorne Blvd.		
Portland,		
Oregon	12866.00	186.56
97214		
	0.00	
541-67-0093		
Sam York		0.00
4713 SW Vermont Street		
Portland,		
Oregon		
97219		
OR 6644529 12866.01 747.01		0.00

 ACTION: Simply can also print mailing labels for your employees. From the Reports menu, click **Employee Labels**. Your screen will show:

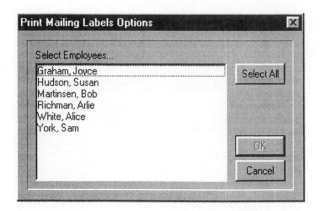

ACTION: Click **Graham, Joyce** to select. Click **OK.** Simply will print the following mailing label:

> Graham, Joyce
> 3456 SE Madison Street
> Portland, Oregon 97214

ACTION: Close the Employees window and return to the home window. Click the **Reports** menu, point to Financials, and click **Trial Balance**. You will get the following:

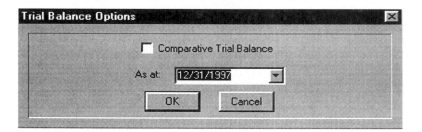

ACTION: Accept the default as at date of 12/31/1997 by clicking **OK.** You will get the following Trial Balance:

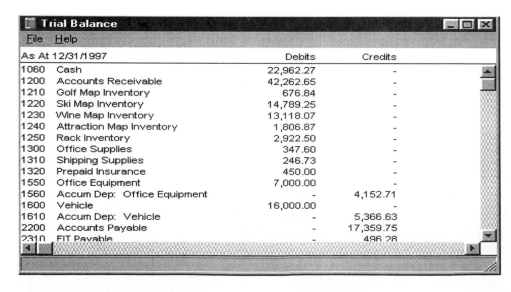

ACTION: Print the trial balance by choosing **Print** from the Trial Balance File menu. Compare your trial balance with the one shown below:

Oregon Explorer Maps/Your Name
Trial Balance As At 12/31/1997

		Debits	Credits
1060	Cash	22,962.27	-
1200	Accounts Receivable	42,262.65	-
1210	Golf Map Inventory	676.84	-
1220	Ski Map Inventory	14,789.25	-
1230	Wine Map Inventory	13,118.07	-
1240	Attraction Map Inventory	1,806.87	-
1250	Rack Inventory	2,922.50	-
1300	Office Supplies	347.60	-
1310	Shipping Supplies	246.73	-
1320	Prepaid Insurance	450.00	-
1550	Office Equipment	7,000.00	-
1560	Accum Dep: Office Equipment	-	4,152.71
1600	Vehicle	16,000.00	-
1610	Accum Dep: Vehicle	-	5,366.63
2200	Accounts Payable	-	17,359.75
2310	FIT Payable	-	496.28
2320	SIT Payable	-	364.24
2330	Social Security Tax Payable	-	790.00
2340	Medicare Tax Payable	-	184.76
2350	FUTA Payable	-	23.24
2360	SUTA Payable	-	495.63
2400	Medical Insurance Payable	-	125.00
2710	Loans Payable	-	0.00
3560	Karen Bailey, Capital	-	78,185.62
3570	Karen Bailey, Drawing	27,500.00	-
4210	Wholesale Golf Map Sales	-	8,791.59
4220	Wholesale Ski Map Sales	-	6,724.19
4230	Wholesale Wine Map Sales	-	6,634.19
4240	Wholesale Attraction Map Sales	-	22,128.97
4310	Distributor Golf Map Sales	-	43,212.79
4320	Distributor Ski Map Sales	-	37,145.84
4330	Distributor Wine Map Sales	-	36,110.84
4340	Distributor Attraction Map Sales	-	123,106.97
4410	Retail Attraction Map Sales	-	0.00
4500	Rack Sales	-	1,636.49
4600	Sales Discounts	876.46	-
4700	Sales Returns and Allowances	2,049.75	-
4810	Interest Income	-	0.00
4820	Bad Check Charges	-	25.00
5010	COGS-Golf Maps	15,714.35	-
5020	COGS-Ski Maps	15,134.38	-
5030	COGS-Wine Maps	13,580.81	-
5040	COGS-Attraction Maps	34,081.08	-
5050	COGS-Racks	1,361.50	-
5060	Purchase Discounts	-	11.89
5070	Purchase Returns and Allowances	0.00	-
5301	Wages	76,466.00	-
5310	Social Security Tax Expense	4,740.89	-
5320	Medicare Tax Expense	1,108.76	-

5330	FUTA Expense	224.00	-
5340	SUTA Expense	2,403.35	-
5400	Phone Expense	1,376.92	-
5410	Postage Expense	976.29	-
5420	Shipping Expense	18,974.32	-
5430	Advertising Expense	10,876.20	-
5440	Vehicle Expense	627.46	-
5450	Utilities Expense	1,176.42	-
5460	Rent Expense	30,000.00	-
5470	Membership and Dues Expense	973.20	-
5480	Subscription Expense	267.50	-
5490	Interest Expense: Loans	0.00	-
5500	Dep. Expense: Office Equipment	1,986.05	-
5510	Dep. Expense: Vehicle	2,566.63	-
5610	Insurance Expense	1,650.00	-
5620	Office Supplies Expense	2,219.95	-
5630	Shipping Supplies Expense	1,011.42	-
5650	Bank Service Charge Expense	295.00	-
5660	Credit Card Fees Expense	23.92	-
5800	Misc. Expense	247.23	-
		393,072.62	393,072.62

 ACTION: Close the Trial Balance window. Make a backup copy of Oregon Explorer Maps' data files. Then choose **Exit** from the home window File menu to end the current work session and return to your Windows desktop.

SUMMARY

This chapter has explored the Payroll components of CA-Simply Accounting for Windows as they would typically be used by a business. Use of the Payroll Journal dialog box to record payroll transactions and to issue payroll checks was explained in detail. In addition, the procedures used to display and print a Payroll Journal, Employee List, Employee Year-to-Date Summary, Employee Quarter-to-Date Summary, Employee Detail report, SUTA Summary, 940 Summary, 941 FIT Summary, 941 Social Security/Medicare Summary, W-2 slips, and employee mailing labels have been demonstrated. By examining the methods used to record Payroll transactions, various integration/linking features of CA-Simply Accounting for Windows were illustrated.

QUESTIONS

QUESTIONS ABOUT THE SOFTWARE

1. In CA-simply Accounting for Windows, all payroll functions are fully integrated with and linked to the General Ledger accounts. Explain this statement and give an example.

2. What are the differences between an Employee Report YTD Summary and an Employee Report Detail?

3. Prior to removing an employee record from the Payroll Ledger, what reports should be printed? Why?

4. What type of information is reported on a 940 Summary report? How frequently is Federal Form 940 filed?

5. What options are available in CA-simply Accounting for Windows for displaying or printing a SUTA Summary report?

6. Name the CA-Simply Accounting for Windows reports that would be used to help prepare Federal Form 941. How frequently are 941 forms filed?

QUESTIONS ABOUT PAYROLL OPERATIONS

7. Name the three reasons why employers must maintain detailed and accurate payroll accounting records.

8. You would like to know the total FUTA tax expense incurred by the business to date this year. Describe two places that you could look within the CA-Simply Accounting for Windows program to answer your question.

9. An employee of the business has requested a pay raise and is under the impression that the total cost of his current position to the company is equal to his monthly salary. How could you use the employee's Employee Year-To-Date Summary report to explain why this impression is incorrect?

EXPLORING ALTERNATIVE SOFTWARE TECHNIQUES

10. Payroll Journal entries can be recorded using either the Automatic Payroll Deductions feature of CA-Simply Accounting for Windows (this method was demonstrated in this chapter) or by entering payroll deductions manually. Sometimes, a company may need to prepare a payroll check with deductions calculated manually even though they normally use the Automatic Payroll Deductions feature. This might occur if a company pays annual bonuses to its employees. To make a payroll entry with deductions calculated manually:

A. If you are paying a bonus, you may want to open the Payroll Ledger and change the employee's pay periods to 1 per year. If you do not change the number of pay periods per year, Simply will calculate taxes on the bonus as if it were part of the employee's regular income for the year.

B. Double-click the **Paychecks** icon on the home window.

C. Click the **Enter Taxes Manually** button on the Payroll Journal toolbar.

D. Select the employee from the Employee List. If the employee selected has a salary or commission amount listed in his or her Payroll Ledger record, the default salary or commission amount and related deductions will appear in these data fields. The **FIT**, **SIT**, **Medicare Tax**, **Social Security Tax**, and **SUTA** fields will be available for editing. (If you have Simply calculate taxes automatically, these fields will not be available for editing.)

E. Fill in or change the fields as required. If you change the amounts in the **Salary** or **Commission** fields, the program does not automatically recalculate the taxes. You may enter the amount of the taxes manually or click the **Recalculate Taxes** button on the toolbar.

F. When the entry is complete, review it to be sure that it is correct by choosing **Display Payroll Entry** from the Payroll Journal Report menu; make any corrections required; then click the **Print** icon on the toolbar. After the check is printed, click the **Post** icon to post the entry.

G. If you set the number of pay periods to 1 for this employee, open the employee's Payroll Ledger record and change it back to the correct number.

The manual payroll deductions calculation feature of CA-Simply Accounting for Windows has been explained in the context of paying an employee an annual bonus. In what other situations might this feature of CA-Simply Accounting for Windows be useful to a business?

TRANSMITTAL

Oregon Explorer Maps   **Name:** _____
Chapter 7

Attach the following documents and reports:

1. Check 1738
2. Check 1739
3. Check 1740
4. Check 1741
5. Check 1741 (corrected check)
6. Payroll Journal 12/31/1997 to 12/31/1997
7. Employee List 12/31/1997
8. Employee Year-to-Date Summary 12/31/1997
9. Employee Detail 1/1/1997 to 12/31/1997
10. SUTA Year-to-Date Summary 12/31/1997
11. 940 Summary 12/31/1997
12. 941 FIT Summary 12/31/1997
13. 941 Social Security/Medicare Summary 12/31/1997
14. W-2 for Sam York
15. Mailing label for Joyce Graham
16. Trial Balance As at 12/31/1997

EXERCISE—Windmill Wheels
(Continued from Chapter 6)

1. Load CA-Simply Accounting for Windows; open the data files for Windmill Wheels (A:\WINDMILL\Windmill.acs); then record the following transactions under the session date of 12/19/1997:

    December 31—Issue a payroll check to Art Roper for his regular salary, deducting $75.00 for medical insurance (Project: none). Print Check 3474.

    December 31—Issue a payroll check to Jennifer Soley for her regular salary, deducting $25.00 for medical insurance (Project: none). Print Check 3475.

    December 31—Issue a payroll check to Annette Watson for her regular salary, deducting $25.00 for medical insurance (Project: none). Print Check 3476.

    December 31—Issue a payroll check to Scott Zoe for 200 regular hours at his regular hourly rate and 10 hours at his overtime hourly rate (Project: none). Print Check 3477.

2. Record the following Payroll Ledger maintenance items:

    December 31—Create a new Payroll Ledger record for Rogello Lopez, 2811 SE 74th Avenue, Portland, Oregon 97206, 503-774-4750;. SSN# 541-8-3227; Birth Date: 12/12/1968; Hire Date: 12/31/1997. Regular Rate: 7.30; Overtime Rate: 10.95; Pay Periods: 12; Tax Table: Oregon; Federal Allowances: 1; Federal Status: Single; State Allowances: 1; State Status: Single.

    December 31—Modify Scott Zoe's address. He has moved to 4944 SW Barbur Blvd., Portland, Oregon 97201, 503-228-5052.

3. Print the following reports:

    1. Employee List 12/31/1997
    2. Payroll Journal 12/31/1997 to 12/31/1997
    3. Employee report (Select All, YTD Summary) 12/31/1997
    4. SUTA Summary (Oregon, YTD) 12/31/1997
    5. 940 Summary (Select All) 12/31/1997
    6. 941 Summary (Select All, FIT) 12/31/1997
    7. 941 Summary (Select All, SS/Med Tax) 12/31/1997
    8. W-2 slip for Scott Zoe
    9. Trial Balance As at 12/31/1997

4. Make a backup of Windmill Wheels' data files. Exit from the program. Complete the Windmill Wheels Transmittal.

TRANSMITTAL

Windmill Wheels   Name: _____
Chapter 7

A. Attach the following documents and reports:

1. Check 3474
2. Check 3475
3. Check 3476
4. Check 3477
5. Employee List 12/31/1997
6. Payroll Journal 12/31/1997 to 12/31/1997
7. Employee Year-to-Date Summary 12/31/1997
8. SUTA Year-to-Date Summary 12/31/1997
9. 940 Summary 12/31/1997
10. 941 FIT Summary 12/31/1997
11. 941 Social Security/Medicare Summary 12/31/1997
12. W-2 for Scott Zoe
13. Trial Balance As at 12/31/1997

B. Refer to your reports to list the amounts requested below:

1. What was Jennifer Soley's net take-home pay for December? $_____

2. Refer to the 940 Summary. How much YTD FUTA tax expense is reported? $_____

3. What is the balance of the Medical Insurance Payable account on 12/31/1997 $_____

4. What is the balance of the Wages account on 12/31/1997? $_____

5. Refer to the 941 Social Security/Medicare Summary report. How much Medicare
    tax expense was incurred for the calendar quarter ending 12/31/1997? $_____

MERCHANDISING BUSINESSES—
INVENTORY, GENERAL, AND PROJECTS

MERCHANDISING BUSINESSES—INVENTORY, GENERAL, AND PROJECTS

LEARNING OBJECTIVES

After studying this chapter, you will be able to:
- Open the Adjustments Journal
- Open the Item Assembly Journal
- Open the Inventory Ledger
- Enter inventory adjustment transactions
- Enter inventory transfer transactions
- Enter project allocations in the Adjustments Journal
- Review and edit Adjustments and Item Assembly Journals transactions
- Post transactions in the Adjustments and Item Assembly Journals
- Create, modify, and remove inventory records using the Inventory Ledger
- Display and print reports from the Adjustments and Item Assembly Journals
- Display and print inventory reports
- Display and print project reports
- Create, modify, and remove projects using the Projects Ledger
- Enter adjusting entries in the General Journal
- Prepare a bank reconciliation
- Display and print a trial balance, an income statement, and a balance sheet
- Perform a year-end closing of the accounting records
- Observe and understand inventory-related and general-related integration/linking accounts

END-OF-PERIOD PROCEDURES

In this chapter, you will continue working with the Oregon Explorer Maps company files. Features of the Inventory, Project, and General components of CA-Simply Accounting for Windows will be discussed in detail. In addition, year-end accounting procedures will be demonstrated. At the conclusion of this chapter, a practice set for Camera Corner will give you an opportunity to work with the Receivables, Payables, Payroll, Inventory, Project, and General components of CA-Simply Accounting for Windows all at the same time to record transactions and to perform the year-end procedures for a merchandising business. Source documents, similar to those illustrated throughout the Oregon Explorer Maps Tutorial are used to represent transactions in the Camera Corner practice set.

ACCOUNTING FOR INVENTORY

Three components of CA-Simply Accounting for Windows are used to account for certain types of inventory transactions and to maintain inventory records: Adjustments Journal, Item Assembly Journal, and Inventory Ledger. The Adjustments Journal is used to record adjustments to inventory items that have been damaged, lost, or become obsolete. As the name indicates, the Item Assembly Journal is used in a manufacturing business to record the components required to make or assemble an item. The Item Assembly Journal is also used to move inventory items from one inventory item record or classification to another. This might occur if two or more inventory items are combined to make a third inventory item or if a single inventory item is divided to make two or more inventory items. In this chapter, we will move items from one inventory item into another as a matter of correcting our records. Consequently, the Adjustments and Item Assembly Journals are used to record nonroutine types of transactions that affect inventory quantities and values. The Inventory Ledger keeps track of the inventory records for all goods and services that a business sells. Each record contains an item number, description, unit of measure, selling price, minimum level, quantity on hand, and value. The record also shows the asset, revenue, and expense accounts associated with each inventory item.

All inventory functions in CA-Simply Accounting for Windows are fully integrated with and linked to the General Ledger. This is done when the linking accounts are identified. For example, when an inventory adjustment is recorded in the Adjustments Journal, the program automatically records the entry in the General Journal, posts the related accounts in the General Ledger, and updates the inventory item's subsidiary record in the Inventory Ledger. Therefore, once an inventory-related transaction is posted, its effect on the overall financial condition of the company is reflected immediately and automatically throughout the company's financial records.

The following chart lists the possible combinations of positive and negative inventory-related entries in the CA-Simply Accounting for Windows Journals, and the effects of these entries on the related Inventory records and General Ledger accounts:

Effects of Inventory-Related Journal Entries on Account Balances

Journal	Notes*		Entry					Effect On:					
				Inventory				General Ledger				Project	
		Qty	Amt	Qty	Value	A/R	Inv	A/P	Rev	Exp	Rev	Exp	
Purchases	1	+	+	+	+		+	+					
	2	0	+	0	+		+	+					
	3	0	-	0	-		-	-					
	4	-	-	-	-		-	-					
Sales	5	+	+	-	-	+	-		+	+	+	+	
	6	-	-	+	+	-	+		-	-	-	-	
	7	+	0	-	-		-			+		+	
Adjust.	8	+	+	+	+		+			-		-	
	8	-	-	-	-		-			+		+	
	8	+	-	+	-		-			+		+	
	8	-	+	-	+		+			-		-	
	9	0	+	0	+		+			-		-	
	9	0	-	0	-		-			+		+	
	10	+	0	+	0								
	10	-	0	-	0								
Transfer	11	+	+	-/+	0		0						
	12	+	+	-/+	+		+			-			
	13	-	-	+/-	0		0						
	14	-	-	+/-	-		-			+			

Legend: (+ Increase), (- Decrease), (0 No change)

*Refer to the following notes for additional information and transaction description.

Notes:
1. Inventory purchase on account.
2. Increased charge for a previous inventory purchase. Inventory quantity unaffected.
3. Decreased charge for a previous inventory purchase (Purchase Discount). Inventory quantity unaffected.

4. Inventory returned to a vendor for credit. (Purchase Return and Allowance)
5. Inventory sale on account.
6. Inventory returned by a customer for credit. (Sales Return and Allowance)
7. Inventory provided to a customer at no charge.
8. Adjustment to inventory quantity and value.
9. Adjustment to inventory value. Quantity unaffected.
10. Adjustment to inventory quantity. Value is unaffected. No journal entry is produced.
11. An inventory transfer without additional costs. Inventory decreases for items transferred out and increases for items transferred in. A journal entry is produced only if the items being transferred involve different General Ledger inventory asset accounts.
12. An inventory transfer with additional costs. Inventory decreases for items transferred out and increases for items transferred in.
13. A reversed inventory transfer (correcting entry), without additional costs. Inventory increases for items transferred out and decreases for items transferred in. A journal entry is only produced if the items being transferred involved different General Ledger inventory asset accounts.
14. A reversed inventory transfer (correcting entry), with additional costs. Inventory increases for items transferred out and decreases for items transferred in.

OREGON EXPLORER MAPS TUTORIAL

The following tutorial is a step-by-step guide to recording adjusting and transfer entries and related project allocations within the Inventory and General components of CA-Simply Accounting for Windows. The methods used to establish inventory records in the Inventory Ledger and projects in the Project Ledger will also be demonstrated. The procedures used to prepare the financial statements, bank reconciliation, and closing the accounting records at the end of the year will be discussed. The procedures required to record merchandising transactions and project allocations in the Receivables and Payables components were discussed in Chapters 5 and 6. Payroll procedures were discussed in Chapter 7. The Oregon Explorer Maps Tutorial will be continued and concluded in this chapter to give you a comprehensive overview of how CA-Simply Accounting for Windows can be used to maintain the accounting records for a merchandising business.

INVENTORY ADJUSTING ENTRIES

At the end of each accounting period, businesses must make adjusting entries to update the accounting records prior to preparing the financial statements. Merchandising businesses need to take a physical count of the inventory remaining on hand at the end of the fiscal year and adjust the perpetual inventory records for any discrepancies that exist between the accounting records and the physical count. Oregon Explorer Maps has completed its annual physical inventory count, and the required adjustments are noted in the following memo:

Oregon Explorer Maps—Document 68   **Session Date: 12/31/1997**

Memo   **Date:** December 31, 1997

Inventory Count per Computerized Records:

Number	Description	Unit	Price	Quantity	Cost	Value
Attr2-D	Explore Oregon-Attractions	Each	2.25	946	0.54	510.85
Attr2-W	Explore Oregon-Attractions	Each	3.00	1,575	0.54	850.52
Golf1	Explore Oregon-Golf	Each	3.00	1,030	0.6907	711.38
RPlast	Plastic Racks	Each	5.95	177	4.9452	875.30
RWire	Wire Racks	Each	4.75	273	3.6984	1,009.65
RWood	Wood Racks	Each	4.95	247	3.9845	984.16
Ski1	Explore Oregon-Ski	Each	3.00	325	0.82	266.50
Ski2-D	Explore Oregon-Ski	Each	2.25	15,900	0.75	11,925.00
Ski2-W	Explore Oregon-Ski	Each	3.00	3,494	0.7499	2,620.25
Wine1	Explore Oregon-Wine	Each	3.00	456	0.76	346.56
Wine2-D	Explore Oregon-Wine	Each	2.25	15,875	0.68	10,794.75
Wine2-W	Explore Oregon-Wine	Each	3.00	2,904	0.68	1,974.72
						32,869.64

Inventory Corrections per Physical Count:

Correction 1 (Item Assembly Journal): Transfer 100 Attr2-W maps to Attr2-D maps at a total cost of $54.00. Comment: Records Correction.

Correction 2 (Adjustments Journal): Decrease Ski1 by 320 maps at a total cost of $266.50. Comment: Dated Inventory. (Project: Ski Map Sales Summary)

Correction 3 (Item Assembly Journal): Transfer 50 Wine2-W maps to Wine2-D maps at a total cost of $34.00. Comment: Records Correction.

Correction 4 (Adjustments Journal): Decrease Wine1 by 450 maps at a total cost of $342.00. Comment: Dated Inventory. (Project: Wine Map Sales Summary)

Item Assembly Journal—Recording Inventory Transfers

In a merchandising business, the Item Assembly Journal is used to record transfers from one inventory item record to another. Journal entries are produced only if the items transferred are associated with different inventory asset accounts and/or there are additional costs associated with the inventory item transfer. Subsidiary inventory item records will reflect the transfer regardless of whether or not a journal entry is produced.

 ACTION: Load CA-Simply Accounting for Windows; open the data files for Oregon Explorer Maps (A:\EXPLORER\Explorer.asc); then leave the session date set at 12/31/1997. The Oregon Explorer Maps home window will appear as shown below:

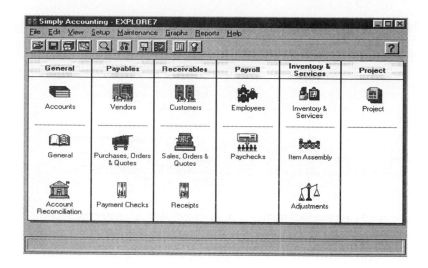

ACTION: Open the Item Assembly Journal dialog box by double-clicking on the **Item Assembly** icon. Your screen will look like this:

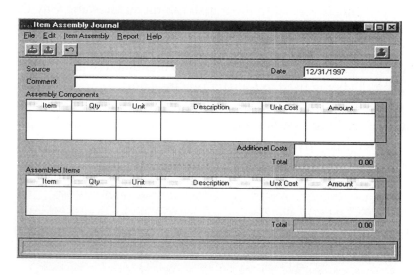

ACTION: Enter the word *Memo* into the **Source** field; press the TAB key; accept the default date of 12/31/1997; press the TAB key. Since this entry is being made to transfer maps from one category to another, enter *Records Correction* into the **Comment** field; then press the TAB key. Your screen will look like this:

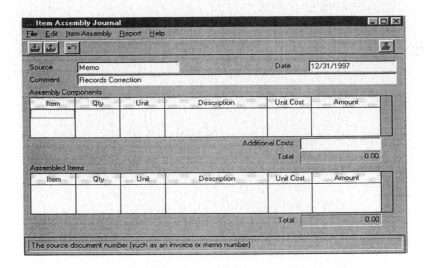

Explanation: The Source text box can be used for any reference number or notation you wish to associate with an inventory transfer and the source document that authorizes the transfer. The Comment text box can be used for comments related to the transfer in much the same way that an explanation is used when journal entries are recorded in a manual accounting system. Note that the flashing insertion point is positioned in the Assembly Components **Item** field. Remember, in a manufacturing business, the assembly components would contain the items used to manufacture an item for sale. In a merchandising business, this feature is being used to transfer one inventory item into another inventory item.

 ACTION: With the flashing insertion point positioned in the Assembly Components **Item** field, you will enter the item that inventory is being transferred from. Press the ENTER key or double-click in the **Item** field with your mouse. Your screen will look like this:

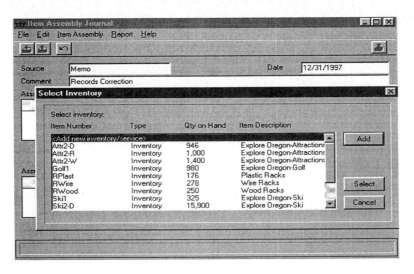

Explanation: The Select Inventory dialog box will appear.

 ACTION: To record the Correction 1 transfer (see Document 68), select the **Attr2-W** inventory item by double-clicking on the item or by highlighting the item and clicking the **Select** button. Your screen will look like this:

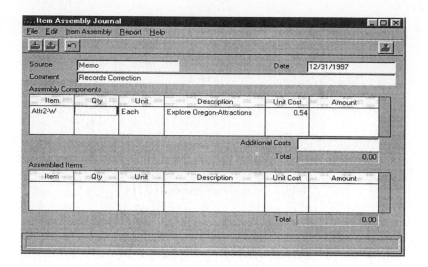

Explanation: The program has automatically completed the **Unit**, **Description**, and **Unit Cost** fields. The unit cost listed is the current average unit cost for this item based on the average cost inventory valuation method used by the CA-Simply Accounting for Windows program. You can change the unit cost if the transfer unit cost differs from the current average unit cost. The flashing insertion point is positioned in the **Qty** field.

 ACTION: With the flashing insertion point positioned in the **Qty** field, enter *100*; then press the TAB key. Your screen will look like this:

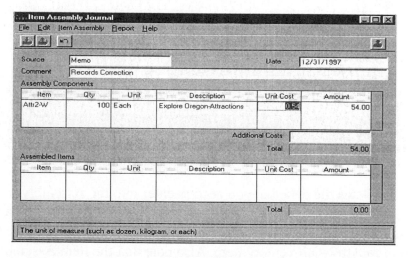

Explanation: The program has automatically multiplied the number entered in the **Qty** field (100) by the amount in the **Unit Cost** field (0.54) and entered the result in the **Amount** field (54.00). The program calculates the amount by multiplying the unit cost by the quantity. If you enter a different amount, the program will calculate the new unit cost by dividing amount by the quantity.

 ACTION: Click in the **Item** field under the Assembled Items portion of the dialog box to position the flashing insertion point in this field, this is where you will enter the item to which the inventory is being transferred. Press the ENTER key to display the Select Inventory dialog box; then select the **Attr2-D** inventory item. Your screen will look like this:

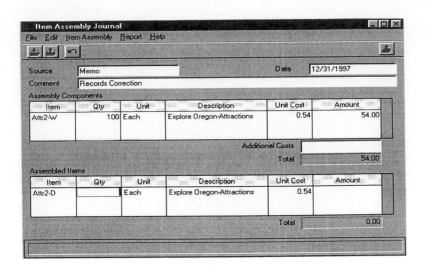

Explanation: The flashing insertion point is positioned in the Assembled Items **Qty** field.

ACTION: Enter *100* into the **Qty** field; then press the TAB key. Your screen will look like this:

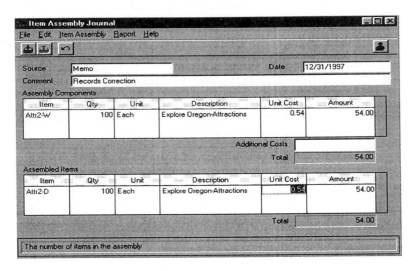

Explanation: This completes the data that you need to enter into the Assembly Item Journal dialog box to record Correction 1 from Document 68. Note that no entry was required in the **Additional Costs** field because there were no additional costs incurred by Oregon Explorer Maps to move these maps from Attr2-W inventory item to Attr2-D inventory item. Also note that the Item Assembly Journal dialog box does not have an allocation column or button. Project allocations can be made only to revenue and expense accounts. Inventory asset accounts are the only type of accounts affected by entries in the Item Assembly Journal. Before you post this entry, you need to verify that the transaction data are correct.

ACTION: Select **Display Item Assembly Journal Entry** from the Item Assembly Report menu. Your screen will look like this:

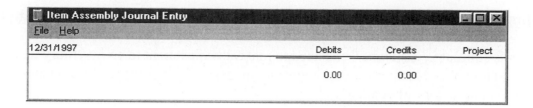

Explanation: No journal entry is produced by this transfer. Journal entries are produced only if the inventory items transferred are associated with different inventory asset accounts and/or there are additional costs associated with the inventory item transfer. The Attr2-W and Attr2-D inventory items are both associated with the Attraction Map Inventory account.

 ACTION: Close the Item Assembly Journal Entry window and return to the Item Assembly Journal. If you have made an error, use the following editing techniques to correct the error:

Editing Tips
Editing an Item Assembly Journal Entry

Move to the field that contains the error by either pressing the TAB key to move forward through each field or the SHIFT and TAB keys together to move to a previous field. This will highlight the selected field information so that you can change it. Alternatively, you can use the mouse to point to a field and drag through the incorrect information to highlight it. Type the correct information; then press the TAB key to enter it.

If an inventory item is incorrect, select the correct item from the Select Inventory Item dialog box after double-clicking on the incorrect item in the **Item** field.

To discard an entry and start over, either choose **Undo Entry** from the Item Assembly Journal Edit menu or click the **Close** button on the title bar. Click the **Yes** button in response to the question, "Are you sure you want to discard this journal entry?"

Review the transaction data for accuracy after any corrections.

It is IMPORTANT TO NOTE that the only way to edit a transaction after it is posted is to reverse the entry and enter the correct transaction. To correct transactions posted in error, see the correction made for Correction 3 to transfer Wine Maps later in the chapter.

 ACTION: After verifying that the transaction data are correct; click the **Post** button to record the transfer. Click the **OK** button on the following dialog box:

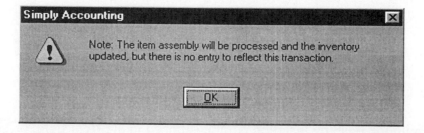

Adjustments Journal—Recording Inventory Adjustments and Project Allocations

The Adjustments Journal is used when you need to make an adjustment to an inventory item. In Correction 2, old and out-of-date inventory items (ski maps) are being removed from stock so an adjustment for this inventory item needs to be made.

ACTION: Close the Item Assembly Journal dialog box; then open the Adjustments Journal dialog box. Your screen will look like this:

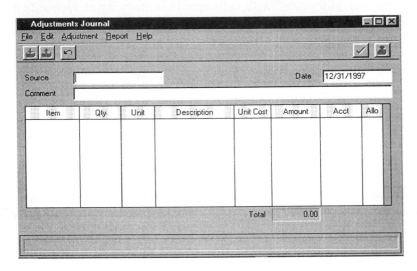

ACTION: Enter *Memo* into the **Source** field; press the TAB key; accept the default date of 12/31/1997; press the TAB key; enter *Dated Inventory* into the **Comment** field; then press the TAB key. Your screen will look like this:

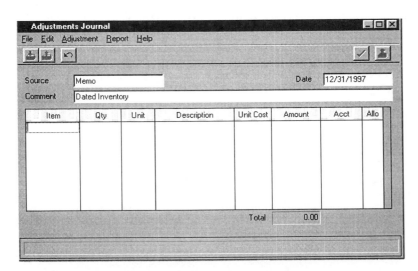

Explanation: The flashing insertion point is positioned in the **Item** field.

ACTION: With the flashing insertion point positioned in the **Item** field, press the ENTER key or double-click in the **Item** field with your mouse. Your screen will look like this:

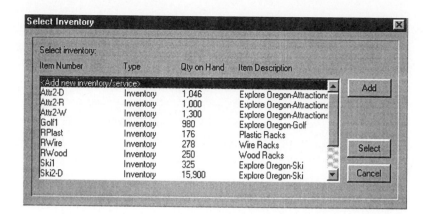

ACTION: To record the Correction 2 adjustment (see Document 68), select the Ski1 inventory item by double-clicking on the item or by highlighting the item and clicking the **Select** button. Your screen will look like this:

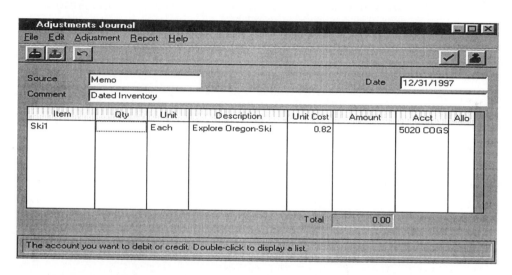

Explanation: The program has automatically completed the **Unit**, **Description**, **Unit Cost**, and **Acct** fields. The unit cost listed is the current average unit cost for this item based on the average cost inventory valuation method used by the CA-Simply Accounting for Windows program. You can change the unit cost if the adjustment unit cost differs from the current average unit cost. The flashing insertion point is positioned in the **Qty** field.

ACTION: With the flashing insertion point positioned in the **Qty** field, enter *-320*; then press the TAB key. Your screen will look like this:

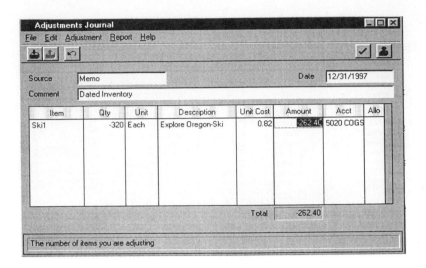

Explanation: The program has automatically multiplied the number entered in the **Qty** field (-320) by the amount in the **Unit Cost** field (0.82) and entered the result in the **Amount** field (-262.40). The program calculates the amount by multiplying the unit cost by the quantity. If you enter a different amount, the program will calculate the new unit cost by dividing amount by the quantity. The **Allo** column and button are now available (no longer dimmed).

ACTION: Click the **Allocate** button on the toolbar. ✓ Allocate 100% of the Ski1 map adjustment to the Ski Map Sales Summary Project. Your screen will look like this:

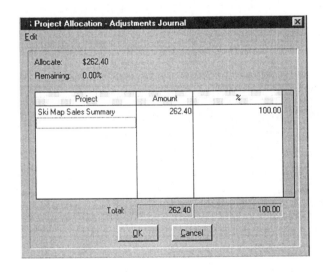

ACTION: Click the **OK** button to allocate the adjustment. Your screen will show the following:

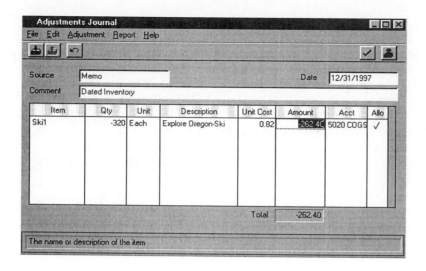

Explanation: This completes the data you need to enter into the Adjustments Journal dialog box to record Correction 2 from Document 68. Before you post this entry, you need to verify that the transaction data and allocations are correct.

 ACTION: Choose **Display Adjustments Journal Entry** from the Adjustments Journal Report menu. Your screen will look like this:

Adjustments Journal Entry			
File Help			
12/31/1997	Debits	Credits	Project
5020 COGS-Ski Maps	262.40	-	
- Ski Map Sales Summary			262.40
1220 Ski Map Inventory	-	262.40	
	262.40	262.40	

Explanation: Oregon Explorer Maps has elected to charge the cost of dated inventory to the cost of goods sold account associated with the inventory item. An alternative approach would be to establish a separate expense account for inventory adjustments. CA-Simply Accounting for Windows facilitates this approach through the use of an optional Adjustments Write-off Inventory integration/linking account. A similar integration/linking option is offered for transfer costs. For more information about these integration/linking options, see Chapter 9. When the cost of goods sold account is used, the standard journal entry for an inventory adjustment is:

	Debit	**Credit**
Cost of Goods Sold	xxx	
Inventory		xxx

Review the journal entry and allocation for accuracy noting any errors.

 ACTION: Close the Adjustments Journal Entry window. If you made an error, use the following editing techniques to correct the error:

Editing Tips
Editing Adjustments Journal Entries and Project Allocations

Move to the field that contains the error by either pressing the TAB key to move forward through each field or the SHIFT and TAB keys together to move to a previous field. This will highlight the selected field information so that you can change it. Alternatively, you can use the mouse to point to a field and drag through the incorrect information to highlight it. Type the correct information; then press the TAB key to enter it.

If an inventory item is incorrect, select the correct item from the Select Inventory Item dialog box after double-clicking on the incorrect item in the **Item** field.

If you have associated an inventory item with an incorrect account number, select the correct account number from the chart of accounts display after double-clicking on the incorrect account number in the **Acct** field.

If you have associated an inventory item with an incorrect project or have allocated an incorrect amount to a project, highlight a field in the incorrectly allocated inventory item line; then click the **Allocate** button or double-click in the **Allo** column to display the Project Allocation dialog box. To correct the project, select the correct project from the Select Project dialog box after double-clicking on the incorrect project in the **Project** field; then click the **OK** button. To correct the allocated amount or percentage, highlight the incorrect amount or percentage; enter the correct amount or percentage; then click the **OK** button.

To discard an entry and start over, either choose **Undo Entry** from the Adjustments Journal Edit menu or double-click the **Exit** button on the title bar. Click the **Yes** button in response to the question, "Are you sure you want to discard this journal entry?"

Review the journal entry and allocations for accuracy after any corrections by choosing **Display Adjustments Journal Entry** from the Adjustments Journal Report menu.

It is IMPORTANT TO NOTE that the only way to edit a transaction after it is posted is to reverse the entry and enter the correct transaction. To correct transactions posted in error, refer to the transactions for Corrections 2 and 4 later in the chapter.

ACTION: After verifying that the journal entry and allocation are correct, click the **Post** button to post the transaction. You will get the following message:

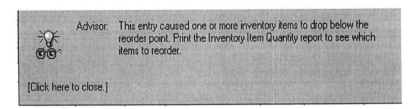

Advisor: This entry caused one or more inventory items to drop below the reorder point. Print the Inventory Item Quantity report to see which items to reorder.

[Click here to close.]

ACTION: Click the **[Click here to close.]** prompt on the Advisor. Close the Adjustments Journal dialog box and return to the home window.

Additional Inventory Adjusting Entries

Refer to Document 68. Record the information for Correction 3 and Correction 4.

ACTION: After you have posted the transaction data associated with Correction 3 and Correction 4 in Document 68, from the home window Reports menu, point to Journal Entries, Adjustments. Your screen will look like this:

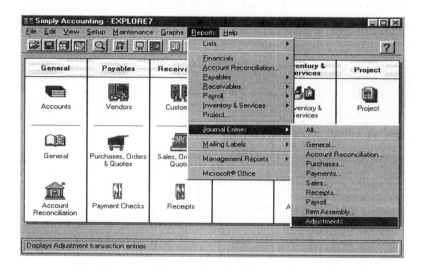

ACTION: Click **Adjustments**. Your screen will show the following:

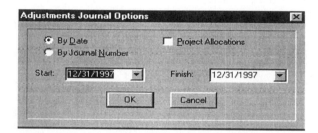

Explanation: The Adjustments Journal Options dialog box appears, asking you to define the information you want displayed.

ACTION: Select **By Date**; check the **Project Allocations** check box; leave the start and finish dates set at 12/31/1997; then click the **OK** button. Your screen will look like this:

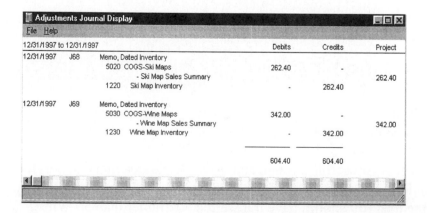

Explanation: Review the display for accuracy, verifying that journal entry dates, account names and numbers, amounts, and allocations are correct. If you have posted an incorrect transaction, refer to the special editing box presented earlier in the chapter.

ACTION: Select **Print** from the Adjustments Journal Display File menu. Compare your report to the one shown below:

Oregon Explorer Maps/Your Name
Adjustments Journal 12/31/1997 to 12/31/1997

				Debits	**Credits**	**Project**
12/31/1997	J41	Memo, Dated Inventory				
		5020	COGS-Ski Maps	262.40	-	
			Ski Map Sales Summary			262.40
		1220	Ski Map Inventory	-	262.40	
12/31/1997	J42	Memo, Dated Inventory				
		5030	COGS-Wine Maps	342.00	-	
			Wine Map Sales Summary			342.00
		1230	Wine Map Inventory	-	342.00	
				604.40	604.40	

ACTION: Close the Adjustments Journal Display window. Double-click the **Inventory & Services** icon on the home window. Click the **Display by Name** button on the Inventory & Services toolbar. You will see the following:

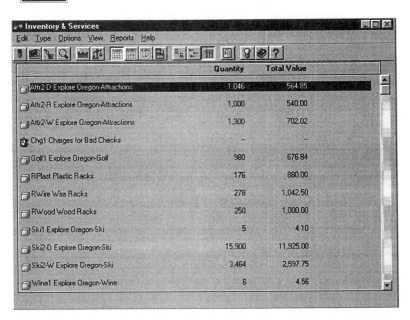

Explanation: You will see a listing of the inventory and service items for the company. In addition, the **Display by Name** button also lists the quantity and total value for each inventory item.

ACTION: As you scroll through and examine the Inventory & Services Ledger, you realize that you should have made the quantity and value for Ski1 and Wine1 equal to zero (0). You also determine that you should have transferred 507 rather than 50 Wine2-W maps to Wine2-D maps, making the Wine2-W quantity 2,400. Close the Inventory & Services Ledger.

▨ **ACTION:** Open the Item Assembly Journal. Your screen will show the following:

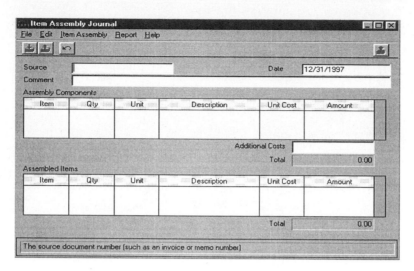

Explanation: You have two ways in which to enter the correction to the Item Assembly Journal: Because the original transaction was used to transfer maps from one category or item to another and did not involve any change in cost or value, you can simply record an additional transfer. The second method would be to reverse the original transfer of 50 Wine2-W maps and re-enter the correct amount of 507 maps. To become familiar with the reversal of the original transaction, we will reverse the original entry and record the correct entry.

▨ **ACTION:** To indicate a correcting entry, enter *Memo COR* as the source. The date remains 12/31/1997. The comment should be *Correcting Entry*. Select **Wine2-W** as the item. Your screen will show the following:

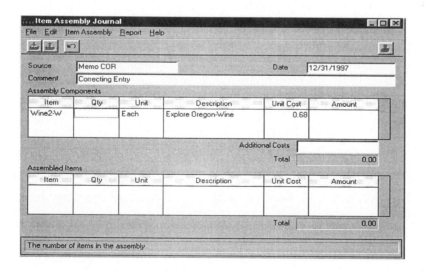

▨ **ACTION:** The cursor should be positioned in the **Qty** column. Enter *-50* in the **Qty** column. Press TAB. Your screen will show the following:

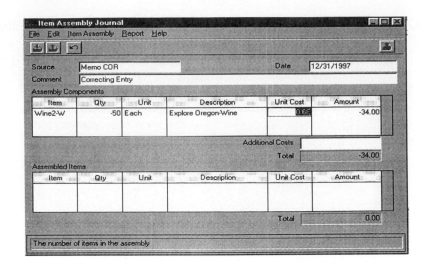

Explanation: When a negative quantity is entered, the amount will also be negative.

ACTION: Click in the **Item** column for Assembled Items. Enter *Wine2-D* as the item and *-50* as the quantity. Press TAB. Your screen will show the following:

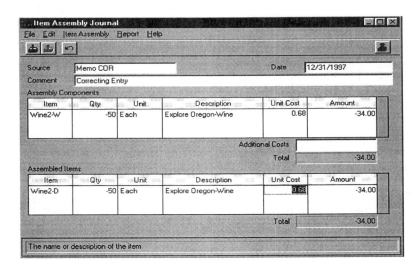

ACTION: Click the **Post** button on the toolbar to record the correction. Close the Item Assembly Journal or click the **Simply Accounting** button on the taskbar to return to the home window. Double-click the **Inventory & Services** icon. Scroll through the item list until you see Wine2-D and Wine2-W. Your screen will show the following:

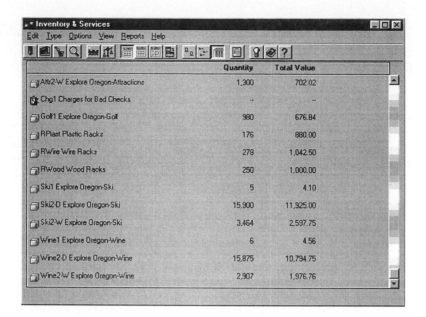

ACTION: Return to the Item Assembly Journal and record the transaction to transfer 507 Wine2-W maps to Wine2-D maps. Use the original comment of *Records Correction*. As you access the Item Selection screen, notice the quantity and value of the inventory item. When the transaction has been entered, your screen will show the following:

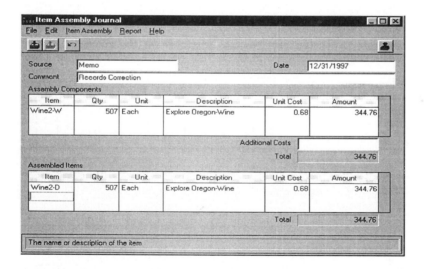

ACTION: Post the transaction, close the Item Assembly Ledger, and open the Inventory & Services Ledger. Scroll through the item list until you see Wine2-D and Wine2-W. Note the change in quantity and value. Your screen will show the following:

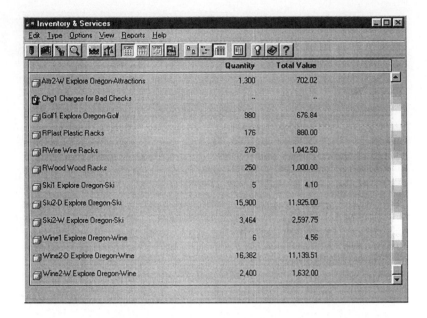

ACTION: Close or minimize the Inventory & Services Ledger. Open the Adjustments Journal. Your screen will show the following:

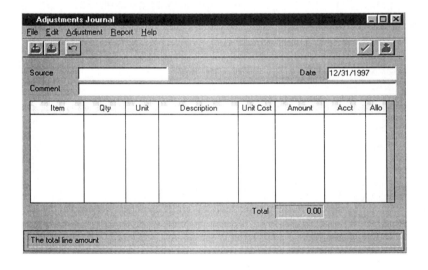

ACTION: Enter *Memo COR* as the source; the date remains 12/31/1997, and the comment is *Dated Inventory Reversal*. Your screen will show the following:

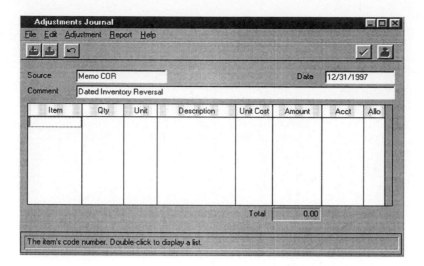

ACTION: Enter *Ski1* as the item. The quantity will be the opposite of the original entry, so enter *320* and press TAB. Allocate the transaction to Ski Map Sales Summary. Your screen will show the following:

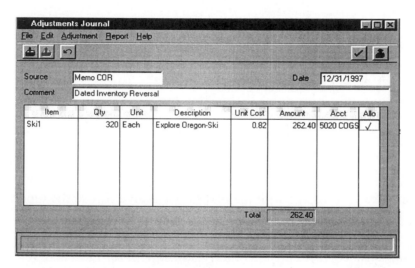

Explanation: Because the original entry was -320, the correction is 320 and the amount is $262.40.

ACTION: A correction may be made in the form of a compound entry because there are two adjustments that need to be corrected. Combine the correction by clicking in the **Item** column beneath Ski1. Select **Wine1** as the item and enter *450* for the quantity. Allocate the transaction to Wine Map Sales Summary and press TAB. Your screen will show the following:

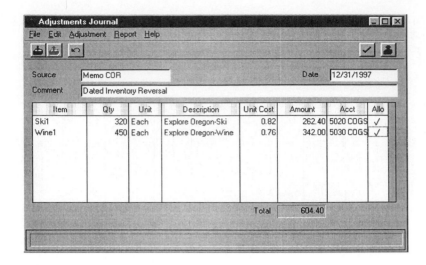

ACTION: Click **Report** on the menu bar. Click **Display Adjustments Journal Entry**. You will see the following report:

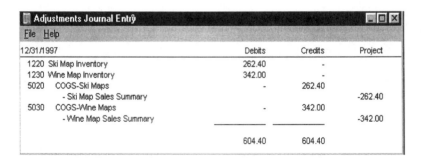

ACTION: Compare your report with the one shown above. Close the report. If you made any errors, correct them. Post the correction.

ACTION: Record the correct dated inventory adjustment for Ski1 and Wine1 as a compound entry. Enter *Memo* as the Source; the date remains 12/31/1997, and the comment is *Dated Inventory*. Access the Select Inventory screen by double-clicking in the **Item** column. Click **Ski1**. Your screen will show the following:

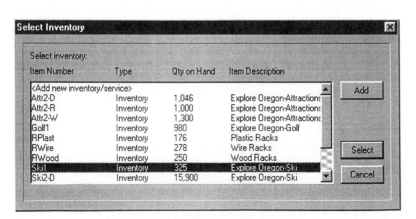

Explanation: Notice the **Qty on Hand** column shows 325 Explore Oregon-Ski maps.

ACTION: Select **Ski1** and enter *-325* for the quantity. Allocate the transaction to Ski Map Sales Summary. Your screen will show the following:

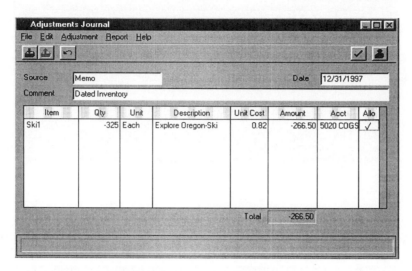

Explanation: The quantity is -325, and the amount is -266.50. This entry should reduce the quantity for Ski1 to zero.

ACTION: Position the cursor in the **Items** column beneath Ski1. Open the Select Item dialog box by double-clicking. Click **Wine1** to highlight. Your screen will show the following:

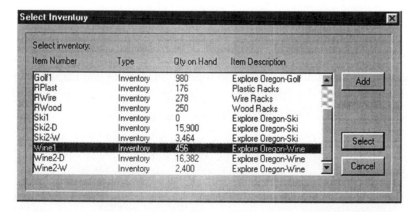

Explanation: Notice that the quantity on hand for Ski1 is 0. The quantity on hand for Wine1 is 456. The next step of the compound entry will make the quantity on hand for Wine1 zero.

ACTION: Select **Wine1** as the item number; enter *-456* in the **Qty** column. Allocate the transaction to the Wine Map Sales Summary. Your screen will show the following:

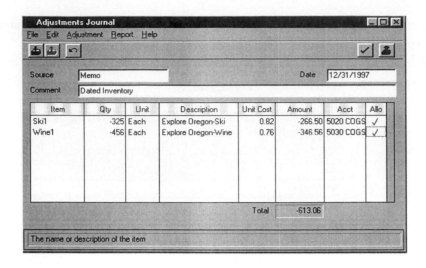

ACTION: Display the Adjustments Journal Entry report. Your report will appear as follows:

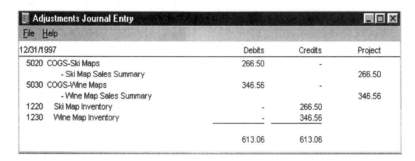

ACTION: Compare your journal entry with the one shown above. Close the Adjustments Journal Entry report and correct any errors you may have made. Post the transaction and close the Adjustments Journal. Open the Inventory & Services Ledger. Scroll through the ledger until you see the Ski and Wine items. Your ledger should appear as shown:

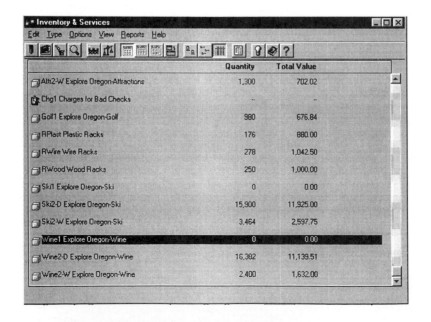

Explanation: Notice that the quantity for Ski1 is 0, the quantity for Wine1 is 0, and the quantity for Wine2-W is 2,400. The corrections and adjustments have been made correctly.

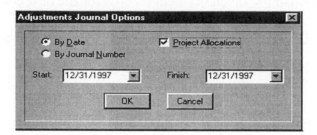

ACTION: Close the Inventory & Services Ledger. Prepare an Adjustments Journal report by clicking **Reports** on the home window menu bar, pointing to Journal Entries, and clicking **Adjustments**. You will get the following dialog box:

ACTION: Prepare the Adjustments Journal report by date for 12/31/1997 to 12/31/1997. Select **Project Allocations**. Click **OK.** Your report will appear as follows:

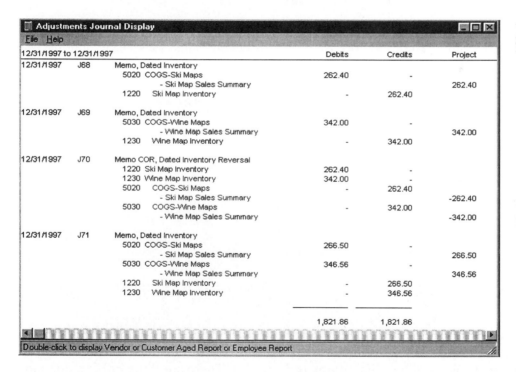

ACTION: Print your report and compare it with the one shown above. Close the Adjustments Journal Report.

INVENTORY LEDGER—MAINTAINING INVENTORY RECORDS

Transactions can be entered only through the Journals components of the program. The Inventory & Services Ledger component is used to maintain item records. Each item record contains an item number, description, unit, price, minimum level, quantity on hand, and value. The record also shows the asset, revenue, and expense accounts associated with or linked to each inventory item. You can create, modify, or remove inventory records through the Inventory & Services Ledger dialog box.

Creating an Inventory Record

The second edition of the Explore Oregon-Golf map is expected to arrive from the printer soon. The accountant would like to establish the inventory item records for the new edition of the map in advance.

Oregon Explorer Maps—Document 69   **Session Date: 12/31/1997**

Memo   **Date:** December 31, 1997

Create a new Inventory Ledger inventory item record as follows:

Item: Golf2 Explore Oregon-Golf; Unit: Each; Selling Price: 3.00; Min. Level: 100; Asset: 1210 Golf Map Inventory; Revenue: 4210 Wholesale Golf Map Sales; Expense: 5010 COGS-Golf Maps

ACTION: Open the Inventory & Services Ledger. Click the **Create** button. 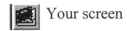 Your screen will look like this:

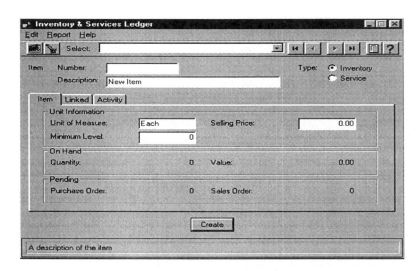

Explanation: A blank ledger dialog box is displayed. There are three information tabs containing fields. The tabs and fields are defined as follows:

Item Tab

Item Number: In the left part of the field, enter the item number or descriptive abbreviation.

Description: Enter a description of the item, up to 35 characters.

Type: Indicate whether the item is an inventory item or a service item.

Unit Information: This section contains information about the size, price, and so forth of the item:

Unit of Measure: Enter the unit of measure by which the item is sold, up to seven characters. For example, enter dozen, gram, gallon, hour, or each.

Selling Price: Enter the selling price per unit. The program fills in this price when you enter a sales invoice, but you can change it on the invoice if you wish.

Minimum Level: Enter the minimum number of units to which the stock on hand can fall before you order new stock. The program uses this number in the Inventory Quantity report to alert you to reorder items that are below the minimum.

On Hand: This section contains information supplied by Simply regarding the number of units on hand and the value of the units on hand. The program updates it every time you buy, sell, transfer, or adjust a quantity of this item.

Pending: This section contains information supplied by Simply regarding the number of items on order.

Linked Tab

Asset: Click the drop-down list arrow to the right of the field to display a list of asset accounts in the General Ledger; then choose the one you want to associate with this inventory item. Through the program's integration/linking feature, the asset account selected will be posted when transactions affecting inventory are recorded in the Sales, Purchases, Adjustments, and Item Assembly Journals.

Revenue: Click the drop-down list arrow to the right of the field to display a list of revenue accounts in the General Ledger; then choose the one you want to associate with this inventory item. Through the program's integration/linking feature, the revenue account selected will be posted when transactions affecting inventory are recorded in the Sales Journal.

C.O.G.S.: Click the drop-down list arrow to the right of the field to display a list of cost of goods sold accounts in the General Ledger; then choose the one you want to associate with this inventory item. Through the program's integration/linking feature, the cost of goods sold account selected will be posted when transactions affecting inventory are recorded in the Sales, Adjustments, and Item Assembly Journals.

Activity Tab

Provide year-to-date and last year historical information regarding the number of transactions, sales, and cost of goods sold for the item.

 ACTION: Enter the available information about the new inventory item into the Inventory & Services Ledger dialog box. Complete the Items tab first. Your screen will look like this:

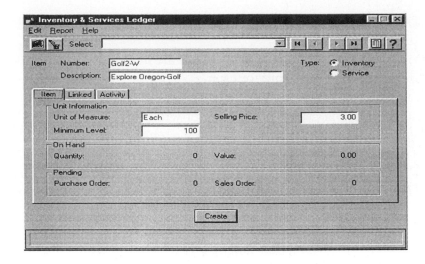

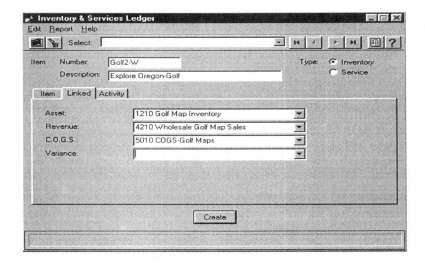

ACTION: Click the **Linked** tab. Refer to the transaction memo and complete the account information to link specific asset, revenue, and cost of goods sold accounts to this item. Your screen will show the following:

ACTION: Click the **Activity** Tab. There is nothing to enter on this tab at this time; however, familiarize yourself with this screen. Review the information on all tabs and verify that the information you entered is correct. If you have made an error, use the following editing techniques to correct the error:

Editing Tips
Editing an Inventory Ledger Record

Move to the field that contains the error by either pressing the TAB key to move forward through each field or the SHIFT and TAB keys together to move to a previous field. This will highlight the selected field information so that you can change it. Alternatively, you can use the mouse to point to a field and drag through the incorrect information to highlight it. Type the correct information; then press the TAB key to enter it.

Click the drop-down list arrows to select field information as required.

To discard a record and start over, choose **Undo Changes** from the Inventory Ledger Edit menu; then click the **Yes** button in response to the question, "Are you sure you want to undo changes to this ledger page?" Alternatively, double-click the **Exit** button on the toolbar; then click the **No** button in response to the question, "Do you still want to create this ledger page?"

It is IMPORTANT TO NOTE that the only way to edit a Inventory Ledger record after it is created is to either modify the record or remove it and create a new Inventory Ledger record.

 ACTION: When the Inventory Ledger page is correct, click the **Create** button.

Explanation: The program has added the new inventory item to Oregon Explorer Maps' records.

Modifying an Inventory Record

If you have an error in an inventory record after you have created it or need to change some information about an inventory item, choose **Find** from the Inventory Ledger Edit menu or click the **Find** button on the toolbar; then choose the inventory item from the list presented. Make corrections as necessary, using the Editing Tips for Editing an Inventory Ledger Record. To accept the changes, either use the scroll bar to move to another ledger page or close the dialog box by clicking the **Exit** button. Note that you can change only descriptive information about an item, such as unit price or minimum level; to change the quantity or value, you must make entries in the Purchases, Sales, Transfers, or Adjustments Journals.

Removing an Inventory Record

You cannot remove an inventory record unless its quantity on hand is zero. If the quantity is not zero, you must wait until journal entries in the Sales, Adjustments, or Item Assembly Journals have changed the quantity to zero. To remove an inventory record, choose **Find** from the Inventory Ledger Edit menu; then choose the inventory item from the list presented or click the drop-down list arrow next to Selection on the Inventory & Services Ledger dialog box. Choose **Remove** from the Inventory Ledger Edit menu or click the **Remove** button on the toolbar. The program will ask you if you are sure you want to remove the inventory record. Click **Yes** to remove it; then close the dialog box by clicking the **Exit** button.

 ACTION: Click the drop-down list arrow for **Select**. Click **Ski1** to highlight. Your screen will show the following:

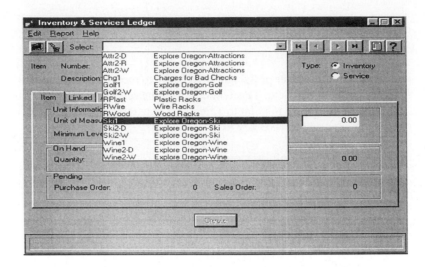

ACTION: Double-click **Ski1** to insert as the ledger item. Click the **Remove** button on the toolbar. You may get the following dialog box:

ACTION: Click **OK.** Close the Inventory & Services Ledger and return to the home window. Click the **Maintenance** menu on the home window menu bar. Point to Clear Inventory Tracking Data. Your screen will show the following:

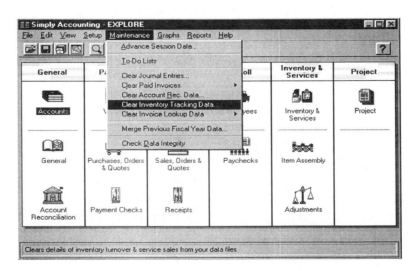

ACTION: Click **Clear Inventory Tracking Data**. You will get the following dialog box:

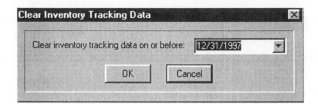

Explanation: When you clear inventory tracking data, additional disk space is made available and the program clears the details of processed invoices. In case you need to look up invoice details later, be sure you have a backup of your data before you clear inventory tracking data.

ACTION: Click **OK** to accept the date of 12/31/1997. You will get the following message:

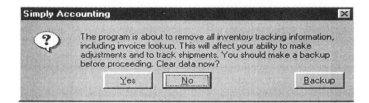

ACTION: If you have not backed up your data recently, click **Backup** and follow previous instructions for creating a backup. When you have a current backup of your data, click **Yes**.

ACTION: Double-click the **Inventory & Services** icon on the home window. Click **Ski1** on the list of Inventory items shown. Click the **Remove** button. You will get the following message:

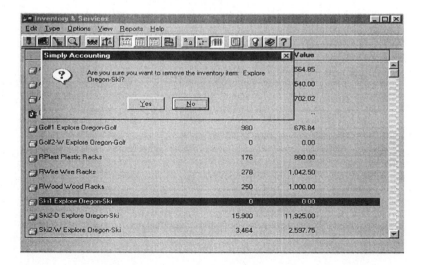

ACTION: Click **Yes**. Ski1 has been removed from the Inventory & Services Ledger. Close the ledger and return to the home window.

Additional Inventory Ledger Maintenance Items

Enter the following additional maintenance items:

Document 70 December 31—Create a new Inventory Ledger inventory item record as follows:

Item: Golf2-D Explore Oregon-Golf; Unit: Each; Selling Price: 2.25; Min. level: 100; Asset: 1210 Golf Map Inventory; Revenue: 4310 Distributor Golf Map Sales; Expense: 5010 COGS-Golf Maps

Document 71 December 31—Remove the Wine1 inventory item record.

INVENTORY REPORTS

A variety of inventory-related reports are available in CA-Simply Accounting for Windows. The program can print or display Inventory List, Inventory Quantity, and Inventory Synopsis reports. Use the scroll bars at the bottom or right side of a displayed report to view reports that contain more text than can be displayed at one time.

 ACTION: Click the home window Reports menu; point to Lists; point to Inventory & Services. Your screen will look like this:

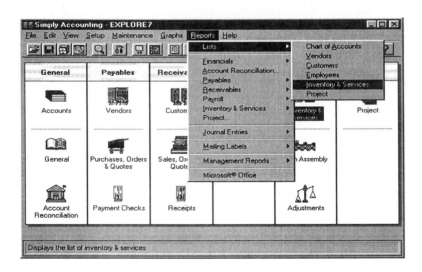

 ACTION: Click **Inventory & Services**. You will see the following list:

```
Inventory and Services List
File  Help

12/31/1997
Attr2-D              Explore Oregon-Attractions                           Inventory
 1240 Attraction Map Inventory  4340 Distributor Attraction Ma... 5040 COGS-Attraction Maps  ...
Attr2-R              Explore Oregon-Attractions                           Inventory
 1240 Attraction Map Inventory  4410 Retail Attraction Map Sa... 5040 COGS-Attraction Maps  ...
Attr2-W              Explore Oregon-Attractions                           Inventory
 1240 Attraction Map Inventory  4240 Wholesale Attraction M... 5040 COGS-Attraction Maps  ...
Chg1                 Charges for Bad Checks                               Service
 ...                  4820 Bad Check Charges          ...                  ...
Golf1                Explore Oregon-Golf                                  Inventory
 1210 Golf Map Inventory  4210 Wholesale Golf Map Sal... 5010 COGS-Golf Maps  ...
Golf2-D              Explore Oregon-Golf                                  Inventory
 1210 Golf Map Inventory  4310 Distributor Golf Map Sales 5010 COGS-Golf Maps  ...
Golf2-W              Explore Oregon-Golf                                  Inventory
 1210 Golf Map Inventory  4210 Wholesale Golf Map Sal... 5010 COGS-Golf Maps  ...
RPlast               Plastic Racks                                        Inventory
 1250 Rack Inventory      4500 Rack Sales          5050 COGS-Racks         ...
RWire                Wire Racks                                           Inventory
 1250 Rack Inventory      4500 Rack Sales          5050 COGS-Racks         ...
RWood                Wood Racks                                           Inventory
 1250 Rack Inventory      4500 Rack Sales          5050 COGS-Racks         ...
Ski2-D               Explore Oregon-Ski                                   Inventory
 1220 Ski Map Inventory   4320 Distributor Ski Map Sales 5020 COGS-Ski Maps ...
Ski2-W               Explore Oregon-Ski                                   Inventory
 1220 Ski Map Inventory   4220 Wholesale Ski Map Sales 5020 COGS-Ski Maps   ...
Wine2-D              Explore Oregon-Wine                                  Inventory
 1230 Wine Map Inventory  4330 Distributor Wine Map Sa... 5030 COGS-Wine Maps ...
Wine2-W              Explore Oregon-Wine                                  Inventory
 1230 Wine Map Inventory  4230 Wholesale Wine Map Sa... 5030 COGS-Wine Maps  ...

Items on file: 14
```

ACTION: Choose **Print** from the Inventory List File menu. Compare your report to the one shown above.

ACTION: Close the Inventory List window; point to Inventory on the Inventory & Services selection on home window Reports menu. Your screen will look like this:

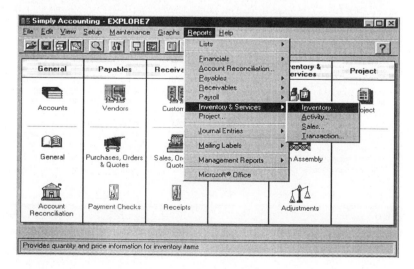

ACTION: Click **Inventory**. You will get the following Inventory Report Options dialog box:

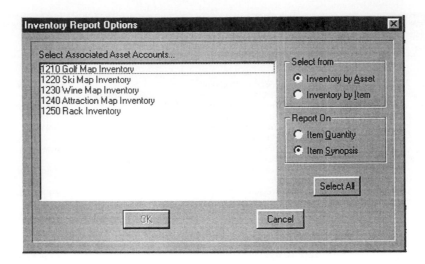

Explanation: The Inventory Report Options dialog box appears, asking you to define the information you want displayed.

You can choose to display items associated with one or more asset accounts (Select from Inventory by Asset), with individual inventory items (Select from Inventory by Item), or for all items (Select All). The Inventory Quantity report shows item number, item description, unit, quantity of stock on hand, minimum stock level, and the number of items that have fallen below the minimum stock level. The Inventory Synopsis report shows item number, item description, unit, price, quantity of stock on hand, cost, and value (quantity multiplied by cost). In addition, the Inventory Synopsis report shows the margin percentage of each inventory item.

   ACTION: Click the **Inventory by Asset** and **Item Synopsis** options; click the **Select All** button; then click the **OK** button. Your screen will look like this:

Inventory Synopsis			Price	Quantity	Cost	Value	Margin (%)
12/31/1997							
Attr2-D	Explore Oregon-Attra...	Each	2.25	1,046	0.54	564.85	76.00
Attr2-R	Explore Oregon-Attra...	Each	4.50	1,000	0.54	540.00	88.00
Attr2-W	Explore Oregon-Attra...	Each	3.00	1,300	0.54	702.02	82.00
Golf1	Explore Oregon-Golf	Each	3.00	980	0.6907	676.84	76.98
Golf2-D	Explore Oregon-Golf	Each	2.25	0	0.0	0.00	100.00
Golf2-W	Explore Oregon-Golf	Each	3.00	0	0.0	0.00	100.00
RPlast	Plastic Racks	Each	5.95	176	5.0	880.00	15.97
RWire	Wire Racks	Each	4.75	278	3.75	1,042.50	21.05
RWood	Wood Racks	Each	4.95	250	4.0	1,000.00	19.19
Ski2-D	Explore Oregon-Ski	Each	2.25	15,900	0.75	11,925.00	66.67
Ski2-W	Explore Oregon-Ski	Each	3.00	3,464	0.7499	2,597.75	75.00
Wine2-D	Explore Oregon-Wine	Each	2.25	16,382	0.68	11,139.51	69.78
Wine2-W	Explore Oregon-Wine	Each	3.00	2,400	0.68	1,632.00	77.33
						32,700.47	

ACTION: Select **Print** from the Inventory Synopsis File menu. Compare your report to the one shown above.

ACTION: Close the Inventory Synopsis window and return to the home window.

ACTION: Choose **Exit** from the home window File menu to end the current work session and return to your Windows desktop.

ALTERNATIVE ACTION: You can continue with the tutorial without exiting from the program if you wish. The next steps are recorded under the same session date as the prior steps. Skip the next ACTION; then continue with the tutorial.

PROJECT LEDGER—MAINTAINING PROJECT RECORDS

Transactions can be entered only through the Journals components of the program. The Project Ledger component is used to maintain project records. Each record contains a project name and start date. The Project Ledger does not have its own journal; allocation information is stored with journal entries in the originating journal. Consequently, the Project Ledger serves only a reporting role in the CA-Simply Accounting for Windows program.

Creating a Project Record

To create a new project, open the Project Ledger; then choose Create from the Project Ledger Edit menu. Enter the requested information:

Project Name: Enter the project name, up to 35 characters.

Start Date: Enter the date the project started or the date you wish to begin accumulating project-related revenue and expense information.

Balance Forward Section

Revenue and Expenses: Enter any revenue or expenses generated by the project as of the end of the previous month.

Click the **Create** button after verifying that all of the information is correct.

Modifying a Project Record

If you have an error in a project record after you have created it or need to change some information about a project, choose the project by clicking the drop-down list arrow for **Select** on the Project Ledger, then choose the project from the list presented. Make corrections as necessary. To accept the changes, either use the scroll bar to move to another ledger page or close the dialog box by clicking the **Exit** button.

Removing a Project Record

You can remove a project record at any time. However, you should not remove a project unless you have printed all the reports that contain information related to that project; after you remove the project, the reports are not available. To remove a project, choose the project by clicking the drop-down list arrow for **Select** on the Project Ledger, then choose the project from the list presented. Click the **Remove** button on the toolbar. The program will ask you if you are sure you want to remove the project record. Click **Yes** to remove it; then close the dialog box.

PROJECT REPORTS

A variety of project reports are available in CA-Simply Accounting for Windows. The program can print or display Project List, Project Summary, and Project Detail reports. Use the scroll bars at the bottom or right side of a displayed report to view reports that contain more text than can be displayed at one time.

ACTION: Load CA-Simply Accounting for Windows; open the data files for Oregon Explorer Maps (A:\EXPLORER\Explorer.asc); leave the session date set at 12/31/1997. The home window for Oregon Explorer Maps will appear.

ACTION: Choose **Lists**, then click **Project** on the home window Reports menu. Your screen will show the following report:

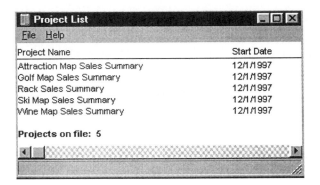

ACTION: Choose **Print** from the Project List File menu. Compare your report to the one shown above.

ACTION: Close the Project List window; then choose **Project** from the home window Reports menu. Your screen will look like this:

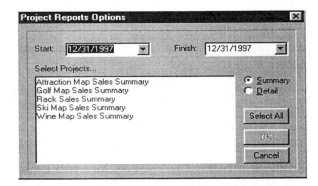

Explanation: The Project Report Options dialog box appears, asking you to define the information you want displayed.

Enter the start and finish dates or accept the dates displayed. The start date must be between the earliest transaction date and the session date inclusive. The finish date must be between the start date and the session date inclusive. Select **Summary** to include totals for revenue and expense accounts, or select **Detail** to include all journal entries as well as totals. Select a project or projects from the list, or choose **Select All**.

 ACTION: Enter *12/1/1997* as the start date; leave the finish date set at 12/31/1997; click the **Detail** option button; click the **Select All** button; click the **OK** button. Your screen will look like this:

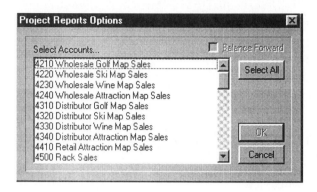

Explanation: A second Project Reports Options dialog box will appear, asking you to further define the information you want displayed.

Select an account or accounts from the Select Accounts list, or choose **Select All** to include all revenue and expense accounts that have project allocations. Check the **Balance Forward** check box to include the balance forward from previous years accumulations for the selected Projects. **Note**: The **Balance Forward** check box is dimmed for Oregon Explorer Maps. The company started using the Project component of CA-Simply Accounting for Windows on December 1; therefore, there are no prior year accumulations to report.

 ACTION: Click the **Select All** button; then click the **OK** button. Your screen will look like this:

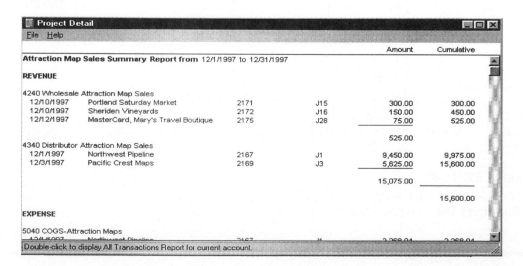

ACTION: Choose **Print** from the Project Detail File menu. Compare your report to the one shown below:

Oregon Explorer Maps/Your Name
Attraction Map Sales Summary Detail Report from 12/1/1997 to 12/31/1997

REVENUE
4240 Wholesale Attraction Map Sales

12/10/1997	Portland Saturday Market	2171	J15	300.00	300.00
12/10/1997	Sheriden Vineyards	2172	J16	150.00	450.00
12/12/1997	MasterCard, Mary's Travel Boutique	2175	J28	75.00	525.00
				525.00	

4340 Distributor Attraction Map Sales

12/1/1997	Northwest Pipeline	2167	J1	9,450.00	9,975.00
12/3/1997	Pacific Crest Maps	2169	J3	5,625.00	15,600.00
				15,075.00	
					15,600.00

EXPENSE
5040 COGS-Attraction Maps

12/1/1997	Northwest Pipeline	2167	J1	2,268.04	2,268.04
12/3/1997	Pacific Crest Maps	2169	J3	1,350.02	3,618.06
12/10/1997	Portland Saturday Market	2171	J15	54.00	3,672.06
12/10/1997	Sheriden Vineyards	2172	J16	27.00	3,699.06
12/12/1997	MasterCard, Mary's Travel Boutique	2175	J28	13.50	3,712.56
				3,712.56	

5439 Advertising Expense

12/14/1997	The Oregon Magazine	927	J37	300.00	4,012.56
					4,012.56

Revenue minus Expense   11,587.44

Oregon Explorer Maps/Your Name
Golf Map Sales Summary Detail Report from 12/1/1997 to 12/31/1997

REVENUE
4210 Wholesale Golf Map Sales

12/12/1997	Visa, <One-time customer>	2174	J27	75.00	75.00
12/12/1997	MasterCard, Mary's Travel boutique	2175	J28	75.00	150.00
				150.00	

4700 Sales Returns and Allowances

12/4/1997	Springwater Country Club	CM56	J6	-6.00	144.00

EXPENSE
4010 COGS-Golf Maps

12/4/1997	Springwater Country Club	CM56	J6	-1.38	-1.38
12/12/1997	Visa, <One-time customer>	2174	J27	17.27	15.89
12/12/1997	MasterCard, Mary's Travel Boutique	2175	J28	17.27	33.16
				33.16	
					33.16

REVENUE minus EXPENSE   110.84

Oregon Explorer Maps/Your Name
Rack Sales Summary Detail Report from 12/1/1997 to 12/31/1997

REVENUE

4500	Rack Sales				
12/1/1997	Northwest Pipeline	2167	J1	190.25	190.25
12/2/1997	Applegate Vineyard Winery	2168	J2	4.75	195.00

12/2/1997	Reversing J2. Correction is J5.	ADJ2168	J4	-4.75	190.25
12/12/1997	Applegate Vineyard Winery	2168	J5	4.95	195.20
12/12/1997	Visa, <One-time customer>	2174	J27	11.90	207.10
12/12/1997	MasterCard, Mary's Travel Boutique	2175	J28	11.90	219.00
				219.00	
					219.00

EXPENSE

5050 COGS-Racks

12/1/19997	Northwest Pipeline	2167	J1	156.25	156.25
12/2/1997	Applegate Vineyard Winery	2168	J2	3.75	160.00
12/2/1997	Reversing J2. Correction is J5.	ADJ2168	J4	-3.75	156.25
12/12/1997	Applegate Vineyard Winery	2168	J5	4.00	160.25
12/12/1997	Visa, <One-time customer>	2174	J27	10.00	170.25
12/12/1997	MasterCard, Mary's Travel Boutique	2175	J28	10.00	180.25
				180.25	
					180.25

REVENUE minus EXPENSE 38.75

Oregon Explorer Maps/Your Name
Ski Map Sales Summary Detail Report from 12/1/1997 to 12/31/1997

REVENUE

4220 Wholesale Ski Map Sales

12/10/1997	Blue Mountain Slopes	2170	J14	165.00	165.00
12/12/1997	MasterCard, Mary's Travel Boutique	2175	J28	75.00	240.00
				240.00	

4320 Distributor Ski Map Sales

12/1/1997	Northwest Pipeline	2167	J1	2,700.00	2,940.00
12/3/1997	Pacific Crest Maps	2169	J3	2,025.00	4,965.00
				4,725.00	

4700 Sales Returns and Allowances

12/5/1997	Lost Lake Lodge	CM58	J8	-15.00	4,950.00
					4,950.00

EXPENSE

5020 COGS-Ski Maps

12/1/1997	Northwest Pipeline	2167	J1	900.00	900.00
12/3/1997	Pacific Crest Maps	2169	J3	675.00	1,575.00
12/5/1997	Lost Lake Lodge	CM58	J8	-4.10	1,570.90
12/10/1997	Blue Mountain Slopes	2170	J14	41.25	1,612.15
12/12/1997	MasterCard, Mary's Travel Boutique	2175	J28	18.75	1,630.90
12/31/1997	Dated Inventory	Memo	J68	262.40	1,893.30
12/31/1997	Dated Inventory Reversal	MemoCOR	J70	-262.40	1,630.90
12/31/1997	Dated Inventory	Memo	J71	266.50	1,897.40
				1,897.40	

5430 Advertising Expense

12/14/1997	Northwest Slopes	8743	J38	1,500.00	3,397.50
					3,397.40

REVENUE minus EXPENSE 1,552.60

Oregon Explorer Maps/Your Name
Wine Map Sales Summary Detail Report from 12/1/1997 to 12/31/1997

REVENUE

4230 Wholesale Wine Map Sales

12/2/1997	Applegate Vineyard Winery	2168	J2	90.00	90.00
12/2/1997	Reversing J2. Correction is J5.	ADJ2168	J4	-90.00	0.00

12/2/1997	Applegate Vineyard Winery	2168	J5	90.00	90.00
12/4/1997	Applegate Vineyard Winery	CM57	J22	-9.00	81.00
12/12/1997	MasterCard, Mary's Travel Boutique	2175	J28	75.00	156.00
				156.00	

4330 Distributor Wine Map Sales

12/1/1997	Northwest Pipeline	2167	J1	2,250.00	2,406.00
12/3/1997	Pacific Crest Maps	2169	J3	1,462.50	3,868.50
				3,712.50	

4700 Sales Returns and Allowances

12/4/1997	Applegate Vineyard Winery	CR57	J7	-9.00	3,859.50
12/4/1997	Reversing J7. Correction is J22.	ADJCR57	J21	9.00	3,868.50
				0.00	
					3,868.50

EXPENSE

5030 COGS-Wine Maps

12/1/1997	Northwest Pipeline	2167	J1	679.98	649.98
12/2/1997	Applegate Vineyard Winery	2168	J2	20.40	700.38
12/3/1997	Pacific Crest Maps	2169	J3	441.99	1,142.37
12/2/1997	Reversing J2. Correction is J5.	ADJ2168	J4	-20.40	1,121.97
12/2/1997	Applegate Vineyard Winery	2168	J5	20.40	1,142.37
12/4/1997	Applegate Vineyard Winery	CR57	J7	-2.28	1,140.09
12/4/1997	Reversing J7. Correction is J22.	ADJCR57	J21	2.28	1,142.37
12/4/1997	Applegate Vineyard Winery	CM57	J22	-2.04	1,140.33
12/12/1997	MasterCard, Mary's Travel Boutique	2175	J28	17.00	1,157.33
12/31/1997	Dated Inventory	Memo	J69	342.00	1,499.33
12/31/1997	Dated Inventory Reversal	MemoCOR	J70	-342.00	1,157.33
12/31/1997	Dated Inventory	Memo	J71	346.56	1,503.89
				1,503.89	

5430 Advertising Expense

12/14/1997	Oregon Wine Press	1497	J39	600.00	2,103.89
					2,103.89

REVENUE minus EXPENSE   1,764.61

▒ **ACTION:** Close the Project Detail window and return to the home window.

▒ **ACTION:** Choose **Exit** from the home window File menu to end the current work session and return to your Windows desktop.

▒ **ALTERNATIVE ACTION:** You can continue with the tutorial without exiting from the program if you wish. The next steps are recorded under the same session date as the prior steps. Skip the next ACTION; then continue with the tutorial.

GENERAL JOURNAL—GENERAL ADJUSTING ENTRIES

At the end of each accounting period, businesses must make adjusting entries to update the accounting records prior to preparing the financial statements. Some businesses choose to make adjusting entries annually, others choose to make adjusting entries monthly. Oregon Explorer Maps records adjusting entries monthly for depreciation, expired insurance, and office supplies used during the past month. The following memo authorizes the noninventory-related adjusting entries for December:

Oregon Explorer Maps—Document 72 **Session Date: 12/31/1997**

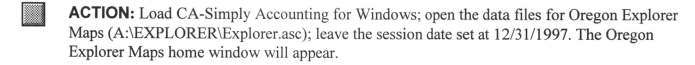

Memo **Date:** December 31, 1997

Record the following adjusting entries for December:

1. Office supplies used, $215.45
2. Shipping supplies used, $176.49
3. Expired prepaid insurance, $150.00
4. Office equipment depreciation, $180.55
5. Vehicle depreciation, $233.33

ACTION: Load CA-Simply Accounting for Windows; open the data files for Oregon Explorer Maps (A:\EXPLORER\Explorer.asc); leave the session date set at 12/31/1997. The Oregon Explorer Maps home window will appear.

ACTION: Open the General Journal; enter the word *Memo* in the **Source** field; press the TAB key; press the TAB key again to accept 12/31/1997 in the **Date** field; enter *Dec. Adj. Entry for Office Supplies* in the **Comment** text box; then press the TAB key. Your screen will look like this:

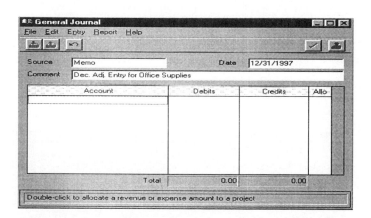

Explanation: A flashing insertion is positioned in the **Account** field.

ACTION: With the flashing insertion point positioned in the **Account** field, either press the ENTER key or double-click in the field with your mouse. Your screen will look like this:

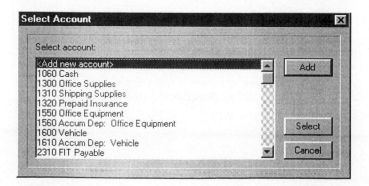

Explanation: The standard journal entry to record office supplies used is:

	Debit	**Credit**
Office Supplies Expense	xxx	
Office Supplies		xxx

The General Journal is used to record a variety of types of journal entries; consequently, you need to select the accounts to be debited and credited from the Select Account dialog box.

ACTION: Select **Office Supplies Expense** (account number 5620) from the Select Account dialog box. Your screen will look like this:

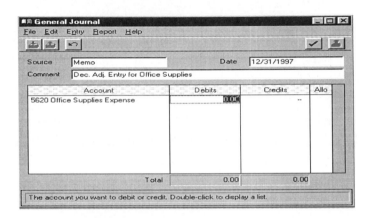

Explanation: The program has positioned the flashing insertion point in the **Debits** field.

ACTION: Enter *215.45* in the **Debits** field; then press the TAB key. Your screen will look like this:

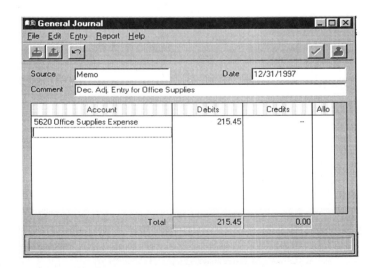

Explanation: The flashing insertion point is positioned in the **Account** field, ready for the selection of the account to be credited for this adjusting entry.

ACTION: With the flashing insertion point positioned in the **Account** field, either press the ENTER key or double-click in the field with your mouse; then select **Office Supplies** (account number 1300) from the Select Account dialog box. Your screen will look like this:

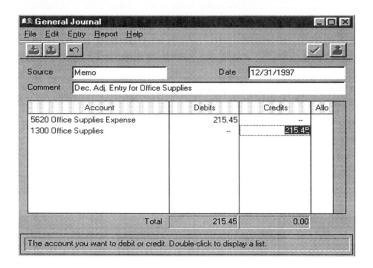

Explanation: The program has offered the same amount as the debit portion of the entry as a default amount in the **Credits** field.

 ACTION: Press the TAB key to accept the default credits amount. Your screen will look like this:

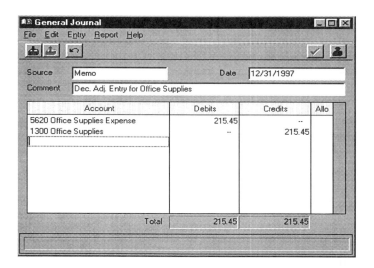

Explanation: This completes the data you need to enter into the General Journal dialog box to record the adjusting entry for office supplies used during the month. You do not need to allocate the December adjusting entries to a project. Due to the manner in which Oregon Explorer Maps uses the Project component of CA-Simply Account for Windows, noninventory-related adjusting entries are not charged to projects. For businesses that choose to allocate General Journal entries to projects, the procedures used to record allocations are identical to those used in the Purchases, Sales, and Adjustments Journals. Before posting this transaction, you need to verify that the transaction data are correct by viewing the journal entry.

OREGON GOLD BANK
2931 SE 25ᵗʰ Street
Portland, OR 97214
(503) 555-1122

Oregon Explorer Maps
2000 SE Hawthorne Blvd.
Portland, OR 97214

Acct. # 123-098			December, 1997
12/1/1997 Beginning Balance			$36,202.94
12/7/1997 Deposit 2138	$18,000.00		54,202.94
12/8/1997 Deposit 2139	11,400.00		65,602.94
12/12/1997 Deposit 2140	602.70		66,205.64
12/12/1997 Deposit 2141	304.95		66,510.59
12/12/1997 Deposit 2142	374.88		66,885.47
12/12/1997 NSF Check		18,000.00	48,885.47
12/16/1997 Check 1726		57.60	48,872.87
12/16/1997 Check 1727C		16,742.00	32,085.87
12/16/1997 Check 1728		250.00	31,835.87
12/16/1997 Check 1729		529.20	31,306.67
12/16/1997 Check 1730		36.75	31,269.92
12/16/1997 Check 1731		16.66	31,253.26
12/16/1997 Check 1732		485.00	30,768.26
12/16/1997 Check 1733		705.00	30,063.26
12/16/1997 Check 1734		192.00	29,871.26
12/16/1997 Check 1735		1,524.27	28,346.99
12/16/1997 Check 1736		361.62	27,985.37
12/16/1997 Check 1737		125.00	27,860.37
12/31/1997 Computer Equip. Loan Pmt.: $29.17 Principal, $53.39 Interest		82.56	27,777.81
12/31/1997 Service Chg. $8 and NSF Fee $15		23.00	27,754.81
12/31/1997 Interest	92.51		27,847.32
12/31/1997 Ending Balance			27,847.32

ACTION: Enter the ending balance from the bank statement into the **End Balance** box in the Work Sheet section of the Account Reconciliation Journal. Your screen should appear as follows:

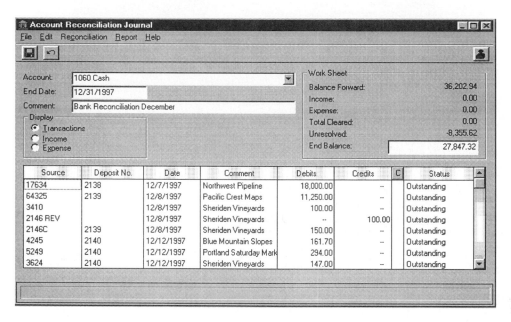

Explanation: The Work Sheet section of the Account Reconciliation Journal shows the balance forward (beginning balance) for the cash account. When the end balance is entered from the bank statement, the unresolved difference between the balance forward and the end balance is automatically calculated by Simply Accounting. When deposits and checks are cleared and when service charges, automatic payments, and interest income are recorded, the amount shown as unresolved should be 0.00.

ACTION: The first item shown on the Bank Reconciliation is the $18,000.00 check from Northwest Pipeline that was returned by the bank marked NSF. Click in the **C** column. This will place a check mark (✔) in the column and change the status from outstanding to cleared. To change the status from cleared to NSF, double-click **Cleared** in the **Status** column to get the Select Transaction Status dialog box as shown below:

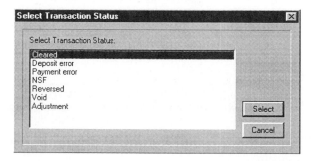

ACTION: Click **NSF** in the Select Transaction Status dialog box; then click the **Select** button. This will change the status of the original entry for Northwest Pipeline to NSF. Your screen will show the following:

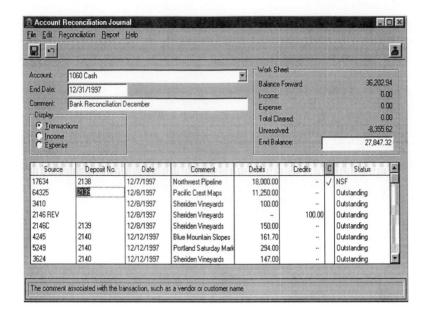

ACTION: Repeat the procedures indicated to change the status of the $18,000.00 credit for Northwest Pipeline to reversed. When these steps have been completed, your screen will appear as follows:

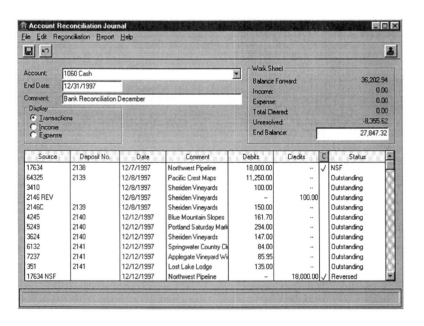

Explanation: The original NSF check and the returned NSF check have been marked with the appropriate NSF and reversed status.

ACTION: Clear Deposit 2139 by comparing the amount shown on the bank statement with the amounts shown in the Account Reconciliation Journal. Add the $11,250.00 for Pacific Crest Maps with the $150 for Sheriden Vineyards. If the two items equal the amount shown on the Bank Statement, click in the **C** column for each of the checks deposited. This will place a check mark in the column and change the status from outstanding to cleared. Once this is complete, your screen will look like the following:

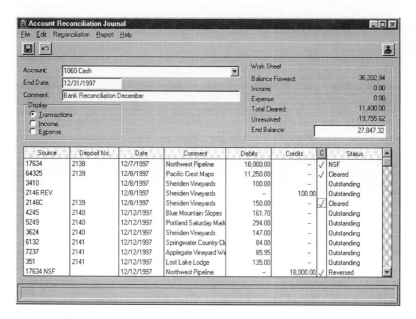

Explanation: Notice the change in the **Status** column from outstanding to cleared. Also notice the changes in the Work Sheet area of the journal. The total cleared is $11,400.00 and the unresolved amount is -$19,755.62

 ACTION: Clear all the items deposited on Deposit 2140 by clicking in the **C** column next to any of the checks deposited on this deposit slip. Then double-click the **C** column heading. This should place check marks next to the $161.70 amount deposited for the check from Blue Mountain Slopes, the $294.00 amount deposited from Portland Saturday Market, and the $147.00 amount deposited for the check from Sheriden Vineyards. Your screen should appear as follows:

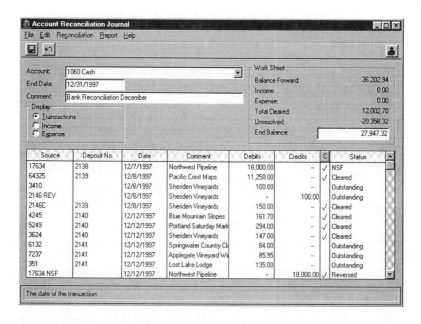

Explanation: The shortcut illustrated above can save time when several items have been deposited on one deposit slip.

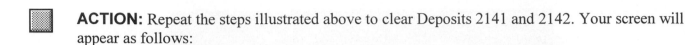

ACTION: Repeat the steps illustrated above to clear Deposits 2141 and 2142. Your screen will appear as follows:

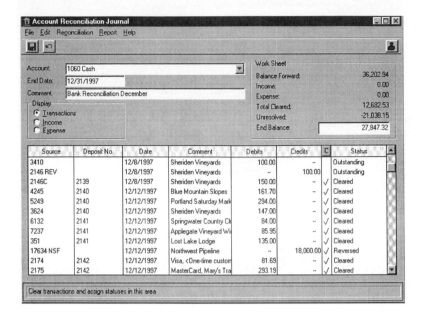

Explanation: All the deposits that were shown on the bank statement have been marked cleared. Notice that the correction made to the transaction for Sheriden Vineyards appears in the Account Reconciliation Journal. Even though the two $100.00 transactions for Sheriden Vineyards were a correction, Simply still records and displays the them as part of the Account Reconciliation Journal so that no cash transaction is hidden. These corrections must also be changed from the outstanding status.

ACTION: To change the status of a correction, the transaction must first be checked and changed from a status of outstanding to cleared. Click the **C** column to mark both of the corrections for Sheriden Vineyards to cleared. Your screen will appear as follows:

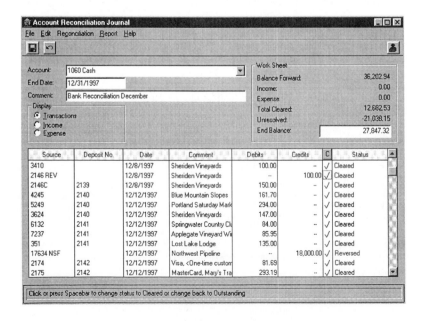

Explanation: Once the status is cleared, it may be changed to something more appropriate.

ACTION: Because the original transaction of $100.00 for Sheriden Vineyards was corrected by using a reversing entry, the status of this transaction should be changed from cleared to reversed. Do this by double-clicking **Cleared** in the **Status** column to get the Select Transaction Status dialog box.

ACTION: Click **Reversed** in the Select Transaction Status dialog box; then click the **Select** button. This will change the status of the original entry for Sally Hall to reversed. Repeat the procedures indicated to change the status of the $100.00 credit for Sheriden Vineyards to adjustment. When these steps have been completed, your screen will appear as follows:

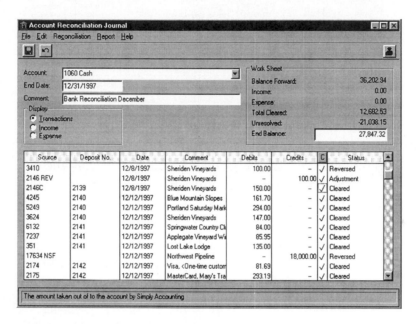

Reconcile the Bank Statement: Clearing Checks

Once the deposits have been reconciled, the next step in the reconciliation process is to clear all the checks that have been processed by the bank.

ACTION: If necessary, use the scroll button next to the **Status** column to scroll down through the transactions until you see the checks. Check 1726 has been cleared by the bank. Clear Check 1726 in the amount of $57.60 by clicking next to the check in the **C** column. This will place a check mark in the column and change the status to cleared. Your screen will appear as follows:

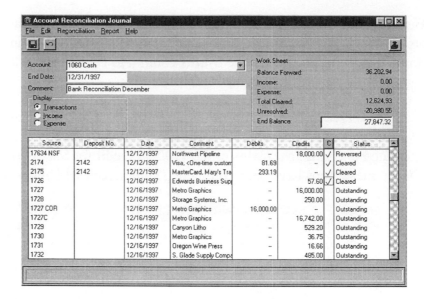

Explanation: The above procedure clears the check that has been paid by the bank and changes the amount for the total cleared and the amount for unresolved. Because all the deposits were cleared first, you may have noticed that the unresolved amount is a negative number. As the checks are cleared, the amount that is unresolved will continue to change.

ACTION: Repeat the steps listed above until all the checks shown on the bank statement have been cleared. When this is complete, your screen will appear as follows:

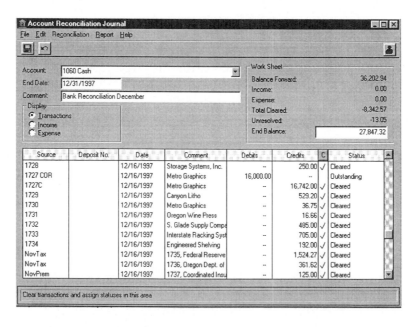

Explanation: All the checks paid by the bank have been cleared; yet, there is still an unresolved amount. As you look at the Account Reconciliation Journal, you will notice that there is a correcting entry that was made but still shows a status of outstanding. Because the $16,000.00 transaction for Metro Graphics was entered in error and subsequently corrected, Check 1727 should have a status of reversed and the debit entry for $16,000.00 that was made to correct the error should have a status of adjustment.

ACTION: To change the status of a correction, the transaction must first be checked and changed from a status of outstanding to cleared. Click the **C** column to mark both of the corrections for Metro Graphics to cleared.

ACTION: Once the status is cleared, it may be changed to something more appropriate. Because the original transaction of $16,000.00 for Metro Graphics was corrected by using a reversing entry, the status of this transaction should be changed from cleared to reversed. Do this by double-clicking **Outstanding** in the **Status** column to get the Select Transaction Status dialog box. Click **Reversed** in the Select Transaction Status dialog box then click the **Select** button. This will change the status of the original entry for Metro Graphics to reversed. Repeat the procedures indicated to change the status of the $16,000.00 debit to Metro Graphics to adjustment. When these steps have been completed, your screen will appear as follows:

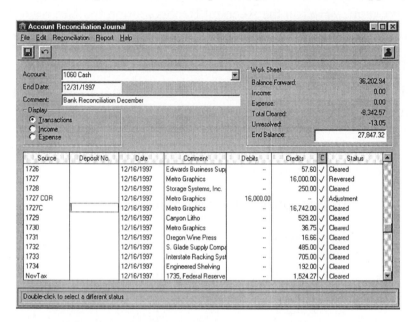

Explanation: At this point, all deposits, cleared checks, and correcting entries have been removed from a status of outstanding. Yet, there is still an amount shown as unresolved. As you look at the Account Reconciliation Journal, you will notice several transactions listed as outstanding. When you look at the bank statement, you will notice amounts listed for an automatic loan payment, a bank service charge, and interest paid by the bank. All of these items must be accounted for as part of the reconciliation process.

Reconcile the Bank Statement: Outstanding Checks and Deposits in Transit

ACTION: There are no deposits that have not cleared the bank, so this month, there are no deposits in transit. If there were, any deposits that did not appear on the bank statement would be deposits in transit and would maintain a status of outstanding. Check 1738 for $1,207.48 to Joyce Graham has not been marked as cleared. Verify that it does not appear on the bank statement. Since it does not, it should maintain a status of outstanding. Repeat the procedure for all the other checks that have not been cleared. A correction is shown for the paycheck for Sam York. Until the check clears for Sam York, you may leave the correcting entry marked outstanding.

Explanation: No change is made to the Account Reconciliation Journal for any checks or deposits that have not yet been cleared by the bank.

Reconcile the Bank Statement: Recording Bank Statement Transactions

The next part of the bank reconciliation requires entering any transaction that appears on the bank statement but does not appear in the Account Reconciliation Journal.

ACTION: Make an entry in the General Journal to record the automatic loan payment for the computer equipment. As stated in the bank statement, the loan payment amount (principal) is $29.17 and the amount of interest paid is $53.39, for a total payment of $82.56. Use *Memo* as the source of the Journal transaction. Save the Account Reconciliation prepared up to this point by clicking the **Save** icon 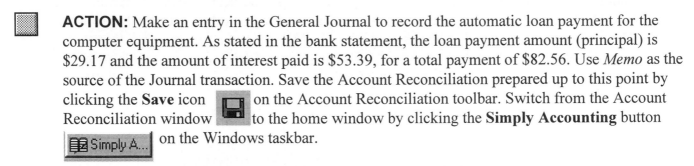 on the Account Reconciliation toolbar. Switch from the Account Reconciliation window to the home window by clicking the **Simply Accounting** button on the Windows taskbar.

Explanation: Clicking the **Simply Accounting** button on the taskbar switches between windows within Simply without having to close the Account Reconciliation Journal.

ACTION: Open the General Journal by double-clicking the **General** icon on the home window. Your screen should look like the following:

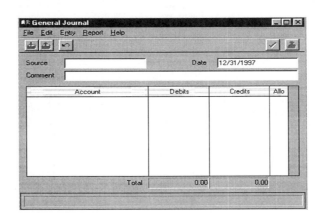

Explanation: A blank General Journal dialog box is on the screen ready to have the adjusting entry recorded for the loan payment.

ACTION: Enter the transaction for the automatic loan payment. The source is *Memo*. The comment is *December Loan Pmt. Computer Equip.* Use the date of 12/31/1997. Because this is a compound entry, you will debit 2710 Loans Payable for $29.17 and you will debit 5490 Interest Expense: Loans for $53.39. When the first debit amount is entered, Simply automatically credits the second account for the same amount. Your screen will appear as follows:

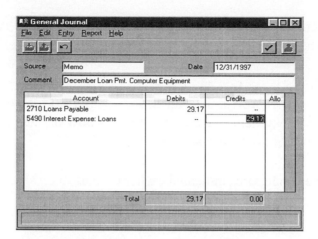

ACTION: Eliminate the credit to Interest Expense by deleting the credit amount, clicking in the **Debit** column, and entering *53.39*. Your screen should look like the following:

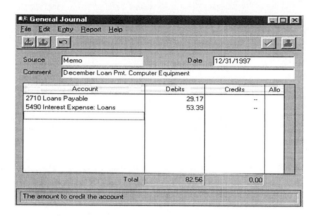

ACTION: Enter *1060 Cash* as the next account used in the transaction. Simply will automatically enter the credit amount of $82.56. Your screen will show the following:

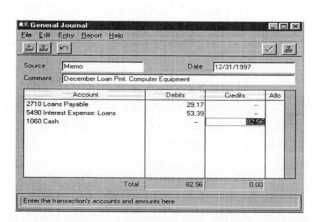

ACTION: TAB to enter the credit amount into the Total box at the bottom of the screen. Compare your transaction to the above. If you have used the correct accounts and amounts, click the **Post** button. When the transaction has been posted, return to the Account Reconciliation Journal by clicking the **Account Reconciliation** button [Account Re...] on the Windows taskbar.

Explanation: If necessary, scroll through the transactions displayed for the cash account until you see the entry for the automatic loan payment. Because the entry is now on the bank statement and in the Account Reconciliation Journal, it must be marked cleared.

ACTION: Follow the procedures indicated earlier to mark the December loan payment as cleared. Your screen should look like the following:

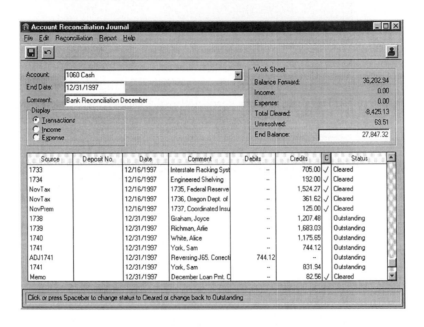

Explanation: The automatic loan payment has been cleared. Yet, there is still an unresolved amount of $69.51, and there are still two items on the bank statement that have not been reconciled.

ACTION: As you look at the bank charges on the bank statement, you will see that there is an $8 service charge and a $15 charge for the NSF check. To record the NSF check charges, return to the General Journal by clicking the **General Journal** button [General Jour...] on the taskbar.

Explanation: When the bank returned the NSF check, an entry was made recording the bank fees and the charge by Oregon Explorer Maps. In this entry, Bad Check Charges, an income account, was credited for all of the fees to be received from Northwest Pipeline. At this time, the amount of the bank fee must be removed from the income account, and cash will be decreased by the bank's deduction to the bank account.

ACTION: The source for the General Journal entry is *Bank Statemnt*, the date is 12/31/1997, and the comment is *NSF Charges*. The account to be debited for $15 is Bad Check Charges. Cash is credited $15. Enter this information and compare your entry with the following:

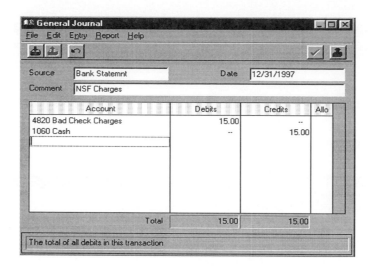

Explanation: This entry removes the amount of the bank's bad check charge from the income account and leaves a $10 balance in the account, which is the amount Oregon Explorer Maps charged Northwest Pipeline for the bad check.

ACTION: Post the General Journal transaction. Close the General Journal and return to the Account Reconciliation window. Mark the transaction as cleared.

Explanation: There are still two items on the bank statement that have not been recorded. In addition to displaying transactions, the Account Reconciliation Journal can also display a window for income or expense. Both the Income display and the Expense display show a window in which up to three transactions may be recorded for items that have been added to or deducted from the account.

ACTION: Enter the $8.00 service charge by clicking **Expense** in the Display area of the Account Reconciliation Journal. Your screen will appear as follows:

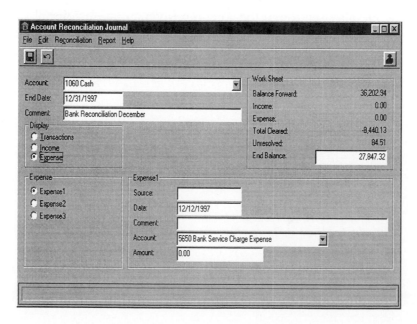

Explanation: The Account Reconciliation Journal displays the screen used to enter expenses. Notice that Expense1 is shown. Simply will allow two other expense transactions to be recorded as part of the bank reconciliation.

  ACTION: Complete the recording of the $8.00 bank service charge. Enter *Bank Statemnt* as the source, *12/31/1997* as the date, *December Service Charge* as the comment, and *8* for the amount. When finished, your screen will show the following:

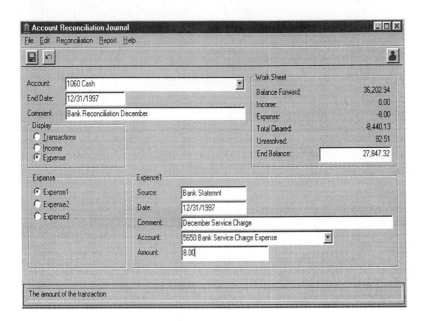

Explanation: The amount of the service charge has been entered. Notice that the unresolved amount is now $92.51. The final item to be entered from the bank statement is the $92.51 interest earned on the account.

  ACTION: In the Display section of the Account Reconciliation Journal window, click **Income**. Income1 should be selected and appear in the Income1 section of the window. If it does not appear automatically, click **Income1** in the Income column. Your screen will appear as follows:

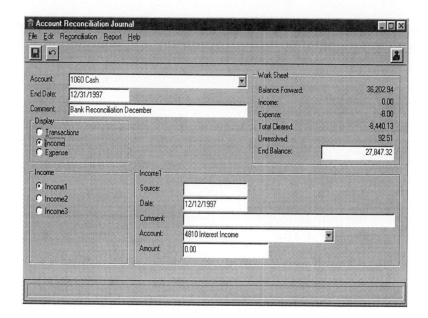

ACTION: Enter the $92.51 interest income received from the bank. Use *Bank Statemnt* as the source, *12/31/1997* as the date, and *December Interest* as the comment. Enter *92.51* as the amount. When complete, your screen should appear as follows:

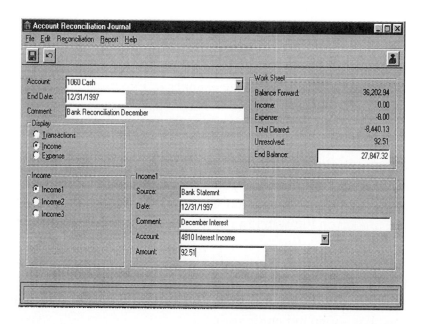

Explanation: All items on the bank statement have been entered. Notice that the unresolved amount is now equal to 0.00.

Reconcile the Bank Statement: Reports, Printing, and Processing

Once you have reconciled every item on the statement and matched or checked everything in the Account Reconciliation window, the unresolved amount will be zero if everything in the reconciliation has been done correctly. When you reconcile an account and process the reconciliation, Simply updates the income and expense accounts you selected and entered in the Account Reconciliation window. In addition, all transactions whose status is no longer outstanding are removed from the Account Reconciliation window. Only the transactions with a status of outstanding remain in the transaction window. Finally, the Account Reconciliation window is updated to prepare for the next reconciliation by advancing the ending date by one month and changing the ending balance in the Work Sheet area to the new balance forward.

To complete the bank reconciliation process, an Account Reconciliation report should be printed so you have a record of your work. This printout should be filed along with the bank statement. The last part of the bank reconciliation is to back up your work.

ACTION: To see the transactions for the service charges and the interest income, click **Report** on the menu bar. Then click **Display Account Reconciliation Journal Entry**. Your screen should appear as follows:

Account Reconciliation Journal Entry		
File Help		
12/31/1997	Debits	Credits
12/31/1997 Bank Statemnt, December Interest		
1060 Cash	92.51	-
4810 Interest Income	-	92.51
12/31/1997 Bank Statemnt, December Service Charge		
1060 Cash	-	8.00
5650 Bank Service Charge Expense	8.00	-
	100.51	100.51

ACTION: Click **File** on the Account Reconciliation Journal Entry menu bar. Click **Print** to print a copy of the journal entries. Close the Account Reconciliation Journal Entry. If your entries do not match the above, make the appropriate changes to Expense1 and/or Income1 to correct. Click the **Save** button on the toolbar to save the transactions recorded.

ACTION: Prior to Processing the Account Reconciliation, it is a good idea to print an Account Reconciliation Detail report. (This report may also be printed after the reconciliation has been processed.) In order to print this report, you need to access the Reports menu on the home window toolbar. Do not close the Account Reconciliation Journal. Click the **Simply Accounting** button [Simply Acco...] on the Windows taskbar.

Explanation: Clicking the button for the home window on the Windows taskbar switches you from one part of the program to another. Notice the Simply Accounting button looks like it is pressed in (this means it is the active window—the one on the screen) and the Account Reconciliation button looks like it is pushed out (it is inactive—open but not in use).

ACTION: Click **Report** on the home window; click **Account Reconciliation.** Your screen will show the following Account Reconciliation Report Options dialog box:

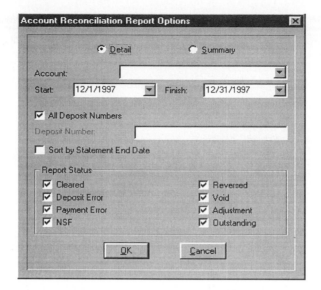

ACTION: Complete the Account Reconciliation Report Options dialog box by clicking the drop-down list arrow for **Accounts**. Click **1060 Cash** and TAB to select. Verify that **Detailed** is selected and that the start date is 12/1/1997 and the finish date is 12/31/1997. When your screen matches the following, click **OK.**

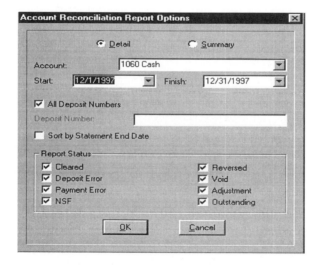

ACTION: The following Account Reconciliation Detail report will appear on your screen:

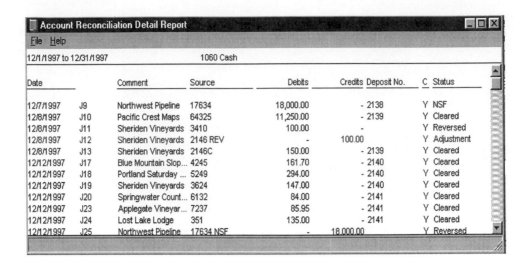

Explanation: This report shows all of the items reconciled on the Transaction display of the Account Reconciliation Journal. The Account Reconciliation Journal Entry report shows the transactions entered on the Income and Expense displays.

ACTION: Click **File** and **Print** to print the report. Compare your report with the one shown below:

Oregon Explorer Maps/Your Name
Account Reconciliation Detail Report 12/1/1997 to 12/31/1997

1060 Cash   Deposit No.: ***all***   By statement end date: N
Cleared: Y, Deposit error: Y, Payment error: Y, NSF: Y, Reversed: Y, Void: Y, Adjustment: Y, Outstanding: Y

Date		Comment	Source	Debits	Credits	Deposit No.	C	Status
12/7/1997	J9	Northwest Pipeline	17634	18,000.00	-	2138	Y	NSF
12/8/1997	J10	Pacific Crest Maps	64325	11,250.00	-	2139	Y	Cleared
12/8/1997	J11	Sheriden Vineyards	3410	100.00	-		Y	Reversed
12/8/1997	J12	Sheriden Vineyards	2146 REV	-	100.00		Y	Adjustment
12/8/1997	J13	Sheriden Vineyards	2146 C	150.00	-	2139	Y	Cleared
12/12/1997	J17	Blue Mountain Slopes	4245	161.70	-	2140	Y	Cleared
12/12/1997	J18	Portland Saturday M...	5249	294.00	-	2140	Y	Cleared
12/12/1997	J19	Sheriden Vineyards	3624	147.00	-	2140	Y	Cleared
12/12/1997	J20	Springwater Country ...	6132	84.00	-	2141	Y	Cleared
12/12/1997	J23	Applegate Vineyard ...	7237	85.95	-	2141	Y	Cleared
12/12/1997	J24	Lost Lake Lodge	351	135.00	-	2141	Y	Cleared
12/12/1997	J25	Northwest Pipeline	17634 NSF	-	18,000.00		Y	Reversed
12/12/1997	J27	Visa, <One-time cust ...	2174	81.69	-	2142	Y	Cleared
12/12/1997	J28	MasterCard, Mary's T ...	2175	293.19	-	2142	Y	Cleared
12/16/1997	J48	Edwards Business S ...	1726	-	57.60		Y	Cleared
12/16/1997	J49	Metro Graphics	1727	-	16,000.00		Y	Reversed
12/16/1997	J50	Storage Systems, Inc.	1728	-	250.00		Y	Cleared
12/16/1997	J51	Metro Graphics	1727 COR	16,000.00	-		Y	Adjustment
12/16/1997	J52	Metro Graphics	1727 C	-	16,742.00		Y	Cleared
12/16/1997	J53	Canyon Litho	1729	-	529.20		Y	Cleared
12/16/1997	J54	Metro Graphics	1730	-	36.75		Y	Cleared
12/16/1997	J55	Oregon Wine Press	1731	-	16.66		Y	Cleared
12/16/1997	J56	S. Glade Supply Co...	1732	-	485.00		Y	Cleared
12/16/1997	J57	Interstate Racking Sy...	1733	-	705.00		Y	Cleared
12/16/1997	J58	Engineered Shelving	1734	-	192.00		Y	Cleared
12/16/1997	J59	1735, Federal Reserv...	NovTax	-	1,524.27		Y	Cleared
12/16/1997	J60	1736, Oregon Dept. o...	NovTax	-	361.62		Y	Cleared
12/16/1997	J61	1737, Coordinated In...	NovPrem	-	125.00		Y	Cleared
12/31/1997	J62	Graham, Joyce	1738	-	1,207.48		N	Outstanding
12/31/1997	J63	Richman, Arlie	1739	-	1,683.03		N	Outstanding
12/31/1997	J64	White, Alice	1740	-	1,175.65		N	Outstanding
12/31/1997	J65	York, Sam	1741	-	744.12		N	Outstanding
12/31/1997	J66	Reversing J65. Corre...	ADJ1741	744.12	-		N	Outstanding
12/31/1997	J67	York, Sam	1741	-	831.94		N	Outstanding
12/31/1997	J78	December Loan Pmt...	Memo	-	82.56		Y	Cleared
12/31/1997	J79	NSF Charges	Bank Statemnt	-	15.00		Y	Cleared

Explanation: If your report does not match, return to the Account Reconciliation window and make any changes necessary.

 ACTION: When all items printed are correct, close the Account Reconciliation Detail report and return to the Account Reconciliation Journal by clicking the **Account Reconciliation** button on the taskbar. Click the **Post** button to process the account reconciliation. When the processing is complete, your screen should show the following:

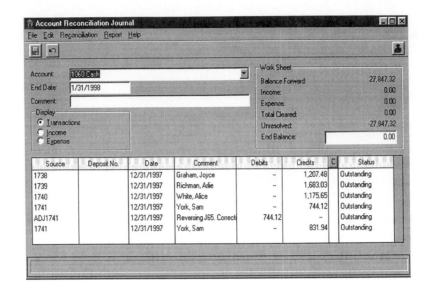

Explanation: The only items shown are the transactions with an outstanding status. Notice that the end date has been changed and that the end balance of the previous reconciliation is now shown as the balance forward on this Account Reconciliation Journal.

ACTION: The bank reconciliation is complete. Close the Account Reconciliation Journal and return to the home window. Back up your work by clicking **File** on the menu bar. Click **Backup**. Name your backup file *A:\Backup\Backup Chapter 8 Bank Reconciliation Complete.* Click **OK** to back up your work.

GENERAL REPORTS AND FINANCIAL STATEMENTS

A variety of General-related reports are available in CA-Simply Accounting for Windows. The procedures required to print and display a General Journal report were demonstrated earlier in this chapter. In addition to the General Journal report, the program can print or display a chart of accounts, general ledger, trial balance, income statement, and balance sheet. Use the scroll bars at the bottom or right side of a displayed report to view reports that contain more text than can be displayed at one time.

ACTION: Choose **Financials**, **Trial Balance** from the home window Reports menu; accept the default date of 12/31/1997; then click the **OK** button. Your screen will show the Trial Balance.

ACTION: Print the Trial Balance by choosing **Print** from the Trial Balance File menu. Compare your trial balance to the one shown below:

Oregon Explorer Maps/Your Name
Trial Balance As At 12/31/1997

		Debits	**Credits**
1060	Cash	22,949.22	-
1200	Accounts Receivable	42,262.65	-
1210	Golf Map Inventory	676.84	-
1220	Ski Map Inventory	14,522.75	-
1230	Wine Map Inventory	12,771.51	-
1240	Attraction Map Inventory	1,806.87	-
1250	Rack Inventory	2,922.50	-

1300	Office Supplies	132.15	-
1310	Shipping Supplies	70.24	-
1320	Prepaid Insurance	300.00	-
1550	Office Equipment	10,000.00	-
1560	Accum Dep: Office Equipment	-	4,333.26
1600	Vehicle	16,000.00	-
1610	Accum Dep: Vehicle	-	5,599.96
2200	Accounts Payable	-	17,359.75
2310	FIT Payable	-	496.28
2320	SIT Payable	-	364.24
2330	Social Security Tax Payable	-	790.00
2340	Medicare Tax Payable	-	184.76
2350	FUTA Payable	-	23.24
2360	SUTA Payable	-	495.63
2400	Medical Insurance Payable	-	125.00
2710	Loans Payable	-	2,970.83
3560	Karen Bailey, Capital	-	78,185.62
3570	Karen Bailey, Drawing	27,500.00	-
4210	Wholesale Golf Map Sales	-	8,791.59
4220	Wholesale Ski Map Sales	-	6,724.19
4230	Wholesale Wine Map Sales	-	6,634.19
4240	Wholesale Attraction Map Sales	-	22,128.97
4310	Distributor Golf Map Sales	-	43,212.79
4320	Distributor Ski Map Sales	-	37,145.84
4330	Distributor Wine Map Sales	-	36,110.84
4340	Distributor Attraction Map Sales	-	123,106.97
4410	Retail Attraction Map Sales	-	0.00
4500	Rack Sales	-	1,636.49
4600	Sales Discounts	876.46	-
4700	Sales Returns and Allowances	2,049.75	-
4810	Interest Income	-	92.51
4820	Bad Check Charges	-	10.00
5010	COGS-Golf Maps	15,714.35	-
5020	COGS-Ski Maps	15,400.88	-
5030	COGS-Wine Maps	13,927.37	-
5040	COGS-Attraction Maps	34,081.08	-
5050	COGS-Racks	1,361.50	-
5060	Purchase Discounts	-	11.89
5070	Purchase Returns and Allowances	0.00	-
5301	Wages	76,466.00	-
5310	Social Security Tax Expense	4,740.89	-
5320	Medicare Tax Expense	1,108.76	-
5330	FUTA Expense	224.00	-
5340	SUTA Expense	2,403.35	-
5400	Phone Expense	1,376.92	-
5410	Postage Expense	976.29	-
5420	Shipping Expense	18,974.32	-
5430	Advertising Expense	10,876.20	-
5440	Vehicle Expense	627.46	-
5450	Utilities Expense	1,176.42	-
5460	Rent Expense	30,000.00	-
5470	Membership and Dues Expense	973.20	-
5480	Subscription Expense	267.50	-
5490	Interest Expense: Loans	53.39	-
5500	Dep. Expense: Office Equipment	2,166.60	-
5510	Dep. Expense: Vehicle	2,799.96	-
5610	Insurance Expense	1,800.00	-
5620	Office Supplies Expense	2,435.40	

5630	Shipping Supplies Expense	1,187.91	-
5650	Bank Service Charge Expense	303.00	-
5660	Credit Card Fees Expense	23.92	-
5800	Misc. Expense	247.23	-
		396,534.84	396,534.84

ACTION: Close the Trial Balance window; then choose **Financials, Income Statement** from the home window Reports menu. Accept 1/1/1997 as the start date; accept 12/31/1997 as the finish date; then click the **OK** button on the Report Options dialog box. The Income Statement will be displayed.

ACTION: Choose **Print** from the Income Statement File menu. Compare your report to the one shown below:

Oregon Explorer Maps
Income Statement 1/1/1997 to 12/31/1997

REVENUE
SALES REVENUE

Wholesale Golf Map Sales	8,791.59	
Wholesale Ski Map Sales	6,724.19	
Wholesale Wine Map Sales	6,634.19	
Wholesale Attraction Map Sales	22,128.97	
Total Wholesale Sales		44,278.94
Distributor Golf Map Sales	43,212.79	
Distributor Ski Map Sales	37,145.84	
Distributor Wine Map Sales	36,110.84	
Distributor Attraction Map Sales	123,106.97	
Total Distributor Sales		239,576.44
Retail Attraction Map Sales	0.00	
Total Retail Sales		0.00
Rack Sales		1,636.49
Sales Discounts		-876.46
Sales Returns and Allowances		-2,049.75
TOTAL SALES REVENUE		282,565.66

OTHER REVENUE

Interest Income	92.51
Bad Check Charges	10.00
TOTAL OTHER REVENUE	102.51

TOTAL REVENUE	282,688.17

EXPENSE
COST OF GOODS SOLD

COGS-Golf Maps	15,714.35
COGS-Ski Maps	15,400.88
COGS-Wine Maps	13,927.37
COGS-Attraction Maps	34,081.08
COGS-Racks	1,361.50
Purchase Discounts	-11.89
Purchase Returns and Allowances	0.00
TOTAL COST OF GOODS SOLD	80,473.29

OPERATING EXPENSES

Wages	76,466.00
Social Security Tax Expense	4,740.89
Medicare Tax Expense	1,108.76
FUTA Expense	224.00
SUTA Expense	2,403.35
Phone Expense	1,376.92
Postage Expense	976.29
Shipping Expense	18,974.32
Advertising Expense	10,876.20
Vehicle Expense	627.46
Utilities Expense	1,176.42
Rent Expense	30,000.00
Membership and Dues Expense	973.20
Subscription Expense	267.50
Interest Expense: Loans	53.39
Dep. Expense: Office Equipment	2,166.60
Dep. Expense: Vehicle	2,799.96
Insurance Expense	1,800.00
Office Supplies Expense	2,435.40
Shipping Supplies Expense	1,187.91
Bank Service Charge Expense	303.00
Credit Card Fees Expense	23.92
Misc. Expense	247.23
TOTAL OPERATING EXPENSES	161,208.72

TOTAL EXPENSE	241,682.01

NET INCOME	40,966.16

 ACTION: Close the Income Statement window; choose **Financials**, **Balance Sheet** from the home window Reports menu; then accept the balance sheet as at date of 12/31/1997 by clicking the **OK** button. Choose **Print** from the Balance Sheet File menu. Compare your balance sheet to the one shown below:

Oregon Explorer Maps/Your Name
Balance Sheet As At 12/31/1997

ASSETS

CURRENT ASSETS

Cash		22,949.22
Accounts Receivable		42,262.65
Golf Map Inventory	676.84	
Ski Map Inventory	14,522.75	
Wine Map Inventory	12,771.51	
Attraction Map Inventory	1,806.87	
Rack Inventory	2,922.50	
Total Inventory		32,700.47
Office Supplies		132.15
Shipping Supplies		70.24
Prepaid Insurance		300.00
TOTAL CURRENT ASSETS		98,414.73

FIXED ASSETS

Office Equipment	10,000.00	
Accum Dep: Office Equipment	-4,333.26	
Net: Office Equipment		5,666.74
Vehicle	16,000.00	
Accum Dep: Vehicle	-5,599.96	
Net: Vehicle		10,400.04
TOTAL FIXED ASSETS		16,066.78
TOTAL ASSETS		114,481.51

LIABILITIES

CURRENT LIABILITIES

Accounts Payable	17,359.75
FIT Payable	496.28
SIT Payable	364.24
Social Security Tax Payable	790.00
Medicare Tax Payable	184.76
FUTA Payable	23.24
SUTA Payable	495.63
Medical Insurance Payable	125.00
TOTAL CURRENT LIABILITIES	19,838.90
TOTAL LIABILITIES	22,809.73

EQUITY

OWNER'S EQUITY

Karen Bailey, Capital	78,185.62
Karen Bailey, Drawing	-27,500.00
Current Earnings	40,968.16
TOTAL OWNER'S EQUITY	91,671.78
TOTAL EQUITY	91,671.78
LIABILITIES AND EQUITY	114,481.51

 ACTION: Close the Balance Sheet window; then choose **Exit** from the home window File menu to end the current work session and return to your Windows desktop.

YEAR-END CLOSING PROCEDURES

At the end of an accounting year, a business must close its revenue and expense accounts to owner's equity. The closing process clears the revenue and expense accounts so that transactions for the following year can be accumulated in these accounts. In addition, if the business uses an owner's drawing account, this temporary owner's equity account must also be closed. CA-Simply Accounting for Windows can automatically close all revenue and expense accounts to owner's equity but does not have the capability of automatically closing an owner's drawing account. Oregon Explorer Maps uses a drawing account; therefore, a closing entry for the drawing account must be entered directly into the General Journal.

All of Oregon Explorer Maps' routine transactions for 1997 have been recorded. The accounting records have also been adjusted for 1997, and the 1997 financial statements and Project reports have been printed. It is time to close the accounting records for the year. In an actual business situation, several other reports, such as a General Journal (including all ledger entries) and a General Ledger (selecting all accounts) would be printed for the entire year, and a backup copy of the company's 1997 data files would be made. In this tutorial, we will omit the printing of these additional reports; however, it is important that you make a backup copy of Oregon Explorer Maps' data files prior to performing the closing procedures.

ACTION: Make a backup copy of Oregon Explorer Maps' data files as previously instructed.

Oregon Explorer Maps—Document 76   **Session Date: 12/31/1997**

Memo   **Date:** December 31, 1997

Close the Karen Bailey, Drawing account to the Karen Bailey, Capital account.

ACTION: Load CA-Simply Accounting for Windows; open the data files for Oregon Explorer Maps (A:\EXPLORER\Explorer.asc); leave the session date set at 12/31/1997. The Oregon Explorer Maps home window will appear.

ACTION: Open the General Journal; then enter the above closing entry. Your screen should agree with the one shown below:

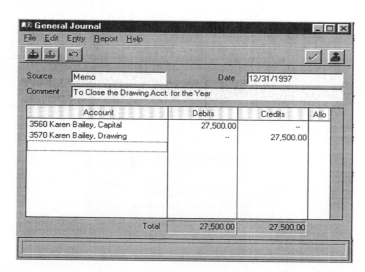

ACTION: Choose **Display General Journal Entry** from the General Journal Report menu. Compare your display to the one shown below:

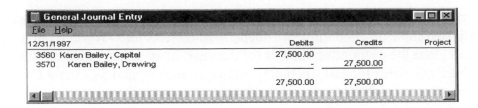

Explanation: Review the journal entry noting any errors.

ACTION: Close the General Journal Entry window. If you made an error, refer to the Editing Tips for Editing General Journal Entries and Project Allocations, which appears in a special box earlier in this chapter, for information on corrective action.

ACTION: After verifying that the journal entry is correct, click the **Post** button to post the closing entry; close the General Journal dialog box. To see the effect of the closing entry, prepare a balance sheet. Scroll through the report until you see the Owner's Equity section. Your Equity section should look like the following:

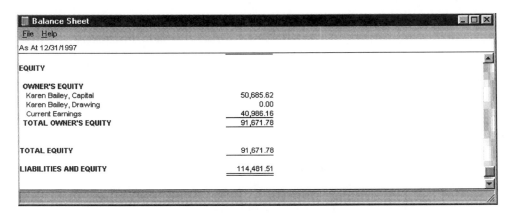

ACTION: Close the Balance Sheet. Choose **Advance Session Date** from the home window Maintenance menu. Your screen will look like this:

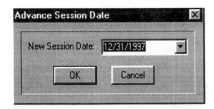

Explanation: The final step in the closing process requires advancing the session date to the first day of the next fiscal year, in this case 1/1/1998. During the closing process, the program will permanently remove all journal entries from all journals and all individual postings of journal entries to the General Ledger accounts. As journal files are cleared, the program will combine all revenue and expense project allocations to balance forward amounts for each project. Individual posting information for revenue and expense allocations will no longer be available. The ending balances for assets, liabilities, and the updated owner's equity accounts will become the beginning balances in 1998 for these accounts. All revenue and expense accounts will show zero balances, and the 1997 income will be transferred to the general integration/linking account designated in the company's data files. Oregon Explorer Maps has established 3560 Karen Bailey, Capital as the general integration/linking account.

 ACTION: Advance the session date to 1/1/1998; click the **OK** button; then click the **OK** button in response to the warning message. You will return to the home window.

Explanation: The warning message stated that the revenue and expense accounts would be closed to an account titled Retained Earnings. This is the account that corporations use to accumulate earnings. Oregon Explorer Maps is a sole proprietorship, and the program will correctly close the revenue and expense accounts to the Karen Bailey, Capital account even though the message used a different account name. The backup copy of Oregon Explorer Maps' data files that you made at the beginning of this section will serve as the backup copy suggested in the warning message.

 ACTION: Choose **Financials**, **Trial Balance** from the home window Reports menu; accept the default as at date of 1/1/1998; click the **OK** button. Choose **Print** from the Trial Balance File menu. Compare your trial balance to the one shown below:

Oregon Explorer Maps/Your Name
Trial Balance As At 1/1/1998

		Debits	Credits
1060	Cash	22,949.22	-
1200	Accounts Receivable	42,262.65	-
1210	Golf Map Inventory	676.84	-
1220	Ski Map Inventory	14,522.75	-
1230	Wine Map Inventory	12,771.51	-
1240	Attraction Map Inventory	1,806.87	-
1250	Rack Inventory	2,922.50	-
1300	Office Supplies	132.15	-
1310	Shipping Supplies	70.24	-
1320	Prepaid Insurance	300.00	-
1550	Office Equipment	10,000.00	-
1560	Accum Dep: Office Equipment	-	4,333.26
1600	Vehicle	16,000.00	-
1610	Accum Dep: Vehicle	-	5,599.96
2200	Accounts Payable	-	17,359.75
2310	FIT Payable	-	496.28
2320	SIT Payable	-	364.24
2330	Social Security Tax Payable	-	790.00
2340	Medicare Tax Payable	-	184.76
2350	FUTA Payable	-	23.24
2360	SUTA Payable	-	495.63
2400	Medical Insurance Payable	-	125.00
2710	Loans Payable	-	2,970.83
3560	Karen Bailey, Capital	-	91,674.78
3570	Karen Bailey, Drawing	-	0.00
4210	Wholesale Golf Map Sales	-	0.00
4220	Wholesale Ski Map Sales	-	0.00
4230	Wholesale Wine Map Sales	-	0.00
4240	Wholesale Attraction Map Sales	-	0.00
4310	Distributor Golf Map Sales	-	0.00
4320	Distributor Ski Map Sales	-	0.00
4330	Distributor Wine Map Sales	-	0.00
4340	Distributor Attraction Map Sales	-	0.00
4410	Retail Attraction Map Sales	-	0.00

4500	Rack Sales	-	0.00
4600	Sales Discounts	-	0.00
4700	Sales Returns and Allowances	-	0.00
4810	Interest Income	-	0.00
4820	Bad Check Charges	-	0.00
5010	COGS-Golf Maps	0.00	-
5020	COGS-Ski Maps	0.00	-
5030	COGS-Wine Maps	0.00	-
5040	COGS-Attraction Maps	0.00	-
5050	COGS-Racks	0.00	-
5060	Purchase Discounts	0.00	-
5070	Purchase Returns and Allowances	0.00	-
5301	Wages	0.00	-
5310	Social Security Tax Expense	0.00	-
5320	Medicare Tax Expense	0.00	-
5330	FUTA Expense	0.00	-
5340	SUTA Expense	0.00	-
5400	Phone Expense	0.00	-
5410	Postage Expense	0.00	-
5420	Shipping Expense	0.00	-
5430	Advertising Expense	0.00	-
5440	Vehicle Expense	0.00	-
5450	Utilities Expense	0.00	-
5460	Rent Expense	0.00	-
5470	Membership and Dues Expense	0.00	-
5480	Subscription Expense	0.00	-
5490	Interest Expense: Loans	0.00	-
5500	Dep. Expense: Office Equipment	0.00	-
5510	Dep. Expense: Vehicle	0.00	-
5610	Insurance Expense	0.00	-
5620	Office Supplies Expense	0.00	-
5630	Shipping Supplies Expense	0.00	-
5650	Bank Service Charge Expense	0.00	-
5660	Credit Card Fees Expense	0.00	-
5800	Misc. Expense	0.00	-
		124,414.73	124,414.73

 ACTION: Close the Trial Balance window; then choose **Exit** from the home window File menu to end the current work session and return to your Windows desktop.

SUMMARY

This chapter has explored the Inventory, Project, and General components of CA-Simply Accounting for Windows as they would typically be used by a merchandising business. Use of the Item Assembly Journal, Adjustments Journal, Inventory Ledger, and Project Ledger to record nonroutine inventory adjustments and to maintain inventory and project records has been explained in detail. In addition, the methods used to display and print an Adjustments Journal, Inventory List, Inventory Report, and Project reports have been demonstrated. The procedures required to display and print the financial statements, perform a bank reconciliation, and close the accounting records at the end of the fiscal year have been explained. By examining the methods used to record inventory-related and general-related transactions and to adjust and close the accounting records at the end of the year, the various integration/linking features of CA-Simply Accounting for Windows were illustrated.

QUESTIONS

QUESTIONS ABOUT THE SOFTWARE

1. In CA-Simply Accounting for Windows, all inventory functions are fully integrated/linked with the General Ledger. Explain this statement and give an example.

2. Why must each inventory item be associated with a specific asset, revenue, and expense account in the CA-Simply Accounting for Windows program?

3. Transactions entered into the Item Assembly Journal for Oregon Explorer Maps did not produce any journal entries. Why?

4. What conditions does the program impose for the removal of an inventory item record?

5. Why is it important to print project reports for all projects prior to advancing the session date to a new fiscal year?

6. The Item Assembly Journal dialog box does not present an Allocate button. Why?

QUESTIONS ABOUT YEAR-END CLOSING PROCEDURES

7. What effect does advancing the session date to a new fiscal year have on the accounting records maintained by the program?

8. Your company has just completed its annual physical count of the inventory on hand. There are several discrepancies between the physical count and the computerized inventory records. You have been asked to investigate these differences. Describe what might be the likely causes for these discrepancies.

9. You are in the process of reviewing a project that the company has been working on for the past three years. You have some questions regarding the expenses associated with the project during the first year. How would you obtain information regarding the expenses associated with the project during the first year?

EXPLORING ALTERNATIVE SOFTWARE TECHNIQUES

10. On December 1, Oregon Explorer Maps decided to begin using the Project component of CA-Simply Accounting for Windows on an experimental basis. Five projects were established:

    1. Attraction Map Sales Summary
    2. Golf Map Sales Summary
    3. Rack Sales Summary
    4. Ski Map Sales Summary
    5. Wine Map Sales Summary

As you worked through the Oregon Explorer Maps Tutorial, revenues and expenses were allocated to each of these projects and detailed project reports were printed as part of Oregon Explorer Maps' year-end procedures. It was Oregon Explorer Maps' plan to evaluate the benefits of using the Project component of CA-Simply Accounting for Windows at the end of December. Prepare a short report describing the advantages and disadvantages of continuing to use the Project component. Comment on how the project reports might be used by the business as they are currently defined, and include any suggestions you may have about defining projects in a different way in the future.

TRANSMITTAL

Oregon Explorer Maps   **Name**_____
Chapter 8

Attach the following documents and reports:

1. Adjustments Journal 12/31/1997 to 12/31/1997
2. Adjustments Journal 12/31/1997 to 12/31/1997 (shows corrections)
3. Inventory & Services List 12/31/1997
4. Inventory Synopsis 12/31/1997
5. Project List 12/31/1997
6. Attraction Map Sales Summary, Detail report 12/1/1997 to 12/31/1997
7. Golf Map Sales Summary, Detail report 12/1/1997 to 12/31/1997
8. Rack Map Sales Summary, Detail report 12/1/1997 to 12/31/1997
9. Ski Map Sales Summary, Detail report 12/1/1997 to 12/31/1997
10. Wine Map Sales Summary, Detail report 12/1/1997 to 12/31/1997
11. General Journal 12/31/1997 to 12/31/1997
12. Account Reconciliation Journal entry 12/31/1997
13. Account Reconciliation Detail report 12/1/1997 to 12/31/1997
14. Trial Balance As at 12/31/1997
15. Income Statement 1/1/1997 to 12/31/1997
16. Balance Sheet As at 12/31/1997
17. Trial Balance As at 1/1/1998

EXERCISE—Windmill Wheels
(CONTINUED FROM CHAPTER 7)

1. Load CA-Simply Accounting for Windows; open the data files for Windmill Wheels (A:\WINDMILL\Windmill.asc); then record the following transactions under the session date of 12/31/1997:

    December 31 —Record the following Inventory adjusting entries:

    A. Transfer 1 road bike to the Tandem Bike Inventory at a total cost of $175.00. Comment: Records Correction. (**Note:** You must override the default unit cost and amount offered in the Assembled Items section of the Item Assembly dialog box and enter *175.00* to record this adjustment correctly.)
    B. Decrease the City Bike inventory by 1 bike at a total cost of $137.50. Comment: Damaged Goods. (Project: Main Store)
    C. Print the Adjustments Journal (with project allocations) 12/31/1997 to 12/31/1997

    December 31 —Create a new Inventory Ledger inventory item record as follows:
    Item: 7 Teen Bike; Unit: Each; Selling Price: 300.00; Min. level: 10; Asset: 1250 Inventory; Revenue: 4250 Sales; Expense: 5050 Cost of Goods Sold

    December 31 — Record the following general adjusting entries (Project: none):

    A. Office equipment depreciation for December in the amount of $50.00.
    B. Store equipment depreciation for December in the amount of $180.00.
    C. Office supplies used during December of $225.95.
    D. Expired insurance for December in the amount of $150.00.
    E. Record the purchase of a computer for $2,599. The computer is considered office equipment and the purchase is being made by taking out a loan. The bank will automatically deduct the payment from the bank account.
    F. Print the General Journal (do not include project allocations) 12/31/1997 to12/31/1997

    December 31—Back up Windmill. Name the file *A:\Backup\12-31 Prior to Bank Reconciliation.*

When the backup is complete, use the following bank statement to complete the reconciliation of Account 1060 Cash. Print the Account Reconciliation Journal entry for 12/31/1997 and the Account Reconciliation Detail report 12/1/1997 to 12/31/1997.

OREGON GOLD BANK 2931 SE 25ᵗʰ Street, Portland, OR 97214			
(503) 555-1122			December, 1997
Windmill Wheels, 13 NW 23ʳᵈ Street, Portland, OR 972140			Acct. # 11-563
12/1/1997 Beginning Balance			$22,634.92
12/3/1997 Deposit 2137	$4,308.50		26,943.42

12/5/1997 Deposit 2138	3,425.00		30,368.42
12/5/1997 Deposit 2139	2,475.00		32,843.42
12/5/1997 Deposit 2140	1,551.00		34,394.42
12/12/1997 Deposit 2141	20,002.00		54,396.42
12/12/1997 Deposit 2142	1,339.50		55,735.92
12/12/1997 NSF Check		$2,250.00	53,485.92
12/15/1997 Check 3467		1,616.12	51,869.80
12/15/1997 Check 3468		384.79	51,485.01
12/15/1997 Check 3469		125.00	51,360.01
12/19/1997 Check 3470		55.80	51,304.21
12/19/1997 Check 3471		661.50	50,642.71
12/26/1997 Check 3472		183.75	50,458.96
12/26/1997 Check 3473		177.91	50,281.05
12/31/1997 Computer Equip. Loan Pmt.: $29.17 Principal, $53.39 Interest		82.56	50,198.49
12/31/1997 Service Chg.		23.00	50,175.49
12/31/1997 Interest	209.06		50,384.55
12/31/1997 Ending Balance			$50,384.55

2. Print the following reports:

   A. Inventory report (Select All, Select Assets, Synopsis) 12/31/1997
   B. Project report (Select All, Detail) 12/1/1997 to 12/31/1997
   C. Trial Balance As at 12/31/1997
   D. Income Statement 1/1/1997 to 12/31/1997
   E. Balance Sheet As at 12/31/1997

3. Make a backup copy of Windmill Wheels' data files.

   December 31 —Record the closing entry for Alton Long's drawing account (Project: none).

4. Advance the session date to 1/1/1998; then print a Trial Balance As at 1/1/1998.

5. Exit from the program and complete the Windmill Wheels Transmittal.

TRANSMITTAL

Windmill Wheels   Name:_____
Chapter 8

A. Attach the following documents and reports:

 1. Adjustments Journal 12/31/1997 to 12/31/1997
 2. General Journal 12/31/1997 to 12/31/1997
 3. Account Reconciliation Journal entry 12/31/1997
 4. Account Reconciliation Detail report 12/1/1997 to 12/31/1997
 5. Inventory Synopsis 12/31/1997
 6. Branch Store Sales Summary Detail report from 12/1/1997 to 12/31/1997
 7. Main Store Sales Summary Detail report from 12/1/1997 to 12/31/1997
 8. Trial Balance As at 12/31/1997
 9. Income Statement 1/1/1997 to 12/31/1997
10. Balance Sheet As at 12/31/1997
11. Trial Balance As at 1/1/1998

B. Refer to your reports to list the amounts requested below:

1. What are total assets on 12/31/1997? $_____

2. What is net income for the year? $_____

3. What is the total value of the Road Bike inventory item on 12/31/1997? $_____

4. What is the balance of the Inventory account on 12/31/1997? $_____

5. What is the balance of Alton Long's Capital account on 1/1/1998? $_____

END-OF-SECTION 2— CAMERA CORNER PRACTICE SET: MERCHANDISING BUSINESS

COMPANY PROFILE

Camera Corner is owned and operated by David Skarra as a sole proprietorship in Portland, Oregon. Products include cameras, lenses, and film. Camera Corner maintains their own accounting records using CA-Simply Accounting for Windows. As a merchandising business with several employees, the company uses the General, Receivables, Payables, Inventory & Services, Payroll, and Project components of the program.

As an employee of Camera Corner, you are responsible for recording Camera Corner's December transactions, and for performing the month-end and year-end accounting procedures using CA-Simply Accounting for Windows. As transactions are recorded, print all items (such as, invoices, receipts, and checks, etc.) that can be printed.

Camera Corner has established the following accounting procedures and policies for use with the CA-Simply Accounting for Windows program.

Sales

Sales are made on a cash, credit card, and credit basis with payment terms of 2/10, net 30 offered to credit customers. When credit sales are made, an invoice is prepared using the CA-Simply Accounting for Windows automatic invoicing preparation feature. You will receive a memo from Mr. Skarra when an invoice needs to be prepared. At the time the invoice is prepared, assign the discount terms of 2/10, net 30. Cash sales are recorded weekly based on Camera Corner's Weekly Cash Sale Summary form. Bank deposits for cash, credit cards, and checks will be made as instructed. Record cash sales in the Sales Journal using the cash sale option and the customer identified as Cash Sales. All sales revenue is distributed to one of Camera Corner's three projects: Camera Sales Summary, Lens Sales Summary, or Film Sales Summary. Receivables Ledger records are created as needed for new credit customers; consequently, the one-time customer option within the CA-Simply Accounting for Windows program is not used except for credit card sales. All details regarding fully paid invoices are retained in the accounting data files.

Credit Memos

Returned merchandise is charged to the Sales Returns and Allowances account and is distributed to one of Camera Corner's three projects: Camera Sales Summary, Lens Sales Summary, or Film Sales Summary. You will receive a memo from Mr. Skarra when a credit memo needs to be prepared.

Cash Receipts and Sales Discounts

Most of Camera Corner's credit customers take advantage of the 2/10, net 30 discount terms. Mr. Skarra will make a notation on each customer's check regarding the amount of the discount allowed. Sales discounts are charged to the sales discounts account and are NOT distributed to projects.

Purchases

Payables Ledger records have been established for those vendors that Camera Corner deals with on a frequent basis. All details of fully paid invoices are retained in the company's accounting data files. Occasionally, the business will make a purchase or receive a bill from a new vendor. The owner, Mr. Skarra, may or may not want to establish a Payables Ledger record for the new vendor and payment may or may not be due immediately. Therefore, Mr. Skarra uses the following notations on vendor invoices, statements, and bills to indicate how he would like the purchase handled.

1. *Approved.* Record purchase in the Purchases Journal under the established vendor's name. Payment is not yet due.
2. *New Vendor.* Create a Payables Ledger record for the vendor.
3. *Issue Check.* Issue a check using the cash purchase option in the Purchases Journal.
4. *One-Time Vendor.* Issue a check using the one-time vendor and cash purchase option in the Purchases Journal.
5. *New Item.* Create a new Inventory Ledger record using the information provided, associating the new item with the appropriate asset, revenue, and expense accounts.

Review Purchases source documents carefully; Mr. Skarra may use more than one notation on a source document.

Expenses paid using the cash purchase option in the Purchases Journal are NOT distributed to projects.

Debit Memos

Debit memos are prepared when merchandise is returned to a vendor for credit. Returned merchandise is charged directly to the inventory account associated with the returned item. You will receive a memo from Mr. Skarra when a debit memo needs to be prepared.

Payments on Account and Purchase Discounts

When Mr. Skarra wants a check issued as a payment on account to a credit vendor, he prepares a memo to that effect. If a payment is being made within the discount period, be sure to take the discount. You will need to prepare a check using the CA-Simply Accounting for Windows automatic check preparation feature and give it to Mr. Skarra to sign and mail.

Cash Payments for Current Liabilities and Draws

Use the cash purchase option in the Purchases Journal to record payments of current liabilities and draws as requested in the memos prepared by Mr. Skarra. You will need to prepare a check using the

CA-Simply Accounting for Windows automatic check preparation feature and give it to Mr. Skarra to sign and mail.

Payroll Checks

Camera Corner uses the CA-Simply Accounting for Windows automatic payroll deductions and check preparation features. Payroll entries are NOT distributed to projects. Employees are paid monthly on the last working day of each month.

Other Information

Purchases of office supplies are debited to the Office Supplies asset account and are adjusted monthly. Journal entries associated with bank reconciliations are recorded in the General Journal, and checks issued to replenish Petty Cash are recorded in the Purchases Journal using the one-time vendor option. Create new General Ledger accounts in the chart of accounts as requested by Mr. Skarra, using the title and number indicated in his memo. Reference numbers for use in the **Check** and **Invoice** fields when using the cash purchase or cash sale options may not always be listed on source documents. Use your best judgment in determining descriptive information for use in these fields.

Month-End and Year-End Accounting Procedures

At the end of each month, Mr. Skarra has you complete a bank reconciliation and record any related journal entries. He also includes a memo at this time informing you of any monthly adjusting entries required. If the month just ending is also the year-end for the business, Mr. Skarra will request that the year-end financial statements be prepared and that his drawing account be closed along with the revenue and expense accounts in preparation for recording transactions in the new fiscal year.

Camera Corner's 12/1/1997 Trial Balance appears below:

Camera Corner/Your Name
Trial Balance As At 12/1/1997

		Debits	Credits
1010	Cash	17,943.20	-
1050	Petty Cash	100.00	-
1200	Accounts Receivable	16,294.55	-
1310	Camera Inventory	52,227.50	-
1320	Lens Inventory	8,545.00	-
1330	Film Inventory	1,653.75	-
1410	Office Supplies	622.30	-
1420	Prepaid Insurance	600.00	-
1550	Office Equipment	4,700.00	-
1560	Accum Dep: Office Equip.	-	2,683.18
1630	Store Equipment	4,000.00	-
1640	Accum Dep: Store Equip.	-	1,341.59
2200	Accounts Payable	-	8,725.00
2310	FIT Payable	-	591.76
2320	SIT Payable	-	384.79
2330	Social Security Tax Payable	-	830.18
2340	Medicare Tax Payable	-	194.18
2350	FUTA Payable	-	23.24
2360	SUTA Payable	-	278.88

2400	Medical Insurance Payable	-	160.00
2710	Loans Payable	-	0.00
3560	David Skarra, Capital	-	65,957.13
3580	David Skarra, Drawing	27,500.00	-
4010	Camera Sales	-	259,683.76
4020	Lens Sales	-	40,673.36
4030	Film Sales	-	12,514.88
4200	Sales Returns & Allow.	396.25	-
4300	Sales Discounts	402.97	-
4450	Interest Income	-	0.00
5010	Cost Of Goods Sold-Cameras	130,246.92	-
5020	Cost of Goods Sold-Lens	20,400.12	-
5030	Cost of Goods Sold-Film	6,276.96	-
5040	Purchase Discounts	0.00	-
5050	Purchase Returns and Allowances	0.00	-
5300	Wages	70,398.00	-
5310	Social Security Tax Expense	4,364.68	-
5320	Medicare Tax Expense	1,020.79	-
5330	FUTA Expense	224.00	-
5340	SUTA Expense	2,186.55	-
5410	Advertising Expense	2,675.00	-
5420	Utilities Expense	1,147.19	-
5430	Deprec Exp: Office Equip.	1,283.26	-
5440	Insurance Expense	2,200.00	-
5450	Rent Expense	12,100.00	-
5460	Office Supplies Expense	1,934.56	-
5470	Deprec Exp: Store Equip.	641.63	-
5480	Phone Expense	762.43	-
5490	Bank Service Charge Expense	330.00	-
5500	Credit Card Fees Expense	0.00	-
5510	Interest Expense: Loans	0.00	-
5550	Miscellaneous Expense	864.32	-
		394,041.93	394,041.93

Packet 1: Week Ending 12/5/1997

The first packet for December contains several source documents and memos that you need to record using CA-Simply Accounting for Windows. Examine each source document carefully, referring to the accounting procedures and policies described earlier if you have questions about how to record a transaction. To begin the practice set, load CA-Simply Accounting for Windows; open the data files for Camera Corner (A:\CAMERA\Camera.asc); then advance the session date to 12/5/1997.

Camera Corner—Document 1   **Session Date: 12/5/1997**

Memo   **Date:** December 1, 1997

Add your name to the company name for Camera Corner. Then, prepare an invoice to Oregon Photo for the sale of 5 Replica cameras (C500), 10 Reflex cameras (C400), and 15 rolls of Captiva 400 film (F400) at our regular sales prices. Terms: 2/10, net 30.

Camera Corner—Document 2   **Session Date: 12/5/1997**

STATEMENT

TO: Camera Corner   **FROM:** Willamette Corporation   **DATE:** December 1, 1997

December 1997 Rent $1,100.00

Approved. Issue Check. DS

Camera Corner—Document 3   **Session Date: 12/5/1997**

Memo   **Date:** December 1, 1997

Prepare Credit Memo 11 to Clark School District for the return of 2 Echo cameras (C100) for a total of $600.00. Use Account 4010.

Camera Corner—Document 4   **Session Date: 12/5/1997**

Mirror Photography   1650
1726 West 9th Street
Vancouver, WA 98660   Dec. 1 , 19 97   98-57
                                               1230

Pay to the
order of   Camera Corner $ 3,562.35

Three thousand five hundred sixty-two and 35/100   Dollars

Washington Federal Bank, P. O. 1762, Vancouver, WA 98665

For Invoice #5876   *Vera Singleton*

Deposit the check, using Deposit Slip 3271.

Camera Corner—Document 5   **Session Date: 12/5/1997**

Memo   **Date:** December 2, 1997

Prepare Debit Memo 27 to Lens Craft for the return of 1 Imagery camera (C200) for a total of $89.50.

Camera Corner—Document 6   **Session Date: 12/5/1997**

Camera Wholesalers
7122 Nob Hill North
San Francisco, CA 94023

CAMERA WHOLESALERS

Invoice # _4896_
To: Camera Corner
7834 SW Capital Hwy.
Portland, OR 97219

Date	Code	Quantity	Description	Unit Price	Amount
12/2/1997	73862	10	Shadow Lens	$ 95.00	$ 950.00
	73914	10	Symbol Lens	100.00	1,000.00
			Terms: N/30	**TOTAL**	**$1,950.00**

Shipping: FOB Destination

Camera Corner—Document 7   **Session Date: 12/5/1997**

Memo   **Date:** December 3, 1997

Purchased a computer and printer for $3,000.00 for use in the office. The monthly loan payment will be automatically deducted on the bank statement.

Camera Corner—Document 8   **Session Date: 12/5/1997**

Memo   **Date:** December 3, 1997

Order 20 rolls of a new sales item: F1000 Captiva 1000; Unit: Roll; Selling Price: $15.95; Minimum Level: 10; Linking Accounts: Asset–1330 Film Inventory, Revenue–4030 Film Sales, Cost of Goods Sold–5030 Cost of Goods Sold-Film. Place the order with Sutterbug Supply, Inc., at $6.75 per roll. Terms: 2/10, net 30.

Camera Corner—Document 9   **Session Date: 12/5/1997**

Memo   **Date:** December 3, 1997

Issue a check in the amount of $1,705.44 to PhotoCraft in payment of Invoice 7226 less a 2% discount.

Camera Corner—Document 10   **Session Date: 12/5/1997**

Memo   **Date:** December 3, 1997

Record a Visa sale to a one-time customer for 10 rolls of Captiva 100 film at $8.95 per roll.

Camera Corner—Document 11   **Session Date: 12/5/1997**

Camera Corner		*Weekly Cash Sales Summary*		**No. 48**	
For Week Ending: 12-5-1997				Approved by: DS	
Item	**Quantity**	**Unit**	**Description**	**Unit Price**	**Amount**
C100	6	Each	Echo	$300.00	$1,800.00
C200	3	Each	Imagery	179.00	537.00
F100	14	Rolls	Captiva 100	8.95	125.30
F200	12	Rolls	Captiva 200	9.95	119.40
				TOTAL	**$2,581.70**

Use Deposit Slip 3272 for the Visa receipt and the weekly cash sales.

Camera Corner—Document 12   **Session Date: 12/5/1997**

Memo

Correct CM11 to Clark School District. Change the account to Account 4200 Sales Returns and Allowances. Print the corrected credit memo.

End-of-Session Procedures

A. Print the following reports:

1. Journal (All entries, By Date, Project Allocations) 12/1/1997 to 12/5/1997
2. Customer Aged report (Select All, Detail, Include Terms) As at 12/5/1997
3. Vendor Aged report (Select All, Detail, Include Terms) As at 12/5/1997
4. Inventory report (Select All, Select Assets, Synopsis) 12/5/1997
5. Income Statement 1/1/1997 to 12/5/1997
6. Trial Balance As at 12/5/1997

B. Make a backup copy of Camera Corner's data files. Exit from the program. Complete the Camera Corner Transmittal.

TRANSMITTAL

Camera Corner   **Name**_____

Packet 1   **Session Date: 12/5/1997**

A. Attach the following documents and reports:

1. Invoice 5882
2. Check 1706
3. CM11
4. Receipt of Check 1650 in Payment of Invoice 5876
5. Purchase Order 1
6. Check 1707
7. Invoice 5883 for Visa sale
8. Sum 48
9. Corrected CM11
10. General Journal 12/1/1997 to 12/5/1997
11. Customer Aged report As at 12/5/1997
12. Vendor Aged report As at 12/5/1997
13. Inventory report 12/5/1997
14. Income Statement 1/1/1997 to 12/5/1997
15. Trial Balance As at 12/5/1997

B. Refer to your reports to list the amounts requested below:

1. Accounts Payable balance $_____

2. Accounts Receivable balance $_____

3. Cash balance $_____

4. Net income $_____

5. Total inventory value $_____

Packet 2: Week Ending 12/12/1997

Load CA-Simply Accounting for Windows; open the data files for Camera Corner (A:\CAMERA\Camera.asc); then advance the session date to 12/12/1997. Record the following transactions:

Camera Corner—Document 13   **Session Date: 12/12/1997**

Memo   **Date:** December 7, 1997

Received Invoice 9004 from Sutterbug along with the full order of F1000 film ordered on Purchase Order 1. Terms 2/10, net 30.

Camera Corner—Document 14   **Session Date: 12/12/1997**

Memo   **Date:** December 7, 1997

Prepare an invoice to Mirror Photography for the sale of 1 Trace lens (L300), 1 Reflex camera (C400), and 5 rolls of Captiva 200 film (F200) at our regular sales prices. Terms: 2/10, net 30.

Camera Corner—Document 15   **Session Date: 12/12/1997**

Memo   **Date:** December 8, 1997

Issue a check in the amount of $1,870.10 to Sutterbug Supply, Inc., in payment of Invoice 8962 less a 2% discount.

Camera Corner—Document 16   **Session Date: 12/121997**

Clark School District 2530 Mill Plain Blvd. Vancouver, WA 98660	6221 Dec. 8 , 19 97 98-57 1230

Pay to the
order of ____ Camera Corner ____ $ 2,373.86

Two thousand three hundred seventy-three and 86/100 _____ Dollars

	Approved D.S.	Invoice #5879	3,034.50
Washington Federal Bank, P. O. 1762, Vancouver, WA 98665		Discount 2%	60.39
		CM 11	600.00
For __ Invoice #5879 __ *Wanda Jackson*			2,373.86

Camera Corner—Document 17   **Session Date: 12/12/1997**

Camera Wholesalers
7122 Nob Hill North
San Francisco, CA 94023

New Item!
Selling Price $250.00 Each
Minimum 20
Number: C600

Invoice #   8571

To: Camera Corner
     7834 SW Capital Hwy.
     Portland, OR 97219

Date	Code	Quantity	Description	Unit Price	Amount
12/10/97	19120	26 each	Glance Camera	$ 125.00	$3,250.00
			Terms: N/30	**TOTAL**	**$3,250.00**

Shipping: FOB Destination

Camera Corner—Document 18   **Session Date: 12/12/1997**

Memo   **Date:** December 10, 1997

Issue a check to Sutterbug Supply, Inc., in payment of Invoice 9004 less a 2% discount.

Camera Corner—Document 19   **Session Date: 12/12/1997**

Memo   **Date:** December 11, 1997

Prepare Debit Memo 28 to National Camera for the return of 1 Glance camera (C600) for a total of $125.00.

Camera Corner—Document 20   **Session Date: 12/12/1997**

Memo   **Date:** December 11, 1997

MasterCard sale to one-time customer for 3 rolls of F1000.

Camera Corner—Document 21   **Session Date: 12/12/1997**

(PN) **Photography Northwest**
833 SW 11th Ave.
Portland, Oregon 97204
Phone: 503-222-3611

Invoice #   7213

To: Camera Corner
     7834 SW Capital Hwy.
     Portland, OR 97219

Date	Description	Amount
12/11/1997	Special Lens Advertising	$400.00
	Terms: Payable on Receipt **TOTAL**	**$400.00**

Approved. Issue Check. D.S.

Camera Corner—Document 22 **Session Date: 12/5/1997**

	Camera Corner	*Weekly Cash Sales Summary*			**No. 49**	
	For Week Ending: 12-12-1997				Approved by: DS	

Item	Quantity	Unit	Description	Unit Price	Amount
L100	7	Each	Shadow Lens	$189.00	$1,323.00
L200	9	Each	Symbol Lens	199.00	1,791.00
C200	6	Each	Imagery	179.00	1,074.00
F100	20	Rolls	Captiva 100	8.95	179.50
				TOTAL	$4,367.00

Use Deposit Slip 3273 for the credit card receipts, checks received, and the weekly cash sales.

Camera Corner—Document 23 **Session Date: 12/12/1997**

Pacific Office Supply
3628 SE 39th Ave.
Portland, Oregon 97214
Phone: 503-222-3611

Invoice # __8267__

To: Camera Corner
7834 SW Capital Hwy.
Portland, OR 97219

Date	Description	Amount
12/12/97	Office Supplies	$326.80
	Terms: Payable on Receipt **TOTAL**	**$326.80**

Approved. Issue Check. D.S.

Camera Corner—Document 24 **Session Date: 12/12/1997**

Memo **Date:** December 12, 1997

Prepare an invoice to Daily News for the sale of 1 Symbol lens (L200), 1 Metaphor camera (C300), and 20 rolls of Captiva 400 film (F400) at our regular sales prices. Terms: 2/10, net 30.

Camera Corner—Document 25   **Session Date: 12/12/1997**

Memo   **Date:** December 12, 1997

Correct an error on DM28. The original debit memo was issued to National Camera. The debit memo should be issued to Camera Wholesalers. Make this correction by using the Adjust Invoice feature for sales invoices, selecting DM28 for National Camera, and changing the quantity to **0**. Post the correction and answer Yes to the dialog box regarding this adjustment. Re-enter a new DM28 with Camera Wholesalers as the vendor. Use the date of December 11 for the transaction.

End-of-Session Procedures

A. Print the following reports:

    1. Journal Entries (By Date, Project Allocation, All Entries) 12/6/1997 to 12/12/1997
    2. Customer Aged report (Select All, Detail, Include Terms) As at 12/12/1997
    3. Vendor Aged report (Select All, Detail, Include Terms) As at 12/12/1997
    4. Inventory report (Select All, Select Assets, Synopsis) 12/12/1997
    5. Income Statement 1/1/1997 to 12/12/1997
    6. Trial Balance As at 12/12/1997

B. Make a backup copy of Camera Corner's data files. Exit from the program. Complete the Camera Corner Transmittal.

TRANSMITTAL

Camera Corner   **Name**_____
Packet 2   **Session Date: 12/12/1997**

A. Attach the following documents and reports:

  1. Invoice 5884
  2. Check 1708
  3. Receipt of Check 6221 in payment of Invoice 5879 (including discount and return)
  4. Check 1709
  5. Invoice 5885 for MasterCard sale
  6. Check 1710
  7. Sum 49
  8. Check 1711
  9. Invoice 5886
10. Journal Entries 12/6/1997 to 12/12/1997
11. Customer Aged report As at 12/12/1997
10. Vendor Aged report As at 12/12/1997
11. Inventory report 12/12/1997
12. Income Statement 1/1/1997 to 12/12/1997
13. Trial Balance As at 12/12/1997

B. Refer to your reports to list the amounts requested below:

1. Accounts Payable balance $_____

2. Accounts Receivable balance $_____

3. Cash balance $_____

4. Net income $_____

5. Total inventory value $_____

Packet 3: Week Ending 12/19/1997

Load CA-Simply Accounting for Windows; open the data files for Camera Corner (A:\CAMERA\Camera.asc); then advance the session date to 12/19/1997. Record the following transactions:

Camera Corner—Document 26　　　　　　　**Session Date: 12/19/1997**

Passport Photos
049 SW Porter Street
Portland, Oregon 97202

821

Dec. 14 , 19 97　　93-57
　　　　　　　　　　1250

Pay to the
order of ____ Camera Corner _____ $ 3,394.20

__Three thousand three hundred ninety-four and 20/100_____Dollars

Portland Regional Bank, P. O. 2789, Portland, OR 97212

For __Invoice 5825__　　　__Pam Quin__

Deposit the check, using Deposit Slip 3274.

Camera Corner—Document 27　　　　　　　**Session Date: 12/19/1997**

PhotoCraft　　　　　　　　　　　　　　Invoice ___7681___
540 Belmont Avenue　　　　　　　　　**To:** Camera Corner
Seattle, WA 98125　　　　　　　　　　　　7834 SW Capital Hwy.
　　　　　　　　　　　　　　　　　　　Portland, OR 97219

Date	Quantity	Description	Unit Price	Amount
12/14/97	200 Rolls	Captiva 400 film	$6.45	$1,290.00

Shipping: FOB Destination	Terms: N/30		TOTAL	$1,290.00

Approved. D.S.

Camera Corner—Document 28　　　　　　　**Session Date: 12/19/1997**

Memo　　　　　　　　　　　　　　**Date:** December 14, 1997

Issue a check in the amount of $4,648.04 to Camera Wholesalers in payment of Invoices 4762 and 4896.

Camera Corner—Document 29   **Session Date: 12/19/1997**

Frame Master   Invoice ___Z721___
1200 Golden Gate Way   **To:** Camera Corner
San Francisco, CA 94023   7834 SW Capital Hwy.
415-989-7433   **Date: 12/15/1997**   Portland, OR 97219

Code	Quantity	Description	Unit Price	Amount
V12	50 Rolls	Captiva 200 Film	$4.95	$247.50

Shipping: FOB Destination	Terms: N/30	TOTAL	$247.50
Approved. D.S.		New Vendor!	

Camera Corner—Document 30   **Session Date: 12/19/1997**

Memo   **Date:** December 15, 1997

Change the name of Account 2340 SUTA Payable to 2340 Medicare Tax Payable. Issue a check to the Federal Reserve Bank for the payment of the November payroll liabilities and taxes as follows:

FIT Payable	$ 591.76
Social Security Tax Payable	830.18
Medicare Tax Payable	194.18
Total Amount Due	$1,616.12

Camera Corner—Document 31   **Session Date: 12/19/1997**

Memo   **Date:** December 15, 1997

Issue a check to the Oregon Dept. of Revenue for the payment of the November SIT Payable in the amount of $384.79.

Camera Corner—Document 32   **Session Date: 12/19/1997**

Mirror Photography   1982
1726 West 9th Street
Vancouver, WA 98660   Dec. 16 , 19 97   98-57
                                                    1230

Pay to the
order of   Camera Corner $ 856.27

Eight hundred fifty-six and 27/100   Dollars

Washington Federal Bank, P. O. 1762, Vancouver, WA 98665

For   Invoice #5884   *Vera Singleton*

Camera Corner—Document 33   **Session Date: 12/19/1997**

Memo   **Date:** December 17, 1997

Create a new "Land" account number 1520 in the chart of accounts.

Camera Corner—Document 34   **Session Date: 12/19/1997**

Memo   **Date:** December 18, 1997

Prepare an invoice to Passport Photos for the sale of 1 Metaphor camera (C300) at our regular sales price. Terms: Net 30.

Camera Corner—Document 35   **Session Date: 12/19/1997**

Camera Corner   *Weekly Cash Sales Summary*   **No. 50**

For Week Ending: 12-19-1997   Approved by: DS

Item	Quantity	Unit	Description	Unit Price	Amount
C500	2	Each	Replica	$899.00	$1,798.00
C400	1	Each	Reflex	599.00	599.00
C600	2	Each	Glance	250.00	500.00
F200	10	Rolls	Captiva 200	9.95	99.50
				TOTAL	**$2,996.50**

Camera Corner—Document 36   **Session Date: 12/19/1997**

> *Memo*   **Date:** December 19, 1997
>
> Please issue a check to David Skarra in the amount of $2,500.00 as a December draw.

Camera Corner—Document 37   **Session Date: 12/19/1997**

> *Memo*   **Date:** December 19, 1997
>
> Bank returned Check 821 in the amount of $3,394.20 Received from Passport Photos as payment in full for Invoice 5825. There is a $25 NSF charge ($15 that the bank will charge and $10 that we charge). Create any necessary accounts and/or items required to record the NSF check. (Use Account 4460 as the account number for Bad Check Charges.)

End-of-Session Procedures

A. Print the following reports:

1. Journal Entries (By Date, Project Allocation, All Entries) 12/13/1997 to 12/19/1997
2. Customer Aged report (Select All, Detail, Include Terms) As at 12/19/1997
3. Vendor Aged report (Select All, Detail, Include Terms) As at 12/19/1997
4. Inventory report (Select All, Select Assets, Synopsis) 12/19/1997
5. Income Statement 1/1/1997 to 12/19/1997
6. Trial Balance As at 12/19/1997

B. Make a backup copy of Camera Corner's data files. Exit from the program. Complete the Camera Corner Transmittal.

TRANSMITTAL

Camera Corner   **Name**_____

Packet 3   **Session Date: 12/19/1997**

A. Attach the following documents and reports:

  1. Receipt of Check 821 in payment of Invoice 5825
  2. Check 1712
  3. Check 1713
  4. Check 1714
  5. Receipt of Check 1982 in payment of Invoice 5884
  6. Invoice 5887
  7. Sum50
  8. Check 1715
  9. Invoice 5888
10. Journal Entries 12/13/1997 to 12/19/1997
11. Customer Aged report As at 12/19/1997
12. Vendor Aged report As at 12/19/1997
13. Inventory report 12/19/1997
14. Income Statement 1/1/1997 to 12/19/1997
15. Trial Balance As at 12/19/1997

B. Refer to your reports to list the amounts requested below:

1. Accounts Payable balance $_____

2. Accounts Receivable balance $_____

3. Cash balance $_____

4. Net income $_____

5. Total inventory value $_____

Packet 4: Week Ending 12/26/1997

Load CA-Simply Accounting for Windows; open the data files for Camera Corner (A:\CAMERA\Camera.asc); then advance the Session date to 12/26/1997. Record the following transactions:

Camera Corner—Document 38   **Session Date: 12/26/1997**

Memo   **Date:** December 21, 1997

Prepare Debit Memo 29 to PhotoCraft for the return of 10 rolls of Captive 400 film (F400) in the amount of $64.50.

Camera Corner—Document 39   **Session Date: 12/26/1997**

Memo   **Date:** December 21, 1997

Prepare an invoice to a new customer, Monarch Prints, 475 Prom Way, Seaside, Oregon, 97138, 503-738-3334, Contact: Sunny Thomas, for the sale of 2 Echo cameras (C100), 1 Trace lens (L300), and 2 rolls of Captiva 100 film (F100) at our regular sales prices. Terms: net 30.

Camera Corner—Document 40   **Session Date: 12/26/1997**

Memo   **Date:** December 22, 1997

Issue a check in the amount of $2,288.95 to Lens Craft in payment of Invoice 6770 less DM27.

Camera Corner—Document 41   **Session Date: 12/26/1997**

Memo   **Date:** December 23, 1997

Prepare Credit Memo 12 to Monarch Prints for the return of 1 Echo camera (C100) for a total of $300.00. Use Account 4010 for the transaction account.

Camera Corner—Document 42   **Session Date: 12/26/1997**

Camera Wholesalers

7122 Nob Hill North ● San Francisco, CA 94023

Date: 12/24/1997

Invoice # 4982

To: Camera Corner

7834 SW Capital Hwy.

Portland, OR 97219

Code	Quantity	Description	Unit Price	Amount
73222	4 Each	Trace Lens	$110.00	$440.00

Shipping: FOB Destination	Terms: N/30		TOTAL	$440.00

Approved. D.S.

Camera Corner—Document 43   **Session Date: 12/26/1997**

Pacific Office Supply

3628 SE 39th Ave.

Portland, Oregon 97214

Phone: 503-222-3611

Invoice 8419

To: Camera Corner

7834 SW Capital Hwy.

Portland, OR 97219

Date	Description	Amount
12/24/97	Office Supplies	$202.05

	Terms: Payable on Receipt	TOTAL	$202.05

Approved. Issue Check. D.S.

Camera Corner—Document 44   **Session Date: 12/26/1997**

National Camera

4970 NE Halsey

Portland, OR 97220

Date: 12/24/1997

New Item!

Selling Price: $400 each

Minimum: 15

Number L400

Invoice 8627

To: Camera Corner

7834 SW Capital Hwy.

Portland, OR 97219

Code	Quantity	Description	Unit Price	Amount
18721	20 Each	Vision Lens	$200.00	$4,000.00

Shipping: FOB Destination	Terms: N/30		TOTAL	$4,000.00

Approved. D.S.

Camera Corner—Document 45   **Session Date: 12/26/1997**

Camera Corner *Weekly Cash Sales Summary*				**No. 51**	
For Week Ending: 12-26-1997				Approved by: DS	

Item	Quantity	Unit	Description	Unit Price	Amount
F100	26	Rolls	Captiva 100	$8.95	$232.70
F200	30	Rolls	Captiva 200	9.95	298.50

C200	10	Each	Imagery	179.00	1,790.00
C100	6	Each	Echo	300	1,800.00
				TOTAL	**$4,121.20**

Use Deposit Slip 3276 for the weekly deposit.

Camera Corner—Document 46   **Session Date: 12/26/1997**

Photography Northwest   **Invoice #__7362__**
PN **833 SW 11ᵗʰ Ave.**   **To:** Camera Corner
Portland, Oregon 97204   7834 SW Capital Hwy.
Phone: 503-222-3611   Portland, OR 97219

Date	Description	Amount
12/26/1997	Special Camera Advertising	$700.00

| | **Terms: Payable on Receipt** | **TOTAL** | **$700.00** |

Approved. Issue Check. D.S.

Camera Corner—Document 47   **Session Date: 12/26/1997**

Memo   **Date:** December 26, 1997

Adjust Credit Memo 12 to Monarch Prints. Use Account 4200 for the transaction account rather than 4010.

End-Of-Session Procedures

A. Print the following reports:

1. Journal Entries (By Date, Project Allocation, All Entries) 12/20/1997 to 12/26/1997
2. Customer Aged report (Select All, Detail, Include Terms) As at 12/26/1997
3. Vendor Aged report (Select All, Detail, Include Terms) As at 12/26/1997
4. Inventory report (Select All, Select Assets, Synopsis) 12/26/1997
5. Income Statement 1/1/1997 to 12/26/1997
6. Trial Balance As at 12/26/1997

B. Make a backup copy of Camera Corner's data files. Exit from the program. Complete the Camera Corner Transmittal.

TRANSMITTAL

Camera Corner   **Name**_____
Packet 4   **Session Date: 12/26/1997**

A. Attach the following documents and reports:

   1. Invoice 5889
   2. Check 1716
   3. CM 12
   4. Check 1717
   5. Sum51
   6. Check 1718
   7. CM12
   8. All Journal Entries 12/20/1997 to 12/26/1997
   9. Customer Aged report As at 12/26/1997
  10. Vendor Aged report As at 12/26/1997
  11. Inventory report 12/26/1997
  12. Income Statement 1/1/1997 to 12/26/1997
  13. Trial Balance As at 12/26/1997

B. Refer to your reports to list the amounts requested below:

1. Accounts Payable balance $_____

2. Accounts Receivable balance $_____

3. Cash balance $_____

4. Net income $_____

5. Total inventory value $_____

Packet 5: Partial Week Ending 12/31/1997

Load CA-Simply Accounting for Windows; open the data files for Camera Corner (A:\CAMERA\Camera.asc); then advance the session date to 12/31/1997. Record the following transactions:

Camera Corner—Document 48　　　　　　　　　　**Session Date: 12/31/1997**

Memo　　　　　　　　　　　　　　　　**Date:** December 28, 1997

Issue a check to PhotoCraft in payment of Invoice 7681 less DM29.

Camera Corner—Document 49　　　　　　　　　　**Session Date: 12/31/1997**

Memo　　　　　　　　　　　　　　　　**Date:** December 29, 1997

Prepare an invoice to Clark School District for the sale of 2 Reflex cameras (C400) and 10 rolls of Captiva 400 film (F400) at our regular sales prices. Terms: 2/10, net 30.

Camera Corner—Document 50　　　　　　**Session Date: 12/31/1997**

Monarch Prints	768
475 Prom Way	
Seaside, Oregon 97138	Dec. 29 , 19 97 93-57 / 1240
Pay to the order of _____ Camera Corner _____	$ 542.90
Five hundred forty-two and 90/100 _____ Dollars	
Coast Bank ✿ P. O. 829 ✿ Seaside, OR 97138	
For __ Invoice 5889 less CM __ *Sunny Thomas*	

Camera Corner—Document 51   **Session Date: 12/31/1997**

Frame Master
1200 Golden Gate Way
San Francisco, CA 94023
415-989-7433   **Date: 12/29/1997**

Invoice # _Z894_
To: Camera Corner
7834 SW Capital Hwy.
Portland, OR 97219

Code	Quantity	Description	Unit Price	Amount
D41	15 Each	Glance Camera	$125.00	$1,875.00

Shipping: FOB Destination	Terms: N/30	TOTAL	$1,875.00

Approved. D.S.

Camera Corner—Document 52   **Session Date: 12/31/1997**

Western Telephone ✳ 4298 SW 10th ✳ Portland, OR ✳ 97205

INVOICE: 69-201   **DATE:** 12-29-97   **DUE DATE:** 1-4-98

CURRENT CHARGES:
WESTERN TELEPHONE CHARGES

Monthly Service and Equipment	$50.50
Itemized Calls	10.78
WESTERN TELEPHONE CURRENT CHARGES	**$61.28**

ITT COMMUNICATION CHARGES

Itemized Calls	21.32
ITT COMMUNICATION CURRENT CHARGES	**$21.32**

TOTAL CURRENT CHARGES Payable upon Receipt   **$82.60**

CUSTOMER INFORMATION: Camera Corner, 7834 SW Capital Hwy, Portland, OR 97210

Approved to record for later payment. DS

Camera Corner—Document 53   **Session Date: 12/31/1997**

Cascade Electric

890 Stark Street ✿ Portland, OR 97214

Camera Corner
7834 SW Capital Hwy., Portland, OR 97219

December Service:
Invoice K010023
Date 12/30/1997
Due 01/04/1998

TOTAL DUE: $85.76

Usage: Meter Number 12-0932   Readings: 58659-39204   Usage 545kWh

Approved to record transaction for payment later. DS

Camera Corner—Document 54　　　　　　　　　　**Session Date: 12/31/1997**

Camera Corner *Weekly Cash Sales Summary* **No. 52**					
For Week Ending: 12-31-1997				Approved by: DS	
Item	**Quantity**	**Unit**	**Description**	**Unit Price**	**Amount**
L400	3	Each	Vision Lens	$400.00	$1,200.00
C500	1	Each	Replica	899.00	899.00
F400	25	Rolls	Captiva 400	12.95	323.75
				TOTAL	**$2,422.75**

Use Deposit Slip 3277 for the weekly deposit.

Camera Corner—Document 55　　　　　　　　　　**Session Date: 12/31/1997**

Memo

Date: December 31, 1997

Please issue a check to replenish petty cash as follows. (Do a QuickAdd to add a vendor named Cash. The Invoice Number is PCash.)

Office Supplies	$ 65.99
Misc. Expense	10.05
David Skarra, Drawing	20.00
	$ 96.04

Camera Corner—Document 56　　　　　　　　　　**Session Date: 12/31/1997**

Memo

Date: December 31, 1997

Please issue payroll checks as follows:

Employee	Salary	Hourly Rate	Hours	Medical Deduction
April Reed	$ 2,275.00			$ 100.00
Jim Sakamoto	1,625.00			30.00
Alexander Webster	1,700.00			30.00
Lupe Yanez		$ 7.50	147	none

Camera Corner—Document 57   **Session Date: 12/31/1997**

Memo   **Date:** December 31, 1997

Reconcile the following bank statement. Make any necessary entries. Print the Account Reconciliation Journal entry and the Account Reconciliation report.

Portland Bank
P. O. 981, Portland, OR 97212

| Statement Date: 12/31/1997 | | Camera Corner | |
| Account: 0113499 | | 7834 SW Capital Hwy. Portland, OR 97219 | |

Description	Deposit	Check	Balance
12/1/1997 Beginning Balance			$17,943.20
12/1/1997 Deposit 3271	$3,562.35		21,505.55
12/3/1997 Check 1707		$1,705.44	19,800.11
12/5/1997 Deposit 3272	2,665.83		22,465.94
12/8/1997 Check 1708		1,870.10	20,595.84
12/10/1997 Check 1709		132.30	20,463.54
12/11/1997 Check 1710		400.00	20,063.54
12/12/1997 Deposit 3273	6,785.84		26,849.38
12/12/1997 Check 1711		326.80	26,522.58
12/14/1997 Deposit 3274	3,394.20		29,916.78
12/14/1997 Check 1712		4,648.04	25,268.74
12/15/1997 Check 1713		1,616.12	23,652.62
12/15/1997 Check 1714		384.79	23,267.83
12/19/1997 Deposit 3275	3,852.77		27,120.60
12/19/1997 Check 1715		2,500.00	24,620.60
12/19/1997 NSF Check		3,394.20	21,226.40
12/22/1997 Check 1716		2,288.95	18,937.45
12/24/1997 Check 1717		202.05	18,735.40
12/26/1997 Deposit 3276	4,121.20		22,856.60
12/26/1997 Check 1718		700.00	22,156.60

12/31/1997 Office Equipment Loan Pmt: $5.36 Principal; $58.24 Interest		63.60	22,093.00
12/31/1997 Interest	62.45		22,155.45
12/31/1997 Charges: NSF Charge $15; Service Charge $25		40.00	22,115.45
12/31/1997 Ending Balance			22,115.45

End-of-Session Procedures

A. Print the following reports:

   1. Journal Entries (By Date, Project Allocation, All Entries) 12/27/1997 to 12/31/1997
   2. Customer Aged report (Select All, Detail, Include Terms) As at 12/31/1997
   3. Vendor Aged report (Select All, Detail, Include Terms) As at 12/31/1997
   4. Inventory report (Select All, Select Assets, Synopsis) 12/31/1997
   5. Income Statement 1/1/1997 to 12/231/1997
   6. Trial Balance As at 12/31/1997

B. Make a backup copy of Camera Corner's data files. Exit from the program. Complete the Camera Corner Transmittal.

TRANSMITTAL

Camera Corner   **Name**_____

Packet 5   **Session Date: 12/31/1997**

A. Attach the following documents and reports:

1. Check 1719
2. Invoice 5890
3. Receipt of Check 768 in payment of Invoice 5889 less CM12
4. Sum52
5. Check 1720
6. Payroll Check 1721
7. Payroll Check 1722
8. Payroll Check 1723
9. Payroll Check 1724
10. Account Reconciliation Journal entry 12/31/1997
11. Account Reconciliation Detail report 12/1/1997 to 1/1/1998
12. All Journal Entries 12/27/1997 to 12/31/1997
13. Customer Aged report As at 12/31/1997
14. Vendor Aged report As at 12/31/1997
15. Inventory Synopsis 12/31/1997
16. Income Statement 1/1/1997 to 12/31/1997
17. Trial Balance As at 12/31/1997

B. Refer to your reports to list the amounts requested below:

1. Accounts Payable balance $_____

2. Accounts Receivable balance $_____

3. Cash balance $_____

4. Net income $_____

5. Total inventory value $_____

Packet 6: Month-End and Year-End Procedures 12/31/1997 and 1/1/1998

A. Load CA-Simply Accounting for Windows; open the data files for Camera Corner (A:\CAMERA\Camera.asc); then leave the session date set at 12/31/1997. Record the adjusting entries authorized by the following memo:

Camera Corner—Document 58   **Session Date: 12/31/1997**

Memo   **Date:** December 31, 1997

Please record the following adjusting entries for December:

1. Decrease the Captiva 200 film (F200) inventory by 10 rolls at a total cost of $49.50. Comment: Damaged Goods. (Project: Film Sales Summary)
2. Expired insurance, $200.00
3. Office supplies used, $256.00
4. Office equipment depreciation, $116.66
5. Store equipment depreciation, $58.33

B. Print the following documents and reports:

1. Journal Entries (By Date, Project Allocation, All Entries) 12/1/1997 to 12/31/1997
2. Employee report (Select All, YTD Summary) 12/31/1997
3. W-2 slips (Select All)
4. Project report (Select All, Detail) 12/1/1997 to 12/31/1997
5. Inventory report (Select All, Select Assets, Synopsis) 12/31/1997
6. Trial Balance As at 12/31/1997
7. Income Statement 1/1/1997 to 12/231/1997
8. Balance Sheet As at 12/31/1997

C. Make a backup copy of Camera Corner's data files.

D. Record the closing entry authorized by the following memo:

Camera Corner—Document 59   **Session Date: 12/31/1997**

Memo   **Date:** December 31, 1997

Please record the entry to close my drawing account for the year.

E. Advance the session date to 1/1/1998.

F. Print a Trial Balance As at 1/1/1998.

G. Exit from the program. Complete the Camera Corner Transmittal.

TRANSMITTAL

Camera Corner   **Name**_____

Packet 6   **Session Date: 12/31/1997 to 1/1/1998**

A. Attach the following documents and reports:

  1. All Journal Entries 12/1/1997 to 12/31/1997
  2. Employee report 12/31/1997
  3. W-2 slips
  4. Project report 12/1/1997 to 12/31/1997
  5. Inventory report 12/31/1997
  6. Trial Balance As at 12/31/1997
  7. Income Statement 1/1/1997 to 12/231/1997
  8. Balance Sheet As at 12/31/1997
  9. Trial Balance As at 1/1/1998
10. Income Statement 1/1/1998 to 1/1/1998
11. Balance Sheet As at 1/1/1998

B. Refer to your reports to list the amounts requested below:

1.   What are total assets at 12/31/1997? $_____

2.   How much is net income for the year? $_____

3.   How much is the total cost of goods sold for the year? $_____

4.   How much did David Skarra withdraw from the business during the year? $_____

5.   How much employer's expense did Camera Corner incur for Lupe Yanez
       for the year? $_____

6.   What is the total inventory value on 12/31/1997? $_____

7.   How much in deductions were withheld from Jim Sakamoto's paychecks
       for the year? $_____

8.   How much is net income for the Camera Sales Summary project
       for December? $_____

9.   What is the balance of the David Skarra, Capital account on 1/1/1998? $_____

10.   How much cumulative revenue was reported for the Film Sales Summary
       project for December? $_____

SECTION 3:

COMPUTERIZING A MANUAL
ACCOUNTING SYSTEM

COMPUTERIZING A MANUAL ACCOUNTING SYSTEM—GENERAL LEDGER, SETTINGS, AND LINKING ACCOUNTS

COMPUTERIZING A MANUAL ACCOUNTING SYSTEM— GENERAL LEDGER, SETTINGS, AND LINKING ACCOUNTS

LEARNING OBJECTIVES

After studying this chapter, you will be able to:
- Create a new set of company data files
- Establish fiscal start, fiscal end, and earliest transaction dates
- Select and establish company settings
- Design and create a chart of accounts
- Enter beginning account balances
- Establish linking accounts
- Make the General Ledger Ready

CONVERT A MANUAL SYSTEM TO A COMPUTERIZED SYSTEM

In this chapter, you will learn how to convert a manual accounting system to a computerized accounting system. The CA-Simply Accounting for Windows program facilitates this process by allowing two modes of program operation: Not Ready and Ready. The program is not ready when it is not integrated/linked and you are setting up the company's accounting records. The program is ready when it is integrated/linked and you are using it for regular accounting. In each of the prior chapters, you were working with the CA-Simply Accounting for Windows program in the Ready mode. You will now have an opportunity to work with the CA-Simply Accounting for Windows program in the Not Ready mode.

CLASSIC CLOCKS TUTORIAL

The following tutorial is a step-by-step guide to converting Classic Clocks' manual accounting system to a computerized accounting system. The procedures required to establish Classic Clocks' customized settings, chart of accounts, beginning account balances, linking accounts, and to make the General Ledger ready for operation will be demonstrated. The Classic Clocks Tutorial will be continued in Chapter 10 and completed in Chapter 11 to give you a comprehensive overview of how to computerize the accounting records of a small merchandising business. In Chapter 10, the procedures required to make Classic Clocks' Payables, Receivables, Payroll, Inventory, and Project Ledgers ready for operation will be discussed. In Chapter 11, the procedures for budgeting will be presented.

Study Tips

To get the most educational value out of the Classic Clocks Tutorial in Chapters 9, 10, and 11, the following study steps are recommended for each chapter:

1. Read the entire chapter.
2. Answer the questions at the end of the chapter.
3. Complete all of the Classic Clocks Tutorial steps (indicated by the word ACTION) in the chapter using your computer. **Hint**: Place a check mark (✔) in the box as you complete each ACTION.
4. Enter all of the additional transactions (represented in narrative form) as they occur throughout the chapter.
5. As you work through the tutorial, compare your displays/reports to those illustrated in the text to determine the accuracy of your work. If you detect an error while working in the Not Ready mode, follow the Editing Tips (highlighted in special boxes) to correct the error. If you detect an error in a posted transaction after making a ledger ready, refer to the procedures presented throughout the chapters to correct the error.
6. Complete the Classic Clocks Tutorial Transmittal located at the end of the chapter.
7. Review the LEARNING OBJECTIVES stated at the beginning of the chapter to ensure that you have accomplished each objective.
8. Complete The Paint Place Exercise at the end of the chapter.

CLASSIC CLOCKS COMPANY PROFILE

Classic Clocks is a sole proprietorship owned by Maria Lindsay in Coeur D'Alene, Idaho. Maria operates a retail store that sells clocks and watches. She has maintained a manual accounting system for her business and would like to covert to a computerized accounting system beginning December 1, 1997. Maria has selected the CA-Simply Accounting for Windows program as the most appropriate software for her business. As a merchandising business with employees, Maria plans to use the General, Receivables, Payables, Inventory, Payroll, and Project Ledgers of the program.

CREATING A COMPANY

A new company is created by using Simply's Setup Wizard. New company data files can be created in the CA-Simply Accounting for Windows program by establishing a company subdirectory, company file name, and path to that company file name while using the wizard. In addition, the fiscal start, fiscal end, earliest transaction dates, and the company address information need to be entered into the program. The company information for Classic Clocks is listed in the following memo:

Classic Clocks—Document 1   **December, 1, 1997**

Memo   **Date:** December 1, 1997

Company Information:

Classic Clocks/Your Name	Fiscal start: 1/1/97	Federal ID: 93-987654
1200 Lakeway	Fiscal end: 12/31/97	State ID: 123456
Coeur D'Alene, Idaho 83814	Earliest Transaction Date: 12/1/1997	
208-555-6349	Fax: 208-555-9436	

ACTION: To create a company, you must open Simply Accounting. When the Select Company window appears, select **Create a new company** and click **OK**.

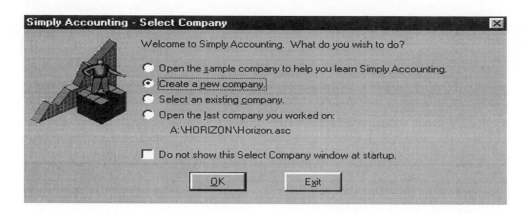

Explanation: The CA-Simply Accounting-Select Company dialog box will appear. Your screen will differ based on the last set of company data files that you accessed and the disk drive you are using to store your student data files.

ACTION: Follow the steps listed on the Setup Wizard to create a company. When finished with one screen, click **Next**. When the setup is complete, you will click the **Finish** button. The first screen in the Wizard will look similar to the following:

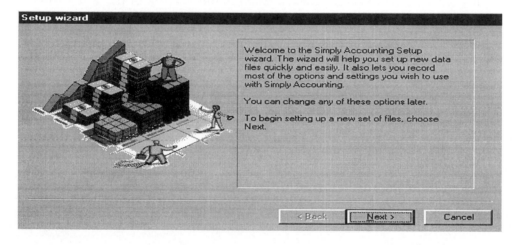

ACTION: Because Classic Clocks has a designated chart of accounts, select **Create a new list of accounts from scratch** and click **Next. Note:** As an aid to creating a business, Simply provides standardized charts of accounts for many different types of companies.

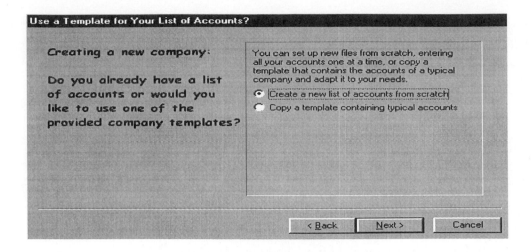

ACTION: The next step is to enter the company name. Be sure to type the storage location of the data as part of the company name. **Note:** Because this is a new company, data files for this company are not located with the other company files on the CD-ROM that came with the text. The company files for all the companies created in this section of the text will be stored on floppy disks. To store the company files on a disk located in drive A, key: *A:\Clocks\Classic Clocks*; to store in drive B, key: *B:\Clocks\Classic Clocks*; to store on your hard disk, key: *C:\Winsim\Clocks\ Classic Clocks*. Your screen will look similar to the following:

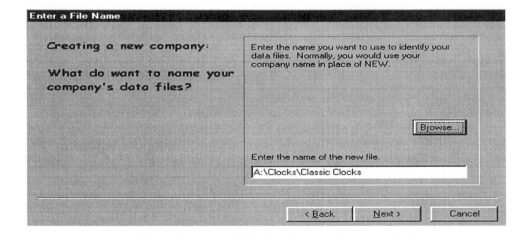

ACTION: Continue with the company creation. If you have keyed the name and location of the company correctly, click **Yes** on the following screen. If not, click **No** and make any necessary corrections.

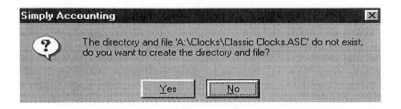

ACTION: Enter *1/1/97* into the **Fiscal Year Start** text box; enter *12/31/97* into the **Fiscal Year End** text box; then enter *12/1/97* into the **Earliest Transaction** text box. **Note**: Simply will enter 1997 as the year. Proofread carefully. The only time you may enter the date of the earliest transaction is when you create the company. Your screen will look like this:

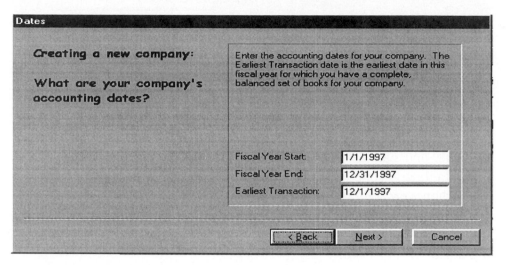

Explanation: The fiscal start date is the first day of your accounting year. The fiscal end date is the last day of your accounting year. The earliest transaction date is the earliest date on which you can process transactions for the fiscal year. You cannot process a transaction with a date that is earlier than the earliest transaction date. The earliest transaction date can be the fiscal start date, the fiscal end date, or any date in between. The only time the earliest transaction date may be entered is when you first set up the program, so it is critical to enter the correct date.

ACTION: The following screen is used to indicate the activities for which you plan to use Simply Accounting. All items are selected, so click **Next** to continue.

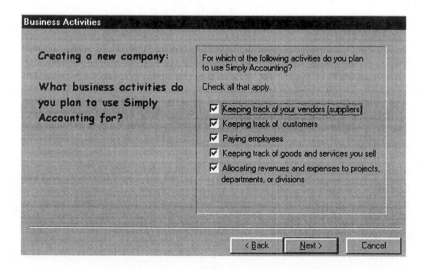

ACTION: On the Company Name and Address screen, enter the company information for Classic Clocks (see Document 1). Your screen should agree with the following:

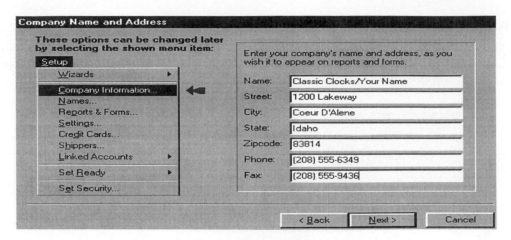

Explanation: The city and state designations in the Company Information dialog box will become the default settings for all city and state fields throughout the CA-Simply Accounting for Windows program. From this point on, whenever a city or state field in any ledger is open for initial data entry, Coeur D'Alene will appear as the default in the **City** field, and Idaho will appear as the default in the **State** field. Note that the educational version of CA-Simply Accounting for Windows packaged with this text is limited to using dates prior to 1998.

COMPANY SETTINGS IN SETUP WIZARD

The CA-Simply Accounting for Windows program presets certain defaults for each ledger and for screen displays and printing functions. Each of these settings can be modified to customize the program to a specific company's needs. Part of the Setup Wizard is designed to customize the settings for the company. Follow the screens presented in the Wizard to enter the following settings modifications:

Classic Clocks—Document 2　　　　　　　　　　　　　　　　　**December 1, 1997**

Memo　　　　　　　　　　　　　　　　　　　　　　**Date:** December 1, 1997

Company settings modifications information for Setup Wizard:

Use accounting terminology. Accept the income and deduction account names for payroll and the project title as Project. Check with your instructor regarding printer setup instructions. Do NOT use cash-basis accounting or the budgeting feature of Simply. Use the check number as the source code for cash purchases and sales. Accept the default values used by Simply Accounting unless information is provided below:

Receivables	**Payables**	**Payroll**	**Inventory**
Sales tax: 8.0%	no changes	SUTA rate: 3.5	Inventory Tracking
		FUTA rate: 0.8	Inventory Lookup

　ACTION: Continue with the Setup Wizard for Classic Clocks. Select **Use Accounting Terms** as the terminology to be used. Your screen will look like this:

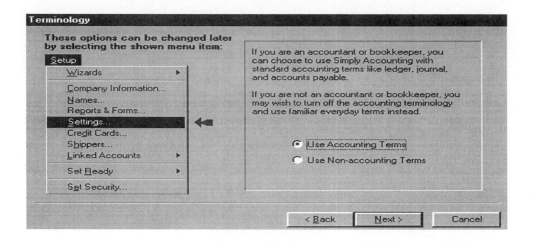

ACTION: Enter the federal and state IDs for Classic Clocks (see Document 1).

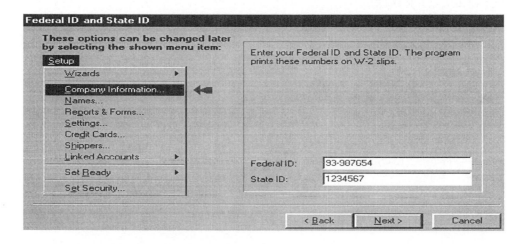

ACTION: Accept the income and deduction names provided by Simply Accounting.

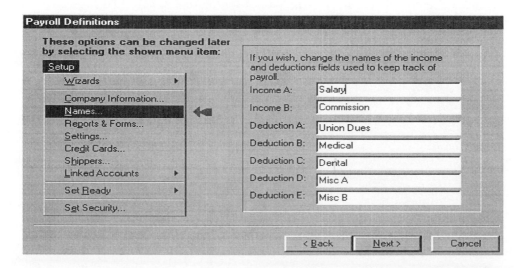

ACTION: Click **Next** to accept the name of the project title as Project.

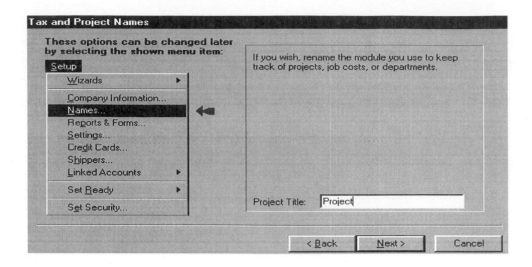

ACTION: Check with your instructor to see if you need to complete the printer setup for your company. If not, click **Next**.

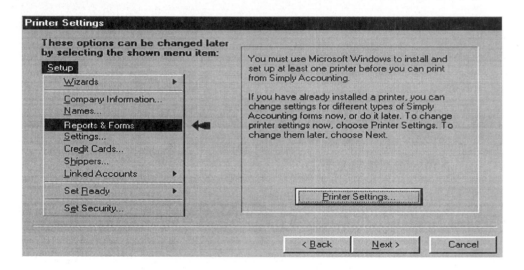

ACTION: Both **Inventory Tracking** and **Invoice Lookup** should be selected. Click **Next**.

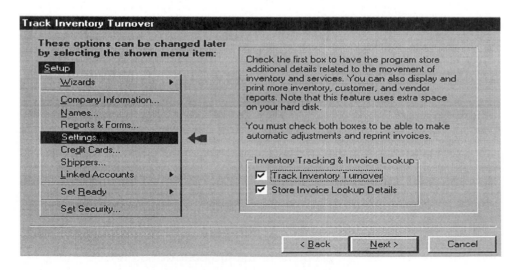

Explanation: Track Inventory Turnover is selected in order to have the program store extra details related to the movement of inventory items and sale of services. For each inventory item or service, the program records the quantity and revenue for goods and services sold for both the current and past year; the number of transactions recorded for the item, for the current and past year; the date of the last sale; and for each inventory item, the cost of goods sold in the current and past year. Store Invoice Lookup Details is selected if you want to be able to look up the details of all sales and purchase invoices, orders, and quotes. You will also be allowed to reprint invoices, orders, or quotes, and trace shipments. Both Inventory Tracking and Invoice Lookup items must be selected in order to make automatic adjustments and reprint invoices.

ACTION: Because cash-basis accounting is not used by most businesses, do not select anything on this screen. Click **Next** to continue.

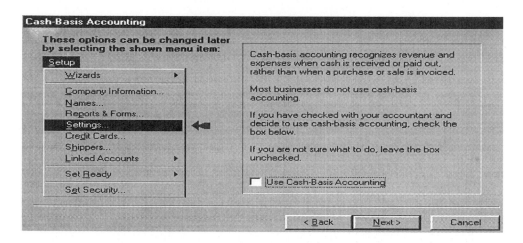

ACTION: At this point, Classic Clocks does not plan to use Simply's Budgeting feature. If budgeting is desired at a later time, settings may be changed at that point.

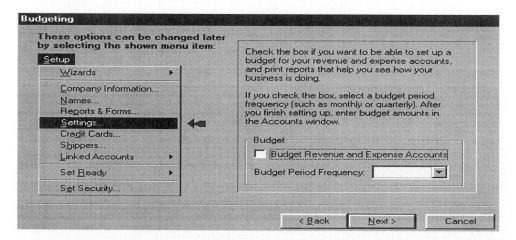

ACTION: In order to reconcile bank and credit card statements with the records in your bank account in Simply Accounting, click **Use Check No. as the Source Code for Cash Purchases and Sales.**

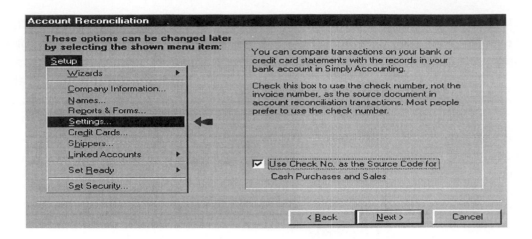

ACTION: Enter *8.0%* as the amount of sales tax charged. There is no freight tax.

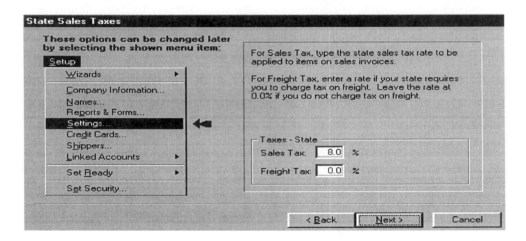

ACTION: On this screen, you will indicate the payroll tax rates Classic Clocks pays for State Disability Insurance, for the State Unemployment Tax Act, and for the Federal Unemployment Tax Act. Leave the SDI rate at 0.0. Enter *3.5* for the SUTA rate and *0.8* for the FUTA rate.

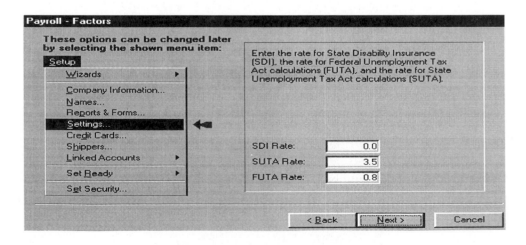

ACTION: Make sure the Automatic Payroll Deductions box is selected. Click **Next**.

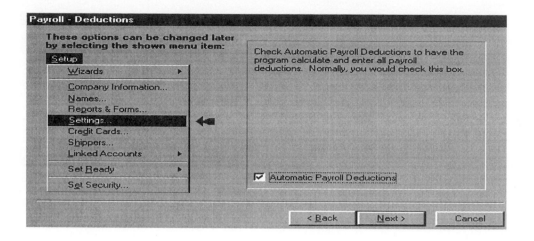

ACTION: No deductions are made prior to calculating taxes. Click **Next** on the screens for deducting union dues, medical, dental, misc. A, and misc. B.

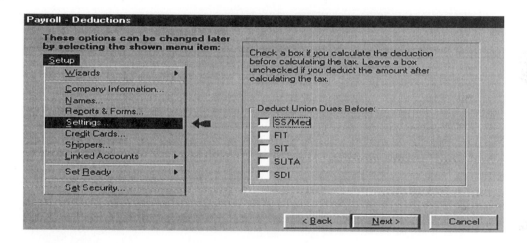

ACTION: Enter the next Invoice number as *5882* and the next Check number as *2840*. Use *1* for all other numbers.

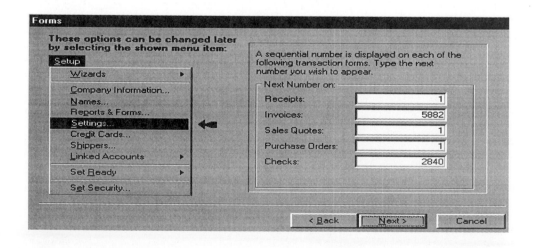

ACTION: The Setup Wizard for Classic Clocks has been completed. Click **Finish** to save the company setup.

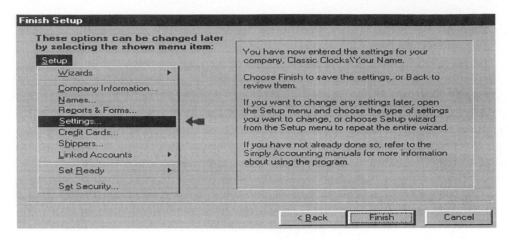

Explanation: The company file is created and saved in the location specified in the Setup Wizard. However, it is not yet ready for use. This is indicated by all the not ready symbols shown on the following screen:

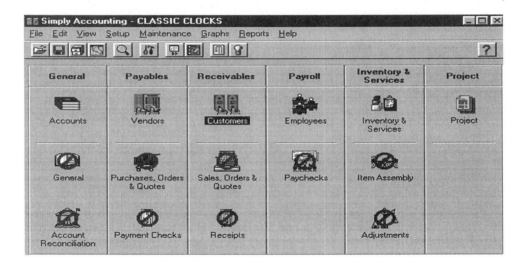

COMPANY SETTINGS NOT INCLUDED IN SETUP WIZARD

In addition to the settings established in the Setup Wizard, there are several more detailed settings to be established. As you go through and establish the additional settings by using Settings from the Setup menu, you will also see the information you entered in the Setup Wizard. Other than the dates entered for begin fiscal year, end fiscal year, and earliest transaction date, all other settings may be changed via the Setup menu.

Classic Clocks—Document 3   **December 1, 1997**

Memo   **Date:** December 1, 1997

Make additional changes to settings using the Settings selection from the Setup menu. There are no changes to be made to for Display, System, Sales Taxes, General, Receivables, Payables, Payroll, Inventory & Services, or E-Mail. Make the following changes to Forms, Comments, and Projects:

Forms: Confirm printing for invoices; confirm printing for checks; accept default for printing company name and address on all items listed.

Comments: Default invoice comment: Thank you for shopping at Classic Clocks!

Projects: Warn if allocation is not complete.

ACTION: Click **Setup** on the menu bar; click **Settings.** You should see the information for the Display tab. Your screen will look like the following:

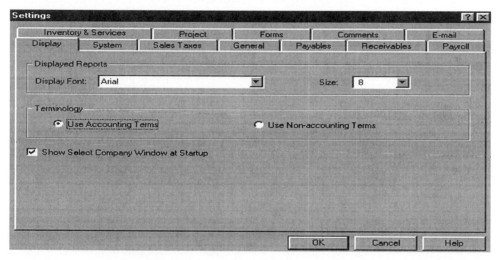

Explanation: Notice the selection of Use Accounting Terms and Show Select Company Window at Startup. These settings were established in the Setup Wizard. Your display font and size may differ from the ones shown above. If your settings have worked well for you while working with the other companies in this text, do not change the settings.

ACTION: Click each of the tabs that do not have any changes listed in Document 3 and review the settings selected in the Setup Wizard. **Note:** The Inventory & Services tab will be explored in greater detail later in the chapter.

ACTION: Click the **Forms** tab and mark the items to confirm printing for invoices and checks (see Document 3).

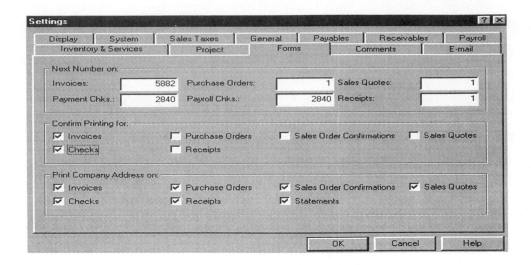

Explanation: Forms settings fields are defined as follows:

Next Number on: Indicates the number you want printed on your next invoice, purchase order, sales quotes, payment checks, payroll checks, and receipts. **Note**: The **Payroll Chks.** number is the same number as the **Payment Chks.** number.

Confirm Printing for: Check any of the boxes if you want the program to warn you if you are about to process an invoice, check, purchase order, receipt, sales order confirmation, or sales quote before it is printed.

Print Company Address on: Check any of the boxes if you want the program to print the company name and address on invoices, checks, purchase orders, receipts, sales order confirmations, statements, or sales quotes.

 ACTION: Verify that all of the Forms settings are correct; then click the **Comments** tab and enter the sales invoice comment provided in Document 3. Your screen will look like this:

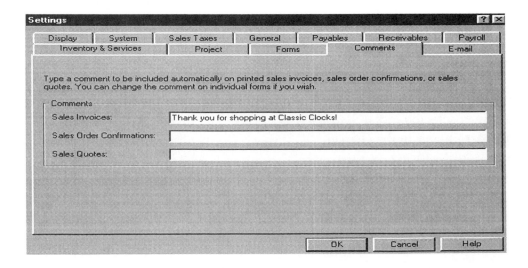

ACTION: Verify that the sales invoice comment is correct; then click **OK** and click the **Inventory & Services** tab. Accept the default selections. Your screen will look like this:

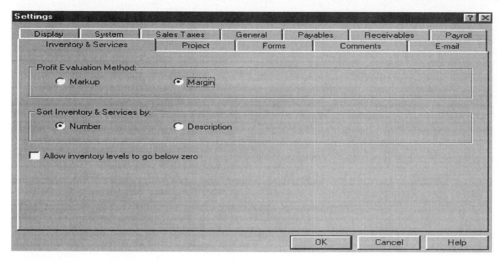

Explanation: The Inventory & Services selections are defined as follows:

Profit Evaluation Method: Markup is selected if the profit on inventory items is to be calculated based on cost; Margin is selected if the profit on inventory items is to be calculated on selling price.

The program calculates markup as follows: $\dfrac{\text{Selling Price - Cost}}{\text{Cost}}$

The program calculates margin as follows: $\dfrac{\text{Selling Price - Cost}}{\text{Selling Price}}$

Sort Inventory & Services by: Number is selected if the program is to sort inventory items by number; Description is selected if the program is to sort inventory items by description. The selection made determines which field will appear first (either Number or Description) when accessing inventory item information.

 ACTION: Click the **Project** tab. Select **Warn if Allocation is not Complete**. Your screen will look like this:

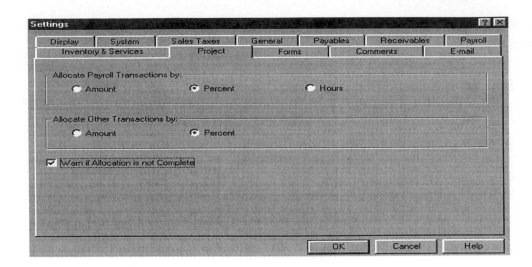

Explanation: The Projects settings fields are defined as follows:

Allocate Payroll Transactions by: Choose the Amount, Percent, or Hours option; then when you allocate a payroll entry to a project, enter the amount, percentage, or hours you wish to allocate. Percent is selected by default.

Allocate Other Transactions by: Choose the Amount or Percent option; then when you allocate an entry, enter the amount or percentage you wish to allocate. Again, the default is Percent.

Warn if Allocation is not Complete: Check this box if you want the program to warn you if you are about to post an entry that has not been fully allocated.

ACTION: Click **OK** to close Settings. Click the **Setup** menu. Note that there is a selection to Set Security. This is an optional feature. It can be used to establish passwords restricting access to ledgers and journals for companies that wish to use password protection as part of their internal accounting controls. **The use of passwords should be avoided for all tutorials, exercises, and practice sets in this text.** If you accidentally open this menu option, click the **Cancel** button. Click the **home window** to exit the Setup menu.

ACTION: Click the **Exit** button to end the current work session and return to your Windows desktop.

ALTERNATIVE ACTION: You can continue with the tutorial without exiting from the program if you wish.

CREATING A CHART OF ACCOUNTS

Maria has made notations on the following income statement and balance sheet to help her understand the CA-Simply Accounting for Windows coding procedure for financial statements. The program uses eight types of "accounts" to create headings and to format and total the account balances on financial statements:

1. Section Heading   4. Subgroup Total   7. Group Total
2. Group Heading   5. Group Account   8. Section Total
3. Subgroup Account   6. Current Earnings

These terms are used only for creating a chart of accounts and for formatting financial statements. They are not related to debits and credits. For example, an account that has a normal debit balance can appear in either the left or right column of a financial statement.

Subgroup accounts and Group accounts are postable accounts. Postable accounts can be assigned opening balances when the program is not ready, and you can post journal entries to these accounts when the program is ready. All other "account" types are nonpostable accounts. Nonpostable accounts are used for financial statement formatting and do not have opening balances or accept journal entries.

Classic Clocks
Income Statement 12/1/1997 to 12/1/1997

REVENUE	—Section Heading		
SALES	—Group Heading		
Clock Sales		$105,763.24	
Watch Sales	⌐Postable Accounts	56,534.26	⌐Group Accounts
Sales Returns & Allow.		(188.63)	
Sales Discounts		(201.15)	
NET SALES	—Group Total	$161,907.72	
TOTAL REVENUE	—Section Total	$161,907.72	
EXPENSES	—Section Heading		
COST OF GOODS SOLD	—Group Heading		
Cost Of Goods Sold-Clocks		$ 52,881.62	
Cost of Goods Sold-Watches		28,267.13	
TOTAL COST OF GOODS SOLD	—Group Total	$ 81,148.75	
OPERATING EXPENSES	—Group Heading		
Wages		$ 32,631.00	
Social Security Tax Expense		2,023.13	
Medicare Tax Expense		473.13	
FUTA Expense		112.00	
SUTA Expense		1,129.01	
Advertising Expense		2,435.00	
Utilities Expense	⌐Postable Accounts	1,147.19	⌐Group Accounts
Deprec Exp: Office Equip.		1,283.26	
Insurance Expense		1,100.00	
Rent Expense		6,600.00	
Office Supplies Expense		934.56	
Deprec Exp: Store Equip.		641.63	
Phone Expense		762.43	
Bank Service Charge Expense		165.00	
Miscellaneous Expense		432.15	
TOTAL OPERATING EXPENSES	—Group Total	$ 51,869.49	
TOTAL EXPENSE	—Section Total	$133,018.24	
NET INCOME		$ 28,889.48	

Classic Clocks
Balance Sheet As At 12/1/1997

ASSETS	—Section Heading		
CURRENT ASSETS	—Group Heading		
Cash		$ 8,424.63	⎤
Petty Cash		100.00	⎬ Group Accounts
Accounts Receivable	⎡Postable Accounts	8,147.27	⎦
Clock Inventory		$20,065.00	⎤ Subgroup Accounts
Watch Inventory		11,648.00	⎦
Total Inventory		31,713.00	—Subgroup Total
Office Supplies	⎡Postable Accounts	311.15	⎤ Group Accounts
Prepaid Insurance	⎦	200.00	⎦
TOTAL CURRENT ASSETS	—Group Total	$48,896.05	
FIXED ASSETS	—Group Heading		
Office Equipment	⎡Postable	$ 4,700.00	⎤ Subgroup Accounts
Accum Dep: Office Equip.	⎦Accounts	(2,683.18)	⎦
Net Office Equipment		2,016.82	—Subgroup Total
Store Equipment	⎡Postable	4,000.00	⎤ Subgroup Accounts
Accum Dep: Store Equip.	⎦Accounts	(1,341.59)	⎦
Net Store Equipment		2,658.41	—Subgroup Total
TOTAL FIXED ASSETS	—Group Total	$ 4,675.23	
TOTAL ASSETS	—Section Total	$53,571.28	
LIABILITIES	—Section Heading		
CURRENT LIABILITIES	—Group Heading		
Accounts Payable		$ 4,362.50	⎤
FIT Payable		255.28	⎥
SIT Payable		124.72	⎥
Social Security Tax Payable		369.64	⎥
Medicare Tax Payable	⎡Postable Accounts	86.44	⎬ Group Accounts
FUTA Payable		6.15	⎥
SUTA Payable		194.15	⎥
Medical Insurance Payable		44.00	⎥
Sales Tax Payable		1,170.90	⎦
TOTAL CURRENT LIABILITIES	—Group Total	$ 6,613.78	
TOTAL LIABILITIES	—Section Total	$ 6,613.78	
EQUITY	—Section Heading		
OWNER'S EQUITY	—Group Heading		
Maria Lindsay, Capital		$42,268.02	⎤ Group Accounts
Maria Lindsay, Drawing		(24,200.00)	⎦
Current Earnings		28,889.48	—Current Earnings
TOTAL OWNER'S EQUITY	—Group Total	$46,957.50	
TOTAL EQUITY	—Section Total	$46,957.50	
LIABILITIES AND EQUITY		$53,571.28	

Section Heading

Section headings correspond to the main sections of the balance sheet and income statement. There are five section headings: Assets, Liabilities, Equity, Revenue, and Expense. Each section heading can contain several group headings. The names of section headings are printed automatically by the program and cannot be changed. Section headings are nonpostable accounts.

Group Heading

Group headings are used to subdivide and to classify groups of accounts within a section. For example, on the Classic Clocks balance sheet, Current Assets appears as a group heading. Group headings are nonpostable accounts. Each group heading must be followed by a group total.

Subgroup Account

A subgroup account is a postable account and is used for accounts whose balances will be subtotaled, rather than included directly in the group total. A subgroup account stores amounts processed in the transaction windows. Balances are shown in the left column of the financial statement. For example, on the Classic Clocks balance sheet, Clock Inventory and Watch Inventory appear as subgroup accounts. A subgroup account must be followed by a subtotal account.

Subgroup Total

A subgroup total account lists the total of all consecutive subgroup accounts that immediately precede it. The subgroup total is calculated automatically by the program and is printed in the right column within a section. For example, the Total Inventory account on the Classic Clocks balance sheet is a subgroup total account. Subgroup total accounts are nonpostable accounts. Each subgroup total must be within a group preceded by a group heading and followed by a group total.

Group Account

A group account is a postable account and is used for amounts included directly in the group total. For example, on the Classic Clock income statement, the expense accounts appear as group accounts. The balance of a group account is printed in the right column within a section and must be followed by a group total.

Current Earnings

Current earnings is a nonpostable account. Its balance is the net difference between the postable revenue account totals and the postable expense account totals. Each time a journal entry that affects a revenue or expense account is posted, the program recalculates the balance in the Current Earnings account. There is only one Current Earnings account; it is printed in the right column within the Equity section of the balance sheet.

Group Total

A group total is a nonpostable account. It is the total of all the group and subgroup total accounts immediately above it up to the preceding group heading. For example, the Total Current Assets account on the Classic Clocks balance sheet is a group total. Group totals are calculated automatically by the program and are printed in the right column within a section. Group totals are themselves totaled in the section total. For example, on the Classic Clocks income statement the group totals Total Cost of Goods Sold and Total Operating Expenses are added to determine the section total, Total Expense.

Section Total

Section totals are nonpostable accounts and correspond to the main sections of the balance sheet and income statement. The program uses five section totals: Total Assets, Total Liabilities, Total Equity, Total Revenue, and Total Expense. Section totals include all group totals for a section. The program prints the names of section totals automatically. You cannot change them.

Account Numbers

To ensure that accounts are listed under the correct section heading and that the program prints the accounts in the right order on financial statements, the CA-Simply Accounting for Windows program uses the following account numbering system:

Asset accounts	1000-1999	Revenue accounts	4000-4999
Liability accounts	2000-2999	Expense accounts	5000-5999
Equity accounts	3000-3999		

Accounts are printed in numerical order within each section. When assigning account numbers, it is a good practice to leave gaps between account numbers so that new related accounts can be inserted in the future.

Account Balances

General Ledger accounts printed on financial statements can have any value, positive or negative, up to $999,999,999.99. Account balances that are contrary to the normal balance for an account are shown with minus signs in the financial statements. For example, the Sales Discount account (a revenue account that would normally have a credit balance) on the Classic Clocks income statement is shown with a minus sign to indicate a debit balance in this account.

GENERAL LEDGER—ENTERING ACCOUNTS AND ACCOUNT BALANCES

Maria has studied the preceding financial statement design information and has created the following memo, listing the accounts and account balances that need to be established in the CA-Simply Accounting for Windows program:

Classic Clocks—Document 4   **December 1, 1997**

Memo   **Date:** December 1, 1997

Balance Sheet Accounts:

Acct. No.	Account Name	Account Balance	Account Type
1000	CURRENT ASSETS		Group heading
1010	Cash	8,424.63	Group account
1050	Petty Cash	100.00	Group account

1200	Accounts Receivable	8,147.27	Group account
1310	Clock Inventory	20,065.00	Subgroup account
1320	Watch Inventory	11,648.00	Subgroup account
1390	Total Inventory		Subgroup total
1410	Office Supplies	311.15	Group account
1420	Prepaid Insurance	200.00	Group account
1490	TOTAL CURRENT ASSETS		Group total
1500	FIXED ASSETS		Group heading
1550	Office Equipment	4,700.00	Subgroup account
1551	Accum. Dep.: Office Equip.	-2,683.18	Subgroup account
1552	Net Office Equipment		Subgroup total
1650	Store Equipment	4,000.00	Subgroup account
1651	Accum Dep: Store Equip.	-1,341.59	Subgroup account
1652	Net Store Equipment		Subgroup total
1690	TOTAL FIXED ASSETS		Group total
2000	CURRENT LIABILITIES		Group heading
2200	Accounts Payable	4,362.50	Group account
2310	FIT Payable	255.28	Group account
2320	SIT Payable	124.72	Group account
2330	Social Security Tax Payable	369.64	Group account
2335	Medicare Tax Payable	86.44	Group account
2340	FUTA Payable	6.15	Group account
2350	SUTA Payable	194.15	Group account
2400	Medical Insurance Payable	44.00	Group account
2500	Sales Tax Payable	1,170.90	Group account
2690	TOTAL CURRENT LIABILITIES		Group total
3000	OWNER'S EQUITY		Group heading
3560	Maria Lindsay, Capital	42,268.02	Group account
3580	Maria Lindsay, Drawing	-24,200.00	Group account
3690	TOTAL OWNER'S EQUITY		Group total

Income Statement Accounts:

Acct. No.	Account Name	Account Balance	Account Type
4000	SALES		Group heading
4010	Clock Sales	105,763.24	Group account
4020	Watch Sales	56,534.26	Group account
4200	Sales Returns & Allowances	-188.63	Group account
4300	Sales Discounts	-201.15	Group account
4390	NET SALES		Group total
5000	COST OF GOODS SOLD		Group heading
5010	Cost Of Goods Sold: Clocks	52,881.62	Group account
5020	Cost of Goods Sold: Watches	28,267.13	Group account
5090	TOTAL COST OF GOODS SOLD		Group total
5200	OPERATING EXPENSES		Group heading
5300	Wages	32,631.00	Group account
5310	Social Security Tax Expense	2,023.13	Group account
5320	Medicare Tax Expense	473.13	Group account
5330	FUTA Expense	112.00	Group account
5340	SUTA Expense	1,129.01	Group account
5410	Advertising Expense	2,435.00	Group account
5420	Utilities Expense	1,147.19	Group account

5430	Depreciation Exp.: Office Equipment	1,283.26	Group account
5440	Insurance Expense	1,100.00	Group account
5450	Rent Expense	6,600.00	Group account
5460	Office Supplies Expense	934.56	Group account
5470	Depreciation Exp.: Store Equipment	641.63	Group account
5480	Telephone Expense	762.43	Group account
5490	Bank Service Charge Expense	165.00	Group account
5500	Miscellaneous Expense	432.15	Group account
5900	TOTAL OPERATING EXPENSES		Group total

ACTION: Load CA-Simply Accounting for Windows; then open the data files for Classic Clocks. Your screen will look like the following:

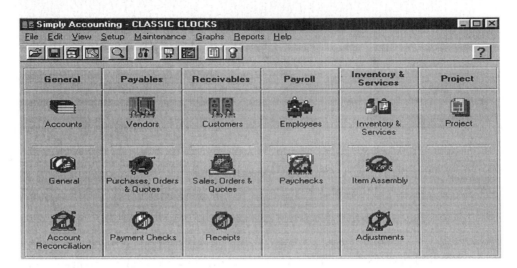

ACTION: Open Accounts in the General section of the screen. Your screen will look like this:

Explanation: All accounts established are shown in this window. Because Current Earnings is the only account that currently exists in the Classic Clocks chart of accounts, it is only account displayed. The Current Earnings account is used to identify the current year's earnings within the equity section of the balance sheet.

ACTION: Choose **Create** from the General Ledger Edit menu or click the **Create** button on the toolbar. Your screen will look like this:

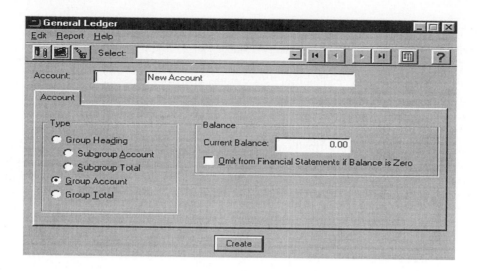

Explanation: A blank General Ledger dialog box is presented, ready for new accounts to be entered. **Note**: Leave the **Omit from Financial Statements if Balance is Zero** check box unchecked for all new accounts.

ACTION: Enter the information about the first new account (1000 CURRENT ASSETS) listed on Document 3. Your screen should agree with the one shown below:

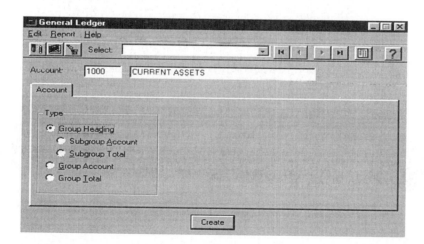

ACTION: Verify that all of the information is correct. If you have made an error, use the following editing techniques to correct the error. Otherwise, click **Create** to create the CURRENT ASSETS Group Heading Account.

Explanation: The program has added the new account to Classic Clocks' chart of accounts and has cleared the General Ledger dialog box in preparation for creating another account.

Editing Tips
Editing a General Ledger Record in the Not Ready Mode

While working with the General Ledger in the Not Ready mode, many of the restrictions that were in place in the Ready mode do not apply. You can create, modify, or remove account information and account balances as needed while working in the Not Ready mode.

If the account you wish to edit does not currently appear in the General Ledger dialog box, click the drop-down list arrow by Select and click the account you wish to delete, or select the account from the chart of accounts display. Modify the General Ledger record as necessary or choose **Remove** from the General Ledger Edit menu. Another method is to select the account you wish to change and click the **Edit** or **Remove** button on the toolbar. Click the **OK** button if you receive a message stating "This account cannot be removed while it is being used as a linking account." Refer to the section titled "Modifying and Removing Linking Accounts" later in this chapter for information on how to remove a linking account from the chart of accounts.

An example of removing the Current Asset account by clicking the account name and clicking **Remove** is shown below:

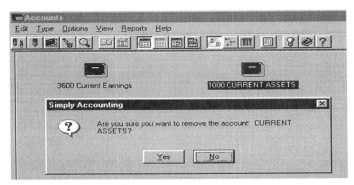

The final step in the removal of the account is to click the **Yes** button on the dialog box.

 ACTION: Create the other accounts that appear in Document 4, using the same procedures used when creating the Current Assets account. Be sure to insert the account balances for all accounts that have a balance shown in Document 4. For accounts such as Accumulated Depreciation, be sure to enter a minus in front of the balance. When all accounts have been added, close the General Ledger dialog box; then choose **Display Chart of Accounts** from the Accounts window Report menu. Your screen will very much like the following report, except the accounts will be listed in one column.

Explanation: Account codes for each type of account are listed on the chart of accounts. The codes are defined as follows: H—Group heading; S—Subgroup total; G—Group account; X—Current earnings; A—Subgroup account; T—Group total.

```
┌──────────────────────────────────────┐
│ ▢ Chart of Accounts                    │
├──────────────────────────────────────┤
│ File   Help                            │
└──────────────────────────────────────┘
```

12/1/1997

ASSETS

1000	**CURRENT ASSETS**	**H**
1010	Cash	G
1050	Petty Cash	G
1200	Accounts Receivable	G
1310	Clock Inventory	A
1320	Watch Inventory	A
1390	Total Inventory	S
1410	Office Supplies	G
1420	Prepaid Insurance	G
1490	**TOTAL CURRENT ASSETS**	**T**
1500	**FIXED ASSETS**	**H**
1550	Office Equipment	A
1551	Accum. Dep.: Office Equip.	A
1552	Net Office Equipment	S
1650	Store Equipment	A
1651	Accum. Dep.: Store Equip.	A
1652	Net Store Equipment	S
1690	**TOTAL FIXED ASSETS**	**T**

LIABILITIES

2000	**CURRENT LIABILITIES**	**H**
2200	Accounts Payable	G
2310	FIT Payable	G
2320	SIT Payable	G
2330	Social Security Tax Payable	G
2335	Medicare Tax Payable	G
2340	FUTA Payable	G
2350	SUTA Payable	G
2400	Medical Insurance Payable	G
2500	Sales Tax Payable	G
2690	**TOTAL CURRENT LIABILITIES**	**T**

EQUITY

3000	**OWNER'S EQUITY**	**H**
3560	Maria Lindsay, Capital	G
3580	Maria Lindsay, Drawing	G
3600	Current Earnings	X
3690	**TOTAL OWNER'S EQUITY**	**T**

REVENUE

4000	**SALES**	**H**
4010	Clock Sales	G
4020	Watch Sales	G
4200	Sales Returns & Allowances	G
4300	Sales Discounts	G
4390	**NET SALES**	**T**

EXPENSE

5000	**COST OF GOODS SOLD**	**H**
5010	Costs of Goods Sold: Clocks	G
5020	Cost of Goods Sold: Watches	G
5090	**TOTAL COST OF GOODS SOLD**	**T**
5200	**OPERATING EXPENSES**	**H**
5300	Wages	G
5310	Social Security Tax Expense	G
5320	Medicare Tax Expense	G
5330	FUTA Expense	G
5340	SUTA Expense	G
5410	Advertising Expense	G
5420	Utilities Expense	G
5430	Depreciation Exp.: Office Equipment	G
5440	Insurance Expense	G
5450	Rent Expense	G
5460	Office Supplies Expense	G
5470	Depreciation Exp.: Store Equipment	G
5480	Telephone Expense	G
5490	Bank Service Charge Expense	G
5500	Miscellaneous Expense	G
5990	**TOTAL OPERATING EXPENSES**	**T**

▨ **ACTION:** Choose **Print** from the Chart of Accounts File menu. Compare your Chart of Accounts to the one shown above. If you detect an error, refer to the Editing Tips for Editing a General Ledger Record in the Not Ready Mode for information on corrective action.

▨ **ACTION:** Close the Chart of Accounts window; then choose **Trial Balance** from the Account window Report menu. If you receive an error message, read the message carefully for information regarding corrective action. Make corrections as required; then repeat this ACTION. Other than appearing in one column, your report will look like this:

🗔 Trial Balance

File   Help

As At 12/1/1997	Debits	Credits
1010 Cash	8,424.63	·
1050 Petty Cash	100.00	·
1200 Accounts Receivable	8,147.27	·
1310 Clock Inventory	20,065.00	·
1320 Watch Inventory	11,648.00	·
1410 Office Supplies	311.15	·
1420 Prepaid Insurance	200.00	·
1550 Office Equipment	4,700.00	·
1551 Accum. Dep.: Office Equip.	·	2,683.18
1650 Store Equipment	4,000.00	·
1651 Accum. Dep.: Store Equip.	·	1,341.59
2200 Accounts Payable	·	4,362.50
2310 FIT Payable	·	255.28
2320 SIT Payable	·	124.72
2330 Social Security Tax Payable	·	369.64
2335 Medicare Tax Payable	·	86.44
2340 FUTA Payable	·	6.15
2350 SUTA Payable	·	194.15
2400 Medical Insurance Payable	·	44.00
2500 Sales Tax Payable	·	1,170.90
3560 Maria Lindsay, Capital	·	42,268.02
3580 Maria Lindsay, Drawing	24,200.00	·

	Debits	Credits
4010 Clock Sales	·	105,763.24
4020 Watch Sales	·	56,534.26
4200 Sales Returns & Allowances	188.63	·
4300 Sales Discounts	201.15	·
5010 Costs of Goods Sold: Clocks	52,881.62	·
5020 Cost of Goods Sold: Watches	28,267.13	·
5300 Wages	32,631.00	·
5310 Social Security Tax Expense	2,023.13	·
5320 Medicare Tax Expense	473.13	·
5330 FUTA Expense	112.00	·
5340 SUTA Expense	1,129.01	·
5410 Advertising Expense	2,435.00	·
5420 Utilities Expense	1,147.19	·
5430 Depreciation Exp.: Office Equipment	1,283.26	·
5440 Insurance Expense	1,100.00	·
5450 Rent Expense	6,600.00	·
5460 Office Supplies Expense	934.56	·
5470 Depreciation Exp.: Store Equipment	641.63	·
5480 Telephone Expense	762.43	·
5490 Bank Service Charge Expense	165.00	·
5500 Miscellaneous Expense	432.15	·
	215,204.07	215,204.07

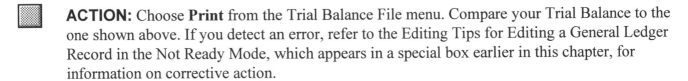 **ACTION:** Choose **Print** from the Trial Balance File menu. Compare your Trial Balance to the one shown above. If you detect an error, refer to the Editing Tips for Editing a General Ledger Record in the Not Ready Mode, which appears in a special box earlier in this chapter, for information on corrective action.

ACTION: Close the Trial Balance window. Prepare an income statement from 1/1/1997 to 12/1/1997 by selecting **Income Statement** from the Accounts window Report menu, verifying the dates shown on the dialog box and clicking **OK**. If you receive an error message, read the message carefully for information regarding corrective action. Make corrections as required; then repeat this ACTION. Except for appearing in one column, your report will look like this:

🗔 Income Statement

File   Help

1/1/1997 to 12/1/1997

REVENUE

SALES

Clock Sales	105,763.24
Watch Sales	56,534.26
Sales Returns & Allowances	-188.63
Sales Discounts	-201.15
NET SALES	161,907.72

TOTAL REVENUE	161,907.72

EXPENSE

COST OF GOODS SOLD

Costs of Goods Sold: Clocks	52,881.62
Cost of Goods Sold: Watches	28,267.13
TOTAL COST OF GOODS SOLD	81,148.75

OPERATING EXPENSES

Wages	32,631.00
Social Security Tax Expense	2,023.13
Medicare Tax Expense	473.13
FUTA Expense	112.00
SUTA Expense	1,129.01
Advertising Expense	2,435.00
Utilities Expense	1,147.19
Depreciation Exp.: Office Equipment	1,283.26
Insurance Expense	1,100.00
Rent Expense	6,600.00
Office Supplies Expense	934.56
Depreciation Exp.: Store Equipment	641.63
Telephone Expense	762.43
Bank Service Charge Expense	165.00
Miscellaneous Expense	432.15
TOTAL OPERATING EXPENSES	51,869.49

TOTAL EXPENSE	133,018.24
NET INCOME	28,889.48

▓ **ACTION:** Choose **Print** from the Income Statement File menu. Compare your Income Statement to the one shown above. If you detect an error, refer to the Editing Tips for Editing a General Ledger Record in the Not Ready Mode, which appears in a special box earlier in this chapter, for information on corrective action.

▓ **ACTION:** Close the Income Statement window; then choose **Balance Sheet** from the Account window Report menu. If you receive an error message, read the message carefully for information regarding corrective action. Make corrections as required; then repeat this ACTION. Other than appearing in one column, your report will look like this:

▓ Balance Sheet

File   Help

As At 12/1/1997
ASSETS

CURRENT ASSETS

Cash		8,424.63
Petty Cash		100.00
Accounts Receivable		8,147.27
Clock Inventory	20,065.00	
Watch Inventory	11,648.00	
Total Inventory		31,713.00
Office Supplies		311.15
Prepaid Insurance		200.00
TOTAL CURRENT ASSETS		48,896.05

FIXED ASSETS

Office Equipment	4,700.00	
Accum. Dep.: Office Equip.	-2,683.18	
Net Office Equipment		2,016.82
Store Equipment	4,000.00	
Accum. Dep.: Store Equip.	-1,341.59	
Net Store Equipment		2,658.41
TOTAL FIXED ASSETS		4,675.23

TOTAL ASSETS   53,571.28

LIABILITIES

CURRENT LIABILITIES

Accounts Payable	4,362.50
FIT Payable	255.28
SIT Payable	124.72
Social Security Tax Payable	369.64
Medicare Tax Payable	86.44
FUTA Payable	6.15
SUTA Payable	194.15
Medical Insurance Payable	44.00
Sales Tax Payable	1,170.90
TOTAL CURRENT LIABILITIES	6,613.78

TOTAL LIABILITIES   6,613.78

EQUITY

OWNER'S EQUITY

Maria Lindsay, Capital	42,268.02
Maria Lindsay, Drawing	-24,200.00
Current Earnings	28,889.48
TOTAL OWNER'S EQUITY	46,957.50

TOTAL EQUITY   46,957.50

LIABILITIES AND EQUITY   53,571.28

▓ **ACTION:** Choose **Print** from the Balance Sheet File menu. Compare your Balance Sheet to the one shown above. If you detect an error, refer to the Editing Tips for Editing a General Ledger Record in the Not Ready mode for information on corrective action.

▓ **ACTION:** Close the Balance Sheet window, the Account window, and the Simply Accounting program to end the current work session and return to your Windows desktop.

▓ **ALTERNATIVE ACTION:** You can continue with the tutorial without exiting from the program if you wish. Close the Balance Sheet and Account windows; skip the next ACTION; continue with the tutorial.

ESTABLISHING LINKING ACCOUNTS

At this stage in the conversion process, Classic Clocks' financial records contain all of the new accounts and account balances that appeared in Document 4. The next step in the conversion process involves identifying the accounts that will be used to integrate or link the General Ledger with the Receivables, Payables, Inventory, and Payroll Ledgers. Linking accounts are used to create the integration links among the ledgers. Maria has determined that the linking accounts listed in the following memo need to be established:

Classic Clocks—Document 5   **December 1, 1997**

Memo   **Date:** December 1, 1997

Linking Account Information:

General Linking Accounts
Bank account: 1010 Cash
Retained earnings: 3560 Maria Lindsay, Capital

Payables Linking Accounts
Accounts payable: 2200 Accounts Payable

Receivables Linking Accounts
Accounts receivable: 1200 Accounts Receivable
Sales tax payable: 2500 Sales Tax Payable
Sales discounts: 4300 Sales Discounts

Inventory Linking Accounts
None

Payroll Linking Accounts
FIT: 2310 FIT Payable
SIT: 2320 SIT Payable SST:
Medicare Tax: 2335 Medicare Tax Payable
SST: 2330 Social Security Tax Payable
FUTA: 2340 FUTA Payable
SUTA: 2350 SUTA Payable
Wages: 5300 Wages
Medicare Tax: 5320 Medicare Tax Expense
SST : 5310 Social Security Tax Expense
FUTA: 5330 FUTA Expense
SUTA: 5340 SUTA Expense
Medical: 2400 Medical Insurance Payable

ACTION: Load CA-Simply Accounting for Windows; open the data files for Classic Clocks; click **Setup** on the menu bar; click **Wizards**; click **Linked accounts**. Your screen will show:

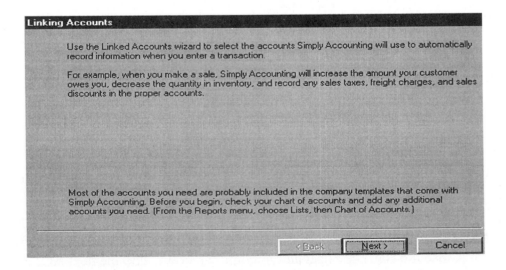

ACTION: Click **Next**. Your screen will look like the following. Because Classic Clocks has only one bank account, click **Next**.

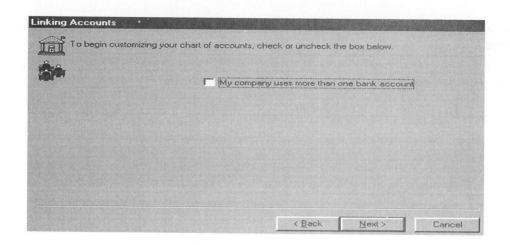

ACTION: Enter *1010 Cash* as the account used to record money paid in and money paid out. Your screen will look like this:

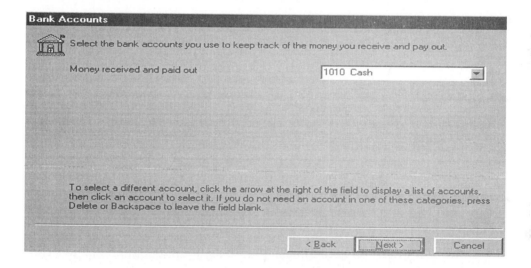

ACTION: Identify account 3560 Maria Lindsay, Capital as the account for retained earnings. Your screen will look like this:

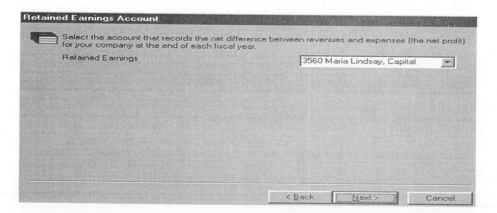

Explanation: The account number assigned to Retained Earnings represents the linking account into which the current year's earnings will be closed when the session date is advanced to the next accounting year. The Retained Earnings account is the account used by corporations to accumulate earnings. Classic Clocks is a sole proprietorship and will want the Retained Earnings designation set to the account number assigned to Maria Lindsay, Capital in the chart of accounts. The Current Earnings account is used to identify the current year's earnings within the equity section of the balance sheet.

 ACTION: Verify that the Retained Earnings account is correct; click **Next**. Complete the screen for Vendors and Purchases by filling in *2200 Accounts Payable* as the account used for the total amount you owe your vendors.

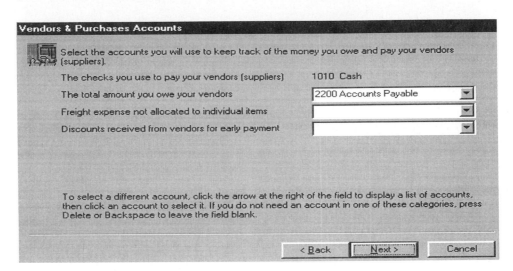

Explanation: Four accounts are identified on the screen for Vendors & Purchases Accounts:

Payables Bank Account: The bank account used to issue checks to vendors. (This linking account designation is automatically inserted by Simply and is required prior to changing the status of the Payables Ledger to ready.)

Accounts Payable: The account to be used to accumulate the total amount owed to vendors. (Its balance is updated automatically by the program each time a purchase or payment is posted for a vendor. This linking account designation is required prior to changing the status of the Payables Ledger to ready.)

Freight: The account used to record freight expense. (This is an optional Payables linking account used to accumulate freight expenses that cannot be allocated to individual items purchased.)

Purchase Discounts: The account to be used to record early payment discounts for vendors. (Purchases will not be eligible for discounts at this time, so the account is blank.)

 ACTION: Verify that the Vendors & Purchases Accounts are correct; click **Next** to continue to establish linking accounts. Your screen will look like this:

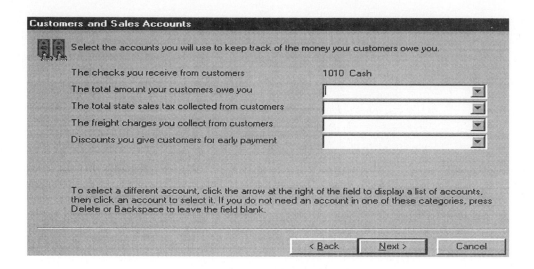

Explanation: There are five Customers and Sales linking accounts.

Receivables Bank Account: This is the bank account used to record checks received from customers. Simply automatically designates the account—1010 Cash. This linking account designation is required prior to changing the status of the Receivables Ledger to ready.

Accounts Receivable: This account accumulates the total amount owed by customers. Its balance is updated automatically by the program each time a sale or receipt is posted for a customer. This linking account designation is required prior to changing the status of the Receivables Ledger to ready.

Sales Tax Payable: This is an optional Customers and Sales/Receivables linking account used to accumulate the total amount of sales tax collected from customers.

Freight Charges: This is an optional Customers and Sales/Receivables linking account used to accumulate freight charges collected from customers.

Sales Discounts: This optional Customers and Sales/Receivables linking account is used to record sales discounts given to customers.

 ACTION: Simply automatically assigns account 1010 Cash as the Receivables bank account. Click the drop-down list arrow to the right of the **The total amount your customers owe you** field; select **1200 Accounts Receivable** from the chart of accounts display; click the drop-down list arrow to the right of the **The total sales tax collected from customers** field; select **2500 Sales Tax Payable** from the chart of accounts display. Classic Clocks does not charge freight, so this field is left blank. Click the drop-down list arrow to the right of **Discounts you give customers for early payment**; select **4300 Sales Discounts**. Your screen will look like this:

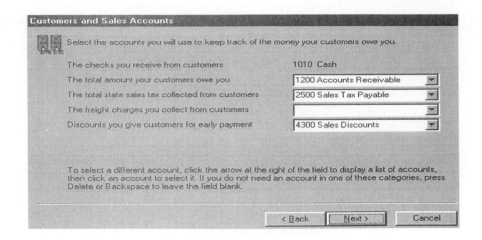

![Customers and Sales Accounts dialog box]

ACTION: Verify that the Customers and Sales/Receivables Linking Accounts are correct; click the **Next** button. Enter the linking accounts for the Payroll Accounts. Click the drop-down list arrow next to each text box. Click the appropriate account for each text box. **FIT is 2310 FIT Payable**, **SIT is 2320 SIT Payable**, **Medicare Tax is 2335 Medicare Tax Payable**, and **SST is 2330 Social Security Tax Payable**. Classic Clocks does not allow employee advances so leave that text box blank. Your screen will look like this:

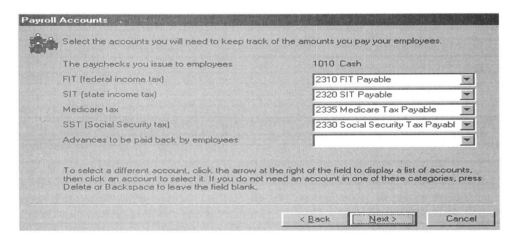

Explanation: All the Payroll Ledger linking accounts are defined as follows:

Payroll Bank: This is the bank account used to record payroll checks. Simply automatically assigns account 1010 Cash for this account. This linking account designation is required prior to changing the status of the Payroll Ledger to ready.

FIT: This account accumulates the total amount of federal income taxes collected from employees. This linking account designation is required prior to changing the status of the Payroll Ledger to ready.

SIT: This is an optional linking account that accumulates the total amount of state income taxes collected from employees.

Medicare Tax: This account accumulates the total amount of Medicare tax collected from employees and the Medicare tax payable by the employer. This linking account designation is required prior to changing the status of the Payroll Ledger to ready.

SST: This account accumulates the total amount of Social Security tax collected from employees and the Social Security tax payable by the employer. This linking account designation is required prior to changing the status of the Payroll Ledger to ready.

Advances: This optional linking account accumulates the total amount of advances extended to employees.

FUTA: This account accumulates the total amount of FUTA payable by the employer. This linking account designation is required prior to changing the status of the Payroll Ledger to ready.

SUTA: This account accumulates the total amount of SUTA payable by the employer and collected from employees in accordance with the requirements of the state. This linking account designation is required prior to changing the status of the Payroll Ledger to ready.

SDI: This account is an optional linking account that accumulates the total amount of state disability insurance collected from employees and payable by the employer in accordance with the requirements of the state.

Local Tax: This account is an optional linking account that accumulates the total amount of local tax collected from employees.

Union, Medical, Dental: These accounts are optional linking accounts that accumulate the total amount of union dues, medical plan premiums, or dental plan premiums collected from employees.

Wages: This account accumulates the gross wages paid to employees. This linking account designation is required prior to changing the status of the Payroll Ledger to ready.

Medicare Tax: This account accumulates the employer's portion of the Medicare tax expense account. This linking account designation is required prior to changing the status of the Payroll Ledger to ready.

Social Security Tax: This account accumulates the employer's portion of the Social Security tax payable account. This linking account designation is required prior to changing the status of the Payroll Ledger to ready.

FUTA: This account accumulates the employer's federal unemployment tax expense. This linking account designation is required prior to changing the status of the Payroll Ledger to ready.

SUTA: This account accumulates the employer's portion of the state unemployment tax expense. This linking account designation is required prior to changing the status of the Payroll Ledger to ready.

SDI: This optional linking account is used to record the employer's portion of the state disability insurance.

ACTION: Continue to complete the payroll linking account screens by clicking the drop-down list arrow to the right of each payroll linking account and selecting the appropriate account (see Document 5) from the chart of accounts display. Your screens should agree with the ones shown below:

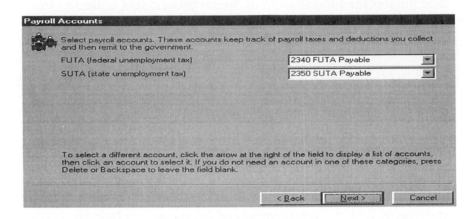

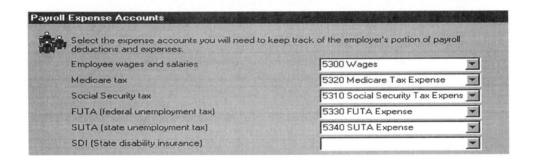

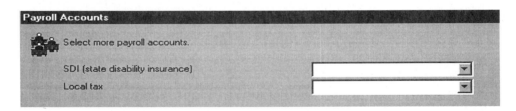

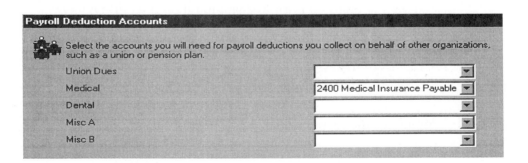

ACTION: Verify that the payroll linking accounts are correct; click the **OK** button. Complete the Inventory Accounts screen using the information provided in Document 5. Your screen will look like this:

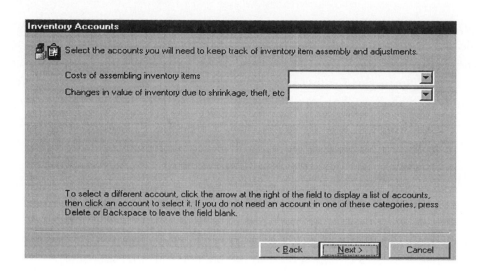

Explanation: Inventory Ledger linking accounts are defined as follows:

Costs of assembling inventory items: This is an optional linking account that accumulates the cost of transferring inventory items from one inventory item record to another.

Changes in value of inventory: This is an optional linking account that accumulates the reduction in value to damaged, lost, or obsolete inventory items.

ACTION: Because Classic Clocks does not plan to use the optional inventory linking accounts, click the **Next** button. Your screen will look like this:

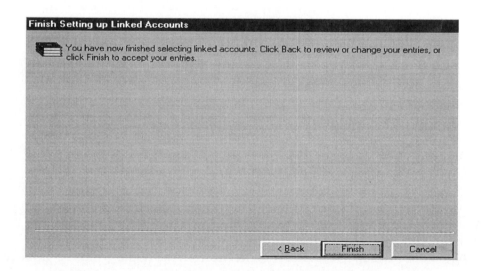

ACTION: Click **Finish** to complete the linking of accounts for Classic Clocks.

MODIFYING AND REMOVING LINKING ACCOUNTS

You can modify linking accounts as needed while working in the Not Ready and Ready modes. Journal entries made while in the Ready mode will be posted automatically to the new linking accounts that you specify. To remove the integration link for an account in the Not Ready and Ready modes, delete the account from the dialog box for the ledger involved. If the account has been designated as a linking account through its association with an inventory item, delete the asset, revenue, or expense account from the Inventory Ledger record for that inventory item. If you are working in the Not Ready mode, you can then remove the account from the chart of accounts if you wish. If you are working in the Ready mode, you cannot remove the account unless its balance is zero and it has not been used since the earliest transaction date.

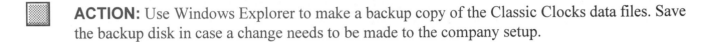

ACTION: Choose **Exit** from the home window File menu to end the current work session and return to your Windows desktop.

ACTION: Use Windows Explorer to make a backup copy of the Classic Clocks data files. Save the backup disk in case a change needs to be made to the company setup.

MAKING THE GENERAL LEDGER READY

You have now established the settings, chart of accounts, account balances, and linking accounts for Classic Clocks in the CA-Simply Accounting for Windows program. You have also made a backup copy of the Classic Clocks data files in the Not Ready mode. The status of the General Ledger can now be changed from not ready to ready.

ACTION: Load CA-Simply Accounting for Windows; then open the data files for Classic Clocks. Your screen will look like this:

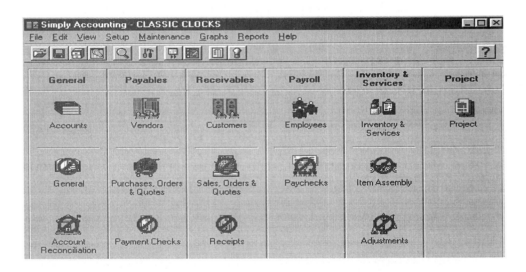

ACTION: Choose **Setup, Set Ready, General** from the home window. Your screen will look like this:

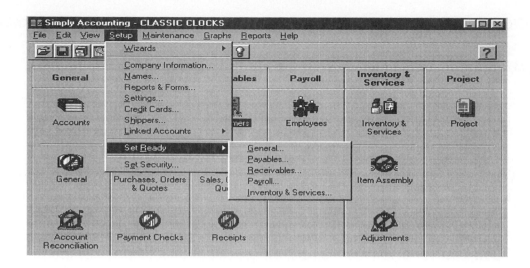

Explanation: Once a ledger has been set ready, you cannot return its status to not ready; consequently, it is extremely important that you make a backup copy of a company's data files prior to changing the status of any ledger from not ready to ready.

   ACTION: Click the **Proceed** button. If you receive an error message, read the message carefully for information on corrective action. Make corrections as required; then repeat this ACTION. If you did not make a backup of your company, do so at this time. Your screen will look like this:

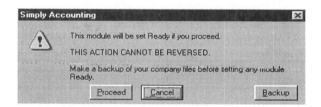

Explanation: The General Journal is now presented in the unlocked position and General Journal entries can be recorded. The program has set the session date equal to the earliest transaction date of 12/1/1997.

BANK RECONCILIATION AND CREDIT CARDS

Once the General Journal is in the Ready mode, the cash account needs to be set up to be reconciled. In addition, if a company wishes to accept credit cards for sales transactions, credit card information, charges, and accounts must be provided to Simply so that credit cards may be accepted as part of a transaction. The credit card setup may be performed at any time; however, it is appropriate to do the setup at this point. Prior to setting up cash for reconciliation and adding the credit card information, the chart of accounts should be evaluated to see if any accounts need to be added.

Classic Clocks—Document 6   **December 1, 1997**

Memo   **Date:** December 1, 1997

Set up the Cash account to be reconciled. Complete the credit card information so that credit cards may be accepted for sales transactions. Create any necessary accounts.

ACTION: Double-click the **Accounts** icon on the home window. Scroll through the list of accounts to see if there are accounts for interest income, bank service charges, and credit card fees.

ACTION: There is an account for bank service charges, but there are no accounts for interest income or credit card fees. Add the two accounts by clicking the **Create** button on the Accounts toolbar. Because interest income is a form of revenue not earned in the direct operation of the business, it should be in a category called Other Income. Create this section. Enter *4400 OTHER INCOME* as a Group Heading. Your screen will show the following:

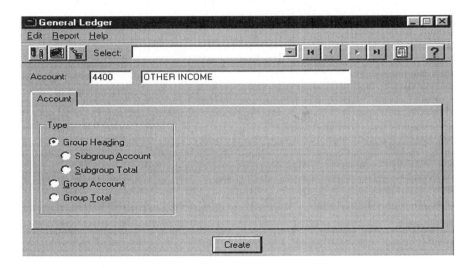

ACTION: Click **Create**. Repeat the procedures above to add the following accounts: 4410 Interest Income as a Group Account, 4490 TOTAL OTHER INCOME, and 5495 Credit Card Fees.

ACTION: Set up the Cash account so it may be reconciled by clicking the drop-down list arrow for **Select**. Click **1010 Cash** to highlight. Click the **Account Reconciliation** tab for the cash account. Click **Save Transactions for Account Reconciliation**. Your screen will show the following:

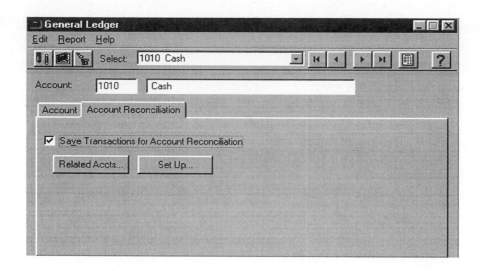

ACTION: Click **Related Accts...** Your screen will show the following:

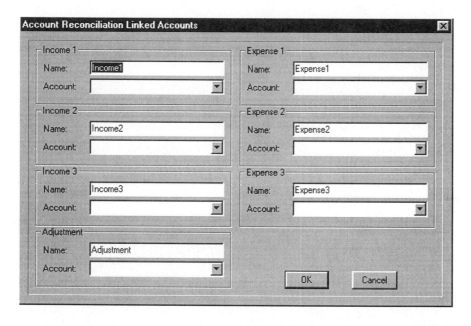

Explanation: This screen allows you to link the reconciliation of the Cash account to specific income and expense accounts that will be used to record interest income, bank service charges, and the like during the account reconciliation.

ACTION: Click the drop-down list arrow for **Account** next to Income 1. Click **4410 Interest Income** to select. Repeat the procedure for Expense 1 to select **5490 Bank Service Charge Expense**. Your screen will show the following:

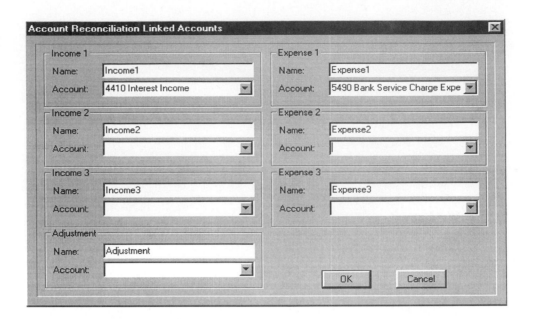

ACTION: Click **OK.** Click the **Set Up** button. Your screen will show the following dialog box:

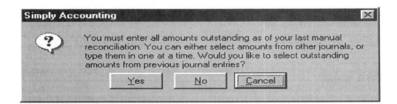

ACTION: Since there are no amounts outstanding, click **No.** The Set Up Account Reconciliation screen appears. Enter the cash balance of *8424.63* into the **Last Reconciled End Balance**. Your screen will appear as follows:

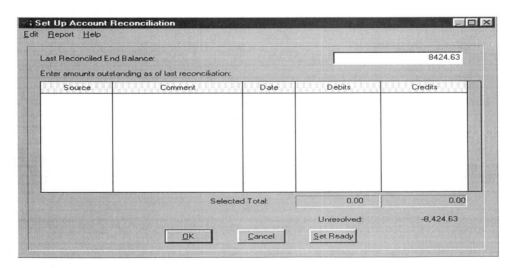

ACTION: Press the TAB key. The unresolved amount will show 0.00. Click the **Set Ready** button.

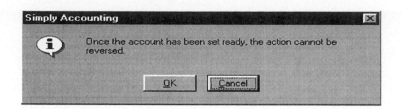

ACTION: Click **OK** on the dialog box. The cash account is now set up for reconciliation. Close the General Ledger. Close Accounts and return to the home window.

ACTION: Click the **Setup** menu on the home window. Click **Credit Cards**. Your screen will show the following Credit Card Information screen:

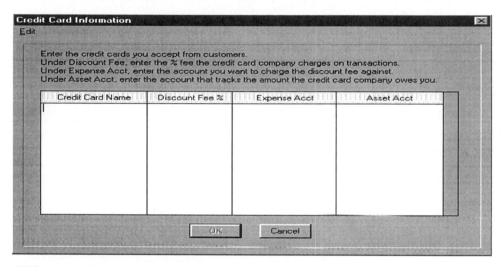

Explanation: This screen is used to enter the name of the credit card being accepted, the fee the bank charges the company for accepting the credit card, the expense account used to record the credit card fee, and the asset account used to record the remaining amount of the transaction.

ACTION: Enter the following information for Visa credit cards: Credit Card Name: Visa; Discount Fee %: 6.00; Expense Account: 5495 Credit Card Fees; Asset Account: 1010 Cash. Repeat the procedures for MasterCard using the same accounts and percentages as the Visa card. When both credit cards have been entered, your screen will show the following:

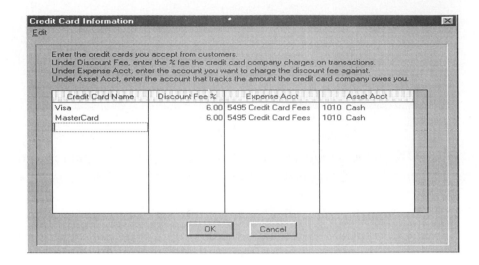

Explanation: Classic Clocks plans to accept bank credit cards rather than cards like American Express. With a bank credit card, the amount of the credit card sale (less fees) would be directly deposited into the company's bank account. If Classic Clocks chose to accept a nonbank credit card, the Asset account debited would be Accounts Receivable (or perhaps Credit Cards Receivable). This would be debited until the actual amount for the credit card sale (less fees) was received from the credit card company. When the payment was received, Cash would be debited and the receivable account would be credited.

   **ACTION:** Click **OK** to record the Credit Card Information and return to the home window.

TRANSACTIONS AND REPORTS

A. Record the following General Journal transactions under the session date of 12/1/1997:

Document 7 December 1—Maria Lindsay made a $1,000 capital contribution to the business.

Document 8 December 1—Increase the Petty Cash account balance by $50.

B. Print the following reports:

General Journal 12/1/1997 to 12/1/1997
Trial Balance As at 12/1/1997

C. Compare your General Journal and Trial Balance to the ones shown below:

Classic Clocks
General Journal 12/1/1997 to 12/1/1997

					Debits	**Credits**
12/1/1997	J1	Memo	Capital Contribution by Owner			
		1010		Cash	1,000.00	-
		3560		Maria Lindsay, Capital	-	1,000.00
12/1/1997	J2	Memo	To Increase Petty Cash Fund			
		1050		Petty Cash	50.00	0.00
		1010		Cash	-	-
					1,050.00	1,050.00

Classic Clocks
Trial Balance As At 12/1/1997

		Debits	Credits
1010	Cash	9,374.63	-
1050	Petty Cash	150.00	-
1200	Accounts Receivable	8,147.27	-
1310	Clock Inventory	20,065.00	-
1320	Watch Inventory	11,648.00	-
1410	Office Supplies	311.15	-
1420	Prepaid Insurance	200.00	-
1550	Office Equipment	4,700.00	-
1551	Accum. Dep: Office Equip.	-	2,683.18
1650	Store Equipment	4,000.00	-
1651	Accum. Dep: Store Equip.	-	1,341.59
2200	Accounts Payable	-	4,362.50
2310	FIT Payable	-	255.28
2320	SIT Payable	-	124.72
2330	Social Security Tax Payable	-	369.64
2335	Medicare Tax Payable	-	86.44
2340	FUTA Payable	-	6.15
2350	SUTA Payable	-	194.15
2400	Medical Insurance Payable	-	44.00
2500	Sales Tax Payable	-	1,170.90
3560	Maria Lindsay, Capital	-	43,268.02
3580	Maria Lindsay, Drawing	24,200.00	-
4010	Clock Sales	-	105,763.24
4020	Watch Sales	-	56,534.26
4200	Sales Returns & Allowances	188.63	-
4300	Sales Discounts	201.15	-
4410	Interest Income	-	0.00
5010	Cost Of Goods Sold-Clocks	52,881.62	-
5020	Cost of Goods Sold-Watches	28,267.13	-
5300	Wages	32,631.00	-
5310	Social Security Tax Expense	2,023.13	-
5320	Medicare Tax Expense	473.13	-
5330	FUTA Expense	112.00	-
5340	SUTA Expense	1,129.01	-
5410	Advertising Expense	2,435.00	-
5420	Utilities Expense	1,147.19	-
5430	Depreciation Exp: Office Equipment	1,283.26	-
5440	Insurance Expense	1,100.00	-
5450	Rent Expense	6,600.00	-
5460	Office Supplies Expense	934.56	-
5470	Depreciation Exp: Store Equipment	641.63	-
5480	Telephone Expense	762.43	-
5490	Bank Service Charge Expense	165.00	-
5495	Credit Card Fees	0.00	-
5500	Miscellaneous Expense	432.15	-
		216,204.07	216,204.07

ACTION: Make a backup copy of the Classic Clocks data files. Choose **Exit** from the home window File menu to end the current work session and return to your Windows desktop.

SUMMARY

This chapter has explored how to work with company data files in the Not Ready mode to customize the CA-Simply Accounting for Windows program to a specific company's needs. The procedures for establishing a company's settings, designing and creating financial statements, and entering initial account balances were discussed and demonstrated. The procedures required to establish linking accounts were also explored. In addition, you learned how to make the General Ledger ready for operation.

QUESTIONS

QUESTIONS ABOUT THE SOFTWARE

1. Explain the difference between the Ready and Not Ready modes of operation in the CA-Simply Accounting for Windows program.

2. When a new set of company data files are created for a company, the program establishes certain default settings for the company. These settings can be customized to meet the needs of a particular company. Describe the procedures used to modify default settings for the Payroll Ledger.

3. What is a group total?

4. Explain how a subgroup total account might be used in formatting a company's financial statements.

5. Define the following terms: *postable account* and *nonpostable account*.

6. What is a linking account? How are linking accounts established in the CA-Simply Accounting for Windows program?

7. What procedures must be followed to remove a linking account from the CA-Simply Accounting for Windows program?

QUESTIONS ABOUT CONVERSION PROCEDURES

8. List the procedures you would follow to create a new set of company data files for a company.

9. Why is it important to make a backup copy of a company's data files prior to changing the status of the General Ledger to ready?

EXPLORING ALTERNATIVE SOFTWARE TECHNIQUES

10. The following dialog box, accessed by choosing **Names** from the home window Setup menu, lets you change the names of several Payroll Ledger fields and the Project Ledger if different names are more suited to the needs of a particular company.

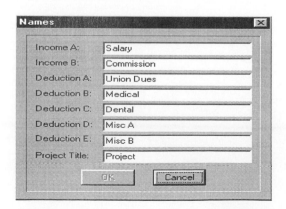

Names fields are defined as follows:

Income A and **Income B:** The default names for these Payroll Ledger fields are Salary and Commission. The amounts in both fields are taxable, and they can be renamed as necessary to record any type of income earned by employees in the business.

Deduction A, **Deduction B**, **Deduction C, Deduction D,** and **Deduction E:** The default names for these Payroll Ledger fields are Union, Medical, Dental, Misc. A, and Misc. B. Enter a more meaningful name for one or more of these fields to correspond with the typical types of voluntary deductions requested by employees.

Project Title: The default name for the Project Ledger is Project. Enter a more meaningful name to describe the profit centers in the business.

Suggest at least one alternative name that a company may decide to use for Income A, Deduction A, and Project Title.

TRANSMITTAL

Classic Clocks   **Name**_____
Chapter 9   **Session Date: 12/1/1997**

Attach the following reports:

1. Chart of Accounts 12/1/1997
2. Trial Balance As At 12/1/1997
3. Income Statement 1/1/1997 to 12/1/1997
4. Balance Sheet As at 12/1/1997
5. General Journal report 12/1/1997 to 12/1/1997 (after the additional transactions have been entered)
6. Trial Balance As at 12/1/1997 (after the additional transactions have been entered)

EXERCISE—The Paint Place

COMPANY PROFILE

The Paint Place is a sole proprietorship owned by Mike Poole in Vancouver, Washington. Mike operates a retail store that sells paint. He has maintained a manual accounting system for his business and would now like to covert to a computerized accounting system beginning December 1, 1997. Mike has selected the CA-Simply Accounting for Windows program as the most appropriate software for his business. As a merchandising business with employees, Mike plans to use the General, Receivables, Payables, Inventory, Payroll, and Project Ledgers of the program.

The objective of this exercise is to make the General Ledger Ready. The Paint Place exercise will be continued at the end of Chapter 10 with instructions on how to make the other ledgers ready.

1. Because this is a new company, data files for this company are not located with the other company files on the CD-ROM that came with the text. The company files for all the companies created in this section of the text will be stored on floppy disks. To create a new subdirectory on your Student Data Files disk for The Paint Place, start Windows; click the **Start** button, point to Programs, click **Windows Explorer**. Click the disk location for the company—**A:**, **B:**, or **C:** (if using C:, also click **Wimsim** folder). Right click on the Contents side of Explorer, point to New, click **Folder**, type *Paint*, press ENTER.

2. Click the **OK** button; click the **Close** button to close Windows Explorer.

3. To create a new set of company data files for The Paint Place, open the CA-Simply Accounting for Windows program; click **Create a new company**, click **OK**. Complete the steps listed in the Setup Wizard to create the new company.

4. You are going to create a new list of accounts from scratch.

5. Determine the location of the Paint folder you created. Enter one of the following into the **Enter a File Name** text box:

   > A:\Paint\Paint.asc (if you are storing your student data files on the disk in drive A)
   > B:\Paint\Paint.asc (if you are storing your student data files on the disk in drive B)
   > C:\Winsim\Paint\Paint.asc (if you are storing your student data files on your hard disk)

6. Click the **Next** button. (If you receive an error message stating "Cannot create company file." click the **OK** button. Check the path you have entered into the **Enter a File Name** text box to ensure that you have entered the path correctly. Make corrections as required; click the **Next** button.) Enter the fiscal start, fiscal end, and earliest transaction dates in the Dates dialog box.

   > Fiscal start: *1/1/97*
   > Fiscal end: *12/31/97*
   > Earliest transaction: *12/1/1997*

7. Click the **Next** button. (If you still receive an error message; click the **OK** button; then click the **Exit** button in the CA-Simply Accounting-Open File dialog box to return to your Windows desktop. Go to the beginning of this exercise and repeat each instruction. The most likely cause for the error message is that you have not created the subdirectory titled Paint on your Student Data Files disk. The CA-Simply Accounting for Windows program cannot create a new set of company data files for The Paint Place until the subdirectory titled Paint is created on your Student Data Files disk.) Make sure all the business activities listed on the next screen have been selected and click **Next**.

8. Complete the Company information by entering the following company information:

    The Paint Place/Your Name
    3559 Plain Way
    Vancouver, Washington 98661

9. The federal ID is *93-209381*, and the state ID is *39281*. Accounting terms will be used. Use the default names provided for Payroll Definitions and Projects title. The printer settings should be correct; however, if you need to adjust the settings, please check with your instructor. Make sure that both items on Track Inventory Turnover are selected. DO NOT select cash basis or use the budgeting feature of Simply. Use the check number as the source code for cash purchases and sales. Accept the default values used by Simply Accounting unless the information is provided below.

Receivables	Payables	Payroll	Inventory
Sales tax: 8.0%	no changes	SUTA rate: 3.5	Inventory Tracking
		FUTA rate: 0.8	Inventory Lookup
		Use Automatic Deductions	

Forms
Next invoice number: 5468
Next check number: 2345

10. Click **Finish** to save the information entered on the Setup Wizard.

11. Make additional changes to settings using the Settings selection from the Setup menu. There are no changes to be made to the settings for Display, System, Sales Taxes, General, Receivables, Payables, Payroll, Inventory & Services, or E-Mail. Make the following changes to Forms, Comments, and Projects:

    Forms: Confirm printing for invoices; Confirm printing for checks; accept default for printing company name and address on all items listed

    Comments: Default invoice comment: The Paint Place thanks you for your business!

    Projects: Warn if allocation is not complete.

12. Mike has listed the account names and balances from The Paint Place's manual accounting system on the following Chart of Accounts Worksheet. Complete the missing information for account numbers, account names, and account types, using the financial statement formatting information provided in this chapter.

Chart of Accounts Worksheet

Acct. No.	Account Name	Account Balance	Account Type
1000	CURRENT ASSETS		
_____	Cash	13,872.94	_____
_____	Petty Cash	100.00	_____
_____	Accounts Receivable	8,259.95	_____
_____	Inventory	28,928.67	_____
_____	Store Supplies	1,622.30	_____
_____	Prepaid Insurance	1,200.00	_____
_____	_____		_____
_____	_____		_____
_____	Office Equipment	2,800.00	_____
_____	Accum Dep: Office Equip.	-1,469.44	_____
_____	_____		_____
_____	Store Equipment	3,500.00	_____
_____	Accum Dep: Store Equip.	-1,916.67	_____
_____	_____		_____
_____	_____		_____
2000	_____		_____
_____	Accounts Payable	4,142.12	_____
_____	FIT Payable	261.73	_____
_____	Social Security Tax Payable	374.98	_____
_____	Medicare Tax Payable	87.70	_____
_____	FUTA Payable	6.98	_____
_____	SUTA Payable	135.52	_____
_____	Sales Tax Payable	217.42	_____
_____	_____		_____
_____	_____		_____
_____	Mike Poole, Capital	36,076.25	_____
_____	Mike Poole, Drawing	-11,000.00	_____
_____	_____		_____
_____	_____		_____
_____	Sales	152,678.45	_____
_____	Sales Returns & Allow.	-144.33	_____
_____	_____		_____
_____	OTHER INCOME		_____
_____	Interest Income	0.00	_____
_____	TOTAL INCOME		_____
_____	_____		_____
_____	Cost of Goods Sold	75,842.65	_____
_____	_____		_____
5200	OPERATING EXPENSES		_____
_____	Advertising Expense	1,945.00	_____
_____	Rent Expense	6,600.00	_____
_____	Cash Short/Over	9.12	_____
_____	Utilities Expense	983.21	_____
_____	Depreciation Exp: Store Equipment	916.63	_____
_____	Depreciation Exp: Office Equipment	702.78	_____
_____	Store Supplies Expense	752.65	_____

_____	Insurance Expense	1,100.00	_____
_____	Bank Service Charge Expense	0.00	_____
_____	Credit Card Fees	0.00	_____
_____	Wages	33,240.00	_____
_____	Social Security Tax Expense	2,060.89	_____
_____	Medicare Tax Expense	481.99	_____
_____	FUTA Expense	112.00	_____
_____	SUTA Expense	1,086.40	_____
_____	Miscellaneous Expense	105.75	_____
_____	_____		_____

13. Load CA-Simply Accounting for Windows; open the data files for The Paint Place (A:\PAINT\Paint.asc); open Accounts on the General section of the screen then create the accounts and enter the account balances listed on your worksheet.

14. Print a Chart of Accounts, Trial Balance, Income Statement, and Balance Sheet. Verify that your data are correct. (If you receive an error message, read the message carefully for information regarding corrective action. Make corrections as required; then print a new, correct Chart of Accounts, Trial Balance, Income Statement, and Balance Sheet.)

15. Based on the information you listed on your Chart of Accounts Worksheet, complete the missing information for account names and numbers for each linking account listed on the following Linking Accounts Worksheet.

Linking Accounts Worksheet

General Linking Account
Bank account: _____
Retained earnings: _____

Payables Linking Accounts
Payables bank account: _____
Accounts payable: _____

Receivables Linking Accounts
Receivables bank account: _____
Accounts receivable: _____
Sales tax payable: _____

Payroll Linking Accounts
Payroll bank: _____
FIT: _____
Medicare Tax: _____
SST: _____
FUTA (Payable):   _____
SUTA (Payable):   _____
Wage: _____
Medicare Tax (Expense):   _____
SST (Expense):   _____
FUTA (Expense):   _____
SUTA (Expense):   _____

Inventory Linking Accounts None

16. Click **Setup**, **Wizards, Linked** accounts on the home window. Enter the linking account information from your Linking Accounts Worksheet.

17. Make a backup copy of The Paint Place data files.

18. Choose **Set Ready**, **General** from the home window Setup menu. Click the **Proceed** button. (If you receive an error message, read the message carefully for information on corrective action. Make corrections as required; then repeat this instruction.)

19. Set up the Cash account for reconciliation. Use Interest Income as the Income 1 account and Bank Service Charges as the Expense 1 account.

20. Create the credit card Information to accept Visa and MasterCard credit cards. Both companies charge a 6% fee. The expense account to use for both cards is Credit Card Fees. The asset account to use for both cards is Cash.

21. Record the following transactions:

    J1: December 1—Mike Poole made a $1,500 capital contribution to the business.

    J2: December 1—Increase the Petty Cash account balance by $50.

22. Print the following reports:

    A.   General Journal (By posting date) 12/1/1997 to 12/1/1997
    B.   Trial Balance As at 12/1/1997

23. Exit from the program. Complete The Paint Place Transmittal.

TRANSMITTAL

The Paint Place   Name_____
Chapter 9   Session Date: 12/1/1997

A. Attach the following reports:

1. Chart of Accounts 12/1/1997
2. Trial Balance As at 12/1/1997
3. Income Statement 1/1/1997 to 12/1/1997
4. Balance Sheet As at 12/1/1997
5. General Journal 12/1/1997 to 12/1/1997 (after the additional transactions have been entered)
6. Trial Balance As at 12/1/1997 (after the additional transactions have been entered)

B. Refer to the Trial Balance As at 12/1/1997 that you printed after entering the additional transactions. List the amounts requested below:

1. What is the balance of the Cash account? $_____

2. What is the balance of the Petty Cash account? $_____

3. What is the balance of the Mike Poole, Capital account? $_____

4. What is the balance of the Accounts Receivable account? $_____

COMPUTERIZING A MANUAL ACCOUNTING SYSTEM—RECEIVABLES, PAYABLES, INVENTORY, PAYROLL, AND PROJECT LEDGERS

COMPUTERIZING A MANUAL ACCOUNTING SYSTEM— RECEIVABLES, PAYABLES, INVENTORY, PAYROLL, AND PROJECT LEDGERS

LEARNING OBJECTIVES

After studying this chapter, you will be able to:
- Enter customer records and historical sales invoices
- Enter vendor records and historical purchase invoices
- Enter inventory item records and historical inventory data
- Enter employee records and historical payroll data
- Create projects
- Make the Receivables, Payables, Inventory, and Payroll Ledgers ready
- Understand the operational restrictions of each ledger in the Ready mode
- Understand the important times for printing reports and making backup copies of company data files

In this chapter, you will continue working with the Classic Clocks company files. The procedures required to prepare the Receivables, Payables, Inventory, Payroll, and Project Ledgers for operation are discussed, and the operational restrictions of each ledger in the Ready mode are presented. Summaries of each step involved in the conversion process and important times for making backup copies of company data files are also provided. At the conclusion of Chapter 11, a comprehensive practice set for Firelight Stoves will give you an opportunity to prepare the General, Receivables, Payables, Inventory, Payroll, and Project Ledgers for operation for a merchandising business. Once each of Firelight Stoves' ledgers are ready, you will have the opportunity to record transactions and perform the year-end closing procedures.

CLASSIC CLOCKS TUTORIAL

The following tutorial is a step-by-step guide to working with the Receivables, Payables, Inventory, and Payroll Ledgers in the Not Ready mode. The methods used to establish customer, vendor, inventory item, employee, and project records will be demonstrated. In addition, the procedures required to enter historical sales invoices, purchase invoices, inventory data, and payroll data are presented. Once the historical financial data for each ledger has been entered, the status of Receivables, Payables, Inventory, and Payroll Ledgers will be changed from not ready to ready. The procedures required to make the General Ledger ready for operation were discussed in Chapter 9. Regardless of the order in which the other ledgers are made ready, the General Ledger must be in the Ready mode prior to changing the status of any other ledger. The Classic Clocks Tutorial will be continued and concluded in Chapter 11 to give you a comprehensive overview of how CA-Simply Accounting for Windows can be used to computerize the manual accounting system of a small merchandising business.

RECEIVABLES LEDGER

Maria Lindsay has assembled the historical sales invoice and address information for each of Classic Clocks' customers. Before the Receivables Ledger can be made ready, each customer's address must be inserted into the program, and each current outstanding invoice for that customer must be recorded. Classic Clocks' manual accounting records currently contain sufficient information regarding prior payments by customers. Therefore, only the current outstanding sales invoices will be recorded in the Receivables Ledger. In the Not Ready mode, the ledgers are not integrated/linked and no journal entries can be recorded. The objective of entering historical sales invoices is to ensure that the total of all outstanding invoices agree with the Accounts Receivable account balance in the General Ledger. The total of all outstanding invoices must be equal to the Accounts Receivable account balance established in the General Ledger before the Receivables Ledger can be changed to ready status.

Classic Clocks—Document 9   **Session Date: 12/1/1997**

Memo   **Date:** December 1, 1997

Customer Information

Heras, Elaine
1395 Salomon Street
Coeur D'Alene, Idaho 83814
Phone: 208-666-2941
Historical Outstanding Sales Invoice: none

Northwest Inns
Corporate Headquarters
1726 West 9th Street
Vancouver, Washington 98660
Phone: 206-667-1254
Fax: 206-667-1250
nwinns@aol.com
Historical Outstanding Sales Invoice:
        5876, 11/28/1997, $3,636.05

Cash Sales
Classic Clocks
1200 Lakeway
Coeur D'Alene, Idaho 83814
Phone: 208-667-5512
Fax: 208-667-5515
Historical Outstanding Sales Invoice: none

Sailing, Jeremy
1824 Coho Road
Coeur D'Alene, Idaho 83814
Phone: 208-663-5601
Historical Outstanding Sales Invoice:
        5853, 11/18/1997, $1,476.67

Sandpoint School District
Wendy Corbett
2530 Mill Plain Blvd.
Sandpoint, Idaho 83860
Phone: 208-662-0078
Fax: 208-662-0075
sandpoint@idaho.edu
Historical Outstanding Sales Invoice:
        5879, 11/29/1997, $3,034.55

Total Historical Outstanding Sales Invoices:
        $ 8,147.27

Note: Leave the **Clear invoices when paid** check box unchecked for each customer. Check the **Print statements for this customer** check box for all customers.

Creating Customer Records

     ACTION: Load CA-Simply Accounting for Windows; open the data files for Classic Clocks (A:\CLOCK\Classic Clocks.asc); leave the session date set at 12/1/1997, and close the To-Do List. The home window for Classic Clocks will appear as shown below:

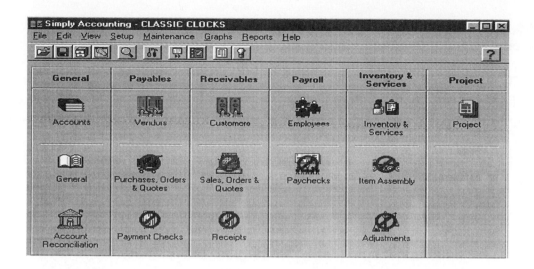

Explanation: The General Journal is presented in the unlocked position, indicating that the General Ledger is ready and that General Journal entries can be recorded. All other journals are presented in the locked position, indicating that all of the other ledgers are currently not ready.

ACTION: In the home window, double-click the **Customers** icon. Your screen will look like this:

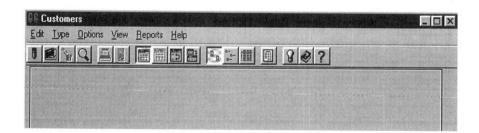

ACTION: Click the **Create** button on the toolbar. Enter the customer information for Heras, Elaine (see Document 9). Your screen should agree with the one shown below:

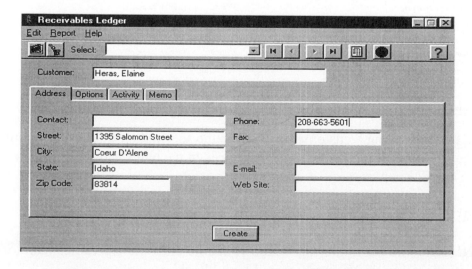

ACTION: Verify that the information correct is correct; then click the **Create** button.

Explanation: A blank Receivables Ledger dialog box is presented ready for other new customer records to be entered.

 ACTION: Enter the information for Classic Clocks' other customers (see Document 9); then select **Display Customer List** from the Receivables Ledger Report menu. Your screen will look like this:

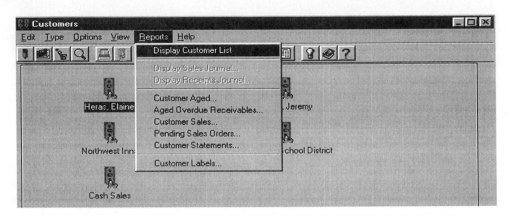

 ACTION: Click the **File** menu on the Customer List; click **Print**. Compare your report to the one shown below:

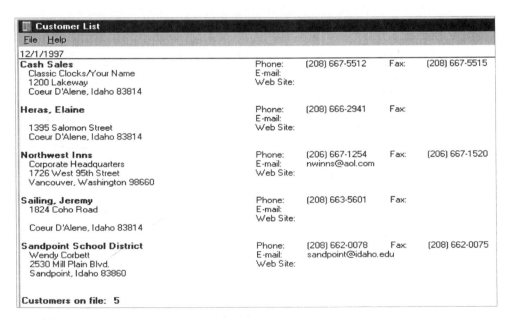

If you made an error in entering a customer record, see the special box titled Editing Tips for Editing a Receivables Ledger Record and Historical Sales Invoices in the Not Ready Mode presented in the following section of this chapter.

Entering Historical Sales Invoices

 ACTION: Close the Customer List window; double-click the **Customer** icon for Sailing, Jeremy on the customers screen. Your screen will look like this:

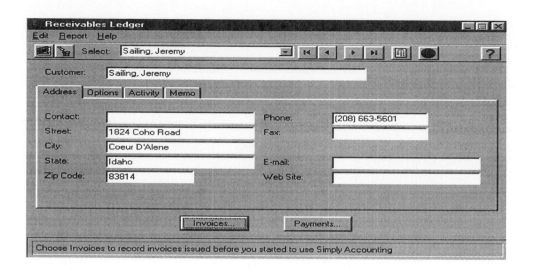

Explanation: Two buttons will appear on your screen: **Invoices** and **Payments**. Use of these buttons will present dialog boxes for entering historical sales invoices and payments for each customer.

ACTION: Click the **Invoices** button. Enter the information about the historical outstanding sales invoice for Sailing, Jeremy (see Document 9). Your screen will look like this:

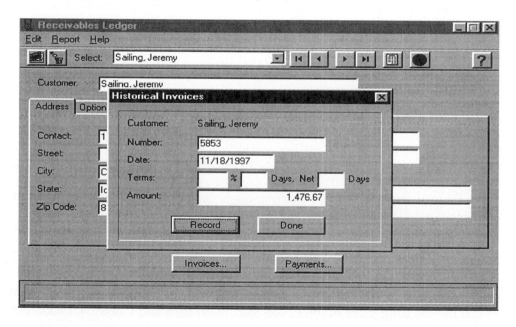

ACTION: Verify that the information is correct; click the **Record** button; click the **Done** button. On the Receivables Ledger screen for Jeremy Sailing, click the **Activity** tab. Your screen will look like this:

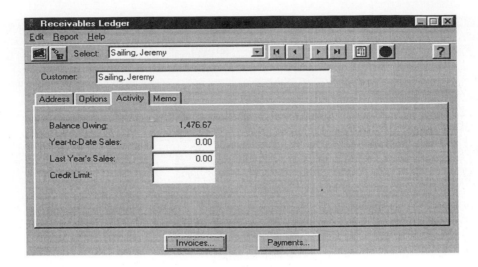

Explanation: Use the following editing techniques to correct errors:

> **Editing Tips:**
> **Editing a Receivables Ledger Record and Historical Sales Invoices in the Not Ready Mode**
>
> While working with the Receivables Ledger in the Not Ready mode, many of the restrictions that were in place in the Ready mode do not apply. You can create, modify, or remove customer records as needed while working in the Not Ready mode.
>
> If the customer record you wish to edit does not currently appear in the Receivables Ledger dialog box, choose **Find** from the Receivables Ledger Edit menu; then select the customer from the customer list display. Modify the customer record as necessary or choose **Remove** from the Receivables Ledger Edit menu. If you remove a customer record, all recorded historical sales and payments for that customer will also be removed.
>
> To edit a recorded historical sales invoice and retain customer address information, check the **Clear invoices when paid** check box for the customer on the Options tab; then click the **Payment** button. Pay the incorrect sales invoice (use any check number you wish; then click the **Record** and **Done** buttons); then uncheck the **Clear invoices when paid** check box for the customer. This will completely remove the invoice from the Receivables Ledger record for this customer. Re-enter the historical sales invoice correctly.

 ACTION: Click the drop-down list **arrow** next to Jeremy's name; click **Northwest Inns**, enter the historical outstanding sales invoices for Northwest Inns and Classic Clocks' other customers (see Document 9).

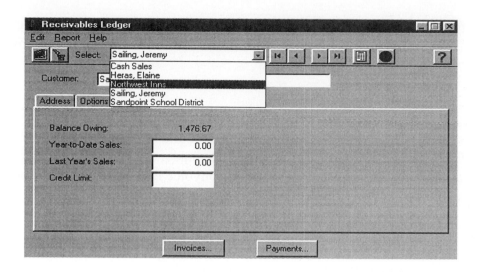

ACTION: Close the Receivables Ledger; choose **Customer Aged** from the Customer window Report menu; click the **Detail** option button; then click the **Select All** and **OK** buttons. Your screen will look like this:

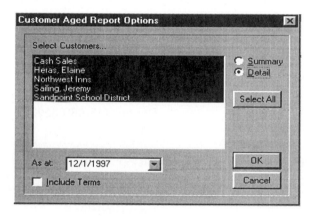

ACTION: Choose **Print** from the Customer Aged Detail File menu. Compare your report to the one shown below:

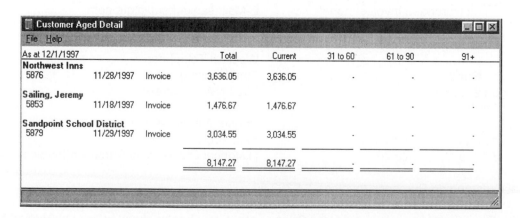

As at 12/1/1997			Total	Current	31 to 60	61 to 90	91+
Northwest Inns							
5876	11/28/1997	Invoice	3,636.05	3,636.05	.	.	.
Sailing, Jeremy							
5853	11/18/1997	Invoice	1,476.67	1,476.67	.	.	.
Sandpoint School District							
5879	11/29/1997	Invoice	3,034.55	3,034.55	.	.	.
			8,147.27	8,147.27	.	.	.

If you made an error in entering a customer record or historical outstanding sales invoice, see the special box titled Editing Tips for Editing a Receivables Ledger Record and Historical Sales Invoices in the Not Ready Mode presented earlier in the chapter.

PAYABLES LEDGER

Maria Lindsay has assembled the historical purchase invoice and address information for each of Classic Clocks' vendors. Before the Payables Ledger can be made ready, each vendor's address must be inserted into the program, and each current outstanding purchase invoice for that vendor must be recorded. Classic Clocks' manual accounting records currently contain sufficient information regarding prior payments made to vendors. Therefore, only the current outstanding purchase invoices will be recorded in the Payables Ledger. In the Not Ready mode, the ledgers are not integrated/linked and no journal entries can be recorded. The objective of entering purchase invoices is to ensure that the total of all outstanding invoices agree with the Accounts Payable account balance in the General Ledger. The total of all outstanding invoices must be equal to the Accounts Payable account balance established in the General Ledger before the Payables Ledger can be changed to ready status.

Classic Clocks—Document 10   **Session Date: 12/1/1997**

Memo   **Date:** December 1, 1997

Vendor Information

True Time Clocks
Alice Anderson
540 Belmont Avenue
Seattle, Washington 98125
Phone: 206-567-9045
Fax: 206-567-9046
Historical Outstanding Purchase Invoice:
      7226, 11/29/1997, $1,740.24

Idaho Electric
Joan Smith
1213 Sixth Avenue
Coeur D'Alene, Idaho 83814
Phone: 208-667-1034
Fax: 208-667-1035
Historical Outstanding Purchase Invoice: none

Watch Works
Cal Nguyen
12014 SW Canyon Road
Beaverton, Oregon 97005
Phone: 503-292-7869
Fax: 503-292-7870
Historical Outstanding Purchase Invoice:
      6770, 11/22/1997, $2,622.26

Clock Wholesalers
Bob Mandel
8321 Trolly Street
San Francisco, California 94023
Phone: 415-989-3522
Fax: 415-989-5400
E-Mail: clocks@xyz.org
Historical Outstanding Purchase Invoice: none

Sagle Office Supply
Pam Gladstone
345 NW 3rd Street
Coeur D'Alene, Idaho 83814
Phone: 208-667-2244
Fax: 208-667-2245
E-Mail: sagleoffsup@gte.com
Historical Outstanding Purchase Invoice: none

Western Telephone
Tom Henning
5623 NW 4th Street
Coeur D'Alene, Idaho 83814
Phone: 208-667-9965
Fax: 208-667-9966
Historical Outstanding Purchase Invoice: none

Total Historical Outstanding Purchase Invoices: $4,362.50

Note: Leave the **Clear invoices when paid** and **Print contact on checks** check boxes unchecked for all vendors.

Creating Vendor Records

ACTION: Close the Customer Aged Detail window. In the home window, double-click the **Vendors** icon. Your screen will look like this:

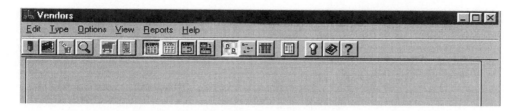

ACTION: Enter the vendor information for True Time Clocks (see Document 10). Verify that the information is correct; then click the **Create** button. Your screen should agree with the one shown below:

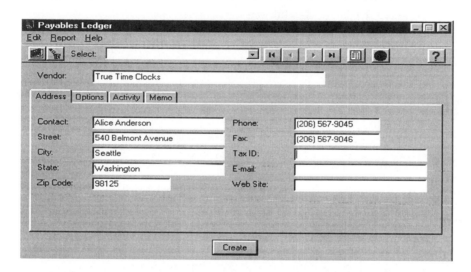

Explanation: Use the following editing techniques to correct errors:

Editing Tips:
Editing a Payables Ledger Record and Historical Purchase Invoices in the Not Ready Mode

While working with the Payables Ledger in the Not Ready mode, many of the restrictions that were in place in the Ready mode do not apply. You can create, modify, or remove vendor records as needed while working in the Not Ready mode.

If the vendor record you wish to edit does not currently appear in the Payables Ledger dialog box, choose **Find** from the Payables Ledger Edit menu; then select the vendor from the vendor list display. Modify the vendor record as necessary or choose **Remove** from the Payables Ledger Edit menu. If you remove a vendor record, all recorded historical purchases and payments for that vendor will also be removed.

To edit a recorded historical vendor invoice and retain vendor address information, check the **Clear invoices when paid** check box for the vendor; then click the **Payment** button. Pay the incorrect purchase invoice (use any check number you wish; then click the **Record** and **Done** buttons); then uncheck the **Clear invoices when paid** check box for the vendor. This will completely remove the invoice from the Payables Ledger record for this vendor. Re-enter the historical purchase invoice correctly.

ACTION: A blank Payables Ledger dialog box should be on the screen. It is ready for the remaining vendor records to be entered. Enter the information for Classic Clocks' other vendors (see Document 10); then select **Display Vendor List** from the Payables Ledger Report menu. Your screen will look like this:

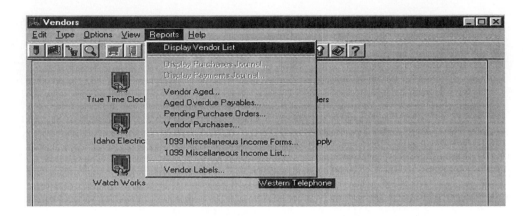

ACTION: Choose **Print** from the Vendor List File menu. Compare your report to the one shown below:

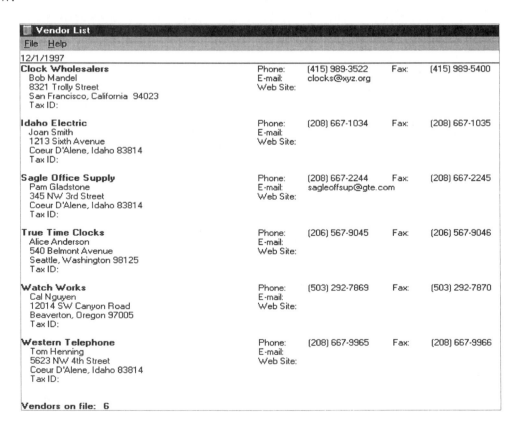

If you made an error in entering a vendor record, see the special box titled Editing Tips for Editing a Payables Ledger Record and Historical Purchases Invoices in the Not Ready Mode presented earlier in this chapter.

Entering Historical Purchase Invoices

■ **ACTION:** Close the Vendor List window; double-click the **Vendor** icon for True Time Clocks on the vendors screen. Your screen will look like this:

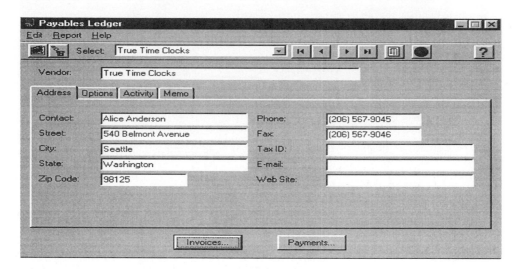

Explanation: Two buttons will appear on your screen: **Invoices** and **Payments**. Use of these buttons will present dialog boxes for entering historical purchase invoices and payments for each vendor.

■ **ACTION:** Click the **Invoices** button. Enter the information about the historical outstanding purchase invoice for True Time Clocks (see Document 10). Your screen will look like this:

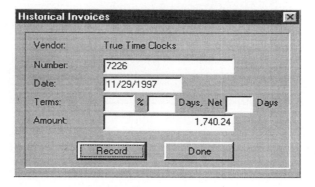

■ **ACTION:** Verify that the information is correct; click the **Record** button; then click the **Done** button. On the Vendor Ledger screen for True Time Clocks, click the **Activity** tab. Your screen will look like this:

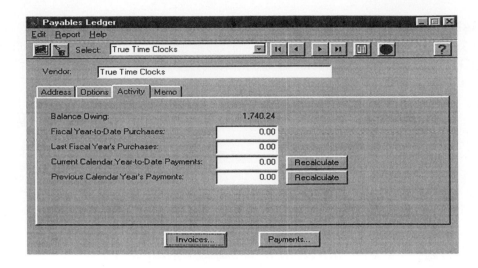

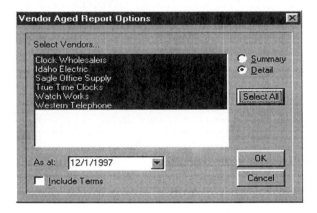

ACTION: Click the drop-down list arrow next to True Time Clocks; click **Watch Works**, enter the historical outstanding purchase invoices for Watch Works (see Document 10). Close the Payables Ledger; choose **Vendor Aged** from the Vendors window Report menu; click the **Detail** option button; then click the **Select All** and **OK** buttons. Your screen will look like this:

ACTION: Choose **Print** from the Vendor Aged Detail File menu. Compare your report to the one shown below:

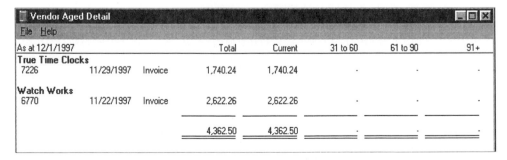

If you made an error in entering a vendor record or historical purchases invoice, see the special shaded box titled Editing Tips for Editing a Payables Ledger Record and Historical Purchase Invoices in the Not Ready Mode presented earlier in this chapter.

■ **ACTION:** Close the Vendor Aged Detail window; close the Vendor screen, choose **Exit** from the home window File menu to end the current work session and return to your Windows desktop.

■ **ALTERNATIVE ACTION:** You can continue with the tutorial without exiting from the program if you wish. Close the Vendor Aged Detail window and the Vendor screen; skip the portion of the next ACTION that discusses opening the program and continue with the tutorial.

INVENTORY LEDGER

Maria Lindsay has assembled the historical information for each of Classic Clocks' inventory items. Before the Inventory Ledger can be made ready, each inventory item must be inserted into the program, and the current quantity and total value of each inventory item must be recorded. In addition, each inventory item must be associated with an asset, revenue, and expense account. Asset, revenue, and expense accounts associated with inventory items are the accounts used to establish the integration link among the Inventory, Receivables, Payables, and General Ledgers. All accounts associated with inventory items in this manner are defined as linking accounts by the program. Consequently, the restrictions for modifying and removing linking accounts discussed in Chapter 9 apply to these accounts.

In the Not Ready mode, the ledgers are not integrated/linked and no journal entries can be recorded. The objective of entering inventory item record information is to ensure that the total value of all inventory items agree with the total of the Inventory account balances in the General Ledger. The total value of all inventory items must be equal to the Inventory account balances established in the General Ledger before the Inventory Ledger can be changed to ready status.

Classic Clocks—Document 11   **Session Date: 12/1/1997**

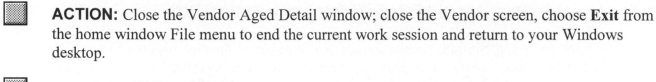

Memo   **Date:** December 1, 1997

Inventory Information

Number	Description	Unit	Selling Price	Min. Level	Quantity	Total Value
C100	Floor Clock	Each	1,190.00	2	10	5,950.00
C200	Chime Clock	Each	300.00	15	35	5,250.00
C300	Cuckoo Clock	Each	350.00	5	15	2,625.00
C400	Mantle Clock	Each	390.00	5	20	3,900.00
C500	School House Clock	Each	78.00	10	60	2,340.00
W100	Silver Watch	Each	118.00	4	12	708.00
W200	Gold Watch	Each	330.00	5	31	5,115.00
W300	Brass Watch	Each	98.00	10	25	1,225.00
W400	Bronze Watch	Each	130.00	10	40	2,600.00
W500	Plastic Watch	Each	40.00	25	100	2,000.00
						31,713.00

Associate each Clock inventory item with the following accounts: <u>Asset</u>: 1310 Clock Inventory; <u>Revenue</u>: 4010 Clock Sales; <u>Expense</u>: 5010 Cost of Goods Sold-Clocks

Associate each Watch inventory item with the following accounts: <u>Asset</u>: 1320 Watch Inventory; <u>Revenue</u>: 4020 Watch Sales; <u>Expense</u>: 5020 Cost of Goods Sold-Watches

Creating Inventory Records and Entering Historical Inventory Data

ACTION: Load CA-Simply Accounting for Windows; open the data files for Classic Clocks (A:\CLOCK\Classic Clocks.asc); leave the session date set at 12/1/1997. In the home window, double-click the **Inventory & Services** icon. Your screen will look like this:

ACTION: Click the **Create** button. 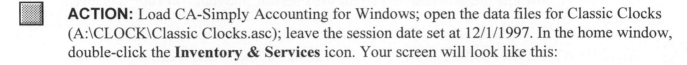 On the Item tab, enter the inventory item information for the Floor Clock (C100) from Document 11. Your screen should agree with the one shown below:

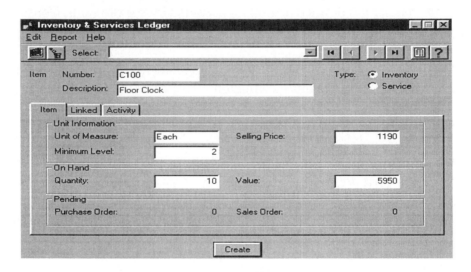

Explanation: Use the following editing techniques to correct errors:

> **Editing Tips:**
> **Editing an Inventory Ledger Record in the Not Ready Mode**
>
> While working with the Inventory Ledger in the Not Ready mode, many of the restrictions that were in place in the Ready mode do not apply. You can create, modify, or remove inventory item records as needed while working in the Not Ready mode.
>
> If the inventory item record you wish to edit does not currently appear in the Inventory Ledger dialog box, choose **Find** from the Inventory Ledger Edit menu; then select the inventory item from the inventory item display. Modify the inventory item record as necessary or choose **Remove** from the Inventory Ledger Edit menu.

ACTION: Verify that the information is correct; then click the **Linked** tab and fill in the account names and numbers to link the item to the appropriate accounts. If your screen matches the following screen, click the **Create** button.

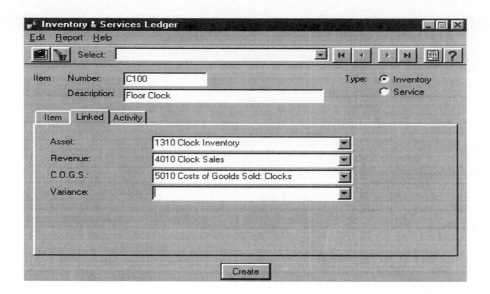

Explanation: A blank Inventory Ledger dialog box is presented ready for other new inventory item records to be entered.

ACTION: Enter the information for the other inventory items (see Document 11); then select **Display Inventory List** from the Inventory & Services Report menu. Your screen will look like this:

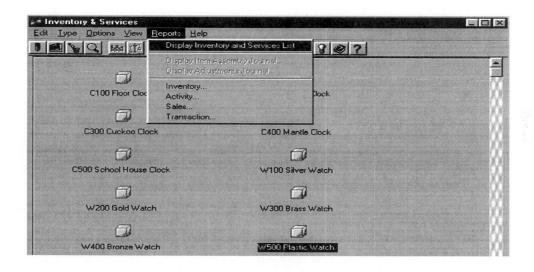

ACTION: Choose **Print** from the Inventory List File menu. Compare your report to the one shown below:

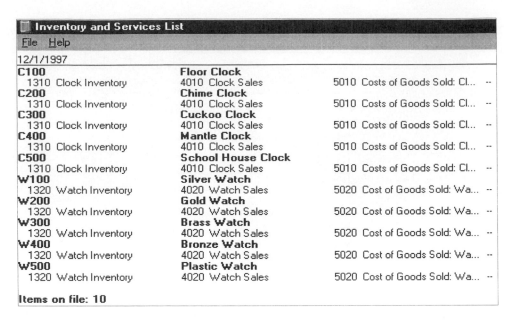

If you made an error entering an inventory item record, see the special box titled Editing Tips for Editing an Inventory Ledger Record in the Not Ready Mode presented earlier in this chapter.

ACTION: Close the Inventory List window; choose **Inventory** from the home window **Report** menu; click **Inventory & Services** and **Inventory**. Your screen will look like this:

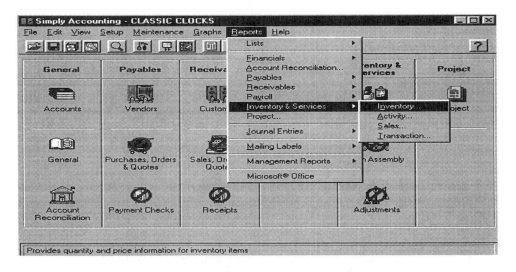

ACTION: On the Inventory Report Options screen, make sure **Select from Inventory by Asset** and **Report on Item Synopsis** are selected, then click the **Select All** and **OK** buttons.

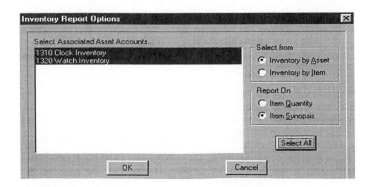

ACTION: Choose **Print** from the Inventory Synopsis File menu. Compare your report to the one shown below:

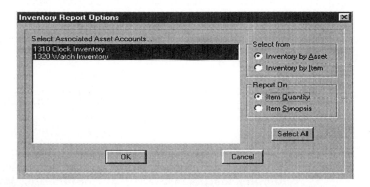

Inventory Synopsis

File Help

12/1/1997

			Price	Quantity	Cost	Value	Margin (%)
C100	Floor Clock	Each	1,190.00	10	595.0	5,950.00	50.00
C200	Chime Clock	Each	300.00	35	150.0	5,250.00	50.00
C300	Cuckoo Clock	Each	350.00	15	175.0	2,625.00	50.00
C400	Mantle Clock	Each	390.00	20	195.0	3,900.00	50.00
C500	School House Clock	Each	78.00	60	39.0	2,340.00	50.00
W100	Silver Watch	Each	118.00	12	59.0	708.00	50.00
W200	Gold Watch	Each	330.00	31	165.0	5,115.00	50.00
W300	Brass Watch	Each	98.00	25	49.0	1,225.00	50.00
W400	Bronze Watch	Each	130.00	40	65.0	2,600.00	50.00
W500	Plastic Watch	Each	40.00	100	20.0	2,000.00	50.00
						31,713.00	

If you made an error entering an inventory item record, see the special box titled Editing Tips for Editing an Inventory Ledger Record in the Not Ready Mode presented earlier in this chapter.

 ACTION: Close the Inventory Synopsis window; on the Inventory Report Options screen, click the **Select from Inventory by Assets** and **Report on Item Quantity** options to select; then click **Select All** and **OK** buttons. Your screen will look like this:

Inventory Report Options

Select Associated Asset Accounts...

1310 Clock Inventory
1320 Watch Inventory

Select from
- ⦿ Inventory by Asset
- ○ Inventory by Item

Report On
- ⦿ Item Quantity
- ○ Item Synopsis

Select All

OK   Cancel

 ACTION: Choose **Print** from the Inventory Quantity File menu. Compare your report to the one shown below:

Inventory Quantity

File Help

12/1/1997

			Quantity	Minimum	On Pur Order	On Sal Order	To Order
C100	Floor Clock	Each	10	2	0	0	-
C200	Chime Clock	Each	35	15	0	0	-
C300	Cuckoo Clock	Each	15	5	0	0	-
C400	Mantle Clock	Each	20	5	0	0	-
C500	School House Clock	Each	60	10	0	0	-
W100	Silver Watch	Each	12	4	0	0	-
W200	Gold Watch	Each	31	5	0	0	-
W300	Brass Watch	Each	25	10	0	0	-
W400	Bronze Watch	Each	40	10	0	0	-
W500	Plastic Watch	Each	100	25	0	0	-

If you made an error entering an inventory item record, see the special box titled Editing Tips for Editing an Inventory Ledger Record in the Not Ready Mode presented earlier in this chapter.

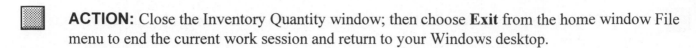

ACTION: Close the Inventory Quantity window; then choose **Exit** from the home window File menu to end the current work session and return to your Windows desktop.

ALTERNATIVE ACTION: You can continue with the tutorial without exiting from the program if you wish. Close the Inventory Quantity window; skip the portion of the next ACTION that discusses opening the program and continue with the tutorial.

PAYROLL LEDGER

Maria Lindsay has assembled the historical payroll information for each of Classic Clocks' employees. Before the Payroll Ledger can be made ready, each employee must be inserted into the program. When a business decides to make the Payroll Ledger ready at any time other than at the beginning of a calendar year, two additional steps are required: (1) enter the employee's quarter-to-date (QTD) information, and (2) enter the employee's year-to-date (YTD) information. If a business decides to make the Payroll Ledger ready at the beginning of a calendar year, these two steps can be omitted because no QTD or YTD payroll information will have yet accumulated for the employees.

Classic Clocks is converting to the CA-Simply Accounting for Windows program as of December 1; each employee's QTD and YTD information will be entered. In the Not Ready mode, the ledgers are not integrated/linked and no journal entries can be recorded. The objective of entering QTD and YTD information is to ensure that the balances in the employee records agree with the payroll accounts in the General Ledger and that the correct QTD and YTD information is reported in the various payroll reports. The total of all payroll information must be equal to the payroll account balances in the General Ledger before the Payroll Ledger can be changed to ready status.

Classic Clocks—Document 12   **Session Date: 12/1/1997**

Memo   **Date:** December 1, 1997

Employee Information
Simmons, Martha
220 NW 2nd Street
Coeur D'Alene, Idaho 83814
Phone: 208-667-3333
SSN: 541 87 7865
Birthdate: 11/13/50
Hire Date: 8/1/96
Pay Periods: 12
Salary: $1,725.00
Tax Table: Idaho
Federal Allowances: 2, Married
State Allowances: 2, Married

QTD Information
Simmons, Martha
Salary: 3,450.00
Medical: 44.00
FIT deduction: 252.50
SIT deduction: 121.26
MedTax deduction: 50.02
SSTax deduction: 213.90
MedTax expense: 50.02
SSTax expense: 213.90
SUTA expense: 107.63

YTD Information
Simmons, Martha
Salary: 18,975.00
Medical: 242.00
FIT deduction: 1,388.75
SIT deduction: 666.93
MedTax deduction: 275.11
SSTax deduction: 1,176.45
MedTax expense: 275.11
SSTax expense: 1,176.45
SUTA expense: 651.05
FUTA expense: 56.00

Welsh, Howard
230 NW Way
Coeur D'Alene, Idaho 83814
Phone: 208-667-5244
SSN: 541 98 6652
Birthdate: 1/25/55
Hire Date: 6/15/96
Pay Periods: 12

Welsh, Howard
Regular: 2,472.00
Medical: 0.00
FIT deduction: 252.06
SIT deduction: 125.06
MedTax deduction: 35.84
SSTax deduction: 153.26
MedTax expense: 35.84

Welsh, Howard
Regular: 13,656.00
Medical: 0.00
FIT deduction: 1,395.33
SIT deduction: 692.55
MedTax deduction: 198.02
SSTax deduction: 846.68
MedTax expense: 198.02

Welsh, Howard Continued
Regular: $8.00
Overtime: $12.00
Tax Table: Idaho
Federal Allowances: 1, Single
State Allowances: 1, Single

Welsh, Howard QTD Continued
SSTax expense: 153.26
SUTA expense: 86.52

Welsh, Howard YTD Continued
SSTax expense: 846.68
SUTA expense: 477.96
FUTA expense: 56.00

Creating Employee Records and Entering Historical Data

ACTION: Load CA-Simply Accounting for Windows; open the data files for Classic Clocks (A:\CLOCK\Classic Clocks.asc); then leave the session date set at 12/1/1997. In the home window, double click the **Employees** icon. Your screen will look like this:

ACTION: On the Payroll Ledger Personal tab, enter the information for employee Martha Simmons (see Document 12). Your screen should agree with the one shown below:

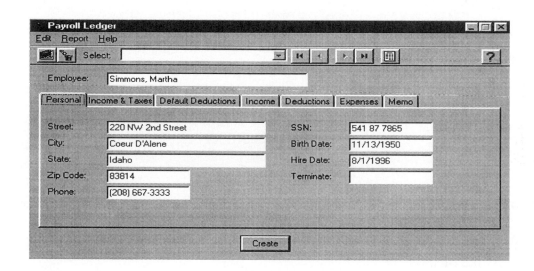

Explanation: Use the following editing techniques to correct errors:

Editing Tips:
Editing a Payroll Ledger Record, QTD, and YTD Information in the Not Ready Mode

While working with the Payroll Ledger in the Not Ready mode, many of the restrictions that were in place in the Ready mode do not apply. You can create, modify, or remove employee records as needed while working in the Not Ready mode.

If the employee record you wish to edit does not currently appear in the Payroll Ledger dialog box, choose **Find** from the Payroll Ledger Edit menu; then select the employee from the employee list display. Modify the employee record as necessary or choose **Remove** from the Payroll Ledger Edit menu. If you remove an employee record, all QTD and YTD information for that employee will also be removed.

To edit QTD or YTD information and retain employee address information, click the **Income**, **Deductions**, or **Expenses** tab for the individual employee and make corrections as required.

ACTION: Using the information for Martha Simmons in Document 12, fill in the information required on the Income & Taxes tab. Your screen will look like this:

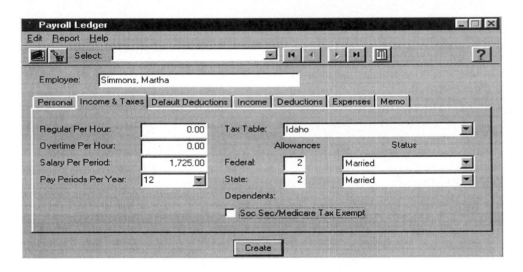

Explanation: This screen is used to provide the information regarding pay rate and tax withholding.

ACTION: There is nothing to complete for Martha on the Default Deductions tab. Your screen will look like this:

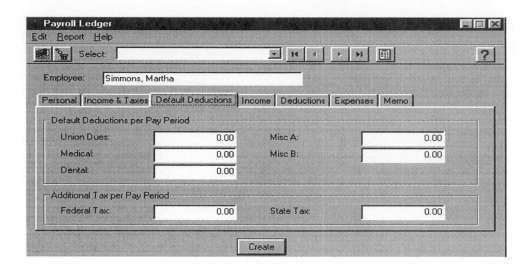

Explanation: If an optional deduction is withheld from an employee's check each pay period, recording the amount on this screen will allow Simply to make the deduction automatically when payroll is processed.

ACTION: Complete the QTD and YTD information required for Martha's income and benefits on the Income tab. Your screen will look like this:

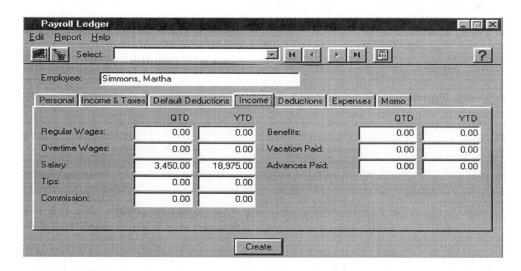

Explanation: Information on this screen is provided for earnings and benefits for the quarter to date and the year to date.

ACTION: Complete the QTD and YTD amounts for deductions withheld from Martha's paycheck. Your screen will look like the one below:

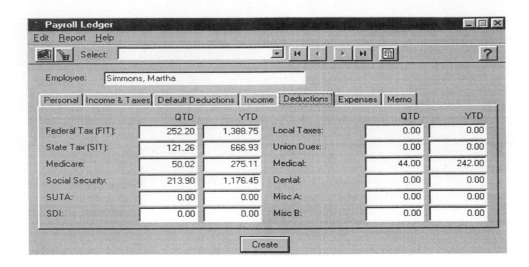

Explanation: This screen is used to complete the quarter-to-date and year-to-date figures for withholdings and deductions made to an employee's paycheck.

ACTION: Record the amount of payroll expenses incurred for Martha Simmons on the Expenses screen. Your screen will look like the following:

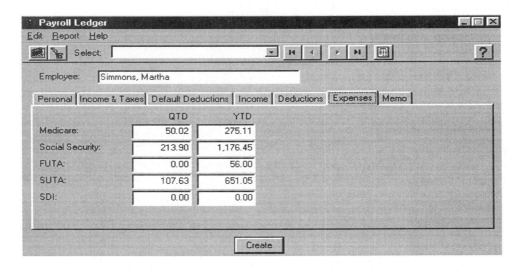

Explanation: The quarter-to-date and year-to-date amounts for payroll expenses for an employee are provided on the Expense tab.

ACTION: No entry is required for Martha on the Memo tab. Check the information entered on all of the tabs for this employee. Correct any errors. When all information provided is correct, click **Create**. Enter the information for Classic Clocks' other employee (see Document 12). Once the information has been entered for Howard Welsh, close the Payroll Ledger screen. Choose **Display Employee List** from the Employee Report menu. Your screen will look like this:

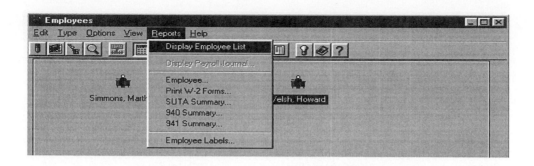

ACTION: Choose **Print** from the Employee List File menu. Compare your report to the one shown below:

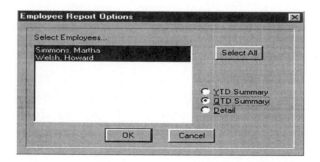

If you made an error entering an employee record, see the special box titled Editing Tips for Editing a Payroll Ledger Record, QTD, and YTD Information in the Not Ready Mode presented earlier in this chapter.

ACTION: Choose **Employee** from the Employee window **Report** menu; click the **QTD Summary** option button; then click the **Select All** and **OK** buttons. Your screen will look like this:

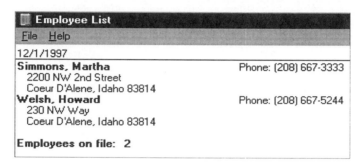

ACTION: Choose **Print** from the Employee Quarter-to-Date Summary File menu. Compare your report to the following:

```
▓ Employee Quarter-to-Date Summary
File  Help
```

12/1/1997
Simmons, Martha

Personal:	**Earnings:**	**Deductions:**
SSN _ _ _ _ _ _ _ _ _ _ _ _ 541 87 7865	Regular _ _ _ _ _ _ _ _ _ _ _ _ _ _ 0.00	FIT _ _ _ _ _ _ _ _ _ _ _ _ _ _ _ _ _ .252.50
Birthdate _ _ _ _ _ _ _ _ _ _ .11/13/1950	Overtime _ _ _ _ _ _ _ _ _ _ _ _ _ _ 0.00	SIT _ _ _ _ _ _ _ _ _ _ _ _ _ _ _ _ .121.26
Hire Date _ _ _ _ _ _ _ _ _ _ _ 8/1/1996	Salary _ _ _ _ _ _ _ _ _ _ _ _ _ _ _ 3,450.00	Medicare Tax _ _ _ _ _ _ _ _ _ _ _ .50.02
Terminate Date _ _ _ _ _ _ _ _ _ _ _ _ _	Tips _ _ _ _ _ _ _ _ _ _ _ _ _ _ _ _ 0.00	Soc Sec Tax _ _ _ _ _ _ _ _ _ _ _ .213.90
Pay Periods _ _ _ _ _ _ _ _ _ _ _ _ .12/yr	Commission _ _ _ _ _ _ _ _ _ _ _ _ 0.00	SUTA _ _ _ _ _ _ _ _ _ _ _ _ _ _ _ _ 0.00
Regular _ _ _ _ _ _ _ _ _ _ _ _ _ .0.00/hr	Benefits _ _ _ _ _ _ _ _ _ _ _ _ _ _ 0.00	SDI _ _ _ _ _ _ _ _ _ _ _ _ _ _ _ _ _ 0.00
Overtime _ _ _ _ _ _ _ _ _ _ _ _ .0.00/hr	Vacation Paid _ _ _ _ _ _ _ _ _ _ _ _ 0.00	Local Taxes _ _ _ _ _ _ _ _ _ _ _ _ 0.00
Salary _ _ _ _ _ _ _ _ _ _ _ 1,725.00/prd	Gross _ _ _ _ _ _ _ _ _ _ _ _ _ _ _ 3,450.00	Union Dues _ _ _ _ _ _ _ _ _ _ _ _ 0.00
SS/Med Tax Exempt _ _ _ _ _ _ _ _ _ No		Medical _ _ _ _ _ _ _ _ _ _ _ _ _ _ .44.00
	Employer's Expense:	Dental _ _ _ _ _ _ _ _ _ _ _ _ _ _ _ 0.00
Tax Table _ _ _ _ _ _ _ _ _ _ _ _ _ .Idaho	Medicare Tax _ _ _ _ _ _ _ _ _ _ _ .50.02	Misc A _ _ _ _ _ _ _ _ _ _ _ _ _ _ _ 0.00
Additional FIT _ _ _ _ _ _ _ _ _ _ 0.00/prd	Soc Sec Tax _ _ _ _ _ _ _ _ _ _ _ 213.90	Misc B _ _ _ _ _ _ _ _ _ _ _ _ _ _ _ 0.00
Federal Allowances _ _ _ _ _ _ _ _ _ _ 2	FUTA _ _ _ _ _ _ _ _ _ _ _ _ _ _ _ _ 0.00	Withheld _ _ _ _ _ _ _ _ _ _ _ _ _ .681.68
Federal Status _ _ _ _ _ _ _ _ _ _ .Married	SUTA _ _ _ _ _ _ _ _ _ _ _ _ _ _ _ 107.63	
Additional SIT _ _ _ _ _ _ _ _ _ 0.00/prd	SDI _ _ _ _ _ _ _ _ _ _ _ _ _ _ _ _ _ 0.00	Advance Paid _ _ _ _ _ _ _ _ _ _ _ 0.00
Dependents _ _ _ _ _ _ _ _ _ _ _ _ _ 0	Expense _ _ _ _ _ _ _ _ _ _ _ _ 371.55	
State Allowances _ _ _ _ _ _ _ _ _ _ .2, 0		Net Pay _ _ _ _ _ _ _ _ _ _ _ _ _ .2,768.32
State Status _ _ _ _ .Married		

Welsh, Howard

Personal:	**Earnings:**	**Deductions:**
SSN _ _ _ _ _ _ _ _ _ _ _ _ 541 98 6652	Regular _ _ _ _ _ _ _ _ _ _ _ _ _ .2,472.00	FIT _ _ _ _ _ _ _ _ _ _ _ _ _ _ _ _ _ .252.06
Birthdate _ _ _ _ _ _ _ _ _ _ _ 1/25/1955	Overtime _ _ _ _ _ _ _ _ _ _ _ _ _ _ 0.00	SIT _ _ _ _ _ _ _ _ _ _ _ _ _ _ _ _ .125.06
Hire Date _ _ _ _ _ _ _ _ _ _ 6/15/1996	Salary _ _ _ _ _ _ _ _ _ _ _ _ _ _ _ 0.00	Medicare Tax _ _ _ _ _ _ _ _ _ _ _ .35.84
Terminate Date _ _ _ _ _ _ _ _ _ _ _ _ _	Tips _ _ _ _ _ _ _ _ _ _ _ _ _ _ _ _ 0.00	Soc Sec Tax _ _ _ _ _ _ _ _ _ _ _ .153.26
Pay Periods _ _ _ _ _ _ _ _ _ _ _ _ .12/yr	Commission _ _ _ _ _ _ _ _ _ _ _ _ 0.00	SUTA _ _ _ _ _ _ _ _ _ _ _ _ _ _ _ _ 0.00
Regular _ _ _ _ _ _ _ _ _ _ _ _ _ .8.00/hr	Benefits _ _ _ _ _ _ _ _ _ _ _ _ _ _ 0.00	SDI _ _ _ _ _ _ _ _ _ _ _ _ _ _ _ _ _ 0.00
Overtime _ _ _ _ _ _ _ _ _ _ _ _ .12.00/hr	Vacation Paid _ _ _ _ _ _ _ _ _ _ _ _ 0.00	Local Taxes _ _ _ _ _ _ _ _ _ _ _ _ 0.00
Salary _ _ _ _ _ _ _ _ _ _ _ _ _ 0.00/prd	Gross _ _ _ _ _ _ _ _ _ _ _ _ _ _ _ 2,472.00	Union Dues _ _ _ _ _ _ _ _ _ _ _ _ 0.00
SS/Med Tax Exempt _ _ _ _ _ _ _ _ _ No		Medical _ _ _ _ _ _ _ _ _ _ _ _ _ _ _ 0.00
	Employer's Expense:	Dental _ _ _ _ _ _ _ _ _ _ _ _ _ _ _ 0.00
Tax Table _ _ _ _ _ _ _ _ _ _ _ _ _ .Idaho	Medicare Tax _ _ _ _ _ _ _ _ _ _ _ .35.84	Misc A _ _ _ _ _ _ _ _ _ _ _ _ _ _ _ 0.00
Additional FIT _ _ _ _ _ _ _ _ _ _ 0.00/prd	Soc Sec Tax _ _ _ _ _ _ _ _ _ _ _ 153.26	Misc B _ _ _ _ _ _ _ _ _ _ _ _ _ _ _ 0.00
Federal Allowances _ _ _ _ _ _ _ _ _ _ 1	FUTA _ _ _ _ _ _ _ _ _ _ _ _ _ _ _ _ 0.00	Withheld _ _ _ _ _ _ _ _ _ _ _ _ _ .566.22
Federal Status _ _ _ _ _ _ _ _ _ _ _ Single	SUTA _ _ _ _ _ _ _ _ _ _ _ _ _ _ _ .86.52	
Additional SIT _ _ _ _ _ _ _ _ _ 0.00/prd	SDI _ _ _ _ _ _ _ _ _ _ _ _ _ _ _ _ _ 0.00	Advance Paid _ _ _ _ _ _ _ _ _ _ _ 0.00
Dependents _ _ _ _ _ _ _ _ _ _ _ _ _ 0	Expense _ _ _ _ _ _ _ _ _ _ _ _ 275.62	
State Allowances _ _ _ _ _ _ _ _ _ _ .1, 0		Net Pay _ _ _ _ _ _ _ _ _ _ _ _ _ .1,905.78
State Status _ _ _ _ .Single		

If you made an error entering an employee record, see the special box titled Editing Tips for Editing a Payroll Ledger Record, QTD, and YTD Information in the Not Ready Mode presented earlier in this chapter.

▓ **ACTION:** Close the Employee Quarter-to-Date Summary window; choose **Employee** from the Employee window Report menu; click the **YTD Summary** option button; then click the **Select All** and **OK** buttons.

▓ **ACTION:** Choose **Print** from the Employee Year-to-Date Summary File menu. Compare your report to the one shown below:

Employee Year-to-Date Summary

File   Help

12/1/1997

Simmons, Martha

Personal:
SSN _ _ _ _ _ _ _ _ _ _ _ _ 541 87 7865
Birthdate _ _ _ _ _ _ _ _ _ 11/13/1950
Hire Date _ _ _ _ _ _ _ _ _ 8/1/1996
Terminate Date _ _ _ _ _ _ _ _ _ _ _
Pay Periods _ _ _ _ _ _ _ _ _ _ _ 12/yr
Regular _ _ _ _ _ _ _ _ _ _ _ .0.00/hr
Overtime _ _ _ _ _ _ _ _ _ _ _ .0.00/hr
Salary _ _ _ _ _ _ _ _ _ _ 1,725.00/prd
SS/Med Tax Exempt _ _ _ _ _ _ _ _ No

Tax Table _ _ _ _ _ _ _ _ _ _ _ _ _ Idaho
Additional FIT _ _ _ _ _ _ _ _ 0.00/prd
Federal Allowances _ _ _ _ _ _ _ _ _ 2
Federal Status _ _ _ _ _ _ _ _ _ Married
Additional SIT _ _ _ _ _ _ _ _ 0.00/prd
Dependents _ _ _ _ _ _ _ _ _ _ _ _ _ 0
State Allowances _ _ _ _ _ _ _ _ _ 2, 0
State Status _ _ _ _ _ Married

Earnings:
Regular _ _ _ _ _ _ _ _ _ _ _ _ _ _ 0.00
Overtime _ _ _ _ _ _ _ _ _ _ _ _ _ 0.00
Salary _ _ _ _ _ _ _ _ _ _ _ 18,975.00
Tips _ _ _ _ _ _ _ _ _ _ _ _ _ _ _ 0.00
Commission _ _ _ _ _ _ _ _ _ _ _ 0.00
Benefits _ _ _ _ _ _ _ _ _ _ _ _ 0.00
Vacation Paid _ _ _ _ _ _ _ _ _ 0.00
Gross _ _ _ _ _ _ _ _ _ _ _ 18,975.00

Employer's Expense:
Medicare Tax _ _ _ _ _ _ _ _ _ 275.11
Soc Sec Tax _ _ _ _ _ _ _ _ 1,176.45
FUTA _ _ _ _ _ _ _ _ _ _ _ _ _ 56.00
SUTA _ _ _ _ _ _ _ _ _ _ _ _ 651.05
SDI _ _ _ _ _ _ _ _ _ _ _ _ _ _ 0.00
Expense _ _ _ _ _ _ _ _ _ _ 2,158.61

Deductions:
FIT _ _ _ _ _ _ _ _ _ _ _ _ _ 1,388.75
SIT _ _ _ _ _ _ _ _ _ _ _ _ _ 666.93
Medicare Tax _ _ _ _ _ _ _ _ 275.11
Soc Sec Tax _ _ _ _ _ _ _ 1,176.45
SUTA _ _ _ _ _ _ _ _ _ _ _ _ 0.00
SDI _ _ _ _ _ _ _ _ _ _ _ _ _ 0.00
Local Taxes _ _ _ _ _ _ _ _ _ 0.00
Union Dues _ _ _ _ _ _ _ _ _ 0.00
Medical _ _ _ _ _ _ _ _ _ _ _ 242.00
Dental _ _ _ _ _ _ _ _ _ _ _ _ 0.00
Misc A _ _ _ _ _ _ _ _ _ _ _ _ 0.00
Misc B _ _ _ _ _ _ _ _ _ _ _ _ 0.00
Withheld _ _ _ _ _ _ _ _ _ _ 3,749.24

Advance Paid _ _ _ _ _ _ _ _ _ 0.00

Net Pay _ _ _ _ _ _ _ _ _ _ 15,225.76

Welsh, Howard

Personal:
SSN _ _ _ _ _ _ _ _ _ _ _ _ 541 98 6652
Birthdate _ _ _ _ _ _ _ _ _ _ 1/25/1955
Hire Date _ _ _ _ _ _ _ _ _ 6/15/1996
Terminate Date _ _ _ _ _ _ _ _ _ _ _
Pay Periods _ _ _ _ _ _ _ _ _ _ _ 12/yr
Regular _ _ _ _ _ _ _ _ _ _ _ .8.00/hr
Overtime _ _ _ _ _ _ _ _ _ _ _ 12.00/hr
Salary _ _ _ _ _ _ _ _ _ _ _ 0.00/prd
SS/Med Tax Exempt _ _ _ _ _ _ _ _ No

Tax Table _ _ _ _ _ _ _ _ _ _ _ _ _ Idaho
Additional FIT _ _ _ _ _ _ _ _ 0.00/prd
Federal Allowances _ _ _ _ _ _ _ _ _ 1
Federal Status _ _ _ _ _ _ _ _ _ Single
Additional SIT _ _ _ _ _ _ _ _ 0.00/prd
Dependents _ _ _ _ _ _ _ _ _ _ _ _ _ 0
State Allowances _ _ _ _ _ _ _ _ _ 1, 0
State Status _ _ _ _ _ Single

Earnings:
Regular _ _ _ _ _ _ _ _ _ _ 13,626.00
Overtime _ _ _ _ _ _ _ _ _ _ _ _ 0.00
Salary _ _ _ _ _ _ _ _ _ _ _ _ _ 0.00
Tips _ _ _ _ _ _ _ _ _ _ _ _ _ _ _ 0.00
Commission _ _ _ _ _ _ _ _ _ _ _ 0.00
Benefits _ _ _ _ _ _ _ _ _ _ _ _ 0.00
Vacation Paid _ _ _ _ _ _ _ _ _ 0.00
Gross _ _ _ _ _ _ _ _ _ _ _ 13,626.00

Employer's Expense:
Medicare Tax _ _ _ _ _ _ _ _ _ 198.02
Soc Sec Tax _ _ _ _ _ _ _ _ _ 846.68
FUTA _ _ _ _ _ _ _ _ _ _ _ _ _ 56.00
SUTA _ _ _ _ _ _ _ _ _ _ _ _ 477.96
SDI _ _ _ _ _ _ _ _ _ _ _ _ _ _ 0.00
Expense _ _ _ _ _ _ _ _ _ _ 1,578.66

Deductions:
FIT _ _ _ _ _ _ _ _ _ _ _ _ _ 1,395.33
SIT _ _ _ _ _ _ _ _ _ _ _ _ _ 692.55
Medicare Tax _ _ _ _ _ _ _ _ 198.02
Soc Sec Tax _ _ _ _ _ _ _ _ 846.68
SUTA _ _ _ _ _ _ _ _ _ _ _ _ 0.00
SDI _ _ _ _ _ _ _ _ _ _ _ _ _ 0.00
Local Taxes _ _ _ _ _ _ _ _ _ 0.00
Union Dues _ _ _ _ _ _ _ _ _ 0.00
Medical _ _ _ _ _ _ _ _ _ _ _ 0.00
Dental _ _ _ _ _ _ _ _ _ _ _ _ 0.00
Misc A _ _ _ _ _ _ _ _ _ _ _ _ 0.00
Misc B _ _ _ _ _ _ _ _ _ _ _ _ 0.00
Withheld _ _ _ _ _ _ _ _ _ _ 3,132.58

Advance Paid _ _ _ _ _ _ _ _ _ 0.00

Net Pay _ _ _ _ _ _ _ _ _ _ 10,493.42

If you made an error entering an employee record, see the special shaded box titled Editing Tips for Editing a Payroll Ledger Record, QTD, and YTD Information in the Not Ready Mode presented earlier in this chapter.

PROJECT LEDGER

New projects can be created in either the Not Ready or Ready mode in the CA-Simply Accounting for Windows program. Classic Clocks would like to establish two projects as listed in the following memo:

Classic Clocks—Document 13   **Session Date: 12/1/1997**

Memo   **Date:** December 1, 1997

Project Information
Name: Clock Sales Summary   Name: Watch Sales Summary
Start date: 12/1/1997   Start date: 12/1/1997

Creating Project Records

ACTION: Close the Employee Year-to-Date Summary window; then double-click the **Project** icon on the home window. Your screen will look like this:

ACTION: Enter the information for the Clock Sales Summary project (see Document 13). Your screen should agree with the one shown below:

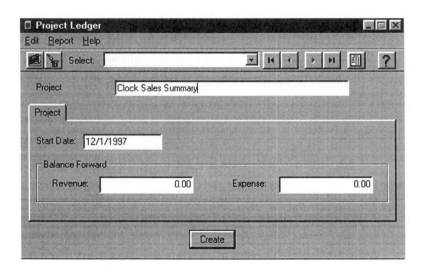

Explanation: Use the following editing techniques to correct errors:

> **Editing Tips:**
> **Editing a Project Record**
>
> The Project Ledger serves only a reporting role in the CA-Simply Accounting for Windows program. It does not have its own journal; allocation information is stored with journal entries in the originating journal. Consequently, its status does not need to be changed from not ready to ready prior to use. You can create, modify, or remove project records at any time.
>
> If the Project Ledger record you wish to edit does not currently appear in the Project Ledger dialog box, choose **Find** from the Project Ledger Edit menu; then select the project from the Project list display. Modify the Project Ledger record as necessary or choose **Remove** from the Project Ledger Edit menu.

ACTION: Click the **Create** button; enter the information for Classic Clocks' other project (see Document 13); then select **Display Project List** from the Project window Report menu. Your screen will look like this:

ACTION: Choose **Print** from the Project List File menu. Compare your report to the one shown below:

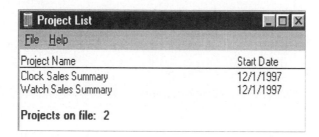

If you made an error entering a project record, see the special box titled Editing Tips for Editing a Project Ledger Record.

ACTION: Close the Project List window and the Project window. Make a backup copy of Classic Clocks' data files. Click the **Exit** button on the home window to end the current work session and return to your Windows desktop.

MAKING THE LEDGERS READY

You have now entered Classic Clocks' historical financial information into each subsidiary ledger. The settings and linking accounts for each ledger have been established, and the General Ledger is in the Ready mode. The next step in the conversion process involves making the subsidiary ledgers ready.

ACTION: Load CA-Simply Accounting for Windows; open the data files for Classic Clocks (A:\CLOCK\Classic Clocks.asc); then leave the session date set at 12/1/1997. The home window for Classic Clocks will appear as shown below:

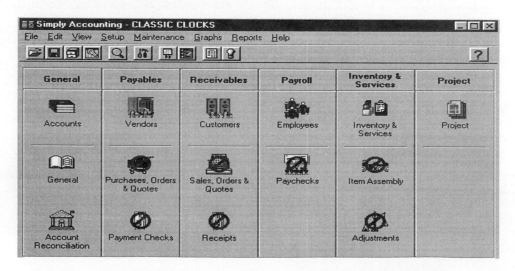

ACTION: Click the **Setup** menu on the home window; point to Set Ready; click **Receivables**. Your screen will look like this:

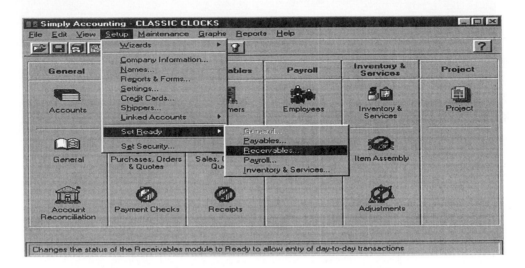

Explanation: Once a ledger has been set ready, you cannot return its status to not ready; consequently, it is extremely important that you make a backup copy of a company's data files prior to changing the status of any ledger from not ready to ready.

ACTION: Click the **Proceed** button as displayed in the following graphic. If you receive an error message, read the message carefully for information regarding corrective action. Make corrections as required; then repeat this ACTION. After you have set Receivables to ready, your screen will look like the second graphic.

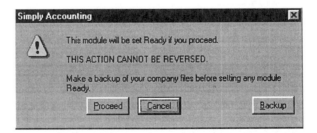

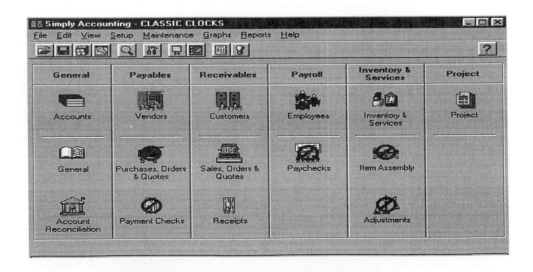

Explanation: The Receivables icons for Sales, Orders & Quotes and Receipts are presented in the unlocked position, indicating that the Receivables Ledger is ready and that sales and receipts entries can be recorded.

ACTION: Repeat the preceding two ACTIONS for the Payables, Payroll and Inventory & Services. When all items have been unlocked, your screen will look like this:

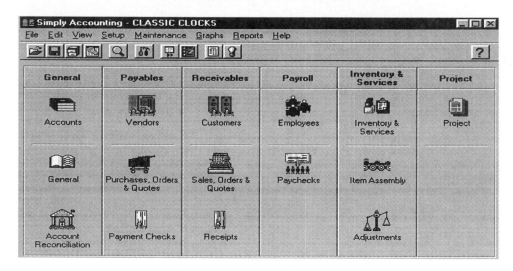

Explanation: When all of the ledgers are ready, all of the corresponding journals will be unlocked and ready to accept journal entries.

ACTION: Choose **Advance Session Date** from the home window Maintenance menu. Advance the session date to 12/31/1997. Click the **OK** button for the message, "The date entered is more than one week past your previous session date of 12/01/1997." Your screens will look like this:

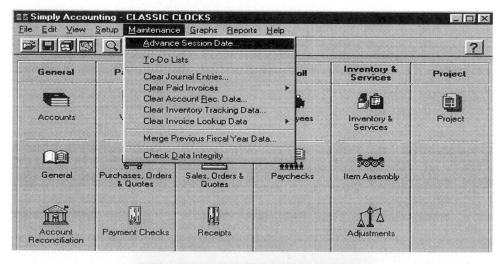

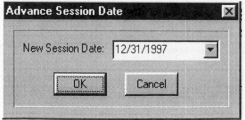

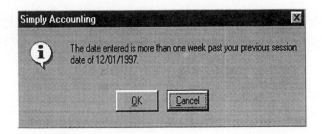

ADDITIONAL TRANSACTIONS AND REPORTS

A. Enter the following transactions under the session date of 12/31/1997:

Document 14 December 28—Sold 1 gold watch (Item W200) to Heras, Elaine (Project: Watch Sales Summary). Print Invoice 5882. Note that the program automatically calculated the 8% sales tax on this invoice.

Document 15 December 29—Received Check 765 from Sailing, Jeremy in the amount of $1,476.67 in full payment of Invoice 5853. (Use Deposit Slip 2240 to deposit the check.)

Document 16 December 30—Received Invoice C1011 from Clock Wholesalers in the amount of $1,190.00 for the purchase of 2 floor clocks (C100). (When an item is for resale, it is not taxed until the final sale. If an SST—state sales tax—amount appears, click in the **S** column and remove the 8.00. This will remove the sales tax.)

Document 17 December 30—Issue Check 2840 to True Time Clocks in full payment of Invoice 7226.

Document 18 December 31—Issue a payroll check to Martha Simmons for her regular salary, deducting $22.00 for medical insurance. Print Check 2841. (Project: none)

B. Print the following reports:

Journal (By posting date, project allocations, All entries) 12/1/1997 to 12/31/1997
Trial Balance As at 12/31/1997

C. Compare your reports to the ones shown below:

All Journal Entries Display

File Help

12/1/1997 to 12/31/1997			Debits	Credits	Project
12/1/1997	J1	Memo, Capital Contribution by Owner			
		1010 Cash	1,000.00	·	
		3560 Maria Lindsay, Capital	·	1,000.00	
12/1/1997	J2	Memo, To Increase Petty Cash Fund			
		1050 Petty Cash	50.00	·	
		1010 Cash	·	50.00	
12/28/1997	J3	5882, Heras, Elaine			
		1200 Accounts Receivable	356.40	·	
		5020 Cost of Goods Sold: Watches	165.00	·	
		- Watch Sales Summary			165.00
		1320 Watch Inventory	·	165.00	
		2500 Sales Tax Payable	·	26.40	
		4020 Watch Sales	·	330.00	
		- Watch Sales Summary			330.00
12/29/1997	J4	765, Sailing, Jeremy			
		1010 Cash	1,476.67	·	
		1200 Accounts Receivable	·	1,476.67	
12/30/1997	J5	C1011, Clock Wholesalers			
		1310 Clock Inventory	1,190.00	·	
		2200 Accounts Payable	·	1,190.00	
12/30/1997	J6	2840, True Time Clocks			
		2200 Accounts Payable	1,740.24	·	
		1010 Cash	·	1,740.24	
12/31/1997	J7	2841, Simmons, Martha			
		5300 Wages	1,725.00	·	
		5310 Social Security Tax Expense	106.95	·	
		5320 Medicare Tax Expense	25.01	·	
		5340 SUTA Expense	60.38	·	
		1010 Cash	·	1,411.03	
		2310 FIT Payable	·	111.88	
		2320 SIT Payable	·	48.13	
		2330 Social Security Tax Payable	·	213.90	
		2335 Medicare Tax Payable	·	50.02	
		2350 SUTA Payable	·	60.38	
		2400 Medical Insurance Payable	·	22.00	
			7,895.65	7,895.65	

Trial Balance

File   Help

As At 12/31/1997	Debits	Credits
1010 Cash	7,700.03	-
1050 Petty Cash	150.00	-
1200 Accounts Receivable	7,027.00	-
1310 Clock Inventory	21,255.00	-
1320 Watch Inventory	11,483.00	-
1410 Office Supplies	311.15	-
1420 Prepaid Insurance	200.00	-
1550 Office Equipment	4,700.00	-
1551 Accum. Dep.: Office Equip.	-	2,683.18
1650 Store Equipment	4,000.00	-
1651 Accum. Dep.: Store Equip.	-	1,341.59
2200 Accounts Payable	-	3,812.26
2310 FIT Payable	-	367.16
2320 SIT Payable	-	172.85
2330 Social Security Tax Payable	-	583.54
2335 Medicare Tax Payable	-	136.46
2340 FUTA Payable	-	6.15
2350 SUTA Payable	-	254.53
2400 Medical Insurance Payable	-	66.00
2500 Sales Tax Payable	-	1,197.30
3560 Maria Lindsay, Capital	-	43,268.02
3580 Maria Lindsay, Drawing	24,200.00	-
4010 Clock Sales	-	105,763.24
4020 Watch Sales	-	56,864.26
4200 Sales Returns & Allowances	188.63	-
4300 Sales Discounts	201.15	-
4410 Interest Income	-	0.00
5010 Costs of Goods Sold: Clocks	52,881.62	-
5020 Cost of Goods Sold: Watches	28,432.13	-
5300 Wages	34,356.00	-
5310 Social Security Tax Expense	2,130.08	-
5320 Medicare Tax Expense	498.14	-
5330 FUTA Expense	112.00	-
5340 SUTA Expense	1,189.39	-
5410 Advertising Expense	2,435.00	-
5420 Utilities Expense	1,147.19	-
5430 Depreciation Exp.: Office Equipment	1,283.26	-
5440 Insurance Expense	1,100.00	-
5450 Rent Expense	6,600.00	-
5460 Office Supplies Expense	934.56	-
5470 Depreciation Exp.: Store Equipment	641.63	-
5480 Telephone Expense	762.43	-
5490 Bank Service Charge Expense	165.00	-
5495 Credit Card Fees	0.00	-
5500 Miscellaneous Expense	432.15	-
	216,516.54	216,516.54

REVIEW OF THE CONVERSION PROCESS

In the process of converting Classic Clocks' manual accounting system to a computerized accounting system using CA-Simply Accounting for Windows, you have performed a variety of tasks and procedures. The following is a summary of those tasks and procedures. The summary may be used as a blueprint for converting any manual accounting system to a computerized system using CA-Simply Accounting for Windows. The following summary assumes that the company wishes to use the General, Receivables, Payables, Inventory, Payroll, and Project Ledgers; that all the company's financial data is available for reference; and that the CA-Simply Accounting for Windows program has been installed.

Step 1: Create a new subdirectory on the data files disk for the new company.

Step 2: Load CA-Simply Accounting for Windows; then enter the path for the new company's data files.

Step 3: Enter the fiscal start, fiscal end, and earliest transaction dates for the new company.

Step 4: Enter the company information.

Step 5: Complete the company settings in Setup Wizard and Settings selection from the Setup Menu for Receivables, Payables, Payroll, Forms, Inventory & Services, Projects, and Comments.

Step 6: Exit from the program.

Step 7: Create a Chart of Accounts Worksheet with the following columns:

Acct. No.	**Account Name**	**Account Balance**	**Account Type**

Step 8: Using the Chart of Accounts Worksheet, create a chart of accounts for the company. Enter the accounts and account balances from the company's trial balance as of the earliest transaction date; then add accounts for group headings, group accounts, group totals, subgroup accounts, and subgroup totals as required.

Step 9: Load CA-Simply Accounting for Windows; open the data files for the company; then create the accounts and enter the account balances listed on your Chart of Accounts Worksheet.

Step 10: Print a Chart of Accounts, Trial Balance, Income Statement, and Balance Sheet. Verify that your data are correct.

Step 11: Create a Linking Accounts Worksheet with the following items:

General Linking Accounts
Bank account
Retained earnings

Payables Linking Accounts
Accounts payable
Freight expense (if applicable)

Receivables Linking Accounts
Accounts receivable
Sales tax payable
Freight revenue (if applicable)
Sales discounts

Inventory Linking Accounts
Transfer costs (if applicable)
Adjustment write-off (if applicable)

Payroll Linking Accounts
FIT (payable)
SIT (payable)
Medicare tax (payable)
SST (payable)
FUTA (payable)
SUTA (payable)

SDI (if applicable)
Local tax (if applicable)
Union deduction (if applicable)
Medical deduction (if applicable)
Dental deduction (if applicable)
Wages (expense)
Medicare tax (expense)
SST (expense)
FUTA (expense)
SUTA (expense)
SDI (expense; if applicable)

Step 12: Refer to your Chart of Accounts Worksheet; enter the linking accounts for the General, Payables, Receivables, Payroll, and Inventory Ledgers on your Linking Accounts Worksheet. Establish the linking accounts listed your Linking Accounts Worksheet.

Step 13: Make a backup copy of the company's data files.

Step 14: Make the General Ledger ready.

Step 15: Open Customers in the Receivables column; enter customer records; enter historical sales invoices and payments; then print a Customer List and a Customer Aged Detail report. Verify that the data are correct.

Step 16: Open Vendors in the Payables column; enter vendor records; enter historical purchase invoices and payments; then print a Vendor List and a Vendor Aged Detail report. Verify that the data are correct.

Step 17: Open Inventory & Services in the Inventory & Services column; enter inventory item records; then print an Inventory List, Inventory Synopsis, and Inventory Quantity report. Verify that the data are correct.

Step 18: Open Employees in the Payroll column; enter employee records; enter QTD and YTD payroll information; then print an Employee List, Employee Quarter-to-Date Summary and Employee Year-to-Date Summary report. Verify that the data are correct.

Step 19: Open the Project Ledger; enter project records; then print a Project List. Verify that the data are correct.

Step 20: Make a backup copy of the company's data files.

Step 21: Make each remaining ledger ready.

Step 22: Exit from the program.

OPERATIONAL RESTRICTIONS IN THE READY MODE

Several operational restrictions in the Ready mode have been discussed throughout this text. This section is intended to summarize those restrictions for a business using the General, Receivables, Payables, Inventory, Payroll, and Project Ledgers.

A. Once the ledgers are ready, the user may specify the date(s) to be associated with most operations. These dates generally must equal or range between the fiscal start date (or earliest transaction date, if it is later than the fiscal year's start) and the session date. Some reports are available only as of the session date. Session date–based reports include the Vendor Aged and Customer Aged reports, Customer Statements, Payroll reports, and Inventory reports.

B. You cannot delete a group account or a subgroup account unless the account has a zero balance and has not been used since the earliest transaction date. Account balances can be changed only through journal entries.

C. You cannot change the account number of a group account or a subgroup account unless the account has not been used since the earliest transaction date.

D. You cannot change a group account or a subgroup account to a group heading, group total, or a subgroup total. To make this change, delete the account; then re-enter the account number and name and specify the correct account type.

E. In the Payables Ledger, you cannot delete a vendor record unless there are no outstanding invoices. Vendor account balances can be changed only through journal entries.

F. In the Receivables Ledger, you cannot delete a customer record unless there are no outstanding invoices. Customer account balances can be changed only through journal entries.

G. In the Inventory Ledger you cannot delete an inventory item record unless there is no stock on hand. Inventory account balances can be changed only through journal entries or through Inventory & Services Adjustments.

H. In the Payroll Ledger, you cannot delete an employee who has outstanding advances. Payroll account balances can be changed only through journal entries. In addition, payroll journal entries are always stored with the session date regardless of the pay period ending date.

AUDIT TRAIL

The CA-Simply Accounting for Windows program is designed to produce a good audit trail of all accounting transactions provided that certain procedures are followed for printing reports at specified intervals. Important times for printing reports have been discussed throughout the text. The following chart summarizes these procedures.

Report	Month-End	Calendar Quarter-End	Calendar Year-End	Fiscal Year-End
Income Statement				
Month-to-date	x			x
Year-to-date	x			x
Balance Sheet	x			x
General Ledger (past month)	x			
	x			
General Journal (past month)	x			x
Accounts Payable				
Purchases Journal (past month)	x			x
Payments Journal (past month)	x			x
Vendor Aged (summary and detail)	x			x
Accounts Receivable				
Sales Journal (past month)	x			x
Receipts Journal (past month)	x			x
Customer Aged (summary and detail)	x			x
Payroll Journal (past month)	x		x	x

Payroll Reports				
Employee QTD Summary		x	x	
Employee YTD Summary		x	x	
W-2 Slips			x	
SUTA Summary		x	x	
940 Summary		x	x	
941 Summary		x	x	
Payroll Register				
Inventory				
Inventory (Quantity and Synopsis)	x			x
Transfers Journal (past month)	x			x
Adjustments Journal	x			x
Chart of Accounts	x			x
Project Report	x			x

BACKUP COPIES

It is important to back up a company's CA-Simply Accounting for Windows data files on a regular basis. Backups ensure that the business has a copy of its accounting data in case the current data become damaged. Backups also allow the company to print historical reports at any time, even after the start of a new month, calendar quarter, calendar year, or fiscal year. Use the backup copy of the company's data for the desired time period instead of the current data to print these reports.

Businesses using the CA-Simply Accounting for Windows program should back up data files at the end of each working session, and before the start of a new month, calendar quarter, calendar year, and fiscal year. It is important to keep a duplicate backup disk of company data and store it offsite. For the purposes of this text, backup copies of company data files have been made less frequently due to the small volume of transactions recorded for each example company.

SUMMARY

This chapter has explored how to work with the Receivables, Payables, Inventory, and Payroll Ledgers in the Not Ready mode. The procedures for entering customer, vendor, employee, project, and inventory data were discussed and demonstrated. The methods used to make the Receivable, Payables, Inventory, and Payroll Ledgers ready for operation were explained. In addition, the restrictions for using each ledger in the Ready mode were discussed, along with the important times for printing certain reports and making backup copies of a company's data files.

QUESTIONS

QUESTIONS ABOUT THE SOFTWARE

1. Which ledger must be made ready before any other ledger?

2. What is the purpose of entering historical purchase invoices in the Payables Ledger?

3. How do you correct an error in a recorded historical sales invoice in the Not Ready mode?

4. Why must each inventory item be associated with an asset, revenue, and expense account?

5. What operational restrictions are placed on customer records once the Receivables Ledger is ready?

6. What operational restrictions are placed on group accounts and subgroup accounts once the General Ledger is ready?

7. To maintain a good audit trail of all accounting transactions, how frequently should General Ledger reports be printed?

QUESTIONS ABOUT CONVERSION PROCEDURES

8. Why is it important to make a backup copy of a company's data files prior to making a ledger ready?

9. Why does the program prevent status changes from not ready to ready when the subsidiary ledger records do not agree with their related General Ledger account balances?

EXPLORING ALTERNATIVE SOFTWARE TECHNIQUES

10. It is important that some thought be given to the date a business plans to convert to a computerized accounting system and how the new computerized accounting system will be implemented. In the examples in this chapter, each business has elected to convert to a computerized accounting system on December 1, with the intention of using the General, Receivables, Payables, Inventory, Payroll, and Project Ledgers. This implementation method (referred to as the Direct Conversion method) was selected to give you an opportunity to work with all aspects of a conversion.

    Alternative approaches to conversion dates and methods of implementation include the following options:

    1. **Parallel Conversion**: The organization operates both the manual and the computerized accounting system in parallel until it is clear that no operating problems are occurring with the new computerized accounting system.

    2. **Phased Conversion:** One or two key ledgers are converted first and are allowed to operate for a period of a few weeks to a month. Once these ledgers are running smoothly, the remaining ledgers are converted. For example, the General and Payroll Ledgers may be implemented first, with the Receivables, Payables, Inventory, and Project Ledgers implemented at a later date.

3. **Pilot Conversion:** An isolated division or department is selected as a test site for full implementation. Later, after the system has proven itself operational and most implementation problems have been solved, the remaining segments of the organization are converted.

4. **Conversion Dates:** The beginning of the fiscal year, fiscal quarter, calendar year, or calendar quarter is selected as the earliest transaction date for conversion purposes.

Prepare a short report, recommending that a business implement a new computerized accounting system on December 1 and operate a parallel manual accounting system for the month of December. Include a discussion of the advantages of these implementation methods in your report.

TRANSMITTAL

Classic Clocks   **Name:** _____
Chapter 10

A. Attach the following documents and reports:

1. Customer List 12/1/1997
2. Customer Aged Detail As at 12/1/1997
3. Vendor List 12/1/1997
4. Vendor Aged Detail As at 12/1/1997
5. Inventory and Services List 12/1/1997
6. Inventory Synopsis 12/1/1997
7. Inventory Quantity 12/1/1997
8. Employee List 12/1/1997
9. Employee Quarter-to-Date Summary 12/1/1997
10. Employee Year-to-Date Summary 12/1/1997
11. Project List 12/1/1997
12. Invoice 5882
13. Receipt of Check 765 in full payment of Invoice 5853
14. Check 2840
15. Check 2841
16. All Journal Entries 12/1/1997 to 12/31/1997
17. Trial Balance As at 12/31/1997

B. Refer to your reports to list the amounts requested below:

1. What is the balance of the Cash account? $_____

2. What is the balance of the Clock Inventory account? $_____

3. What is the balance of the Wages account? $_____

4. What is the balance of the Accounts Receivable account? $_____

5. What is the balance of the Accounts Payable account? $_____

EXERCISE—The Paint Place
(CONTINUED FROM CHAPTER 9)

Mike Poole would now like to make ready the Receivables, Payables, Inventory, and Payroll Ledgers for The Paint Place.

A. Load CA-Simply Accounting for Windows; open The Paint Place data files (A:\PAINT\Paint.asc); then leave the session date set at 12/1/1997.

B. Enter the customer records and outstanding historical sales invoices:

Anderson, Elaine
1726 West 9th Street
Vancouver, Washington 98660
206-457-1633
Historical outstanding sales invoice:
       No. 5459, 11/24/1997, $2,293.05

Cash Sales
The Paint Place
3459 Plain Way
Vancouver, Washington 98661
206-229-4512
Historical outstanding sales invoice: none

Kerns, Jake
8921 NW 99th Street
Vancouver, Washington 98665
206-783-1112
Historical outstanding sales invoice:
       No. 5443, 11/21/1997, $2,675.95

Young, Wes
1522 SE 1st Street
Camas, Washington 98607
206-723-1100
Historical outstanding sales invoice:
       No. 5467, 11/29/1997, $3,290.95

Total outstanding historical sales invoices: $8,259.95

Note: Leave the **Clear invoices when paid** check box unchecked for each customer. Check the **Print statements for this customer** check box for all customers.

C. Print a Customer List and Customer Aged Detail report. Verify that the data are correct.

D. Enter the vendor records and outstanding historical purchase invoices.

Painters Supply
12014 SW Canyon Road
Beaverton, Oregon 97005
503-246-8612
Historical outstanding purchase invoice:
       No. CC556, 11/14/1997, $975.34

Vantage Tints
7122 Nob Hill North
San Francisco, California 94023
415-989-2345
Historical outstanding purchase invoice:
       No. E5657, 11/29/1997, $1,116.33

Wholesale Paints
540 Belmont Avenue
Seattle, Washington 98125
206-345-1032
Historical outstanding purchase invoice:
       No. 6723, 11/21/1997, $2,050.45

Total outstanding purchase invoices: $4,142.12

Note: Leave the **Clear invoices when paid** and **Print contact on checks** check boxes unchecked for all vendors.

E. Print a Vendor List and Vendor Aged Detail report. Verify that the data are correct.

F. Enter the inventory item records and historical inventory data.

Number	Description	Unit	Selling Price	Min. Level	Quantity	Total Value
1	Latex Flat	Gallon	16.95	300	642	4,795.74
2	Latex Semi-Gloss	Gallon	16.95	200	1,066	7,963.02
3	Latex High-Gloss	Gallon	16.95	200	600	4,482.00
4	Oil High-Gloss	Gallon	17.95	200	801	7,184.97
5	Oil Semi-Gloss	Gallon	17.95	200	502	4,502.94
						28,928.67

Link all items to Asset: 1300 Inventory; Revenue: 4010 Sales; COGS: 5010 Cost of Goods Sold

G. Print an Inventory List, Inventory Synopsis, and Inventory Quantity report. Verify that the data are correct.

H. Enter the employee records, QTD, and YTD payroll information.

Employee Information

Smith, Billie
P. O. Box 4171
Vancouver, Washington 98662
Phone: 206-253-3831
SSN: 542 62 0002
Birthdate: 4/23/54
Hire date: 7/1/96
Pay periods: 12
Salary: $1,800.00

Tax table: Washington
Federal allowances: 2, Married

Marshall, Bob
2909 F Street
Vancouver, Washington 98663
Phone: 206-693-1294
SSN: 541 88 3331
Birthdate: 5/21/59
Hire date: 3/1/96
Pay periods: 12
Regular: $8.00
Overtime: $12.00
Tax table: Washington
Federal allowances: 1, Single

Quarter-to-Date (QTD) Information

Smith, Billie
Salary: 3,600.00
FIT deduction: 275.00
Medicare tax deduction: 52.20
SST deduction: 223.20
Medicare tax expense: 52.20
SST expense: 223.20
SUTA expense: 49.00

Marshall, Bob
Regular: 2,472.00
FIT deduction: 252.06
Medicare tax deduction: 35.85
SST deduction: 153.27
Medicare tax expense: 35.85
SST expense: 153.27
SUTA expense: 86.52

Year-to-Date (YTD) Information

Smith, Billie	Marshall, Bob
Salary: 19,800.00	Regular: 13,440.00
FIT deduction: 1,512.50	FIT deduction: 1,362.93
Medicare tax deduction: 287.10	Medicare tax deduction: 194.89
SST deduction: 1,227.60	SST deduction: 833.29
Medicare tax expense: 287.10	Medicare tax expense: 194.89
SST expense: 1,227.60	SST expense: 833.29
SUTA expense: 616.00	SUTA expense: 470.40
FUTA expense: 56.00	FUTA expense: 56.00

I.   Print an Employee List, Employee Quarter-to-Date Summary, and Employee Year-to-Date Summary report. Verify that the data are correct.

J.   Enter the project records:

Name: Branch Store Sales	Name: Main Store Sales
Start date: 12/1/1997	Start date: 12/1/1997

K.   Print a Project List. Verify that the data are correct.

L.   Make a backup copy of The Paint Place data files.

M.   Make the Receivables, Payables, Inventory, and Payroll Ledgers ready.

N.   Advance the session date to 12/31/1997. Record the following transactions:

December 28—Sold 5 gallons of oil high-gloss (Item 4) to Jake Kerns (Project: Main Store Sales). Print Invoice 5468. Note that the program has automatically calculated the 8% sales tax on this invoice.

December 28—Issue Check 2345 to Painters Supply in full payment of Invoice CC556.

December 29—Received Check 4521 from Wes Young in the amount of $3,290.95 in full payment of Invoice 5467. (Use Deposit Slip 1875 to deposit this check.)

December 30—Received Invoice 6845 from Wholesale Paints in the amount of $1,494.00 for the purchase of 200 gallons of latex high-gloss (Item 3). (There is no sales tax on this invoice.)

December 31—Issue a payroll check to Billie Smith for her regular salary. Print Check 2346. (Project: none)

O.   Print the following reports:

1.   Journal (By posting date, project allocations, All entries) 12/1/1997 to 12/31/1997
2.   Trial Balance As at 12/31/1997

Q.   Exit from the program. Complete The Paint Place Transmittal.

TRANSMITTAL

The Paint Place   **Name:**_____
Chapter 10

A. Attach the following documents and reports:

1. Customer List 12/1/1997
2. Customer Aged Detail As at 12/1/1997
3. Vendor List 12/1/1997
4. Vendor Aged Detail As at 12/1/1997
5. Inventory and Services List 12/1/1997
6. Inventory Synopsis 12/1/1997
7. Inventory Quantity 12/1/1997
8. Employee List 12/1/1997
9. Employee Quarter-to-Date Summary 12/1/1997
10. Employee Year-to-Date Summary 12/1/1997
11. Project List 12/1/1997
12. Invoice 5468
13. Check 2345
14. Receipt of Check 4521 in payment of Invoice 5467
14. Check 2346
15. Journal 12/1/1997 to 12/31/1997
16. Trial Balance As at 12/31/1997

B. Refer to your reports to list the amounts requested below:

1. What is the balance of the Cash account? $_____

2. What is the balance of the Inventory account? $_____

3. What is the balance of the Wages account? $_____

4. What is the balance of the Accounts Receivable account? $_____

5. What is the balance of the Accounts Payable account? $_____

COMPUTERIZING A MANUAL ACCOUNTING SYSTEM— BUDGETING

COMPUTERIZING A MANUAL ACCOUNTING SYSTEM— BUDGETING

LEARNING OBJECTIVES

After studying this chapter, you will be able to:
- Establish settings to use the budgeting features of CA-Simply Accounting
- Enter budget data
- Change budget amounts
- Prepare budgeting reports showing percentage differences
- Prepare budgeting reports showing dollar differences
- Prepare graphs that show actual performance compared to the budget

BUDGETING IS A NECESSITY

A business must plan its operations and needs to know if the company is performing up to expectations. This helps the owners/managers identify strengths and weaknesses in the business and becomes a basis for adding or deleting product lines, employees, or facilities. One way in which a business can evaluate its performance is by budgeting. A budget is an estimate of projected income and expenses and is developed based on past performances and current expectations. A budget helps a company identify its future plans and expectations and evaluate whether or not performance is in line with expectations.

CLASSIC CLOCKS TUTORIAL

The following tutorial is a step-by-step guide to working with the budgeting process and the procedures used in Simply Accounting to set up budgeting for revenue and expense accounts. This chapter will conclude the use of the Classic Clocks tutorial and the training in computerizing a company.

BUDGETING

A budget can be established for revenue and expense accounts for a month, a bimonthly period, a quarter, a semiannual period, or for the entire year. If a budget period is changed, the amount budgeted will also be changed. For example, if an item is budgeted at $1,200 for the year and the budget is changed to monthly, the monthly amount budgeted will be $100.

Classic Clocks—Document 19   **Session Date: 12/31/1997**

Memo

Date: December 1, 1997

Select the budgeting option from Settings on the Setup menu.

▨ **ACTION:** Load CA-Simply Accounting for Windows; open the data files for Classic Clocks (A:\CLOCK\Classic Clocks.asc); leave the session date set at 12/31/1997, and close the To-Do List. The home window for Classic Clocks will appear.

▨ **ACTION:** On the Setup menu, choose **Settings**. Select the **General** tab. Your screen will show the following:

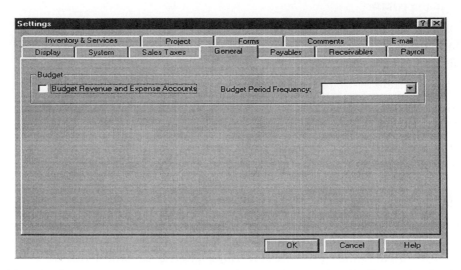

Explanation: This tab allows you to turn on the budget option and to indicate the budget period frequency.

▨ **ACTION:** Click **Budget Revenue and Expense Accounts** to select. Click the drop-down list arrow next to **Budget Period Frequency**. Your screen will show:

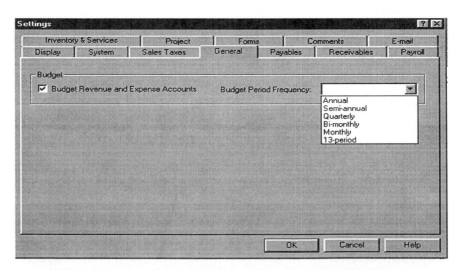

Explanation: Several period options are available: annual, semiannual, quarterly, bimonthly, monthly, and 13-period.

▨ **ACTION:** Click **Annual** to select it as the budget period frequency. Click **OK.** You will get the following dialog box:

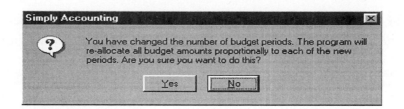

ACTION: Click **Yes**. Close Settings and return to the home window.

Classic Clocks—Document 20   **Session Date: 12/31/1997**

Memo   **Date:** December 1, 1997

Provide the following annual budget amounts to the Revenue and Expense accounts indicated:

Revenue Accounts:		Operating Expense Accounts Continued	
Clock Sales	100,000.00	FUTA Expense	118.00
Watch Sales	60,000.00	SUTA Expense	1,245.00
Sales Returns and Allowances	-200.00	Advertising Expense	2,500.00
Sales Discounts	-500.00	Utilities Expense	1,200.00
Interest Income	425.00	Depreciation Exp.: Office Equipment	1,283.26
		Insurance Expense	1,200.00
Cost of Goods Sold Accounts		Rent Expense	6,600.00
Cost of Goods Sold: Clocks	53,000.00	Office Supplies Expense	950.00
Cost of Goods Sold: Watches	30,000.00	Depreciation Exp.: Store Equipment	641.63
		Telephone Expense	800.00
Operating Expense Accounts		Bank Service Charge Expense	160.00
Wages	36,000.00	Credit Card Fees	960.00
Social Security Tax Expense	2,235.00	Miscellaneous Expense	425.00
Medicare Tax Expense	523.00		

ACTION: Double-click the **Accounts** icon on the home window. Scroll through the accounts. Click **Clock Sales** to select the account. Click the **Edit** button on the toolbar. Your screen will show the following:

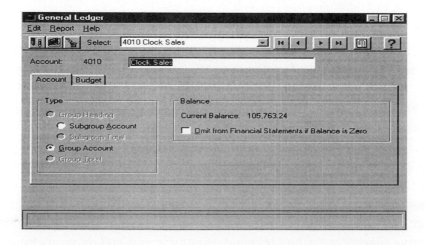

ACTION: Click the **Budget** tab for the Clock Sales account. Click **Budget this Account** and enter *100,000.00* into the **Amount** text box. Press TAB. Your screen will appear as follows:

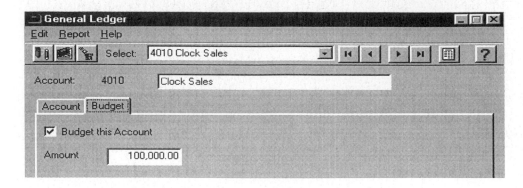

ACTION: Click the drop-down list arrow for **Select** (next to 4010 Clock Sales). You will get a list of all the accounts as shown:

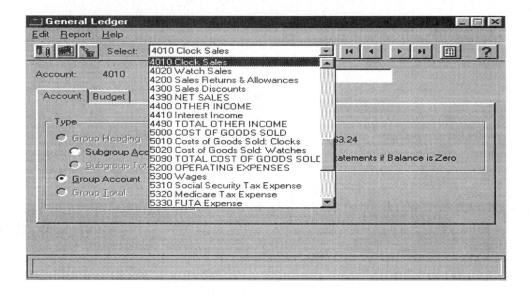

Explanation: When the drop-down list arrow is clicked, the budget information for Clock Sales is saved as part of the account.

ACTION: Click **Watch Sales**. Repeat the steps used to record the budget information for Clock Sales. Continue this procedure for all revenue and expense accounts indicated in the memo.

ACTION: When all the budget items have been recorded, close the General Ledger edit screen and return to the Accounts screen.

PREPARE REPORTS USING BUDGET AMOUNTS

Once accounts have been given projected budget amounts, several reports that reflect the amount budgeted and the actual amount of revenue and expenses may be prepared. The income statement is one of the most informative reports regarding revenue, expenses, and budget projections.

Classic Clocks—Document 21   **Session Date: 12/31/1997**

Memo   **Date:** December 1, 1997

Prepare an Income Statement showing a Comparison of Actual to Budget. Print the report two ways: Actual vs. Budget with a percent difference and Actual vs. Budget with a dollar difference.

ACTION: Click the **Reports** menu on the menu bar. Point to Financials, click **Income Statement**. You will get the following screen:

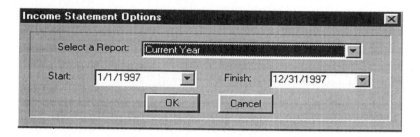

ACTION: Click the drop-down list arrow for **Select a Report**. Click **Comparison of Actual to Budget (Current).** Your screen will show the following dialog box:

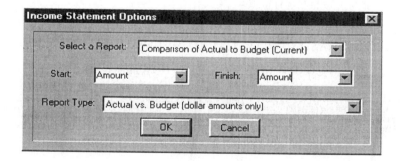

ACTION: Click the drop-down list arrow for **Report Type**. Click **Actual vs. Budget (with a percent difference).** Click **OK.** You will get the following report:

Income Statement

File   Help

Comparison of Actual to Budget	Actual to 12/31/1997	Budget	Percent
REVENUE			
SALES			
Clock Sales	105,763.24	100,000.00	5.76
Watch Sales	56,864.26	60,000.00	-5.23
Sales Returns & Allowances	-188.63	-200.00	-5.69
Sales Discounts	-201.15	-500.00	-59.77
NET SALES	162,237.72	159,300.00	1.84
OTHER INCOME			
Interest Income	0.00	425.00	-100.00
TOTAL OTHER INCOME	0.00	425.00	-100.00
TOTAL REVENUE	162,237.72	159,725.00	1.57
EXPENSE			
COST OF GOODS SOLD			
Costs of Goods Sold: Clocks	52,881.62	53,000.00	-0.22
Cost of Goods Sold: Watches	28,432.13	30,000.00	-5.23
TOTAL COST OF GOODS SOLD	81,313.75	83,000.00	-2.03
OPERATING EXPENSES			
Wages	34,356.00	36,000.00	-4.57
Social Security Tax Expense	2,130.08	2,235.00	-4.69
Medicare Tax Expense	498.14	523.00	-4.75
FUTA Expense	112.00	118.00	-5.08
SUTA Expense	1,189.39	1,245.00	-4.47
Advertising Expense	2,435.00	2,500.00	-2.60
Utilities Expense	1,147.19	1,200.00	-4.40
Depreciation Exp.: Office Equipment	1,283.26	1,283.26	0.00
Insurance Expense	1,100.00	1,200.00	-8.33
Rent Expense	6,600.00	6,600.00	0.00
Office Supplies Expense	934.56	950.00	-1.63
Depreciation Exp.: Store Equipment	641.63	641.63	0.00
Telephone Expense	762.43	800.00	-4.70
Bank Service Charge Expense	165.00	160.00	3.13
Credit Card Fees	0.00	960.00	-100.00
Miscellaneous Expense	432.15	425.00	1.68
TOTAL OPERATING EXPENSES	53,786.83	56,840.89	-5.37
TOTAL EXPENSE	135,100.58	139,840.89	-3.39
NET INCOME	27,137.14	19,884.11	36.48

Explanation: This report shows the actual amount received in Revenue and Expense accounts for the current year and the amount budgeted for the current year. In the third column, the percentage difference between the actual and budgeted amounts is shown.

 ACTION: Print your report and compare it with the one shown above. Close the Income Statement. Prepare an Income Statement showing the actual vs. budget with a dollar difference. Your screen will show the following report:

Income Statement

File   Help

Comparison of Actual to Budget	Actual to 12/31/1997	Budget	Difference
REVENUE			
SALES			
Clock Sales	105,763.24	100,000.00	5,763.24
Watch Sales	56,864.26	60,000.00	-3,135.74
Sales Returns & Allowances	-188.63	-200.00	11.37
Sales Discounts	-201.15	-500.00	298.85
NET SALES	162,237.72	159,300.00	2,937.72
OTHER INCOME			
Interest Income	0.00	425.00	-425.00
TOTAL OTHER INCOME	0.00	425.00	-425.00
TOTAL REVENUE	162,237.72	159,725.00	2,512.72
EXPENSE			
COST OF GOODS SOLD			
Costs of Goods Sold: Clocks	52,881.62	53,000.00	-118.38
Cost of Goods Sold: Watches	28,432.13	30,000.00	-1,567.87
TOTAL COST OF GOODS SOLD	81,313.75	83,000.00	-1,686.25
OPERATING EXPENSES			
Wages	34,356.00	36,000.00	-1,644.00
Social Security Tax Expense	2,130.08	2,235.00	-104.92
Medicare Tax Expense	498.14	523.00	-24.86
FUTA Expense	112.00	118.00	-6.00
SUTA Expense	1,189.39	1,245.00	-55.61
Advertising Expense	2,435.00	2,500.00	-65.00
Utilities Expense	1,147.19	1,200.00	-52.81
Depreciation Exp.: Office Equipment	1,283.26	1,283.26	0.00
Insurance Expense	1,100.00	1,200.00	-100.00
Rent Expense	6,600.00	6,600.00	0.00
Office Supplies Expense	934.56	950.00	-15.44
Depreciation Exp.: Store Equipment	641.63	641.63	0.00
Telephone Expense	762.43	800.00	-37.57
Bank Service Charge Expense	165.00	160.00	5.00
Credit Card Fees	0.00	960.00	-960.00
Miscellaneous Expense	432.15	425.00	7.15
TOTAL OPERATING EXPENSES	53,786.83	56,840.89	-3,054.06
TOTAL EXPENSE	135,100.58	139,840.89	-4,740.31
NET INCOME	27,137.14	19,884.11	7,253.03

Explanation: This report shows the same amounts for the Actual and Budget columns; however, the difference is displayed in a dollar amount.

 ACTION: Print the Income Statement and compare it with the one shown above. Close the Income Statement.

CHANGE BUDGET INFORMATION

Budget amounts and periods may be changed while working in Simply Accounting. To change a budget period, return to the Settings for General on the Setup menu. To change a budget amount, return to the individual account on the Accounts window.

Classic Clocks—Document 22   **Session Date: 12/31/1997**

Memo   **Date:** December 31, 1997

Change the budget amount for advertising expense to $2,400.00. Change the budget period to monthly. Prepare an Income Statement for December to December showing actual vs. budgeted amounts with a percentage difference.

ACTION: Edit the Advertising Expense Account. Click the **Budget** tab and change the amount to *2,400.00*. Your screen will show the following:

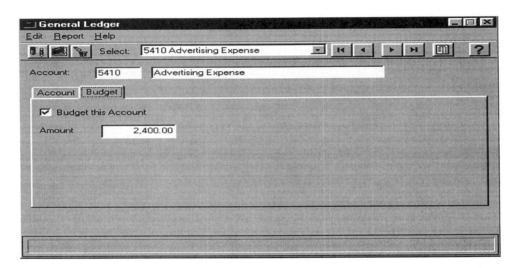

ACTION: Close the General Ledger and the Accounts window and return to the home window. Click the **Setup** menu on the menu bar. Click the **General** tab and change the budget frequency to monthly. Your screen will show the following:

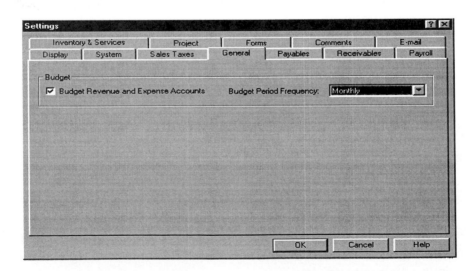

ACTION: Click **OK.** Click **Yes** on the dialog box regarding changing the budget periods. Return to the Advertising Expense account Budget tab. It will show the following:

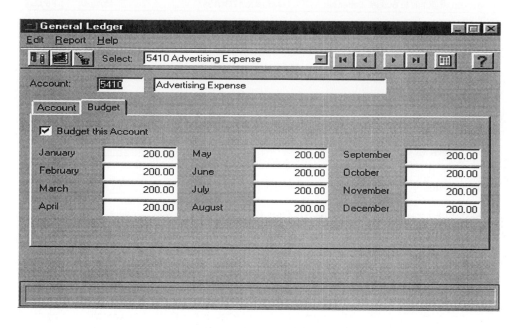

Explanation: Simply recalculated the $2,400.00 budgeted amount for the year into 12 equal amounts.

PREPARE REPORTS WITH UPDATED BUDGET AMOUNTS

When budget amounts are changed, the changes will be reflected in the reports prepared. Because very few transactions have been entered for Classic Clocks since it was converted to a computerized system, many of the results shown in the monthly report will show a big discrepancy between the actual amount and the budgeted amount. If all the transactions for Classic Clocks for the month of December had been recorded, this discrepancy would not appear.

 ACTION: Prepare an Income Statement that is a comparison of actual to budget (current) for December to December. The report type should be Actual vs. Budget (with percent difference). Your Income Statement Options dialog box should appear as follows:

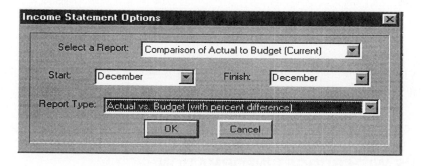

ACTION: When your dialog box appears as the above, click **OK.** Print and compare your Income Statement with the one shown below:

Income Statement

File   Help

Comparison of Actual to Budget December	Actual to 12/31/1997	Budget	Percent
REVENUE			
SALES			
Clock Sales	0.00	8,333.33	-100.00
Watch Sales	330.00	5,000.00	-93.40
Sales Returns & Allowances	0.00	-16.67	-100.00
Sales Discounts	0.00	-41.67	-100.00
NET SALES	330.00	13,274.99	-97.51
OTHER INCOME			
Interest Income	0.00	35.42	-100.00
TOTAL OTHER INCOME	0.00	35.42	-100.00
TOTAL REVENUE	330.00	13,310.41	-97.52
EXPENSE			
COST OF GOODS SOLD			
Costs of Goods Sold: Clocks	0.00	4,416.67	-100.00
Cost of Goods Sold: Watches	165.00	2,500.00	-93.40
TOTAL COST OF GOODS SOLD	165.00	6,916.67	-97.61
OPERATING EXPENSES			
Wages	1,725.00	3,000.00	-42.50
Social Security Tax Expense	106.95	186.25	-42.58
Medicare Tax Expense	25.01	43.58	-42.61
FUTA Expense	0.00	9.83	-100.00
SUTA Expense	60.38	103.75	-41.80
Advertising Expense	0.00	200.00	-100.00
Utilities Expense	0.00	100.00	-100.00
Depreciation Exp.: Office Equipment	0.00	106.94	-100.00
Insurance Expense	0.00	100.00	-100.00
Rent Expense	0.00	550.00	-100.00
Office Supplies Expense	0.00	79.17	-100.00
Depreciation Exp.: Store Equipment	0.00	53.47	-100.00
Telephone Expense	0.00	66.67	-100.00
Bank Service Charge Expense	0.00	13.33	-100.00
Credit Card Fees	0.00	80.00	-100.00
Miscellaneous Expense	0.00	35.42	-100.00
TOTAL OPERATING EXPENSES	1,917.34	4,728.41	-59.45
TOTAL EXPENSE	2,082.34	11,645.08	-82.12
NET INCOME	-1,752.34	1,665.33	-205.22

Explanation: The big discrepancy between the actual amount of the revenue and expense items is due to the fact that not all transactions were entered for the month of December.

ACTION: Close the Income Statement and return to the home window.

PREPARE GRAPHS WITH BUDGET INFORMATION

In addition to reports, Simply Accounting displays budget information in a graphical format. Several graphs are available to show budget information.

ACTION: Click the **Graphs** menu on the home window menu bar. You will see the following list of graphs available in CA-Simply Accounting:

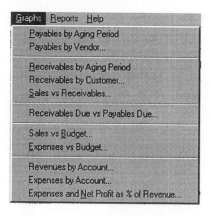

ACTION: Click **Sales vs Budget** on the Graph menu. All the Revenue accounts will be displayed. Click **Clock Sales** and **Watch Sales**. Click **OK.** Print the graph and compare it with the following graph:

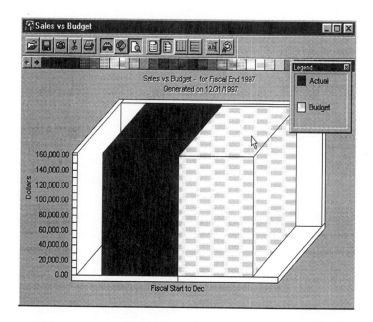

Explanation: The graph displays the actual amount of revenue for both selected accounts in one column and the budgeted amount of revenue for both selected accounts in the other column. Several changes may be made to the graph display.

ACTION: Remove the legend by clicking the **Show/Hide Legend** button on the toolbar. Change the color of a column by pointing to the color you would like to use and dragging it down to the appropriate column. Your cursor will turn into a can of paint. When you release the cursor, the column will change into the color selected. Remove the legend, change the colors of the graph columns (your choice), and print the graph.

ACTION: Close the Sales vs. Budget graph. Prepare an Expenses vs Budget graph. Select all of the accounts. Print the graph. Your graph will look like the following:

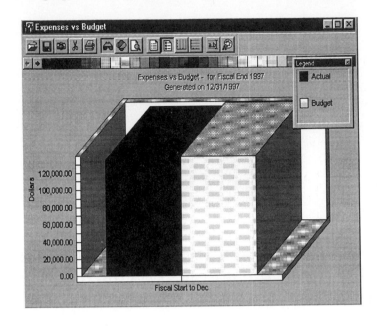

ACTION: Close the Expenses vs Budget graph. Back up your data. Close Simply Accounting.

SUMMARY

Budgeting can provide a company with information on the results of its operations. This helps a company in planning for expansion, reduction, financing, and other operational decisions that must be made in a business. Once a company has selected the use of the budgeting option and provided budget projections, reports and graphs showing the results of operations vs. budgets may be prepared.

QUESTIONS

QUESTIONS ABOUT THE SOFTWARE

1. Does budgeting have to be set up when the company is configured?

2. What are the budget frequency periods that may be selected?

3. What are the steps involved in selecting and setting up budgeting?

4. What is an advantage of preparing a graph rather than displaying information in a written report?

5. Why would a company want to include budgeting in its setup?

6. What happens to budget amounts when a budget period is changed from annual to monthly?

7. Where is budget information provided for an individual account?

QUESTIONS ABOUT BUDGET REPORTS

8. Name the three ways in which an Income Statement can be prepared to include budget data.

9. To prepare an Income Statement with actual vs. budget for the month of December, what would the start and finish months be?

EXPLORING ALTERNATIVE SOFTWARE TECHNIQUES

10. A budget amount may be increased or decreased by manually inserting the adjusted figures. CA-Simply Accounting software also allows all budgeted accounts to be increased or decreased by a certain percentage. Explain the advantages and disadvantages of each method of providing budget amounts.

TRANSMITTAL

Classic Clocks   **Name:** _____
Chapter 11

Attach the following documents and reports:

1. Income Statement: Comparison of Actual to Budget for Fiscal End 1997 (Percent Difference)
2. Income Statement: Comparison of Actual to Budget for Fiscal End 1997 (Dollar Amount)
3. Income Statement: Comparison of Actual to Budget December for Fiscal End 1997
4. Graph: Sales vs. Budget for Fiscal End 1997
5. Graph: Sales vs. Budget for Fiscal End 1997 (Revised)
6. Graph: Expenses vs. Budget for Fiscal End 1997

EXERCISE—The Paint Place
(CONTINUED FROM CHAPTER 10)

Mike Poole would like to add budgeting to the company setup.

A. Load CA-Simply Accounting for Windows; open The Paint Place data files (A:\PAINT\Paint.asc); then leave the session date set at 12/1/1997.

B. Set up budgeting and select a budget frequency of annual.

C. Add the following budget amounts:

Revenue Accounts:		Operating Expense Accounts Continued	
Sales	150,000.00	Depreciation Exp.: Store Equipment	916.63
Sales Returns and Allowances	-200.00	Depreciation Exp.: Office Equipment	702.78
Other Income	75.00	Store Supplies Expense	750.00
		Insurance Expense	1,100.00
Cost of Goods Sold Accounts		Bank Service Charge Expense	125.00
Cost of Goods Sold	75,000.00	Credit Card Fees	900.00
		Wages	35,000.00
Operating Expense Accounts		Social Security Tax Expense	2,200.00
Advertising Expense	2,000.00	Medicare Tax Expense	510.00
Rent Expense	6,600.00	FUTA Expense	100.00
Cash Short/Over	25.00	SUTA Expense	1,200.00
Utilities Expense	1,000.00	Miscellaneous Expense	425.00

D. Print the following reports:

1. Income Statement: Comparison of Actual to Budget for Fiscal End 1997 (Percent Difference)
2. Income Statement: Comparison of Actual to Budget for Fiscal End 1997 (Dollar Amount)

E. Change the budget frequency to monthly.

F. Print the following reports:

1. Income Statement: Comparison of Actual to Budget December for Fiscal End 1997 (Percent Difference)
2. Graph: Sales vs. Budget for Fiscal End 1997 (Sales Account only)
3. Graph: Expenses vs. Budget for Fiscal End 1997 (Select All)

G. Back up your work. Exit the program. Complete the Paint Place Transmittal.

TRANSMITTAL

The Paint Place   **Name:**_____
Chapter 11

A. Attach the following reports:

1. Income Statement: Comparison of Actual to Budget for Fiscal End 1997 (Percent Difference)
2. Income Statement: Comparison of Actual to Budget for Fiscal End 1997 (Dollar Amount)
3. Income Statement: Comparison of Actual to Budget December for Fiscal End 1997
4. Graph: Sales vs. Budget for Fiscal End 1997
5. Graph: Expenses vs. Budget for Fiscal End 1997

B. Refer to your reports to list the amounts requested below:

1. What is the percent difference in sales for the fiscal year?   _____

2. What is the dollar difference in sales for the fiscal year? $_____

3. What is the percent difference in net income for the fiscal year?   _____

4. What is the dollar difference in net income for the fiscal year? $_____

5. What is the percent difference in net income for the month of December?   _____

END-OF-SECTION 3—FIRELIGHT STOVES: PRACTICE SET

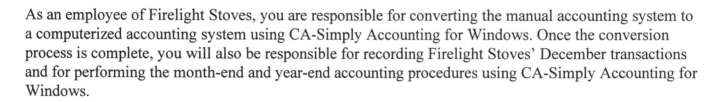

COMPANY PROFILE

Firelight Stoves is a sole proprietorship owned by Janice Cook in Vancouver, Washington. Janice operates a retail store that sells various types of stoves. She has maintained a manual accounting system for her business and would now like to covert to a computerized accounting system beginning December 1, 1997. Janice has selected the CA-Simply Accounting for Windows program as the most appropriate software for her business. As a merchandising business with employees, Janice plans to use the General, Receivables, Payables, Inventory, Payroll, and Project Ledgers of the program.

As an employee of Firelight Stoves, you are responsible for converting the manual accounting system to a computerized accounting system using CA-Simply Accounting for Windows. Once the conversion process is complete, you will also be responsible for recording Firelight Stoves' December transactions and for performing the month-end and year-end accounting procedures using CA-Simply Accounting for Windows.

STAGE 1: MAKING THE GENERAL LEDGER READY

1. Because you are creating a new company, the company file for Firelight Stoves is not on the CD-Rom that accompanies the text. You will be creating this file on a disk. Create a new set of company data files for Firelight Stoves. Load CA-Simply Accounting for Windows; on the Select Company screen, click **Create a new Company**. Complete the Setup Wizard. Indicate that you will create a chart of accounts from scratch. The name of the company file will be:

   A:\Stoves\Stoves.asc (if you are storing your student data files on the disk in drive A)
   B:\Stoves\Stoves.asc (if you are storing your student data files on the disk in drive B)
   C:\Winsim\Stoves\Stoves.asc (if you are storing your student data files on your hard disk)

2. Click the **Next** button; then enter the following dates in the **Company Dates** dialog box:

   Fiscal start: 1/1/1997; fiscal end: 12/31/1997; earliest transaction: 12/1/1997

3. You plan to use all the business activities available. Use accounting terms. The company information is:

   Firelight Stoves/Your Name
   2000 East Evergreen
   Vancouver, Washington 98661
   Telephone: 206-555-3265
   Fax: 206-555-5632

   Federal ID: 93-653109
   State ID: 39128

4. Payroll definitions remain as shown. The project name is Project. If necessary, change the printer settings; otherwise, click **Next** on the printer settings screen.

5. Select Track Inventory Turnover and Store Invoice Lookup Details. DO NOT use cash-basis accounting. Select **Budget Revenue and Expense Accounts**. Use an annual period for budgeting. Use the check number as the source code for cash purchases and sales.

6. The following tax and payroll information will be used: state sales tax, 8%; SUTA, 3.5%; FUTA, 0.8%; Automatic Payroll Deductions, none.

7. Use the following form numbers: Next Number On: Receipts 1; Invoices 5882; Sales Quotes 1; Purchase Orders 1; Checks 1706.

8. Once the company file has been created, go to Settings on the Setup menu. Do the following: Confirm printing for invoices and checks; enter the default invoice comment: *Firelight Stoves thanks you for your business!*

9. Janice has listed the account names and balances from Firelight Stoves' manual accounting system on the following Chart of Accounts Worksheet. Complete the missing information, using the financial statement formatting information provided in Chapter 9.

Chart of Accounts Worksheet

Acct. No.	Account Name	Account Balance	Account Type	Budget Amount
___	Cash	7,561.32	___	
___	Petty Cash	100.00	___	
___	Accounts Receivable	10,294.55	___	
___	Inventory	33,523.50	___	
___	Office Supplies	1,962.43	___	
___	Prepaid Insurance	500.00	___	
___	_____		___	
___	Office Equipment	5,400.00	___	
___	Accum Dep: Office Equipment	-2,747.21	___	
___	Store Equipment	2,100.00	___	
___	Accum Dep: Store Equipment	-830.55	___	
___	_____		___	
___	Accounts Payable	5,725.00	___	
___	FIT Payable	264.43	___	
___	Social Security Tax Payable	377.20	___	
___	Medicare Tax Payable	95.38	___	
___	FUTA Payable	6.98	___	
___	SUTA Payable	134.40	___	
___	Sales Tax Payable	1,110.38	___	
___	TOTAL CURRENT LIABILITIES		___	
___	LONG-TERM LIABILITIES			
___	Loans Payable	3,500.00	___	
___	_____		___	

_____	Janice Cook, Capital	33,850.21	_____	
_____	Janice Cook, Drawing	-12,100.00	_____	
_____			_____	
_____	_____		_____	
_____	Sales	162,678.45	_____	165,678.00
	Sales Returns and Allowances	-1,185.00	_____	-1,200.00
_____	Sales Discounts	-1,835.75	_____	-1,900.00
_____	_____		_____	
_____	Interest Income	250.00	_____	275.00
_____			_____	
_____	_____		_____	
_____	Cost of Goods Sold	81,391.00	_____	82,310.00
_____	Purchase Discounts	-750.00	_____	-900.00
_____	_____		_____	
5150	Advertising Expense	2,365.00	_____	2,400.00
_____	Rent Expense	8,250.00	_____	9,000.00
_____	Utilities Expense	1,576.43	_____	1,720.00
_____	Depreciation Exp: Store Equipment	397.22	_____	433.33
_____	Depreciation Exp: Office Equipment	1,313.88	_____	1433.32
_____	Office Supplies Expense	832.65	_____	910.00
_____	Insurance Expense	1,100.00	_____	1,200.00
5290	Interest Expense: Loans	250.00	_____	275.00
5310	Bank Service Charges	235.00	_____	260.00
_____	Credit Card Fees	928.00	_____	1,100.00
_____	Wages	33,258.00	_____	36,300.00
_____	Social Security Tax Expense	2,061.99	_____	2,250.00
_____	Medicare Tax Expense	482.24	_____	500.00
_____	FUTA Expense	112.00	_____	125.00
_____	SUTA Expense	1,085.28	_____	1,200.00
_____	Miscellaneous Expense	118.95	_____	130.00
_____	_____		_____	

10. Enter the account balances and budget amounts listed on your Chart of Accounts Worksheet. Print a Chart of Accounts, Trial Balance, Income Statement (comparison of actual to budget, dollar amounts only), and Balance Sheet. Verify that your data are correct. (If you receive an error message, read the message carefully for information regarding corrective action. Make corrections as required; then reprint your reports.)

11. Based on the information you listed on your Chart of Accounts Worksheet, complete the following Linked Accounts Worksheet.

Linked Accounts Worksheet

General Linked Account
Retained earnings: _____

Payables Linked Accounts
Payables bank account: _____
Accounts payable: _____
Purchase discount: _____

Inventory Linked Accounts
None

Receivables Linked Accounts
Receivables bank account: _____
Accounts receivable: _____
Sales tax payable: _____

Payroll Linked Accounts
Payroll bank: _____

Payables:	Expenses:
FIT: _____	Wage: _____
MedTax: _____	MedTax: _____
SSTax: _____	SSTax : _____
FUTA: _____	FUTA: _____
SUTA: _____	SUTA: _____

12. Enter the linked account information from your Linked Accounts Worksheet. Make a backup copy of the Firelight Stoves data files.

13. Set the General module ready from the home window Setup menu. Click the **Proceed** button on the dialog box. If you receive an error message, read the message carefully for information on corrective action. Make corrections as required; then repeat this instruction.

14. Record the following transactions:

December 1—Janice Cook made a $1,500 capital contribution to the business. Use Deposit Slip 1701.
December 1—Increase the Petty Cash account balance by $50.

15. Print the following reports:

    A. Journal (By date, All Entries) 12/1/1997 to 12/1/1997
    B. Trial Balance As at 12/1/1997

16. Back up your work. Exit from the program.

17. Complete the Firelight Stoves Transmittal.

TRANSMITTAL

Firelight Stoves   Name_____
Stage 1: Making the General Ledger Ready

A. Attach the following reports:

1. Chart of Accounts 12/1/1997
2. Trial Balance As at 12/1/1997
3. Income Statement (comparison of actual to budget) 1/1/1997 to 12/1/1997
4. Balance Sheet As at 12/1/1997
5. Journal 12/1/1997 to 12/1/1997
6. Trial Balance As at 12/1/1997 (after the additional transactions have been entered)

B. Refer to the Trial Balance As at 12/1/1997 that you printed after entering the additional transactions. List the amounts requested below:

1. What is the balance of the Cash account? $_____

2. What is the balance of the Petty Cash account? $_____

3. What is the balance of the Janice Cook, Capital account? $_____

4. What is the balance of the Accounts Receivable account? $_____

5. What is the balance of the Accounts Payable account? $_____

STAGE 2: MAKING THE SUBSIDIARY LEDGERS READY

Janice Cook would now like you to make the Receivables, Payables, Inventory, and Payroll Ledgers ready for Firelight Stoves.

A. Load CA-Simply Accounting for Windows; open the data files for Firelight Stoves (A:\STOVE\Stoves.asc); then leave the session date set at 12/1/1997.

B. Enter the customer records and outstanding historical sales invoices. (All invoices have 2/10, net 30 for the terms. Enter the terms on the same screen as the invoice information.)

Alice White Designs
3987 West Evergreen
Vancouver, Washington 98661
206-236-9712
Historical outstanding sales invoice:
    No. 5825, 11/2/1997, 2/10 Net 30, $2,394.20

Cash Sales
Firelight Stoves
2000 East Evergreen
Vancouver, Washington 98661
206-555-3265
Historical outstanding sales invoice: none

Construction Contractors
10234 NW 99th Street
Vancouver, Washington 98665
206-783-5533
Historical outstanding sales invoice:
    No. 5672, 6/9/1997, 2/10 Net 30, $2,001.50

Creative Housing
1643 SE 31st Street
Camas, Washington 98607
206-723-2370
Historical outstanding sales invoice:
    No. 5876, 11/28/1997, 2/10 Net 30, $1,635.05

Nancy Powers, Interiors
1824 SE Salmon Street
Vancouver, Washington 98661
206-236-7721
Historical outstanding sales invoice:
    No. 5821, 10/31/1997, 2/10 Net 30, $2,229.25

Northwest Warmth
3122 West 9th Street
Vancouver, Washington 98660
206-457-1443
Historical outstanding sales invoice:
    No. 5879, 11/29/1997, 2/10 Net 30, $2,034.55

Total historical outstanding sales invoices: $10,294.55

Note: Leave the **Clear invoices when paid** check box unchecked for each customer. Check the **Print statements for this customer** check box for all customers.

C. Print a Customer List and a Customer Aged Detail report (include terms). Verify the data.

D. Enter the vendor records and outstanding historical purchase invoices (including terms where given).

Cascade Electric
890 Stark Avenue
Vancouver, Washington 98665
206-232-1292
Historical outstanding purchase invoice: none

Contractor's Gazette
977 SW 11th Avenue
Portland, Oregon 97205
503-222-3611
Historical outstanding purchase invoice: none

Cook, Janice
3219 West 99th Street
Vancouver, Washington 98660
206-457-2312
Historical outstanding purchase invoice: none

Federal Reserve Bank
Vancouver Branch
P.O. Box 3436
Vancouver, Washington 98661
206-226-1149
Historical outstanding purchase invoice: none

Housewarmers
345 California Street
San Francisco, California 94023
415-989-3412
Historical outstanding purchase invoice:
    No. 6770, 11/22/1997, Net 30, $1,378.45

National Stove
4970 Halsey
Vancouver, Washington 98661
206-222-9543
Historical outstanding purchase invoice: none

Rocky Mountain Heating
120 Summit Blvd.
New York, New York 10019
718-246-8612
Historical outstanding purchase invoice:
    No. 4762, 11/14/1997, Net 30, $1,698.04

Walker's Woodstoves
345 Spokane Road
Seattle, Washington 98125
206-345-4511
Historical outstanding purchase invoice:
    No. 7226, 11/29/1997, 3/10 Net 30, $740.24

Western Telephone
4298 10th Avenue
Vancouver, Washington 98665
206-222-3500
Historical outstanding purchase invoice: none

Lloyd Corporation
1679 Timothy Lane
Vancouver, Washington 98662
206-222-7854
Historical outstanding purchase invoice: none

Pacific Office Supply
3638 M Street
Vancouver, Washington 98664
206-645-1234
Historical outstanding purchase invoice: none

Stove Wholesalers
3295 North Field
Denver, Colorado 80227
719-423-9997
Historical outstanding purchase invoice:
    No. 8692, 11/30/1997, 2/10 Net 30, $1,908.27

Washington Dept. of Revenue
P.O. Box 14800
Seattle, Washington 98168
206-378-3390
 Historical outstanding purchase invoice: none

Total historical outstanding purchase invoices: $5,725.00

Note: Leave the **Clear invoices when paid** and **Print contact on checks** check boxes unchecked.

E. Print a Vendor List and Vendor Aged Detail report (include terms). Verify the data.

F. Enter the inventory item records and historical inventory data.

Number	Description	Unit	Selling Price	Min. Level	Quantity	Total Value
1	Glow Stove	Each	650.00	10	39	10,998.00
2	Mini-Glow Stove	Each	175.00	5	11	830.50
3	Little Spark	Each	225.00	5	10	840.00
4	Blaze Stove	Each	825.00	15	33	10,230.00
5	Cook Stove	Each	950.00	10	25	10,625.00
						33,523.50

Associate each inventory item with the following accounts:
    Asset: Inventory   **Revenue:** Sales   **COGS:** Cost of Goods Sold

G. Print an Inventory List, Inventory Synopsis, and Inventory Quantity report. Verify the data.

H. Enter the employee records, QTD, and YTD payroll information.

Employee Information	Quarter-to-Date (QTD) Information	Year-to-Date (YTD) Information
Meyer, Theresa	Salary: 3,650.00	Salary: 19,850.00
P.O. Box 9800	FIT deduction: 282.50	FIT deduction: 1,520.00
Vancouver, Washington 98662	Medicare Tax deduction: 52.93	Medicare Tax deduction: 287.83
Phone: 206-252-8931	Soc Sec Tax deduction: 226.30	Soc Sec Tax deduction: 1,230.70
SSN: 541 48 2002	Medicare Tax expense: 52.93	Medicare Tax expense: 287.83
Birthdate: 8/29/54	Soc Sec Tax expense: 226.30	Soc Sec Tax expense: 1,230.70
Hire date: 6/1/91		FUTA expense: 56.00
Salary: $1,850.00	SUTA expense: 49.00	SUTA expense: 616.00
Pay periods: 12		
Tax table: Washington		
Federal allowances: 2, Married		
Zenner, Kevin	Regular: 2,440.00	Regular: 13,408.00
2302 K Street	FIT deduction: 247.26	FIT deduction: 1,358.13
Vancouver, Washington 98663	Medicare Tax deduction: 35.37	Medicare Tax deduction: 194.41
Phone: 206-693-2783	Soc Sec Tax deduction: 151.27	Soc Sec Tax deduction: 831.29
SSN: 542 34 5331	Medicare Tax expense: 35.37	Medicare Tax expense: 194.41
Birthdate: 7/2/59	Soc Sec Tax expense: 151.27	Soc Sec Tax expense: 831.29
Hire date: 2/1/91		FUTA expense: 56.00
Regular: $8.00	SUTA expense: 86.40	SUTA expense: 469.28
Overtime: $12.00		
Pay periods: 12		
Tax table: Washington		
Federal allowances: 1, Single		

I. Print an Employee List, Employee Quarter-to-Date Summary, and Employee Year-to-Date Summary report. Verify that the data are correct.

J. Enter the project record: Name: Trade Show Sales Summary; Start date: 12/1/1997

K. Print a Project List. Verify that the data are correct.

L. Make a backup copy of the Firelight Stoves data files.

M. Make the Receivables, Payables, Inventory, and Payroll Ledgers Ready. If you receive an error message, read the message carefully for information on corrective action. Make corrections as required; then repeat this instruction.

N. Set up the Cash account so it can be reconciled. The Income1 account is Interest Income. The Expense1 account is Bank Service Charges.

O. The company will accept Visa and MasterCard credit cards. Firelight Stoves is charged a 6% fee for each credit card. The accounts to be used are Credit Card Fees and Cash.

P. Make another backup copy of the Firelight Stoves data files. Exit from the program.

Q. Complete the Firelight Stoves Transmittal.

TRANSMITTAL

Firelight Stoves   Name_____
Stage 2: Making the Subsidiary Ledgers Ready

A. Attach the following reports:

   1. Customer List 12/1/1997
   2. Customer Aged Detail As at 12/1/1997
   3. Vendor List 12/1/1997
   4. Vendor Aged Detail As at 12/1/1997
   5. Inventory and Services List 12/1/1997
   6. Inventory Synopsis 12/1/1997
   7. Inventory Quantity 12/1/1997
   8. Employee List 12/1/1997
   9. Employee Quarter-to-Date Summary 12/1/1997
10. Employee Year-to-Date Summary 12/1/1997
11. Project List 12/1/1997

B. Refer to your reports to list the amounts requested below:

1. How much is Theresa Meyer's net pay year-to-date? $_____

2. How much is the total value of inventory? $_____

3. What is the Customer Aged Detail total? $_____

4. What is the Vendor Aged Detail total? $_____

5. How much is Kevin Zenner's net pay quarter-to-date? $_____

STAGE 3: RECORDING TRANSACTIONS FOR THE WEEK ENDING 12/5/1997

Firelight Stoves has established the following accounting procedures and policies for use with the CA-Simply Accounting for Windows program.

Sales

Sales are made on a cash and credit basis with payment terms of 2/10, net 30 offered to credit customers. When credit sales are made, an invoice is prepared using the CA-Simply Accounting for Windows automatic invoicing preparation feature. You will receive a memo from Janice when an invoice needs to be prepared. Cash sales are recorded weekly based on Firelight Stoves' Weekly Cash Sale Summary form. Record cash sales in the Sales Journal, using the cash sale option and the customer identified as Cash Sales. Record the weekly deposit of cash sales into the Cash Account Reconciliation. Accept the automatically calculated sales tax amount for all cash and credit sales. Receivables Ledger records are created as needed for new credit customers; consequently the one-time customer option within the CA-Simply Accounting for Windows program is not used except for credit card sales. All details regarding fully paid invoices are retained in the accounting data files.

Credit Memos

Returned merchandise is charged to the Sales Returns and Allowances account. Accept the automatically calculated sales tax amount for all returned merchandise. You will receive a memo from Janice when a credit memo needs to be prepared.

Cash Receipts and Sales Discounts

Most of Firelight Stoves' credit customers take advantage of the 2/10, net 30 discount terms. If taken, sales discounts are charged to the Sales Discounts account.

Purchases

Payables Ledger records have been established for those vendors that Firelight Stoves deals with on a frequent basis. All details of fully paid invoices are retained in the company's accounting data files. Occasionally, the business will make a purchase or receive a bill from a new vendor. The owner, Janice, may or may not want to establish a Payables Ledger record for the new vendor and payment may or may not be due immediately. Therefore, Janice uses the following notations on vendor invoices, statements, and bills to indicate how she would like the purchase handled.

1. *Approved.* Record purchase in the Purchases Journal under the established vendor's name. Payment is not yet due.
2. *New Vendor.* Create a Payables Ledger record for the vendor.
3. *Issue Check.* Issue a check using the cash purchase option in the Purchases Journal.
4. *One-Time Vendor.* Issue a check, using the one-time vendor and cash purchase options in the Purchases Journal.
5. *New Item.* Create a new Inventory Ledger record, using the information provided, associating the new item with the appropriate asset, revenue, and expense accounts.

Review Purchases source documents carefully; Janice may use more than one notation on a source document.

Debit Memos

Debit memos are prepared when merchandise is returned to a vendor for credit. Returned merchandise is charged directly to the inventory account associated with the returned item. You will receive a memo from Janice when a debit memo needs to be prepared.

Payments on Account and Purchase Discounts

When Janice wants a check issued as a payment on account to a credit vendor, she prepares a memo to that effect. If a purchase discount can be taken, always take it. You will prepare checks using the CA-Simply Accounting for Windows automatic check preparation feature.

Cash Payments for Current Liabilities and Draws

Use the cash purchase option in the Purchases Journal to record payments of current liabilities and draws as requested in the memos prepared by Janice. You will prepare checks using the CA-Simply Accounting for Windows automatic check preparation feature.

Payroll Checks

Firelight Stoves uses the CA-Simply Accounting for Windows automatic payroll deductions and check preparation features. The state of Washington does not assess an income tax on employees. Employees are paid monthly on the last working day of each month.

Projects and Distributions

Firelight Stoves has a single project: Trade Show Sales Summary. Revenues earned and expenses incurred due to trade show participation are allocated to the Trade Show Sales Summary project. Janice will make a notation on the source document indicating if the revenue or expense is associated with a trade show. Revenue and expenses associated with retail store operations are NOT allocated to a project.

Other Information

Purchases of office supplies are debited to the Office Supplies asset account and are adjusted monthly. Journal entries associated with bank reconciliations are recorded in the General Journal, and checks issued to replenish petty cash are recorded in the Purchases Journal using the one-time vendor option. Create new General Ledger accounts in the chart of accounts as requested by Janice using the title and number indicated in her memo. Reference numbers for use in the **Check** and **Invoice** fields when using the cash purchase or cash sale options may not always be listed on source documents. Use your best judgment in determining descriptive information for use in these fields.

Month-End and Year-End Accounting Procedures

At the end of each month, complete a bank reconciliation and enter any related journal entries. In addition, a memo will be issued informing you of any monthly adjusting entries required. If the month just ending is also the year-end for the business, Janice will request that the year-end financial statements be prepared and that her drawing account be closed along with the revenue and expense accounts in preparation for recording transactions in the new fiscal year.

The first packet for December contains several source documents and memos that you need to record using CA-Simply Accounting for Windows. Examine each source document carefully, referring to the accounting procedures and policies described earlier if you have questions about how to record a transaction. To begin recording transactions, load CA-Simply Accounting for Windows; open the data files for Firelight Stoves (A:\STOVES\Stoves.asc); then advance the session date to 12/5/1997.

Firelight Stoves—Document 1   **Session Date: 12/5/1997**

Memo   **Date:** December 1, 1997

Prepare an invoice to Nancy Powers, Interiors for the sale of 5 Blaze stoves (Item 4) at the regular sales price plus tax. Terms 2/10, net 30.

Firelight Stoves—Document 2   **Session Date: 12/5/1997**

STATEMENT

TO: Firelight Stoves   **FROM:** Lloyd Corporation   **DATE:** 12-1-1997

December, 1997 Rent..$750.00

Approved. Issue check.   J. C.

Firelight Stoves—Document 3   **Session Date: 12/5/1997**

Memo   **Date:** December 1, 1997

Prepare Credit Memo 11 to Northwest Warmth for the return of 1 Little Spark stove (Item 3), -$225.00 plus tax. (Use Account 4010 as the transaction account.)

Firelight Stoves—Document 4   **Session Date: 12/5/1997**

Memo   **Date:** December 1, 1997

Received Check 11678 from Creative Housing for $1,602.35 in full payment of Invoice 5876.

Firelight Stoves—Document 5   **Session Date: 12/5/1997**

Memo   **Date:** December 2, 1997

Prepare Debit Memo 27 to Housewarmers for the return of 1 Glow stove (Item 1) for a total of -$282.00.

Firelight Stoves—Document 6   **Session Date: 12/5/1997**

Rocky Mountain Heating   **Invoice: 4896**   **Date:** December 2, 1997

10 Mini-Glow Stoves   @$75.50 each   Total: $755.00

    Approved JC   Terms Net 30

Firelight Stoves—Document 7   **Session Date: 12/5/1997**

Memo   **Date:** December 3, 1997

Issue a check in the amount of $718.03 to Walker's Woodstoves in payment of Invoice 7226 less discount.

Firelight Stoves—Document 8   **Session Date: 12/5/1997**

<u>**Weekly Cash Sales Summary**</u>					**Date:** December 5, 1997		**No. 48**	
Item 2	Quantity 1	Unit	Each	Mini-Glow Stove	Selling Price $175.00		Amount $175.00	
3	2		Each	Little Spark Stove	225.00		450.00	
5	3		Each	Cook Stove	950.00		<u>2,850.00</u>	
				8% Sales Tax			<u>278.00</u>	
Use Deposit Slip 1702. Include checks received.						TOTAL	<u>$3,753.00</u>	

End-of-Session Procedures

A. Print the following reports:
1. Journal (By date, Project allocations, All entries) 12/1/1997 to 12/5/1997
2. Customer Aged report (Select All, Detail, include Terms) As At 12/5/1997
3. Vendor Aged report (Select All, Detail, include Terms) As At 12/5/1997
4. Inventory report (Select All, Select Assets, Synopsis) 12/5/1997
5. Income Statement (current year) 1/1/1997 to 12/5/1997
6. Trial Balance As at 12/5/1997

B. Make a backup copy of the Firelight Stoves data files. Exit from the program. Complete the Firelight Stoves Transmittal.

TRANSMITTAL

Firelight Stoves   **Name**_____
Stage 3: Session Date 12/5/1997

A. Attach the following documents and reports:

1. Invoice 5882
2. Check 1706
3. CM11
4. Receipt of Check 11678 in payment of Invoice 5876
5. Check 1707
6. Sum48
7. All Journal Entries 12/1/1997 to 12/5/1997
8. Customer Aged report As at 12/5/1997
9. Vendor Aged report As at 12/5/1997
10. Inventory Synopsis 12/5/1997
11. Income Statement 1/1/1997 to 12/5/1997
12. Trial Balance As at 12/5/1997

B. Refer to your reports to list the amounts requested below:

1. Accounts Payable balance $_____

2. Accounts Receivable balance $_____

3. Cash balance $_____

4. Net income $_____

5. Total inventory value $_____

STAGE 4: RECORDING TRANSACTIONS FOR THE WEEK ENDING 12/12/1997

Load CA-Simply Accounting for Windows; open the data files for Firelight Stoves
(A:\STOVES\Stoves.asc); then advance the session date to 12/12/1997. Record the following
transactions:

Firelight Stoves—Document 9   **Session Date: 12/12/1997**

Memo   **Date:** December 7, 1997

Prepare an invoice to Creative Housing for the sale of 1 Cook stove (Item 5) at our regular sales price plus tax.
Terms: 2/10, net 30.

Firelight Stoves—Document 10   **Session Date: 12/12/1997**

Memo   **Date:** December 8, 1997

Issue a check in the amount of $1,870.10 to Stove Wholesalers in payment of Invoice 8692 less a 2% discount.

Firelight Stoves—Document 11   **Session Date: 12/12/1997**

Memo   **Date:** December 9, 1997

Received Check 6221 from Northwest Warmth for $1,750.86 in full payment of Invoice 5879. (Take discount and
apply CM11.)

Firelight Stoves—Document 12   **Session Date: 12/12/1997**

National Stove   **Invoice: 8571**   **Date:** December 10, 1997

5   Arc Burner Stove   @$250.00 each   Total: $1,250.00
     Approved JC   New Item: Selling Price $525.00, Minimum: 3, Item Number: 6   Terms Net 30

Firelight Stoves—Document 13   **Session Date: 12/12/1997**

Memo   **Date:** December 11, 1997

Prepare Debit Memo 28 to National Stove for the return of 1 Arc Burner stove (Item 6) for a total of -$250.00.

Firelight Stoves—Document 14   **Session Date: 12/12/1997**

Contractor's Gazette   **Invoice: 7213**   **Date:** December 11, 1997

   Trade Show Advertising   Total: $400.00
Approved. Issue check. JC   Allocate to Trade Show Sales Summary Project   Terms Payable on Receipt

---

Firelight Stoves—Document 15   **Session Date: 12/12/1997**

Weekly Cash Sales Summary   **Date:** December 12, 1997   **No. 49**

Item	6	Quantity	1	Unit	Each	Arc Burner Stove	Selling Price $525.00	Amount $525.00
	3		2		Each	Little Spark Stove	225.00	450.00
						8% Sales Tax		78.00

Use Deposit Slip 1703. Include checks received.   TOTAL $1,053.00

Firelight Stoves—Document 16   **Session Date: 12/12/1997**

Pacific Office Supply   **Invoice: 8267**   **Date:** December 12, 1997

   Office Supplies   Total: $316.80
   Approved. Issue check. JC   Terms Payable on Receipt

Firelight Stoves—Document 17   **Session Date: 12/12/1997**

Memo   **Date:** December 12, 1997

Prepare an invoice to Construction Contractors for the sale of 1 Arc Burner stove (Item 6) at our regular sales price plus tax. Terms 2/10, net 30.

End-Of-Session Procedures

A. Print the following reports:

1. Journal (By date, Project allocations, All entries) 12/6/1997 to 12/12/1997
2. Customer Aged report (Select All, Detail, Include Terms) As at 12/12/1997
3. Vendor Aged report (Select All, Detail, Include Terms) As at 12/12/1997
4. Inventory report (Select All, Select Assets, Synopsis) 12/12/1997
5. Inventory report (Select All, Select Assets, Quantity) 12/12/1997
6. Income Statement (current year) 1/1/1997 to 12/12/1997
7. Trial Balance As at 12/12/1997

B. Make a backup copy of the Firelight Stoves data files. Exit from the program. Complete the Firelight Stoves Transmittal.

TRANSMITTAL

Firelight Stoves   Name_____
Stage 4: Session Date 12/12/1997

A. Attach the following reports:

1. Invoice 5883
2. Check 1708
3. Receipt of Check 6221 in payment of Invoice 5879
4. Check 1709
5. Sum49
6. Check 1710
7. Invoice 5884
8. Journal Entries 12/6/1997 to 12/12/1997
9. Customer Aged Detail report As at 12/12/1997
10. Vendor Aged Detail report As at 12/12/1997
11. Inventory Synopsis 12/12/1997
12. Inventory Quantity 12/12/1997
13. Income Statement 1/1/1997 to 12/12/1997
14. Trial Balance As at 12/12/1997

B. Refer to your reports to list the amounts requested below:

1. Accounts Payable balance $_____

2. Accounts Receivable balance $_____

3. Cash balance $_____

4. Net income $_____

5. Total inventory value $_____

STAGE 5: RECORDING TRANSACTIONS FOR THE WEEK ENDING 12/19/1997

Load CA-Simply Accounting for Windows; open the data files for Firelight Stoves
(A:\STOVES\Stoves.asc); then advance the session date to 12/19/1997. Record the following
transactions:

Firelight Stoves—Document 18   **Session Date: 12/19/1997**

Memo   **Date:** December 13, 1997
Correct CM11. The Sales Returns and Allowances should have been used as the transaction account.

Firelight Stoves—Document 19   **Session Date: 12/19/1997**

Memo   **Date:** December 13, 1997
Prepare Purchase Order 1 to new vendor: Gas Stoves Limited, 351 Geary Street, San Francisco, CA 94023,
415-989-4343. Order 6 Arc Burner stoves at $250.00 each for a total of $1,500.00. Terms Net 30.

Prepare Purchase Order 2 to Walker's Woodstoves for 10 Little Spark stoves at $84.00 each. For a total of
$840.00. Terms 3/15, net 30.

Firelight Stoves—Document 20   **Session Date: 12/19/1997**

Walker's Woodstoves   **Invoice: 7681**   **Date:** December 14, 1997

10   Little Spark Stove   @$84.00 each   Total: $840.00
     Approved JC   Received from Purchase Order 2   Terms 3/15, net 30

Firelight Stoves—Document 21   **Session Date: 12/19/1997**

Memo   **Date:** December 14, 1997
Issue a check in the amount of $2,453.04 to Rocky Mountain Heating in payment of Invoices 4762 and 4896.

Firelight Stoves—Document 22   **Session Date: 12/19/1997**

Gas Stoves Limited   **Invoice: Z721**   **Date:** December 15, 1997

6   Arc Burner Stove   @$250.00 each   Total: $1,500.00
     Approved JC   Received from Purchase Order 1   Terms net 30

Firelight Stoves—Document 23   **Session Date: 12/19/1997**

Memo   **Date:** December 15, 1997
Issue a check for $737.01 to the Federal Reserve Bank for the payment of the November payroll liabilities and
taxes as follows: FIT Payable $264.43; Social Security Tax Payable $377.20; Medicare Tax Payable $95.38.

Issue a check for $1,110.38 to the Washington Dept. of Revenue for the payment of the November sales tax.

Firelight Stoves—Document 24   **Session Date: 12/19/1997**

Memo   **Date:** December 16, 1997
Received Check 11982 from Creative Housing for $1,005.48 in full payment of Invoice 5883. (Take discount.)

Firelight Stoves—Document 25   **Session Date: 12/19/1997**

Memo   **Date:** December 17, 1997
Create a new account 1520 Land in the chart of accounts.

Firelight Stoves—Document 26   **Session Date: 12/19/1997**

Memo   **Date:** December 18, 1997

Prepare an invoice to Alice White Designs for 1 Cook stove (Item 5) at our regular sales price plus tax. Terms 2/10, net 30.

Firelight Stoves—Document 27   **Session Date: 12/19/1997**

Weekly Cash Sales Summary   **Date:** December 19, 1997   **No. 50**

Item 4	Quantity 1	Unit	Each	Blaze Stove	Selling Price $825.00	Amount $825.00
1	2		Each	Glow Stove	650.00	1,300.00
				8% Sales Tax		170.00
Use Deposit Slip 1704. Include checks received.					TOTAL	$2,295.00

Firelight Stoves—Document 28   **Session Date: 12/19/1997**

Memo   **Date:** December 19, 1997

Please issue a check to Janice Cook in the amount of $1,100.00 as a December draw.

End-of-Session Procedures

A. Print the following reports:

1. Journal (By date, Project Allocations All entries) 12/1/1997 to 12/19/1997
2. Customer Aged report (Select All, Detail, Terms) As at 12/19/1997
3. Vendor Aged report (Select All, Detail, Terms) As at 12/19/1997
4. Inventory report (Select All, Select Assets, Synopsis) 12/19/1997
5. Inventory report (Select All, Select Assets, Quantity) 12/19/1997
6. Income Statement (current year) 1/1/1997 to 12/19/1997
7. Trial Balance As at 12/19/1997

B. Make a backup copy of the Firelight Stoves data files. Exit from the program. Complete the Firelight Stoves Transmittal.

TRANSMITTAL

Firelight Stoves   **Name**_____
Stage 5: Session Date 12/19/1997

A. Attach the following documents and reports:

  1. CM11 (Corrected)
  2. Purchase Order 1
  3. Purchase Order 2
  4. Check 1711
  5. Check 1712
  6. Check 1713
  7. Receipt of Check 11982 in payment of Invoice 5883
  8. Invoice 5885
  9. Sum50
 10. Check 1714
 11. Journal Entries 12/1/1997 to 12/19/1997
 12. Customer Aged Detail As at 12/19/1997
 13. Vendor Aged Detail As at 12/19/1997
 14. Inventory Synopsis report 12/19/1997
 15. Inventory Quantity report 12/19/1997
 16. Income Statement 1/1/1997 to 12/19/1997
 17. Trial Balance As at 12/19/1997

B. Refer to your reports to list the amounts requested below:

1. Accounts Payable balance $_____

2. Accounts Receivable balance $_____

3. Cash balance $_____

4. Net income $_____

5. Total inventory value $_____

STAGE 6: RECORDING TRANSACTIONS FOR THE WEEK ENDING 12/26/1997

Load CA-Simply Accounting for Windows; open the data files for Firelight Stoves
(A:\STOVES\Stoves.asc); then advance the session date to 12/26/1997. Record the following
transactions:

Firelight Stoves—Document 29   **Session Date: 12/26/1997**

Memo   **Date:** December 21, 1997

Prepare Purchase Order 3 to Rocky Mountain Heating for 4 cook stoves @ $425 each. Total $1,700.00

Firelight Stoves—Document 30   **Session Date: 12/26/1997**

Memo   **Date:** December 21, 1997

Prepare Debit Memo 29 to Walker's Woodstoves for the return of 2 Little Spark stoves (Item 3), total -$168.00.

Firelight Stoves—Document 31   **Session Date: 12/26/1997**

Memo   **Date:** December 21, 1997

Prepare an invoice to a new customer, Atlas Remodeling, 310 Long Avenue, Kelso, Washington 98626,
206-425-9660, for the sale of 2 Mini-Glow stoves (Item 2) at our regular sales price plus tax. Terms 2/10, net 30.

Firelight Stoves—Document 32   **Session Date: 12/26/1997**

Memo   **Date:** December 22, 1997

Issue a check in the amount of $1,096.45 to Housewarmers in payment of Invoice 6770 less DM27.

Firelight Stoves—Document 33   **Session Date: 12/26/1997**

Memo   **Date:** December 23, 1997

Prepare Credit Memo 12 to Atlas Remodeling for the return of 1 Mini-Glow stove (Item 2) for $175.00 plus tax.
(Use Sales Returns and Allowances for the account.)

Firelight Stoves—Document 34   **Session Date: 12/26/1997**

Rocky Mountain Heating   **Invoice: 4982**   Date: December 24, 1997

4   Cook Stove   @$425.00 each   Total: $1,700.00
     Approved JC   Received from Purchase Order 3   Terms net 30

Firelight Stoves—Document 35   **Session Date: 12/26/1997**

Pacific Office Supply   **Invoice: 8419**   Date: December 24, 1997

     Office Supplies   Amount: $102.05
     Approved. Issue check. JC   Terms: Payable Upon Receipt

Firelight Stoves—Document 36   **Session Date: 12/26/1997**

National Stove   **Invoice: 8627**   Date: December 24, 1997

2   Little Spark Stove   @$84.00 each   Total: $168.00
     Approved JC   Terms: net 30

Firelight Stoves—Document 37   **Session Date: 12/26/1997**

Weekly Cash Sales Summary   **Date:** December 26, 1997   **No. 51**

Item 4   Quantity 1   Unit   Each   Blaze Stove   Selling Price $825.00   Amount $825.00
                                                    8% Sales Tax   66.00
                                                                                         TOTAL $891.00

Firelight Stoves—Document 38   **Session Date: 12/26/1997**

Trade Show Cash Sales Summary   **Date:** December 26, 1997   **No. TSum4**

Item 1   Quantity 7   Unit   Each   Glow Stove   Selling Price $650.00   Amount $4,550.00
                                                    8% Sales Tax   364.00
Distribute to Trade Show Sales Summary   TOTAL $4,914.00
Use Deposit Slip 1705. Include Sum 51.

Firelight Stoves—Document 39   **Session Date: 12/26/1997**

Contractor's Gazette   **Invoice: 7362**   **Date:** December 26, 1997

Trade Show Advertising   Total Amount: $700.00
Approved. Issue Check JC   Distribute to Trade Show Sales Summary Project   Terms Payable Upon Receipt

End-of-Session Procedures

A. Print the following reports:

1. Journal (By date, Project allocations, All entries) 12/20/1997 to 12/26/1997
2. Customer Aged report (Select All, Detail, Terms) As at 12/26/1997
3. Vendor Aged report (Select All, Detail, Terms) As at 12/26/1997
4. Inventory report (Select All, Select Assets, Synopsis) 12/26/1997
5. Inventory report (Select All, Select Assets, Quantity) 12/26/1997
6. Income Statement (current year) 1/1/1997 to 12/26/1997
7. Trial Balance As at 12/26/1997

B. Make a backup copy of the Firelight Stoves data files. Exit from the program. Complete the Firelight Stoves Transmittal.

TRANSMITTAL

Firelight Stoves   Name_____
Stage 6: Session Date 12/26/1997

A. Attach the following documents and reports:

1. Purchase Order 3
2. Invoice 5886
3. Check 1715
4. CM12
5. Check 1716
6. Sum51
7. TSum4
8. Check 1717
9. Journal entries 12/20/1997 to 12/26/1997
10. Customer Aged Detail As at 12/26/1997
11. Vendor Aged Detail As at 12/26/1997
12. Inventory Synopsis 12/26/1997
13. Inventory Quantity 12/26/1997
14. Income Statement 1/1/1997 to 12/26/1997
15. Trial Balance As at 12/26/1997

B. Refer to your reports to list the amounts requested below:

1. Accounts Payable balance $_____

2. Accounts Receivable balance $_____

3. Cash balance $_____

4. Net income $_____

5. Total inventory value $_____

STAGE 7: RECORDING TRANSACTIONS FOR THE PARTIAL WEEK ENDING 12/31/1997

Load CA-Simply Accounting for Windows; open the data files for Firelight Stoves (A:\STOVE\stove.asc); then advance the session date to 12/31/1997. Record the following transactions:

Firelight Stoves—Document 40   **Session Date: 12/31/1997**

Memo   **Date:** December 27, 1997
Prepare an invoice to Northwest Warmth for 1 Arc Burner stove (Item 6) at our regular sales price plus tax.

Firelight Stoves—Document 41   **Session Date: 12/31/1997**

Memo   **Date:** December 28, 1997
Prepare Invoice for credit card sale of 1 Blaze stove to a one-time customer using a Visa.

Firelight Stoves—Document 42   **Session Date: 12/31/1997**

Memo   **Date:** December 28, 1997
Issue a check to Walker's Woodstoves in payment of Invoice 7681 less DM29 and a 3% discount.

Firelight Stoves—Document 43   **Session Date: 12/31/1997**

Memo   **Date:** December 28, 1997
Received Check 2930 from Nancy Powers, Interiors for $2,229.25 in full payment of Invoice 5821. Use Deposit Slip 1706 to deposit the check.

Firelight Stoves—Document 44   **Session Date: 12/31/1997**

Memo   **Date:** December 29, 1997
Check 2930 for $2,229.25 from Nancy Powers, Interiors was returned by the bank marked NSF. Charge $35 fees for NSF check. Create any necessary accounts and/or items required to record the NSF check.

Firelight Stoves—Document 45   **Session Date: 12/31/1997**

Memo   **Date:** December 29, 1997
Prepare Invoice for credit card sale of 1 Little Spark stove to a one-time customer using a MasterCard.

Firelight Stoves—Document 46   **Session Date: 12/31/1997**

Memo   **Date:** December 29, 1997
Received Check 768 from Atlas Remodeling for $181.44 in full payment of Invoice 5886. (Less CM12 and discount.)

Firelight Stoves—Document 47   **Session Date: 12/31/1997**

Gas Stoves Limited	**Invoice: Z894**	**Date:** December 29, 1997
1 Cook Stove	$425.00 each	Amount: $425.00
Approved. JC		Terms: net 30

Firelight Stoves—Document 48   **Session Date: 12/31/1997**

Western Telephone	**Invoice: 69-201**	**Date:** December 29, 1997
Monthly Telephone Charges		Amount: $102.48
Approved. JC		Terms: Net 30

Firelight Stoves—Document 49　　　　　　　　　**Session Date: 12/31/1997**

Cascade Electric　　　　**Invoice: K010023**　**Date:** December 30, 1997

Monthly Electricity Charges　　　　　　　　　Total Due $98.65

Approved. JC

　　　　　　　　　　　　　　　　　　　　　　　　　　Terms: Net 30

Firelight Stoves—Document 50　　　　　　　　　**Session Date: 12/31/1997**

Weekly Cash Sales Summary　　**Date:** December 31, 1997　　**No. 52**

Item	2	Quantity	2	Unit	Each	Mini-Glow Stove	Selling Price $175.00	Amount $350.00
	5		1		Each	Cook Stove	950.00	950.00
						8% Sales Tax		104.00

Use Deposit Slip 1707. Include undeposited checks and credit card receipts　　TOTAL　　$1,404.00

Firelight Stoves—Document 51　　　　　　　　　**Session Date: 12/31/1997**

Memo　　　　　　　　　　　　　　　　**Date:** December 31, 1997

Please issue payroll checks as follows: Theresa Meyer $1,850.00 Salary; Kevin Zenner 154 hrs. at $8.00 per hr.

Firelight Stoves—Document 52　　　　　　　　　**Session Date: 12/31/1997**

Memo　　　　　　　　　　　　　　　　**Date:** December 31, 1997

Use the following bank statement and reconcile the Cash account. Record the adjustment in the journal for the bad check charge by the bank. Print Reconciliation Journal Entry report and Reconciliation report.

Washington State Bank, P. O. 981, Vancouver, WA 98660

Statement Date: 12/31/1997　　　　　　　　　　　　**Account: 01199**

Firelight Stoves, 2000 East Evergreen, Vancouver, WA 98661

12/1/1997 Beginning Balance			$7,561.32
12/1/1997 Deposit 1701	$1,500.00		9,061.32
12/1/1997 Withdrawal		$ 50.00	9,011.32
12/1/1997 Check 1706		750.00	8,261.32
12/3/1997 Check 1707		718.03	7,543.29
12/5/1997 Deposit 1702	5,355.35		12,898.64
12/8/1997 Check 1708		1,870.10	11,028.54
12/11/1997 Check 1709		400.00	10,628.54
12/12/1997 Deposit 1703	2,803.86		13,432.40
12/12/1997 Check1710		316.80	13,115.60
12/14/1997 Check 1711		2,453.04	10,662.56
12/15/1997 Check 1712		737.01	9,925.55
12/15/1997 Check 1713		1,110.38	8,815.17
12/19/1997 Deposit 1704	3,300.48		12,115.65
12/19/1997 Check 1714		1,100.00	11,015.65

12/22/1997 Check 1715		1,096.45	9,919.20
12/24/1997 Check 1716		102.05	9,817.15
12/26/1997 Deposit 1705	5,805.00		15,622.15
12/26/1997 Check 1717		700.00	14,922.15
12/28/1997 Deposit 1706	2,229.25		17,151.40
12/28/1997 NSF Check		2,229.25	14,922.15
12/31/1997 Interest	62.45		14,984.60
12/31/1997 Charges: NSF Charge $15; Service Charge $25		40.00	14,944.60
12/31/1997 Ending Balance			14,944.60

End-of-Session Procedures

A. Print the following reports:

1. Journal (By date, Project allocations, All entries) 12/27/1997 to 12/31/1997
2. Customer Aged report (Select All, Detail, Terms) As at 12/31/1997
3. Vendor Aged report (Select All, Detail, Terms) As at 12/31/1997
4. Inventory report (Select All, Select Assets, Synopsis) 12/31/1997
5. Inventory report (Select All, Select Assets, Quantity) 12/31/1997
6. Income Statement (current year) 1/1/1997 to 12/31/1997
7. Trial Balance As at 12/31/1997

B. Make a backup copy of the Firelight Stoves data files. Exit from the program. Complete the Firelight Stoves Transmittal.

TRANSMITTAL

Firelight Stoves   Name_____
Stage 7: Session Date 12/31/1997

A. Attach the following documents and reports:

1. Invoice 5887
2. Invoice 5888
3. Check 1718
4. Receipt of Check 2930 in payment of Invoice 5821
5. Invoice 5889
6. Invoice 5890
7. Receipt of Check 768 in payment of Invoice 5886
8. Sum52
9. Payroll Check 1719
10. Payroll Check 1720
11. Account Reconciliation Journal entry
12. Account Reconciliation Detail report
13. Journal entries 12/27/1997 to 12/31/1997
14. Customer Aged Detail As at 12/31/1997
15. Vendor Aged Detail As at 12/31/1997
16. Inventory Synopsis 12/31/1997
17. Inventory Quantity 12/31/1997
18. Income Statement 1/1/1997 to 12/31/1997
19. Trial Balance As at 12/31/1997

B. Refer to your reports to list the amounts requested below:

1. Accounts Payable balance $_____

2. Accounts Receivable balance $_____

3. Cash balance $_____

4. Net income $_____

5. Total inventory value $_____

STAGE 8: MONTH-END AND YEAR-END PROCEDURES 12/31/1997 AND 1/1/1998

Load CA-Simply Accounting for Windows; open the data files for Firelight Stoves (A:\STOVES\Stoves.asc); then leave the session date set at 12/31/1997. Record the adjusting entries authorized by the following memo:

Firelight Stoves—Document 53   **Session Date: 12/31/1997**

Memo   **Date:** December 31, 1997

Please record the following adjusting entries for December:
1. Decrease the Mini-Glow stove (Item 2) by 1 stove at a total cost of $75.50. Comment: Damaged Goods
2. Expired insurance, $100.00
3. Office supplies used, $513.35
4. Office equipment depreciation, $119.44
5. Store equipment depreciation, $36.11

A. Print the following documents and reports:

1. Journal (By date, Project allocations, All entries) 12/1/1997 to 12/31/1997
2. Employee report (Select All, YTD Summary) 12/31/1997
3. W-2 slips (Select All)
4. Project report (Select All, Detail) 12/1/1997 to 12/31/1997
5. Inventory report (Select All, Select Assets, Synopsis) 12/31/1997
6. Trial Balance As at 12/31/1997
7. Income Statement (Comparison of Actual to Budget, Using Dollar Amounts) 1/1/1997 to 12/31/1997
8. Balance Sheet As at 12/31/1997

B. Make a backup copy of the Firelight Stoves data files.

C. Record the closing entry authorized by the following memo:

Firelight Stoves—Document 54   **Session Date: 12/31/1997**

Memo   **Date:** December 29, 1997

Please record the entry to close my Drawing account for the year.

D. Advance the session date to 1/1/1998.

E. Print a Trial Balance As at 1/1/1998 and Income Statement 1/1/1998 to 1/1/1998.

F. Exit from the program.

G. Complete the Firelight Stoves Transmittal.

TRANSMITTAL

Firelight Stoves   Name_____
Stage 8: Session Date 12/31/1997 and 1/1/1998

A. Attach the following documents and reports:

1. Journal Entries 12/1/1997 to 12/31/1997
2. Employee Year-to-Date report 12/31/1997
3. W-2 slips
4. Project report 12/1/1997 to 12/31/1997
5. Inventory Synopsis 12/31/1997
6. Trial Balance As at 12/31/1997
7. Income Statement (Comparison of Actual to Budget) 1/1/1997 to 12/31/1997
8. Balance Sheet As at 12/31/1997
9. Trial Balance As at 1/1/1998
10. Income Statement (current year) 1/1/1998 to 1/1/1998

B. Refer to your reports to list the amounts requested below:

1. What are total assets at 12/31/1997? $_____

2. How much is net income for 1997? $_____

3. How much is the total cost of goods sold for the year? $_____

4. How much did Janice Cook withdraw from the business during the year? $_____

5. How much employer's expense did Firelight Stoves incur for Theresa
   Meyer for the year? $_____

6. What is the total inventory value on 12/31/1997? $_____

7. How much in deductions were withheld from Kevin Zenner's payroll
   checks for the year? $_____

8. What is the amount of revenue minus expense for trade show sales? $_____

9. What is the balance of the Janice Cook, Capital account on 1/1/1998? $_____

10. What was the difference between the budgeted amount of net income and
    the actual net income for 1997? $_____

APPENDIX: EXPORTING DATA, DYNAMIC DATA EXCHANGE (DDE), AND MICROSOFT OFFICE INTEGRATION

LEARNING OBJECTIVES

This appendix:
- Discusses the Export feature
- Discusses the DDE feature with the Windows version of Excel or Lotus
- Uses the Export feature in Microsoft office

SHARING DATA AMONG PROGRAMS

The Export and Dynamic Data Exchange (DDE) features of CA-Simply Accounting for Windows facilitate the sharing of accounting information between the accounting program and other software applications. These features significantly enhance an accountant's productivity by eliminating the need to re-enter accounting data for use in a word processing, spreadsheet, or database program. The Export feature allows you to share accounting data at a single point in time. The DDE feature allows you to dynamically link accounting data to another application so that the data is updated continually as new transactions are recorded in the accounting program.

MICROSOFT OFFICE INTEGRATION

In addition to being able to export information to other programs, Simply can export information directly into Microsoft Word, Excel, and Access. Simply contains preformatted documents designed to be used in an office. Some of these documents are form letters to vendors and customers that allow information from Simply Accounting records to be merged into a letter. Preformatted Excel spreadsheets are also contained in Simply Accounting. For example, Simply contains a Physical Inventory Worksheet that is ready for accounting data to be exported into it.

EXPORTING REPORTS

CA-Simply Accounting for Windows can export the same reports that it displays. The exported files created by the program can be used by other programs such as spreadsheets and word processors.

You can export reports in the following formats:

- Comma Separated Values (CSV)
- Lotus 123 Version 1
- Lotus 123 Version 2
- Lotus Symphony

- Microsoft Excel
- SuperCalc
- Text File (ASCII)

ACTION: Load CA-Simply Accounting for Windows; open the data files for Classic Clocks that you used in Chapter 11 (A:\CLOCKS\Classic Clocks.asc); leave the session date set at 12/31/1997. The home window will appear on the screen. From the home window **Report** menu, point to Lists, click **Chart of Accounts**. Click **File** on the Chart of Accounts menu bar. Point to Export. Your screen should be similar to the following:

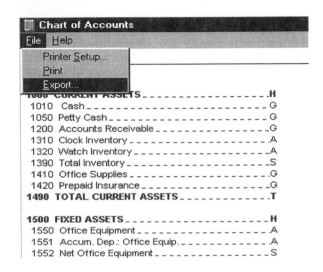

ACTION: Click **Export**. Complete the Export Selection dialog box so that it looks like the following:

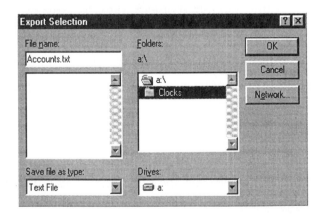

ACTION: Click **OK** on the Export Selection screen. Close the Chart of Accounts window; then choose **Exit** from the home window File menu to end the current work session and return to your Windows desktop. Open a word processing program (Word is used in this illustration); then open the file named A:\accounts.txt. Your screen will look similar to the one shown below:

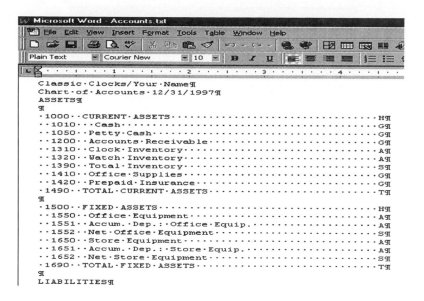

Explanation: You can now edit the chart of accounts to incorporate this information into a word processing document without having to type in the chart of accounts information.

ACTION: Save your document in your word processing program; print your document; then exit your word processing program and return to Simply Accounting.

ACTION: On the Report Menu; point to Financials; click **Trial Balance**. Click the **File** menu on the Trial Balance. Click **Export** and complete the Export Selection so that it appears as follows:

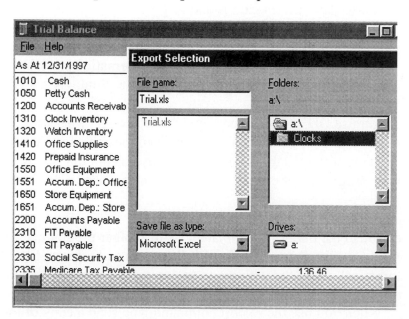

ACTION: Click **OK** on the Export Selection screen. Close the Trial Balance, then choose **Exit** from the home window File menu to end the current work session and return to your Windows desktop. Open a spreadsheet program (Excel is used in this illustration); then open the file named A:\trial.xls. Your screen will look similar to the one shown below:

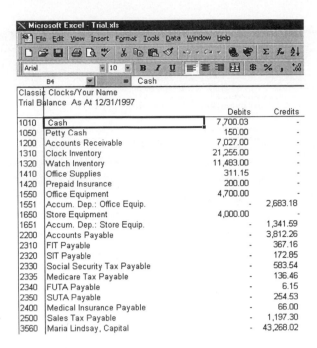

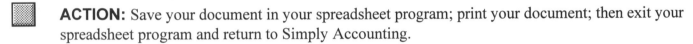

ACTION: Save your document in your spreadsheet program; print your document; then exit your spreadsheet program and return to Simply Accounting.

DYNAMIC DATA EXCHANGE

With DDE, you can send CA-Simply Accounting for Windows data to other Windows programs. DDE establishes an ongoing link between the CA-Simply Accounting for Windows program and another program where the most up-to-date information is exchanged.

A Windows program can send information via DDE or receive information, or both, depending on its capabilities. In Windows terminology, a program that sends information is a DDE server. A program that receives information is a DDE client. CA-Simply Accounting for Windows is a DDE server.

Typically, a business might use DDE to send accounting data to a spreadsheet or word processing program. The data can then be manipulated in a way that is not possible in CA-Simply Accounting for Windows. The current data is still available in the CA-Simply Accounting for Window program, but it is also available in the other program. For example, a business might use DDE to create a budget or do ratio analysis.

With DDE, you first establish the budget or ratio analysis in another program; save the new file; then establish the link between CA-Simply Accounting for Windows and the new file. When you open the new file later, it is automatically updated with the most current CA-Simply Accounting for Windows data. Both DDE and the Export command in CA-Simply Accounting for Windows allow you to send data to other programs. When you use the Export command, you send a copy of the data at a single point in time. To update the data, you must send out the information again. Export sends out any CA-Simply Accounting for Windows report, including journal reports. DDE transfers only ledger data. It is best to use the Export function if you want to use a report, a simple variation of a report, or journal data. Use DDE to use CA-Simply Accounting for Windows data in a form that is not available in a report, and if you want the data to be updated continually without having to repeat commands every time the accounting data changes. The programs to which you want to send data need to know where to find the CA-Simply Accounting for Windows program. Before you use DDE, you must add the location of the CA-Simply Accounting for Windows program to the DOS PATH command in your AUTOEXEC.BAT file. **Always use extreme caution when modifying your system's AUTOEXEC.BAT file.** Because changes to the Autoexec.bat file are required, DDE is discussed but not used in this text.

To transfer information using DDE, you must first create a link between CA-Simply Accounting for Windows and another Windows program. A link establishes an ongoing conversation between the two programs, allowing the exchange of data. For example, if a company had created a spreadsheet document for budgets and linked it to Simply Accounting, as amounts changed in Simply for specified or linked accounts, the same amounts would appear in the linked document. This is illustrated in the following Linked Budget:

Furniture Mart   **Linked Budget**

Account	Description	Current Balance	Budget	Variance
4000	SALES			
4010	Sales	183,878.45	200,000.00	-16,121.55
4020	Sales Returns & Allow.	-1,585.00	-2,000.00	415.00
4030	Sales Discounts	-1,928.58	-2,000.00	71.42
4390	NET SALES	180,364.87	196,000.00	-15,635.13
5000	COST OF GOODS SOLD			
5010	Cost of Goods Sold	90,267.88	100,000.00	-9,732.12
5040	TOTAL COST OF GOODS SOLD	90,267.88	100,000.00	-9,732.12
5045	OPERATING EXPENSES			
5050	Advertising Expense	3,465.00	3,500.00	-35.00
5070	Rent Expense	9,000.00	9,000.00	0.00
5090	Utilities Expense	1,777.56	1,700.00	77.56
5110	Deprec Exp: Store Equip.	433.33	433.33	0.00
5130	Deprec Exp: Office Equip.	1,433.32	1,433.32	0.00
5150	Office Supplies Expense	1,346.00	1,200.00	146.00
5170	Insurance Expense	1,200.00	1,200.00	0.00
5400	Wages	36,340.00	35,000.00	1,340.00
5410	Social Security Tax Expense	2,253.07	2,170.00	83.07
5420	Medicare Tax Expense	526.93	507.50	19.43
5430	FUTA Expense	112.00	112.00	0.00
5440	SUTA Expense	1,128.40	1,128.40	0.00
5500	Miscellaneous Expense	170.07	250.00	-79.93
5590	TOTAL OPERATING EXPENSES	59,185.68	57,634.55	1,551.13
	Net Income	30,911.31	38,365.45	-7,454.14

Example Transaction for December 31, 1997: Sold to Dan Dunes Designs, 1 couch (Item 5), at the regular sales price and sales tax percentage.

If the preceding transaction was entered the Sales and Cost of Goods Sold sections of the Excel report would change and appear as follows:

Furniture Mart   **Linked Budget**

Account	Description	Current Balance	Budget	Variance
4000	SALES			
4010	Sales	184,828.45	200,000.00	-15,171.55
4020	Sales Returns & Allow.	-1,585.00	-2,000.00	415.00
4030	Sales Discounts	-1,928.58	-2,000.00	71.42
4390	NET SALES	181,314.87	196,000.00	-14,685.13
5000	COST OF GOODS SOLD			
5010	Cost Of Goods Sold	90,692.88	100,000.00	-9,307.12
5040	TOTAL COST OF GOODS SOLD	90,692.88	100,000.00	-9,307.12
5045	OPERATING EXPENSES			

Explanation: The Sales and Cost of Goods Sold accounts have been updated to reflect the sale to Dan Dunes Designs. The variance between the current account balances and the budgeted account balances has been recalculated automatically.

MICROSOFT OFFICE AND SIMPLY ACCOUNTING INTEGRATION

CA-Simply Accounting comes with several documents that have been prepared for Microsoft Office programs. These documents use information from Simply directly in the Office document. All Microsoft Office documents that come with Simply Accounting retrieve information from the SIMPLY.MDB file that is stored on the drive where you installed Simply Accounting. In this section, SIMPLY.MDB will be created and will be used in an Excel document.

 ACTION: Load CA-Simply Accounting for Windows; open the data files for Classic Clocks (A:\CLOCKS\Classic Clocks.asc); leave the session date set at 12/31/1997. The home window will appear on the screen. On the home window Report menu, click **Microsoft® Office**. You will get a list of all the Office documents that come with Simply Accounting in the following:

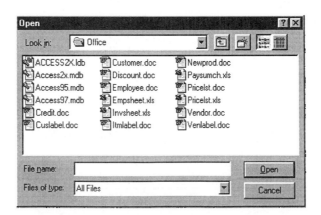

ACTION: Click **Pricelst.xls**; click **Open**. Click **Yes** on the following dialog box:

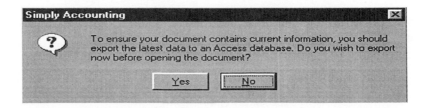

ACTION: Click **Next** on the Export to Microsoft Access dialog box. On the second screen, make sure **Typical Export** is selected and click **Next**, click **Finish** on the final screen. The following Excel screen appears on your window:

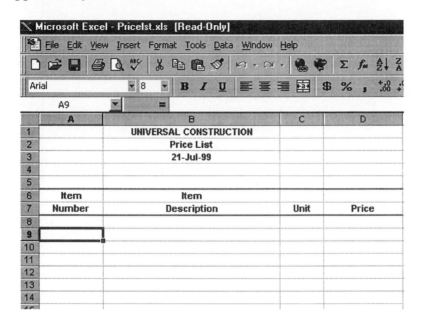

ACTION: Click the **Start** menu and open Microsoft Access. Your screen should show the following:

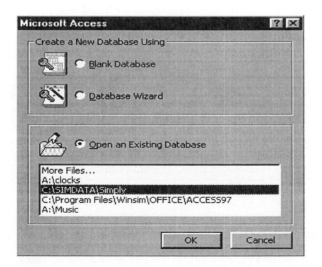

ACTION: Click **SIMDATA\Simply** to highlight (as above); click **OK.** You may get the following:

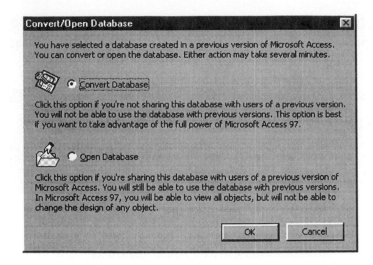

Explanation: If you get this screen, it is indicating that the file needs to be converted for a different version of Access. Check with your instructor to see what version of Microsoft Office you are using; select Convert Database or Open Database and click **OK**.

ACTION: When Access is opened, scroll thorough the list of tables; click **InvAndServPriceLis**t. You will get the following:

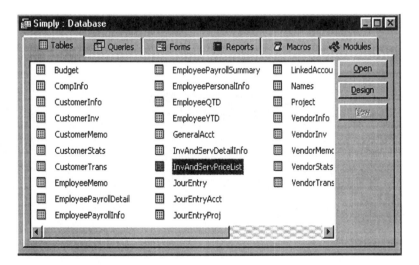

ACTION: Click the **Open** button. The InvAndServPriceList Table appears on the screen. Drag through the cells to highlight as shown. Click the **Copy** button on the Access toolbar. (This copies the highlighted cells to the Windows Clipboard.)

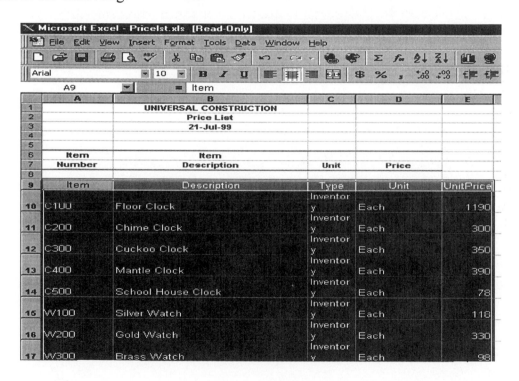

ACTION: Return to Excel by clicking the **Excel** button ![Microsoft...] on the taskbar. Click in Cell A9; click the **Paste** button ![paste icon] on the Excel toolbar. Your screen should appear similar to the following:

ACTION: Click anywhere on the Excel document to remove the highlighting. Print the document. Exit Excel, Access, and Simply, and return to Windows.

SUMMARY

This appendix has explored the Export, Dynamic Data Exchange (DDE), and Microsoft Office integration features of CA-Simply Accounting for Windows as they would typically be used by a business. Both DDE and the Export command in CA-Simply Accounting for Windows allow you to send data to other programs. When you use the Export feature, you send a copy of a report at a single point in time. When you use the DDE feature, data are updated continually as new transactions are recorded in the accounting program. The integration of CA-Simply Accounting and Microsoft Office

recorded in the accounting program. The integration of CA-Simply Accounting and Microsoft Office allows a company to use information from the accounting files in documents that have been created for use by Office programs. The Export, DDE, and Microsoft Office integration features facilitate the sharing of accounting data with other applications so that accountants and other computer users can continue to use the power of the computer to analyze and interpret the financial condition of a business.

INDEX

Note: S1 pages are between Chapters 4 and 5; S2 pages are between Chapters 8 and 9; and S3 pages are after Chapter 11.

ACCPAC International, Inc.
END USER LICENSE AGREEMENT AND LIMITED PRODUCT WARRANTY

CAREFULLY READ THE FOLLOWING TERMS AND CONDITIONS. YOUR OPENING OF THE PROGRAM PACKAGE OR INITIALIZATION OF THE SOFTWARE WILL INDICATE YOUR ACCEPTANCE. IF YOU DO NOT AGREE WITH THESE TERMS AND CONDITIONS YOU SHOULD PROMPTLY RETURN THE COMPLETE PACKAGE AND YOUR MONEY WILL BE REFUNDED.

ACCPAC International, Inc. ("ACCPAC") provides this Program and licenses its use to you. You are responsible for selecting the Program to achieve your intended results and for the installation, use and results obtained from the Program.

THE PROGRAM, INCLUDING ITS CODE, DOCUMENTATION, APPEARANCES, STRUCTURE AND ORGANIZATION, IS A PROPRIETARY PRODUCT OF ACCPAC AND IS PROTECTED BY COPYRIGHT AND OTHER LAWS. TITLE TO THE PROGRAM, OR ANY COPY, MODIFICATION OR MERGED PORTION OF THE PROGRAM, SHALL AT ALL TIMES REMAIN WITH ACCPAC.

1. **License-The following restricted rights are granted:**
    a.   This Program is licensed to you solely for your use on a single computer or on a single computer network system for your own individual use. Even though copies of the Program may be provided on media of different sizes, you may not use both sizes simultaneously on different computers. The Program may be transferred to and used on another computer, so long as the Program is de-installed on the original computer, and shall under no circumstance be used on more than one computer at a time. If designated for use on a network system, the Program may only be used in conjunction with the LanPak for the Program.
    b.   You may either: (i) make one copy of the Program solely for backup or archival purposes in support of your permitted use of the Program, or (ii) transfer the Program to a single hard disk provided you keep the original solely for backup or archival purposes.
    c.   You may transfer the Program together with this license to another person, but only if the other person agrees to accept the terms and conditions of this Agreement. If you transfer the Program and the License, you must at the same time transfer all copies of the Program and its documentation to the same person or destroy those not transferred. Any such transfer terminates your license, but you agree that you shall continue to keep all ACCPAC materials confidential.

2. **Restrictions-Without the prior written consent of ACCPAC, you may not:**
    a.   TRANSFER OR RENT THE PROGRAM OR USE, COPY OR MODIFY THE PROGRAM, IN WHOLE OR IN PART, EXCEPT AS EXPRESSLY PERMITTED IN THIS LICENSE.
    b.   DECOMPILE, REVERSE ASSEMBLE OR OTHERWISE REVERSE ENGINEER THE PROGRAM, EXCEPT TO THE EXTENT THE FOREGOING RESTRICTION IS EXPRESSLY PROHIBITED UNDER APPLICABLE LAW.
    c.   REPRODUCE, DISTRIBUTE OR REVISE THE PROGRAM DOCUMENTATION.
    d.   USE ANY PROGRAM THAT IS DESIGNATED IN ITS DOCUMENTATION AS A "RUNTIME" PROGRAM FOR APPLICATION DEVELOPMENT PURPOSES.
    e.   USE THE PROGRAM TO PROVIDE FACILITY MANAGEMENT, SERVICE BUREAU OR OTHER ACCESS AND USE OF THE PROGRAM TO THIRD PARTIES.

IF YOU FAIL TO COMPLY WITH ANY OF THE TERMS OF THIS LICENSE, YOUR LICENSE WILL BE AUTOMATICALLY TERMINATED. SUCH TERMINATION SHALL BE IN ADDITION TO AND NOT IN LIEU OF ANY CRIMINAL, CIVIL OR OTHER REMEDIES AVAILABLE TO ACCPAC.

3. **Limited Warranty**
    ACCPAC warrants that the Program will substantially perform the functions or generally conform to the Program's specifications published by ACCPAC and included in this package under normal use for a period of 90 days from the date of delivery to you.

    ACCPAC warrants that the media on which the Program is furnished will be free from defects in materials and workmanship, under normal use, for a period of 90 days from date of delivery to you.
    ACCPAC does not warrant that the functions contained in the Program will meet your requirements or that the operation of the Program will be entirely error free or appear precisely as described in the Program documentation.

    EXCEPT AS SPECIFICALLY STATED IN THIS LICENSE, THE PROGRAM IS PROVIDED AND LICENSED "AS IS" WITHOUT WARRANTY OF ANY KIND, WHETHER EXPRESSED OR IMPLIED, INCLUDING BUT NOT LIMITED TO THE IMPLIED WARRANTIES OF MERCHANTABILITY AND FITNESS FOR A PARTICULAR PURPOSE.

ACCPAC SHALL NOT BE BOUND BY OR LIABLE FOR ANY OTHER REPRESENTATIONS OR WARRANTIES, WHETHER WRITTEN OR ORAL, WITH RESPECT TO THE PROGRAM MADE BY ANY THIRD PARTY, INCLUDING AN AUTHORIZED RESELLER OR ITS AGENTS, EMPLOYEES OR REPRESENTATIVES, NOR SHALL YOU BE DEEMED A THIRD PARTY BENFICIARY OF ANY OBLIGATIONS OF ACCPAC TO AN AUTHORIZED RESELLER.

4. **Limitations of Remedies and Liability**
    To the maximum extent permitted by applicable law, the remedies described below are accepted by you as your only remedies.

    ACCPAC's entire liability and your exclusive remedies shall be:

    a.   If the Program does not substantially perform the functions or generally conform to the Program's specifications published by ACCPAC, you may, within 90 days after delivery, write to ACCPAC to report a significant defect. ACCPAC's only responsibility will be to use its best efforts, consistent with industry standards, to cure the defect. If ACCPAC is unable to correct the defect within 90 days after receiving your report, you may terminate your license and this Agreement by returning all copies of the Program with proof of purchase and your money will be refunded.
    b.   If the Program media is defective, within 90 days of delivery, you may return it with a copy of your proof of purchase, and ACCPAC will replace it.

TO THE MAXIMUM EXTENT PERMITTED BY APPLICABLE LAW, IN NO EVENT WILL ACCPAC BE LIABLE TO YOU FOR ANY SPECIAL, INCIDENTAL, INDIRECT OR CONSEQUENTIAL DAMAGES (INCLUDING DAMAGES FOR LOST PROFITS, BUSINESS INTERRUPTION, LOST INFORMATION LOSS OF RECORDED DATA OR OTHER PECUNIARY LOSS), ARISING OUT OF THE USE OR INABILITY TO USE THE PROGRAM, EVEN IF ACCPAC OR AN AUTHORIZED RESELLER HAD BEEN ADVISED OF THE POSSIBILITY OF SUCH DAMAGES.

5. **General**
    This program is provided with "Restricted Rights." Use, duplication or disclosure by the U.S. Government is subject to the restrictions set forth in 48 CFR 52.227-10 (c) (1) and (2) or DFARS 252.227-7013 (c) (1) (ii) or applicable successor provisions.

    The manufacturer is ACCPAC International, Inc.

    You are required to observe the relevant U.S. Export Administration Regulations and may not re-export the Program in violation of these or other applicable export laws or regulations.

    If any provision of this license is held to be unenforceable, the enforceability of the remaining provisions shall in no way be affected or impaired thereby. This Agreement and any disputes arising hereunder shall be governed by the laws of the State of California, United States of America, without regard to conflicts of laws principles. The parties hereby expressly exclude the application of the U.N. Convention on Contracts for the International Sale of Goods to the Agreement.

    Any questions concerning this License should be referred in writing to ACCPAC International, Inc., 6700 Koll Center Parkway, 3rd Floor, Pleasanton, CA 94566.

YOU ACKNOWLEDGE THAT YOU HAVE READ THIS LICENSE AND, BY OPENING THE PROGRAM OR PACKET, OR INSTALLING THE PROGRAM, YOU INDICATE YOUR ACCEPTANCE OF ITS TERMS AND CONDITIONS. YOU ALSO AGREE THAT, UNLESS SPECIFICALLY COVERED BY ANOTHER WRITTEN LICENSE AGREEMENT WITH ACCPAC, THIS LICENSE IS THE COMPLETE AGREEMENT BETWEEN US AND THAT IT SUPERSEDES ANY INFORMATION YOU RECEIVED RELATING TO THE SUBJECT MATTER OF THIS AGREEMENT